UNDERSTANDING FICTION

UNDERSTANDING

FICTION

THIRD EDITION

Cleanth Brooks

Robert Penn Warren

PRENTICE-HALL, INC., ENGLEWOOD CLIFFS, NEW JERSEY 07632

Library of Congress Cataloging in Publication Data

Brooks, Cleanth   ed.
    Understanding fiction.

    1. Fiction—History and criticism.   2. Short
stories.   I.   Warren, Robert Penn   joint ed.
II. Title.
PN3355.B74 1979   808.3   78-27116
ISBN 0-13-936690-3

Editorial/production supervision and interior design by Robb Reavill
Cover design by A Good Thing, Inc.
Manufacturing buyers: Phil Galea, Harry P. Baisley

Printed in the United States of America

10   9   8   7   6   5   4   3   2   1

PRENTICE-HALL INTERNATIONAL, INC., *London*
PRENTICE-HALL OF AUSTRALIA PTY. LIMITED, *Sydney*
PRENTICE-HALL OF CANADA, LTD., *Toronto*
PRENTICE-HALL OF INDIA PRIVATE LIMITED, *New Delhi*
PRENTICE-HALL OF JAPAN, INC., *Tokyo*
PRENTICE-HALL OF SOUTHEAST ASIA PTE. LTD., *Singapore*
WHITEHALL BOOKS LIMITED, *Wellington, New Zealand*

ACKNOWLEDGMENTS

SHERWOOD ANDERSON, "Death in the Woods." Reprinted by permission of Harold Ober Associates Incorporated. Copyright 1926 by the American Mercury, Inc. Renewed 1953 Eleanor Copenhaver Anderson.

MARCEL AYMÉ, "Dermuche." From *Across Paris and Other Stories,* translated by Norman Denny. Copyright Editions Gallimard 1947. Reprinted by permission of Editions Gallimard.

ISAAC BABEL, "Crossing into Poland," from *Collected Stories.* Reprinted by permission of S. G. Phillips, Inc., from *The Collected Stories of Isaac Babel.* Copyright © 1955 by S. G. Phillips, Inc.

JAMES BALDWIN, "The Rockpile," excerpted from the book *Going to Meet the Man* by James Baldwin. Copyright © 1965 by James Baldwin. Reprinted by permission of The Dial Press.

DONALD BARTHELME, "The Balloon," from *Unspeakable Practices, Unnatural Acts,* by Donald Barthelme. Copyright © 1966, 1968 by Donald Barthelme. This story appeared originally in *The New Yorker.*

JORGE LUIS BORGES, "The Meeting." From *The Aleph and Other Stories 1933–1969* by Jorge Luis Borges, edited and translated by Norman Thomas de Giovanni. English translation copyright © 1968, 1969, 1970 by Emece Editores, S.A., and Norman Thomas de Giovanni; © 1970 by Jorge Luis Borges, Adolph BioCasares and Norman Thomas de Giovanni. Reprinted by permission of the publishers, E. P. Dutton.

ANTON CHEKHOV, "Vanka." From *The Portable Chekhov* edited by Avrahm Yarmolinsky. Copyright 1947, © 1975 by The Viking Press, Inc. Reprinted by permission of The Viking Press.

COLETTE, "The Bitch," from *Creatures Great and Small* by Colette, translated by Enid McLeod, Copyright 1951 by Martin Secker & Warburg Ltd. Reprinted with the permission of Farrar, Straus & Giroux, Inc., and Martin Secker & Warburg Limited.

JOHN COLLIER, "De Mortuis," from *Fancies and Goodnight.* © 1942, Renewal © 1969 by John Collier. Reprinted by permission of the Harold Matson Co., Inc.

JULIO CORTÁZAR, "Continuity of Parks." From *End of the Game and Other Stories* by Julio Cortázar, translated by Paul Blackburn. Copyright © 1963, 1967 by Random House, Inc. Reprinted by permission of Pantheon Books, a Division of Random House, Inc.

STEPHEN CRANE, "The Bride Comes to Yellow Sky." From *Stephen Crane: An Omnibus,* Alfred A. Knopf, Inc., 1952.

RALPH ELLISON, "The Battle Royal." Copyright 1947 by Ralph Ellison. Reprinted from *Shadow and Act,* by Ralph Ellison, by permission of Random House, Inc.

WILLIAM FAULKNER, "A Rose for Emily." Copyright 1930 and renewed 1958 by William Faulkner. Reprinted from *Selected Short Stories of William Faulkner,* by permission of Random House, Inc.

F. SCOTT FITZGERALD, "Winter Dreams," by F. Scott Fitzgerald is reprinted from *Stories of F. Scott Fitzgerald* with the permission of Charles Scribner's Sons. Copyright 1922 Frances Scott Fitzgerald Lanahan.

ERNEST HEMINGWAY, "The Killers," by Ernest Hemingway is reprinted from *Men without Women* with the permission of Charles Scribner's Sons. Copyright 1927 Charles Scribner's Sons.

JAMES JOYCE, "Araby." From *Dubliners* by James Joyce. Originally published by B. W. Huebsch, Inc. in 1916. Copyright © 1967 by the Estate of James Joyce. All rights reserved. Reprinted by permission of The Viking Press.

RUDYARD KIPLING, "The Man Who Would Be King." By permission of The National Trust and the Macmillan Co. of London and Basingstoke.

DORIS LESSING, "Black Madonna," from *African Stories.* Copyright © 1951, 1953, 1954, 1957, 1958, 1962, 1963, 1964, 1965. Reprinted by permission of Simon & Schuster, a Division of Gulf & Western Corporation, and Curtis Brown Ltd.

RING LARDNER, "Haircut," by Ring Lardner is reprinted from *The Love Nest and Other Stories* with the permission of Charles Scribner's Sons. Copyright 1925 Ellis A. Lardner.

D. H. LAWRENCE, "Tickets, Please." From *The Complete Stories of D. H. Lawrence,* Vol. II. Copyright 1922 by Thomas B. Seltzer, Inc., 1950 by Frieda Lawrence. Reprinted by permission of The Viking Press.

BERNARD MALAMUD, "The Magic Barrel," from *The Magic Barrel* by Bernard Malamud. Copyright © 1954, 1958 by Bernard Malamud. Reprinted with the permission of Farrar, Straus & Giroux, Inc.

CARSON MCCULLERS, "The Sojourner," from *Collected Short Stories and the Novel, The Ballad of the Sad Cafe* by Carson McCullers. Copyright 1955 by Carson McCullers. Reprinted by permission of Houghton Mifflin Company.

JOYCE CAROL OATES, "29 Inventions." Reprinted from *Marriages and Infidelities* by Joyce Carol Oates by permission of the publisher, Vanguard Press, Inc. Copyright © 1968, 1969, 1970, 1971, 1972 by Joyce Carol Oates.

FLANNERY O'CONNOR, "A Good Man Is Hard To Find," Copyright, 1953, by Flannery O'Connor. Reprinted from her volume *A Good Man Is Hard To Find and Other Stories* by permission of Harcourt Brace Jovanovich Inc.

FRANK O'CONNOR, "The Drunkard," Copyright © 1951, 1956 by Frank O'Connor. Reprinted from *The Stories of Frank O'Connor.* Reprinted by permission of Alfred A. Knopf, Inc., and Joan Daves. First appeared in *The New Yorker.*

PIRANDELLO, "War." Reprinted by permission of Toby Cole, New York, agent for the estate of Luigi Pirandello.

KATHERINE ANNE PORTER, "Noon Wine." Copyright, 1936, 1964, by Katherine Anne Porter. Reprinted from her volume *Pale Horse, Pale Rider* by permission of Harcourt Brace Jovanovich, Inc. " 'Noon Wine': The Sources" excerpted from the book *The Collected Essays and Occasional Writings of Katherine Anne Porter* by Katherine Anne Porter. Copyright ©1956 by Katherine Anne Porter. First published in *Yale Review.* Reprinted by permission Delacorte Press/Seymour Lawrence.

ALAIN ROBBE-GRILLET, "The Secret Room." Reprinted from *Snapshots* by permission of Calder and Boyars Ltd, Publishers, and Grove Press, Inc. Copyright © 1968 by Grove Press, Inc.

JESSE STUART, "Love." Reprinted by permission of Jesse Stuart.

PETER TAYLOR, "The Hand of Emmagene." Copyright © 1975 by Peter Taylor. Reprinted from *In the Miro District and Other Stories,* by Peter Taylor, by permission of Alfred A. Knopf, Inc.

JAMES THURBER, "The Secret Life of Walter Mitty." Copr. © 1942 James Thurber. Copr. © 1970 Helen Thurber. From *My World—And Welcome To It,* published by Harcourt Brace Jovanovich, New York. Originally printed in *The New Yorker.*

JEAN TOOMER, "Fern" is reprinted from *Cane* by Jean Toomer, with the permission of Liveright Publishing Corporation. Copyright 1923 by Boni & Liveright. Copyright renewed 1951 by Jean Toomer.

IVAN TURGENEV, "The District Doctor." From *The Novels and Stories of Ivan Turgenieff,* International Edition, translated by Isabel Hopgood, Charles Scribner's Sons, 1903, 1904.

JOHN UPDIKE, "A&P." Copyright © 1962 by John Updike. Reprinted from *Pigeon Feathers and Other Stories,* by John Updike, by permission of Alfred A. Knopf, Inc. Originally appeared in *The New Yorker.*

ROBERT PENN WARREN, "Blackberry Winter." From *Circus in the Attic and Other Stories,* copyright, 1947, 1975, by Robert Penn Warren. Reprinted by permission of Harcourt Brace Jovanovich, Inc.

EUDORA WELTY, "No Place for You, My Love." From *The Bride of the Innisfallen and Other Stories,* © 1955, by Eudora Welty. Reprinted by permission of Harcourt Brace Jovanovich, Inc. "How I Write." From the *Virginia Quarterly Review,* Spring 1955. By permission of the *Virginia Quarterly Review.*

THOMAS WOLFE, "The Far and the Near" from *From Death to Morning* is reprinted with permission of Charles Scribner's Sons. Copyright 1935 International Magazine Company. First published under the title "The Cottage by the Tracks."

RICHARD WRIGHT, "The Man Who Was Almost a Man" from *Eight Men* by Richard Wright (World). Copyright © 1961, 1940 by Richard Wright. By permission of Harper & Row, Publishers, Inc.

Contents

6 FICTION AND HUMAN EXPERIENCE, *293*

7 STORIES FOR READING, *383*

Preface

It is fairly easy to compile a very good anthology of short fiction. For one thing, there are a number of pieces that have become, as it were, classics—more, in fact, than any ordinary collection could accommodate, and enough, even, to provide for a number of anthologies of special-interest stories about, for instance, love, dogs, childhood, or ethnic affiliation. The word *anthology*, of Greek origin, means a gathering of flowers; and there are more than enough blooms to go around.

An anthology for teaching—a textbook—involves many different considerations. And this is a textbook. But even the stories in a textbook anthology should not give less pleasure than those in any other—except when a poor example is inserted for pedagogical reasons. In fact, if a textbook fulfills its purpose of deepening the comprehension and sharpening the taste of the student, it should provide, in the end, more pleasure than the ordinary anthology can. A spectator who really understands football or baseball certainly enjoys witnessing a game more than one who scarcely knows the rules of the game.

There are, however, no rules for the good story. There are, instead, certain general principles, indicated here by the headings of sections 1 to 4. But an understanding of such principles (here gained through the study of, and debate about, individual stories) is aimed at bringing the reader closer to the true center of successful fiction—to a sense of the relation of the story to life meaningfully lived. Even the type of plot or characterization chosen, though sometimes seeming to be merely technical, has, as we try to indicate, a deep psychological basis. Of course, one aspect of this relationship becomes obvious in section 6, entitled "Fiction and Human Experience," in which three authors attempt to explain the origin of one of their stories—how a germ of early suggestion, or a complex of such early suggestions, might eventuate in a deeper and fuller interpretation of a seemingly casual experience.

In this edition there has been a thorough overhauling of all the material included in past editions. When a story previously included has served its purpose as well as any other we could find, we have kept it. That is, mere novelty has never been our criterion. We have, fortunately, found some stories that do offer better, or more interesting, examples of various principles. Though in sections 1 through 4 we have continued our discussions of the relation of method and meaning, we retain in section 7 (with some changes) stories without commentary or questions so that students may encounter stories as they would in real life—freestanding and a challenge to the interest and a sense of their meaning. To summarize the changes: We have twenty-one new stories in this edition out of a total of fifty-one.

An entirely new feature is section 5, "The New Fiction." During the twentieth century changes in scientific theory and in society have naturally affected the assumptions behind a certain amount of fiction. New scientific views of space and time, and continuing developments in psychology, have suggested basic differences, and from whatever sources, there has been a new emphasis on the disturbed and the sadistic—or what is sometimes (to revive a term used in the eighteenth century for such material) called the *Gothic*. So we have offered examples from Barthelme, Cortázar, Taylor, and others to document such changes.

The second edition of *Understanding Fiction* contained an appendix called "Technical Problems and Principles in the Composition of Fiction." Clearly, this was directed to those courses (of which there were many) in which the emphasis was on the writing of short stories. We have dropped this material, including it in the Teacher's Manual, because we believe that when the text is used as a basis for actual writing, the teacher, as thee best judge of a class, will know when special questions should be raised and related to stories or sections. And the teacher's individual application and elaboration of the principles that we have been forced to treat in more or less synoptic form will prove invaluable to that class.

A final word: It should be clear from even a cursory look at this edition that here, even more than before, we have clung to our generally inductive method as the best way of giving the sense of participation to the student and of making the process of learning one of natural extension and building.

We are deeply grateful to Katherine Anne Porter and Eudora Welty for writing especially for *Understanding Fiction* their accounts of the background of their stories included. The number of users of this book whose comments have been invaluable to us in revision is too great for listing here. But we should make special reference of gratitude to David Milch, of Yale University, to Claude Conyers, for his meticulous copy editing, and to Robb Reavill, of Prentice-Hall, Inc.

C.B.
R.P.W.

UNDERSTANDING FICTION

1
Intentions and Elements of Fiction

As soon as the cave man had leisure to sit around the fire while darkness covered the world beyond, fiction was born. In words, he relived, shivering with fear or gloating in victory, the events of the hunt; he recounted the past history of the tribe; he narrated the deeds of heroes and men of cunning; he told of marvels; he struggled in myths to explain the world and fate; he glorified himself in daydreams converted to narrative. In the sophisticated modern world, many of the elements involved in the cave man's fireside tales have led to branches of speculation and study—history, literature, physics, theology, and psychology, for instance—and we find in our fiction many of the original impulses at work. We find them at work, however, not in the abstract—as we find them in the textbook of psychology or philosophy—but in images of life in the process of being lived as in fiction or drama. Fiction, as we enter into it imaginatively, broadens our experience and increases our knowledge of the possibilities of the self. Fiction is a vital image of life in motion—it is an *imaginative enactment of life*—and, as such, it is an extension of our own lives.

It is well to remind ourselves that fiction goes back to prehistory and that it embodies some of our deepest needs and interests. But it is well to remind ourselves, too, that fiction has, over the ages, become a complex art, as different from the fireside tale as Michelangelo's frescoes in the Sistine Chapel are from the animal paintings in prehistoric caves.

So let us consider modern practice and the elements that go into it. We must remember that fiction changes as the world changes, that each age produces its own kind of fiction. More important, we must remember that, though in our world of technology, change is generally taken to mean progress, change in the world of art (and fiction is primarily an art) does not *necessarily* mean progress; nobody would think that the last best seller is necessarily superior to Homer or to Shakespeare. More generally, we expect fluctuation, and sometimes decline. So in considering fiction here we are concerned with both the new *and* the old, with both their differences and their similarities. We are trying, insofar as possible, to find continuing principles. *But our main purpose here is not to give a history of the short story. It is to deepen our understanding of, and consequently our pleasure in, the various forms of fiction.*

Let us begin by looking at three basic elements found in all the compositions that we generally agree to call fiction: action, character, and theme.

1

THE ATTACK ON THE FORT

Francis Parkman

SIX years ago, a fellow named Jim Beckworth, a mongrel of French, American, and Negro blood, was trading for the Fur Company, in a large village of the Crows. Jim Beckworth was last summer at St. Louis. He is a ruffian of the worst stamp, bloody and treacherous, without honor or honesty; such at least is the character he bears upon the prairie. Yet in his case the standard rules of character fail, for though he will stab a man in his sleep, he will also perform most desperate acts of daring; such, for instance, as the following: While he was in the Crow village, a Blackfoot war-party, between thirty and forty in number, came stealing through the country, killing stragglers and carrying off horses. The Crow warriors got upon their trail and pressed them so closely that they could not escape, at which the Blackfeet, throwing up a semi-circular breastwork of logs at the foot of a precipice, coolly awaited their approach. The logs and sticks, piled four or five feet high, protected them in front. The Crows might have swept over the breastwork and exterminated their enemies; but though outnumbering them tenfold, they did not dream of storming the little fortification. Such a proceeding would be altogether repugnant to their notions of warfare. Whooping and yelling, and jumping from side to side like devils incarnate, they showered bullets and arrows upon the logs; not a Blackfoot was hurt, but several Crows, in spite of their leaping and dodging, were shot down. In this childish manner, the fight went on for an hour or two. Now and then a Crow warrior, in an ecstasy of valor and vainglory, would scream forth his war song, boast himself the bravest and greatest of mankind, grasp his hatchet, rush up, strike it upon the breastwork, and then, as he retreated to his companions, fall dead under a shower of arrows; yet no combined attack was made. The Blackfeet remained secure in their entrenchment. At last Jim Beckworth lost patience.

"You are all fools and old women," he said to the Crows; "come with me, if any of you are brave enough, and I will show you how to fight."

He threw off his trapper's frock of buckskin and stripped himself naked, like the Indians themselves. He left his rifle on the ground, took in his hand a small light hatchet, and ran over the prairie to the right, concealed by a hollow from the eyes of the Blackfeet. Then climbing up the rocks, he gained the top of the precipice behind them. Forty or fifty young Crow warriors followed him. By the cries and whoops that rose from below, he knew that the Blackfeet were just beneath him; and running forward, he leaped down the rock into the midst of them. As he fell he caught one by the long loose hair, and dragging him down, tomahawked him; then grasping another by the belt at his waist, he struck him also a stunning blow, and gaining his feet, shouted the Crow war cry. He swung his hatchet so fiercely around him that the astonished Blackfeet bore back and gave him room. He might, had he chosen, have

2

leaped over the breastwork and escaped; but this was not necessary, for with devilish yells the Crow warriors came dropping in quick succession over the rock among their enemies. The main body of the Crows, too, answered the cry from the front, and rushed up simultaneously. The convulsive struggle within the breastwork was frightful; for an instant the Blackfeet fought and yelled like pent-up tigers; but the butchery was soon complete, and the mangled bodies lay piled together under the precipice. Not a Blackfoot made his escape.

DISCUSSION

Let us make two preliminary observations on this *anecdote* (see Glossary). First, it is allegedly true; it is not made up. Second, Parkman wrote it not primarily because it was spirited and interesting in itself but because it illustrated one aspect of the life he wanted to describe to the people back home. These observations raise two questions. First, would this anecdote be an acceptable piece of fiction if, instead of using fact, Parkman had simply made it up out of his head? Second, would it be an acceptable piece of fiction if Parkman had written it not to instruct his readers but because it was interesting in itself?

We must answer no to the first question because, though fiction is not tied to fact, it may use fact. Many pieces of fiction make as much use of historical fact as does this. We must answer no to the second question because, though many pieces of fiction are written with a desire to instruct the reader, they are not written with the purpose to instruct the reader merely about matters of fact.

If we are not debarred from calling this anecdote fiction because it is true and not because the author's avowed purpose was to instruct the reader, why, then, is it not to be considered a piece of acceptable fiction? To answer this question, we must look at the nature of the anecdote itself.

The anecdote proper is simply the account of a spirited piece of action that, as a piece of action, is unified. That is, we have the situation precipitating the fight, the cunning defense by the Blackfeet that creates a problem for the attacking Crows, the failure of the Crows to solve their problem, then the daring solution by Beckworth. The anecdote, as action, is unified because it presents problem and solution, because it has a beginning, a middle, and an end. Our curiosity about the outcome is satisfied. But this outcome does not satisfy fully the interest that we bring to fiction. For one thing, the action recorded in this anecdote is purely external; it does not sufficiently involve the character and motive of human action. The only item of psychological interest is that Beckworth "lost patience."

Let us look at another example, in which the emphasis is on character: Samuel Clemens' brief account of an old Mississippi River steamboat pilot.

CAPTAIN ISAIAH SELLERS

Samuel Clemens

WE had some talk about Captain Isaiah Sellers, now many years dead. He was a fine man, a high-minded man, and greatly respected both ashore and on the river. He was very tall, well built, and handsome; and in his old age—as I remember him—his hair was as black as an Indian's, and his eye and hand were as strong and steady and his nerve and judgment as firm and clear as anybody's, young or old, among the fraternity of pilots. He was the patriarch of the craft; he had been a keelboat pilot before the day of steamboats; and a steamboat pilot before any other steamboat pilot, still surviving at the time I speak of, had ever turned a wheel. Consequently, his brethren held him in the sort of awe in which illustrious survivors of a bygone age are always held by their associates. He knew how he was regarded, and perhaps this fact added some trifle of stiffening to his natural dignity, which had been sufficiently stiff in its original state.

He left a diary behind him; but apparently it did not date back to his first steamboat trip, which was said to be 1811, the year the first steamboat disturbed the waters of the Mississippi. . . .

Whenever Captain Sellers approached a body of gossiping pilots, a chill fell there, and talking ceased. For this reason: whenever six pilots were gathered together, there would always be one or two newly fledged ones in the lot, and the elder ones would be always "showing off" before these poor fellows; making them sorrowfully feel how callow they were, how recent their nobility, and how humble their degree, by talking largely and vaporously of old-time experiences on the river; always making it a point to date everything back as far as they could, so as to make the new men feel their newness to the sharpest degree possible, and envy the old stagers in the like degree. And how these complacent baldheads *would* swell, and brag, and lie, and date back—ten, fifteen, twenty years, and how they did enjoy the effect produced upon the marveling and envying youngsters!

And perhaps just at this happy stage of the proceedings, the stately figure of Captain Isaiah Sellers, that real and only genuine Son of Antiquity, would drift solemnly into the midst. Imagine the size of the silence that would result on the instant! And imagine the feelings of those baldheads, and the exultation of their recent audience, when the ancient captain would begin to drop casual and indifferent remarks of a reminiscent nature—about islands that had disappeared, and cut-offs that had been made, a generation before the oldest baldhead in the company had ever set his foot in a pilot-house!

Many and many a time did this ancient mariner appear on the scene in the above fashion, and spread disaster and humiliation around him. If one might believe the pilots, he always dated his islands back to the misty dawn of river history; and he never used the same island twice; and never did he employ an island that still existed, or give one a name which anybody present was old enough to have heard of before. If you might believe the pilots, he was always conscientiously particular about little details; never spoke of "the state of Mississippi" for instance—no, he would say, "When the state of Mississippi was where Arkansas now is"; and would never speak of Louisiana or Missouri in a general way, and leave an incorrect impression in your mind—no, he would say, "When Louisiana was up the river farther," or "When Missouri was on the Illinois side."

DISCUSSION

In this sketch Captain Isaiah is treated humorously, though affectionately, as a repository of stories about the river. His stories are obviously marvelous and grandiose and put those told by the other pilots very much in the shade. As Clemens (Mark Twain) develops his sketch, he places little stress on the captain's stories as absorbing tales of adventure in their own right. They are rather legends about the "misty dawn of river history," and Twain more than hints that they are fabulous rather than real.

It is easy, however, to imagine that some of these stories of life on the river, told with a different inflection, might become the material of serious fiction involving moral conflict, heroism, or ethical decisions agonizingly made. After all, as Twain tells us, Captain Isaiah was a high-minded man with an iron hand "as strong and steady and [a] nerve and judgment as firm and clear as anybody's." And in a further paragraph he refers to Captain Isaiah as "a man who . . . would have stayed [at the pilot wheel] till he burned to a cinder, if duty required it." So much for the possibility of the captain's figuring in a heroic tale of the river. But it is also easy to see how Captain Isaiah might figure in a humorous story whose spirit would be close to that of this character sketch. One can imagine his exposing some boaster of deeds of derring-do on the Mississippi or perhaps his outdoing him with a superior boasting of his own. We can even imagine a story of pathos, as Captain Isaiah suddenly discovers that he has come to be regarded as a relic, something left over from another, outdated time.

If in "Captain Isaiah Sellers" we have only the potential of action and a minimum of what we may call thematic emphasis, let us now turn to an extreme example of narrative that reduces action and character to the sole purpose of illustrating a point, of defining a theme. A biblical *parable* (see Glossary) will give us a perfect example. Let us look at the parable of the sower, in chapter 4 of Mark:

> Hearken; Behold, there went out a sower to sow:
> And it came to pass, as he sowed, some fell by the way side, and the fowls of the air came and devoured it up.
> And some fell on stony ground, where it had not much earth; and immediately it sprang up, because it had no depth of earth;
> But when the sun was up, it was scorched; and because it had no root, it withered away.

> And some fell among thorns, and the thorns grew up, and choked it, and it yielded no fruit.
>
> And other fell on good ground, and did yield fruit that sprang up and increased; and it brought forth, some thirty, and some sixty, and some an hundred.

Later, Jesus explains and interprets the parable to his disciples:

> The sower soweth the word.
>
> And these are they by the way side, where the word is sown; but when they have heard, Satan cometh immediately, and taketh away the word that was sown in their hearts.
>
> And these are they likewise which are sown on stony ground; who, when they have heard the word, immediately receive it with gladness;
>
> And have no root in themselves, and so endure but for a time; afterward, when affliction or persecution ariseth for the word's sake, immediately they are offended.
>
> And these are they which are sown among thorns, such as hear the word,
>
> And the cares of this world, and the deceitfulness of riches, and the lusts of other things entering in, choke the word, and it becometh unfruitful.
>
> And these are they which are sown on good ground; such as hear the word, and receive *it*, and bring forth fruit, some thirtyfold, some sixty, and some an hundred.

The biblical parable is, however, only one example of the type of fictional narrative we now discuss. Perhaps the best-known examples of the type in its secular form are Aesop's fables, which have come down to us from ancient times. His fables, it is quite obvious, give us fantastic situations in which animals are actuated by human motivations, speak like human beings, and reveal themselves as rather transparent instances of certain human types. But Aesop's fables usually express a fairly explicit comment on life that can be expressed as a moral. For example, a popular translation of the fable of the fox and the grapes concludes with the moral tag "It is easy to despise what you cannot get."

Forms of the *fable* (see Glossary) are found in many languages, in primitive or sophisticated forms, and some modern fiction is slanted toward the "moral" in an insistent or a subtle way. Again, some modern fiction quite complexly, even ironically, uses the sense of the fable. One example we shall soon come to is "Young Goodman Brown," by Nathaniel Hawthorne, which though a piece of fiction, has the inner content of a fable. But we should remember that most modern fiction, however deeply significant it may be and however serious a comment it may make on human values, tends to do so through the realization of idea in character *and* plot *and* theme as intertwined.

Each of the three following stories is a rather extreme example of one of the types we have been discussing: the story of action, the story of personality, and the story of theme. But, as we have already remarked, a story, to be successful, must be a unity. Let us try to see how, in the stories that follow, the most emphasized element is intertwined with others.

GRAMIGNA'S LOVER

Giovanni Verga

DEAR Farina,[1] I'm sending you here not a story, but the outlines of a story. So it will have at least the merit of being brief, and of being true—a human document, as they say nowadays; interesting, perhaps, for you and for those who would study the great book of the heart. I'll tell it you just as I picked it up in the lanes among the fields, more or less in the same simple and picturesque words of the people who told it to me, and you, I am sure, will prefer to stand face to face with the naked, honest fact rather than have to look for it between the lines of the book, or to see it through the author's lens. The simple human fact will always set us thinking; it will always have the virtue of *having really happened*, the virtue of real tears, of fevers and sensations which have really passed through the flesh. The mysterious process by which the passions knot themselves together, interweave, ripen, develop in their own way underground, in their own tortuous windings that often seem contradictory, this will still constitute for a long time to come the attractive power of the psychological phenomenon which we call the theme of a story, and which modern analysis seeks to follow with scientific exactitude. I shall only tell you the beginning and the end of the story I am sending you to-day, but for you that will be enough, and perhaps one day it will be enough for everybody.

Nowadays we work out differently the artistic process to which we owe so many glorious works of art, we are more particular about trifles, and more intimate; we are willing to sacrifice the grand effect of the catastrophe, or of the psychological crisis, which was visioned forth with almost divine intuition by the great artists of the past, to the logical development, and hence we are necessarily less startling, less dramatic, but not less fatal; we are more modest, if not more humble; but the conquests in psychological truth made by us will be not less useful to the art of the future. Shall we never arrive at such perfection in the study of the passions, that it will be useless to prosecute further that study of the inner man? The science of the human heart, which will be the fruit of the new art, will it not develop to such a degree and to such an extent all the resources of the imagination that the novels and stories of the future will merely record *the various facts* of the case?

But in the meantime I believe that the triumph of the novel, that most complete and most human of all works of art, will be reached when the affinity and the cohesion of all its parts will be so complete that the process of the creation will remain a mystery, a mystery as great as that of the development of the human passions; and that the harmony of its form will be so perfect, the sincerity of its content so evident, its method and its *raison d'être* so necessary, that the hand of the artist will remain absolutely invisible, and the novel will have the effect of real happening, and the work of art will seem *to have made itself*, to have matured and

---

[1]The recipient of Verga's letter, in which form the story is cast.

7

come forth spontaneously like a natural event, without preserving any point of contact with its author; so that it may not show in any of its living forms any imprint of the mind in which it was conceived, any shadow of the eye which visioned it, any trace of the lips that murmured the first words, like the *fiat* of the Creator; let it stand by itself, in the single fact that it is as it must be and has to be, palpitating with life and immutable as a bronze statue, whose creator has had the divine courage to eclipse himself and to disappear in his immortal work.

Several years ago, down there along the Simoneto, they were in pursuit of a brigand, a fellow called Gramigna, if I'm not mistaken; a name accursed as the grass[2] which bears it, and which had left the terror of its fame behind it from one end of the province to the other. Carabiniers, soldiers, and mounted militia followed him for two months, without ever succeeding in setting their claws in him: he was alone, but he was worth ten men, and the ill weed threatened to take root. Add to this that harvest time was approaching, the hay was already spread in the fields, the ears of wheat were already nodding yes! to the reapers who had the sickle already in their hand, yet none the less there was not a proprietor who dared poke his nose over the hedges of his own land, for fear of seeing Gramigna crouching between the furrows, his gun between his legs, ready to blow the head off the first man who came prying into his affairs. Hence the complaints were general. Then the Prefect summoned all the officers of the police, of the carabiniers, and of the mounted militia, and addressed a few words to them that made them prick up their ears. The next day there was a general upheaval: patrols, small bands of armed men, outposts everywhere, in every ditch and behind every dry-stone wall; they drove him before them like an accursed beast across all the province, by day and by night, on foot, on horseback, by telegraph. Gramigna slipped through their hands, and replied with bullets if they got too close on his heels. In the open country, in the villages, in the farmsteads, under the bough-shelter of the inns, in the clubs and meeting-places, nothing was spoken of but him, Gramigna, and of that ferocious hunt, of that desperate flight; the horses of the carabiniers fell dead tired; the militiamen threw themselves down exhausted in every stable; the patrol slept standing; only he, Gramigna, was never tired, never slept, always fled, scrambled down the precipices, slid through the corn, ran on all-fours through the cactus thicket, extricated himself like a wolf down the dry beds of the streams. The principal theme of conversation in the clubs, and on the village door-steps, was the devouring thirst which the pursued man must suffer, in the immense plain dried up under the June sun. The idlers widened their eyes when they spoke of it.

Peppa, one of the handsomest girls of Licodia, was at that time going to marry Neighbour Finu, "Tallow-candle" as they called him, who had his own bit of land and a bay mule in his stable, and was a tall lad, handsome as the sun, who could carry the banner of Saint Margaret as if he were a pillar, without bending his loins.

Peppa's mother wept with satisfaction at her daughter's good for-

---

[2]A root-spreading grass, used as cattle feed by poor peasants.

tune, and spent her time turning over the bride's trousseau in the chest, all white goods, and four of each, "good enough for a queen," and ear-rings that hung to her shoulders, and golden rings for all the ten fingers of her hands; she had as much gold as St. Margaret herself, and they were going to get married just on St. Margaret's day, that fell in June, after the hay-harvest. Tallow-candle left his mule at Peppa's door every evening as he returned from the fields, and went in to say to her that the crops were wonderful, if Gramigna didn't set fire to them, and that the little corn-chamber that opened its gate-door opposite the bed would never be big enough for all the grain this harvest, and that it seemed to him a thousand years, till he could take his bride home, seated behind him on the bay mule.

But one fine day Peppa said to him: "You can leave your mule out of it; I'm not going to get married."

Poor Tallow-candle was thunderstruck, and the old woman began to tear her hair as she heard her daughter turning down the best match in the village.

"It's Gramigna I care for," the girl said to her mother, "and I don't want to marry anybody but him."

"Ah!" The mother rushed around the house, screaming, with her grey hair flying loose like a very witch. "Ah! that fiend has even got in here to bewitch my girl for me."

"No," replied Peppa, her eyes fixed and hard as steel. "No, he's not been here."

"Where have you seen him?"

"I've not seen him. I've heard about him. Hark, though! I can feel him here, till it burns me."

It caused a great talk in the village, though they tried to keep it dark. The goodwives who had envied Peppa the prosperous cornfields, the bay mule, and the fine lad who carried St. Margaret's banner without bending his loins, went round telling all kinds of ugly stories, that Gramigna came to her at night in the kitchen, and that they had seen him hidden under the bed. The poor mother had lit a lamp to the souls in Purgatory, and even the priest had been to Peppa's house, to touch her heart with his stole, and drive out that devil of a Gramigna who had taken possession of it. Through it all she insisted that she had not so much as set eyes on the fellow; but that she saw him at nights in her dreams, and in the morning she got up with her lips parched as if she were feeling in her own body all the thirst he must be suffering.

Then the old woman shut her up in the house, so that she should hear no more talk about Gramigna, and she covered up all the cracks in the house-door' with pictures of the saints. Peppa listened behind the blessed pictures to all that was said outside in the street, and she went white and red, as if the devil were blowing all hell in her face.

At last she heard say that they had tracked down Gramigna to the cactus thickets at Palagonia.–"They've been firing for two hours!" the goodwives said. "There's one carabinier dead, and more than three of the militia wounded. But they fired such showers of bullets on him that this time they've found a pool of blood, where he was."

Then Peppa crossed herself before the old woman's bed-head, and escaped out of the window.

Gramigna was among the prickly-pear cactuses of Palagonia, nor had they been able to dislodge him from that cover for rabbits, torn, wounded though he was, pale with two days' fasting, parched with fever, and his gun levelled: as he saw her coming, resolute, through the thickets of the cactus, in the dim gleam of dawn, he hesitated a moment whether to fire or not.–"What do you want?" he asked her. "What have you come here for?"

"I've come to stay with you," she said to him, looking at him steadily. "Are you Gramigna?"

"Yes, I am Gramigna. If you've come to get those twenty guineas blood-money, you've made a mistake."

"No, I've come to stay with you," she replied.

"Go back!" he said. "You can't stay with me, and I don't want anybody staying with me. If you've come after money you've mistaken your man, I tell you, I've got nothing, see you! It's two days since I even had a bit of bread."

"I can't go back home now," she said. "The road is full of soldiers."

"Clear out! What do I care! Everybody must be looking out for their own skin."

While she was turning away from him, like a dog driven off with kicks, Gramigna called to her.–"Listen! Go and fetch me a bottle of water from the stream down there. If you want to stay with me, you've got to risk your skin."

Peppa went without a word, and when Gramigna heard the firing he began to laugh bitingly, saying to himself: "That was meant for me!"– But when he saw her coming back, a little later, with the flask under her arm, herself pale and bleeding, he first threw himself on her and snatched the bottle, and then when he had drunk till he was out of breath, he asked her:

"You got away then,? How did you manage?"

"The soldiers were on the other side, and the cactuses were thick this side."

"They've made a hole in you, though. Is it bleeding under your clothes?"

"Yes."

"Where are you wounded?"

"In the shoulder."

"That doesn't matter. You can walk."

Thus he gave her permission to stay with him. She followed him, her clothes torn, her body burning with the fever of her wound, shoeless, and she went to get him a flask of water or a hunk of bread, and when she came back empty-handed, in the thick of the firing, her lover, devoured by hunger and by thirst, beat her. At last, one night when the moon was shining on the cactus grove, Gramigna said to her: "They are coming!" and he made her lie down flat, at the bottom of the cleft in the rock, and then he fled to another place. Among the cactus clumps continual firing was heard, and the darkness flushed here and there with brief flames. All at once Peppa heard a noise of feet near her and she looked up to see Gramigna returning, dragging a broken leg, and leaning against the broad stems of the cactus to load his gun. "It's all up!" he said to her. "They'll get me now"—and what froze her blood more than anything was the glitter in his eyes that made him look like a madman. Then when he fell on the dry branches like a bundle of wood, the militiamen were on him in a heap.

Next day they dragged him through the streets of the village on a cart, all torn and blood-stained. The people who pressed forward to see him began to laugh when they saw how little he was, pale and ugly like a figure in a Punch-and-Judy show. And it was for him that Peppa had left Neighbour Finu, the "Tallow-candle"! Poor Tallow-candle, he went and hid himself as if the shame was his, and Peppa was led away between the soldiers, handcuffed, as if she were another robber, she who had as much gold as Saint Margaret herself. Peppa's poor old mother had to sell "all the white goods," of the trousseau, and the golden ear-rings, and the rings for the ten fingers, to pay the lawyers to get off her child; then she had to take her back into the house, poor, sick, disgraced, and herself as ugly now as Gramigna, and with Gramigna's child at her breast. But when they gave her back her daughter, at the end of the trial, the poor old woman repeated her *Ave Maria*, there in the darkening twilight of the naked barracks, among all the carabiniers, and it was as if they had given her a treasure, poor old thing, for this was all she had, and she wept like a fountain with relief. Peppa, on the contrary, seemed as if she had no more tears, and she said nothing, nor was she ever seen in the village, in spite of the fact that the two women had to go and earn their bread labouring. People said that Peppa had learned her trade out in the thickets, and that she went stealing at night. The truth was, she stayed lurking shut up in the kitchen like a wild beast, and she only came forth when her old woman was dead, worn out with hard work, and the house had to be sold.

"You see!" said Tallow-candle, who still cared for her. "I could knock my head against the stones when I think of all the misery you've brought on yourself and on everybody else."

"It's true," replied Peppa. "I know it! It was the will of God."

After she had sold the house and the few bits of furniture that remained to her, she left the village, in the night, as she had returned to it, without once turning back to look at the roof, under which she had slept for so many years; she went to fulfil the will of God in the city, along with her boy, settling near the prison where Gramigna was shut up. She could see nothing but the iron gratings of the windows, on the great mute façade, and the sentinels drove her off, if she stood to gaze searchingly for some sign of him. At last they told her he'd been gone from there for some time, that they'd taken him away over the sea, handcuffed and with the basket round his neck. She didn't say anything. She didn't change her quarters, because she didn't know where to go, and had nobody to go to. She eked out a living doing small jobs for the soldiers and the keepers of the prison, as if she too had been a part of that great, gloomy, silent building; and then she felt for the carabiniers who had taken

Gramigna from her, in the cactus thicket, and who had broken his leg with a bullet, a sort of respectful tenderness, a sort of brute admiration of brute force. On feast days, when she saw them with their scarlet tuft of feathers sticking up in front of their hats, and with glittering epaulettes, all standing erect and square in their dress uniforms of dark-blue with the scarlet stripes, she devoured them with her eyes, and she was always about the barracks, sweeping out the big general rooms, and polishing boots, till they called her "the carabinier's shoe-rag." Only when she saw them fasten on their weapons after nightfall, and set off two by two, their trousers turned up, the revolver at their stomach; or when they mounted on horseback, under the street-lamp that made their rifles glitter, and she heard the tread of horses lose itself in the distance, and the clink of sabres; then every time she turned pale, and as she shut the stable door she shuddered; and when her youngster was playing about with the other urchins on the level ground in front of the prison, running between the legs of the soldiers, and the other brats shouted after him: "Gramigna's kid! Gramigna's kid!" she got in a rage, and ran after them, throwing stones at them.

DISCUSSION

This story is in the form of a letter to a friend of Verga. It is very short, presumably because Verga sensed that his friend would seize on the "middle" that he says is missing—and he says, in fact, that presumably such an act of participatory imagination will eventually be "enough for everybody"—that is, when they have learned to sense the inner motivations and feelings of fiction and not to depend on mere explanation or intrusion by the author.[3]

In other words, Verga seeks to involve the reader's own creative power in the story itself.

To return to the story: we use it here as an introduction because it is, superficially at least, a story emphasizing action, violent physical action—the massive hunt across the parched countryside of Sicily for the outlaw Gramigna. This is the story that day by day unfolds as it is told "in the villages, in the farmsteads, under the bough-shelter of the inns, in the clubs and meeting-places." But to Gramigna's tale of outlawry is grafted the tale of another kind of "outlawry." The beautiful young Peppa, engaged to the pride of the village, Finu, who is both prosperous and "handsome as the sun," announces that she is in love not with Finu but with the outlaw Gramigna, who is being hunted day and night, and whom she has never seen. Finally, when word comes that he has been surrounded and wounded and is cut off from water, she flees to him, to be received not gratefully but gruffly, and in the end to be wounded, left pregnant, and outcast, when Gramigna is taken and jailed, eventually to be sent off to a prison.

[3]The whole question of *realism* and *imagination* (see Glossary) is suggested here, as is the relation of the author to his material.

There is action enough here, certainly, but there is a mystery in the story beyond the action, the mystery that the author leaves in the untold "middle" of the story. What kind of "outlawry" draws Peppa to seek the hunted Gramigna? What is the nature of the "love" that makes her forfeit respectability, comfort, prosperity, Finu's true adoration for her, all for an outlaw she has never seen—and who, as far as we ever know, cares nothing for her? What makes her remain, through isolation and poverty, faithful to the end, in her strange way, to her outlaw, as she throws stones at the brats who tease her son, shouting at him, "Gramigna's kid"?

So the story of action is a story of character and psychology after all, and a story of theme, leaving us to ponder a mysterious question about the nature of love, a question involving the relation of love to ease and risk, to receiving and giving.

But can we sort out these elements of action, character, and theme as distinct elements in the story? No, they are all aspects of the same massive event. They are part of a vital unity.

1. Clearly, most young girls would not act as Peppa does. They would settle down happily with Finu and village conventionality. What does Peppa expect from love that is different? How do you assess the value of her expectations?

2. What are we to make of the relation of Peppa and Gramigna? What are we to make of their first encounter? Later on, she is to have a child by him, yet in any sense can we assume that he "loves" her?

3. If you were to write the story on a larger scale, what would you put into the mysterious and missing "middle"? What do you now make of Peppa's basic attitude at the end? Is it one of regret, bitterness, acceptance of fate, a change of values?

THE SECRET LIFE OF WALTER MITTY

James Thurber

"WE'RE going through!" The Commander's voice was like thin ice breaking. He wore his full-dress uniform, with the heavily braided white cap pulled down rakishly over one cold gray eye. "We can't make it, sir. It's spoiling for a hurricane, if you ask me." "I'm not asking you, Lieutenant Berg," said the Commander. "Throw on the power lights! Rev her up to 8,500! We're going through!" The pounding of the cylinders increased; ta-pocketa-pocketa-pocketa-*pocketa-pocketa*. The Commander stared at the ice forming on the pilot window. He walked over and twisted a row of complicated dials. "Switch on No. 8 auxiliary!" he shouted. "Switch on No. 8 auxiliary!" repeated Lieutenant Berg. "Full strength in No. 3 turret!" shouted the Commander. "Full strength in No. 3 turret!" The crew, bending to their various tasks in the huge, hurtling eight-engined Navy hydroplane, looked at each other and grinned. "The Old Man'll get us through," they said to one another. "The Old Man ain't afraid of Hell!" . . .

"Not so fast! You're driving too fast!" said Mrs. Mitty. "What are you driving so fast for?"

"Hmm?" said Walter Mitty. He looked at his wife, in the seat beside him, with shocked astonishment. She seemed grossly unfamiliar, like a strange woman who had yelled at him in a crowd. "You were up to fifty-five," she said. "You know I don't like to go more than forty. You were up to fifty-five." Walter Mitty drove on toward Waterbury in silence, the roaring of the SN202 through the worst storm in twenty years of Navy flying fading in the remote, intimate airways of his mind. "You're tensed up again," said Mrs. Mitty. "It's one of your days. I wish you'd let Dr. Renshaw look you over."

Walter Mitty stopped the car in front of the building where his wife went to have her hair done. "Remember to get those overshoes while I'm having my hair done," she said. "I don't need overshoes," said Mitty. She put her mirror back into her bag. "We've been all through that," she said, getting out of the car. "You're not a young man any longer." He raced the engine a little. "Why don't you wear your gloves? Have you lost your gloves?" Walter Mitty reached in a pocket and brought out the gloves. He put them on, but after she had turned and gone into the building and he had driven on to a red light, he took them off again. "Pick it up brother!" snapped a cop as the light changed, and Mitty hastily pulled on his gloves and lurched ahead. He drove around the streets aimlessly for a time, and then he drove past the hospital on his way to the parking lot.

. . . "It's the millionaire banker. Wellington McMillan," said the pretty nurse. "Yes?" said Walter Mitty, removing his gloves slowly. "Who has the case?" "Dr. Renshaw and Dr. Benbow, but there are two specialists here, Dr. Remington from New York and Dr. Pritchard-Mitford from London. He flew over." A door opened down a long, cool corridor and Dr. Renshaw came out. He looked distraught and haggard. "Hello, Mitty," he said. "We're having the devil's own time with McMillan, the millionaire banker and close personal friend of Roosevelt. Obstreosis of the ductal tract. Tertiary. Wish you'd take a look at him." "Glad to." said Mitty.

In the operating room there were whispered introductions: "Dr. Remington, Dr. Mitty. Dr. Pritchard-Mitford, Dr. Mitty." "I've read your book on streptothricosis," said Pritchard-Mitford, shaking hands. "A brilliant performance, sir." "Thank you," said Walter Mitty. "Didn't know you were in the States, Mitty," grumbled Remington. "Coals to Newcastle, bringing Mitford and me up here for a tertiary." "You are very kind," said Mitty. A huge, complicated machine, connected to the operating table, with many tubes and wires, began at this moment to go pocketa-pocketa-pocketa. "The new anaesthetizer is giving way!" shouted an interne. "There is no one in the East who knows how to fix it!" "Quiet, man!" said Mitty, in a low, cool voice. He sprang to the machine, which was now going pocketa-pocketa-queep-pocketa-queep. He began fingering delicately a row of glistening dials. "Give me a fountain pen!" he snapped. Someone handed him a fountain pen. He pulled a faulty piston out of the machine and inserted the pen in its place. "That will hold for ten minutes," he said. "Get on with the operation." A nurse hurried over and whispered to Renshaw, and Mitty saw the man turn pale. "Coreopsis has set in," said Renshaw nervously. "If you would take over, Mitty?" Mitty looked at him and at the craven figure of Benbow, who drank, and at the grave, uncertain faces of the two great specialists. "If you wish," he said. They slipped a white gown on him; he adjusted a mask and drew on thin gloves; nurses handed him shining . . .

"Back it up, Mac! Look out for that Buick!" Walter Mitty jammed on the brakes. "Wrong lane, Mac," said the parking-lot attendant, looking at Mitty closely. "Gee. Yeh," muttered Mitty. He began cautiously to back out of the lane marked "Exit Only." "Leave her sit there," said the attendant. "I'll put her away." Mitty got out of the car. "Hey, better leave the key." "Oh," said Mitty, handing the man the ignition key. The attendant vaulted into the car, backed it up with insolent skill, and put it where it belonged.

They're so damn cocky, thought Walter Mitty, walking along Main Street; they think they know everything. Once he had tried to take his chains off, outside New Milford, and he had got them wound around the axles. A man had had to come out in a wrecking car and unwind them, a young grinning garage man. Since then Mrs. Mitty always made him drive to a garage to have the chains taken off. The next time, he thought, I'll wear my right arm in a sling; they won't grin at me then. I'll have my right arm in a sling and they'll see I couldn't possibly take the chains off myself. He kicked at the slush on the sidewalk. "Overshoes," he said to himself, and he began looking for a shoe store.

When he came out into the street again, with the overshoes in a box under his arm, Walter Mitty began to wonder what the other thing was his wife had told him to get. She had told him, twice before they set out from their house for Waterbury. In a way he hated these weekly trips to town—he was always getting something wrong. Kleenex, he thought, Squibb's, razor blades? No. Toothpaste, toothbrush, bicarbonate, carborundum, initiative, and referendum? He gave it up. But she should remember it. "Where's the what's-its-name?" she would ask. "Don't tell me you forgot the what's-its-name." A newsboy went by shouting something about the Waterbury trial.

. . . "Perhaps this will refresh your memory." The District Attorney suddenly thrust a heavy automatic at the quiet figure on the witness stand. "Have you ever seen this before?" Walter Mitty took the gun and examined it expertly. "This is my Webley-Vickers 50.80," he said calmly. An excited buzz ran around the courtroom. The judge rapped for order. "You are a crack shot with any sort of firearms, I believe?" said the District Attorney, insinuatingly. "Objection!" shouted Mitty's attorney. "We have shown that the defendant could not have fired the shot. We have shown that he wore his right arm in a sling on the night of the fourteenth of July." Walter Mitty raised his hand briefly and the bickering attorneys were stilled. "With any known make of gun," he said evenly, "I could have killed Gregory Fitzhurst at three hundred feet *with my left hand*." Pandemonium broke loose in the courtroom. A woman's scream rose above the bedlam and suddenly a lovely, dark-haired girl was in Walter Mitty's arms. The District Attorney struck at her savagely. Without rising from his chair, Mitty let the man have it on the point of the chin. "You miserable cur!" . . .

"Puppy biscuit," said Walter Mitty. He stopped walking and the buildings of Waterbury rose up out of the misty courtroom and surrounded him again. A woman who was passing laughed. "He said 'Puppy biscuit'" she said to her companion. "That man said 'Puppy biscuit' to himself." Walter Mitty hurried on. He went into an A. & P., not the first one he came to but a smaller one farther up the street. "I want some biscuit for small, young dogs," he said to the clerk. "Any special brand, sir?" The greatest pistol shot in the world thought a moment. "It says 'Puppies Bark for It' on the box," said Walter Mitty.

His wife would be through at the hairdresser's in fifteen minutes, Mitty saw in looking at his watch, unless they had trouble drying it; sometimes they had trouble drying it. She didn't like to get to the hotel first; she would want him to be there waiting for her as usual. He found a big leather chair in the lobby, facing a window, and he put the overshoes and the puppy biscuit on the floor beside it. He picked up an old copy of *Liberty* and sank down into the chair. "Can Germany Conquer the World through the Air?" Walter Mitty looked at the pictures of bombing planes and of ruined streets.

. . . "The cannonading has got the wind up in young Raleigh, sir," said the sergeant. Captain Mitty looked up at him through tousled hair. "Get him to bed," he said wearily, "with the others. I'll fly alone." "But you can't, sir," said the sergeant anxiously. "It takes two men to handle that bomber and the Archies are pounding hell out of the air. Von Richtman's circus is between here and Saulier." "Somebody's got to get that ammunition dump," said Mitty. "I'm going over. Spot of brandy?" He poured a drink for the sergeant and one for himself. War thundered and whined around the dugout and battered at the door. There was a rending of wood and splinters flew through the room. "A bit of a near thing," said Captain Mitty carelessly. "The box barrage is closing in," said the sergeant. "We only live once, sergeant," said Mitty, with his faint, fleeting smile. "Or do we?" He poured another brandy and tossed it off. "I never see a man could hold his brandy like you, sir," said the sergeant. "Begging your pardon, sir." Captain Mitty stood up and strapped on his huge Webley-Vickers automatic. "It's forty kilometers through hell, sir," said the sergeant. Mitty finished one last brandy. "After all," he said softly, "what isn't?" The pounding of the cannon increased; there was the rat-tat-tatting of machine guns, and from somewhere came the menacing pocketa-pocketa-pocketa of the new flame-throwers. Walter Mitty walked to the door of the dugout humming *"Auprès de Ma Blonde."* He turned and waved to the sergeant. "Cheerio!" he said. . . .

Something struck his shoulder. "I've been looking all over this hotel for you," said Mrs. Mitty. "Why do you have to hide in this old chair? How did you expect me to find you?" "Things close in," said Walter Mitty vaguely. "What?" Mrs. Mitty said. "Did you get the what's-its-name? The puppy biscuit? What's in that box?" "Overshoes," said Mitty. "Couldn't you have put them on in the store?" "I was thinking," said Walter Mitty. "Does it ever occur to you that I am sometimes thinking?" She looked at him. "I'm going to take your temperature when I get you home," she said.

They went out through the revolving doors that made a faintly derisive whistling sound when you pushed them. It was two blocks to the parking lot. At the drugstore on the corner she said, "Wait here for me. I forgot something. I won't be a minute." She was more than a minute. Walter Mitty lighted a cigarette. It began to rain, rain with sleet in it. He stood up against the wall of the drugstore, smoking. . . . He put his shoulders back and his heels together. "To hell with the handkerchief," said Walter Mitty scornfully. He took one last drag on his cigarette and snapped it away. Then, with that faint, fleeting smile playing about his lips, he faced the firing squad; erect and motionless, proud and disdainful, Walter Mitty the Undefeated, inscrutable to the last.

DISCUSSION

This story may seem to be merely another character sketch, and not fiction at all. True, certain things do happen here, but are the happenings meaningful? Mr. Mitty, a suburbanite, drives his wife into the center for some shopping. After having been reproved for driving too fast, he lets her out at the hairdresser's and leaves his car at the parking lot. He buys a pair of overshoes and a box of dog biscuit, then goes to the lobby of the hotel where his wife is to meet him. On their way back to the parking lot, his wife remembers something that she needs to buy in the drugstore and the story ends as Mr. Mitty waits for her outside. If we call this the "action" of the story, then indeed precious little happens. And if we go on to say that Mr. Mitty's daydreaming, which actually makes up most of the story, is not really connected with the action at all, being a direct expression of character, then the case for denying that the story is fiction becomes rather grave. It looks as if the very sketchy "plot" is simply a convenient rack on which to hang the various manifestations of Mr. Mitty's interior life. Looking at the story in this way, we may be tempted to deny that Thurber's story constitutes that revelation of character *through* action that we have said is essential to fiction.

There is a sense, of course, in which the foregoing account of the story is true: the whole narrative *is* constructed to reveal the character of the man, and aside from that revelation, very little does happen. Yet, it will not be difficult to show that it is a genuine piece of fiction after all.

In the first place, the author never once makes a direct comment upon Walter Mitty's character. We have no difficulty, it is true, in deducing what kind of figure Mitty cuts in the eyes of the parking-lot attendant or of the woman who passes him as he mutters "puppy biscuit." But the author never tells us in his own person what we are to think. He is really quite objective in his report of what happens. We learn what people think of Walter Mitty through the actions and comments of those people—not through any summary made by the author.

In the second place, when it comes to a matter of the way in which Mitty sees himself, that too is mediated through "action." We see Mitty at his business of daydreaming. We see how Mrs. Mitty's mention of the family physician, Dr. Renshaw, sends Mitty into a fantasy in which he becomes the medical hero in the operating room of a great hospital, or how his withering retort to the district attorney, "You miserable cur"—itself a part of one of his daydreams—suddenly reminds him that it is puppy biscuit that he is to remember to purchase.

Most important of all, however, the "action," trivial though it is, gives point and meaning to Mitty's daydreams. It indicates the motivation for these fantasies by revealing Mitty's need to escape from the world in which he lives. It is a world in which his own role is that of the husband henpecked by an overbearing and unimaginative wife who evidently long ago effactually suppressed Mr. Mitty's yearnings for the heroic and venturesome. The "action" in this little story effectively dramatizes this relationship, and though the events in question are in themselves commonplace—Mitty's driving at 55 miles an hour or Mitty's protest at wearing overshoes—they illuminate the very core of Mitty's life.

What attitude are we to take toward Walter Mitty? The situation portrayed is in essence that of the henpecked husband of the comic strips. Yet the effect aimed at here is not so blatant as that of a comic strip. Walter Mitty, though his daydreams embody the stalest of clichès of adventure fiction and the movies, is not made farcically grotesque. He is allowed a certain kind of pathos, even though his creator is obviously amused by his ineffectuality. Are we to take him rather seriously, then, and see in his plight the imprisonment of a high-hearted soul condemned to frustration? Scarcely that, either. The nature of the daydreams and the way that they are grotesquely piled up one upon another effectually prevent our taking the plight of Walter Mitty really seriously. But the reader will need no special help in deciding how to "take" this story. Here again the "action" of the story serves to suggest the proper blend of sympathy and amusement with which we are to view Mr. Mitty. Far from telling us what to feel, the author gives us a dramatic presentation of a few hours of Mr. Mitty's life and leaves it up to us to make our own inferences.

Instead of asking what attitude we should take toward Walter Mitty, we might put this question by asking what the *tone* (see Glossary) of the story is. The tone is the reflection in the makeup of the story of the author's attitudes—toward his material and toward his reader. The tone of a story may be characterized as grave or gay, reserved or ebullient, straightforward or mocking, merry or melancholy, solemn, playful, prim, sentimental—and one might continue through a hundred other adjectives. Actually, however, the tone of most stories will usually be too special and too complicated to be adequately described by any one adjective. The tone of Thurber's story, for example, is one of amused playfulness, but we have seen that it has nothing of scorn in it and that it even allows for a trace of pathos.

Tone as a term used to characterize style derives from "tone of the voice." The tone in which a thing is uttered modifies what is said and may even reverse the meaning. "He's a fine fellow," delivered in a sarcastic tone, means that the speaker does not think that the person in question is a fine fellow at all. In our spoken language, we are constantly giving exact qualifications to what our words literally say by the tone in which we say them. The literary artist usually cannot read us his work aloud; yet if he is an artist, he can control very powerfully and exactly the way we are to "take" what he puts on the page. In the stories that follow, the problem of tone is frequently a matter of primary importance. We shall often have to ask what the tone of a passage or of a whole story is. (If we are thinking primarily not of the story but of the author we may prefer to transpose our question from the tone of the story to the attitude of the author.)

1. In its distortion, the portrait of Walter Mitty may be regarded as a kind of caricature. In this instance is the distortion, like that employed by a good cartoonist, justified? Does it, even through distortion or exaggeration, make a convincing reference to actuality?

2. May the last sentence of the story be said to be an appropriate conclusion? Literally, of course, this sentence refers to the pose Mitty assumes in the particular fantasy in which he is absorbed, but can it be said to apply at another level? Is there a sense in which Walter Mitty is indeed "the Undefeated, inscrutable to the last"? and inscrutable to whom?

3. Consider the function of the following items in making for the humorous effect: Mitty's fondness for the syllables "pocketa-pocketa" as expressive of certain sounds; the *alliteration* (see Glossary) involved in such phrases as "sir, said the sergeant"; the use, in the parts of the story that recount Mitty's various fantasies, of *clichès* (see Glossary) drawn from thriller stories.

YOUNG GOODMAN BROWN

Nathaniel Hawthorne

YOUNG Goodman Brown[1] came forth at sunset into the street at Salem village; but put his head back, after crossing the threshold, to exchange a parting kiss with his young wife. And Faith, as the wife was aptly named, thrust her own pretty head into the street, letting the wind play with the pink ribbons of her cap while she called to Goodman Brown.

"Dearest heart," whispered she, softly and rather sadly, when her lips were close to his ear, "prithee put off your journey until sunrise and sleep in your own bed to-night. A lone woman is troubled with such dreams and such thoughts that she's afeard of herself sometimes. Pray tarry with me this night, dear husband, of all nights in the year."

"My love and my Faith," replied young Goodman Brown, "of all nights in the year, this one night must I tarry away from thee. My jour-

---

[1]The term "Goodman" was used of a respectable and prosperous citizen without reference to blood.

ney, as thou callest it, forth and back again, must needs be done 'twixt now and sunrise. What, my sweet, pretty wife, dost thou doubt me already, and we but three months married?"

"Then God bless you!" said Faith, with the pink ribbons; "and may you find all well when you come back."

"Amen!" cried Goodman Brown. "Say thy prayers, dear Faith, and go to bed at dusk, and no harm will come to thee."

So they parted; and the young man pursued his way until, being about to turn the corner by the meeting-house, he looked back and saw the head of Faith still peeping after him with a melancholy air, in spite of her pink ribbons.

"Poor little Faith!" thought he, for his heart smote him. "What a wretch am I to leave her on such an errand! She talks of dreams, too. Methought as she spoke there was trouble in her face, as if a dream had warned her what work is to be done to-night. But no, no; 't would kill her to think it. Well, she's a blessed angel on earth; and after this one night I'll cling to her skirts and follow her to heaven."

With this excellent resolve for the future, Goodman Brown felt himself justified in making more haste on his present evil purpose. He had taken a dreary road, darkened by all the gloomiest trees of the forest, which barely stood aside to let the narrow path creep through, and closed immediately behind. It was all as lonely as could be; and there is this peculiarity in such a solitude, that the traveler knows not who may be concealed by the innumerable trunks and the thick boughs overhead; so that with lonely footsteps he may yet be passing through an unseen multitude.

"There may be a devilish Indian behind every tree," said Goodman Brown to himself; and he glanced fearfully behind him as he added, "What if the devil himself should be at my very elbow!"

His head being turned back, he passed a crook of the road, and, looking forward again, beheld the figure of a man, in grave and decent attire, seated at the foot of an old tree. He arose at Goodman Brown's approach and walked onward side by side with him.

"You are late, Goodman Brown," said he. "The clock of the Old South was striking as I came through Boston, and that is full fifteen minutes agone."

"Faith kept me back a while," replied the young man, with a tremor in his voice, caused by the sudden appearance of his companion, though not wholly unexpected.

It was now deep dusk in the forest, and deepest in that part of it where these two were journeying. As nearly as could be discerned, the second traveler was about fifty years old, apparently in the same rank of life as Goodman Brown, and bearing a considerable resemblance to him, though perhaps more in expression than features. Still they might have been taken for father and son. And yet, though the elder person was as simply clad as the younger, and as simple in manner too, he had an indescribable air of one who knew the world, and who would not have felt abashed at the governor's dinner table or in King William's court, were it possible that his affairs should call him thither. But the only thing about him that could be fixed upon as remarkable was his staff, which bore the likeness of a great black snake, so curiously wrought that it might almost be seen to twist and wriggle itself like a living serpent. This, of course, must have been an ocular deception, assisted by the uncertain light.

"Come, Goodman Brown," cried his fellow-traveler, "this is a dull place for the beginning of a journey. Take my staff, if you are so soon weary."

"Friend," said the other, exchanging his slow pace for a full stop, "having kept covenant by meeting thee here, it is my purpose now to return whence I came. I have scruples touching the matter thou wot'st of."

"Sayest thou so?" replied he of the serpent, smiling apart. "Let us walk on, nevertheless, reasoning as we go; and if I convince thee not thou shalt turn back. We are but a little way in the forest yet."

"Too far! too far!" exclaimed the goodman, unconsciously resuming his walk. "My father never went into the woods on such an errand, nor his father before him. We have been a race of honest men and good Christians since the days of the martyrs; and shall I be the first of the name of Brown that ever took his path and kept"—

"Such company, thou wouldst say," observed the elder person, interpreting his pause. "Well said, Goodman Brown! I have been as well acquainted with your family as with ever a one among the Puritans; and that's no trifle to say. I helped your grandfather, the constable, when he lashed the Quaker woman so smartly through the streets of Salem; and it was I that brought your father a pitch-pine knot, kindled at my own hearth, to set fire to an Indian village, in King Philip's war.[2] They were my good friends, both; and many a pleasant walk have we had along this path, and returned merrily after midnight. I would fain be friends with you for their sake."

"If it be as thou sayest," replied Goodman Brown, "I marvel they never spoke of these matters; or, verily, I marvel not, seeing that the least rumor of the sort would have driven them from New England. We are a people of prayer, and good works to boot, and abide no such wickedness."

"Wickedness or not," said the traveler with the twisted staff, "I have a very general acquaintance here in New England. The deacons of many a church have drunk the communion wine with me; the selectmen of divers towns make me their chairman; and a majority of the Great and General Court are firm supporters of my interest. The governor and I, too—But these are state secrets."

"Can this be so?" cried Goodman Brown, with a stare of amazement at his undisturbed companion. "Howbeit, I have nothing to do with the governor and council; they have their own ways, and are no rule for a simple husbandman like me. But, were I to go on with thee, how should I meet the eye of that good old man, our minister, at Salem village? Oh, his voice would make me tremble both Sabbath day and lecture day."

Thus far the elder traveler had listened with due gravity; but now

[2]King Philip, chief of the Wampanoog Indians, alarmed by the expansion of Puritan colonies, set out, in 1675, to massacre the intruders. After much pitiless violence on both sides, Philip was defeated and hunted down and killed.

burst into a fit of irrepressible mirth, shaking himself so violently that his snake-like staff actually seemed to wriggle in sympathy.

"Ha! ha! ha!" shouted he again and again; then composing himself, "Well, go on, Goodman Brown, go on; but, prithee, don't kill me with laughing."

"Well, then, to end the matter at once," said Goodman Brown, considerably nettled, "there is my wife, Faith. It would break her dear little heart; and I'd rather break my own."

"Nay, if that be the case," answered the other, "e'en go thy ways, Goodman Brown. I would not for twenty old women like the one hobbling before us that Faith should come to any harm."

As he spoke he pointed his staff at a female figure on the path, in whom Goodman Brown recognized a very pious and exemplary dame, who had taught him his catechism in youth, and was still his moral and spiritual adviser, jointly with the minister and Deacon Gookin.

"A marvel, truly, that Goody Cloyse[3] should be so far in the wilderness at nightfall," said he. "But with your leave, friend, I shall take a cut through the woods until we have left this Christian woman behind. Being a stranger to you, she might ask whom I was consorting with and whither I was going."

"Be it so," said his fellow-traveler. "Betake you the woods, and let me keep the path."

Accordingly the young man turned aside, but took care to watch his companion, who advanced softly along the road until he had come within a staff's length of the old dame. She, meanwhile, was making the best of her way, with singular speed for so aged a woman, and mumbling some indistinct words—a prayer doubtless—as she went. The traveler put forth his staff and touched her withered neck with what seemed the serpent's tail.

"The devil!" screamed the pious old lady.

"Then Goodly Cloyse knows her old friend?" observed the traveler, confronting her and leaning on his writhing stick.

"Ah, forsooth, and is it your worship indeed?" cried the good dame. "Yea, truly it is, and in the very image of my old gossip, Goodman Brown, the grandfather of the silly fellow that now is. But—would your worship believe it?—my broomstick hath strangely disappeared, stolen, as I suspect, by that unhanged witch, Goody Cory, and that, too, when I was all anointed with the juice of smallage, and cinquefoil, and wolf's bane"—

"Mingled with fine wheat and the fat of a new-born babe," said the shape of old Goodman Brown.

"Ah, your worship knows the recipe," cried the old lady, cackling aloud. "So, as I was saying, being all ready for the meeting, and no horse to ride on, I made up my mind to foot it; for they tell me there is a nice young man to be taken into communion to-night. But now your good worship will lend me your arm, and we shall be there in a twinkling."

---

[3]Cloyse, like Carrier, who appears later in the story, was condemned for witchcraft in 1692. One of Hawthorne's ancestors was of the court that gave the death sentence.

"That can hardly be," answered her friend. "I may not spare you my arm, Goody Cloyse; but here is my staff, if you will."

So saying, he threw it down at her feet, where, perhaps, it assumed life, being one of the rods which its owner had formerly lent to the Egyptian magi.[4] Of this fact, however, Goodman Brown could not take cognizance. He had cast up his eyes in astonishment, and, looking down again, beheld neither Goody Cloyse nor the serpentine staff, but this fellow-traveler alone, who waited for him as calmly as if nothing had happened.

"That old woman taught me my catechism," said the young man; and there was a world of meaning in this simple comment.

They continued to walk onward, while the elder traveler exhorted his companion to make good speed and persevere in the path, discoursing so aptly that his arguments seemed rather to spring up in the bosom of his auditor than to be suggested by himself. As they went, he plucked a branch of maple to serve for a walking stick, and began to strip it of the twigs and little boughs, which were wet with evening dew. The moment his fingers touched them they became strangely withered and dried up as with a week's sunshine. Thus the pair proceeded, at a good free pace, until suddenly, in a gloomy hollow of the road, Goodman Brown sat himself down on the stump of a tree and refused to go any farther.

"Friend," said he, stubbornly, "my mind is made up. Not another step will I budge on this errand. What if a wretched old woman do choose to go to the devil when I thought she was going to heaven: is that any reason why I should quit my dear Faith and go after her?"

"You will think better of this by and by," said his acquaintance, composedly. "Sit here and rest yourself a while; and when you feel like moving again, there is my staff to help you along."

Without more words, he threw his companion the maple stick, and was as speedily out of sight as if he had vanished into the deepening gloom. The young man sat a few moments by the roadside, applauding himself greatly, and thinking with how clear a conscience he should meet the minister in his morning walk, nor shrink from the eye of good old Deacon Gookin. And what calm sleep would be his that very night, which was to have been spent so wickedly, but so purely and sweetly now, in the arms of Faith! Amidst these pleasant and praiseworthy meditations, Goodman Brown heard the tramp of horses along the road, and deemed it advisable to conceal himself within the verge of the forest, conscious of the guilty purpose that had brought him thither, though now so happily turned from it.

On came the hoof tramps and the voices of the riders, two grave old voices, conversing soberly as they drew near. These mingled sounds appeared to pass along the road, within a few yards of the young man's hiding-place; but, owing doubtless to the depth of the gloom at that particular spot, neither the travelers nor their steeds were visible. Though their figures brushed the small boughs by the wayside, it could not be

---

[4]When the staff of Aaron, brother to Moses, was cast before Pharaoh, it turned into a serpent. At this the magi of Pharaoh cast down their staves (which had been provided according to Hawthorne's story by Satan), which showed the same miraculous power. See Exodus 7.

seen that they intercepted, even for a moment, the faint gleam from the strip of bright sky athwart which they must have passed. Goodman Brown alternately crouched and stood on tiptoe, pulling aside the branches and thrusting forth his head as far as he durst without discerning so much as a shadow. It vexed him the more, because he could have sworn, were such a thing possible, that he recognized the voices of the minister and Deacon Gookin, jogging along quietly, as they were wont to do, when bound to some ordination or ecclesiastical council. While yet within hearing, one of the riders stopped to pluck a switch.

"Of the two, reverend sir," said the voice like the deacon's, "I had rather miss an ordination dinner than to-night's meeting. They tell me that some of our community are to be here from Falmouth and beyond, and others from Connecticut and Rhode Island, besides several of the Indian powwows, who, after their fashion, know almost as much deviltry as the best of us. Moreover, there is a goodly young woman to be taken into communion."

"Mighty well, Deacon Gookin!" replied the solemn old tones of the minister. "Spur up, or we shall be late. Nothing can be done, you know, until I get on the ground."

The hoofs clattered again; and the voices, talking so strangely in the empty air, passed on through the forest, where no church had ever been gathered or solitary Christian prayed. Whither, then, could these holy men be journeying so deep into the heathen wilderness? Young Goodman Brown caught hold of a tree for support, being ready to sink down on the ground, faint and overburdened with the heavy sickness of his heart. He looked up to the sky, doubting whether there really was a heaven above him. Yet there was the blue arch, and the stars brightening in it.

"With heaven above and Faith below, I will yet stand firm against the devil!" cried Goodman Brown.

While he still gazed upward into the deep arch of the firmament and had lifted his hands to pray, a cloud, though no wind was stirring, hurried across the zenith and hid the brightening stars. The blue sky was still visible, except directly overhead, where this black mass of cloud was sweeping swiftly northward. Aloft in the air, as if from the depths of the cloud, came a confused and doubtful sound of voices. Once the listener fancied that he could distinguish the accents of towns-people of his own, men and women, both pious and ungodly, many of whom he had met at the communion table, and had seen others rioting at the tavern. The next moment, so indistinct were the sounds, he doubted whether he had heard aught but the murmer of the old forest, whispering without a wind. Then came a stronger swell of those familiar tones, heard daily in the sunshine at Salem village, but never until now from a cloud of night. There was one voice, of a young woman, uttering lamentations, yet with an uncertain sorrow, and entreating for some favor, which, perhaps, it would grieve her to obtain; and all the unseen multitude, both saints and sinners, seemed to encourage her onward.

"Faith!" shouted Goodman Brown, in a voice of agony and desperation; and the echoes of the forest mocked him, crying, "Faith! Faith!" as if bewildered wretches were seeking her all through the wilderness.

The cry of grief, rage, and terror was yet piercing the night, when the unhappy husband held his breath for a response. There was a scream, drowned immediately in a louder murmur of voices, fading into far-off laughter, as the dark cloud swept away, leaving the clear and silent sky above Goodman Brown. But something fluttered lightly down through the air and caught on the branch of a tree. The young man seized it, and beheld a pink ribbon.

"My Faith is gone!" cried he, after one stupefied moment. "There is no good on earth; and sin is but a name. Come, devil; for to thee is this world given."

And, maddened with despair, so that he laughed loud and long, did Goodman Brown grasp his staff and set forth again, at such a rate that he seemed to fly along the forest path rather than to walk or run. The road grew wilder and drearier and more faintly traced, and vanished at length, leaving him in the heart of the dark wilderness, still rushing onward with the instinct that guides mortal man to evil. The whole forest was peopled with frightful sounds—the creaking of the trees, the howling of wild beasts, and the yell of Indians; while sometimes the wind tolled like a distant church bell, and sometimes gave a broad roar around the traveler, as if all Nature were laughing him to scorn. But he was himself the chief horror of the scene, and shrank not from its other horrors.

"Ha! ha! ha!" roared Goodman Brown when the wind laughed at him. "Let us hear which will laugh loudest. Think not to frighten me with your deviltry. Come witch, come wizard, come Indian powwow, come devil himself, and here comes Goodman Brown. You may as well fear him as he fear you."

In truth, all through the haunted forest there could be nothing more frightful than the figure of Goodman Brown. On he flew among the black pines, brandishing his staff with frenzied gestures, now giving vent to an inspiration of horrid blasphemy, and now shouting forth such laughter as set all the echoes of the forest laughing like demons around him. The fiend in his own shape is less hideous than when he rages in the breast of man. Thus sped the demoniac on his course, until, quivering among the trees, he saw a red light before him, as when the felled trunks and branches of a clearing have been set on fire, and throw up their lurid blaze against the sky, at the hour of midnight. He paused, in a lull of the tempest that had driven him onward, and heard the swell of what seemed a hymn, rolling solemnly from a distance with the weight of many voices. He knew the tune; it was a familiar one in the choir of the village meeting-house. The verse died heavily away, and was lengthened by a chorus, not of human voices, but of all the sounds of the benighted wilderness pealing in awful harmony together. Goodman Brown cried out, and his cry was lost to his own ear by its unison with the cry of the desert.

In the interval of silence he stole forward until the light glared full upon his eyes. At one extremity of an open space, hemmed in by the dark wall of the forest, arose a rock, bearing some rude, natural resemblance either to an altar or a pulpit, and surrounded by four blazing pines, their tops aflame, their stems untouched, like candles at an evening meeting. The mass of foliage that had overgrown the summit of the rock was all on fire, blazing high into the night and fitfully illuminating the whole field. Each pendent twig and leafy festoon was in a blaze. As the red light arose and fell, a numerous congregation alternately shone forth, then disappeared in shadow, and again grew, as it were, out of the darkness, peopling the heart of the solitary woods at once.

"A grave and dark-clad company," quoth Goodman Brown.

In truth they were such. Among them, quivering to and fro between gloom and splendor, appeared faces that would be seen next day at the council board of the province, and others which, Sabbath after Sabbath, looked devoutly heavenward, and benignantly over the crowded pews, from the holiest pulpits in the land. Some affirm that the lady of the governor was there. At least there were high dames well known to her, and wives of honored husbands, and widows, a great multitude, and ancient maidens, all of excellent repute, and fair young girls, who trembled lest their mothers should espy them. Either the sudden gleams of light flashing over the obscure field bedazzled Goodman Brown, or he recognized a score of the church members of Salem village famous for their especial sanctity. Good old Deacon Gookin had arrived, and waited at the skirts of that venerable saint, his revered pastor. But, irreverently consorting with these grave, reputable, and pious people, these elders of the church, these chaste dames and dewy virgins, there were men of dissolute lives and women of spotted fame, wretches given over to all mean and filthy vice, and suspected even of horrid crimes. It was strange to see that the good shrank not from the wicked, nor were the sinners abashed by the saints. Scattered also among their pale-faced enemies were the Indian priests, or powwows, who had often scared their native forest with more hideous incantations than any known to English witchcraft.

"But where is Faith?" thought Goodman Brown; and, as hope came into his heart, he trembled.

Another verse of the hymn arose, a slow and mournful strain, such as the pious love, but joined to words which expressed all that our nature can conceive of sin, and darkly hinted at far more. Unfathomable to mere mortals is the lore of fiends. Verse after verse was sung; and still the chorus of the desert swelled between like the deepest tone of a mighty organ; and with the final peal of that dreadful anthem there came a sound, as if the roaring wind, the rushing streams, the howling beasts, and every other voice of the unconcerted wilderness were mingling and according with the voice of guilty man in homage to the prince of all. The four blazing pines threw up a loftier flame, and obscurely discovered shapes and visages of horror on the smoke wreaths above the impious assembly. At the same moment the fire on the rock shot redly forth and formed a glowing arch above its base, where now appeared a figure. With reverence be it spoken, the figure bore no slight similitude, both in garb and manner, to some grave divine of the New England churches.

"Bring forth the converts!" cried a voice that echoed through the field and rolled into the forest.

At the word, Goodman Brown stepped forth from the shadow of the trees and approached the congregation, with whom he felt a loathful brotherhood by the sympathy of all that was wicked in his heart. He could have well-nigh sworn that the shape of his own dead father beckoned him to advance, looking downward from a smoke wreath, while a woman, with dim features of despair, threw out her hand to warn him back. Was it his mother? But he had no power to retreat one step, nor to resist, even in thought, when the minister and good old Deacon Gookin seized his arms and led him to the blazing rock. Thither came also the slender form of a veiled female, led between Goody Cloyse, that pious teacher of the catechism, and Martha Carrier, who had received the devil's promise to be queen of hell. A rampant hag was she. And there stood the proselytes beneath the canopy of fire.

"Welcome, my children," said the dark figure, "to the communion of your race. Ye have found thus young your nature and your destiny. My children, look behind you!"

They turned; and flashing forth, as it were, in a sheet of flame, the fiend worshippers were seen; the smile of welcome gleamed darkly on every visage.

"There," resumed the sable form, "are all whom ye have reverenced from youth. Ye deemed them holier than yourselves, and shrank from your own sin, contrasting it with their lives of righteousness and prayerful aspirations heavenward. Yet here are they all in my worshipping assembly. This night it shall be granted you to know their secret deeds: how hoary-bearded elders of the church have whispered wanton words to the young maids of their households; how many a woman, eager for widows' weeds, has given her husband a drink at bedtime and let him sleep his last sleep in her bosom; how beardless youths have made haste to inherit their fathers' wealth; and how fair damsels—blush not, sweet ones—have dug little graves in the garden, and bidden me, the sole guest, to an infant's funeral. By the sympathy of your human hearts for sin ye shall scent out all the places—whether in church, bed-chamber, street, field, or forest—where crime has been committed, and shall exult to behold the whole earth one stain of guilt, one mighty blood spot. Far more than this. It shall be yours to penetrate, in every bosom, the deep mystery of sin, the fountain of all wicked arts, and which inexhaustibly supplies more evil impulses than human power—than my power at its utmost—can make manifest in deeds. And now, my children, look upon each other."

They did so; and, by the blaze of the hell-kindled torches, the wretched man beheld his Faith, and the wife her husband, trembling before that unhallowed altar.

"Lo, there ye stand, my children," said the figure, in a deep and solemn tone, almost sad with its despairing awfulness, as if his once angelic nature could yet mourn for our miserable race. "Depending upon one another's hearts, ye had still hoped that virtue were not all a dream. Now are ye undeceived. Evil is the nature of mankind. Evil must be your only happiness. Welcome again, my children, to the communion of your race."

"Welcome," repeated the fiend worshippers, in one cry of despair and triumph.

And there they stood, the only pair, as it seemed who were yet hesitating on the verge of wickedness in this dark world. A basin was hollowed, naturally, in the rock. Did it contain water, reddened by the lurid light? or was it blood? or, perchance, a liquid flame? Herein did the shape of evil dip his hand and prepare to lay the mark of baptism upon their foreheads, that they might be partakers of the mystery of sin, more conscious of the secret guilt of others, both in deed and thought, than they could now be of their own. The husband cast one look at his pale wife and Faith at him. What polluted wretches would the next glance show them to each other, shuddering alike at what they disclosed and what they saw!

"Faith! Faith!" cried the husband, "look up to heaven, and resist the wicked one."

Whether Faith obeyed he knew not. Hardly had he spoken when he found himself amid calm night and solitude, listening to a roar of the wind which died heavily away through the forest. He staggered against the rock, and felt it chill and damp; while a hanging twig, that had been all on fire, besprinkled his cheek with the coldest dew.

The next morning young Goodman Brown came slowly into the street of Salem village, staring around him like a bewildered man. The good old minister was taking a walk along the graveyard to get an appetite for breakfast and meditate his sermon, and bestowed a blessing, as he passed, on Goodman Brown. He shrank from the venerable saint as if to avoid an anathema. Old Deacon Gookin was at domestic worship, and the holy words of his prayer were heard through the open window. "What God doth the wizard pray to?" quoth Goodman Brown. Goody Cloyse, that excellent old Christian, stood in the early sunshine at her own lattice, catechizing a little girl who had brought her a pint of morning's milk. Goodman Brown snatched away the child as from the grasp of the fiend himself. Turning the corner by the meeting-house, he spied the head of Faith, with the pink ribbons, gazing anxiously forth, and bursting into such joy at sight of him that she skipped along the street and almost kissed her husband before the whole village. But Goodman Brown looked sternly and sadly into her face, and passed on without a greeting.

Had Goodman Brown fallen asleep in the forest and only dreamed a wild dream of a witch-meeting?

Be it so if you will; but, alas! it was a dream of evil omen for young Goodman Brown. A stern, a sad, a darkly meditative, a distrustful, if not a desperate man did he become from the night of that fearful dream. On the Sabbath day, when the congregation were singing a holy psalm, he could not listen because an anthem of sin rushed loudly upon his ear and drowned all the blessed strain. When the minister spoke from the pulpit with power and fervid eloquence, and, with his hand on the open Bible, of the sacred truths of our religion, and of saint-like lives and triumphant deaths, and of future bliss or misery unutterable, then did Goodman Brown turn pale, dreading lest the roof should thunder down upon the gray blasphemer and his hearers. Often, awaking suddenly at midnight, he shrank from the bosom of Faith; and at morning or eventide, when the family knelt down at prayer, he scowled and muttered to himself, and gazed sternly at his wife, and turned away. And when he had lived long, and was born to his grave a hoary corpse, followed by Faith, an aged woman, and children and grandchildren, a goodly procession, besides neighbors not a few, they carved no hopeful verse upon his tombstone, for his dying hour was gloom.

DISCUSSION

The setting of this story—Salem village in the very late seventeenth century—gives the reader a firm grounding in place and time. The element of witchcraft which seems so odd to the modern reader, was actually a firm belief of the period, and the witch trials (and the names of some of the victims) provide plausibility to the atmosphere of the story.[5]

But in contrast to such historical realism we are early given some hint of the fantastic beyond the beliefs of the period. It is odd, is it not, that Faith has been offered no excuse for her new husband's journey, which will leave her alone, he says, this "of all nights of the year"? And an equally fantastic suggestion has just been found in Faith's statement: "A lone woman is troubled with such dreams and such thoughts that she's afeard of herself sometimes. Pray, tarry with me this night, dear husband, of all nights in the year." What is so special about this night? Further, after the husband has left her, he thinks "Well, she's a blessed angel on earth; and after this one night, I'll cling to her skirts and follow her to heaven." Remembering the story "Gramigna's Lover," we reflect that Sicily, and the affair of Gramigna, may be far enough from our world, but they are strange in a very different way.

Clearly, we have left the realm of ordinary realism when young Goodman Brown enters the forest, which early Puritans thought to have been a haunt of natural and supernatural evil. Though they have been presented as a "real" forest and journey, we have hints that they have philosophical or psychological symbolism. When the real devil appears, that is strange enough, but when we realize his resemblance to Brown, and later to Brown's father, we find suggested a "communion" of evil in the blood—a communion that in the end turns out to be universal. The communion with young Goodman Brown is more intimate later, for the devil's arguments seemed rather to spring up in the bosom of the auditor than to be suggested by himself. Can it ever be said that, in a sense, the forest is the inwardness of young Goodman Brown, and that all takes place there?

The journey into the forest toward the great "initiation" into the evil

---

[5]Hawthorne, in the lonely years when he lived in an upper room in his widowed mother's house in Salem, during which he was preparing to be a writer, steeped himself, among other things, in the colonial history of New England. His own family connection with the witch trials has already been mentioned in a footnote.

"communion of the race" does have a growth of suspense, as does a story of action, but the suspense is directed at a philosophical point and not toward the resolution of an action. Even Goodman Brown's hesitation and hope of turning back is not, we sense, based on a woman named Faith, but on the other meaning of the word, on Faith as an allegorical figure. That "faith" enables him to let the minister and Deacon Gookin ride on.

For even though his resolution is weakened by the appearance of the minister and the deacon, he catches a glimpse of a patch of blue evening sky and stars, and cries out: "With heaven above and Faith below, I will stand firm against the devil!"

At this moment, however, a cloud sweeps over the blue and a sound of many voices bursts out, many familiar, among them the voice of a young woman uttering a lamentation, which Brown recognizes as that of Faith. Then he cries her name, and the forest echoes "as if bewildered wretches were seeking her all through the wilderness." This, of course, seems to imply that all in the communion of evil seek, after all, only faith. Meanwhile, Faith's pink ribbon has come fluttering down; and grasping it, Brown bursts into maniacal laughter and rushes through the forest toward the spot of fearful initiation. That is to say, the actual woman Faith may also be of the communion of evil—which has already been hinted at in her fear of dreams during her husband's absence.

There, after the blasphemous ritual, the proselytes are presented to the dark figure, who concludes his speech of welcome: "Depending upon one another's hearts, ye had still hoped that virtue was not all a dream. Now are ye undeceived. Evil is the nature of mankind. Welcome again, my children, to the communion of your race." At the climax, Faith is presented for the mark of baptism.

At the sight young Goodman Brown cries out for her to resist, but he cannot know the end, for suddenly he is alone, listening to the roar of wind disappearing into the forest. Next morning he has found his way back to the village, where all lead their lives as before, the virtuous and unvirtuous, those in truth and those in deception.

The story is left as a question. Had it been merely a dream? In any case, young Goodman Brown has lost his confidence in life. He continues to live with Faith, though without faith, and dies at a ripe age, with children and grandchildren, but with no sentiment of hope on his tomb. His life has been a meaningless charade.

What is the parable saying? At one level it asks, and does not answer, a fundamental question about human nature, a question that has been asked again and again throughout history. Is man naturally evil—as, for example, in the doctrine of Original Sin? Or is he naturally good, as has been held by various sects, but most notably by the French philosopher Rousseau? Or in one modern version, is virtue the result of good environment, and evil the result of bad environment? Are evil and good merely the results of conditioning? In any case, the story is a parable asking a perennial question, in which each generation answers in its own terms.

Can we say that the story by-passes the question of vice and virtue as absolutes—that human nature is a complex thing and that man must live in the effort to make his own definition by faith? In which case, can we hazard that Goodman Brown is the total idealist who cannot live life as it necessarily is?

2
What Plot Reveals

Earlier, in connection with "The Attack on the Fort," we raised the question of the relation of fact and fiction. Though Parkman's anecdote is presumably true, that was not the reason we found it unacceptable as fiction. We know, indeed, that much work accepted as fiction involves fact or may be substantially fact. The real distinction is not "fact" as opposed to "fiction"—as common usage has it—but something much more complex. Such a consideration lies behind the whole question of plot.

We can approach the distinction by considering the writer of history. The historian or biographer deals with facts, and presumably only with facts. But even he *must* interpret his facts. History does not write itself, and the study of history is a hotbed of controversy, of competing interpretations. But the historian insists on the authenticity of the facts that he means to interpret. He claims that his "truth" is one of *correspondence* (see Glossary) with fact, and to establish such a truth is his aim—though, as we have said, his facts must be interpreted. On the other hand, the writer of fiction (even though he may deal with historical materials very faithfully) does not feel bound to precise correspondence with fact; rather he feels bound by a truth of *coherence* (see Glossary) and by "coherence" we here mean the significant relation of all the elements in the fiction. Plot, character, theme—certainly—but a thousand other factors as well, including his selection of facts. And always we must keep in mind that real life—or historical records—never give the fiction writer what he needs—*all* he needs—to create the illusion and his own interpretation of life. The imagined *inwardness* of life being lived, and the moral ("moral" in the broadest sense) of that process must finally depend on imagination and on the significance of the coherence of the whole work. We may summarize crudely (making allowance for the overlaps that occur in relation to fact) as follows: the historian is concerned to discover the pattern implied by the facts (and the significance); the fiction writer may choose *or* "create" facts in accordance with the pattern of human action and values that he wishes to present.

Let us ponder this distinction, as underlying all that is to follow.

Ordinarily, when we speak of "the action of a story," we mean the string of events that constitute the story. In other words, "action" serves as a rough equivalent of what we commonly think of as "plot." When we talk in this fashion we are thinking of the string of events as somehow separable from the characters involved in the events and separable from the main theme—even though we know that, in fact, we cannot really separate an act from the person who commits it, or an act from its meaning. Our minds are in the habit of making such distinctions, abstractions, and analyses, for we need them in dealing with our daily lives and those of others.

When we come to fiction, however, it is necessary to insist on a sharp distinction between *action* and *plot* (see Glossary).

As for action, we do not mean a single event (Goodman Brown went into the forest), but a series of events moving through time and exhibiting unity and significance. Such a series can be regarded as moving through three logical stages: the beginning, the middle, and the end.

The beginning of an action always presents us with a situation in which there is some element of instability, some conflict or contrast (which may be specified or implied, or even, for the moment, ignored). The middle of an action exhibits the development of conflict and the readjustment of forces as they struggle to settle into a new kind of stability. The end of an action shows that some point of stability has been reached (however temporarily); the conflicts among forces that have been brought into play have been resolved. At dawn of the day of the Battle of Waterloo, the fate of Europe hung in balance; at sunset Napoleon was a broken man. On June 7, 1776, Richard Henry Lee of Virginia presented to the Continental Congress a resolution declaring that "these United Colonies are, and of right ought to be, free and independent States"; on July 4 the Declaration of Independence was signed. When Tom Smith, a wealthy, middle-aged banker, met Evelyn Pembroke, he immediately recognized her vain and frivolous nature, but that recognition could not overcome the attraction she exerted; and all of Morristown was surprised when Smith, the very pillar of respectability, was arrested for embezzlement. In each of these actions, two historical and one fictional, we recognize the movement of conflict through time to a point of rest, or resolution.

In these actions we recognize, too, unity and significance; something is settled. But the nature of the thing settled may depend on a point of view. The Battle of Waterloo may be regarded as a completed action, but it may also be regarded as one event in a broader action, in, say, the rise of the British Empire. Or we may regard our imaginary action, say, the account of the banker and the vain Evelyn Pembroke, not as a fulfilled action, but as merely an episode in the life of one of the two persons concerned, or even in the life of, say, Smith's son.

When we come to plot we are concerned with a writer's selection and arrangement of facts drawn from an action (real or imaginary)—a selection and arrangement that determine the unity and significance of the fiction. *Plot, then, is the meaningful manipulation of action.* The teller of a story, whether in idle conversation or in the serious business of writing a novel, cannot possibly use all the thousands of facts involved in the action. He has to *select* the facts that seem to him useful for his particular purpose.

For the storyteller, facts have two kinds of usefulness. A fact (real or imaginary) is useful if it is vivid, that is, if it stirs the imagination to accept the story. One vivid fact may suddenly make a whole passage of narrative seem real to us. A fact is also useful if it indicates, directly or indirectly, the line of development pursued in a story, that is, if it indicates how one thing leads to another, or what the movement of events means. Vividness and significance—these are the tests of usefulness in selection. But the two tend to merge. The vivid detail that catches the imagination helps to create the special quality, the "feel" of a story, and this "feel," this *atmosphere* (see Glossary) is an element of the meanings.

So if we examine fiction we are continually faced with questions about facts. Why was a particular fact selected? What led the writer to use some facts and reject others? How might the choice of other available facts have made a very different story? (Remember that here a "fact" may be imaginary.)

Answers to such questions are always complicated, but the questions are worth pondering. They may lead us toward the full meaning of a story.

After a writer has selected his facts, there comes the question of order. Thus far we have thought of the action as existing in all of its intricate detail out in the world, with all of its components disposed in their actual chronological order. Yet many stories—indeed, in a strict sense, all stories—violate in one way or another the strict chronological sequence of an action as thought of in the actual world. To take an example, no writer can give simultaneously in his narrative two things that occur simultaneously in the action. His order of narration is bound to be artificial. To take another example, the beginning of a story may, or may not, happen to pick up the beginning of the action that it presents. The plot may plunge us into the very middle of things, and then, stage by stage, take us back to the beginning of the action. Or there may be a complicated interweaving of times. The accompanying chart of a hypothetical story indicates this notion.

Sequence of Action: a b c d e f g h i j k l m n o p q r s t u v w x y z

SEQUENCE OF PLOT: F A B H I J E R S T V Y Z

We can see, in our chart, that the plot does not use all the facts of the action, and that the chronological order has been scrambled. The plot, then, is the structure of the action *as presented* in a piece of fiction. It represents the treatment the storyteller makes of the events of his action.

In discussing the nature of an action we have necessarily touched on unity and significance. Let us now return to these topics with more special reference to plot.

When we say "*a* novel," "*a* story," or "*a* plot," we instinctively imply the idea of unity. We imply that the parts, the various individual events, hang together. To begin with, there is the matter of cause and effect. In any story we expect to find one thing bringing on another. If we can detect no reasonable connection between them, if there is no "logic" whatever, we lose interest. Every story must indicate some basis for the relation among its parts, for the story itself is a *particular writer's way of saying how you can make sense of human experience.*

Cause and effect constitute one of the ways of saying this. In works of fiction, however, we cannot think of cause as a mechanical thing—as though one event were one domino knocking over the next one in a long series. The events are human events; that is, they involve human responses to changing situations, including the possibility of action taken to change existing situations. Many nonhuman things may enter into the logic of a story—the weather that ruins a crop, the iceberg that sinks a ship, the explosion that wrecks a mine, the nail lost from the shoe of the horse of the king's messenger—but in the end the central logic we are concerned with is the logic of human motivation. How do human needs and passions work themselves out? Plot, then, is character in action.

Logic, including the logic of *motivation*, (see Glossary), binds the events of a plot together into a unity. This unity is, of course, a dynamic unity. It is a unity involving change: no change, no story. At the beginning of a story we find, as we have earlier said, a situation with some element of instability in it. At the end of the story, we find that things have become stable once more. Something has been settled: Jim Beckworth has captured the Blackfoot fort; Walter Mitty, we have come to know, will never wake up from his dream; Goodman Brown has discovered the complexity of human nature. This movement from instability toward stability involves, as we have said, certain natural stages—the beginning, the middle, and the end.

When we come to consider how these natural stages are treated in terms of plot, we find that we need some special terms. The beginning of the plot action is called the *exposition* (see Glossary)—the "setting forth" of the assumptions from which the story will develop. The middle is called the *complication* (see Glossary), for it presents the increasing difficulty encountered in the movement toward stability. If, for example, a character moves easily toward his triumph, or his ruin, there is really no story. It is no story to tell how a barrel rolls downhill. The story interest inheres in the resistances encountered and overcome, or not overcome—in the logic by which resistance evokes responses that, in their turn, encounter or create new resistances to be dealt with. The complication moves toward a moment, an event, when something has to happen, when something has to crack. This moment is the point of highest tension, the moment when the story turns toward its solution. This is called the *climax* (see Glossary). The story, then, is the story of *conflict* developing logically through the stages of the complication.

The end—the *denouement* (see Glossary)—gives us the outcome of the conflict, the solution to the problem, the basis of a new stability. We realize, of course, that the basis of stability now reached may be only provisional and temporary, that something may come along to upset the hard-won stability. If, for example, we have the story of a stormy courtship and "boy gets girl" in the end, we know that, except in the fairy-tale formula of "and they lived happily ever after," no promise is made of an end to all conflict, all struggle, all problems. The denouement simply gives us the settling of a particular action—the courtship—which is the story that the author has elected to tell.

The meaning of the settlement, however, always reaches beyond the particular action. And this idea takes us back to the question of significance in plot. Insofar, of course, as the development of a plot exhibits logic, it is already exhibiting significance—it is telling us, or showing us, something about human nature and human conduct. The conclusion that stems from this logic aims to give us not only an evaluation of the particular experience related in the story, but a *generalized* evaluation. Always the end of a successful story leaves us with an attitude to take toward life in general. The story embodies a comment on human values—on what is good or bad in human nature and human conduct, on what attitude one may take, finally, toward life and the business of living. That is, any particular story will always appear, in our imagination and feelings, as an image, however shadowy, of the meaning of experience.

The way the meaning is presented may vary from instance to instance. There may be a perfectly explicit general statement, more or less complete—as we will soon find in the epigraph of "The Man Who Would Be King" at the end of this section. Or a story may use *symbolism* (see Glossary) that can be read back into statement as we shall do in our comment on the end of the story. Even when the denouement may seem merely to wind up events and avoid interpretation, we shall find that the story, if it is a successful one, will turn us back toward some basic quality in the story itself; and we shall find that that quality may have subtly modified our feelings and attitudes. It may have enlarged our sympathies—as does "Vanka," by Chekhov—so that we may now more readily regard other people with charity and humility. Or it may have given us a liberating sense of the comedy of experience—as "The Drunkard" by Frank O'Connor. Or the story may conclude on a note of savage satire or chilling irony. Always, however, we expect in fiction an idea about, some stance toward, experience, and if we do not get it we are dissatisfied. We feel cheated. We don't know what the shooting has been about. We feel, in other words, that the story is incoherent—the plot has not fulfilled itself, even though stage by stage the logic of motivation, and the like, may have been seeming to work itself out. We do not like to be preached at, but we do demand a sense of meaningfulness.

So our discussion of plot brings us back to theme, just as it has already led us, in discussing motivation, to the question of character. And that is only natural, for a good story is, after all, a unity. It is consistent within itself. The world of imagination that it presents is—to repeat a term we have already used—*coherent*.

We have tried to indicate something of the function of the parts of a plot, and something of the relation among them. Let us ask the next question: are we to be concerned with any particular *proportion* among the parts? The answer is no.

In some pieces of fiction—whether novels or stories—a great deal of exposition may be required. There may be a great weight of the past behind the moment of crisis, and if we are to understand the story, we must understand what lies behind it. Or we may need to know something of a special world that may be unfamiliar to us.

Sometimes a story needs a long and elaborate denouement. In one sense "The Man Who Would Be King," we shall see, ends when Dravot walks boldly out on the bridge and yells, "Cut, you beggars!" But a good deal of space, and a good deal of narrative, is required before we have the full implications of that moment. Think, however, how little is required to end the story of Walter Mitty. Of course, one story is longer than the other, and more complicated, but even so, there is a fundamental difference that has little to do with the question of length as such. "The Man Who Would Be King" is a story giving the development of a character, and when the development is over it requires some time and some elaboration for its full weight to be felt. John Collier's "De Mortuis," as we shall see, is concerned with a shocking revelation at the end. The shock is the point. If we were to spin out the denouement, we should lose the sense of shock, and add nothing significant. The story does have weighty implications, but they do not need to be elaborated; their force depends on the shock.

What all this amounts to is simple: proportion is not mechanically determined. It depends on the materials of the particular story and the kind of story the writer is trying to make of those materials. As we read, we must try to sense the needs of the situation, and try to understand the intention of the writer.

One more question presents itself in regard to the divisions of a plot: are we to expect to find a sharp line between the exposition and complication, or between complication and denouement? There may, of course, be sharp division, and sometimes the sharpness contributes greatly to the effect—as in "Vanka." But, as we have indicated on our little chart distinguishing between action and plot, there is sometimes considerable interpenetration between one part and another, and especially between exposition and complication, but climax and denouement may sometimes seem to merge. There may be certain advantages, for example, in presenting an element of complication very early, at the very start perhaps, to catch the reader's attention, even before he can get the full import of the event before him. And sometimes a piece of exposition may be withheld until fairly late until the reader feels the need for it and it will come with dramatic force. Our principle here, again, is one of tact, of flexibility. There is no hard and fast rule. As readers, we must try to see how sharp separations or intricate interpenetrations among the parts of a plot are related to the final effect.

In this section we shall not confine ourselves to reading and discussing stories in which the element of plot is strongly marked—stories, for example, like "The Man Who Would Be King." We shall, in fact, read some stories whose plots seem slight. This is a reasonable procedure, for we are concerned here to see how the element of plot, whether strongly marked or recessive, works in relation to other aspects of fiction.

Furthermore, we shall not confine ourselves to stories in which the plot exhibits significant order. We shall look at some instances in which the events are not in significant order, in which they do not adequately embody human values—instances, in short, in which the plot is incoherent. Of all the stories we read in this book we shall be asking questions. Is the plot coherent? Does it make sense? If it does not make sense, in what particular way does it fail? We must, in other words, constantly consider the relation of plot to character and theme.

But not only to character and theme. Stories and novels are composed in words, and so we shall have to think a little about the relation of plot to the resources of language that the writer uses well or badly. Problems of coherence, as we shall see, arise here too.

THE FURNISHED ROOM

O. Henry

RESTLESS, shifting, fugacious as time itself is a certain vast bulk of the population of the red brick district of the lower West Side. Homeless, they have a hundred homes. They flit from furnished room to furnished room, transients forever—transients in abode, transients in heart and mind. They sing "Home, Sweet Home" in ragtime; they carry their *lares et penates* in a bandbox; their vine is entwined about a picture hat; a rubber plant is their fig tree.

Hence the houses of this district, having had a thousand dwellers, should have a thousand tales to tell, mostly dull ones, no doubt; but it would be strange if there could not be found a ghost or two in the wake of all these vagrant guests.

One evening after dark a young man prowled among these crumbling red mansions, ringing their bells. At the twelfth he rested his lean hand baggage upon the step and wiped the dust from his hatband and forehead. The bell sounded faint and far away in some remote, hollow depths.

To the door of this, the twelfth house whose bell he had rung, came a housekeeper who made him think of an unwholesome, surfeited worm that had eaten its nut to a hollow shell and now sought to fill the vacancy with edible lodgers.

He asked if there was a room to let.

"Come in," said the housekeeper. Her voice came from her throat; her throat seemed lined with fur. "I have the third floor, back, vacant since a week back. Should you wish to look at it?"

The young man followed her up the stairs. A faint light from no particular source mitigated the shadows of the halls. They trod noiselessly upon a stair carpet that its own loom would have foresworn. It seemed to have become vegetable; to have degenerated in that rank, sunless air to lush lichen or spreading moss that grew in patches to the staircase and was viscid under the foot like organic matter. At each turn of the stairs were vacant niches in the wall. Perhaps plants had once been set within them. If so, they had died in that foul and tainted air. It may be that statues of the saints had stood there, but it was not difficult to conceive that imps and devils had dragged them forth in the darkness and down to the unholy depths of some furnished pit below.

"This is the room," said the housekeeper, from her furry throat. "It's a nice room. It ain't often vacant. I had some most elegant people in it last summer—no trouble at all, and paid in advance to the minute. The water's at the end of the hall. Sprowls and Mooney kept it three months. They done a vaudeville sketch. Miss B'retta Sprowls—you may have heard of her—oh, that was just the stage names—right there over the dresser is where the marriage certificate hung, framed. The gas is here, and you see there is plenty of closet room. It's a room everybody likes. It never stays idle long."

"Do you have many theatrical people rooming here?" asked the young man.

"They comes and goes. A good proportion of my lodgers is connected with the theaters. Yes, sir, this is the theatrical district. Actor people never stays long anywhere. I get my share. Yes, they comes and they goes."

He engaged the room, paying for a week in advance. He was tired, he said, and would take possession at once. He counted out the money. The room had been made ready, she said, even to towels and water. As the housekeeper moved away he put, for the thousandth time, the question that he carried at the end of his tongue.

"A young girl—Miss Vashner—Miss Eloise Vashner—do you remember such a one among your lodgers? She would be singing on the stage, most likely. A fair girl, of medium height and slender, with reddish, gold hair and a dark mole near her left eyebrow."

"No, I don't remember the name. Them stage people has names they change as often as their rooms. They comes and they goes. No, I can't call that one to mind."

No. Always no. Five months of ceaseless interrogation and the inevitable negative. So much time spent by day in questioning managers, agents, schools, and choruses; by night among the audiences of theaters from all-star casts down to music halls so low that he dreaded to find what he most hoped for. He who had loved her best had tried to find her. He was sure that since her disappearance from home this great, water-girt city held her somewhere, but it was like a monstrous quicksand, shifting its particles constantly, with no foundation, its upper granules of today buried tomorrow in ooze and slime.

The furnished room received its latest guest with a first glow of pseudo-hospitality, a hectic, haggard, perfunctory welcome like the specious smile of a demirep. The sophistical comfort came in reflected gleams from the decayed furniture, the ragged brocade upholstery of a couch and two chairs, a foot-wide cheap pier glass between the two windows, from one or two gilt picture frames and a brass bedstead in a corner.

The guest reclined, inert, upon a chair, while the room, confused in speech as though it were an apartment in Babel, tried to discourse to him of its divers tenantry.

A polychromatic rug like some brilliant-flowered rectangular, tropical islet lay surrounded by a billowly sea of soiled matting. Upon the gray-papered wall were those pictures that pursue the homeless one from house to house—The Huguenot Lovers, The First Quarrel, The

Wedding Breakfast, Psyche at the Fountain. The mantel's chastely severe outline was ingloriously veiled behind some pert drapery drawn rakishly askew like the sashes of the Amazonian ballet. Upon it was some desolate flotsam cast aside by the room's marooned when a lucky sail had borne them to a fresh port—a trifling vase or two, pictures of actresses, a medicine bottle, some stray cards out of a deck.

One by one, as the characters of a cryptograph become explicit, the little signs left by the furnished room's procession of guests developed a significance. The threadbare space in the rug in front of the dresser told that lovely women had marched in the throng. The tiny finger prints on the wall spoke of little prisoners trying to feel their way to sun and air. A splattered stain, raying like the shadow of a bursting bomb, witnessed where a hurled glass or bottle had splintered with its contents against the wall. Across the pier glass had been scrawled with a diamond in staggering letters the name "Maire." It seemed that the succession of dwellers in the furnished room had turned in fury—perhaps tempted beyond forebearance by its garish coldness—and wreaked upon it their passions. The furniture was chipped and bruised; the couch, distorted by bursting springs, seemed a horrible monster that had been slain during the stress of some grotesque convulsion. Some more potent upheaval had cloven a great slice from the marble mantel. Each plank in the floor owned its particular cant and shriek as from a separate and individual agony. It seemed incredible that all this malice and injury had been wrought upon the room by those who had called it for a time their home; and yet it may have been the cheated home instinct surviving blindly, the resentful rage at false household gods that had kindled their wrath. A hut that is our own we can sweep and adorn and cherish.

The young tenant in the chair allowed these thoughts to file, softshod, through his mind, while there drifted into the room furnished sounds and furnished scents. He heard in one room a tittering and incontinent, slack laughter; in others the monologue of a scold, the rattling of dice, a lullaby, and one crying dully; above him a banjo tinkled with spirit. Doors banged somewhere; the elevated trains roared intermittently; a cat yowled miserably upon a back fence. And he breathed the breath of the house—a dank savor rather than a smell—a cold, musty effluvium as from underground vaults mingled with the reeking exhalations of linoleum and mildewed and rotten woodwork.

Then, suddenly, as he rested there, the room was filled with the strong, sweet odor of mignonette. It came as upon a single buffet of wind with such sureness and fragrance and emphasis that it almost seemed a living visitant. And the man cried aloud: "What, dear?" as if he had been called, and sprang up and faced about. The rich odor clung to him and wrapped him around. He reached out his arms for it, all his senses for the time confused and commingled. How could one be peremptorily called by an odor? Surely it must have been a sound. But, was it not the sound that had touched, that had caressed him?

"She has been in this room," he cried, and he sprang to wrest from it a token, for he knew he would recognize the smallest thing that had belonged to her or that she had touched. This enveloping scent of mignonette, the odor that she had loved and made her own—whence came it?

The room had been but carelessly set in order. Scattered upon the flimsy dresser scarf were half a dozen hairpins—those discreet, indistinguishable friends of womankind, feminine of gender, infinite of mood and uncommunicative of tense. These he ignored, conscious of their triumphant lack of identity. Ransacking the drawers of the dresser, he came upon a discarded, tiny, ragged handkerchief. He pressed it to his face. It was racy and insolent with heliotrope; he hurled it to the floor. In another drawer he found odd buttons, a theater program, a pawnbroker's card, two lost marshmallows, a book on the divination of dreams. In the last was a woman's black satin hairbow, which halted him, poised between ice and fire. But the black satin hair bow also is femininity's demure, impersonal, common ornament and tells no tales.

And then he traversed the room like a hound on the scent, skimming the walls, considering the corners of the bulging matting on his hands and knees, rummaging mantel and tables, the curtains and hangings, the drunken cabinet in the corner, for a visible sign, unable to perceive that she was there beside, around, against, within, above him, clinging to him, wooing him, calling him so poignantly through the finer senses that even his grosser ones became cognizant of the call. Once again he answered loudly: "Yes, dear!" and turned, wildeyed, to gaze on vacancy, for he could not yet discern form and color and love and outstretched arms in the odor of mignonette. Oh, God! whence that odor, and since when have odors had a voice to call? Thus he groped.

He burrowed in crevices and corners, and found corks and cigarettes. These he passed in passive contempt. But once he found in a fold of the matting a half-smoked cigar, and this he ground beneath his heel with a green and trenchant oath. He sifted the room from end to end. He found dreary and ignoble small records of many a peripatetic tenant; but of her whom he sought, and who may have lodged there, and whose spirit seemed to hover there, he found no trace.

And then he thought of the housekeeper.

He ran from the haunted room downstairs and to a door that showed a crack of light. She came out to his knock. He smothered his excitement as best he could.

"Will you tell me, madam," he besought her, "who occupied the room I have before I came?"

"Yes, sir. I can tell you again. 'Twas Sprowls and Mooney, as I said. Miss B'retta Sprowls it was in the theaters, but Missis Mooney she was. My house is well known for respectability. The marriage certificate hung, framed, on a nail over—"

"What kind of a lady was Miss Sprowls—in looks, I mean?"

"Why, black-haired, sir, short, and stout, with a comical face. They left a week ago Tuesday."

"And before they occupied it?"

"Why, there was a single gentleman connected with the draying business. He left owing me a week. Before him was Missis Crowder and her two children that stayed four months; and back of them was old Mr.

Doyle, whose sons paid for him. He kept the room six months. That goes back a year, sir, and further I do not remember."

He thanked her and crept back to his room. The room was dead. The essence that had vivified it was gone. The perfume of mignonette had departed. In its place was the old, stale odor of moldy house furniture, of atmosphere in storage.

The ebbing of his hope drained his faith. He sat staring at the yellow, singing gaslight. Soon he walked to the bed and began to tear the sheets into strips. With the blade of his knife he drove them tightly into every crevice around windows and door. When all was snug and taut, he turned out the light, turned the gas full on again, and laid himself gratefully upon the bed.

It was Mrs. McCool's night to go with the can for beer. So she fetched it and sat with Mrs. Purdy in one of those subterranean retreats where housekeepers foregather and the worm dieth seldom.

"I rented out my third floor, back, this evening," said Mrs. Purdy, across a fine circle of foam. "A young man took it. He went up to bed two hours ago."

"Now, did ye, Mrs. Purdy, ma'am?" said Mrs. McCool, with intense admiration. "You do be a wonder for rentin' rooms of that kind. And did ye tell him, then?" she concluded in a husky whisper laden with mystery.

"Rooms," said Mrs. Purdy, in her furriest tones, "are furnished for to rent. I did not tell him, Mrs. McCool."

"'Tis right ye are, ma'am; 'tis by rentin' rooms we kape alive. Ye have the rale sense for business, ma'am. There be many people will rayjict the rentin' of a room if they be tould a suicide has been after dyin' in the bed of it."

"As you say, we has our living to be making," remarked Mrs. Purdy.

"Yis, ma'am; 'tis true. 'Tis just one wake ago this day I helped ye lay out the third floor, back. A pretty slip of a colleen she was to be killin' herself wid the gas—a swate little face she had, Mrs. Purdy, ma'am."

"She'd a-been called handsome, as you say," said Mrs. Purdy, assenting but critical, "but for that mole she had a-growin' by her left eyebrow. Do fill up your glass again, Mrs. McCool."

DISCUSSION

This story is obviously divided into two parts. The first part, which ends with the death of the lodger, concerns his failure in the search for his sweetheart, the odor of mignonette, the lie of the landlady, and the suicide; the second part concerns the revelation, by the landlady to her crony, that his sweetheart had, a week earlier, committed suicide in the same room. What accounts for the fact that O. Henry felt it necessary to treat the story in this fashion? What holds the two parts of the story together? What is the central meaning of this plot?

The most interesting question has to do with the young man's motivation. In one sense, O. Henry has deliberately made the problem of his motivation more difficult by withholding the information that the young man does not know that his sweetheart is dead; indeed, in the room, he gets, with the scent of mignonette, a renewed hope. Why then, under these circumstances does he commit suicide? Presumably, the explanation is this: he has been searching fruitlessly for five months; he is, we are told, tired—and, we assume, not only momentarily tired physically, but spiritually weary. Indeed, we are told: "He was sure that since her disappearance from home this great, water-girt city held her somewhere, but it was like a monstrous quicksand, shifting its particles constantly, with no foundation, its upper granules of today buried tomorrow in ooze and slime." But we are not supposed to believe, even so, that he would have necessarily turned on the gas this particular evening, except in despair at the loss of hope raised by the scent of mignonette. This is the author's account of the motivation of the suicide.

But is the motivation, as presented, really convincing? That will depend on the character of the man. What sort of man is he? Actually, O. Henry tells us very little about him except that he is young, has searched for his sweetheart for five months, and is tired. Especially does the question of the man's character, and state of mind, come up in the incident in which he notices the odor of mignonette. Did he really smell it? Did he merely imagine that he smelled it? "And he breathed the breath of the house . . . a cold, musty effluvium . . . mingled with the reeking exhalations of linoleum and mildewed and rotten woodwork. Then, suddenly, as he rested there, the room was filled with the strong, sweet odor of mignonette. It came as upon a single buffet of wind."

The suddenness with which he notices the odor, the fact that he can find no source for the odor, and finally the complete disappearance of the odor, all tend to imply that he merely imagines it. But over against this view, we have the testimony of the landlady that the sweetheart had actually occupied the room. This question is crucial for the young man's lapse into acute despair. If the odor is real, the author must convince his reader that it exists; if it is imaginary, the author must convince his reader that the psychological condition of the young man will account for its apparent existence. These are the tests the reader must apply to the situation. We have already pointed out that there is some evidence on both sides of the question. The reader must, of course, decide for himself which explanation must be taken, and more important, whether the explanation is convincing, and renders the action credible. The author, perhaps, weighs the evidence toward the presence of the real odor. If this is the case, how are we to account for the fact that the search reveals no source of it, especially since the odor is so overpoweringly strong? Or, perhaps the author has in mind some idea that the odor provokes a mystical communion between the two lovers. But this does not relieve the fiction writer from the necessity for furnishing some sort of specific clue to his meaning. (Moreover, if we are to take the whole experience as an hallucination, the author is certainly not relieved from providing some clear motivation for the event.) In other words, the author is playing with his reader—"mystifying him."

To sum up: it is obvious enough, from the detailed description of the room, that O. Henry is trying to suggest a ground for the man's experience in the nature of the room itself. That is, the room in its disorder, its squalor, its musty smell, its rubbish and debris of nameless lives, reflects the great city, in which his sweetheart has been lost, and in which all humanity seems to become degraded and brutalized. O. Henry wants to suggest the contrast between what the sordid surroundings mean to the hero and what the odor of mignonette means to him. As the girl is lost somewhere in the great city, so the odor is lost somewhere in the room. After the young man is told that the girl has not been there, and after he has been unable to find the source of the odor, the room itself is supposed to become a sort of overwhelming symbol for the futility of his effort. This intention on the part of the author may be sound enough, but the fact that we see what the intention is does not mean that the intention has been carried out. The whole effect of the story depends on the incident of the odor, and we have seen that the handling of this detail is confused. What we have is a faintly symbolic suggestion that the sourceless odor, standing for the young man's finally thwarted hope, is in contrast to the sordidness of the room, and the contrast is too much for him.

Such is the psychological frailty of the story. But resting upon his rather thin and sketchy characterization of the young man, the author chooses to give a turn to the plot by a last-minute surprise. In the second part of the story the landlady tells her crony that she has lied to the young man about the girl.

What is the effect of this revelation? It is intended, obviously, to underline the "irony of fate," to illustrate the hardheartedness of the city in which the young man finds himself, to justify the young man's overwhelming sense that the girl has been in the room, and, all in all, to pull the story together. For the sympathetic reader this conclusion is supposed to suggest that the bonds of love stretch across the confusion and squalor of the great city, and that, in a sense, the young man has finally succeeded in his search, for the lovers are at last united in death. The young man finds, as it were, the proper room in the great city in which to die.

But is the story really pulled together? The end of the story depends on the lie. But are the lives of the lovers altered by the lie? Does the lie cause the death of the young man? It is conceivable that, had the landlady told the truth, the shock of the information might have saved the young man from suicide, but this is the merest speculation. The character, as given in the story, commits suicide in despair when the landlady tells him that the girl has not been there; the landlady's telling him that the girl is irretrievably lost, is dead, would presumably have had the same effect. Or would that fact have saved him?

Actually, is there any point in the lie except to trick the reader—to provide the illusion of a meaningful ending? Whatever irony lies in the ending is based on a farfetched coincidence, and does not depend on the fact that the woman said one thing rather than another. (Readers who are inclined to accept the conclusion of the story as meaningful might try reconstructing the story with the young man's calling at the door, finding with horror that his sweetheart has committed suicide there a week before, renting the room, and turning on the gas. We would then still have the ironical coincidence and a sort of union of the lovers, but the story would seem very tame and flat.) O. Henry, by withholding certain information and thus surprising us with it at the end, has simply tried to give the reader the illusion that the information was meaningful. The irony, in the story as we have it, simply resides in a trick played on the reader rather than in a trick that fate has played on the young man.

Readers who feel that the end of this story is a shabby trick will be able to point out other symptoms of cheapness: the general thinness of characterization, the cluttered and sometimes mawkish description, the wheedling tone taken by the author, and the obvious play for emotional sympathy in such writing as the following: "Oh, God! whence that odor, and since when have odors had a voice to call?" In other words, we can readily surmise that the trickery involved in the surprise ending may be an attempt to compensate for defects within the body of the story itself. The straining to stir the emotions of the reader, the mawkish and wheedling tone—all are attempts to make up for a lack of logic, a lack of coherence, in the story itself. *Sentimentality* (see Glossary) often springs from such a lack of coherence—emotionalism without reference to a reasonable occasion for it.

A trick of plot does not make a story. A surprise ending may appear in a very good story, but only if the surprise has been prepared for, so that, upon second thought, the reader realizes that it is, after all, a logical and meaningful development from what has gone before, and not merely a device employed by the author to give him an easy way out of his difficulties. The same principle applies to *coincidence* (see Glossary) in general. Coincidences do occur in real life, sometimes quite startling ones, and in one sense every story is based on a coincidence—namely, that the particular events happen to occur together, that such and such characters happen to meet, for example, at such and such a moment under such and such circumstances. But since fiction is concerned with a logic of character and action, coincidence, insofar as it is purely illogical, has little place in fiction. Truth can afford to be stranger than fiction, because truth is "true"—is acceptable on its own merits—but the happenings of fiction, as we have seen, must justify themselves in terms of logical connection with other elements in fiction and in terms of meaningfulness. Certainly coincidence is never acceptable when it is used to solve the problem of a story—to bail the author out of his difficulties.

Can you think of a more honest and effective way for these basic materials to be turned into a story? Do not write a new version; simply mull over the possibilities.

VANKA

Anton Chekhov

VANKA Zhukov, a boy of nine, who had been for three months apprenticed to Alyahin the shoemaker, was sitting up on Christmas Eve. Waiting till his master and mistress and the workmen had gone to the midnight service, he took out of his master's cupboard a bottle of ink and a pen with a rusty nib, and, spreading out a crumpled sheet of paper in front of him, began writing. Before forming the first letter he several times looked round fearfully at the door and the windows, stole a glance at the dark ikon, on both sides of which stretched shelves full of lasts, and heaved a broken sigh. The paper lay on the bench while he knelt before it.

"Dear grandfather, Konstantin Makaritch," he wrote, "I am writing you a letter. I wish you a happy Christmas, and all blessings from God Almighty. I have neither father nor mother, you are the only one left me."

Vanka raised his eyes to the dark ikon on which the light of his candle was reflected, and vividly recalled his grandfather, Konstantin Makaritch, who was night watchman to a family called Zhivarev. He was a thin but extraordinarily nimble and lively little old man of sixty-five, with an everlastingly laughing face and drunken eyes. By day he slept in the servants' kitchen, or made jokes with the cooks; at night, wrapped in an ample sheepskin, he walked round the grounds and tapped with his little mallet. Old Kashtanka and Eel, so-called on account of his dark colour and his long body like a weasel's, followed him with hanging heads. This Eel was exceptionally polite and affectionate, and looked with equal kindness on strangers and his own masters, but had not a very good reputation. Under his politeness and meekness was hidden the most Jesuitical cunning. No one knew better how to creep up on occasion and snap at one's legs, to slip into the store-room, or steal a hen from a peasant. His hind legs had been nearly pulled off more than once, twice he had been hanged, every week he was thrashed till he was half dead, but he always revived.

At this moment grandfather was, no doubt, standing at the gate, screwing up his eyes at the red windows of the church, stamping with his high felt boots, and joking with the servants. His little mallet was hanging on his belt. He was clasping his hands, shrugging with the cold, and, with an aged chuckle, pinching first the housemaid, then the cook.

"How about a pinch of snuff?" he was saying, offering the women his snuff-box.

The women would take a sniff and sneeze. Grandfather would be indescribably delighted, go off into a merry chuckle, and cry:

"Tear it off, it has frozen on!"

They give the dogs a sniff of snuff too. Kashtanka sneezes, wriggles her head, and walks away offended. Eel does not sneeze, from politeness, but wags his tail. And the weather is glorious. The air is still, fresh, and transparent. The night is dark, but one can see the whole village with its white roofs and coils of smoke coming from the chimneys, the trees silvered with hoar frost, the snowdrifts. The whole sky spangled with gay twinkling stars, and the Milky Way is as distinct as though it had been washed and rubbed with snow for a holiday. . . .

Vanka sighed, dipped his pen, and went on writing:

"And yesterday I had a wigging. The master pulled me out into the yard by my hair, and whacked me with a boot-stretcher because I accidentally fell asleep while I was rocking their brat in the cradle. And a week ago the mistress told me to clean a herring, and I began from the tail end, and she took the herring and thrust its head in my face. The workmen laugh at me and send me to the tavern for vodka, and tell me to steal the master's cucumbers for them, and the master beats me with anything that comes to hand. And there is nothing to eat. In the morning they give me bread, for dinner, porridge, and in the evening, bread again; but as for tea, or soup, the master and mistress gobble it all up themselves. And I am put to sleep in the passage, and when their wretched brat cries I get no sleep at all, but have to rock the cradle. Dear grandfather, show the divine mercy, take me away from here, home to the village. It's more than I can bear. I bow down to your feet, and will pray to God for you for ever, take me away from here or I shall die."

Vanka's mouth worked, he rubbed his eyes with his black fist, and gave a sob.

"I will powder your snuff for you," he went on. "I will pray for you, and if I do anything you can thrash me like Sidor's goat. And if you think I've no job, then I will beg the steward for Christ's sake to let me clean his boots, or I'll go for a shepherd-boy instead of Fedka. Dear grandfather, it is more than I can bear, it's simply no life at all. I wanted to run away to the village, but I have no boots, and I am afraid of the frost. When I grow up big I will take care of you for this, and not let anyone annoy you, and when you die I will pray for the rest of your soul, just as for my mammy's.

"Moscow is a big town. It's all gentlemen's houses, and there are lots of horses, but there are no sheep, and the dogs are not spiteful. The lads here don't go out with the star, and they don't let anyone go into the choir, and once I saw in a shop window fishing-hooks for sale, fitted ready with the line and for all sorts of fish, awfully good ones, there was even one hook that would hold a forty-pound sheat-fish. And I have seen shops where there are guns of all sorts, after the pattern of the master's guns at home, so that I shouldn't wonder if they are a hundred roubles each. . . . And in the butchers' shops there are grouse and woodcocks and fish and hares, but the shopmen don't say where they shoot them.

"Dear grandfather, when they have the Christmas tree at the big house, get me a gilt walnut, and put it away in the green trunk. Ask the young lady Olga Ignatyevna, say it's for Vanka."

Vanka gave a tremulous sigh, and again stared at the window. He remembered his grandfather always went into the forest to get the Christmas tree for his master's family, and took his grandson with him. It was a merry time! Grandfather made a noise in his throat, the forest crackled with the frost, and looking at them Vanka chortled too. Before chopping down the Christmas tree, grandfather would smoke a pipe, slowly take a pinch of snuff, and laugh at frozen Vanka. . . . The young fir trees, covered with hoar frost, stood motionless, waiting to see which of them was to die. Wherever one looked, a hare flew like an arrow over the snowdrifts. . . . Grandfather could not refrain from shouting: "Hold him, hold him . . . hold him! Ah, the bob-tailed devil!"

When he had cut down the Christmas tree, grandfather used to drag it to the big house, and there set to work to decorate it. . . . The young lady, who was Vanka's favourite, Olga Ignatyevna, was the busiest of all. When Vanka's mother Pelageya was alive, and a servant in the big house, Olga Ignatyevna used to give him goodies, and having nothing better to do, taught him to read and write, to count up to a hundred, and even to dance a quadrille. When Pelageya died, Vanka had been transferred to the servants' kitchen to be with his grandfather, and from the kitchen to the shoemaker's in Moscow.

"Do come, dear grandfather," Vanka went on with his letter. "For Christ's sake, I beg you, take me away. Have pity on an unhappy orphan like me; here everyone knocks me about, and I am fearfully hungry; I can't tell you what misery it is, I am always crying. And the other day the master hit me on the head with a last, so that I fell down. My life is wretched, worse than any dog's. . . . I send greetings to Alyona, one-eyed Yegorka, and the coachman, and don't give my concertina to anyone. I remain, your grandson, Ivan Zhukov. Dear grandfather, do come."

Vanka folded the sheet of writing-paper twice, and put it into an envelope he had bought the day before for a kopek. . . . After thinking a little, he dipped the pen and wrote the address:

To grandfather in the village.

Then he scratched his head, thought a little, and added: *Konstantin Makaritch.* Glad that he had not been prevented from writing, he put on his cap and, without putting on his little greatcoat, ran into the street as he was in his shirt. . . .

The shopmen at the butcher's, whom he had questioned the day before, told him that letters were put in post-boxes, and from the boxes were carried about all over the earth in mailcarts with drunken drivers and ringing bells. Vanka ran to the nearest post-box, and thrust the precious letter in the slit. . . .

An hour later, lulled by sweet hopes, he was sound asleep. . . . He dreamed of the stove. On the stove was sitting his grandfather, swinging his bare legs, and reading the letter to the cooks. . . .

By the stove was Eel, wagging his tail.

DISCUSSION

Here is a very odd story—certainly, in its structure. In the opening paragraph little Vanka begins to write his letter, and the act of the writing is the main action of the story. The content of the letter, the story of Vanka's short history and present misery, is almost purely expository, the explanation for the occasion of the letter. Then comes the denouement: the sudden turn as the improperly addressed letter, carrying all little Vanka's hopes, is dropped into the post box. Then in the closing paragraphs, which serve as a kind of accent, Vanka dreams of the letter, safe at its destination, being read aloud by his grandfather.

The emphasis of this story is on extreme pathos, with all the dangers of sentimentality. Imagine a treatment that would simply trace, in almost chronological order, all the miseries of Vanka until he sits alone on Christmas Eve, praying in his cold little hole of a room. Told thus, the story would be no story at all, merely a kind of sentimental sketch. Or suppose the letter were properly addressed and sent off to the grandfather, who cannot break the articles of apprenticeship, and so Vanka is treated worse than ever. What a poor story that would be!

It is the lack of a proper address—a last touch of pathetic ignorance—that gives the story its shape. And this is the shape of a bitterly ironical joke, with a snapper, a turn, that calls for no explanation, that implies all that lies ahead, but in the shape of a joke. The snapper of O. Henry's "The Furnished Room" is like a joke too. It is not the sharp turn that is bad; it is the fact of the insistence (and the confused insistence) on the pathos that is at the base of O. Henry's failure. In contrast, note the naive factuality of Chekhov's story. Here the shape of the joke works to mitigate the sentimentality threatening the story. It changes the tone. It hardens, in a way, the reader's heart.

There is, however, a *paradox* here (see Glossary). We have the joke of the address; we know that the letter will not reach Vanka's grandfather. But whom does it reach? It reaches the reader—you and you and you. It is, after all, a letter from all the little Vankas in the world to us all, and so the "trick ending" is something more than a trick, after all. And here we may see some explanation of the odd structure of the story, of the long, disproportionate element of exposition.

How do you think O. Henry would have told this story?

DE MORTUIS

John Collier

DR. RANKIN was a large and rawboned man on whom the newest suit at once appeared outdated, like a suit in a photograph of twenty years ago. This was due to the squareness and flatness of his torso, which might have been put together by a manufacturer of packing cases. His face also had a wooden and a roughly constructed look; his hair was wiglike and resentful of the comb. He had those huge and clumsy hands which can be an asset to a doctor in a small upstate town where people still retain a rural relish for paradox, thinking that the more apelike the paw, the more precise it can be in the delicate business of a tonsillectomy.

This conclusion was perfectly justified in the case of Dr. Rankin. For example, on this particular fine morning, though his task was nothing more ticklish than the cementing over of a large patch on his cellar floor, he managed those large and clumsy hands with all the unflurried certainty of one who would never leave a sponge within or create an unsightly scar without.

The doctor surveyed his handiwork from all angles. He added a touch here and a touch there till he had achieved a smoothness altogether professional. He swept up a few last crumbs of soil and dropped them into the furnace. He paused before putting away the pick and shovel he had been using; and found occasion for yet another artistic sweep of his trowel, which made the new surface precisely flush with the surrounding floor. At this moment of supreme concentration, the porch door upstairs slammed with the report of a minor piece of artillery, which, appropriately enough, caused Dr. Rankin to jump as if he had been shot.

The Doctor lifted a frowning face and an attentive ear. He heard two pairs of heavy feet clump across the resonant floor of the porch. He heard the house door opened and the visitors enter the hall, with which his cellar communicated by a short flight of steps. He heard whistling and then the voices of Buck and Bud crying, "Doc! Hi, Doc! They're biting!"

Whether the Doctor was not inclined for fishing that day, or whether, like others of his large and heavy type, he experienced an especially sharp, unsociable reaction on being suddenly startled, or whether he was merely anxious to finish undisturbed the job in hand and proceed to more important duties, he did not respond immediately to the inviting outcry of his friends. Instead, he listened while it ran its natural course, dying down at last into a puzzled and fretful dialogue.

"I guess he's out."

"I'll write a note—say we're at the creek, to come on down."

"We could tell Irene."

"But she's not here, either. You'd think *she'd* be around."

"Ought to be, by the look of the place."

"You said it, Bud. Just look at this table. You could write your name—"

"Sh-h-h! Look!"

Evidently the last speaker had noticed that the cellar door was ajar and that a light was shining below. Next moment the door was pushed wide open and Bud and Buck looked down.

"Why Doc! There you are!"

"Didn't you hear us yelling?"

The Doctor, not too pleased at what he had overheard, nevertheless smiled his rather wooden smile as his two friends made their way down the steps. "I thought I heard someone," he said.

"We were bawling our heads off," Buck said. "Thought nobody was home. Where's Irene?"

"Visiting," said the Doctor. "She's gone visiting."

"Hey, what goes on?" said Bud. "What are you doing? Burying one of your patients, or what?"

"Oh, there's been water seeping up through the floor," said the Doctor. "I figured it might be some spring opened up or something."

"You don't say!" said Bud, assuming instantly the high ethical standpoint of the realtor. "Gee, Doc, I sold you this property. Don't say I fixed you up with a dump where there's an underground spring."

"There was water" said the Doctor.

"Yes, but, Doc, you can look on that geological map the Kiwanis Club got up. There's not a better section of subsoil in the town."

"Looks like he sold you a pup," said Buck, grinning.

"No," said Bud. "Look. When the Doc came here he was green. You'll admit he was green. The things he didn't know!"

"He bought Ted Webber's jalopy," said Buck.

"He'd have bought the Jessop place if I'd let him," said Bud. "But I wouldn't give him a bum steer."

"Not the poor, simple city slicker from Poughkeepsie," said Buck.

"Some people would have taken him," said Bud. "Maybe some people did. Not me. I recommended this property. He and Irene moved straight in as soon as they were married. I wouldn't have put the Doc on to a dump where there'd be a spring under the foundations."

"Oh, forget it," said the Doctor, embarrassed by this conscientiousness. "I guess it was just the heavy rains."

"By gosh!" Buck said, glancing at the besmeared point of the pickaxe. "You certainly went deep enough. Right down into the clay, huh?"

"That's four feet down, the clay," Bud said.

"Eighteen inches," said the Doctor.

"Four feet, said Bud. "I can show you on the map."

"Come on. No arguments," said Buck. "How's about it, Doc? An hour or two at the creek, eh? They're biting."

"Can't do it boys," said the Doctor. "I've got to see a patient or two."

"Aw, live and let live, Doc," Bud said. "Give 'em a chance to get better. Are you going to depopulate the whole darn town?"

The Doctor looked down, smiled, and muttered, as he always did when this particular jest was trotted out. "Sorry, boys," he said. "I can't make it."

"Well," said Bud, disappointed, "I suppose we'd better get along. How's Irene?"

"Irene?" asked the Doctor. "Never better. She's gone visiting. Albany. Got the eleven o'clock train."

"Eleven o'clock?" said Buck. "For Albany?"

"Did I say Albany?" said the Doctor. "Watertown, I meant."

"Friends in Watertown?" Buck asked.

"Mrs. Slater," said the Doctor. "Mr. and Mrs. Slater. Lived next door to 'em when she was a kid, Irene said, over on Sycamore Street."

"Slater?" said Bud. "Next door to Irene. Not in *this* town."

"Oh, yes," said the Doctor. "She was telling me all about them last night. She got a letter. Seems this Mrs. Slater looked after her when her mother was in the hospital one time."

"No," said Bud.

"That's what she told me," said the Doctor. "Of course, it was a good many years ago."

"Look, Doc," said Buck. "Bud and I were raised in this town. We've known Irene's folks all our lives. We were in and out of their house all the time. There was never anybody next door called Slater."

"Perhaps," said the Doctor, "she married again, this woman. Perhaps it was a different name."

Bud shook his head.

"What time did Irene go to the station?" Buck asked.

"Oh, about a quarter of an hour ago," said the Doctor.

"You didn't drive her?" said Buck.

"She walked," said the Doctor.

"We came down Main Street," Buck said. "We didn't meet her."

"Maybe she walked across the pasture," said the Doctor.

"That's a tough walk with a suitcase," said Buck.

"She just had a couple of things in a little bag," said the Doctor.

Bud was still shaking his head.

Buck looked at Bud, and then at the pick, at the new, damp cement on the floor. "Jesus Christ!" he said.

"Oh, God, Doc!" Bud said. "A guy like you!"

"What in the name of heaven are you two bloody fools thinking?" asked the Doctor. "What are you trying to say?"

"A spring!" said Bud. "I ought to have known right away it wasn't any spring."

The Doctor looked at his cement-work, at the pick, at the large worried faces of his two friends. His own face livid. "Am I crazy?" he said. "Or are you? You suggest that I've—that Irene—my wife—oh, go on! Get out! Yes, go and get the sheriff. Tell him to come here and start digging. You—get out!"

Bud and Buck looked at each other, shifted their feet, and stood still again.

"Go on," said the Doctor.

"I don't know," said Bud.

"It's not as if he didn't have the provocation," Buck said.

"God knows," Bud said.

"God knows," Buck said. "You know. I know. The whole town knows. But try telling it to a jury."

The Doctor put his hand to his head. "What's that?" he said. "What is it? Now what are you saying? What do you mean?"

"If this ain't being on the spot!" said Buck. "Doc, you can see how it is. It takes some thinking. We've been friends right from the start. Damn good friends."

"But we've got to think," said Bud. "It's serious. Provocation or not, there's a law in the land. There's such a thing as being an accomplice."

"You were talking about provocation," said the Doctor.

"You're right, " said Buck. "And you're our friend. And if ever it could be called justified—"

"We've got to fix this somehow," said Bud.

"Justified?" said the Doctor.

"You were bound to get wised up sooner or later," said Buck.

"We could have told you," said Bud. "Only—what the hell?"

"We could," said Buck. "And we nearly did. Five years ago. Before ever you married her. You hadn't been here six months, but we sort of cottoned to you. Thought of giving you a hint. Spoke about it. Remember, Bud?"

Bud nodded. "Funny," he said. "I came right out in the open about that Jessop property. I wouldn't let you buy that, Doc. But getting married, that's something else again. We could have told you."

"We're that much responsible," Buck said.

"I'm fifty," said the Doctor. "I suppose it's pretty old for Irene."

"If you was Johnny Weissmuller at the age of twenty-one, it wouldn't make any difference," said Buck.

"I know a lot of people think she's not exactly a perfect wife," said the Doctor. "Maybe she's not. She's young. She's full of life."

"Oh, skip it!" said Buck sharply, looking at the raw cement. "Skip it, Doc, for God's sake."

The Doctor brushed his hand across his face. "Not everybody wants the same thing," he said. "I'm a sort of dry fellow. I don't open up very easily. Irene—you'd call her gay."

"You said it," said Buck.

"She's no housekeeper," said the Doctor. "I know it. But that's not the only thing a man wants. She's enjoyed herself."

"Yeah," said Buck. "She did."

"That's what I love," said the Doctor. "Because I'm not that way myself. She's not very deep, mentally. All right. Say she's stupid. I don't care. Lazy. No system. Well, I've got plenty of system. She's enjoyed herself. It's beautiful. It's innocent. Like a child."

"Yes. If that was all," Buck said.

"But," said the Doctor, turning his eyes full on him, "You seem to know there was more."

"Everybody knows it," said Buck.

"A decent straightforward guy comes to a place like this and marries the town floozy," Bud said bitterly. "And nobody'll tell him. Everybody just watches."

"And laughs," said Buck. "You and me, Bud, as well as the rest."

"We told her to watch her step," said Bud. "We warned her."

"Everybody warned her," said Buck, "But people get fed up. When it got to truck-drivers—"

"It was never us, Doc," said Bud, earnestly. "Not after you came along, anyway."

"The town'll be on your side," said Buck.

"That won't mean much when the case comes to trial in the county seat," said Bud.

"Oh!" cried the Doctor, suddenly. "What shall I do? What shall I do?"

"It's up to you, Bud," said Buck. "I can't turn him in."

"Take it easy, Doc," said Bud. "Calm down. Look, Buck. When we came in here the street was empty, wasn't it?"

"I guess so," said Buck. "Anyway, nobody saw us come down cellar."

"And we haven't been down," Bud said, addressing himself forcefully to the Doctor. "Get that, Doc? We shouted upstairs, hung around a minute or two, and cleared out. But we never came down into this cellar."

"I wish you hadn't," the Doctor said heavily.

"All you have to do is say Irene went out for a walk and never came back," said Buck. "Bud and I can swear we saw her headed out of town with a fellow in a—well, say in a Buick sedan. Everybody'll believe that, all right. We'll fix it. But later. Now we'd better scram."

"And remember, now. Stick to it. We never came down here and we haven't seen you today," said Bud. "So long!"

Buck and Bud ascended the steps, moving with a rather absurd degree of caution. "You'd better get that . . . that thing covered up," Buck said over his shoulder.

Left alone, the Doctor sat down on an empty box, holding his head with both hands. He was still sitting like this when the porch door slammed again. This time he did not start. He listened. The house door opened and closed. A voice cried, "Yoo-hoo! Yoo-hoo! I'm back."

The Doctor rose slowly to his feet. "I'm down here, Irene!" he called.

The cellar door opened. A young woman stood at the head of the steps. "Can you beat it?" she said. "I missed the damn train."

"Oh!" said the Doctor. "Did you come back across the field?"

"Yes, like a fool," she said. "I could have hitched a ride and caught the train up the line. Only I didn't think. If you'd run me over to the junction, I could still make it."

"Maybe," said the Doctor. "Did you meet anyone coming back?"

"Not a soul," she said. "Aren't you finished with that old job yet?"

"I'm afraid I'll have to take it all up again," said the Doctor. "Come down here, my dear, and I'll show you."

DISCUSSION

This story, like "The Furnished Room," involves coincidence and has a trick ending. But are those two things more acceptable here than in "The Furnished Room"? Perhaps we can best answer the question by considering the difference between the pretensions of the two stories.

"The Furnished Room" aspires to be a serious story. O. Henry wants us to feel the pathos and irony of life, the brutality and anonymity of the great city in contrast with the loves and hopes of the lost individuals. The story aims to stir our emotions and evoke our sympathies.

"De Mortuis," on the other hand, is a kind of extended joke. It deals with serious materials, the betrayal of a simple, decent man by an immoral wife, and his murder of her, but the emphasis is not on the human passions and suffering. The treatment is the treatment to be found in a joke, and the point, in a way, lies in the contrast between the potentially serious, even tragic, human situation, on the one hand, and the reversal and punch of the joke, on the other. It's a great joke on Irene. Just wait till she gets downstairs! Won't she be surprised! Well, she had it coming. She stepped into it that time. We have the comic effect—the liberation from the demands of sympathy and seriousness. A suddenly justified liberation for our holiday, as some psychologists would put it.

As a matter of fact, the joke isn't merely on Irene. There is a joke on everybody, on Buck and Bud, who unwittingly get the thing worked up, and on the doctor himself. Life has some rather grim little jokes, the story implies, but the best thing to do is to recognize them as jokes and laugh at them. Even the fact of coincidence—Bud and Buck just happen to drop in at the right time, Irene just happens to miss the train and come back, unseen, across the pasture—are consistent with the comic effect. We accept the coincidences as the machinery of the joke life is playing—for the illogic of life, not the logic, is what gives us the comedy. Poor Irene, and the others, are caught in the improbable coincidences and the unexpected turn, and we laugh at the fact. No appeal has been made to our sympathies. The tone is one of calm detachment, coolly reportorial. We are not involved in the human situation. The fact of the unreported seriousness and the suffering merely gives a grim little edge to the comedy.

To sum up, it is the particular comic tone that makes us accept the coincidences and the trick ending. By tone, as we have already suggested, we mean the impression that the author gives of his attitude toward his subject and his reader. Collier here takes life as a sardonic joke, full of traps and tricks. Careful, Irene, dear, watch that banana peel. It's right there before your eyes.

1. Try to distinguish between exposition and complication in "De Mortuis." Can you point out any elements of exposition that are withheld until complication has begun?

2. Suppose Collier had interpolated toward the end of the story a passage in which the doctor remembers his loneliness before his marriage, dwells on certain moments of tenderness of which Irene had been capable, shudders at the horror of the impulse that seizes him, then steels himself to the act. How would this change the effect of the story? What would be the effect on the tone? Would the story still be coherent?

3. What value for the story does the first paragraph have?

AN OCCURRENCE AT OWL CREEK BRIDGE

Ambrose Bierce

A MAN stood upon a railroad bridge in northern Alabama, looking down into the swift water twenty feet below. The man's hands were behind his back, the wrists bound with a cord. A rope closely encircled his neck. It was attached to a stout cross-timber above his head and the slack fell to the level of his knees. Some loose boards laid upon the sleepers supporting the metals of the railway supplied a footing for him and his executioners—two private soldiers of the Federal army, directed by a sergeant who in civil life may have been a deputy sheriff. At a short remove upon the same temporary platform was an officer in the uniform of his rank, armed. He was a captain. A sentinel at each end of the bridge stood with his rifle in the position known as "support," that is to say, vertical in front of the left shoulder, the hammer resting on the forearm thrown straight across the chest—a formal and unnatural position, enforcing an erect carriage of the body. It did not appear to be the duty of these two men to know what was occurring at the center of the bridge; they merely blockaded the two ends of the foot planking that traversed it.

Beyond one of the sentinels nobody was in sight; the railroad ran straight away into a forest for a hundred yards, then, curving, was lost to view. Doubtless there was an outpost farther along. The other bank of the stream was open ground—a gentle acclivity topped with a stockade of vertical tree trunks, loopholed for rifles, with a single embrasure through which protruded the muzzle of a brass cannon commanding the bridge. Midway of the slope between the bridge and fort were the spectators—a single company of infantry in line, at "parade rest," the butts of the rifles on the ground, the barrels inclining slightly backward against the right shoulder, the hands crossed upon the stock. A lieutenant stood at the right of the line, the point of his sword upon the ground, his left hand resting upon his right. Excepting the group of four at the center of the bridge, not a man moved. The company faced the bridge, staring stonily, motionless. The sentinels, facing the banks of the stream, might have been statues to adorn the bridge. The captain stood with folded arms, silent, observing the work of his subordinates, but making no sign. Death is a dignitary who when he comes announced is to be received with formal manifestations of respect, even by those most familiar with him. In the code of military etiquette silence and fixity are forms of deference.

The man who was engaged in being hanged was apparently about thirty-five years of age. He was a civilian, if one might judge from his habit, which was that of a planter. His features were good—a straight nose, firm mouth, broad forehead, from which his long, dark hair was combed straight back, falling behind his ears to the collar of his well-fitting frock coat. He wore a mustache and pointed beard, but no whiskers; his eyes were large and dark gray, and had a kindly expression which one would hardly have expected in one whose neck was in the hemp. Evidently this was no vulgar assassin. The liberal military code makes provision for hanging many kinds of persons, and gentlemen are not excluded.

The preparations being complete, the two private soldiers stepped aside and each drew away the plank upon which he had been standing. The sergeant turned to the captain, saluted and placed himself immediately behind that officer, who in turn moved apart one pace. These movements left the condemned man and the sergeant standing on the two ends of the same plank, which spanned three of the crossties of the bridge. The end upon which the civilian stood almost, but not quite, reached a fourth. This plank had been held in place by the weight of the captain; it was now held by that of the sergeant. At a signal from the former the latter would step aside, the plank would tilt and the condemned man go down between two ties. The arrangement commended itself to his judgment as simple and effective. His face had not been covered nor his eyes bandaged. He looked a moment at his "unsteadfast footing," then let his gaze wander to the swirling water of the stream racing madly beneath his feet. A piece of dancing driftwood caught his attention and his eyes followed it down the current. How slowly it appeared to move! What a sluggish stream!

He closed his eyes in order to fix his last thoughts upon his wife and children. The water, touched to gold by the early sun, the brooding mists under the banks at some distance down the stream, the fort, the soldiers, the piece of drift—all had distracted him. And now he became conscious of a new disturbance. Striking through the thought of his dear ones was a sound which he could neither ignore nor understand, a sharp, distinct, metallic percussion like the stroke of a blacksmith's hammer upon the anvil; it had the same ringing quality. He wondered what it was, and whether immeasurably distant or near by—it seemed both. Its recurrence was regular, but as slow as the tolling of a death knell. He awaited each stroke with impatience and—he knew not why—apprehension. The intervals of silence grew progressively longer; the delays became maddening. With their greater infrequency the sounds increased in strength and sharpness. They hurt his ear like the thrust of a knife; he feared he would shriek. What he heard was the ticking of his watch.

He unclosed his eyes and saw again the water below him. "If I could free my hands," he thought, "I might throw off the noose and spring into the stream. By diving I could evade the bullets and, swimming vigorously, reach the bank, take to the woods and get away home. My home, thank God, is as yet outside their lines; my wife and little ones are still beyond the invader's farthest advance."

As these thoughts, which have here to be set down in words, were flashed into the doomed man's brain rather than evolved from it the captain nodded to the sergeant. The sergeant stepped aside.

Peyton Farquhar was a well-to-do planter, of an old and highly respected Alabama family. Being a slave owner and like other slave owners a politician, he was naturally an original secessionist and ardently devoted to the Southern cause. Circumstances of an imperious nature, which is unnecessary to relate here, had prevented him from taking service with the gallant army that had fought the disastrous campaigns ending with the fall of Corinth, and he chafed under the inglorious restraint, longing for the release of his energies, the larger life of the soldier, the opportunity for distinction. That opportunity, he felt, would come, as it comes to all in war time. Meanwhile he did what he could. No service was too humble for him to perform in aid of the South, no adventure too perilous for him to undertake if consistent with the character of a civilian who was at heart a soldier, and who in good faith and without too much qualification assented to at least a part of the frankly villainous dictum that all is fair in love and war.

One evening while Farquhar and his wife were sitting on a rustic bench near the entrance to his grounds, a gray-clad soldier rode up to the gate and asked for a drink of water. Mrs. Farquhar was only too happy to serve him with her own white hands. While she was fetching the water her husband approached the dusty horseman and inquired eagerly for news from the front.

"The Yanks are repairing the railroads," said the man, "and are getting ready for another advance. They have reached the Owl Creek bridge, put it in order and built a stockade on the north bank. The commandant has issued an order, which is posted everywhere, declaring that any civilian caught interfering with the railroad, its bridges, tunnels or trains will be summarily hanged. I saw the order."

"How far is it to the Owl Creek bridge?" Farquhar asked.

"About thirty miles."

"Is there no force on this side of the creek?"

"Only a picket post half a mile out, on the railroad, and a single sentinel at this end of the bridge."

"Suppose a man—a civilian and student of hanging—should elude the picket post and perhaps get the better of the sentinel," said Farquhar, smiling, "what could he accomplish?"

The soldier reflected. "I was there a month ago," he replied. "I observed that the flood of last winter had lodged a great quantity of driftwood against the wooden pier at this end of the bridge. It is now dry and would burn like tow."

The lady had now brought the water, which the soldier drank. He thanked her ceremoniously, bowed to her husband and rode away. An hour later, after nightfall, he re-passed the plantation, going northward in the direction from which he had come. He was a Federal scout.

As Peyton Farquhar fell straight downward through the bridge he lost consciousness and was as one already dead. From this state he was awakened—ages later, it seemed to him—by the pain of a sharp pressure up his throat, followed by a sense of suffocation. Keen, poignant agonies seemed to shoot from his neck downward through every fiber of his body and limbs. These pains appeared to flash along well-defined lines of ramification and to beat with an inconceivably rapid periodicity. They seemed like streams of pulsating fire heating him to an intolerable temperature. As to his head, he was conscious of nothing but a feeling of fullness—of congestion. These sensations were unaccompanied by thought. The intellectual part of his nature was already effaced; he had power only to feel, and feeling was torment. He was conscious of motion. Encompassed in a luminous cloud, of which he was now merely the fiery heart, without material substance, he swung through unthinkable arcs of oscillation, like a vast pendulum. Then all at once, with terrible suddenness, the light about him shot upward with the noise of a loud splash; a frightful roaring was in his ears, and all was cold and dark. The power of thought was restored; he knew that the rope had broken and he had fallen into the stream. There was no additional strangulation; the noose about his neck was already suffocating him and kept the water from his lungs. To die of hanging at the bottom of a river!—the idea seemed to him ludicrous. He opened his eyes in the darkness and saw above him a gleam of light, but how distant, how inaccessible! He was still sinking, for the light became fainter and fainter until it was a mere glimmer. Then it began to grow and brighten, and he knew that he was rising toward the surface—knew it with reluctance, for he was now very comfortable. "To be hanged and drowned," he thought "that is not so bad; but I do not wish to be shot. No; I will not be shot; that is not fair."

He was not conscious of an effort, but a sharp pain in his wrist apprised him that he was trying to free his hands. He gave the struggle his attention, as an idler might observe the feat of a juggler, without interest in the outcome. What splendid effort! What magnificent, what superhuman strength! Ah, that was a fine endeavor! Bravo! The cord fell away; his arms parted and floated upward, the hands dimly seen on each side in the growing light. He watched them with a new interest as first one and then the other pounced upon the noose at his neck. They tore it away and thrust it fiercely aside, its undulations resembling those of a water snake. "Put it back, put it back!" He thought he shouted these words to his hands, for the undoing of the noose had been succeeded by the direst pang that he had yet experienced. His neck ached horribly; his brain was on fire; his heart, which had been fluttering faintly, gave a great leap, trying to force itself out at his mouth. His whole body was wracked and wrenched with an insupportable anguish! But his disobedient hands gave no heed to the command. They beat the water vigorously with quick, downward strokes, forcing him to the surface. He felt his head emerge; his eyes were blinded by the sunlight; his chest expanded convulsively, and with a supreme and crowning agony his lungs engulfed a great draught of air, which instantly he expelled in a shriek!

He was now in full possession of his physical senses. They were, indeed, preternaturally keen and alert. Something in the awful disturbance of his organic system had so exalted and refined them that they made record of things never before perceived. He felt the ripples upon his face and heard their separate sounds as they struck. He looked at the forest on the bank of the stream, saw the individual trees, the leaves and the veining of each leaf—saw the very insects upon them: the locusts, the brilliant-bodied flies, the gray spiders stretching their webs from twig to twig. He noted the prismatic colors in all the dew-drops upon a million blades of grass. The humming of the gnats that danced above the eddies of the stream, the beating of the dragonflies' wings, the strokes of the water spiders' legs, like oars which had lifted their boat—all these made audible music. A fish slid along beneath his eyes and he heard the rush of its body parting the water.

He had come to the surface facing down the stream; in a moment the visible world seemed to wheel slowly round, himself the pivotal point, and he saw the bridge, the fort, the soldiers upon the bridge, the captain, the sergeant, the two privates, his executioners. They were in silhouette against the blue sky. They shouted and gesticulated, pointing at him. The captain had drawn his pistol, but did not fire; the others were unarmed. Their movements were grotesque and horrible, their forms gigantic.

Suddenly he heard a sharp report and something struck the water smartly within a few inches of his head, spattering his face with spray. He heard a second report, and saw one of the sentinels with his rifle at his shoulder, a light cloud of blue smoke rising from the muzzle. The man in the water saw the eye of the man on the bridge gazing into his own through the sights of the rifle. He observed that it was a gray eye and remembered having read that gray eyes were keenest, and that all famous marksmen had them. Nevertheless, this one had missed.

A counter-swirl had caught Farquhar and turned him half round; he was again looking into the forest on the bank opposite the fort. The sound of a clear, high voice in a monotonous singsong now rang out behind him and came across the water with a distinctness that pierced and subdued all other sounds even the beating of the ripples in his ears. Although no soldier, he had frequented camps enough to know the dread significance of that deliberate, drawling, aspirated chant, the lieutenant on shore was taking a part in the morning's work. How coldly and pitilessly—with what an even, calm intonation, presaging, and enforcing tranquillity in the men—with what accurately measured intervals fell those cruel words:

"Attention, company! . . . Shoulder arms! . . . Ready! . . . Aim! . . . Fire!"

Farquhar dived—dived as deeply as he could. The water roared in his ears like the voice of Niagara, yet he heard the dulled thunder of the volley and, rising again toward the surface, met shining bits of metal, singularly flattened, oscillating slowly downward. Some of them touched him on the face and hands, then fell away, continuing their descent. One lodged between his collar and neck; it was uncomfortably warm and he snatched it out.

As he rose to the surface, gasping for breath, he saw that he had been a long time under water; he was perceptibly farther down stream—nearer to safety. The soldiers had almost finished reloading; the metal ramrods flashed all at once in the sunshine as they were drawn from the barrels, turned in the air, and thrust into their sockets. The two sentinels fired again, independently and ineffectually.

The hunted man saw all this over his shoulder; he was now swimming vigorously with the current. His brain was as energetic as his arms and legs; he thought with the rapidity of lightning.

"The officer," he reasoned, "will not make that martinet's error a second time. It is as easy to dodge a volley as a single shot. He has probably already given the command to fire at will. God help me, I cannot dodge them all!"

An appalling splash within two yards of him was followed by a loud, rushing sound, *diminuendo*, which seemed to travel back through the air to the fort and died in an explosion which stirred the very river to its deeps! A rising sheet of water curved over him, fell down upon him, blinded him, strangled him! The cannon had taken a hand in the game. As he shook his head free from the commotion of the smitten water he heard the deflected shot humming through the air ahead, and in an instant it was cracking and smashing the branches in the forest beyond.

"They will not do that again," he thought; "the next time they will use a charge of grape. I must keep my eye upon the gun; the smoke will apprise me—the report arrives too late; it lags behind the missile. That is a good gun."

Suddenly he felt himself whirled round and round—spinning like a top. The water, the banks, the forests, the now distant bridge, fort and men—all were commingled and blurred. Objects were represented by their colors only; circular horizontal streaks of color—that was all he saw. He had been caught in a vortex and was being whirled on with a velocity of advance and gyration that made him giddy and sick. In a few moments he was flung upon the gravel at the foot of the left bank of the stream—the southern bank—and behind a projecting point which concealed him from his enemies. The sudden arrest of his motion, the abrasion of one of his hands on the gravel, restored him, and he wept with delight. He dug his fingers into the sand, threw it over himself in handfuls and audibly blessed it. It looked like diamonds, rubies, emeralds; he could think of nothing beautiful which it did not resemble. The trees upon the bank were giant garden plants; he noted a definite order in their arrangement, inhaled the fragrance of their blooms. A strange, roseate light shone through the spaces among their trunks and the wind made in their branches the music of Aeolian harps. He had no wish to perfect his escape—was content to remain in that enchanting spot until retaken.

A whiz and rattle of grapeshot among the branches high above his head roused him from his dream. The baffled cannoneer had fired him a random farewell. He sprang to his feet, rushed up the sloping bank, and plunged into the forest.

All that day he traveled, laying his course by the rounding sun. The forest seemed interminable; nowhere did he discover a break in it, not even a woodman's road. He had not known that he lived in so wild a region. There was something uncanny in the revelation.

By nightfall he was fatigued, footsore, famishing. The thought of his wife and children urged him on. At last he found a road which led him in what he knew to be the right direction. It was as wide and straight as a city street, yet it seemed untraveled. No fields bordered it, no dwelling anywhere. Not so much as the barking of a dog suggested human habitation. The black bodies of the trees forced a straight wall on both sides, terminating on the horizon in a point, like a diagram in a lesson in perspective. Overhead, as he looked up through this rift in the wood, shone great golden stars looking unfamiliar and grouped in strange constellations. He was sure they were arranged in some order which had a secret and malign significance. The wood on either side was full of singular noises, among which—once, twice, and again—he distinctly heard whispers in an unknown tongue.

His neck was in pain and lifting his hand to it he found it horribly swollen. He knew that it had a circle of black where the rope had bruised it. His eyes felt congested; he could no longer close them. His tongue was swollen with thirst; he relieved its fever by thrusting it forward from between his teeth into the cold air. How softly the turf had carpeted the untraveled avenue—he could no longer feel the roadway beneath his feet!

Doubtless, despite his suffering, he had fallen asleep while walking, for now he sees another scene—perhaps he has merely recovered from a delirium. He stands at the gate of his own home. All is as he left it, and all bright and beautiful in the morning sunshine. He must have traveled the entire night. As he pushes open the gate and passes up the wide white walk, he sees a flutter of female garments; his wife, looking fresh and cool and sweet, steps down from the veranda to meet him. At the bottom of the steps she stands waiting, with a smile of ineffable joy, an attitude of matchless grace and dignity. Ah, how beautiful she is! He springs forward with extended arms. As he is about to clasp her he feels a stunning blow upon the back of the neck; a blinding white light blazes all about him with the sound like the shock of a cannon—then all is darkness and silence!

Peyton Farquhar was dead; his body, with a broken neck, swung gently from side to side beneath the timbers of the Owl Creek bridge.

DISCUSSION

This story, like "The Furnished Room," "Vanka," and "De Mortuis," involves a surprise ending, an ironical turn. The basic question that such stories raise is this: is the surprise ending justified; is it validated by the body of the story; is it, in other words, a mere trick, or is it expressive and functional?

Perhaps the best way to clear the ground for a consideration of this basic question is to raise another question, which will no doubt occur to many readers of this story: is it possible for a man in the last moment of his life to have a vision of the sort that Peyton Farquhar has as he falls from Owl Creek bridge? Readers may be inclined to judge this story in terms of their acceptance or rejection of the psychological realism of the incident. But is it possible to have absolutely convincing evidence on this point? Isn't the fact of the vision something that, in itself, can be accepted without too much strain on the reader's credulity? But there is a much more important consideration to be taken into account. Even if we could arrive at a completely satisfying decision about the psychological realism of the incident, would this fact actually determine the nature of our judgment concerning the story? For reasons suggested below, it would not determine our judgment, and therefore preoccupation with this question is likely to prove a red herring—is likely to distract us from the real problem.

Suppose that we assume for the moment that the incident is psychologically valid; there remain these questions to be answered:

1. Why does the author withhold from the reader the knowledge that the dying man's vision is merely a vision?

2. Is any revelation of character or other significant effect accomplished thereby?

3. Does the withholding of this information throw any light on the development of a theme for the story?

4. There is an irony generated by the end of the story, but is it a meaningful irony?

These questions lead us to observe that, basically, fiction is concerned with people. One of the interests we take in it arises from the presentation of human character and human experience as merely human. Both the common and the uncommon human character or experience interest us; the common because we share in it, and the uncommon because it wakes us to marvel at new possibilities. But it is a great—and not uncommon—error to equate the presentation of character as such, or experience as such, with the specific meaning of fiction. Fiction, as we have tried to indicate in section 1, involves a theme, an idea, an interpretation, an attitude toward life developed and embodied in the piece of fiction. Directly or indirectly, through the experience of the characters in the piece of fiction, an evaluation is made—an evaluation that is assumed to have some claim to a general validity.

The plot that depends on some peculiarity of human psychology—as does "An Occurrence at Owl Creek Bridge"—may give us a shock of surprise, but it does not carry a fictional meaning. The peculiar quirk of psychology—the "case study"—must also involve some significant human evaluation, some broadening or deepening of our human attitudes, if it is to be acceptable as fiction. Fiction involves all kinds of human characters and human experiences, common and uncommon, but it is concerned to do more than make a clinical report, medical or psychological. We must keep this firmly in mind. Fiction involves what—understood in its broadest dimension—is a moral concern. It is not concerned with mere peculiarities, quirks or happy (or unhappy) accidents as such.

CROSSING INTO POLAND

Isaac Babel

THE Commander of the VI Division reported: Novgorod-Volynsk was taken at dawn today. The Staff had left Krapivno, and our baggage train was spread out in a noisy rearguard over the highroad from Brest to Warsaw built by Nicholas I upon the bones of peasants.

Fields flowered around us, crimson with poppies; a noontide breeze played in the yellowing rye; on the horizon virginal buckwheat rose like the wall of a distant monastery. The Volyn's peaceful stream moved away from us in sinuous curves and was lost in the pearly haze of the birch groves; crawling between flowery slopes, it wound weary arms through a wilderness of hops. The orange sun rolled down the sky like a lopped-off head, and mild light glowed from the cloud gorges. The standards of the sunset flew above our heads. Into the cool of evening dripped the smell of yesterday's blood, of slaughtered horses. The blackened Zbruch roared, twisting itself into foamy knots at the falls. The bridges were down, and we waded across the river. On the waves rested a majestic moon. The horses were in to the cruppers, and the noisy torrent gurgled among hundreds of horses' legs. Somebody sank, loudly defaming the Mother of God. The river was dotted with the square black patches of the wagons, and was full of confused sounds, of whistling and singing, that rose above the gleaming hollows, the serpentine trails of the moon.

Far on in the night we reached Novograd. In the house where I was billeted I found a pregnant woman and two red-haired, scraggy-necked Jews. A third, huddled to the wall with his head covered up, was already asleep. In the room I was given I discovered turned-out wardrobes, scraps of women's fur coats on the floor, human filth, fragments of the occult crockery the Jews use only once a year, at Eastertime.

"Clear this up," I said to the woman. "What a filthy way to live!" The two Jews rose from their places and, hopping on their felt soles, cleared the mess from the floor. They skipped about noiselessly, monkey-fashion, like Japs in a circus act, their necks swelling and twisting. They put down for me a feather bed that had been disemboweled, and I lay down by the wall next to the third Jew, the one who was asleep. Faint-hearted poverty closed in over my couch.

Silence overcame all. Only the moon, clasping in her blue hands her round, bright, carefree face, wandered like a vagrant outside the window.

I kneaded my numbed legs and, lying on the ripped-open mattress, fell asleep. And in my sleep the Commander of the VI Division appeared to me; he was pursuing the Brigade Commander on a heavy stallion, fired at him twice between the eyes. The bullets pierced the Brigade Commander's head, and both his eyes dropped to the ground. "Why did you turn back the brigade?" shouted Savitsky, the Divisional Commander, to the wounded man—and here I woke up, for the pregnant woman was groping over my face with her fingers.

"Good sir," she said, "you're calling out in your sleep and you're tossing to and fro. I'll make you a bed in another corner, for you're pushing my father about."

She raised her thin legs and rounded belly from the floor and removed the blanket from the sleeper. Lying on his back was an old man, a dead old man. His throat had been torn out and his face cleft in two; in his beard blue blood was clotted like a lump of lead.

"Good sir," said the Jewess, shaking up the feather bed, "the Poles cut his throat, and he begging them: 'Kill me in the yard so that my daughter shan't see me die.' But they did as suited them. He passed away in this room, thinking of me.—And now I should wish to know," cried the woman with sudden and terrible violence, "I should wish to know where in the whole world you would find another father like my father?"

DISCUSSION

1. In the second paragraph, images of the beauty of nature (fields "crimson with poppies," "the yellowing rye," the "peaceful stream," "the pearly haze of the birch groves") are mixed with marks of violence ("the smell of yesterday's blood," the roaring of the river, the oaths). What re-

lation do you sense between this paragraph and the rest of the story? Notice in this connection, the description of the moon outside the window in the fifth paragraph.

2. In the fourth paragraph, what do you make of the narrator's attitude toward the Jews, particularly the woman? Suppose the narrator took a sympathetic tone. What difference would this make for the story?

3. Why does the woman think that no other father in the world could match hers? Why does she utter this thought "with sudden and terrible violence" and not, say, with a wail and outburst of tears? What difference would that make?

4. Here, again, we find a sudden turn at the end. Is it justifiable? Is it grounded in earlier details and tone in the story? Even the "violence"?

5. Suppose this story were developed at considerable length and detail. Would that impair the effect?

So far in this section we have generally dealt with stories more or less sharply focused on a single turn, a shift of plot that makes the point of the story. Though all fiction moves toward a point at which the disturbed equilibrium (which generates the story) is reestablished and a new meaning emerges, many pieces of fiction are much more complex than those we have been considering, requiring more than a simple turn to dramatize the emergence of the new meaning, the new equilibrium. In the stories that follow we shall find varying degrees of complication in plot, and sometimes not one turn but several, occurring in dramatic order.

THE NECKLACE

Guy de Maupassant

SHE was one of those pretty and charming girls who are sometimes, as if by a mistake of destiny, born in a family of clerks. She had no dowry, no expectations, no means of being known, understood, loved, wedded by any rich and distinguished man; and she let herself be married to a little clerk at the Ministry of Public Instruction.

She dressed plainly because she could not dress well, but she was as unhappy as though she had really fallen from her proper station, since with women there is neither caste nor rank: and beauty, grace, and charm act instead of family and birth. Natural fineness, instinct for what is elegant, suppleness of wit, are the sole hierarchy, and make from women of the people the equals of the very greatest ladies.

She suffered ceaselessly, feeling herself born for all the delicacies and all the luxuries. She suffered from the poverty of her dwelling, from the wretched look of the walls, from the worn-out chairs, from the ugliness of the curtains. All those things, of which another woman of her rank would never even have been conscious, tortured her and made her angry. The sight of the little Breton peasant who did her humble housework aroused in her regrets which were despairing, and distracted dreams. She thought of the silent antechambers hung with Oriental tapestry, lit by tall bronze candelabra, and of the two great footmen in knee breeches who sleep in the big armchairs, made drowsy by the heavy warmth of the hot-air stove. She thought of the long *salons* fitted up with ancient silk, of the delicate furniture carrying priceless curiosities, and of the coquettish perfumed boudoirs made for talks at five o'clock with intimate friends, with men famous and sought after, whom all women envy and whose attention they all desire.

When she sat down to dinner, before the round table covered with a tablecloth three days old, opposite her husband, who uncovered the soup tureen and declared with an enchanted air, "Ah, the good *pot-au-feu!* I don't know anything better than that," she thought of dainty dinners, of shining silverware, of tapestry which peopled the walls with ancient personages and with strange birds flying in the midst of a fairy forest; and she thought of delicious dishes served on marvelous plates, and of the whispered gallantries which you listen to with a sphinxlike smile, while you are eating the pink flesh of a trout or the wings of a quail.

She had no dresses, no jewels, nothing. And she loved nothing but that; she felt made for that. She would so have liked to please, to be envied, to be charming, to be sought after.

She had a friend, a former schoolmate at the convent, who was rich, and whom she did not like to go and see any more, because she suffered so much when she came back.

But one evening, her husband returned home with a triumphant air, and holding a large envelope in his hand.

"There," said he. "Here is something for you."

She tore the paper sharply, and drew out a printed card which bore these words:

The Minister of Public Instruction and Mme. Georges Ramponneau request the honor of M. and Mme. Loisel's company at the palace of the Ministry on Monday evening, January eighteenth."

Instead of being delighted, as her husband hoped, she threw the invitation on the table with disdain, murmuring:

"What do you want me to do with that?"

"But, my dear, I thought you would be glad. You never go out, and this is such a fine opportunity. I had awful trouble to get it. Everyone wants to go; it is very select, and they are not giving many invitations to clerks. The whole official world will be there."

She looked at him with an irritated glance, and said, impatiently:

"And what do you want me to put on my back?"

He had not thought of that; he stammered:

"Why, the dress you go to the theater in. It looks very well, to me."

He stopped, distracted, seeing his wife was crying. Two great tears descended slowly from the corners of her eyes toward the corners of her mouth. He stuttered:

"What's the matter? What's the matter?"

But by violent effort, she had conquered her grief, and she replied, with a calm voice, while she wiped her wet cheeks:

"Nothing. Only I have no dress and therefore I can't go to this ball.

Give your card to some colleague whose wife is better equipped than I."

He was in despair. He resumed:

"Come, let us see, Mathilde. How much would it cost, a suitable dress, which you could use on other occasions, something very simple?"

She reflected several seconds, making her calculations and wondering also what sum she could ask without drawing on herself an immediate refusal and a frightened exclamation from the economical clerk.

Finally, she replied, hesitatingly:

"I don't know exactly, but I think I could manage it with four hundred francs."

He had grown a little pale because he was laying aside just that amount to buy a gun and treat himself to a little shooting next summer on the plain of Nanterre, with several friends who went to shoot larks down there, of a Sunday.

But he said:

"All right. I will give you four hundred francs. And try to have a pretty dress."

The day of the ball drew near, and Mme. Loisel seemed sad, uneasy, anxious. Her dress was ready, however. Her husband said to her one evening:

"What is the matter? Come, you've been so queer these last three days."

And she answered:

"It annoys me not to have a single jewel, not a single stone, nothing to put on. I shall look like distress. I should almost rather not go at all."

He resumed:

"You might wear natural flowers. It's very stylish at this time of the year. For ten francs you can get two or three magnificent roses."

She was not convinced.

"No; there's nothing more humiliating than to look poor among other women who are rich."

But her husband cried:

"How stupid you are! Go look up your friend Mme. Forestier, and ask her to lend you some jewels. You're quite thick enough with her to do that."

She uttered a cry of joy:

"It's true. I never thought of it."

The next day she went to her friend and told of her distress.

Mme. Forestier went to a wardrobe with a glass door, took out a large jewel-box, brought it back, opened it, and said to Mme. Loisel:

"Choose, my dear."

She saw first of all some bracelets, then a pearl necklace, then a Venetian cross, gold and precious stones of admirable workmanship. She tried on the ornaments before the glass, hesitated, could not make up her mind to part with them, to give them back. She kept asking:

"Haven't you any more?"

"Why, yes. Look. I don't know what you like."

All of a sudden she discovered, in a black satin box, a superb necklace of diamonds, and her heart began to beat with an immoderate desire. Her hands trembled as she took it. She fastened it around her throat, outside her high-necked dress, and remained lost in ecstasy at the sight of herself.

Then she asked, hesitating, filled with anguish:

"Can you lend me that, only that?"

"Why, yes, certainly."

She sprang upon the neck of her friend kissed her passionately, then fled with her treasure.

The day of the ball arrived. Mme. Loisel made a great success. She was prettier than them all, elegant, gracious, smiling, and crazy with joy. All the men looked at her, asked her name, endeavored to be introduced. All the attachés of the Cabinet wanted to waltz with her. She was remarked by the minister himself.

She danced with intoxication, with passion, made drunk by pleasure, forgetting all, in the triumph of her beauty, in the glory of her success, in a sort of cloud of happiness composed of all this homage, of all this admiration, of all these awakened desires, and of that sense of complete victory which is so sweet to a woman's heart.

She went away about four o'clock in the morning. Her husband had been sleeping since midnight, in a little deserted anteroom, with three other gentlemen whose wives were having a very good time. He threw over her shoulders the wraps which he had brought, modest wraps of common life, whose poverty contrasted with the elegance of the ball dress. She felt this, and wanted to escape so as not to be remarked by the other women, who were enveloping themselves in costly furs.

Loisel held her back.

"Wait a bit. You will catch cold outside. I will go and call a cab."

But she did not listen to him, and rapidly descended the stairs. When they were in the street they did not find a carriage; and they began to look for one, shouting after the cabmen whom they saw passing by at a distance.

They went down toward the Seine, in despair, shivering with cold. At last they found on the quay one of those ancient noctambulant coupés which, exactly as if they were ashamed to show their misery during the day, are never seen round Paris until after nightfall.

It took them to their door in the Rue des Martyrs, and once more, sadly, they climbed up homeward. All was ended, for her. And as to him, he reflected that he must be at the Ministry at ten o'clock.

She removed the wraps which covered her shoulders, before the glass, so as once more to see herself in all her glory. But suddenly she uttered a cry. She no longer had the necklace around her neck!

Her husband, already half undressed, demanded:

"What is the matter with you?"

She turned madly towards him:

"I have—I have—I've lost Mme. Forestier's necklace."

He stood up, distracted.

"What!—how?—impossible!"

And they looked in the folds of her dress, in the folds of her cloak, in her pockets, everywhere. They did not find it.

He asked:

"You're sure you had it on when you left the ball?"

"Yes, I felt it in the vestibule of the palace."

"But if you had lost it in the street we should have heard it fall. It must be in the cab."

"Yes. Probably. Did you take his number?"

"No. And you, didn't you notice it?"

"No."

They looked, thunderstruck, at one another. At last Loisel put on his clothes.

"I shall go back on foot," said he, "over the whole route which we have taken to see if I can find it."

And he went out. She sat waiting on a chair in her ball dress, without strength to go to bed, overwhelmed, without fire, without a thought.

Her husband came back about seven o'clock. He had found nothing.

He went to Police Headquarters, to the newspaper offices, to offer a reward; he went to the cab companies—everywhere, in fact, whither he was urged by the least suspicion of hope.

She waited all day, in the same condition of mad fear before this terrible calamity.

Loisel returned at night with a hollow, pale face; he had discovered nothing.

"You must write to your friend," said he, "that you have broken the clasp of her necklace and that you are having it mended. That will give us time to turn round."

She wrote at his dictation.

At the end of a week they had lost all hope.

And Loisel, who had aged five years, declared:

"We must consider how to replace that ornament."

The next day they took the box which had contained it, and they went to the jeweler whose name was found within. He consulted his books.

"It was not I, madame, who sold that necklace; I must simply have furnished the case."

Then they went from jeweler to jeweler, searching for a necklace like the other, consulting their memories, sick both of them with chagrin and anguish.

They found, in a shop at the Palais Royal, a string of diamonds which seemed to them exactly like the one they looked for. It was worth forty thousand francs. They could have it for thirty-six.

So they begged the jeweler not to sell it for three days yet. And they made a bargain that he should buy it back for thirty-four thousand francs, in case they found the other one before the end of February.

Loisel possessed eighteen thousand francs which his father had left him. He would borrow the rest.

He did borrow, asking a thousand francs of one, five hundred of another, five louis here, three louis there. He gave notes, took up ruinous obligations, dealt with usurers and all the race of lenders. He compromised all the rest of his life, risked his signature without even knowing if he could meet it; and, frightened by the pains yet to come, by the black misery which was about to fall upon him, by the prospect of all the physical privation and of all the moral tortures which he was to suffer, he went to get the new necklace, putting down upon the merchant's counter thirty-six thousand francs.

When Mme. Loisel took back the necklace, Mme. Forestier said to her, with a chilly manner:

"You should have returned it sooner; I might have needed it."

She did not open the case, as her friend had so much feared. If she had detected the substitution, what would she have thought, what would she have said? Would she not have taken Mme. Loisel for a thief?

Mme. Loisel now knew the horrible existence of the needy. She took her part, moreover, all of a sudden, with heroism. That dreadful debt must be paid. She would pay it. They dismissed their servant; they changed their lodgings; they rented a garret under the roof.

She came to know what heavy housework meant and the odious cares of the kitchen. She washed the dishes, using her rosy nails on the greasy pots and pans. She washed the dirty linen, the shirts, and the dishcloths, which she dried upon a line; she carried the slops down to the street every morning, and carried up the water, stopping for breath at every landing. And, dressed like a woman of the people, she went to the fruiterer, the grocer, the butcher, her basket on her arm, bargaining, insulted, defending her miserable money sou by sou.

Each month they had to meet some notes, renew others, obtain more time.

Her husband worked in the evening making a fair copy of some tradesman's accounts, and late at night he often copied manuscript for five sous a page.

And this life lasted for ten years.

At the end of ten years, they had paid everything, everything, with the rates of usury, and the accumulations of the compound interest.

Mme. Loisel looked old now. She had become the woman of impoverished households—strong and hard and rough. With frowsy hair, skirts askew, and red hands, she talked loud while washing the floor with great swishes of water. But sometimes, when her husband was at the office, she sat down near the window, and she thought of that gay evening of long ago, of that ball where she had been so beautiful and so fêted.

What would have happened if she had not lost that necklace? Who knows? Who knows? How little a thing is needed for us to be lost or to be saved!

But, one Sunday, having gone to take a walk in the Champs Elysées to refresh herself from the labor of the week, she suddenly perceived a woman who was leading a child. It was Mme. Forestier, still young, still beautiful, still charming.

Mme. Loisel felt moved. Was she going to speak to her? Yes, certainly. And now that she had paid, she was going to tell her all about it. Why not?

She went up.

"Good-day, Jeanne."

The other, astonished to be familiarly addressed by this plain good-wife, did not recognize her at all, and stammered:

"But—madam!—I do not know—You must be mistaken."

"No. I am Mathilde Loisel."

Her friend uttered a cry.

"Oh, my poor Mathilde! How you are changed!"

"Yes, I have had days hard enough, since I have seen you, days wretched enough—and that because of you!"

"Of me! How so?"

"Do you remember that diamond necklace which you lent me to wear at the ministerial ball?"

"Yes. Well?"

"Well, I lost it."

"What do you mean? You brought it back."

"I brought you back another just like it. And for this we have been ten years paying. You can understand that it was not easy for us, us who had nothing. At last it is ended, and I am very glad."

Mme. Forestier had stopped.

"You say that you bought a necklace of diamonds to replace mine?"

"Yes. You never noticed it, then! They were very like."

And she smiled with a joy which was proud and naïve at once.

Mme. Forestier, strongly moved, took her two hands.

"Oh, my poor Mathilde! Why, my necklace was paste. It was worth at most five hundred francs!"

DISCUSSION

This story, too, ends with a surprising turn: the heroine, after years of privation and struggle caused by the loss of the borrowed necklace, learns that the jewels had, after all, been valueless. At first thought this revelation may seem to be a trick, just as the conclusion of "The Furnished Room" is a trick. On second thought, however, it may not be. To determine whether it is or not, investigate the following questions.

   1. Has Maupassant made use of the fact that the jewels are paste as a starting point from which to develop his story, or has he used it as merely a piece of trickery to provide a surprise ending? In other words, is there a really important difference between the fundamental fact that the jewels are paste and the fact that Mme. Loisel eventually learns this? Would there be an irony in the story even if she had never learned the true nature of the jewels?

   2. Some people, having lost a borrowed diamond necklace, would have made a clean breast of the situation at once, but Mme. Loisel never even considers confessing her loss. Is her failure to do so adequately motivated? Is her pride a true and admirable pride or merely a false pride? Or is there an ironical mixture of the two? Her actions subsequent to the loss of the necklace are presumably conditioned by her character. Are these two elements logically related in the story?

   3. Does the fundamental meaning of the story depend on the fact

of the loss of the necklace, whether paste or real? In other words, is not Mathilde Loisel the sort of woman who, in one way or another, would have wasted her life on some sort of vanity? (In this connection reread the first paragraph of the story.) Does not Maupassant use the loss of the necklace as a means to speed up and intensify a process already inherent in Mme. Loisel's character? If this can be maintained, then does not the falsity of the jewels become a kind of symbol for the root situation of the story? That is, does not the "falsity" of the jewels stand as a symbol for the falsity of the values by which Mme. Loisel once lived?

4. Have we any evidence that the author intended to indicate a regeneration of the heroine? If so, what are we to make of the fact that she discovers in the end that she has now paid for "real" jewels?

5. We may say that the irony of "De Mortuis" is based on a general view of life, the surprising and comic way in which things happen, and that the irony of "Young Goodman Brown" is based on a general view of human nature, the doubleness of human nature. The irony of "The Necklace" is based on something more specific. How would you describe it?

6. Mme. Forestier's revelation that the original necklace was paste carries to us, the readers, the point of the story. What does it carry to Mme. Loisel?

This story gives us a good chance to consider the problem of the treatment of time in fiction. The story takes Mme. Loisel from youth to middle age. Her girlhood is passed over in one sentence in the first paragraph, and the early years of marriage are treated in the second to the fifth paragraphs. Then the time of the ball is treated at considerable length in five direct scenes, the conversation about the dress, the conversation about the jewels, the visit to Mme. Forestier, the ball itself, the search for the lost necklace. Then the time of deprivation and payment, ten years, occupies a page or so. Then comes the denouement, the encounter with Mme. Forestier in the park.

There is, we see, a sort of balance between the long periods of time treated by summary, and the short periods, treated more or less dramatically by direct rendering. In treating the long periods, in which the eye sweeps, as it were, over a panorama, the writer needs to hit on the important fact, or the essential feeling of the period. He needs to distill the thing fundamental to the story—the character of the young Mathilde Loisel, or the way she lived through the ten years of deprivation. In the dramatic—or scenic—treatment the need, however, is to show the process of the movement through the time involved, how there is, step by step, a development; how, for example, Mme. Loisel decides to speak to her old friend in the park, how she accosts her, how she discovers the unexpected joy in the thought that the necklace she had bought had successfully deceived Mme. Forestier, how Mme. Forestier makes the revelation that, for us, will carry the burden of meaning: the "joy" of Mme. Loisel, her pride in a profound accomplishment—however momentary. The scene, in other words, gives the "close-ups" of time, and the summary gives the "long shots."

Often in a summary a writer must give more than mere summary. After all, he is writing fiction, and fiction wants to give the feeling of life, not merely the bare facts. Let us notice how even in the relatively bare summary in which Maupassant presents the years of hardship, he manages by a few specific touches to make us sense the quality of the life of the Loisels. Madame Loisel scraped "her rosy nails on the greasy pots and pans." When she carried up her household water every morning, she had to stop "for breath at every landing." She had become, Maupassant tells us, "strong and hard and rough." Then he writes: "With frowsy hair, skirts askew, and red hands, she talked loud while washing the floor with great swishes of water." It all comes alive with the phrase "great swishes of water." We *see* that.

Some pieces of fiction, even some novels, can proceed almost entirely by scenes, by direct presentation. For instance, "De Mortuis" gives us a single little segment of time, with only a minimum of summarized exposition from the past. Many stories and almost all novels, however, must swing back and forth between more or less direct treatments and narrative summary with more or less of description and analysis thrown in. It is well to begin to notice how these two basic kinds of treatment (with the various shadings and combinations) are related. We must ask ourselves how much the feeling of a particular story, the logic of its telling, the effect it has on us, are related to the writer's handling of this question of time. Again, there is no rule. We must try to inspect our own reactions as carefully and candidly as possible, and try to imagine what would be the effect, in instance after instance, if a different method were used.

WAR

Luigi Pirandello

THE passengers who had left Rome by the night express had to stop until dawn at the small station of Fabriano in order to continue their journey by the small old-fashioned local joining the main line with Sulmona.

At dawn, in a stuffy and smoky second-class carriage in which five people had already spent the night, a bulky woman in deep mourning was hoisted in—almost like a shapeless bundle. Behind her, puffing and moaning, followed her husband—a tiny man, thin and weakly, his face death-white, his eyes small and bright and looking shy and uneasy.

Having at last taken a seat he politely thanked the passengers who had helped his wife and who had made room for her; then he turned round to the woman trying to pull down the collar of her coat, and politely inquired:

"Are you all right, dear?"

The wife, instead of answering, pulled up her collar again to her eyes, so as to hide her face.

"Nasty world," muttered the husband with a sad smile.

And he felt it his duty to explain to his traveling companions that the poor woman was to be pitied, for the war was taking away from her her only son, a boy of twenty to whom both had devoted their entire life, even breaking up their home at Sulmona to follow him to Rome, where he had to go as a student, then allowing him to volunteer for war with an assurance, however, that at least for six months he would not be sent to the front and now, all of a sudden, receiving a wire saying that he was due to leave in three days' time and asking them to go and see him off.

The woman under the big coat was twisting and wriggling, at times growling like a wild animal, feeling certain that all those explanations would not have aroused even a shadow of sympathy from those people who—most likely—were in the same plight as herself. One of them, who had been listening with particular attention, said: "You should thank God that your son is only leaving now for the front. Mine has been sent there the first day of the war. He has already come back twice wounded and been sent back again to the front."

"What about me? I have two sons and three nephews at the front," said another passenger.

"Maybe, but in our case it is our *only* son," ventured the husband.

"What difference can it make? You may spoil your only son with excessive attentions, but you cannot love him more than you would all your other children if you had any. Paternal love is not like bread that can be broken into pieces and split amongst the childen in equal shares. A father gives *all* his love to each one of his children without discrimination, whether it be one or ten, and if I am suffering now for my two sons, I am not suffering half for each of them but double . . ."

"True . . . true . . ." sighed the embarrassed husband, "but suppose (of course we all hope it will never be your case) a father has two sons at the front and he loses one of them, there is still one left to console him . . . while . . ."

"Yes," answered the other, getting cross, "a son left to console him but also a son left for whom he must survive, while in the case of the father of an only son if the son dies the father can die too and put an end to his distress. Which of the two positions is the worse? Don't you see how my case would be worse than yours?"

"Nonsense," interrupted another traveler, a fat, red-faced man with bloodshot eyes of the palest gray.

He was panting. From his bulging eyes seemed to spurt inner violence of an uncontrolled vitality which his weakened body could hardly contain.

"Nonsense," he repeated, trying to cover his mouth with his hand so as to hide the two missing front teeth. "Nonsense. Do we give life to our children for our own benefit?"

The other travelers stared at him in distress. The one who had his son at the front since the first day of the war sighed: "You are right. Our children do not belong to us, they belong to the Country. . . ."

"Bosh," retorted the fat traveler. " Do we think of the Country when we give life to our children? Our sons are born because . . . well, because they must be born and when they come to life they take our own life with them. This is the truth. We belong to them but they can never belong to us. And when they reach twenty they are exactly what we were at their age. We too had a father and mother, but there were so many other things as well . . . girls, cigarettes, illusions, new ties . . . and the Country, of course, whose call we would have answered—when we were twenty—even if father and mother had said no. Now at our age, the love of our Country is still great, of course, but stronger than it is the love for our children. Is there any one of us here who wouldn't gladly take his son's place at the front if he could?"

There was a silence all round, everybody nodding as to approve.

"Why then," continued the fat man, "shouldn't we consider the feelings of our children when they are twenty? Isn't it natural that at their age they should consider the love for their Country (I am speaking of decent boys, of course) even greater than the love for us? Isn't it natural that it should be so, as after all they must look upon us as upon old boys who cannot move any more and must stay at home? If Country exists, if Country is a natural necessity, like bread, of which each of us must eat in order not to die of hunger, somebody must go to defend it. And our sons go, when they are twenty, and they don't want tears, because if they die, they die inflamed and happy (I am speaking, of course, of decent boys). Now, if one dies young and happy, without having the ugly sides of life, the boredom of it, the pettiness, the bitterness of disillusion . . . what more can we ask for him? Everyone should stop crying; everyone should laugh as I do . . . or at least thank God—as I do—because my son, before dying sent me a message saying that he was dying satisfied at having ended his life in the best way he could have wished. That is why, as you see, I do not even wear mourning. . . ."

He shook his light fawn coat as to show it; his livid lip over his missing teeth was trembling, his eyes were watery and motionless, and soon after he ended with a shrill laugh which might well have been a sob.

"Quite so . . . quite so . . ." agreed the others.

The woman who, bundled in a corner under her coat, had been sitting and listening had—for the last three months—tried to find in the words of her husband and her friends something to console her in her deep sorrow, something that might show her how a mother should resign herself to send her son not even to death but to a probably dangerous life. Yet not a word had she found amongst the many which had been said . . . and her grief had been greater in seeing that nobody—as she thought—could share her feelings.

But now the words of the traveler amazed and almost stunned her. She suddenly realized that it wasn't the others who were wrong and could not understand her but herself who could not rise up to the same height of those fathers and mothers willing to resign themselves, without crying, not only to the departure of their sons but even to their death.

She lifted her head, she bent over from her corner trying to listen with great attention to the details which the fat man was giving to his companions about the way his son had fallen as a hero, for his King and his Country, happy and without regrets. It seemed to her that she had stumbled into a world she had never dreamt of, a world so far unknown to her and she was so pleased to hear everyone joining in congratulating that brave father who could so stoically speak of his child's death.

Then suddenly, just as if she had heard nothing of what had been said and almost as if waking up from a dream, she turned to the old man, asking him:

"Then . . . is your son really dead?"

Everybody stared at her. The old man, too, turned to look at her, fixing his great, bulging, horribly watery light gray eyes, deep in her face. For some little time he tried to answer, but words failed him. He looked at her, almost as if only then—at that silly, incongruous question—he had suddenly realized at last that his son was really dead—gone for ever—for ever. His face contracted, became horribly distorted, then he snatched in haste a handkerchief from his pocket and, to the amazement of everyone, broke into harrowing, heart-rending, uncontrollable sobs.

DISCUSSION

This story may seem peculiarly lacking in action, if by the term we mean physical action. After the woman has been "hoisted" into the compartment and her shy, apologetic husband has climbed in after her, there is no physical movement indicated except the wriggling and twisting of the woman under her coat, the attempt of the old man to cover his mouth with his hand when he talks in order to conceal the fact that two of his teeth are missing, his shaking of his fawn-colored overcoat to show that he does not wear mourning, the woman's bending forward to listen to the old man, the turning of all eyes upon the woman when she finally asks the old man about his son, and the contortion of his face as he tries to answer. These physical actions are important in the story, but their importance lies in the fact that they are clues to the feelings and attitudes of the persons involved in the story. They do not, in other words, actually constitute the plot.

The plot itself is constituted of the conflicts among the various attitudes held by the characters toward the subject: the giving of children to the country. The form, then, is almost the form of a debate—different points of view are stated and argued, one after another. But this is not a debate for the mere sake of debate. The persons involved are persons for whom the issue is very real; they have sons in the war, and one man, the old man in the fawn-colored overcoat, has already lost his son. That is, the debate is dramatically meaningful for the participants.

The two extreme positions in the debate are held by the woman and the old man. The woman says nothing, but we know what her position is: "The woman under the big coat was twisting and wriggling, at times growling like a wild animal, feeling certain that all those explanations would not have aroused even a shadow of sympathy from those people who—most likely—were in the same plight as herself." Her grief has a kind of immediacy, like physical pain; it is beyond reasoning or discussion; she can only twist as in pain or utter meaningless animal-like sounds. The other extreme position, that of the old man whose son has been killed, is the most fully stated. He argues that one does not, in the first place, have children for one's own benefit; that, in the second place, a son, being young and idealistic, is more drawn by love of country than by love of parents; that if a son dies for his country he dies happy—if he is "decent"; that one who dies young and happy has been spared the ugly side of life, boredom, pettiness, disillusion; that, therefore, a parent whose son has died heroically should be happy and laugh, as he says he does, or should at least thank God. That is, the old man has completely argued away, philosophized away, all of the fundamental sense of loss and grief. Such are the two extremes of attitude.

Now, what may be called the plot pattern of the story depends upon the opposition between these two extreme views. But it is not a static opposition—a mere statement of difference. Both views are modified—even reversed.

First, the woman, who had been unable to take consolation from her husband or her friends, because, as she felt, nobody could share her feelings, begins to take consolation from the words of the stranger. He has actually lost a son, and therefore he must know, must be able to share, her own feelings. He must be wise, because his loss is greater than hers, for her son is yet alive. Furthermore, the very violence of the old man's position, its difference from all the views given her by husband and friends, its absolute denial of grief by its heroic terms, make her feel that she has "stumbled into a world she had never dreamt of." It seems incredible to her that a man whose son is really dead can speak thus of his loss. So "almost as if waking up from a dream" she asks him, "Then . . . is your son really dead?"

Presumably, if the man should say, simply, "Yes, he is dead," she would be prepared to accept, for the moment at least, his position. If the man could assure her once more that the son is "really" dead, then she could try to imitate his heroic attitude. She, too, would be able to face the fact of death.

But her question, which provides the climax, the focal point of the story, reveals something to the old man, just as his previous words have revealed something to her. So, as in the first place, we find her position modified by him, we find now, in the second place, his position modified by her. When she utters the words "really dead" everybody "stares" at her—as though she has said something out of place, something impolite and embarrassing, as though she had divulged some horrible and shocking secret. The old man stares at her too, and cannot answer. For the first time, he realizes that his son is "really dead—gone for ever—for ever." He is caught now in the abject, animal-like, unreasoning misery, in which she had previously been held, and bursts into sobs.

The story then, depends on a conflict between the basic, personal, unformulable emotion on the one hand, and systems, codes, reason, ideal compensations, and interpretations on the other. There is here an ironical contrast, an irreconcilable contrast—or a contrast, that, if reconcilable, is reconcilable only by the greatest effort. The equilibrium of the man who has made the reconciliation is upset, we see, by the slightest touch, by the woman's "silly, incongruous"—but fundamental—question. Are we to assume, therefore, that the author is simply saying that codes, systems, reason, obligations, ideals do not matter, that the only thing that matters is the fact of personal emotion? It seems not. If so, why would he illustrate the powerful appeal the old man's words make to the woman sunk in grief? No, it seems that Pirandello is putting, in dramatic terms, a basic conflict in human experience—is saying that the two terms of the opposition are always in existence and that neither can be ignored.

Let us turn again to the plot pattern of the story: the movement away from the two extreme positions of the woman and the old man, the process of mutual modification focused, finally, on the question she asks him. In other words, we have, in a sense, two "stories" within a story—the story of the woman's change of attitude and the story of the old man's change of attitude. Each of the two persons seems, when introduced, to be firmly fixed in a special attitude. How are we to account for the changes? Are the changes prepared for and made acceptable in the story?

We have some analysis of the woman's change. It is the novelty, the heroic quality, of the consolation offered by the old man, that attracts her. Further, the fact that he has really lost a son makes her feel that he will "understand" her. But we have no such explicit analysis of the change on the part of the old man. His change of attitude comes as a surprise. But does he not overstate his case in the earlier part of the story? Is there not an inkling of the fact that he is trying to argue against himself rather than against other people? Is there not a hint of hysteria? In this connection one might investigate the following sentence, which comes just after he has said that he does not even wear mourning: "He shook his light fawn coat as to show it; his livid lip over his missing teeth was trembling, his eyes were watery and motionless, and soon after he ended with a shrill laugh which might well have been a sob." Then, we may take the attitude of the woman herself as a kind of preparation for the old man's final change. She represents, as it were, the opposite pole of experience, but an undeniable pole.

The foregoing analysis of the story is not complete. Certain other questions are important for a full interpretation and for an understanding of the author's method.

1. What is the importance of the physical actions in the story? How do they offer clues to the feelings and attitudes of the characters? Consider, for instance, the fact that the old man at first tries to cover his mouth but later forgets to do so.

2. What is the significance of the words we have italicized in the following sentence? "The old man, too, turned to look at her, fixing his great, bulging, *horribly* watery light gray eyes, *deep* in her face."

3. Imagine another version of this story. Suppose that the old man, whose son is merely at the front, argues with the other people in the compartment, and persuades them, as in the present version of the story; at a station, he receives a telegram saying that his son has been killed, whereupon he bursts into "heart-rending, uncontrollable sobs" while they stare at him in amazement. Why would such a version be inferior to the story as Pirandello tells it?

THE MAN WHO WOULD BE KING

Rudyard Kipling

Brother to a Prince and fellow to a beggar if he be found worthy.

THE law, as quoted, lays down a fair conduct of life, and one not easy to follow. I have been a fellow to a beggar again and again under circumstances which prevented either of us finding out whether the other was worthy. I have still to be brother to a Prince, though I once came near to kinship with what might have been a veritable King and was promised the reversion of a Kingdom—army, law courts, revenue and policy all complete. But, today, I greatly fear that my King is dead, and if I want a crown I must go and hunt it for myself.

The beginning of everything was in a railway train upon the road to Mhow from Ajmir. There had been a Deficit in the Budget which necessitated traveling, not Second-class, which is only half as dear as First-class, but by Intermediate, which is very awful indeed. There are no cushions in the Intermediate class, and the population are either Intermediate, which is Eurasian, or native, which for a long night journey is nasty, or Loafer, which is amusing though intoxicated. Intermediates do not patronize refreshment rooms. They carry their food in bundles and pots, and buy sweets from the native sweetmeat-sellers, and drink the roadside water. That is why in the hot weather Intermediates are taken out of the carriages dead, and in all weathers are most properly looked down upon.

My particular Intermediate happened to be empty till I reached Nasirabad, when a huge gentleman in shirt sleeves entered, and, following the custom of Intermediates, passed the time of day. He was a wanderer and a vagabond like myself, but with an educated taste for whisky. He told tales of things he had seen and done, of out-of-the-way corners of the Empire into which he had penetrated, and of adventures in which he risked his life for a few days' food. "If India was filled with men like you and me, not knowing more than the crows where they'd get their next day's rations, it isn't seventy millions of revenue the land would be paying—it's seven hundred millions," said he; and as I looked at his mouth and chin I was disposed to agree with him. We talked politics—the politics of Loaferdom that sees things from the underside where the lath and plaster is not smoothed off—and we talked postal arrangements because my friend wanted to send a telegram back from the next station to Ajmir, which is the turning-off place from the Bombay to the Mhow line as you travel westward. My friend had no money beyond eight annas which he wanted for dinner, and I had no money at all, owing to the hitch in the Budget before-mentioned. Further, I was going into a wilderness where, though I should resume touch with the Treasury, there were no telegraph offices. I was, therefore, unable to help him in any way.

"We might threaten a Stationmaster, and make him send a wire on tick," said my friend, "but that'd mean inquiries for you and for me, and I've got my hands full these days. Did you say you are traveling back along this line within any days?"

"Within ten," I said.

"Can't you make it eight?" said he. "Mine is rather urgent business."

"I can send your telegram within ten days if that will serve you," I said.

"I couldn't trust the wire to fetch him now I think of it. It's this way. He leaves Delhi on the twenty-third for Bombay. That means he'll be running through Ajmir about the night of the twenty-third."

"But I'm going into the Indian Desert," I explained.

"Well *and* good," said he. "You'll be changing at Marwar Junction to get into Jodhpore territory—you must do that—and he'll be coming through Marwar Junction in the early morning of the twenty-fourth by the Bombay Mail. Can you be at Marwar Junction on that time? 'Twon't be inconveniencing you because I know that there's precious few pickings to be got out of these Central India States—even though you pretend to be correspondent of the *Backwoodsman*."

"Have you ever tried that trick?" I asked.

"Again and again, but the Residents find you out, and then you get escorted to the Border before you've time to get your knife into them. But about my friend here. I *must* give him a word o' mouth to tell him what's come to me or else he won't know where to go. I would take it more than kind of you if you was to come out of Central India in time to catch him at Marwar Junction, and say to him, 'He has gone South for the week.' He'll know what that means. He's a big man with a red beard, and a great swell he is. You'll find him sleeping like a gentleman with all his luggage round him in a Second-class compartment. But don't you be afraid. Slip down the window, and say, 'He has gone South for the week,' and he'll tumble. It's only cutting your time of stay in those parts by two days. I ask you as a stranger—going to the West," he said, with emphasis.

"Where have *you* come from?" said I.

"From the East," said he, "and I am hoping that you will give him the message on the Square—for the sake of my Mother as well as your own."

Englishmen are not usually softened by appeals to the memory of their mothers, but for certain reasons, which will be fully apparent, I saw fit to agree.

"It's more than a little matter," said he, "and that's why I ask you to do it—and now I know that I can depend on you doing it. A Second-class carriage at Marwar Junction, and a red-haired man asleep in it. You'll be sure to remember. I get out at the next station, and I must hold on there till he comes or sends me what I want."

"I'll give him the message if I catch him," I said, "and for the sake of your Mother as well as mine I'll give you a word of advice. Don't try to run the Central India States just now as the correspondent of the *Backwoodsman*. There's a real one knocking about here, and it might lead to trouble."

"Thank you," said he, simply, "and when will the swine be gone? I can't starve because he's ruining my work. I wanted to get hold of the Degumber Rajah down here about his father's widow, and give him a jump."

"What did he do to his father's widow, then?"

"Filled her up with red pepper and slippered her to death as she hung from a beam. I found that out myself, and I'm the only man that would dare going into the State to get hush money for it. They'll try to poison me, same as they did in Chortumna when I went on the loot there. But you'll give the man at Marwar Junction my message?"

He got out at a little roadside station, and I reflected. I had heard, more than once, of men personating correspondents of newspapers and bleeding small Native States with threats of exposure, but I had never met any of the caste before. They lead a hard life, and generally die with great suddenness. The Native States have a wholesome horror of English newspapers, which may throw light on their peculiar methods of government, and do their best to choke correspondents with champagne, or drive them out of their mind with four-in-hand barouches. They do not understand that nobody cares a straw for the internal administration of Native States so long as oppression and crime are kept within decent limits, and the ruler is not drugged, drunk, or diseased from one end of the year to the other. Native States were created by Providence in order to supply picturesque scenery, tigers, and tall writing. They are the dark places of the earth, full of unimaginable cruelty, touching the Railway and the Telegraph on one side, and, on the other, the days of Harun-al-Raschid. When I left the train I did business with divers Kings, and in eight days passed through many changes of life. Sometimes I wore dress clothes and consorted with Princes and Politicals, drinking from crystal and eating from silver. Sometimes I lay out upon the ground and devoured what I could get, from a plate made of a flapjack, and drank the running water, and slept under the same rug as my servant. It was all in the day's work.

Then I headed for the Great Indian Desert upon the proper date, as I had promised, and the night Mail set me down at Marwar Junction, where a funny little, happy-go-lucky, native-managed railway runs to Jodhpore. The Bombay Mail from Delhi makes a short halt at Marwar. She arrived as I got in, and I had just time to hurry to her platform and go down the carriages. There was only one Second-class on the train. I slipped in the window, and looked down upon a flaming red beard, half covered by a railway rug. That was my man, fast asleep, and I dug him gently in the ribs. He woke with a grunt, and I saw his face in the light of the lamps. It was a great and shining face.

"Tickets again?" said he.

"No," said I. "I am to tell you that he is gone South for the week. He is gone South for the week!"

The train had begun to move out. The red man rubbed his eyes. "He has gone South for the week," he repeated. "Now that's just like his impidence. Did he say that I was to give you anything?—'Cause I won't."

"He didn't," I said, and dropped away, and watched the red lights die out in the dark. It was horribly cold, because the wind was blowing off the sands. I climbed into my own train—not an Intermediate Carriage this time—and went to sleep.

If the man with the beard had given me a rupee I should have kept it as a memento of a rather curious affair. But the consciousness of having done my duty was my only reward.

Later on I reflected that two gentlemen like my friends could not do any good if they foregathered and personated correspondents of newspapers, and might, if they "stuck up" one of the little rat-trap states of Central India or Southern Rajputana, get themselves into serious difficulties. I therefore took some trouble to describe them as accurately as I could remember to people who would be interested in deporting them; and succeeded, so I was later informed, in having them headed back from Degumber borders.

Then I became respectable, and returned to an Office where there were no Kings and no incidents except the daily manufacture of a newspaper. A newspaper office seems to attract every conceivable sort of person, to the prejudice of discipline. Zenana-mission ladies arrive, and beg that the Editor will instantly abandon all his duties to describe a Christian prize-giving in a back-slum of a perfectly inaccessible village; Colonels who have been overpassed for commands sit down and sketch the outline of a series of ten, twelve, or twenty-four leading articles on Seniority *versus* Selection; missionaries wish to know why they have not been permitted to escape from their regular vehicles of abuse and swear at a brother missionary under special patronage of the editorial We; stranded theatrical companies troop up to explain that they cannot pay for their advertisements, but on their return from New Zealand or Tahiti will do so with interest; inventors of patent punkah-pulling machines, carriage couplings, and unbreakable swords and axletrees call with specifications in their pockets and hours at their disposal; tea companies enter and elaborate their prospectuses with the office pens; secretaries of ball committees clamor to have the glories of their last dance more fully expounded; strange ladies rustle in and say, "I want a hundred lady's cards printed *at once*, please," which is manifestly part of an Editor's duty; and every dissolute ruffian that ever tramped the Grand Trunk Road makes it his business to ask for employment as a proofreader. And, all the time, the telephone bell is ringing madly, and Kings are being killed on the Continent, and Empires are saying—"You're another," and Mister Gladstone is calling down brimstone upon the British Dominions, and the little black copy boys are whining, "*kaa-pi chay-ha-yeh*" (copy wanted) like tired bees, and most of the paper is as blank as Modred's shield.

But that is the amusing part of the year. There are other six months wherein none ever come to call, and the thermometer walks inch by inch up to the top of the glass, and the office is darkened to just above reading light, and the press machines are red-hot of touch, and nobody writes anything but accounts of amusements in the Hill stations or obituary notices. Then the telephone becomes a tinkling terror, because it tells you of the sudden deaths of men and women that you knew intimately, and the prickly heat covers you as with a garment, and you sit down and write: "A slight increase of sickness is reported from the Khuda Janta Khan District. The outbreak is purely sporadic in its nature, and, thanks to the energetic efforts of the District authorities, is now almost at an end. It is, however, with deep regret we record the death, etc."

Then the sickness really breaks out, and the less recording and reporting the better for the peace of the subscribers. But the Empires and the Kings continue to divert themselves as selfishly as before, and the Foreman thinks that a daily paper really ought to come out once in twenty-four hours, and all the people at the Hill stations in the middle of their amusements say, "Good gracious! Why can't the paper be more sparkling? I'm sure there's plenty going on up here."

That is the dark half of the moon, and, as the advertisements say, "must be experienced to be appreciated."

It was in that season, and a remarkably evil season, that the paper began running the last issue of the week on Saturday night, which is to say, Sunday morning, after the custom of a London paper. This was a great convenience, for immediately after the paper was put to bed, the dawn would lower the thermometer from 96° to almost 84° for half an hour, and in that chill—you have no idea how cold is 84° on the grass until you begin to pray for it—a very tired man could set off to sleep ere the heat roused him.

One Saturday night it was my pleasant duty to put the paper to bed alone. A King or courtier or a courtesan or a community was going to die or get a new Constitution, or do something that was important on the other side of the world, and the paper was to be held open till the latest possible minute in order to catch the telegram. It was a pitchy black night, as stifling as a June night can be, and the *loo*, the red-hot wind from the westward, was booming among the tinder-dry trees and pretending that the rain was on its heels. Now and again a spot of almost boiling water would fall on the dust with the flop of a frog, but all our weary world knew that was only pretense. It was a shade cooler in the press room than the office, so I sat there, while the type clicked and clicked and the nightjars hooted at the windows, and the all but naked compositors wiped the sweat from their foreheads and called for water. The thing that was keeping us back, whatever it was, would not come off, though the *loo* dropped and the last type was set, and the whole round earth stood still in the choking heat, with its finger on its lip, to wait the event. I drowsed, and wondered whether the telegraph was a blessing, and whether this dying man, or struggling people, was aware of the inconvenience the delay was causing. There was no special reason beyond the heat and worry to make tension, but as the clock hands crept up to three o'clock and the machines spun their flywheels two or three times to see that all was in order, before I said the word that would set them off, I could have shrieked aloud.

Then the roar and rattle of the wheels shivered the quiet into little bits. I rose to go away, but two men in white clothes stood in front of me. The first one said, "It's him!" The second said, "So it is!" And they both laughed almost as loudly as the machinery roared, and mopped their foreheads. "We see there was a light burning across the road and we were sleeping in that ditch there for coolness, and I said to my friend here, 'The office is open. Let's come along and speak to him as turned us back from the Degumber State,' " said the smaller of the two. He was the man I had met in the Mhow train, and his fellow was the red-bearded man of Marwar Junction. There was no mistaking the eyebrows of the one or the beard of the other.

I was not pleased, because I wished to go to sleep, not to squabble with loafers. "What do you want?" I asked.

"Half an hour's talk with you cool and comfortable, in the office," said the red-bearded man. "We'd *like* some drink—the Contrack doesn't begin yet, Peachey, so you needn't look—but what we really want is advice. We don't want money. We ask you as a favor, because you did us a bad turn about Degumber."

I led from the press room to the stifling office with the maps on the walls, and the red-haired man rubbed his hands. "That's something like," said he. "This was the proper shop to come to. Now, Sir, let me introduce to you Brother Peachey Carnehan, that's him, and Brother Daniel Dravot, that is *me*, and the less said about our professions the better, for we have been most things in our time. Soldier, sailor, compositor, photographer, proofreader, street preacher, and correspondents of the *Backwoodsman* when we thought the paper wanted one. Carnehan is sober, and so am I. Look at us first and see that's sure. It will save you cutting into my talk. We'll take one of your cigars apiece, and you shall see us light."

I watched the test. The men were absolutely sober, so I gave them each a tepid peg.

"Well *and* good," said Carnehan of the eyebrows, wiping the froth from his mustache. "Let me talk now, Dan. We have been all over India, mostly on foot. We have been boiler-fitters, engine-drivers, petty contractors, and all that, and we have decided that India isn't big enough for such as us."

They certainly were too big for the office. Dravot's beard seemed to fill half the room and Carnehan's shoulders the other half, as they sat on the big table. Carnehan continued: "The country isn't half worked out because they that governs it won't let you touch it. They spend all their blessed time in governing it, and you can't lift a spade, nor chip a rock, nor look for oil, nor anything like that without all the Government saying, 'Leave it alone and let us govern.' Therefore, such as it is, we will let it alone, and go away to some other place where a man isn't crowded and can come to his own. We are not little men, and there is nothing that we are afraid of except Drink, and we have signed a Contrack on that. *Therefore*, we are going away to be Kings."

"Kings in our own right," muttered Dravot.

"Yes, of course," I said. "You've been tramping in the sun, and it's a very warm night, and hadn't you better sleep over the notion? Come to-morrow."

"Neither drunk nor sunstruck, " said Dravot. "We have slept over the notion half a year, and require to see Books and Atlases, and we have decided that there is only one place now in the world that two strong men can Sar-a-*whack*. They call it Kafiristan. By my reckoning it's the top right-hand corner of Afghanistan, not more than three hundred miles from Peshawar. They have two and thirty heathen idols there, and we'll be the thirty-third. It's a mountainous country, and the women of those parts are very beautiful."

"But that is provided against in the Contrack," said Carnehan. "Neither Women nor Liqu-or, Daniel."

"And that's all we know, except that no one has gone there, and they fight, and in any place where they fight, a man who knows how to drill men can always be a King. We shall go to those parts and say to any King we find, 'D'you want to vanquish your foes?' and we will show him how to drill men; for that we know better than anything else. Then we will sub-vert that King and seize his Throne and establish a Dy-nasty."

"You'll be cut to pieces before you're fifty miles across the Border," I said. "You have to travel through Afghanistan to get to that country. It's one mass of mountains and peaks and glaciers, and no Englishman has been through it. The people are utter brutes, and even if you reached them you couldn't do anything."

"That's more like," said Carnehan. "If you could think us a little more mad we would be more pleased. We have come to you to know about this country, to read a book about it, and be shown maps. We want you to tell us that we are fools and to show us your books." He turned to the bookcases.

"Are you at all in earnest?" I said.

"A little," said Dravot, sweetly. "As big a map as you have got, even if it's all blank where Kafiristan is, and any books you've got. We can read, though we aren't very educated."

I uncased the big thirty-two-miles-to-the-inch map of India, and two smaller Frontier maps, hauled down volume INF-KAN of the *Encyclopaedia Britannica*, and the men consulted them.

"See here!" said Dravot, his thumb on the map. "Up to Jagdallak, Peachey and me know the road. We was there with Roberts's Army. We'll have to turn off to the right at Jagdallak through Laghmann territory. Then we get among the hills—fourteen thousand feet—fifteen thousand—it will be cold work there, but it don't look very far on the map."

I handed him Wood on the *Sources of the Oxus*. Carnehan was deep n the Encyclopaedia.

"They're a mixed lot," said Dravot, reflectively; "and it won't help us to know the names of their tribes. The more tribes the more they'll fight, and the better for us. From Jagdallak to Ashang. H'mm!"

"But all the information about the country is as sketchy and inaccu-rate as can be," I protested. "No one knows anything about it really. Here's the file of the United Services' Institute. Read what Bellew says."

"Blow Bellew!" said Carnehan. "Dan, they're an all-fired lot of heathens, but this book here says they think they're related to us English."

I smoked while the men poured over Raverty, Wood, the maps, and the Encyclopaedia.

"There is no use your waiting," said Dravot, politely. "It's about four o'clock now. We'll go before six o'clock if you want to sleep, and we won't steal any of the papers. Don't you sit up. We're two harmless lunatics and if you come, tomorrow evening, down to the Serai we'll say good-by to you."

"You *are* two fools," I answered. "You'll be turned back at the Frontier or cut up the minute you set foot in Afghanistan. Do you want any money or a recommendation down-country? I can help you to the chance of work next week."

"Next week we shall be hard at work ourselves, thank you," said Dravot. "It isn't so easy being a King as it looks. When we've got our Kingdom in order we'll let you know, and you can come up and help us to govern it."

"Would two lunatics make a Contrack like that?" said Carnahan, with subdued pride, showing me a greasy half-sheet of note paper on which was written the following. I copied it, then and there, as a curiosity:

This Contract between me and you pursuing witnesseth in the name of God— Amen and so forth.

(One)   That me and you will settle this matter together: i.e.; to be Kings of Kafiristan.

(Two)   That you and me will not , while this matter is being settled, look at any Liquor, nor any Woman, black, white or brown, so as to get mixed up with one or the other harmful.

(Three)   That we conduct ourselves with dignity and discretion and if one of us gets into trouble the other will stay by him.

Signed by you and me this day.

Peachey Taliaferro Carnehan.

Daniel Dravot.

Both Gentlemen at Large.

"There was no need for the last article," said Carnehan, blushing modestly; "but it looks regular. Now you know the sort of men that Loafers are—we are Loafers, Dan, until we get out of India—and do you think that we would sign a Contrack like that unless we was in earnest? We have kept away from the two things that make life worth having."

"You won't enjoy your lives much longer if you are going to try this idiotic adventure. Don't set the office on fire," I said, "and go away before nine o'clock."

I left them still poring over the maps and making notes on the back of the "Contrack." "Be sure to come down to the Serai tomorrow," were their parting words.

The Kumharsen Serai is the great four-square sink of humanity where the strings of camels and horses from the North load and unload. All the nationalities of Central Asia may be found there, and most of the folk of India proper. Balkh and Bokhara there meet Bengal and Bombay, and try to draw eyeteeth. You can buy ponies, turquoises, Persian pussy-cats, saddlebags, fat-tailed sheep, and musk in the Kumharsen Serai, and get many strange things for nothing. In the afternoon I went down there to see whether my friends intended to keep their word or were lying about drunk.

A priest attired in fragments of ribbons and rags stalked up to me, gravely twisting a child's paper whirligig. Behind was his servant bending under the load of a crate of mud toys. The two were loading up two camels, and the inhabitants of the Serai watched them with shrieks of laughter.

"The priest is mad," said a horse-dealer to me. "He is going up to Kabul to sell toys to the Amir. He will either be raised to honor or have his head cut off. He came in here this morning and has been behaving madly ever since."

"The witless are under the protection of God," stammered a flat-cheeked Usbeg in broken Hindi. "They foretell future events."

"Would they could have foretold that my caravan would have been cut up by the Shinwaris almost within shadow of the Pass!" grunted the Eusufzai agent of a Rajputana trading house whose goods had been feloniously diverted into the hands of other robbers just across the Border, and whose misfortunes were the laughingstock of the bazaar. "Ohé, priest, whence come you and whither do you go?"

"From Roum have I come," shouted the priest, waving his whirligig; "from Roum, blown by the breath of a hundred devils across the sea! O thieves, robbers, liars, the blessing of Pir Khan on pigs, dogs, and perjurers! Who will take the Protected of God to the North to sell charms that are never still to the Amir? The camels shall not gall, the sons shall not fall sick, and the wives shall remain faithful while they are away, of the men who give me place in their caravan. Who will assist me to slipper the King of the Roos with a golden slipper with a silver heel? The protection of Pir Khan be upon his labors!" He spread out the skirts of his gaberdine and pirouetted between the lines of tethered horses.

"There starts a caravan from Peshawar to Kabul in twenty days, *Huzrut*," said the Eusufzai trader. "My camels go therewith. Do thou also go and bring us good luck."

"I will go even now!" shouted the priest. "I will depart upon my winged camels, and be at Peshawar in a day! Ho! Hazar Mir Khan," he yelled to his servant, "drive out the camels, but let me first mount my own."

He leaped on the back of his beast as it knelt, and, turning round to me, cried, "Come thou also, Sahib, a little along the road, and I will sell thee a charm—an amulet that shall make thee King of Kafiristan."

Then the light broke upon me, and I followed the two camels out of the Serai till we reached open road and the priest halted.

"What d'you think o' that?" said he in English. "Carnehan can't talk their patter, so I've made him my servant. He makes a handsome servant. 'Tisn't for nothing that I've been knocking about the country for fourteen years. Didn't I do that talk neat? We'll hitch on to a caravan at

Peshawar till we get to Jagdallak, and then we'll see if we can get donkeys for our camels, and strike into Kafiristan. Whirligigs for the Amir, O Lor'! Put your hand under the camel bags and tell me what you feel."

I felt the butt of a Martini, and another and another.

"Twenty of 'em," said Dravot, placidly. "Twenty of 'em, and amunition to correspond, under the whirligigs and the mud dolls."

"Heaven help you if you are caught with those things!" I said. "A Martini is worth her weight in silver among the Pathans."

"Fifteen hundred rupees of capital—every rupee we could beg, borrow, or steal—are invested on these two camels," said Dravot. "We won't get caught. We're going through the Khyber with a regular caravan. Who'd touch a poor mad priest?"

"Have you got everything you want?" I asked, overcome with astonishment.

"Not yet, but we shall soon. Give us a memento of your kindness, Brother. You did me a service yesterday, and that time in Marwar. Half my Kingdom shall you have, as the saying is." I slipped a small charm compass from my watch chain and handed it up to the priest.

"Good-by," said Dravot, giving me hand cautiously. "It's the last time we'll shake hands with an Englishman these many days. Shake hands with him, Carnehan," he cried, as the second camel passed me.

Carnehan leaned down and shook hands. Then the camels passed away along the dusty road, and I was left alone to wonder. My eye could detect no failure in the disguises. The scene in Serai attested that they were complete to the native mind. There was just the chance, therefore, that Carnehan and Dravot would be able to wander through Afghanistan without detection. But, beyond, they would find death, certain and awful death.

Ten days later a native friend of mine, giving me the news of the day from Peshawar, wound up his letter with: "There has been much laughter here on account of a certain mad priest who is going in his estimation to sell pretty gauds and insignificant trinkets which he ascribes as great charms to H. H. The Amir of Bokhara. He passed through Peshawar and associated himself to the Second Summer caravan that goes to Kabul. The merchants are pleased, because through superstition they imagine that such mad fellows bring good fortune."

The two, then, were beyond the Border, I would have prayed for them, but, that night, a real King died in Europe, and demanded an obituary notice.

The wheel of the world swings through the same phases again and again. Summer passed and winter thereafter, and came and passed again. The daily paper continued and I with it, and upon the third summer there fell a hot night, a night issue, and a strained waiting for something to be telegraphed from the other side of the world, exactly as had happened before. A few great men had died in the past two years, the machines worked with more clatter, and some of the trees in the Office garden were few feet taller. But that was all the difference.

I passed over to the press room, and went through just such a scene as I have already described. The nervous tension was stronger than it had been two years before, and I felt the heat more acutely. At three o'clock I cried, "Print off," and turned to go, when there crept to my chair what was left of a man. He was bent into a circle, his head was sunk between his shoulders, and he moved his feet one over the other like a bear. I could hardly see whether he walked or crawled—this rag-wrapped, whining cripple who addressed me by name, crying that he was come back. "Can you give me a drink?" he whimpered. "For the Lord's sake, give me a drink!"

I went back to the office, the man followed with groans of pain, and I turned up the lamp.

"Don't you know me?" he gasped, dropping into a chair, and he turned his drawn face, surmounted by a shock of gray hair, to the light.

I looked at him intently. Once before I had seen eyebrows that met over the nose in an inch-broad black band, but for the life of me I could not tell where.

"I don't know you," I said, handing him the whisky. "What can I do for you?"

He took a gulp of the spirit raw, and shivered in spite of the suffocating heat.

"I've come back," he repeated; "and I was the King of Kafiristan—me and Dravot—crowned Kings we was! In this office we settled it—you setting there and giving us the books. I am Peachey—Peachey Taliaferro Carnehan, and you've been setting here ever since—O Lord!"

I was more than a little astonished, and expressed my feelings accordingly.

"It's true," said Carnehan, with a dry cackle, nursing his feet, which were wrapped in rags. "True as gospel. Kings we were, with crowns upon our heads—me and Dravot—poor Dan—oh, poor, poor Dan, that would never take advice, not though I begged of him!"

"Take the whisky," I said, "and take your own time. Tell me all you can recollect of everything from beginning to end. You got across the border on your camels, Dravot dressed as a mad priest and you his servant. Do you remember that?"

"I ain't mad—yet, but I shall be that way soon. Of course I remember. Keep looking at me, or maybe my words will go all to pieces. Keep looking at me in my eyes and don't say anything."

I leaned forward and looked into his face as steadily as I could. He dropped one hand upon the table and I grasped it by the wrist. It was twisted like a bird's claw, and upon the back was a ragged, red, diamond-shaped scar.

"No, don't look there. Look at *me*," said Carnehan.

"That comes afterwards, but for the Lord's sake don't distrack me. We left with that caravan, me and Dravot, playing all sorts of antics to amuse the people we were with. Dravot used to make us laugh in the evenings when all the people was cooking their dinners—cooking their dinners, and . . . what did they do then? They lit little fires with sparks that went into Dravot's beard, and we all laughed—fit to die. Little red fires they was, going into Dravot's big red beard—so funny." His eyes left mine and he smiled foolishly.

"You went as far as Jagdallak with that caravan," I said, at a venture, "after you had lit those fires. To Jagdallak, where you turned off to try to get into Kafiristan."

"No, we didn't neither. What are you talking about? We turned off before Jagdallak, because we heard the roads was good. But they wasn't good enough for our two camels—mine and Dravot's. When we left the caravan, Dravot took off all his clothes and mine too, and said we would be heathen, because the Kafirs didn't allow Mohammedans to talk to them. So we dressed betwixt and between, and such a sight as Daniel Dravot I never saw yet nor expect to see again. He burned half his beard, and slung a sheepskin over his shoulder, and shaved his head into patterns. He shaved mine too, and made me wear outrageous things to look like a heathen. That was in a most mountaineous country, and our camels couldn't go along any more because of the mountains. They were tall and black, and coming home I saw them fight like wild goats—there are lots of goats in Kafiristan. And these mountains, they never keep still, no more than goats. Always fighting they are, and don't let you sleep at night."

"Take some more whisky," I said, very slowly. "What did you and Daniel Dravot do when the camels could go no further because of the rough roads that led into Kafiristan?"

"What did which do? There was a a party called Peachey Taliaferro Carnehan that was with Dravot. Shall I tell you about him? He died out there in the cold. Slap from the bridge fell old Peachey, turning and twisting in the air like a penny whirligig that you can sell to the Amir. No; they was two for three ha'pence, those whirligigs, or I am much mistaken and woeful sore. And then these camels were no use, and Peachey said to Dravot, 'For the Lord's sake, let's get out of this before our heads are chopped off,' and with that they killed the camels all among the mountains, not having anything in particular to eat, but first they took off the boxes with the guns and the ammunition, till two men came along driving four mules. Dravot up and dances in front of them, singing, 'Sell me four mules.' Says the first man, 'If you are rich enough to buy, you are rich enough to rob'; but before ever he could put his hand to his knife, Dravot breaks his neck over his knee, and the other party runs away. So Carnehan loaded the mules with the rifles that was taken off the camels, and together we starts forward into those bitter cold mountaineous parts, and never a road broader than the back of your hand."

He paused for a moment, while I asked him if he could remember the nature of the country through which he had journeyed.

"I am telling you as straight as I can, but my head isn't as good as it might be. They drove nails through it to make me hear better how Dravot died. The country was mountaineous and the mules were most contrary, and the inhabitants was dispersed and solitary. They went up and up, and down and down, and that other party, Carnehan, was imploring of Dravot not to sing and whistle so loud, for fear of bringing down the tremenjus avalanches. But Dravot says that if a King couldn't sing it wasn't worth being King, and whacked the mules over the rump, and never took no heed for ten cold days. We came to a big level valley all among the mountains, and the mules were near dead, so we killed them, not having anything in special for them or us to eat. We sat upon the boxes, and played odd and even with the cartridges that was jolted out.

"Then ten men with bows and arrows ran down that valley, chasing twenty men with bows and arrows and the row was tremenjus. They was fair men—fairer than you or more—with yellow hair and remarkable well built. Says Dravot, unpacking the guns, 'This is the beginning of the business. We'll fight for the ten men,' and with that he fires two rifles at the twenty men, and drops one of them at two hundred yards from the rock where we was sitting. The other men began to run, but Carnehan and Dravot sits on the boxes picking them off at all ranges, up and down the valley. Then we goes up to the ten men that had run across the snow too, and they fires a footy little arrow at us. Dravot he shoots above their heads and they all falls down flat. Then he walks over and kicks them, and then he lifts them up and shakes hands all around to make them friendly like. He calls them and gives them the boxes to carry, and waves his hand for all the world as though he was King already. They takes the boxes and him across the valley and up the hill into a pine wood on the top, where there was half a dozen big stone idols. Dravot he goes to the biggest—a fellow they call Imbra—and lays a rifle and a cartridge at his feet, rubbing his nose respectful with his own nose, patting him on the head, and saluting in front of it. He turns round to them men and nods his head, and says, 'That's all right. I'm in the know too, and all these old jim-jams are my friends.' Then he opens his mouth and points down it, and when the first man brings him food, he says 'No'; and when the second man brings him food, he says 'No'; but when one of the old priests and the boss of the village brings him food, he says 'Yes'; very haughty, and eats it slow. That was how we came to our first village, without any trouble, just as though we had tumbled from the skies. But we tumbled from one of those damned rope bridges, you see, and you couldn't expect a man to laugh much after that."

"Take some more whisky and go on," I said. "That was the first village you came into. How did you get to be King?"

"I wasn't King," said Carnehan. "Dravot he was the King, and a handsome man he looked with the gold crown on his head and all. Him and the other party stayed in that village, and every morning Dravot sat by the side of old Imbra, and the people came and worshiped. That was Dravot's order. Then a lot of men came into the valley, and Carnehan and Dravot picks them off with the rifles before they knew where they was, and runs down into the valley and up again the other side, and finds another village, same as the first one, and the people all falls down flat on their faces, and Dravot says, 'Now what is the trouble between you two villages?' and the people points to a woman, as fair as you or me, that was carried off, and Dravot takes her back to the first village and counts up the dead—eight there was. For each dead man Dravot pours a little milk on the ground and waves his arms like a whirligig and 'That's all right,' says he. Then he and Carnehan takes the big boss of each village by the arm and walks them down into the valley, and shows them how to scratch a line with a spear right down the valley, and gives each a sod of turf from both sides o' the line. Then all the people comes down and shouts like the devil and all, and Dravot says, 'Go and dig the land, and be fruitful and multiply,' which they did, though they didn't understand. Then we asks the names of things in their lingo—bread and water and fire and idols and such, and Dravot leads the priest of each village up to the idol, and says he must sit there and judge the people, and if anything goes wrong he is to be shot.

"Next week they was all turning up the land in the valley as quiet as bees and much prettier, and the priests heard all the complaints and told Dravot in dumb show what it was about. 'That's just the beginning,' says Dravot. 'They think we're Gods.' He and Carnehan picks out twenty good men and shows them how to click off a rifle, and form fours, and advance in line, and they was very pleased to do so, and clever to see the hang of it. Then he takes out his pipe and his 'baccy-pouch and leaves one at one village and one at the other, and off we two goes to see what was to be done in the next valley. That was all rock, and there was a little village there, and Carnehan says, 'Send 'em to the old valley to plant,' and takes 'em there and gives 'em some land that wasn't took before. They were a poor lot, and we blooded 'em with a kid before letting 'em into the new Kingdom. That was to impress the people, and then they settled down quiet, and Carnehan went back to Dravot, who had got into another valley, all snow and ice and most mountaineous. There was no people there, and the Army got afraid, so Dravot shoots one of them, and goes on till he finds some people in a village, and the Army explains that unless the people wants to be killed they had better not shoot their little matchlocks; for they had matchlocks. We makes friends with the priest and I stays there alone with two of the Army, teaching the men how to drill, and a thundering big Chief comes across the snow with kettledrums and horns twanging, because he heard there was a new God kicking about. Carnehan sights for the brown of the men half a mile across the snow and wings one of them. Then he sends a message to the Chief that, less he wished to be killed, he must come and shake hands with me and leave his arms behind. The Chief comes alone first, and Carnehan shakes hands with him and whirls his arms about, same as Dravot used, and very much surprised that Chief was, and strokes my eyebrows. Then Carnehan goes alone to the Chief, and asks him in dumb show if he had an enemy he hated. 'I have,' says the Chief. So Carnehan weeds out the pick of his men, and sets the two of the Army to show them drill, and at the end of two weeks the men can maneuver about as well as Volunteers. So he marches with the Chief to a great big plain on the top of a mountain, and the Chief's men rushes into a village and takes it; we three Martinis firing into the brown of the enemy. So we took that village too, and I gives the Chief a rag from my coat and says, 'Occupy till I come'; which was scriptural. By way of a reminder, when me and the Army was eighteen hundred yeards away, I drops a bullet near him standing on the snow, and all the people falls flat on their faces. Then I sends a letter to Dravot, wherever he be by land or by sea."

At the risk of throwing the creature out of train I interrupted, "How could you write a letter up yonder?"

"The letter?—Oh!—The letter! Keep looking at me between the

eyes, please. It was a string-talk letter, that we'd learned the way of it from a blind beggar in the Punjab."

I remember that there had once come to the office a blind man with a knotted twig and a piece of string which he wound round the twig according to some cipher of his own. He could, after the lapse of days or hours, repeat the sentence which he had reeled up. He had reduced the alphabet to eleven primitive sounds; and tried to teach me his method, but failed.

"I sent that letter to Dravot," said Carnehan; "and told him to come back because this Kingdom was growing too big for me to handle, and then I struck for the first valley, to see how the priests were working. They called the village we took along with the Chief, Bashkai, and the first village we took, Er-Heb. The priests at Er-Heb was doing all right, but they had a lot of pending cases about land to show me, and some men from another village had been firing arrows at night. I went out and looked for that village and fired four rounds at it from a thousand yards. That used all the cartridges I cared to spend, and I waited for Dravot, who had been away two or three months, and I kept my people quiet.

"One morning I heard the devil's own noise of drums and horns, and Dan Dravot marches down the hill with his Army and a tail of hundreds of men, and—which was the most amazing—a great gold crown on his head. 'My Gord, Carnehan,' says Daniel, 'this is a tremenjus business, and we've got the whole country as far as it's worth having. I am the son of Alexander by Queen Semiramis, and you're my younger brother and a God too! It's the biggest thing we've ever seen. I've been marching and fighting for six weeks with the Army, and every footy little village for fifty miles has come in rejoiceful; and more than that, I've got the key of the whole show, as you'll see, and I've got a crown for you! I told 'em to make two of 'em at a place called Shu, where the gold lies in the rock like suet in mutton. Gold I've seen, and turquoise I've kicked out of the cliffs, and there's garnets in the sands of the river, and here's a chunk of amber that a man brought me. Call up all the priests and, here, take your crown.'

"One of the men opens a black hair bag and I slips the crown on. It was too small and too heavy, but I wore it for the glory. Hammered gold it was—five pound weight, like a hoop of a barrel.

"'Peachey,' says Dravot, 'we don't want to fight no more. The Craft's the trick, so help me!' and he brings forward that same Chief that I left at Bashkai—Billy Fish we called him afterwards, because he was so like Billy Fish that drove the big tank engine at Mach on the Bolan in the old days. 'Shake hands with him,' says Dravot, and I shook hands and nearly dropped, for Billy Fish gave me the Grip. I said nothing, but tried him with the Fellow Craft Grip. He answers, all right, and I tried the Master's Grip, but that was a slip. 'A Fellow Craft he is!' I says to Dan. 'Does he know the word?' 'He does,' says Dan, 'and all the priests know. It's a miracle! The Chiefs and the priests can work a Fellow Craft Lodge in a way that's very like ours, and they've cut the marks on the rocks, but they don't know the Third Degree, and they've come to find out. It's Gord's Truth. I've known these long years that the Afghans knew up to the Fellow Craft Degree, but this is a miracle. A God and a Grand Master of the Craft am I, and a Lodge in the Third Degree I will open, and we'll raise the head priests and the Chiefs of the villages.'

"'It's against all the law,' I says, 'holding a Lodge without warrant from anyone; and we never held any office in any Lodge.'

"'It's a master stroke of policy,' says Dravot. 'It means running the country as easy as a four-wheeled bogy down a down grade. We can't stop to inquire now, or they'll turn against us. I've forty Chiefs at my heel, and passed and raised according to their merit they shall be. Billet these men on the villages and see that we run up a Lodge of some kind. The temple of Imbra will do for the Lodge room. The women must make aprons as you show them. I'll hold a levee of chiefs tonight and Lodge tomorrow!'

"I was fair run off my legs, but I wasn't such a fool as not to see what a pull this Craft business gave us. I showed the priests' families how to make aprons of the degrees, but for Dravot's apron the blue border and marks was made of turquoise lumps on white hide, not cloth. We took a great square stone in the temple for the Master's chair, and little stones for the officers' chairs, and painted the black pavement with white squares, and did what we could to make things regular.

"At the levee which was held that night on the hillside with big bonfires, Dravot gives out that him and me were Gods and sons of Alexander, and Past Grand Masters in the Craft, and was come to make Kafiristan a country where every man should eat in peace and drink in quiet, and specially obey us. Then the Chiefs come round to shake hands, and they was so hairy and white and fair it was just shaking hands with old friends. We gave them names according as they was like men we had known in India—Billy Fish, Holly Dilworth, Pikky Kergan that was Bazaar-master when I was at Mhow, and so on and so on.

"The most amazing miracle was at Lodge next night. One of the old priests was watching us continuous, and I felt uneasy, for I knew we'd have to fudge the Ritual, and I didn't know what the men knew. The old priest was a stranger come in from beyond the village of Bashkai. The minute Dravot puts on the Master's apron that the girls had made for him, the priest fetches a whoop and a howl, and tried to overturn the stone that Dravot was sitting on. 'It's all up now,' I says. 'That comes of meddling with the Craft without warrant!' Dravot never winked an eye, not when ten priests took and tilted over the Grand Master's chair—which was to say the stone of Imbra. The priest begins rubbing the bottom end of it to clear away the black dirt, and presently, he shows all the other priests the Master's Mark, same as was on Dravot's apron, cut into the stone. Not even the priests of the temple of Imbra knew it was there. The old chap falls flat on his face at Dravot's feet and kisses 'em. 'Luck again,' says Dravot, across the Lodge to me, 'they say it's the missing Mark that no one could understand the why of. We're more than safe now.' Then he bangs the butt of his gun for a gavel and says, 'By virtue of the authority vested in me by my own right hand and the help of Peachey, I declare myself Grand Master of all Freemasonry in Kafiristan in this the Mother Lodge o' the country, and the King of Kafiristan equally with Peachey!' At that he puts on his crown and I puts on mine—I was doing Senior Warden—and we opens the Lodge in most ample form. It was a amazing miracle! The priests moved in Lodge through the first two degrees almost without telling, as if the memory was coming back to them. After that, Peachey and Dravot raised such as was worthy—high priests and Chiefs of far-off villages. Billy Fish was the first, and I can tell you we scared the soul out of him. It was not in any way according to Ritual, but it served our turn. We didn't raise more than ten of the biggest men, because we didn't want to make the Degree common. And they was clamoring to be raised.

"'In another six months,' says Dravot, 'we'll hold another Communication and see how you are working.' Then he asks them about their villages, and learns that they was fighting one against the other and were fair sick and tired of it. And when they wasn't doing that they was fighting with the Mohammedans. 'You can fight those when they come into our country,' says Dravot. 'Tell off every tenth man of your tribes for a Frontier guard, and send two hundred at a time to this valley to be drilled. Nobody is going to be shot or speared at any more so long as he does well, and I know that you won't cheat me because you're white people—sons of Alexander—and not like common, black Mohammedans. You are *my* people and by God,' says he, running off into English at the end, 'I'll make a damned fine Nation of you, or I'll die in the making!'

"I can't tell all we did for the next six months because Dravot did a lot I couldn't see the hang of, and he learned their lingo in a way I never could. My work was to help the people plow, and now and again go out with some of the Army and see what the other villages were doing, and make 'em throw rope bridges across the ravines which cut up the country horrid. Dravot was very kind to me, but when he walked up and down in the pine wood pulling that bloody red beard of his with both fists I knew he was thinking plans I could not advise him about, and I just waited for orders.

"But Dravot never showed me disrespect before the people. They were afraid of me and the Army, but they loved Dan. He was the best of friends with the priests and the Chiefs; but anyone could come across the hills with a complaint and Dravot would hear him out fair, and call four priests together and say what was to be done. He used to call in Billy Fish from Bashkai, and Pikky Kergan from Shu, and an old Chief we called Kafuzelum—it was like enough to his real name—and hold councils with 'em when there was any fighting to be done in small villages. That was his Council of War, and the four priests of Bashkai, Shu, Khawak, and Madora was his Privy Council. Between the lot of them they sent me, with forty men and twenty rifles, and sixty men carrying turquoises, into the Ghorband country to buy those hand-made Martini rifles, that come out of the Amir's workshops at Kabul, from one of the Amir's Herati regiments that would have sold the very teeth out of their mouths for turquoises.

"I stayed in Ghorband a month, and gave the Governor there the pick of my baskets for hush money, and bribed the Colonel of the regiment some more, and, between the two and the tribespeople, we got more than a hundred hand-made Martinis, a hundred good Kohat Jezails that'll throw to six hundred yards, and forty man-loads of very bad ammunition for the rifles. I came back with what I had, and distributed 'em among the men that the Chiefs sent to me to drill. Dravot was too busy to attend to those things, but the old Army that we first made helped me, and we turned out five hundred men that could drill, and two hundred that knew how to hold arms pretty straight. Even those corkscrewed, hand-made guns was a miracle to them. Dravot talked big about powder shops and factories, walking up and down in the pine wood when the winter was coming on.

"'I won't make a nation,' says he. 'I'll make an Empire! These men aren't niggers; they're English! Look at their eyes—look at their mouths. Look at the way they stand up. They sit on chairs in their own houses. They're the Lost Tribes, or something like it, and they've grown to be English. I'll take a census in the spring if the priests don't get frightened. There must be a fair two million of 'em in these hills. The villages are full o' little children. Two million people—two hundred and fifty thousand fighting men—and all English! They only want the rifles and a little drilling. Two hundred and fifty thousand men, ready to cut in on Russia's right flank when she tries for India! Peachey, man', he says, chewing his beard in great hunks, 'we shall be Emperors—Emperors of the Earth! Rajah Brooke will be a suckling to us. I'll treat with the Vice-roy on equal terms. I'll ask him to send me twelve picked English—twelve that I know of—to help us govern a bit. There's Mackray, Sergeant-pensioner at Segowli—many's the good dinner he's given me, and his wife a pair of trousers. There's Donkin, the Warder of Tounghoo Jail; there's hundreds that I could lay my hand on if I was in India. The Vice-roy shall do it for me. I'll send a man through in the spring for those men, and I'll write for a dispensation from the Grand Lodge for what I've done as Grand Master. That—and all the Sniders that'll be thrown out when the native troops in India take up the Martini. They'll be worn smooth, but they'll do for fighting in these hills. Twelve English, a hundred thousand Sniders run through the Amir's country in driblets—I'd be content with twenty thousand in one year—and we'd be an Empire. When everything was shipshape, I'd hand over the crown—this crown I'm wearing now—to Queen Victoria on my knees, and she'd say, "Rise up, Sir Daniel Dravot." Oh, it's big! It's big, I tell you! But there's so much to be done in every place—Bashkai, Khawak, Shu, and everywhere else.'

"'What is it?' I says. 'There are no more men coming to be drilled this autumn. Look at those fat, black clouds. They're bringing the snow.'

"'It isn't that, ' says Daniel, putting his hand very hard on my shoulder; 'and I don't wish to say anything that's against you, for no other living man would have followed me and made me what I am as you have done. You're a first-class Commander-in-chief, and the people know you; but—it's a big country, and somehow you can't help me, Peachey, in the way I want to be helped.'

"'Go to your blasted priests, then!' I said, and I was sorry when I made that remark, but it did hurt me sore to find Daniel talking so superior when I'd drilled all the men, done all he told me.

"'Don't let's quarrel, Peachey,' says Daniel, without cursing. 'You're a King, too, and the half of this Kingdom is yours; but can't you see, Peachey, we want cleverer men than us now—three or four of 'em, that we can scatter about for our Deputies. It's a hugeous great State, and I can't always tell the right thing to do, and I haven't time for all I want to do, and here's the winter coming on and all.' He put half his beard into his mouth, and it was as red as the gold of his crown.

"'I'm sorry, Daniel,' says I. 'I've done all I could. I've drilled the men and shown the people how to stack their oats better; and I've brought in those tinware rifles from Ghorband—but I know what you're driving at. I take it Kings always feel oppressed that way.'

"'There's another thing too,' says Dravot, walking up and down. 'The winter's coming and these people won't be giving much trouble and if they do we can't move about. I want a wife.'

"'For Gord's sake leave the women alone!' I says. 'We've both got all the work we can, though I *am* a fool. Remember the Contrack, and keep clear o' women.'

"'The Contrack only lasted till such time as we was Kings; and Kings we have been these months past,' says Dravot, weighing his crown in his hand. 'You go get a wife too, Peachey—a nice, strappin', plump girl that'll keep you warm in the winter. They're prettier than English girls, and we can take the pick of 'em. Boil 'em once or twice in hot water, and they'll come as fair as chicken and ham.'

"'Don't tempt me!' I says. 'I will not have any dealings with a woman not till we are a dam' site more settled than we are now. I've been doing the work o' two men, and you've been doing the work o' three. Let's lie off a bit, and see if we can get some better tobacco from Afghan country and run in some good liquor; but no women.'

"'Who's talking o' *women?*' says Dravot. 'I said *wife*—a Queen to breed a King's son for the King. A Queen out of the strongest tribe, that'll make them your blood brothers, and that'll lie by your side and tell you all the people thinks about you and their own affairs. That's what I want.'

"'Do you remember that Bengali woman I kept at Mogul Serai when I was a plate layer?' says I. 'A fat lot o' good she was to me. She taught me the lingo and one or two other things; but what happened? She ran away with the Station Master's servant and half my month's pay. Then she turned up at Dadur Junction in tow of a half-caste, and had the impidence to say I was her husband—all among the drivers in the running shed!'

"'We're done with that,' says Dravot. 'These women are whiter than you or me, and a Queen I will have for the winter months.'

"'For the last time o' asking, Dan, do *not*', I says. 'It'll only bring us harm. The Bible says that Kings ain't to waste their strength on women, 'specially when they've got a new raw Kingdom to work over.'

"'For the last time of answering, I will,' said Dravot, and he went away through the pine trees looking like a big red devil. The low sun hit his crown and beard on one side and the two blazed like hot coals.

"But getting a wife was not as easy as Dan thought. He put it before the Council, and there was no answer till Billy Fish said that he'd better ask the girls. Dravot damned them all round. 'What's wrong with me?' he shouts, standing by the idol Imbra. 'Am I a dog or am I not enough of a man for your wenches? Haven't I put the shadow of my hand over this country? Who stopped the last Afghan raid?' It was me really, but Dravot was too angry to remember. 'Who brought your guns? Who repaired the bridges? Who's the Grand Master of the sign cut in the stone?' and he thumped his hand on the block that he used to sit on in Lodge, and at Council, which opened like Lodge always. Billy Fish said nothing, and no more did the others. 'Keep your hair on, Dan,' said I; 'and ask the girls. That's how it's done at Home, and these people are quite English.'

"'The marriage of the King is a matter of State,' says Dan, in a white-hot rage, for he could feel, I hope, that he was going against his better mind. He walked out of the Council room, and the others sat still, looking at the ground.

"'Billy Fish,' says I to the Chief of Bashkai, 'what's the difficulty here? A straight answer to a true friend.' 'You know,' says Billy Fish. 'How should a man tell you who know everything? How can daughters of men marry Gods or Devils? It's not proper.'

"I remembered something like that in the Bible; but if, after seeing us as long as they had, they still believed we were Gods, it wasn't for me to undeceive them.

"'A God can do anything,' says I. 'If the King is fond of a girl he'll not let her die.' 'She'll have to,' said Billy Fish. 'There are all sorts of Gods and Devils in these mountains, and now and again a girl marries one of them and isn't seen any more. Besides, you two know the Mark cut in the stone. Only the Gods know that. We thought you were men till you showed the sign of the Master.'

"I wished then that we had explained about the loss of the genuine secrets of a Master Mason at the first go-off; but I said nothing. All that night there was a blowing of horns in a little dark temple halfway down the hill, and I heard a girl crying fit to die. One of the priests told us that she was being prepared to marry the King.

"'I'll have no nonsense of that kind,' says Dan. 'I don't want to interfere with your customs, but I'll take my own wife.' 'The girl's a little bit afraid,' says the priest. 'She thinks she's going to die, and they are aheartening of her up down in the temple.'

"'Hearten her very tender then,' says Dravot, 'or I'll hearten you with the butt of a gun so that you'll never want to be heartened again.' He licked his lips, did Dan, and stayed up walking about more than half the night, thinking of the wife that he was going to get in the morning. I wasn't any means comfortable, for I knew that dealings with a woman in foreign parts, though you was a crowned King twenty times over, could not but be risky. I got up very early in the morning while Dravot was asleep, and I saw the priests talking together in whispers, and the Chiefs talking together too, and they looked at me out of the corners of their eyes.

"'What's up, Fish?' I says to the Bashkai man, who was wrapped up in his furs and looking splendid to behold.

"'I can't rightly say,' says he; 'but if you can induce the King to drop all this nonsense about marriage, you'll be doing him and me and yourself a great service.'

"'That I do believe,' says I. 'But sure, you know, Billy, as well as me, having fought against and for us, that the King and me are nothing more than two of the finest men that God Almighty ever made. Nothing more, I do assure you.'

"'That may be,' says Billy Fish, 'and yet I should be sorry if it was.' He sinks his head upon his great fur cloak for a minute and thinks. 'King,' says he, 'be you man or God or Devil, I'll stick by you today. I have twenty of my men with me, and they will follow me. We'll go to Bashkai until the storm blows over.'

"A little snow had fallen in the night, and everything was white except the greasy fat clouds that blew down and down from the north. Dravot came out with his crown on his head, swinging his arms and stamping his feet, and looking more pleased than Punch.

"'For the last time, drop it, Dan,' says I in a whisper. 'Billy Fish here says that there will be a row.'

"'A row among my people!' says Dravot. 'Not much. Peachey, you're a fool not to get a wife too. Where's the girl?' says he, with a voice as loud as the braying of a jackass. 'Call up all the Chiefs and priests, and let the Emperor see if his wife suits him.'

"The was no need to call anyone. They were all there leaning on their guns and spears round the clearing in the center of the pine wood. A deputation of priests went down to the temple to bring up the girl, and the horns blew up fit to wake the dead. Billy Fish saunters round and gets as close to Daniel as he could, and behind him stood his twenty men with matchlocks. Not a man of them under six feet. I was next to Dravot, and behind me was twenty men of the regular Army. Up comes the girl, and a strapping wench she was, covered with silver and turquoises, but white as death, and looking back every minute at the priests.

"'She'll do,' said Dan, looking her over. 'What's to be afraid of, lass? Come and kiss me.' He puts his arm round her. She shuts her eyes, gives a bit of a squeak, and down goes her face in the side of Dan's flaming red beard."

" 'The slut's bitten me!' says he, clapping his hand to his neck, and, sure enough, his hand was red with blood. Billy Fish and two of his matchlock-men catches hold of Dan by the shoulders and drags him into the Bashkai lot, while the priests howl in their lingo, 'Neither God nor Devil, but a man!' I was all taken aback, for a priest cut at me in front and the Army behind began firing into the Bashkai men.

"'God A-mighty!' says Dan. 'What is the meaning o' this?'

"'Come back! Come away!' says Billy Fish, 'Ruin and Mutiny is the matter. We'll break for Bashkai if we can.'

"I tried to give some sort of orders to my men—the men o' the regular Army—but it was no use, so I fired into the brown of 'em with an English Martini and drilled three beggars in a line. The valley was full of shouting, howling creatures, and every soul was shrieking, 'Not a God not a Devil, but only a man!' The Bashkai troops stuck to Billy Fish all they we worth, but their matchlocks wasn't half as good as the Kabul Breechloaders, and four of them dropped. Dan was bellowing like a bull, for he was very wrathy; and Billy Fish had a hard job to prevent him running out at the crowd. 'We can't stand,' says Billy Fish. 'Make a run for it down the valley! The whole place is against us.' The matchlock-men ran, and we went down the valley in spite of Dravot's protestations. He was swearing horribly and crying out that he was a King. The priests rolled great stones on us, and the regular Army fired hard, and there wasn't more than six men, not counting Dan, Billy Fish, and Me, that came down to the bottom of the valley alive.

"Then they stopped firing and the horns in the temple blew again. 'Come away—for Gord's sake come away!' says Billy Fish. 'They'll send runners out to all the villages before ever we get to Bashkai. I can protect you there, but I can't do anything now.'

"My own notion is that Dan began to go mad in his head from that hour. He stared up and down like a stuck pig. Then he was all for walking back alone and killing the priests with his bare hands; which he could have done. 'An Emperor am I,' says Daniel, 'and next year I shall be a Knight of the Queen.'

"'All right, Dan,' says I; 'but come along now while there's time.'

"'It's your fault,' says he, 'for not looking after your Army better. There was mutiny in the midst, and you didn't know—you damned engine-driving, plate-laying, missionary's-pass-hunting hound!' I was too heartsick to care, though it was all his foolishness that brought the smash.

"'I'm sorry, Dan,' says I, 'but there's no accounting for natives. This business is our Fifty-Seven. Maybe we'll make something out of it yet, when we've got to Bashkai.'

"'Let's get to Bashkai, then,' says Dan, 'and, by God, when I come back here again I'll sweep the valley so there isn't a bug in a blanket left!'

"We walked all that day, and all that night Dan was stumping up and down on the snow, chewing his beard and muttering to himself.

"'There's no hope o' getting clear,' said Billy Fish. 'The priests will have sent runners to the villages to say that you are only men. Why didn't you stick on as Gods till things was more settled? I'm a dead man,' says Billy Fish, and he throws himself down on the snow and begins to pray to his Gods.

"Next morning we was in a cruel bad country—all up and down, no level ground at all, and no food either. The six Bashkai men looked at Billy Fish hungrywise as if they wanted to ask something, but they said never a word. At noon we came to the top of a flat mountain all covered with snow, and when we climbed up into it, behold, there was an Army in position waiting in the middle!

"'The runners have been very quick,' says Billy Fish, with a little bit of a laugh. 'They are waiting for us.'

"Three or four men began to fire from the enemy's side, and a chance shot took Daniel in the calf of the leg. That brought him to his senses. He looks across the snow at the Army, and sees the rifles that we had brought into the country.

"'We're done for,' says he. 'They are Englishmen, these people—and it's my blasted nonsense that has brought you to this. Get back, Billy Fish, and take your men away; you've done what you could, and now cut for it. Carnehan,' says he, 'shake hands with me and go along with Billy. Maybe they won't kill you. I'll go and meet 'em alone. It's me that did it. Me, the King!'

"'Go!' says I. 'Go to Hell, Dan! I'm with you here. Billy Fish, you clear out, and we two will meet those folk.'

"'I'm a Chief,' says Billy Fish, quite quiet. 'I stay with you. My men can go.'

"The Bashkai fellows didn't wait for a second word, but ran off, and Dan and Me and Billy Fish walked across to where the drums were drumming and the horns were horning. It was cold—awful cold. I've got that cold in the back of my head now. There's a lump of it there."

The punkah coolies had gone to sleep. Two kerosene lamps were blazing in the office, and the perspiration poured down my face and splashed on the blotter as I leaned forward. Carnehan was shivering, and I feared that his mind might go. I wiped my face, took a fresh grip of the piteously mangled hands, and said, "What happened after that?"

The momentary shift in my eyes had broken the clear current.

"What was you pleased to say?" whined Carnehan. "They took them without any sound. Not a little whisper all along the snow, not though the King had knocked down the first man that set hand on him—not though old Peachey fired his last cartridge into the brown of 'em. Not a single solitary sound did those swines make. They just closed up tight, and I tell you their furs stunk. There was a man called Billy Fish, a good friend of us all, and they cut his throat, Sir, then and there, like a pig; and the King kicks up the bloody snow and says, 'We've had a dashed fine run for our money. What's coming next?' But Peachey, Peachey Taliaferro, I tell you, Sir, in confidence as betwixt two friends, he lost his head, Sir. No, he didn't neither. The King lost his head, so he did, all along o' one of those cunning rope bridges. Kindly let me have the paper cutter, Sir. It tilted this way. They marched him a mile across that snow to a rope bridge over a ravine with a river at the bottom. You may have seen such. They prodded him behind like an ox. 'Damn your eyes!' says the King. 'D'you suppose I can't die like a gentleman?' He turns to Peachey—Peachey that was crying like a child. 'I've brought you to this, Peachey,' says he. 'Brought you out of your happy life to be killed in Kafiristan, where you was late Commander-in Chief of the Emperor's forces. Say you forgive me, Peachey,' 'I do,' says Peachey, 'Fully and freely do I forgive you, Dan.' 'Shake hands, Peachey,' says he. 'I'm going now.' Out he goes, looking neither right nor left, and when he was plumb in the middle of those dizzy dancing ropes, 'Cut, you beggars,' he shouts; and they cut, and old Dan fell, turning round and round and round, twenty thousand miles, for he took half an hour to fall till he struck the water, and I could see his body caught on a rock with the gold crown close beside.

"But do you know what they did to Peachey between two pine trees?

They crucified him, Sir, as Peachey's hands will show. They used wooden pegs for his hands and his feet; and he didn't die. He hung there and screamed, and they took him down next day, and said it was a miracle that he wasn't dead. They took him down—poor old Peachey that hadn't done them any harm—that hadn't done them any . . ."

He rocked to and fro and wept bitterly, wiping his eyes with the back of his scarred hands and moaning like a child for ten minutes.

"They was cruel enough to feed him up in the temple, because they said he was more of a God than old Daniel that was a man. Then they turned him out on the snow, and told him to go home, and Peachey came home in about a year, begging along the roads quite safe; for Daniel Dravot he walked before and said, 'Come along, Peachey, It's a big thing we're doing.' The mountains they danced at night, and the mountains they tried to fall on Peachey's head, but Dan he held up his hand, and he never let go of Dan's head. They gave it to him as a present in the temple, to remind him not to come again, and though the crown was pure gold, and Peachey was starving, never would Peachey sell the same. You knew Dravot, Sir! You knew Right Worshipful Brother Dravot! Look at him now!"

He fumbled in the mass of rags round his bent waist; brought out a black horsehair bag embroidered with silver thread; and shook therefrom on to my table—the dried, withered head of Daniel Dravot! The morning sun that had long been paling the lamps struck the red beard and blind sunken eyes; struck, too, a heavy circlet of gold studded with raw turqoises, that Carnehan placed tenderly on the battered temples.

"You behold now," said Carnehan, "The Emperor in his habit as he lived—the King of Kafiristan with his crown upon his head. Poor old Daniel that was a monarch once!"

I shuddered, for, in spite of defacements manifold, I recognized the head of the man of Marwar Junction. Carnehan rose to go. I attempted to stop him. He was not fit to walk abroad. "Let me take away the whisky, and give me a little money," he gasped. "I was a King once. I'll go to the Deputy Commissioner and ask to set in the Poorhouse till I get my health. No, thank you, I can't wait till you get a carriage for me. I've urgent private affairs—in the South—at Marwar."

He shambled out of the office and departed in the direction of the Deputy Commissioner's house. That day at noon I had occasion to go down the blinding hot Mall, and I saw a crooked man crawling along the white dust of the roadside, his hat in his hand, quavering dolorously after the fashion of street-singers at Home. There was not a soul in sight, and he was out of all possible earshot of the houses. And he sang through his nose, turning his head from right to left:

> *The Son of Man goes forth to war,*
> *A golden crown to gain;*
> *His blood-red banner streams afar—*
> *Who follows in his train?*

I waited to hear no more, but put the poor wretch into my carriage and drove him off to the nearest missionary for eventual transfer to the Asylum. He repeated the hymn twice while he was with me, whom he did not in the least recognize, and I left him singing it to the missionary.

Two days later I inquired after his welfare of the Superintendent of the Asylum.

"He was admitted suffering from sunstroke. He died early yesterday morning," said the Superintendent. "Is it true that he was half an hour bareheaded in the sun at midday?"

"Yes," said I, "but do you happen to know if he had anything upon him by any chance when he died?"

"Not to my knowledge," said the Superintendent.

And there the matter rests.

DISCUSSION

At first glance, this seems to be merely a story of adventure in a far-off and exotic place. There are journeys, mysterious strangers, battles, pagan temples, madness, a crucifixion. The reader's curiosity about the turn of events is whetted by many cunning devices for provoking suspense. For instance, the first stranger's mysterious message leads to the red-bearded man in the second-class carriage. The trader and his servant in the bazaar turn out to be the adventurers ready for their journey. Or, to go further, in the *episode* (see Glossary) concerning the mark on the stone, everything hangs for a moment in the balance until the mark is disclosed. Kipling, in other words, not only plays on the reader's curiosity about the final outcome, but plays up our suspense as to the outcome of the individual steps in the story's development. Curiosity is constantly exploited.

Furthermore, we can see how, in this story in which plot seems to be so dominant in interest, one incident is caused by another. For instance, the marriage causes the discovery that brings on the ruin of the kings. But though we can link up the various episodes into a chain of cause and effect, we can see that this chain really depends upon the characters themselves.

Again, considered superficially, the matter of motivation seems to present little difficulty. Many men desire riches and power, as do Peachey and Dravot; and it may seem that we need go no further into the matter in our discussion of the motivation. (Indeed, this is as far as most adventure stories do go in presenting motivation.) But we can see that in this story, the motivation is more complicated. For example, as the kings acquire their power, the simple desire for riches and power, especially for Dravot, begins to change. There is a growing sense of responsibility for, and pride in, the people that they rule. Dravot begins to talk about bringing in skilled administrators, recognizing with an unexpected kind of humility that the business of kingship is more complicated than he had thought. He even begins to dream of turning over his kingdom to Queen Victoria—of taking his place in history as one of the Empire Builders. Actually, it is this development of character that proves to be one of the factors leading to his downfall, for the desire for marriage is not merely his simple human desire for companionship—though this is present—but it is also a desire to found a royal line, to leave someone to rule the kingdom after his death. The wedding, therefore, must be public, with due ceremony and ritual.

The adventure itself has gone hand in hand with a development of character. That is, the men we meet at the beginning of the story are the kind who, as outcasts, see "things from the underside where the lath and plaster is not smoothed off." But Dravot does not die like an outcast: "They prodded him behind like an ox. 'Damn your eyes!' says the King. 'you suppose I can't die like a gentleman?'" He does die "like a gentlemen," like a king and like a man. And even Peachey, whose position is subordinate to Dravot's throughout the story, participates in this new dignity. He comes back through the wild mountains, through terrors and hardships, but he never relinquishes the bag containing the head of the King and the crown, the symbol of kingship. So, paradoxically, the two outcasts, the "loafers," become most truly kings in the moment when their false kingship is taken from them and they become fully men. That is, when external kingship is lost, internal kingship is achieved.

This idea may prompt us to look back again at the meaning of the situation that brings about the ruin of the adventure. The natives have thought of them as gods—not as human kings. The power of Peachey and Dravot is, thus, that of the king-as-god, not that of the king-as-man. But Dravot, the king-as-god, wants to be a man—he has human instincts that the mere exercise of godlike power cannot satisfy. He wants to have power, to be a god (for, to have power over the natives, he must be a god, as we discover), and he longs to be a man. This is the dilemma he is caught in, and the dilemma that ruins him. The story at this point shows itself to be in a sense, then, a study of kingship; and there is a continuation of this study of kingship in the account of Dravot's death, where, as we have seen, Dravot achieves another kind of kingship and the nature of kingship is redefined.

Perhaps the general point may be summarized as follows. The loafers are impelled by a dream of kingship, but not a kingship hedged about by constitutional limitations, not a kingship dependent upon a mere social arrangement, not a kingship with a mere figurehead or symbol for the power of the state, but a "real" kingship of absolute power. Such power depends upon their remaining aloof from humanity as gods; yet they are men, and man, not even for power, will forfeit his humanity. It is ironical that Dravot finally exercises his godlike power only in order to become a man—to satisfy his basic human desires. This step brings ruin, but there is a further irony in the fact that Dravot becomes most truly kingly at the moment of his ruin. Especially is this true for the reader who sees simply a kind of tawdry showmanship and deception in the parade of godlike power over the ignorant tribesmen, but who admires the way Dravot meets his death. Thus the story involves a contrast between kinds of kingship, between kinds of power, external and internal, power over others and power over oneself.

This account of "The Man Who Would Be King" does not, of course, provide a full interpretation of the story. Various aspects of *point of view* (see Glossary) and other technical matters should be considered (see the discussion pages 109–10). The questions that follow are only a few of those that should be raised in a full analysis of the story. The student should choose several of these topics as exercises and write a full discussion of one of them.

1. Why is it appropriate that Peachey should be heard singing the particular hymn that he sings? Is it in his character to sing this particular hymn? How is the hymn related to the "meaning" of the story? Define the ironies involved in this incident.

2. Is Billy Fish loyal to Dravot as "god" or as "man"? What light does the fact of his loyalty shed on the rest of the story?

3. Is the contract signed by Dravot and Peachey humorous, pathetic, or heroic?

4. How does the fact that this story is told by a first-person narrator help us to define the characters? As a matter of fact, there are two narrators, the newspaper man and Peachey. What is the logic behind this?

5. What is the significance of the crucifixion of Peachey?

3
What Character Reveals

The stories in this section may be considered with a special view to the problem of character in fiction. But, as we have had occasion to observe several times before this, fiction never deals with character in isolation, for what a man is determines what he does, and it is primarily through what he does that we who observe him know what he is.

The proof of the inextricable interweaving of character and action may be most readily seen by a glance back at the stories in the preceding section. Though our attention was focused there upon problems of plot, we found that we could not discuss these stories without going into the problems of character. We had constantly to ask whether the actions performed were "in character"; that is, whether they were psychologically credible.

Though plot and character interpenetrate each other, there is some justification for stressing one problem at a time: let us consider here some of the problems of characterization. We may begin with the problem of exposition. In some fundamental sense, every character in fiction must resemble ourselves; that is, he or she must be recognizably human even as we are. But some characters are obviously much more special than others, and require much fuller characterization. In "The Secret Life of Walter Mitty" we encounter an easily recognized type. Dravot in "The Man Who Would Be King" is a man quite outside the average reader's common acquaintance, and if he is to seem real, he must be convincingly presented. The fact that Dravot is a man of action, not an introspective man, makes the author's task easier. If the character's inward life is more complicaed and significant than his outer, more special problems of presentation may arise.

How shall the author present his character? Directly, with a summary of his traits and characteristics, or indirectly (that is, through dialogue and action)? The very nature of fiction suggests that the second method is its characteristic means, yet direct presentation is constantly used in fiction, often effectively. Much depends upon the underlying purpose of the story and much depends upon matters of scope and scale. If the author made every presentation of character indirectly, insisting that each character gradually unfold himself through natural talk and gesture and action, the procedure might become intolerably boring. "The Necklace" indicates how direct presentation—and even summary presentation—can be properly and effectively used. (Look back at the first three paragraphs of this story on page 66.) But when he comes to the significant scenes of the story, the author of "The Necklace" discards summary in favor of dramatic presentation.

The danger of direct presentation is that it tends to forfeit the vividness of drama and the reader's imaginative participation. Direct, descriptive presentation works best, therefore, with rather flat and typical characters, or as a means to get rapidly over more perfunctory materials. When direct presentation of character becomes also direct comment on a character, the author may find himself "telling" us what to feel and think rather than "rendering" a scene for our imaginative participation. In "The Furnished Room," for example, O. Henry tends to "editorialize" on the hero's motives and beliefs, and constant plucking at the reader's sleeve and nudging him to sympathize with the hero's plight may become so irritating that the whole scene seems falsified. Yet in D. H. Lawrence's "Tickets, Please," a story near the end of this section, we shall see that direct commentary—and even explicit interpretation of the characters' motives—can on occasion be effectively used by an author.

The contrast between rather ordinary characters and out-of-the-way characters can be used to suggest the opposing extremes that bound the domain of fiction. The ordinary and typical characters tend to be secondary in a story. We tend to seek the "individualized" character, even if he seems common in many ways. If the poorly individualized character tends to be prominent, then the story is probably tilted toward fable or parable. (*Completely* flat characters, mere types, would, of course, probably take us out of fiction altogether. Even if every hero does at some level represent all of us, no seriously developed story can be about as pure an abstraction as our common humanity.)

At the opposite extreme, we find the fictional character who is so eccentric, so much out of the way, so perverse, that he ceases to be humanly credible. Fiction at this point passes off imperceptibly into the psychiatric case study. This is not to put narrow limits upon what the artist can do. If one looks deep enough, any character reveals complexities and eccentricities. Even madness is not to be automatically ruled out of the subject matter of fiction. In "A Rose for Emily," a story in section 4, William Faulkner tells of a character perverted to the point of madness; yet many people will feel that the story has a large human significance, and is not merely a clinician's report. Behind the "madness" lurks a meaning.

The domain of fiction is, then, the world of credible human beings, admittedly an amazingly diverse and varied world. Since it is the world of human beings, it can be presented concretely and dramatically. What is excludes at either end is the world of pure abstraction: economic man, Mrs. Average Housewife, the typical American, *Homo sapiens*; and at the other extreme, the mere freak, the psychological monster, the report from the psychiatrist's casebook. (But of course an artist may be able to put Mrs. Average Housewife or the young man with the classic Oedipus complex into a successful story. To do so, of course, he must satisfy more than a scientific and statistical interest: the abstraction must be made credible and significant in some broad "moral" sense.

From what has been said already, it is plain that an author's selection of modes of character presentation will depend upon a number of things. His decision on when to summarize traits or events, on when to describe directly, and on when to allow the character to express his feelings through dialogue and action, will depend upon the general end of the story and upon the way in which the action of the story is to be developed from a beginning, through a complicating middle, to an inevitable end.

One of the most important modes for character revelation is, of course, speech—the ways that characters talk. The laconic soldier, the querulous charwoman, the shy convent-school girl, the garrulous barkeep, the pedantic professor—all have their own vocabularies and their ways of putting words together. An author, in order to be convincing, must have his characters speak "in character," and his normal way of presenting an unusual character is to give us the flavor of his dialect and idiom, for instance, notice the characteristic language of Peachey and Dravot.

This use of speech is a rich resource for dramatic presentation. But again, if used incessantly it might kill a story by making it too talky. Indirect discourse, like character summary and character description, is a quicker way of getting over the ground, and in fiction has its very important uses. Notice, for example, in "War" that the husband's explanation of why his wife is to be pitied is very properly indirect discourse: "And he felt it his duty to explain . . . that the poor woman was to be pitied, for the war was taking away from her her only son," But the speeches of the old man who argues for the sublimity of sacrificing one's son for one's country are given as direct discourse. The importance of the old man's speeches to the story, the need for dramatic vividness, the very pace of the story—all call for direct discourse. Thus we have "'Nonsense,' interrupted another traveler," and so on.

So important is character to fiction that one way to approach the basic pattern of a story is to ask "Whose story is this?" In other words, it usually is the first importance to see whose fortunes are at stake. Sometimes the answer is quite obvious. In "The Secret Life of Walter Mitty," for example, it is very easy to see that this is Mr. Mitty's story and not Mrs. Mitty's. Her only function is to throw light upon her husband's situation. Mrs. Mitty undoubtedly has a story—who of us has not?—and James Thurber might have elected to tell it. But he has not done so here. It is easy to see that this is Mr. Mitty's story, but it is not so easy to see whose story it is that is related in "The Man Who Would Be King." One is inclined to say that is it Dravot's story. He is pictured as the dominant member of the pair; it is he who rises to the heroic gesture at the end and who dies like a king. Yet one could at least argue that this is Peachey's story, since he too learns the nature of kingship through witnessing Dravot's heroic action and since, magnificently loyal to the memory of Dravot, he acts out a heroic role himself. But even when it is not easy to say—or even important to determine—precisely whose story it is, the question is usually worth putting. To entertain the question is to throw light upon the relation of character with character.

One further word about the Dravot-Peachey relationship: we shall encounter in this text stories that belong primarily to a "Peachey"—that is, to an observer of the action who unconsciously participates in and interprets the meaning that a "Dravot" initiates. For what "happens" in a story is not necessarily some external thing. An internal thing—a shifted relationship, a change of heart—may decisively change someone's life.

Let us return to "Young Goodman Brown" to observe characters that have very little to individualize them. Both the husband and the wife scarcely exist beyond the roles they play as the loving young couple, each believing in the "goodness" of the other. The story depends on what happens in the forest—*in general*—rather than on a special quality. It approaches fable, or parable, with interest in character reduced to a minimum.

In our earlier discussion of plot we had a good deal to say about conflict in fiction. Conflict has the closest relation to character, for we cannot remain long interested in conflicts between impersonal forces. If conflicts between animals strike us as interesting, that is because we can rather easily project ourselves into them. We actually make some such projection even in the instance of a man's conflict with the elements or with some other inanimate force. A man who is fighting a fire or trying to beat his way through a great storm, or who is trying to hold out against hunger and pain is likely to treat the impersonal force as if it were another being—the Enemy.

Man's contest with external forces is the simplest kind of struggle and finally the least interesting. Few stories deal with it in purity. The great and typical human conflicts is one human being's conflict with other human beings. This is the stuff most fiction is made of. Here we find typical stories of the hero defeating the villain, of the true lover winning out over the wealthy roué, of the amateur detective outwitting the clever murderer. These are the standard contests of our more popular fiction. But in this general category of one human being against another, we also find stories of greater sensitivity and depth and penetration. For human beings, being the mixture of good and bad that we are, frequently find themselves at cross purposes and in conflict—not only with outsiders but with aspects of their own natures. Indeed, the more mature examples of conflict between character and character shade off into the third category that has to do with man's conflict with himself.

We can illustrate this last statement by referring to some of the stories that you have already read. "The Man Who Would Be King" is an "action" story, and the conflict is primarily a conflict between Dravot and the wild tribesmen upon whom he means to impose his will. But even in this story, a more important and significant conflict is an inward event. The conflict between his appetites and his growing sense of statesmanship costs Dravot his kingdom. And it is through another inward event, Dravot's conquest of himself, that his final spiritual victory comes. One can also illustrate the importance of inward conflict from Pirandello's story "War." Ostensibly the conflict is between the fervent old man's attitude toward sacrificing his son for his country and the attitudes of his apprehensive, all-too-human companions in the railway compartment. The old man's passionate arguments prevail over the minds of the others; but in persuading them, he discovers for the first time that he has never really persuaded himself.

Earlier in this book we argued for the importance of the truth of coherence as distinguished from the truth of correspondence. Since a work of literature does not pretend to be a factual document of actual events, but a typical and representative "action," the demands of truth of correspondence tend to be limited to correspondence to human nature and to the human norms. Within the story or poem itself we are primarily and unremittingly concerned with truth of coherence—with how the parts cohere into a total meaningful pattern.

Nowhere are the claims for coherence asserted more plainly than in the matter of character presentation. A character must be credible—must make sense, must be able to command our belief. True, the character in question may be an eccentric; he may be brutally criminal; he may even be mad. But his thoughts and actions must ultimately be coherent. If the characters in a story simply don't make sense, we have to reject the story. But we must remember that the kind of sense a character must make is his own kind, not our kind. For example, a more sensible, less proud woman than Mathilde Loisel in "The Necklace" might have made a clean breast of things to her friend and been spared the terrible and unnecessary consequences, but it is the coherence of Mme. Loisel's character that Maupassant must persuade us of. If he does not persuade us that his Mme. Loisel is really capable of accepting, and persisting through, the life of hardship that comes with the loss of the necklace, then the story itself is incredible. An obvious test of fiction then is to ask if the motives and actions of its characters are rendered coherent. It is the glory of fiction that great artists have been able to render coherent so many strange and out-of-the-way, often apparently self-contradictory, examples of human nature.

TENNESSEE'S PARTNER

Bret Harte

I DO not think that we ever knew his real name. Our ignorance of it certainly never gave us any social inconvenience, for at Sandy Bar in 1854 most men were christened anew. Sometimes these appellatives were derived from some distinctiveness of dress, as in the case of "Dungaree Jack"; or from some peculiarity of habit, as shown in "Saleratus Bill," so called from an undue proportion of that chemical in his daily bread; or from some unlucky slip, as exhibited in "The Iron Pirate," a mild, inoffensive man, who earned that baleful title by his unfortunate mispronunciation of the term "iron pyrites." Perhaps this may have been the beginning of a rude heraldry; but I am constrained to think that it was because a man's real name in that day rested solely upon his own unsupported statement. "Call yourself Clifford, do you?" said Boston, addressing a timid newcomer with infinite scorn; "hell is full of such Cliffords!" He then introduced the unfortunate man, whose name happened to be really Clifford, as "Jay-bird Charley"—an unhallowed inspiration of the moment that clung to him ever after.

But to return to Tennessee's Partner, whom we never knew by any other than this relative title. That he had ever existed as a separate and distinct individuality we only learned later. It seems that in 1853 he left Poker Flat to go to San Francisco, ostensibly to procure a wife. He never got any farther than Stockton. At that place he was attracted by a young person who waited upon the table at the hotel where he took his meals. One morning he said something to her which caused her to smile not unkindly, to somewhat coquettishly break a plate of toast over his upturned, serious, simple face, and to retreat to the kitchen. He followed her, and emerged a few moments later, covered with more toast and victory. That day week they were married by a justice of the peace, and returned to Poker Flat. I am aware that something more might be made of this episode, but I prefer to tell it as it was current at Sandy Bar—in the gulches and barrooms—where all sentiment was modified by a strong sense of humor.

Of their married felicity but little is known, perhaps for the reason that Tennessee, then living with his partner, one day took occasion to say something to the bride on his own account, at which, it is said, she smiled not unkindly and chastely retreated—this time as far as Marysville, where Tennessee followed her, and where they went to housekeeping without the aid of a justice of the peace. Tennessee's Partner took the loss of his wife simply and seriously, as was his fashion. But to everybody's surprise, when Tennessee one day returned from Marysville, without his partner's wife—she having smiled and retreated with somebody else—Tennessee's Partner was the first man to shake his hand and greet him with affection. The boys who had gathered in the cañon to see the shooting were naturally indignant. Their indignation might have found vent in sarcasm but for a certain look in Tennessee's Partner's eye that indicated a lack of humorous appreciation. In fact, he was a grave man, with a steady application to practical detail which was unpleasant in a difficulty.

Meanwhile a popular feeling against Tennessee had grown up on the Bar. He was known to be a gambler; he was suspected to be a thief. In these suspicions Tennessee's Partner was equally compromised; his continued intimacy with Tennessee after the affair above quoted could only be accounted for on the hypothesis of a copartnership of crime. At last Tennessee's guilt became flagrant. One day he overtook a stranger on his way to Red Dog. The stranger afterward related that Tennessee beguiled the time with interesting anecdote and reminiscence, but illogically concluded the interview in the following words: "And now, young man, I'll trouble you for your knife, your pistols, and your money. You see your weppings might get you into trouble at Red Dog, and your money's a temptation to the evilly disposed. I think you said your address was San Francisco. I shall endeavor to call." It may be stated here that Tennessee had a fine flow of humor, which no business preoccupation could wholly subdue.

This exploit was his last. Red Dog and Sandy Bar made common cause against the highwayman. Tennessee was hunted in very much the same fashion as his prototype, the grizzly. As the toils closed around him, he made a desperate dash through the Bar, emptying his revolver at the crowd before the Arcade Saloon, and so on up Grizzly Cañon; but at its farther extremity he was stopped by a small man on a gray horse. The men looked at each other a moment in silence. Both were fearless, both self-possessed and independent; and both types of a civilization that in the seventeenth century would have been called heroic, but in the nineteenth simply "reckless."

"What have you got there?—I call," said Tennessee, quietly.

"Two bowers and an ace," said the stranger, as quietly, showing two revolvers and a bowie knife.

"That takes me," returned Tennessee; and, with this gambler's epigram, he threw away his useless pistol, and rode back with his captor.

It was a warm night. The cool breeze which usually sprang up with the going down of the sun behind the chaparral-crested mountain was that evening withheld from Sandy Bar. The little cañon was stifling with heated resinous odors, and the decaying driftwood on the Bar sent forth faint, sickening exhalations. The feverishness of the day and its fierce passions still filled the camp. Lights moved restlessly along the bank of the river, striking no answering reflection from its tawny current. Against the blackness of the pines the windows of the old loft above the express office stood out staringly bright; and through their curtainless panes the loungers below could see the forms of those who were even then deciding the fate of Tennessee. And above all this, etched on the dark firmament, rose the Sierra, remote and passionless, crowned with remoter passionless stars.

The trial of Tennessee was conducted as fairly as was consistent with a judge and jury who felt themselves to some extent obliged to justify, in their verdict, the previous irregularities of arrest and indictment. The law of Sandy Bar was implacable, but not vengeful. The excitement and personal feelings of the chase were over; with Tennessee safe in their hands, they were ready to listen patiently to any defense, which they were already satisfied was insufficient. There being no doubt in their own minds, they were willing to give the prisoner the benefit of any that might exist. Secure in the hypothesis that he ought to be hanged on general principles, they indulged him with more latitude of defense than his reckless hardihood seemed to ask. The judge appeared to be more anxious than the prisoner, who, otherwise unconcerned, evidently took a grim pleasure in the responsibility he had created. "I don't take any hand in this yer game," had been his invariable, but good-humored reply to all questions. The judge—who was also his captor—for a moment vaguely regretted that he had not shot him "on sight" that morning, but presently dismissed this human weakness as unworthy of the judicial mind. Nevertheless, when there was a tap at the door, and it was said that Tennessee's Partner was there on behalf of the prisoner, he was admitted at once without question. Perhaps the younger members of the jury, to whom the proceedings were becoming irksomely thoughtful, hailed him as a relief.

For he was not, certainly, an imposing figure. Short and stout, with a square face, sunburned into a preternatural redness, clad in a loose duck "jumper" and trousers streaked and splashed with red soil, his aspect under any circumstances would have been quaint, and was now even ridiculous. As he stooped to deposit at his feet a heavy carpetbag he was carrying, it became obvious, from partially developed legends and inscriptions, that the material with which his trousers had been patched had been originally intended for a less ambitious covering. Yet he advanced with great gravity, and after having shaken the hand of each person in the room with labored cordiality, he wiped his serious perplexed face on a red bandana handkerchief, a shade lighter than his complexion, laid his powerful hand upon the table to steady himself, and thus addressed the judge:

"I was passin' by," he began, by way of apology, "and I thought I'd just step in and see how things was gittin' on with Tennessee thar—my pardner. It's a hot night. I disremember any sich weather before on the Bar."

He paused a moment, but nobody volunteering any other meteorological recollection, he again had recourse to his pocket handkerchief, and for some moments mopped his face diligently.

"Have you anything to say on behalf of the prisoner?" said the judge finally.

"Thet's it," said Tennessee's Partner, in a tone of relief. "I come yar as Tennessee's pardner—knowing him nigh on four year, off and on, wet and dry, in luck and out o' luck. His ways ain't aller my ways, but thar ain't any p'ints in that young man, thar ain't any liveliness as he's been up to, as I don't know. And you sez to me, sez you—confidential-like, and between man and man—sez you, 'Do you know anything in his behalf?' and I sez to you, sez I—confidential-like, as between man and man—'What should a man know of his pardner?'"

"Is this all you have to say?" asked the judge impatiently, feeling, perhaps, that a dangerous sympathy of humor was beginning to humanize the court.

"Thet's so," continued Tennessee's Partner. "It ain't for me to say anything agin' him. And now, what's the case? Here's Tennessee wants money, wants it bad, and doesn't like to ask it of his old pardner. Well, what does Tennessee do? He lays for a stranger, and he fetches that stranger; and you lays for *him*, and you fetches *him*; and the honors is easy. And I put it to you, bein' a fa'r-minded man, and to you, gentlemen all, as fa'r-minded men, ef this isn't so."

"Prisoner," said the judge, interrupting, "have you any questions to ask this man?"

"No! no!" continued Tennessee's Partner, hastily. "I play this yer hand alone. To come down to the bedrock, it's just this: Tennessee, thar, has played it pretty rough and expensive-like on a stranger, and on this yer camp. And now, what's the fair thing? Some would say more, some would say less. Here's seventeen hundred dollars in coarse gold and a watch,—it's about all my pile,—and call it square!" And before a hand could be raised to prevent him, he had emptied the contents of the carpetbag upon the table.

For a moment his life was in jeopardy. One or two men sprang to their feet, several hands groped for hidden weapons, and a suggestion to "throw him from the window" was only overridden by a gesture from the judge. Tennessee laughed. And apparently oblivious of the excitement, Tennessee's Partner improved the opportunity to mop his face again with his handkerchief.

When order was restored, and the man was made to understand, by the use of forcible figures and rhetoric, that Tennessee's offense could not be condoned by money, his face took a more serious and sanguinary hue, and those who were nearest to him noticed that his rough hand trembled slightly on the table. He hesitated a moment as he slowly returned the gold to the carpetbag, as if he had not yet entirely caught the elevated sense of justice which swayed the tribunal, and was perplexed with the belief that he had not offered enough. Then he turned to the judge, and saying, "This yer is a lone hand, played alone, and without my pardner," he bowed to the jury and was about to withdraw, when the judge called him back:

"If you have anything to say to Tennessee, you had better say it now."

For the first time that evening the eyes of the prisoner and his strange advocate met. Tennessee smiled, showed his white teeth, and saying, "Euchred, old man!" held out his hand. Tennessee's Partner took it in his own, and saying, "I just dropped in as I was passin' to see how things was gettin' on," let the hand passively fall, and adding that "it was a warm night," again mopped his face with his handkerchief, and without another word withdrew.

The two men never again met each other alive. For the unparalleled insult of a bribe offered to Judge Lynch—who, whether bigoted weak, or narrow, was at least incorruptible—firmly fixed in the mind of that mythical personage any wavering determination of Tennessee's fate; and at the break of day he was marched, closely guarded, to meet it at the top of Marley's Hill.

How he met it, how cool he was, how he refused to say anything, how perfect were the arrangements of the committee, were all duly reported, with the addition of a warning moral and example to all future evil-doers, in the *Red Dog Clarion*, by its editor, who was present, and to whose vigorous English I cheerfully refer the reader. But the beauty of that midsummer morning, the blessed amity of earth and air and sky, the awakened life of the free woods and hills, the joyous renewal and promise of Nature, and above all, the infinite serenity that thrilled through each, was not reported, as not being a part of the social lesson. And yet, when the weak and foolish deed was done, and a life, with its possibilities and responsibilities, had passed out of the misshapen thing that dangled between earth and sky, the birds sang, the flowers bloomed, the sun shone, as cheerily as before; and possibly the *Red Dog Clarion* was right.

Tennessee's Partner was not in the group that surrounded the ominous tree. But as they turned to disperse, attention was drawn to the singular appearance of a motionless donkey cart halted at the side of the road. As they approached, they at once recognized the venerable Jenny and the two-wheeled cart as the property of Tennessee's Partner, used by him in carrying dirt from his claim; and a few paces distant the owner of the equipage himself, sitting under a buckeye tree, wiping the perspiration from his glowing face. In answer to an inquiry, he said he had come for the body of the "diseased," "if it was all the same to the committee." He didn't wish to "hurry anything"; he could "wait." He was not working that day; and when the gentlemen were done with the "diseased," he would take him. "Ef thar is any present," he added, in his simple, serious way, "as would care to jine in the fun'l, they kin come." Perhaps it was from a sense of humor, which I have already intimated as a feature of Sandy Bar—perhaps it was from something even better than that, but two thirds of the loungers accepted the invitation at once.

It was noon when the body of Tennessee was delivered into the hands of his partner. As the cart drew up to the fatal tree, we noticed that it contained a rough oblong box,—apparently made from a section of sluicing,—and half filled with bark and the tassels of pine. The cart was further decorated with slips of willow, and made fragrant with buckeye blossoms. When the body was deposited in the box, Tennessee's Partner drew over it a piece of tarred canvas, and gravely mounting the narrow seat in front, with his feet upon the shafts, urged the little donkey forward. The equipage moved slowly on, at that decorous pace which was habitual with Jenny even under less solemn circumstances. The men—half curiously, half jestingly, but all good-humoredly— strolled along beside the cart, some in advance, some a little in the rear of the homely catafalque. But whether from the narrowing of the road or some present sense of decorum, as the cart passed on, the company fell to the rear in couples, keeping step, and otherwise assuming the external show of a formal procession. Jack Folinsbee, who had at the outset played a funeral march in dumb show upon an imaginary trombone, desisted from a lack of sympathy and appreciation—not having, perhaps, your true humorist's capacity to be content with the enjoyment of his own fun.

The way led through Grizzly Cañon, by this time clothed in funereal drapery and shadows. The redwoods, burying their moccasined feet in the red soil, stood Indian file along the track, trailing an uncouth benediction from their bending boughs upon the passing bier. A hare, surprised into helpless inactivity, sat upright and pulsating in the ferns by the roadside, as the cortege went by. Squirrels hastened to gain a secure outlook from higher boughs; and the bluejays, spreading their wings, fluttered before them like outriders, until the outskirts of Sandy Bar were reached, and the solitary cabin of Tennessee's Partner.

Viewed under more favorable circumstances, it would not have been a cheerful place. The unpicturesque site, the rude and unlovely outlines, the unsavory details, which distinguish the nest-building of the California miner, were all here, with the dreariness of decay superadded. A few paces from the cabin there was a rough enclosure, which, in the brief days of Tennessee's Partner's matrimonial felicity, had been used as a garden, but was now overgrown with fern. As we approached it, we were surprised to find that what we had taken for a recent attempt at cultivation was the broken soil about an open grave.

The cart was halted before the enclosure, and rejecting the offers of assistance with the same air of simple self-reliance he had displayed throughout, Tennessee's Partner lifted the rough coffin on his back, and deposited it unaided within the shallow grave. He then nailed down the board which served as a lid, and mounting the little mound of earth beside it, took off his hat and slowly mopped his face with his handkerchief. This the crowd felt was a preliminary to speech, and they disposed themselves variously on stumps and boulders, and sat expectant.

"When a man," began Tennessee's Partner slowly, "has been running free all day, what's the natural thing for him to do? Why, to come home. And if he ain't in a condition to go home, what can his best friend do? Why, bring him home. And here's Tennessee has been running free, and we brings him home from his wandering." He paused and picked up a fragment of quartz, rubbed it thoughtfully on his sleeve and went on: "It ain't the first time I've packed him on my back, as you see'd me now. It ain't the first time that I brought him to this yer cabin when he couldn't help himself; it ain't the first time that I and Jinny have waited for him on yon hill, and picked him up and so fetched him home, when he couldn't speak and didn't know me. And now that it's the last time, why"—he paused, and rubbed the quartz gently on his sleeve—"you see it's sort of rough on his pardner. And now, gentlemen," he added abruptly, picking up his long-handled shovel, "the fun'l's over; and my thanks, and Tennessee's thanks, to you for your trouble."

Resisting any proffers of assistance, he began to fill in the grave, turning his back upon the crowd, that after a few moments' hesitation gradually withdrew. As they crossed the little ridge that hid Sandy Bar from view, some, looking back, thought they could see Tennessee's Partner, his work done, sitting upon the grave, his shovel between his knees, and his face buried in his red bandana handkerchief. But it was argued by others that you couldn't tell his face from his handkerchief at that distance, and this point remained undecided.

In the reaction that followed the feverish excitement of that day, Tennessee's Partner was not forgotten. A secret investigation had cleared him of any complicity in Tennessee's guilt, and left only a suspicion of his general sanity. Sandy Bar made a point of calling on him, and proferring various uncouth but well-meant kindnesses. But from that day his rude health and great strength seemed visibly to decline; and when the rainy season fairly set in, and the tiny grass blades were beginning to peep from the rocky mount above Tennessee's grave, he took to his bed.

One night, when the pines beside the cabin were swaying in the storm and trailing their slender fingers over the roof, and the roar and rush of the swollen river were heard below, Tennessee's Partner lifted his head from the pillow, saying, "It is time to go for Tennessee; I must put Jinny in the cart"; and would have risen from his bed but for the restraint of his attendant. Struggling, he still pursued his singular fancy: "There, now, steady, Jinny—steady, old girl. How dark it is! Look out for the ruts—and look out for him, too, old gal. Sometimes, you know, when he's blind drunk, he drops down right in the trail. Keep on straight up to the pine on the top of the hill. Thar! I told you so!—thar he is—coming this way, too—all by himself, sober, and his face a-shining. Tennessee! Pardner!"

And so they met.

DISCUSSION

This is the story of a man's intense loyalty to his friend. The man Tennessee actually steals his partner's wife, but the friendship of the men survives even this severe test: they become reconciled, and later after Tennessee has been executed for highway robbery, his partner claims the body, buries it with such rites of decency as he can contrive, and soon himself wastes away and dies. What makes this display of loyalty even more remarkable is that Tennessee's partner is not a man to whom we would ordinarily ascribe much delicacy of feeling. Not that this latter point invalidates the story. Other writers have remarked upon the intensity and rightness of the feelings of simple and "unliterary" persons. To take an instance from a contemporary writer, Ernest Hemingway frequently allows his "tough" and "hard-boiled" characters to reveal a sensitivity that belies their apparent callousness.

The difficulty with this story has to do with the credibility of the actions of Tennessee's partner. Do we really believe that he would act so magnanimously? That will depend upon our understanding of his character; and that in turn will have to do with Bret Harte's presentation of the psychological steps by which Tennessee's partner arrives at the actions in question. In any case, the episode of the wife-stealing will be the hardest to accept.

The community, in this instance, certainly expected trouble: according to the primitive code the loss of honor that Tennessee's partner has suffered definitely demands bloodletting. Moreover, the partner is a man who evidently sees everything in very concrete and personal terms—witness his conduct at the trial in which he shows that he has no conception of abstract justice, and the relation of a man to his wife is a very personal and concrete relation. How could this man forgive Tennessee? (If, of course, he had regarded his wife as a mere chattel, then the whole meaning of his act of forgiveness is lost, for the conflict— between affection for his friend on the one hand and affection for his wife on the other—disappears from the situation.) But Bret Harte has really dodged this psychological problem. Even though it is plain that he meant the burial scene and not the wife-stealing episode to be the climax of the story, we still have a right to ask that the wife-stealing episode be credibly developed. In fact, if it is not made credible, the whole story loses its point.

What else does Bret Harte give us in preparation for the climactic burial scene? He gives us the scene of attempted bribery. The purpose of this scene seems to be to indicate the partner's naiveté with regard to the conventions of society, to the nature of law, and even to the concept of abstract justice itself. Apparently, he honestly sees the situation Tennessee has fallen into as one that can be settled by a money payment. The stranger will be compensated for his losses and will be given something for his trouble. Perhaps there is the implication that he is attempting to bribe the court. Indeed, the judge proceeds to give the man a lecture on the nature of law: "the man was made to understand . . . that Tennessee's offense could not be condoned by money." But another purpose of

118

the scene is to develop the idea of the partner's doglike devotion: he is willing to sacrifice his "pile" for his friend.

For what, after all, does this court incident intend to prepare us? It is, of course, not merely for the incident of the burial, as such. For someone among the rough citizenry would have buried the hanged man in any case, and perhaps with a kind of elemental pity. (Tennessee, has, for instance, certain qualities that would extort special admiration in this primitive community—a courage and coolness dramatized several times in the story.) The intended high point in the story is the funeral oration, which Tennessee's partner delivers to the camp. It is here that our full sense of the pathos is supposed to emerge.

But if such pathos is to emerge to the full, and is to be meaningful, the author must have persuaded us (1) that it is logical for this particular character to deliver the oration under the circumstances and (2) that this oration brings to focus elements of interpretation and meaning implicit in previous incidents.

But there are more difficulties. First, the partner, whose life had been dominated by a merely personal attachment to his friend and who had been completely incapable of understanding why his friend had to be hanged (as indicated by the bribery scene), would more probably have felt a sullen resentment against the men who had done his friend to death for, in his eyes, no good reason. (He can be under no illusion the spectators have come to the funeral out of love for Tennessee.) Under such circumstances would he give this oration?

Second, assuming that the partner would have delivered the oration, would he have said what Bret Harte makes him say? For example, would he have apologized to the spectators and have thanked them for their trouble? Notice that Bret Harte does not intend for us to take this as the bitter irony of a hurt man, but as a manifestation of a kind of Christlike forgiveness. The partner is almost too good to be true. The whole attempt is an appeal to sentiment.

Notice further, in this connection, what Bret Harte has the partner say in his delirium as he dies of a broken heart. Here, even the language becomes unrealistic; it is entirely out of the partner's idiom. For example, would he have said "There, now, steady, Jinny—steady, old girl. How dark it is!" Isn't it more likely that he would have said "It's dark as hell"? or "God-a-mighty, it's dark!" Why does Bret Harte break out of the partner's idiom? Because he is straining for a highly emotional effect, and feeling that the realistic language is not good enough, he resorts to "poeticizing" the character. The same thing is true of the symbolic reference, in the dying speech, to the pine tree on the top of the hill.

But other examples of such strain are to be found earlier in the story. Take, for example, the description of nature as the partner carries the body to the place of burial: "The way led through Grizzly Cañon, by this time clothed in funereal drapery and shadows. The redwoods, burying moccasined feet in the red soil, stood in Indian file along the track, trailing an uncouth benediction from their bending boughs upon the passing bier." Nature, apparently, is sympathetic with the partner's grief. Like him, it can give only an "uncouth benediction," but it expresses its brooding sympathy as best it can. One recognizes that a writer may legitimately use description of nature as a device for defining the atmosphere of a piece of fiction, or may even use it as specific symbolism. But it should be quite clear that Bret Harte here is not using it legitimately. It is used here to give a false heightening to the pathos of the scene, and the description is as "poeticized" as is the partner's dying speech. For example, the description of the redwoods "burying their moccasined feet in the red soil" is completely irrelevant and represents an attempt at fanciful decoration; it is another instance of the author's straining for effects that, he seems to feel, are not adequately supported by the situation in itself.

The presence of this straining for an emotional effect is one of the surest symptoms that one is dealing with a case of sentimentality. In its general sense, as we have seen, sentimentality may be defined as an emotional response in excess of the occasion—or without relevance to the occasion. We speak of a person who weeps at some trivial occurrence as being sentimental. Such a person lacks a sense of proportion and gets a morbid enjoyment from an emotional debauch for its own sake. When we apply the term to a piece of literature, a story, for instance, we usually mean that the author intends for the reader to experience an intense emotion that is actually not justified by the materials of the story.

One symptom of sentimentality is, as we have said, the author's straining to heighten and prettify and poeticize his language quite apart from the dramatic issues involved in the story.

A second symptom frequently to be found is "editorializing" on the part of the author—pointing out to the reader what he should feel, nudging the reader to respond—devices that would not be necessary if the story could make its own case. (For example, Bret Harte comments on the hanging as follows: "And yet, when the weak and foolish deed was done, and a life, with its possibilities and responsibilities, had passed out of the misshapen thing that dangled between earth and sky, the birds sang, the flowers bloomed, the sun shone, as cheerily as before.")

A third symptom is the tendency to dodge the real issues that should prepare for the final effect of a story. That is, an author who is primarily concerned with giving an emotional effect may not be too scrupulous about the means adopted to that end. For example, in this story Bret Harte is so thoroughly obsessed with the pathos of the partner's loyalty that he has devoted no thought to the precise nature of the basis of that loyalty. As has already been pointed out, he does not bring the wife-stealing episode into real focus. By skimping it and moving toward the final effort at pathos, he has made the whole story seem anticlimactic and illogical. Either he was so little interested in the psychology of the situation that he did not investigate it, or he was aware that the issues involved were too complicated for him to handle.

This story raises a basic question of character: has not Bret Harte taken a theme—which, perhaps, he had seen successfully employed for pathetic effects in other fiction—and attempted to trick it out with a new romantic setting, touches of local color (such as descriptions of the community and bits of dialect), and poeticized writing, without ever grounding the story in a presentation of the real psychological issues involved—without, in other words, trying to understand his main character?

1. Compare the relation of Tennessee and his partner with that of Dravot and Peachey in "The Man Who Would Be King." How did Kipling avoid sentimentality?

2. Compare the "editorializing" of O. Henry in "The Furnished Room" with that of Bret Harte in this story. What is the function of the "editorializing" in each?

3. Discuss the question of sentimentality in "Vanka." Did Chekhov avoid sentimentality? If so, how?

ARABY

James Joyce

NORTH Richmond Street, being blind, was a quiet street except at the hour when the Christian Brothers' School set the boys free. An uninhabited house of two stories stood at the blind end, detached from its neighbors in a square ground. The other houses of the street, conscious of decent lives within them, gazed at one another with brown imperturbable faces.

The former tenant of our house, a priest, had died in the back drawing room. Air, musty from having been long enclosed, hung in all the rooms, and the waste room behind the kitchen was littered with old useless papers. Among these I found a few paper-covered books, the pages of which were curled and damp: *The Abbot*, by Walter Scott, *The Devout Communicant*, and *The Memoirs of Vidocq*. I liked the last best because its leaves were yellow. The wild garden behind the house contained a central apple tree and a few straggling brushes under one of which I found the late tenant's rusty bicycle pump. He had been a very charitable priest; in his will he had left all his money to institutions and the furniture of his house to his sister.

When the short days of winter came dusk fell before we had well eaten our dinners. When we met in the street the houses had grown somber. The space of sky above us was the color of ever-changing violet and towards it the lamps of the street lifted their feeble lanterns. The cold air stung us and we played till our bodies glowed. Our shouts echoed in the silent street. The career of our play brought us through the dark muddy lanes behind the houses where we ran the gauntlet of the rough tribes from the cottages, to the back doors of the dark odorous stables where a coachman smoothed and combed the horse or shook music from the buckled harness. When we returned to the street, light from the kitchen windows had filled the areas. If my uncle was seen turning the corner we hid in the shadow until we had seen him safely housed. Or if Mangan's sister came out on the doorstep to call her brother in to his tea we watched her from our shadow peer up and down the street. We waited to see whether she would remain or go in and, if she remained, we left our shadow and walked up to Mangan's steps resignedly. She was waiting for us, her figure defined by the light from the half-opened door. Her brother always teased her before he obeyed and I stood by the railings looking at her. Her dress swung as she moved her body and the soft rope of her hair tossed from side to side.

Every morning I lay on the floor in the front parlor watching her door. The blind was pulled down to within an inch of the sash so that I could not be seen. When she came out on the doorstep my heart leaped. I ran to the hall, seized my books and followed her. I kept her brown figure always in my eye and, when we came near the point at which our ways diverged, I quickened my pace and passed her. This happened morning after morning. I had never spoken to her, except for a few casual words, and yet her name was like a summons to all my foolish blood.

Her image accompanied me even in places the most hostile to romance. On Saturday evenings when my aunt went marketing I had to go to carry some of the parcels. We walked through the flaring streets, jostled by drunken men and bargaining women, amid the curses of laborers, the shrill litanies of shop boys who stood on guard by the barrels of pigs' cheeks, the nasal chanting of street singers, who sang a *come-all-you* about O'Donovan Rossa, or a ballad about the troubles in our native land. These noises converged in a single sensation of life for me: I imagined that I bore my chalice safely through a throng of foes. Her name sprang to my lips at moments in strange prayers and praises which I myself did not understand. My eyes were often full of tears (I could not tell why) and at times a flood from my heart seemed to pour itself out into my bosom. I thought little of the future. I did not know whether I would ever speak to her or not or, if I spoke to her, how I could tell her of my confused adoration. But my body was like a harp and her words and gestures were like fingers running upon the wires.

One evening I went into the back drawing room in which the priest had died. It was a dark rainy evening and there was no sound in the house. Through one of the broken panes I heard the rain impinge upon the earth, the fine incessant needles of water playing in the sodden beds. Some distant lamp or lighted window gleamed below me. I was thankful that I could see so little. All my senses seemed to desire to veil themselves and, feeling that I was about to slip from them, I pressed the palms of my hands together until they trembled, murmuring: *"O love! O love!"* many times.

At last she spoke to me. When she addressed the first words to me I was so confused that I did not know what to answer. She asked me was I going to *Araby*. I forgot whether I answered yes or no. It would be a splendid bazaar, she said; she would love to go.

"And why can't you?" I asked.

While she spoke she turned a silver bracelet round and round her wrist. She could not go, she said, because there would be a retreat that week in her convent. Her brother and two other boys were fighting for their caps and I was alone at the railings. She held one of the spikes, bowing her head towards me. The light from the lamp opposite our door caught the white curve of her neck, lit up her hair that rested there and, falling, lit up the hand upon the railing. It fell over one side of her dress and caught the white border of a petticoat, just visible as she stood at ease.

"It's well for you," she said.

"If I go," I said, "I will bring you something."

What innumerable follies laid waste my waking and sleeping thoughts after that evening! I wished to annihilate the tedious intervening days. I chafed against the work of school. At night in my bedroom and by day in the classroom her image came between me and the page I strove to read. The syllables of the word *Araby* were called to me through the silence in which my soul luxuriated and cast an Eastern enchantment over me. I asked for leave to go to the bazaar on Saturday night. My aunt was surprised and hoped it was not some Freemason affair. I answered few questions in class. I watched my master's face pass from amiability to sternness; he hoped I was not beginning to idle. I could not call my wandering thoughts together. I had hardly any patience with the serious work of life which, now that it stood between me and my desire, seemed to me child's play, ugly monotonous child's play.

On Saturday morning I reminded my uncle that I wished to go to the bazaar in the evening. He was fussing at the hall stand, looking for the hat brush, and answered me curtly:

"Yes, boy, I know."

As he was in the hall I could not go into the front parlor and lie at the window. I left the house in bad humor and walked slowly towards the school. The air was pitilessly raw and already my heart misgave me.

When I came home to dinner my uncle had not yet been home. Still it was early. I sat staring at the clock for some time and, when its ticking began to irritate me, I left the room. I mounted the staircase and gained the upper part of the house. The high cold empty gloomy rooms liberated me and I went from room to room singing. From the front window I saw my companions playing below in the street. Their cries reached me weakened and indistinct and, leaning my forehead against the cool glass, I looked over at the dark house where she lived. I may have stood there for an hour, seeing nothing but the brown-clad figure cast by my imagination, touched discreetly by the lamplight at the curved neck, at the hand upon the railings and at the border below the dress.

When I came downstairs again I found Mrs. Mercer sitting at the fire. She was an old garrulous woman, a pawnbroker's widow, who collected used stamps for some pious purpose. I had to endure the gossip of the tea table. The meal was prolonged beyond an hour and still my uncle did not come. Mrs. Mercer stood up to go: she was sorry she couldn't wait any longer, but it was after eight o'clock and she did not like to be out late, as the night air was bad for her. When she had gone I began to walk up and down the room, clenching my fists. My aunt said:

"I'm afraid you may put off your bazaar for this night of Our Lord."

At nine o'clock I heard my uncle's latchkey in the hall door. I heard him talking to himself and heard the hall stand rocking when it had received the weight of his overcoat. I could interpret these signs. When he was midway through his dinner I asked him to give me the money to go to the bazaar. He had forgotten.

"The people are in bed and after their first sleep now," he said.

I did not smile. My aunt said to him energetically:

"Can't you give him the money and let him go? You've kept him late enough as it is."

My uncle said he was very sorry he had forgotten. He said he believed in the old saying: "All work and no play makes Jack a dull boy." He asked me where I was going and, when I had told him a second time he asked me did I know *The Arab's Farewell to His Steed*. When I left the kitchen he was about to recite the opening lines of the piece to my aunt.

I held a florin tightly in my hand as I strode down Buckingham Street towards the station. The sight of the streets thronged with buyers and glaring with gas recalled to me the purpose of my journey. I took my seat in a third-class carriage of a deserted train. After an intolerable delay the train moved out of the station slowly. It crept onward among ruinous houses and over the twinkling river. At Westland Row Station a crowd of people pressed to the carriage doors; but the porters moved them back, saying that it was a special train for the bazaar. I remained alone in the bare carriage. In a few minutes the train drew up beside an improvised wooden platform. I passed out on to the road and saw by the lighted dial of a clock that it was ten minutes to ten. In front of me was a large building which displayed the magical name.

I could not find any sixpenny entrance and, fearing that the bazaar would be closed, I passed in quickly through a turnstile, handing a shilling to a weary-looking man. I found myself in a big hall girdled at half its height by a gallery. Nearly all the stalls were closed and the greater part of the hall was in darkness. I recognized a silence like that which pervades a church after a service. I walked into the center of the bazaar timidly. A few people were gathered about the stalls which were still open. Before a curtain, over which the words *Café Chantant* were written in colored lamps, two men were counting money on a salver. I listened to the fall of the coins.

Remembering with difficulty why I had come I went over to one of the stalls and examined porcelain vases and flowered tea sets. At the door of the stall a young lady was talking and laughing with two young gentlemen. I remarked their English accents and listened vaguely to their conversation.

"O, I never said such a thing!"

"O, but you did!"

"O, but I didn't!"

"Didn't she say that?"

"Yes, I heard her."

"O, there's a . . . fib!"

Observing me, the young lady came over and asked me did I wish to buy anything. The tone of her voice was not encouraging; she seemed to have spoken to me out of a sense of duty. I looked humbly at the great jars that stood like eastern guards at either side of the dark entrance to the stall and murmured:

"No, thank you."

The young lady changed the position of one of the vases and went back to the two young men. They began to talk of the same subject. Once or twice the young lady glanced at me over her shoulder.

I lingered before her stall, though I knew my stay was useless, to make my interest in her wares seem the more real. Then I turned away slowly and walked down the middle of the bazaar. I allowed the two pennies to fall against the sixpence in my pocket. I heard a voice call from one end of the gallery that the light was out. The upper part of the hall was now completely dark.

Gazing up into the darkness I saw myself as a creature driven and derided by vanity; and my eyes burned with anguish and anger.

DISCUSSION

On what may be called the simplest level this is a story of a boy's disappointment. A great part of the story, however, does not directly concern itself with the boy's love affair, but with the world in which he lives—the description of his street, the information about the dead priest and the priest's abandoned belongings, the relations with the aunt and uncle. These matters seem to come very naturally into the story; that is, they may be justified individually in the story on realistic grounds. If such elements served *merely* as "setting" or *only* as atmosphere, then the story would be overloaded with nonfunctional material. Obviously, however, for any reader except the most casual, these items do have a function. If we find in what way these apparently irrelevant items in "Araby" are related to each other and to the disappointment of the boy, we shall have defined the theme of the story.

What, then, is the relation of the boy's disappointment to such matters as the belongings of the dead priest, the fact that he stands apart talking to the girl while his friends are quarreling over the cap, the gossip over the tea table, the uncle's lateness, and so on? One thing that is immediately suggested by the mention of these things is the boy's growing sense of isolation, the lack of sympathy between him and his friends, teachers, and family. He says, "I imagined that I bore my chalice safely through a throng of foes." For instance, when the uncle is standing in the hall, the boy could not go into the front parlor and lie at the window; or at school his ordinary occupations began to seem "ugly monotonous child's play." But this sense of isolation has, also, moments that are almost triumphant. The porters at the station wave the crowds back, "saying that it was a special train for the bazaar" and was not for them. The boy is left alone in the bare carriage, but he is going to "Araby," moving triumphantly toward some romantic and exotic fulfillment. The metaphor of the chalice implies the same kind of precious secret triumph. It is not only the ordinary surrounding world, however, from which he is cruelly or triumphantly isolated. He is also isolated from the girl herself. He talks to her only once, and then is so confused that he does not know how to answer her. But the present he hopes to bring her from Araby would somehow serve as a means of communicating his feelings to her, a symbol for their relationship in the midst of the inimical world.

In the last scene at the bazaar, there is a systematic, though subtle, preparation for the final realization on the part of the boy. There is the "improvised wooden platform" in contrast with the "magical name" displayed above the building. Inside, most of the stalls are closed. The "young lady" and young men who talk together are important in the preparation. They pay the boy no mind, except insofar as the "young lady" is compelled by her position as clerk to ask him what he wants. But her tone is "not encouraging." She, too, belongs to the inimical world. But she, also, belongs to a world he is trying to penetrate: she and her admirers are on terms of easy intimacy—an intimacy in contrast to his relation to Mangan's sister. It is an exotic, rich world into which he cannot penetrate: he can only look "humbly at the great jars that stood like eastern guards at either side of the dark entrance to the stall." Ironically, the "young lady" and her admirers, far from realizing that they are on holy, guarded ground, indulge in trivial, easy banter, which seems to defile and cheapen the secret world from which the boy is barred. How do we know this? It is not stated, but the contrast between the conversation of the young lady and her admirers, and the tone of the sentence about the "great jars" indicates such an interpretation.

Such scenes, then, help to point up and particularize the general sense of isolation suggested by the earlier descriptive materials, and thereby to prepare for the last sentence of the story, in which, under the sudden darkness of the cheap barnlike bazaar, the boy sees himself as "a creature driven and derided by vanity," while his eyes burn with "anguish and anger."

We have seen how the apparently casual incidents and items of description do function in the story to build up the boy's sense of intolerable isolation, his sense of being isolated from the common world in so sacred a precinct. But this is only part of the function of this material. The careful reader will have noticed how many references, direct or indirect, there are to religion and the ritual of the church. We have the dead priest, the Christian Brothers' School, the aunt's hope that the bazaar is not "some Freemason affair," her mention, when the uncle has been delayed, of "this night of Our Lord." At one level, these references merely indicate the type of community in which the impressionable boy is growing up. But there are other, less obvious, references, which relate more intimately to the boy's experience. Even the cries of the shop boys for him are "shrill litanies." He imagines that he bears a "chalice safely through a throng of foes." When he is alone the name of Mangan's sister springs to his lips "in strange prayers and praises." For this reason, when he speaks of his "confused adoration," we see that the love of the girl takes on, for him, something of the nature of a mystic, religious experience. The use of the very word *confused* hints of the fact that romantic love and religious love are mixed up in his mind.

The boy is isolated from a world that seems ignorant of, and even hostile to, his love. In a sense he knows that his aunt and uncle are good and kind, but they do not understand him. He had once found satisfaction in the society of his companions and in his schoolwork, but he has become impatient with both. But there is also a sense in which he accepts his isolation and is even proud of it. The world not only does not understand his secret but would cheapen and contaminate it. The metaphor of the chalice borne through a throng of foes, supported as it is by the body of the story, suggests a sort of consecration like that of the religious devotee. The implications of the references to religion, then, help define the boy's attitude and indicate why, for him, so much is staked upon the journey to the bazaar. It is interesting to note, therefore, that the first overt indication of his disillusionment and disappointment is expressed in a metaphor involving a church: "Nearly all the stalls were closed and the greater part of the hall was in darkness. I recognized a silence like that which pervades a church after a service. . . . Two men were counting money on a salver. I listened to the fall of the coins." And this episode, of course, is an echo of the money-changers in the Temple at Jerusalem (Mark 11:15); so here we have the idea that the contamination of the world has invaded the very temple of love. (The question may arise as to whether this is not reading too much into the passage. But whatever interpretation is to be made of the particular incident, it is by just such suggestion and implication that closely wrought stories, such as this one, are controlled by their authors and embody their fundamental meaning.)

Is this a sentimental story? It is about an adolescent love affair, about "puppy love," which is usually not taken seriously and is often an occasion for amusement. The boy of the story is obviously investing casual incidents with a meaning they do not deserve; he himself admits, in the end, that he has fallen into self-deception. How does the author avoid the charge that he has taken the matter overseriously?

The answer to this question would involve a consideration of the point of view from which the story is told. It is told by the hero himself, but after a long lapse of time, after he has reached maturity. This fact, it is true, is not stated in the story, but the style itself is not that of an adolescent boy. It is a formal and complicated style, rich in subtle implications. In other words, the man is looking back upon the boy, detached and judicial. For instance, the boy, in the throes of the experience, would never have said of himself: "I had never spoken to her, except for a few casual words, and yet her name was like a summons to all my foolish blood." The man knows, as it were, that the behavior of the boy was, in a sense, foolish. The emotions of the boy are confused. He has unraveled the confusion long after, knows that it existed and why it existed.

If the man has unraveled the confusions of the boy, why is the event still significant to him? Is he merely dwelling on the pathos of adolescent experience? It seems, rather, that he sees in the event, as he looks back on it, a foreshadowing of a problem that has run through later experience. The discrepancy between the real and the ideal scarcely exists for the child, but it is a constant problem, in all sorts of terms, for the adult.

This story is about a boy's first confrontation of that problem—that is, about his growing up. The man may have made adjustments to this problem, and may have worked out certain provisional solutions, but, looking back, he still recognizes it as a problem, and an important one. The sense of isolation and disillusion that sprang from the boy's experience—though it may seem trivial—becomes not less but more aggravated and fundamental in the adult's experience. So, the story is not merely an account of a stage in the process of growing up; it does not merely represent a clinical interest in the psychology of growing up. It is a symbolic rendering of a central conflict in mature experience.

1. What does the boy have in common with the dead priest? Suppose that the dead man had been a shopkeeper, a lawyer, or anyone else who did not "carry a chalice." Would that have made any difference in the story?

2. Children are supposed to have more imagination than adults. What has happened when, for the boy, his previous occupations seem to be "ugly monotonous child's play"?

3. There is in this story a relatively small amount of dramatically rendered material. Can you say why? Is this fact consistent with the general tone and meaning of the story?

4. Think how easy it would have been to make this a sentimental, tear-jerking story about the disappointment of "first love." In this connection, comment on the "distancing" of the time of the telling from the time of the event and the tone of analysis. Comment on style in this connection.

THE DISTRICT DOCTOR

Ivan Turgenev

ONE day in autumn on my way back from a remote part of the country I caught cold and fell ill. Fortunately the fever attacked me in the district town at the inn; I sent for the doctor. In half-an-hour the district doctor appeared, a thin, dark-haired man of middle height. He prescribed me the usual sudorific, ordered a mustard plaster to be put on, very deftly slid a five-ruble note up his sleeve, coughing drily and looking away as he did so, and then was getting up to go home, but somehow fell into talk and remained. I was exhausted with feverishness; I foresaw a sleepless night, and was glad of a little chat with a pleasant companion. Tea was served. My doctor began to converse freely. He was a sensible fellow, and expressed himself with vigour and some humour. Queer things happen in the world: you may live a long while with some people, and be on friendly terms with them, and never once speak openly with them from your soul; with others you scarcely have time to get acquainted, and all at once you are pouring out to him or he to you—all your secrets, as though you were at confession. I don't know how I gained the confidence of my new friend—anyway, with nothing to lead up to it, he told me a rather curious incident;and here I will report his tale for the information of the indulgent reader. I will try to tell it in the doctor's own words.

"You don't happen to know," he began in a weak and quavering voice (the common result of the use of unmixed Berezov snuff); "you don't happen to know the judge here, Mylov, Pavel Lukich? . . . You don't know him? . . . Well, it's all the same." (He cleared his throat and rubbed his eyes.) "Well, you see, the thing happened, to tell you exactly without mistake, in Lent, at the very time of the thaws. I was sitting at his house—our judge's, you know—playing preference.[1] Our judge is a good fellow, and fond of playing preference. Suddenly," (the doctor made frequent use of this word, suddenly) "they tell me, 'There's a servant asking for you.' I say 'What does he want?' They say 'He has brought a note—it must be from a patient.' 'Give me the note,' I say. So it is from a patient—well and good—you understand—it's our bread and butter. . . . But this is how it was: a lady, a widow, writes to me; she says, 'My daughter is dying. Come, for God's sake!' she says, 'and the horses have been sent for you!' . . . Well, that's all right. But she was twenty miles from town, and it was midnight out of doors, and the roads in such a state, my word! And as she was poor herself, one could not expect more than two silver rubles, and even that problematic; and perhaps it might only be a matter of a roll of linen and a sack of oatmeal in payment. However, duty, you know, before everything: a fellow-creature may be dying. I hand over my cards at once to Kalliopin, the member of the provincial commission, and return home. I look; a wretched little trap was standing at the steps, with peasant's horses, fat—too fat—and their coats as shaggy as felt; and the coachman sitting with his cap off out of respect. Well, I think to myself, 'It's clear, my friend, these patients aren't rolling in riches.' . . . You smile; but I tell you, a poor man like me has to take everything into consideration. . . . If the coachman sits like a prince, and doesn't touch his cap, and even sneers at you behind his beard, and flicks his whip—then you may bet on six rubles. But this case, I saw, had a very different air. However, I think there's no help for it; duty before everything. I snatch up the most necessary drugs, and set off. Will you believe it? I only just managed to get there at all. The road was infernal: streams, snow, watercourses, and the dyke had suddenly burst there—that was the worst of it! However, I arrived at last. It was a little thatched house. There was a light in the windows; that meant they expected me. I was met by an old lady, very venerable, in a cap. 'Save her!' she says; 'she is dying.' I say, 'Pray don't distress yourself—where is the invalid?' 'Come this way.' I see a clean little room, a lamp in the corner; on the bed a girl of twenty, unconscious. She was in a burning heat, and breathing heavily—it was fever. There were two other girls, her sisters, scared and in tears. 'Yesterday,' they tell me, 'she was perfectly well and had a good appetite; this morning she complained of her head, and this evening, suddenly, you see, like this.' I say again: 'Pray don't be uneasy.' It's a doctor's duty, you know—and I went up to her and bled her, told them to put on a mustard plaster, and prescribed a mixture. Meantime I

---

[1] A card game resembling whist.

looked at her, you know—there, by God! I had never seen such a face!—she was a beauty, in a word! I felt quite shaken by pity. Such lovely features; such eyes! . . . But, thank God! she became easier; she fell into a perspiration, seemed to come to her senses, looked round, smiled, and passed her hand over her face. . . . Her sisters bent over her. They ask, 'How are you?' 'All right,' she says, and turns away. I looked at her; she had fallen asleep. 'Well,' I say, 'now the patient should be left alone.' So we all went out on tiptoe; only a maid remained, in case she was wanted. In the parlour there was a samovar standing on the table, and a bottle of rum; in our profession one can't get on without it. They gave me tea; asked me to stop the night. . . . I consented: where could I go, indeed, at that time of night? The old lady kept groaning. 'What is it?' I say; 'she will live; don't worry yourself; you had better take a little rest yourself; it is about two o'clock.' 'But will you send to wake me if anything happens?' 'Yes, yes.' The old lady went away, and the girls too went to their own rooms; they made up a bed for me in the parlour. Well, I went to bed—but I could not get to sleep, for a wonder! for in reality I was very tired. I could not get my patient out of my head. At last I could not put up with it any longer; I got up suddenly; I think to myself, 'I will go and see how the patient is getting on.' Her bedroom was next to the parlour. Well, I got up, and gently opened the door—how my heart beat! I looked in: the servant was asleep, her mouth wide open, and even snoring, the wretch! but the patient lay with her face towards me, and her arms flung wide apart, poor girl! I went up to her . . . when suddenly she opened her eyes and stared at me! 'Who is it? who is it?' I was in confusion. 'Don't be alarmed, madam,' I say; 'I am the doctor; I have come to see how you feel.' 'You the doctor?' 'Yes, the doctor; your mother sent for me from the town; we have bled you, madam; now pray go to sleep, and in a day or two, please God! we will set you on your feet again.' 'Ah, yes, yes doctor, don't let me die . . . please, please.' 'Why do you talk like that? God bless you!' She is in a fever again, I think to myself; I felt her pulse; yes, she was feverish. She looked at me, and then took me by the hand. 'I will tell you why I don't want to die; I will tell you. . . . Now we are alone; and only, please don't you . . . not to anyone . . . Listen . . . ! I bent down; she moved her lips quite to my ear; she touched my cheek with her hair—I confess my head went round—and began to whisper. . . . I could make out nothing of it. . . . Ah, she was delirious! . . . She whispered and whispered, but so quickly, and as if it were not in Russian; at last she finished, and shivering dropped her head on the pillow, and threatened me with her finger: 'Remember, doctor, to no one.' I calmed her somehow, gave her something to drink, waked the servant, and went away."

At this point the doctor again took snuff with exasperated energy, and for a moment seemed stupefied by its effects.

"However," he continued, "the next day, contrary to my expectations, the patient was no better. I thought and thought, and suddenly decided to remain there, even though my other patients were expecting me. . . . And you know one can't afford to disregard that; one's practice suffers if one does. But, in the first place, the patient was really in danger; and secondly, to tell the truth, I felt strongly drawn to her. Besides, I liked the whole family. Though they were really badly off, they were singularly, I may say, cultivated people. . . . Their father had been a learned man, an author; he died, of course, in poverty, but he had managed before he died to give his children an excellent education; he left a lot of books too. Either because I looked after the invalid very carefully, or for some other reason; anyway, I can venture to say all the household loved me as one of the family. . . . Meantime the roads were in a worse state than ever; all communications, so to say, were cut off completely; even medicine could with difficulty be got from the town. . . . The sick girl was not getting better . . . Day after day, and day after day . . . but . . . here. . . ." (The doctor made a brief pause.) "I declare I don't know how to tell you." . . . (He again took snuff, coughed, and swallowed a little tea.) "I will tell you without beating about the bush. My patient . . . how should I say? . . . Well she had fallen in love with me . . . or, no, it was not that she was in love . . . however . . . really, how should one say?" (The doctor looked down and grew red.) "No," he went on quickly, "in love, indeed! A man should not over-estimate himself. She was an educated girl, clever and well-read, and I had even forgotten my Latin, one may say, completely. As to appearance" (the doctor looked himself over with a smile) "I am nothing to boast of there either. But God Almighty did not make me a fool; I don't take black for white; I know a thing or two; I could see very clearly, for instance, that Aleksandra Andreyevna—that was her name—did not feel love for me, but had a friendly, so to say, inclination—a respect or something for me. Though she herself perhaps mistook this sentiment, anyway this was her attitude; you may form your own judgment of it. But," added the doctor, who had brought out all these disconnected sentences without taking breath, and with obvious embarrassment, "I seem to be wandering rather—you won't understand anything like this. . . . There with your leave, I will relate it all in order."

He drank a glass of tea, and began in a calmer voice.

"Well, then. My patient kept getting worse and worse. You are not a doctor, my good sir; you cannot understand what passes in a poor fellow's heart, especially at first, when he begins to suspect that the disease is getting the upper hand of him. What becomes of his belief in himself? You suddenly grow so timid it's indescribable. You fancy then that you have forgotten everything you knew, and that the patient has no faith in you, and that other people begin to notice how distracted you are, and tell you the symptoms with reluctance; that they are looking at you suspiciously, whispering. . . . Ah! it's horrid! There must be a remedy, you think, for this disease, if one could find it. Isn't this it? You try—no, that's not it! You don't allow the medicine the necessary time to do good. . . . You clutch at one thing, then at another. Sometimes you take up a book of medical prescriptions—here it is, you think! Sometimes, by Jove, you pick one out by chance, thinking to leave it to fate. . . . But meantime a fellow creature's dying, and another doctor would have saved him. 'We must have a consultation,' you say; 'I will not take the responsibility on myself.' And what a fool you look at such times! Well, in time you learn to bear it; it's nothing to you. A man has died—but it's not your fault; you treated him by the rules. But what's still more torture to you is to see blind faith in you, and to feel yourself that you are not able to be of use. Well, it was just this blind faith that the whole of Aleksandra Andreyevna's family had in me; they had forgotten to think that their daughter was in danger. I, too, on my side assure them that it is nothing, but meantime my heart sinks into my boots. To add to our troubles, the roads were in such a state that the coachman was gone for whole days together to get medicine. And I never left the patient's room; I could not tear myself away; I tell her amusing stories, you know, and play cards with her. I watch by her side at night. The old mother thanks me with tears in her eyes; but I think to myself, 'I don't deserve your gratitude.' I frankly confess to you—there is no object in concealing it now—I was in love with my patient. And Aleksandra Andreyevna had grown fond of me; she would not sometimes let any one be in her room but me. She began to talk to me, to ask me questions; where I had studied, how I lived, who are my people, whom I go to see. I feel that she ought not to talk; but to forbid her to—to forbid her resolutely, you know—I could not. Sometimes I held my head in my hands, and asked myself, 'What are you doing, villain?' . . . And she would take my hand and hold it, give me a long, long look, and turn away, sigh, and say, 'How good you are!' Her hands were so feverish, her eyes so large and languid. . . . 'Yes,' she says, 'you are a good, kind man; you are not like our neighbours. . . . No, you are not like that. . . . Why did I not know you till now!' 'Aleksandra Andreyevna, calm yourself,' I say. . . . 'I feel, believe me, I don't know how I have gained . . . but there, calm yourself. . . . All will be right; you will be well again.' And meanwhile I must tell you," continued the doctor, bending forward and raising his eyebrows, "that they associated very little with the neighbours, because the smaller people were not on their level, and pride hindered them from being friendly with the rich. I tell you, they were an exceptionally cultivated family, so you know it was gratifying for me. She would only take her medicine from my hands . . . she would lift herself up, poor girl, with my aid, take it, and gaze at me. . . . My heart felt as if it were bursting. And meanwhile she was growing worse and worse, worse and worse, all the time; she will die, I think to myself; she must die. Believe me, I would sooner have gone to the grave myself; and here were her mother and sisters watching me, looking into my eyes . . . and their faith in me was wearing away. 'Well, how is she?' 'Oh, all right, all right!' All right, indeed! My mind was failing me. Well, I was sitting one night alone again by my patient. The maid was sitting there too, and snoring away in full swing; I can't find fault with the poor girl, though! she was worn out too. Aleksandra Andreyevna had felt very unwell all the evening; she was very feverish. Until midnight she kept tossing about; at last she seemed to fall asleep; at least, she lay still without stirring. The lamp was burning in the corner before the holy image. I sat there, you know, with my head bent; I even dozed a little. Suddenly it seemed as though someone touched me on the side; I turned round. . . . Good God! Aleksandra Andreyevna was gazing with intent eyes at me . . . her lips parted, her cheeks seemed burning. 'What is it?' 'Doctor, shall I die?' 'Merciful heavens!' 'No, doctor, no; please don't tell me I shall live . . . don't say so. . . . If you knew. . . . Listen! For God's sake don't conceal my real position,' and her breath came so fast. 'If I can know for certain that I must die . . . then I will tell you all—all!' 'Aleksandra Andreyevna, I beg!' 'Listen! I have not been asleep at all . . . I have been looking at you a long while. . . . For God's sake! . . . I believe in you; you are a good man, an honest man; I entreat you by all that is sacred in the world—tell me the truth! If you knew how important it is for me. . . . Doctor, for God's sake tell me. . . . Am I in danger?' 'What can I tell you, Aleksandra Andreyevna pray?' 'For God's sake, I beseech you!' 'I can't conceal from you,' I say, 'Aleksandra Andreyevna; you are certainly in danger; but God is merciful.' 'I shall die, I shall die.' And it seemed as though she were pleased; her face grew so bright; I was alarmed. 'Don't be afraid, don't be afraid! I am not frightened by death at all.' She suddenly sat up and leaned on her elbow. 'Now . . . yes, now I can tell you that I thank you with my whole heart . . . that you are kind and good—that I love you!' I stared at her, like one possessed; it was terrible for me, you know. 'Do you hear, I love you!' 'Aleksandra Andreyevna, how have I deserved—"No, no, you don't—you don't understand me.' . . . And suddenly she stretched out her arms, and taking my head in her hands, she kissed it. . . . Believe me, I almost screamed aloud. . . . I threw myself on my knees, and buried my head in the pillow. She did not speak; her fingers trembled in my hair; I listen; she is weeping. I began to soothe her, to assure her. . . . I really don't know what I did say to her. 'You will wake up the girl,' I say to her; 'Aleksandra Andreyevna, I thank you . . . believe me . . . calm yourself.' 'Enough, enough!' she persisted, 'never mind all of them; let them wake, then; let them come in—it does not matter; I am dying, you see. . . . And what do you fear? Why are you afraid? Lift up your head. . . . Or, perhaps you don't love me; perhaps I am wrong. . . . In that case, forgive me.' 'Aleksandra Andreyevna, what are you saying! . . . I love you, Aleksandra Andreyevna.' She looked straight into my eyes, and opened her arms wide. 'Then take me in your arms.' I tell you frankly, I don't know how it was I did not go mad that night. I feel that my patient is killing herself; I see that she is not fully herself; I understand, too, that if she did not consider herself on the point of death she would never have thought of me; and, indeed, say what you will, it's hard to die at twenty without having known love; this was what was torturing her; this was why, in despair, she caught at me—do you understand now? But she held me in her arms, and would not let me go. 'Have pity on me, Aleksandra Andreyevna, and have pity on yourself,' I say. 'Why,' she says, 'what is there to think of? You know I must die.' . . . This she repeated incessantly. . . . 'If I knew that I should return to life, and be a proper young lady again, I should be ashamed . . . of course, ashamed . . . but why now?' 'But who has said you will die?' 'Oh, no, leave off! you will not deceive me; you don't know how to lie—look at your face.' . . . 'You shall live, Aleksandra Andreyevna; I will cure you; we will ask your mother's blessing . . . we will be united— we will be happy.' 'No, no, I have your word; I must die . . . you have promised me . . . you have told me.' . . . It was cruel for me—cruel for many reasons. And see what trifling things can do sometimes; it seems nothing at all, but it's painful. It occurred to her to ask me, what is my name; not my surname, but my first name. I must needs be so unlucky as to be called Trifon. Yes, indeed; Trifon Ivanich. Every one in the house called me doctor. However, there's a help for it. I say, 'Trifon, madam.' She frowned, shook her head, and muttered something in French—ah, something unpleasant, of course!—and then she laughed—disagreeably too. Well, I spent the whole night with her in this way. Before morning I went away, feeling as though I were mad. When I went again into her room it was daytime, after morning tea. Good God! I could scarcely recognise her; people are laid in their grave looking better than that. I swear to you, on my honour, I don't understand—I absolutely don't understand—now, how I lived through that experience. Three days and nights my patient still lingered on. And what nights! What things she said to me! And on the last night—only imagine to yourself—I was sitting near her, and kept praying to God for one thing only: 'Take her,' I said, 'quickly, and me with her.' Suddenly the old mother comes unexpectedly into the room. I had already the evening before told her—the mother—there was little hope, and it would be well to send for a priest. When the sick girl saw her mother she said: 'It's very well you have come; look at us, we love one another—we have given each other our word.' 'What does she say, doctor? what does she say?' I turned livid. 'She is wandering,' I say; 'the fever.' But she: 'Hush, hush; you told me something quite different just now, and have taken my ring. Why do you pretend? My mother is good—she will forgive—she will understand—and I am dying. . . . I have no need to tell lies; give me your hand.' I jumped up and ran out of the room. The old lady, of course, guessed how it was.

"I will not, however, weary you any longer, and to me, too, of course, it's painful to recall all this. My patient passed away the next day. God rest her soul!" the doctor added, speaking quickly and with a sigh. "Before her death she asked her family to go out and leave me alone with her."

"'Forgive me,' she said; 'I am perhaps to blame towards you . . . my illness . . . but believe me, I have loved no one more than you . . . do not forget me . . . keep my ring.'"

The doctor turned away; I took his hand.

"Ah!" he said, "let us talk of something else, or would you care to play preference for a small stake? It is not for people like me to give way to exalted emotions. There's only one thing for me to think of; how to keep the children from crying and the wife from scolding. Since then, you know, I have had time to enter into lawful wedlock, as they say. . . . Oh . . . I took a merchant's daughter—seven thousand for her dowry. Her name's Akulina; it goes well with Trifon. She is an illtempered woman, I must tell you, but luckily she's asleep all day. . . . Well, shall it be preference?"

We sat down to preference for halfpenny points. Trifon Ivanich won two rubles and a half from me, and went home late, well pleased with his success.

DISCUSSION

"The District Doctor," like "Araby," is a story of love, but it bears a peculiar relation to Joyce's story. With Joyce, we have an account of first love
and its disappointment as told by a mature man looking back on his first
adolescent attachment. With Turgenev, we have something that might
be thought of, in a way, as a splintering of Joyce's story into three related
stories. The first splinter story is that of the young girl who, knowing that
she is to die and feeling that she must not die without having known love,
falls in love with the simple, decent, not particularly attractive young
doctor, with the funny name, and at last gives him her ring. The second
splinter story is that of the doctor, now a modest, middle-aged man, who
had, when young, fallen in love, against all common sense, with his dying
patient—caught in the same dream of an ideal love beyond the reach of
death and the accidents of common life. And there is, too, really a third
splinter story: the subsequent life of the doctor, who, after having had
the glimpse of an ideal love (clearly beyond the common world), has
gone on with his duty to his humdrum practice and has eventually married an ill-tempered woman (presumably for her dowry). We can here
assume that the doctor's later life is a common one, corresponding basically, if not in detail, with that of the narrator of "Araby," who looks back
on his trip to the bazaar as a key symbol of his later life and disillusion-
ments.

1. Describe the doctor as he now is, and his attitude toward life. Describe him as he must have been at the time of the story he tells. Draw
evidence from the story. Make special reference to the ending.
2. Observe that the point of view is complicated here—a story
within a story, and within a story: first, that of the author (who is given a
personality and the hint of a story, however limited); second, that of the
patient (who tells what we may call the central story); and third, that of
the doctor (who tells his own experience). Can you see any reason for
this method?
3. Can you think of any plausible reason why the doctor should now
tell the story of his youth to the author? Would he have been more likely
to tell an old friend or a crony at the bar of the inn? Or some acquaintance in the community?
4. What indication do we have of the author's response (as a character) to the story? What may it suggest about the life of the author (as the
first patient in the story)?
5. Suppose the story ended at the moment when the author shows
his response. What would be the effect? What might be lost, or gained?
Discuss the question of sentimentality in this regard.
6. Try to state the issue, or theme, behind "The District Doctor."
7. Let your imagination play over the materials of the story. For instance, suppose that the young girl had never been the doctor's patient,
or that she had simply died soon after his arrival. Can you imagine that
either circumstance might have made a difference in the attitude of the
woman whom he eventually married?

THE SOJOURNER

Carson McCullers

THE twilight border between sleep and waking was a Roman one this morning: splashing fountains and arched, narrow streets, the golden lavish city of blossoms and age-soft stone. Sometimes in this semi-consciousness he sojourned again in Paris, or German war rubble, or a Swiss skiing and a snow hotel. Sometimes, also, in a fallow Georgia field at hunting dawn. Rome it was this morning in the yearless region of dreams.

John Ferris awoke in a room in a New York hotel. He had the feeling that something unpleasant was awaiting him—what it was, he did not know. The feeling, submerged by matinal necessities, lingered even after he had dressed and gone downstairs. It was a cloudless autumn day and the pale sunlight sliced between the pastel skyscrapers. Ferris went into the next-door drugstore and sat at the end booth next to the window glass that overlooked the sidewalk. He ordered an American breakfast with scrambled eggs and sausage.

Ferris had come from Paris to his father's funeral which had taken place a week before in his home town in Georgia. The shock of death had made him aware of youth already passed. His hair was receding and the veins in his now naked temples were pulsing and prominent and his body was spare except for an incipient belly bulge. Ferris had loved his father and the bond between them had once been extraordinarily close—but the years had somehow unraveled this filial devotion; the death, expected for a long time, had left him with an unforseen dismay. He had stayed as long as possible to be near his mother and brothers at home. His plane for Paris was to leave the next morning.

Ferris pulled out his address book to verify a number. He turned the pages with growing attentiveness. Names and addresses from New York, the capitals of Europe, a few faint ones from his home state in the South. Faded, printed names, sprawled drunken ones. Betty Wills: a random love, married now. Charlie Williams: wounded in the Hürtgen Forest, unheard of since. Grand old Williams—did he live or die? Don Walker: a B.T.O. in television, getting rich. Henry Green: hit the skids after the war, in a sanitarium now, they say. Cozie Hall: he had heard that she was dead. Heedless, laughing Cozie—it was strange to think that she too, silly girl, could die. As Ferris closed the address book, he suffered a sense of hazard, transience, almost of fear.

It was then that his body jerked suddenly. He was staring out of the window when there, on the sidewalk, passing by, was his ex-wife. Elizabeth passed quite close to him, walking slowly. He could not understand the wild quiver of his heart, nor the following sense of recklessness and grace that lingered after she was gone.

Quickly Ferris paid his check and rushed out to ·the sidewalk. Elizabeth stood on the corner waiting to cross Fifth Avenue. He hurried toward her meaning to speak, but the lights changed and she crossed the

136

street before he reached her, but he found himself lagging unaccountably. Her fair hair was plainly rolled, and as he watched her Ferris recalled that once his father had remarked that Elizabeth had a "beautiful carriage." She turned at the next corner and Ferris followed, although by now his intention to overtake her had disappeared. Ferris questioned the bodily disturbance that the sight of Elizabeth aroused in him, the dampness of his hands, the hard heartstrokes.

It was eight years since Ferris had last seen his ex-wife. He knew that long ago she had married again. And there were children. During recent years he had seldom thought of her. But at first, after the divorce, the loss had almost destroyed him. Then after the anodyne of time, he had loved again, and then again. Jeannine, she was now. Certainly his love for his ex-wife was long since past. So why the unhinged body, the shaken mind? He knew only that his clouded heart was oddly dissonant with the sunny, candid autumn day. Ferris wheeled suddenly and, walking with long strides, almost running, hurried back to the hotel.

Ferris poured himself a drink, although it was not yet eleven o'clock. He sprawled out in an armchair like a man exhausted, nursing his glass of bourbon and water. He had a full day ahead of him as he was leaving by plane the next morning for Paris. He checked over his obligations: take luggage to Air France, lunch with his boss, buy shoes and an overcoat. And something—wasn't there something else? Ferris finished his drink and opened the telephone directory.

His decision to call his ex-wife was impulsive. The number was under Bailey, the husband's name, and he called before he had much time for self-debate. He and Elizabeth had exchanged cards at Christmastime, and Ferris had sent a carving set when he received the announcement of her wedding. There was no reason *not* to call. But as he waited, listening to the ring at the other end, misgiving fretted him.

Elizabeth answered; her familiar voice was a fresh shock to him. Twice he had to repeat his name, but when he was identified, she sounded glad. He explained he was only in town for that day. They had a theater engagement, she said—but she wondered if he would come by for an early dinner. Ferris said he would be delighted.

As he went from one engagement to another, he was still bothered at odd moments by the feeling that something necessary was forgotten. Ferris bathed and changed in the late afternoon, often thinking about Jeannine: he would be with her the following night. "Jeannine," he would say, "I happened to run into my ex-wife when I was in New York. Had dinner with her. And her husband, of course. It was strange seeing her after all these years."

Elizabeth lived in the East Fifties, and as Ferris taxied uptown he glimpsed at intersections the lingering sunset, but by the time he reached his destination it was already autumn dark. The place was a building with a marquee and a doorman, and the apartment was on the seventh floor.

"Come in, Mr. Ferris."

Braced for Elizabeth or even the unimagined husband, Ferris was astonished by the freckled red-haired child; he had known of the children, but his mind had failed somehow to acknowledge them. Surprise made him step back awkwardly.

"This is our apartment," the child said politely. "Aren't you Mr. Ferris? I'm Billy. Come in."

In the living room beyond the hall, the husband provided another surprise; he too had not been acknowledged emotionally. Bailey was a lumbering red-haired man with a deliberate manner. He rose and extended a welcoming hand.

"I'm Bill Bailey. Glad to see you. Elizabeth will be in, in a minute. She's finishing dressing."

The last words struck a gliding series of vibrations, memories of the other years. Fair Elizabeth, rosy and naked before her bath. Half-dressed before the mirror of her dressing table, brushing her fine, chestnut hair. Sweet, casual intimacy, the soft-fleshed loveliness indisputably possessed. Ferris shrank from the unbidden memories and compelled himself to meet Bill Bailey's gaze.

"Billy, will you please bring that tray of drinks from the kitchen table?"

The child obeyed promptly, and when he was gone Ferris remarked conversationally, "Fine boy you have there."

"We think so."

Flat silence until the child returned with a tray of glasses and a cocktail shaker of Martinis. With the priming drinks they pumped up conversation: Russia, they spoke of, and the New York rainmaking, and the apartment situation in Manhattan and Paris.

"Mr. Ferris is flying all the way across the ocean tomorrow," Bailey said to the little boy who was perched on the arm of his chair, quiet and well behaved. "I bet you would like to be a stowaway in his suitcase."

Billy pushed back his limp bangs. "I want to fly in an airplane and be a newspaperman like Mr. Ferris." He added with sudden assurance, "That's what I would like to do when I am big."

Bailey said, "I thought you wanted to be a doctor."

"I do!" said Billy. "I would like to be both. I want to be a atom-bomb scientist too."

Elizabeth came in carrying in her arms a baby girl.

"Oh, John!" she said. She settled the baby in the father's lap. "It's grand to see you. I'm awfully glad you could come."

The little girl sat demurely on Bailey's knees. She wore a pale pink crepe de Chine frock, smocked around the yoke with rose, and a matching silk hair ribbon tying back her pale soft curls. Her skin was summer tanned and her brown eyes flecked with gold and laughing. When she reached up and fingered her father's horn-rimmed glasses, he took them off and let her look through them a moment. "How's my old Candy?"

Elizabeth was very beautiful, more beautiful perhaps than he had ever realized. Her straight clean hair was shining. Her face was softer, glowing and serene. It was a madonna loveliness, dependent on the family ambiance.

"You've hardly changed at all," Elizabeth said, "but it has been a long time."

"Eight years." His hand touched his thinning hair self-consciously while further amenities were exchanged.

Ferris felt himself suddenly a spectator—an interloper among these Baileys. Why had he come? He suffered. His own life seemed so solitary, a fragile column supporting nothing amidst the wreckage of the years. He felt he could not bear much longer to stay in the family room.

He glanced at his watch. "You're going to the theater?"

"It's a shame," Elizabeth said, "but we've had this engagement for more than a month. But surely, John, you'll be staying home one of these days before long. You're not going to be an expatriate, are you?"

"Expatriate," Ferris repeated. "I don't much like the word."

"What's a better word?" she asked.

He thought for a moment. "Sojourner might do."

Ferris glanced again at his watch, and again Elizabeth apologized. "If only we had known ahead of time—"

"I just had this day in town. I came home unexpectedly. You see, Papa died last week."

"Papa Ferris is dead?"

"Yes, at Johns Hopkins. He had been sick there nearly a year. The funeral was down home in Georgia."

"Oh, I'm so sorry, John. Papa Ferris was always one of my favorite people."

The little boy moved from behind the chair so that he could look into his mother's face. He asked, "Who is dead?"

Ferris was oblivious to apprehension; he was thinking of his father's death. He saw again the outstretched body on the quilted silk within the coffin. The corpse flesh was bizarrely rouged and the familiar hands lay massive and joined above a spread of funeral roses. The memory closed and Ferris awakened to Elizabeth's calm voice.

"Mr. Ferris's father, Billy. A really grand person. Somebody you didn't know."

"But why did you call him *Papa* Ferris?"

Bailey and Elizabeth exchanged a trapped look. It was Bailey who answered the questioning child. "A long time ago," he said, "your mother and Mr. Ferris were once married. Before you were born—a long time ago."

"Mr. Ferris?"

The little boy stared at Ferris, amazed and unbelieving. And Ferris's eyes, as he returned the gaze, were somehow unbelieving too. Was it indeed true that at one time he had called this stranger, Elizabeth, Little Butterduck during nights of love, that they had lived together, shared perhaps a thousand days and nights and—finally—endured in the misery of a sudden solitude the fiber by fiber (jealousy, alcohol and money quarrels) destruction of the fabric of married love?

Bailey said to the children, "It's somebody's suppertime. Come on now."

"But Daddy! Mamma and Mr. Ferris—I—"

Billy's everlasting eyes—perplexed and with a glimmer of hostility—reminded Ferris of the gaze of another child. It was the young son of Jeannine—a boy of seven with a shadowed little face and knobby knees whom Ferris avoided and usually forgot.

"Quick march!" Bailey gently turned Billy toward the door. "Say good night now, son."

"Good night, Mr. Ferris." He added resentfully, "I thought I was staying up for the cake."

"You can come in afterward for the cake," Elizabeth said. "Run along now with Daddy for your supper."

Ferris and Elizabeth were alone. The weight of the situation descended on those first moments of silence. Ferris asked permission to pour himself another drink and Elizabeth set the cocktail shaker on the table at his side. He looked at the grand piano and noticed the music on the rack.

"Do you still play as beautifully as you used to?"

"I still enjoy it."

"Please play, Elizabeth."

Elizabeth arose immediately. Her readiness to perform when asked had always been one of her amiabilities; she never hung back, apologized. Now as she approached the piano there was the added readiness of relief.

She began with a Bach prelude and fugue. The prelude was as gaily iridescent as a prism in a morning room. The first voice of the fugue, an announcement pure and solitary, was repeated intermingling with a second voice, and again repeated within an elaborated frame, the multiple music, horizontal and serene, flowed with unhurried majesty. The principal melody was woven with two other voices, embellished with countless ingenuities—now dominant, again submerged, it had the sublimity of a single thing that does not fear surrender to the whole. Toward the end, the density of the material gathered for the last enriched insistence on the dominant first motif and with a chorded final statement the fugue ended. Ferris rested his head on the chair back and closed his eyes. In the following silence a clear, high voice came from the room down the hall.

"Daddy, how *could* Mamma and Mr. Ferris—" A door was closed.

The piano began again—what was this music? Unplaced, familiar, the limpid melody had lain a long while dormant in his heart. Now it spoke to him of another time, another place—it was the music Elizabeth used to play. The delicate air summoned a wilderness of memory. Ferris was lost in the riot of past longings, conflicts, ambivalent desires. Strange that the music, catalyst for this tumultuous anarchy, was so serene and clear. The singing melody was broken off by the appearance of the maid.

"Miz Bailey, dinner is out on the table now."

Even after Ferris was seated at the table between his host and hostess, the unfinished music still overcast his mood. He was a little drunk.

"*L'improvisation de la vie humaine*," he said. "There's nothing that makes you so aware of the improvisation of human existence as a song unfinished. Or an old address book."

"Address book?" repeated Bailey. Then he stopped, noncommittal and polite.

"You're still the same old boy, Johnny," Elizabeth said with a trace of the old tenderness.

It was a Southern dinner that evening, and the dishes were his old favorites. They had fried chicken and corn pudding and rich, glazed candied sweet potatoes. During the meal, Elizabeth kept alive a conversation when the silences were overlong. And it came about that Ferris was led to speak of Jeannine.

"I first knew Jeannine last autumn—about this time of the year—in Italy. She's a singer and she had an engagement in Rome. I expect we will be married soon.'

The words seemed so true, inevitable, that Ferris did not at first acknowledge to himself the lie. He and Jeannine had never in that year spoken of marriage. And indeed, she was still married—to a White Russian money-changer in Paris from whom she had been separated for five years. But it was too late to correct the lie. Already Elizabeth was saying: "This really makes me glad to know. Congratulations, Johnny."

He tried to make the amends with truth. "The Roman autumn is so beautiful. Balmy and blossoming." He added, "Jeannine has a little boy of six. A curious trilingual little fellow. We go to the Tuileries sometimes."

A lie again. He had taken the boy once to the gardens. The sallow foreign child in shorts that bared his spindly legs had sailed his boat in the concrete pond and ridden the pony. The child had wanted to go in to the puppet show. But there was not time, for Ferris had an engagement at the Scribe Hotel. He had promised they would go to the guignol another afternoon. Only once had he taken Valentin to the Tuileries.

There was a stir. The maid brought in a white-frosted cake with pink candles. The children entered in their night clothes. Ferris still did not understand.

"Happy birthday, John," Elizabeth said. "Blow out the candles."

Ferris recognized his birthday date. The candles blew out lingeringly and there was the smell of burning wax. Ferris was thirty-eight years old. The veins in his temples darkened and pulsed visibly.

"It's time you started for the theater."

Ferris thanked Elizabeth for the birthday dinner and said the appropriate good-byes. The whole family saw him to the door.

A high, thin moon shone above the jagged, dark skyscrapers. The streets were windy, cold. Ferris hurried to Third Avenue and hailed a cab. He gazed at the nocturnal city with the deliberate attentiveness of departure and perhaps farewell. He was alone. He longed for flighttime and the coming journey.

The next day he looked down on the city from the air, burnished in sunlight, toylike, precise. Then America was left behind and there was only the Atlantic and the distant European shore. The ocean was milky pale and placid beneath the clouds. Ferris dozed most of the day. Toward dark he was thinking of Elizabeth and the visit of the previous evening. He thought of Elizabeth among her family with longing, gentle envy and inexplicable regret. He sought the melody, the unfinished air, that had so moved him. The cadence, some unrelated tones, were all that remained; the melody itself evaded him. He had found instead the first voice of the fugue that Elizabeth had played—it came to him inverted mockingly and in a minor key. Suspended above the ocean the anxieties of transience and solitude no longer troubled him and he thought of his father's death with equanimity. During the dinner hour the plane reached the shore of France.

At midnight Ferris was in a taxi crossing Paris. It was a clouded night and mist wreathed the lights of the Place de la Concorde. The midnight bistros gleamed on the wet pavements. As always after a trans-ocean flight the change of continents was too sudden. New York at morning, this midnight Paris. Ferris glimpsed the disorder of his life: the succession of cities, of transitory loves; and time, the sinister glissando of the years, time always.

"*Vite! Vite!*" he called in terror. "*Dèpêchez-vous.*"

Valentin opened the door to him. The little boy wore pajamas and an outgrown red robe. His grey eyes were shadowed and, as Ferris passed into the flat, they flickered momentarily.

"*J'attends Maman.*"

Jeannine was singing in a night club. She would not be home before another hour. Valentin returned to a drawing, squatting with his crayons over the paper on the floor. Ferris looked down at the drawing—it was a banjo player with notes and wavy lines inside a comic-strip balloon.

"We will go again to the Tuileries."

The child looked up and Ferris drew him closer to his knees. The melody, the unfinished music that Elizabeth had played, came to him suddenly. Unsought, the load of memory jettisoned—this time bringing only recognition and sudden joy.

"Monsieur Jean," the child said, "did you see him?"

Confused, Ferris thought only of another child—the freckled, family-loved boy. "See who, Valentin?"

"Your dead papa in Georgia." The child added, "Was he okay?"

Ferris spoke with rapid urgency: "We will go often to the Tuileries. Ride the pony and we will go into the guignol. We will see the puppet show and never be in a hurry any more."

"Monsieur Jean," Valent in said. "The guignol is now closed."

Again, the terror, the acknowledgment of wasted years and death. Valentin, responsive and confident, still nestled in his arms. His cheek touched the soft cheek and felt the brush of the delicate eyelashes. With inner desperation he pressed the child close—as though an emotion as protean as his love could dominate the pulse of time.

DISCUSSION

1. New York, where most of this story is laid, is merely one of Ferris's stopping places. But why is his return to America, and to his home in Georgia, significant for the story?

2. What is the relation between Ferris's looking over an old ad-

dress book and his unexpected glimpse of Elizabeth? Can it be said that this glimpse changes his view of New York? (Think of this scene as the opening of the story. What would be lost?)

3. We are told that Ferris's "decision" to call Elizabeth was "impulsive," not inspected and debated. But what lies behind this "impulse"? When do we know this?

4. What is the significance of the paragraph beginning "As he went from one engagement to another, he was still bothered"?

5. Why is Ferris "astonished" by the red-haired boy who lets him into the Bailey apartment? Hadn't he known that Elizabeth had children by her second marriage?

6. What is the relation between the sight of the red-haired boy and Ferris's sudden images of Elizabeth at her bath and dressing table with his other "unbidden memories"?

7. Locate several points at which the idea of the passage of time emerges. What is the effect on Ferris? What does he expect from the passage of time?

8. What is the significance of Valentin for the story? Especially in the last scene. Why is it important that Ferris is greeted by Valentin instead of Jeannine?

9. Why does Ferris lie about an impending marriage with Jeannine?

10. Upon his return to the apartment in Paris, what does Ferris discover? Or does he deceive himself? Or is the question to be left open in the story?

11. What does the title mean in relation to the story?

THE DRUNKARD

Frank O'Connor

IT was a terrible blow to Father when Mr. Dooley on the terrace died. Mr. Dooley was a commercial traveller with two sons in the Dominicans and a car of his own, so socially he was miles ahead of us, but he had no false pride. Mr. Dooley was an intellectual, and, like all intellectuals the thing he loved best was conversation, and in his own limited way Father was a well-read man and could appreciate an intelligent talker. Mr. Dooley was remarkably intelligent. Between business acquaintances and clerical contacts, there was very little he didn't know about what went on in town, and evening after evening he crossed the road to our gate to explain to Father the news behind the news. He had a low, palavering voice and a knowing smile, and Father would listen in astonishment, giving him a conversational lead now and again, and then stump triumphantly in to Mother with his face aglow and ask: "Do you know what Mr. Dooley is after telling me?" Ever since, when somebody has given me some bit of information off the record I have found myself on the point of asking: "Was it Mr. Dooley told you that?"

Till I actually saw him laid out in his brown shroud with the rosary beads entwined between his waxy fingers I did not take the report of his death seriously. Even then I felt there must be a catch and that some summer evening Mr. Dooley must reappear at our gate to give us the lowdown on the next world. But Father was very upset, partly because Mr. Dooley was about one age with himself, a thing that always gives a distinctly personal turn to another man's demise; partly because now he would have no one to tell him what dirty work was behind the latest scene at the Corporation. You could count on your fingers the number of men in Blarney Lane who read the papers as Mr. Dooley did, and none of these would have overlooked the fact that Father was only a laboring man. Even Sullivan, the carpenter, a mere nobody, thought he was a cut above Father. It was certainly a solemn event.

"Half past two to the Curragh," Father said meditatively, putting down the paper.

"But you're not thinking of going to the funeral?" Mother asked in alarm.

"'Twould be expected," Father said, scenting opposition. "I wouldn't give it to say to them."

"I think," said Mother with suppressed emotion, "it will be as much as anyone will expect if you go to the chapel with him."

("Going to the chapel," of course, was one thing, because the body was removed after work, but going to a funeral meant the loss of a half-day's pay.)

"The people hardly know us," he added.

"God between us and all harm," Father replied with dignity, "we'd be glad if it was our own turn."

To give Father his due, he was always ready to lose a half day for the sake of an old neighbor. It wasn't so much that he liked funerals as that he was a conscientious man who did as he would be done by; and nothing could have consoled him so much for the prospect of his own death as the assurance of a worthy funeral. And, to give Mother her due, it wasn't the half-day's pay she begrudged, badly as we could afford it.

Drink, you see, was Father's great weakness. He could keep steady for months, even for years, at a stretch, and while he did he was as good as gold. He was first up in the morning and brought the mother a cup of tea in bed, stayed at home in the evenings and read the paper; saved money and bought himself a new blue serge suit and bowler hat. He laughed at the folly of men who, week in and week out, left their hard-earned money with the publicans; and sometimes, to pass an idle hour, he took pencil and paper and calculated precisely how much he saved each week through being a teetotaller. Being a natural optimist he sometimes continued his calculation through the whole span of his prospective existence and the total was breathtaking. He would die worth hundreds.

If I had only known it, this was a bad sign; a sign he was becoming stuffed up with spiritual pride and imagining himself better than his neighbors. Sooner or later, the spiritual pride grew till it called for some form of celebration. Then he took a drink—not whisky, of course; nothing like that—just a glass of some harmless drink like lager beer. That was the end of Father. By the time he had taken the first he already realized that he had made a fool of himself, took a second to forget it and a third to forget that he couldn't forget, and at last came home reeling drunk. From this on it was "The Drunkard's Progress," as in the moral prints. Next day he stayed in from work with a sick head while Mother went off to make his excuses at the works, and inside a fortnight he was poor and savage and despondent again. Once he began he drank steadily through everything down to the kitchen clock. Mother and I knew all the phases and dreaded all the dangers. Funerals were one.

"I have to go to Dunphy's to do a half-day's work," said Mother in distress. "Who's to look after Larry?"

"I'll look after Larry," Father said graciously. "The little walk will do him good."

There was no more to be said, though we all knew I didn't need anyone to look after me, and that I could quite well have stayed at home and looked after Sonny, but I was being attached to the party to act as a brake on Father. As a brake I had never achieved anything, but Mother still had great faith in me.

Next day, when I got home from school, Father was there before me and made a cup of tea for both of us. He was very good at tea, but too heavy in the hand for anything else; the way he cut bread was shocking. Afterwards, we went down the hill to the church. Father wearing his best blue serge and bowler cocked to one side of his head with the least suggestion of the masher. To his great joy he discovered Peter Crowley among the mourners. Peter was another danger signal, as I knew well from certain experiences after Mass on Sunday morning: a mean man, as Mother said, who only went to funerals for the free drinks he could get at them. It turned out that he hadn't even known Mr. Dooley! But Father had a sort of contemptuous regard for him as one of the foolish people who wasted their good money in public-houses when they could be saving it. Very little of his own money Peter Crowley wasted!

It was an excellent funeral from Father's point of view. He had it all well studied before we set off after the hearse in the afternoon sunlight.

"Five carriages!" he exclaimed. "Five carriages and sixteen covered cars! There's one alderman, two councillors and 'tis unknown how many priests. I didn't see a funeral like this since Willie Mack, the publican, died."

"Ah, he was well liked," said Crowley in his husky voice.

"My goodness, don't I know that?" snapped Father. "Wasn't the man my best friend? Two nights before he died—only two nights—he was over telling me of the goings-on about the housing contract. Them fellows in the Corporation are night and day robbers. But even I never imagined he was as well connected as that."

Father was stepping out like a boy, pleased with everything: the other mourners, and the fine houses along Sunday's Well. I knew the danger signals were there in full force: a sunny day, a fine funeral, and a distinguished company of clerics and public men were bringing out all the natural vanity and flightiness of Father's character. It was with something like genuine pleasure that he saw his old friend lowered into the grave; with the sense of having performed a duty and the pleasant awareness that however much he would miss poor Mr. Dooley in the long summer evenings, it was he and not poor Mr. Dooley who would do the missing.

"We'll be making tracks before they break up," he whispered to Crowley as the gravediggers tossed in the first shovelfuls of clay, and away he went, hopping like a goat from grassy hump to hump. The drivers, who were probably in the same state as himself, though without months of abstinence to put an edge on it, looked up hopefully.

"Are they nearly finished, Mick?" bawled one.

"All over now bar the last prayers," trumpeted Father in the tone of one who brings news of great rejoicing.

The carriages passed us in a lather of dust several hundred yards from the public-house, and Father, whose feet gave him trouble in hot weather, quickened his pace, looking nervously over his shoulder for any sign of the main body of mourners crossing the hill. In a crowd like that a man might be kept waiting.

When we did reach the pub the carriages were drawn up outside, and solemn men in black ties were cautiously bringing out consolation to mysterious females whose hands reached out modestly from behind the drawn blinds of the coaches. Inside the pub there were only the drivers and a couple of shawly women. I felt if I was to act a brake at all, this was the time, so I pulled Father by the coattails.

"Dadda, can't we go home now?" I asked.

"Two minutes now," he said, beaming affectionately. "Just a bottle of lemonade and we'll go home."

This was a bribe, and I knew it, but I was always a child of weak character. Father ordered lemonade and two pints. I was thirsty and swallowed my drink at once. But that wasn't Father's way. He had long months of abstinence behind him and an eternity of pleasure before. He took out his pipe, blew through it, filled it, and then lit it with loud pops, his eyes bulging above it. After that he deliberately turned his back on the pint, leaned one elbow on the counter in the attitude of a man who did not knw there was a pint behind him, and deliberately brushed the tobacco from his palms. He had settled down for the evening. He was steadily working through all the important funerals he had ever attended. The carriages departed and the minor mourners drifted in till the pub was half full.

"Dadda," I said, pulling his coat again, "can't we go home now?"

"Oh, your mother won't be in for a long time yet," he said benevolently enough. "Run out in the road and play, can't you?"

It struck me as very cool, the way grown-ups assumed that you could play all by yourself on a strange road. I began to get bored as I had so often been bored before. I knew Father was quite capable of lingering there till nightfall. I knew I might have to bring him home, blind drunk, down Blarney Lane, with all the old women at their doors, saying: "Mick Delaney is on it again." I knew that my mother would be half crazy with anxiety; that next day Father wouldn't go out to work; and before the end of the week she would be running down to the pawn with the clock under her shawl. I could never get over the lonesomeness of the kitchen without a clock.

I was still thirsty. I found if I stood on tiptoe I could just reach Father's glass, and the idea occurred to me that it would be interesting to know what the contents were like. He had his back to it and wouldn't notice. I took down the glass and sipped cautiously. It was a terrible disappointment. I was astonished that he could even drink such stuff. It looked as if he had never tried lemonade.

I should have advised him about lemonade but he was holding forth himself in great style. I heard him say that bands were a great addition to a funeral. He put his arms in the position of someone holding a rifle in reverse and hummed a few bars of Chopin's Funeral March. Crowley nodded reverently. I took a longer drink and began to see that porter might have its advantages. I felt pleasantly elevated and philosophic. Father hummed a few bars of the Dead March in *Saul*. It was a nice pub and a very fine funeral, and I felt sure that poor Mr. Dooley in Heaven must be highly gratified. At the same time I thought they might have given him a band. As Father said, bands were a great addition.

But the wonderful thing about porter was the way it made you stand aside, or rather float aloft like a cherub rolling on a cloud, and watch yourself with your legs crossed, leaning against a bar counter, not worrying about trifles but thinking deep, serious, grown-up thoughts about life and death. Looking at yourself like that, you couldn't help thinking after a while how funny you looked, and suddenly you got embarrassed and wanted to giggle. But by the time I had finished the pint, that phase too had passed; I found it hard to put back the glass, the counter seemed to have grown so high. Melancholia was supervening again.

"Well," Father said reverently, reaching behind him for his drink, "God rest the poor man's soul, wherever he is!" He stopped, looked first at the glass, and then at the people round him. "Hello," he said in a fairly good-humoured tone, as if he were just prepared to consider it a joke, even if it was in bad taste, "who was at this?"

There was silence for a moment while the publican and the old women looked first at Father and then at his glass.

"There was no one at it, my good man," one of the women said with an offended air. "Is it robbers you think we are?"

"Ah, there's no one here would do a thing like that, Mick," said the publican in a shocked tone.

"Well, someone did it," said Father, his smile beginning to wear off.

"If they did, they were them that were nearer it," said the woman darkly, giving me a dirty look; and at the same moment the truth began to dawn on Father. I suppose I must have looked a bit starry-eyed. He bent and shook me.

"Are you all right, Larry?" he asked in alarm.

Peter Crowley looked down at me and grinned.

"Could you beat that?" he exclaimed in a husky voice.

I could, and without difficulty. I started to get sick. Father jumped back in holy terror that I might spoil his good suit, and hastily opened the back door.

"Run! run! run!" he shouted.

I saw the sunlit wall outside with the ivy overhanging it, and ran. The intention was good but the performance was exaggerated, because I lurched right into the wall, hurting it badly, as it seemed to me. Being always very polite, I said "Pardon" before the second bout came on me. Father, still concerned for his suit, came up behind and cautiously held me while I got sick.

"That's a good boy!" he said encouragingly. "You'll be grand when you get that up."

Begor, I was not grand! Grand was the last thing I was. I gave one unmerciful wail out of me as he steered me back to the pub and put me sitting on the bench near the shawlies. They drew themselves up with an offended air, still sore at the suggestion that they had drunk his pint.

"God help us!" moaned one, looking pityingly at me, "isn't it the likes of them would be fathers?"

"Mick," said the publican in alarm, spraying sawdust on my tracks, "that child isn't supposed to be in here at all. You'd better take him home quick in case a bobby would see him."

"Merciful God!" whimpered Father, raising his eyes to heaven and clapping his hands silently as he only did when distraught, "what misfortune was on me? Or what will his mother say? . . . If women might stop at home and look after their children themselves!" he added in a snarl for the benefit of the shawlies. "Are them carriages all gone, Bill?"

"The carriages are finished long ago, Mick," replied the publican.

"I'll take him home," Father said despairingly. . . . "I'll never bring you out again," he threatened me. "Here," he added, giving me the clean handkerchief from his breast pocket, "Put that over your eyes."

The blood on the handkerchief was the first indication I got that I was cut, and instantly my temple began to throb and I set up another howl.

"Whisht, whisht, whisht!" Father said testily, steering me out the door. "One'd think you were killed. That's nothing. We'll wash it when we get home."

"Steady now, old scout!" Crowley said, taking the other side of me. "You'll be all right in a minute."

I never met two men who knew less about the effects of drink. The first breath of fresh air and the warmth of the sun made me groggier than ever and I pitched and rolled between wind and tide till Father started to whimper again.

"God Almighty, and the whole road out! What misfortune was on me didn't stop at my work! Can't you walk straight?"

I couldn't. I saw plain enough that, coaxed by the sunlight, every woman old and young in Blarney Lane was leaning over her half-door or sitting on her doorstep. They all stopped gabbling to gape at the strange spectacle of two sober, middle-aged men bringing home a drunken small boy with a cut over his eye. Father, torn between the shamefast desire to get me home as quick as he could, and the neighborly need to explain that it wasn't his fault, finally halted outside Mrs. Roche's. There was a gang of old women outside a door at the opposite side of the road. I didn't like the look of them from the first. They seemed altogether too interested in me. I leaned against the wall of Mrs. Roche's cottage with my hands in my trousers pockets, thinking mournfully of poor Mr. Dooley in his cold grave on the Curragh, who would never walk down the road again, and, with great feeling, I began to sing a favorite song of Father's.

> *Though lost to Minonia and cold in the grave*
> *He returns to Kincora no more.*

"Wisha, the poor child!" Mrs. Roche said. "Haven't he a lovely voice, God bless him!"

That was what I thought myself, so I was the more surprised when Father said "Whisht!" and raised a threatening finger at me. He didn't seem to realize the appropriateness of the song, so I sang louder than ever.

"Whisht, I tell you!" he snapped, and then tried to work up a smile for Mrs. Roche's benefit. "We're nearly home now. I'll carry you the rest of the way."

But, drunk and all as I was, I knew better than to be carried home ignominiously like that.

"Now," I said severely, "can't you leave me alone? I can walk all right. 'Tis only my head. All I want is a rest."

"But you can rest at home in bed," he said viciously, trying to pick me up, and I knew by the flush on his face that he was very vexed.

"Ah, Jasus," I said crossly, "what do I want to go home for? Why the hell can't you leave me alone?"

For some reason the gang of old women at the other side of the road thought this very funny. They nearly split their sides over it. A gassy fury began to expand in me at the thought that a fellow couldn't have a drop taken without the whole neighborhood coming out to make game of him.

"Who are ye laughing at?" I shouted, clenching my fists at them. "I'll make ye laugh at the other side of yeer faces if ye don't let me pass."

They seemed to think this funnier still; I had never seen such ill-mannered people.

"Go away, ye bloody bitches!" I said.

"Whisht, whisht, whisht, I tell you!" snarled Father, abandoning all pretense of amusement and dragging me along behind him by the hand. I was maddened by the women's shrieks of laughter. I was maddened by Father's bullying. I tried to dig in my heels but he was too powerful for me, and I could only see the women by looking back over my shoulder.

"Take care or I'll come back and show ye!" I shouted. "I'll teach ye to let decent people pass. Fitter for ye to stop at home and wash yeer dirty faces."

"'Twill be all over the road," whimpered Father. "Never again, never again, not if I lived to be a thousand!"

To this day I don't know whether he was forswearing me or the drink. By way of a song suitable to my heroic mood I bawled "The Boys of Wexford," as he dragged me in home. Crowley, knowing he was not safe, made off and Father undressed me and put me to bed. I couldn't sleep because of the whirling in my head. It was very unpleasant, and I got sick again. Father came in with a wet cloth and mopped up after me. I lay in a fever, listening to him chopping sticks to start a fire. After that I heard him lay the table.

Suddenly the front door banged open and Mother stormed in with Sonny in her arms, not her usual gentle, timid self, but a wild, raging woman. It was clear that she had heard it all from the neighbors.

"Mick Delaney," she cried hysterically, "what did you do to my son?"

"Whisht, woman, whisht, whisht!" he hissed, dancing from one foot to the other. "Do you want the whole road to hear?"

"Ah," she said with a horrifying laugh, "the road knows all about it by this time. The road knows the way you filled your unfortunate inno-cent child with drink to make sport for you and that other rotten, filthy brute."

"But I gave him no drink," he shouted, aghast at the horrifying in-terpretation the neighbors had chosen to give his misfortune. "He took it while my back was turned. What the hell do you think I am?"

"Ah," she replied bitterly, "everyone knows what you are now. God forgive you, wasting our hard-earned few ha'pence on drink, and bring-ing up your child to be a drunken corner-boy like yourself."

Then she swept into the bedroom and threw herself on her knees by the bed. She moaned when she saw the gash over my eye. In the kitchen Sonny set up a loud bawl on his own, and a moment later Father appeared in the bedroom door with his cap over his eyes, wearing an expression of the most intense self-pity.

"That's a nice way to talk to me after all I went through," he whined. "That's a nice accusation, that I was drinking. Not one drop of drink crossed my lips the whole day. How could it when he drank it all? I'm the one that ought to be pitied, with my day ruined on me, and I after being made a show for the whole road."

But next morning, when he got up and went out quietly to work with his dinner-basket, Mother threw herself on me in the bed and kissed me. It seemed it was all my doing, and I was being given holiday till my eye got better.

"My brave little man!" she said with her eyes shining. "It was God did it you were there. You were his guardian angel."

DISCUSSION

In this amusing story, there is a reversal of roles. It is not the father who comes reeling down the street, the scandal of the family and the talk of the neighbors, as the appalled little son tries to lead him home and put him mercifully out of sight. It is the little boy who is un-steady on his feet, singing off key, calling the neighbor women "bloody bitches"—to the horror of the appalled father. If the story simply presented us with this topsy-turvy situation and let it go at that, it would amount to no more than a joke that was momentarily amusing. It would not be very much of a story and it would not even wear well as a joke. For even a joke, if it is to continue to seem funny, must be rooted in a true perception of human nature.

The reversal of the roles of father and son in this story is not a momentary trick. If we think back a bit, we shall see that the reversal is assumed throughout the story. On the important matter of his father's weakness for drink, Larry, the little boy, takes his mother's viewpoint. His is the adult concern for an essentially good but childishly weak character who must be protected from himself. Larry is apprehensive and worried. He knows what "signs" are ominous. He knows all too well what the consequences of the first drink will be. His consciousness continues to be suffused with this kind of concern for his father until the beer finally takes effect upon *him*, and for the first time in the story, his apprehensions melt away.

Throughout the story it is the father who has the childlike guilessness—and the charm that frequently accompanies such guilessness. Consider his delight in the funeral: "It was an excellent funeral from Father's point of view." He exclaims that there are "five carriages and sixteen covered cars!" Later, as Larry remarks, "It was with something like genuine pleasure that he saw his old friend lowered into the grave; with the sense of having performed a duty and the pleasant awareness that however much he would miss poor Mr. Dooley in the long summer evenings, it was he and not Mr. Dooley who would do the missing." Later still, he tells the waiting coachmen that the service at the grave is nearly over: "'All over now bar the last prayers,' trumpeted Father in the tone of one who brings news of great rejoicing." And how happily a few minutes later he settles down in the pub as he gets ready to break his long drought!

If Larry's father were a more calculating man, or even a more self-conscious man, the special quality of the humor would be lost, for we would have to take a different attitude toward him. If it is his simplicity and his naiveté that cause troubles, they go far toward relieving him of adult responsibility for them. He is a man more sinned against than sinning—and nowhere more so than when he has to face the "horrifying interpretations" of the neighbor women that he has got his own son drunk. The character of the father thus has everything to do with the point of the story and even with the matter of whether or not we find the story genuinely funny. Though "all occasions inform against him," he has the consciousness of outraged innocence.

The most amusing instance of the general reversal of roles occurs on the way home from the pub, when the father does not forcibly shut up the noisy, tipsy little boy, but pleads with him to be reasonable and quiet just as Larry himself might have pleaded with the drunken father—if our normal expectations about this particular expedition had been realized. But this most amusing of the reversals is also rooted in the father's character: a more cruel man, a more brutal man, would have forced the boy to hush. He would thus have eliminated the humorous exchanges, and the suppression of these—and perhaps also the harshness by which they were suppressed—would have deprived the scene of its humor.

The most startling of the reversals (the one that caps the story) is the twist at the end in which the episode of juvenile delinquency becomes Providential and the little boy drunkenly weaving down the street becomes in the mother's eyes a "guardian angel" guiding aright the steps of the weak father. We laugh at the mother—the way in which she has expressed her commendation is almost as startling as the phrasings of Mrs. Malaprop—and yet what she says is, from her point of view, quite right: Larry has been a little "man." He has saved the family one of the usual visits to the pawnbroker.

1. Is the episode in which Larry drinks his father's pint of beer made plausible? Is this the sort of thing that Larry usually does? Is it credible that the father should have neglected his pint long enough for the child to drink it?

2. Are the observations made by Larry upon his father too sophisticated for a child to make? Is this story being told by Larry soon after the events described, or long after, when Larry has become a man?

3. The exposition in this story is managed very skillfully. Comment upon it. What is gained by delaying the introduction of the father's propensity to drink?

4. What is the importance of the fact that Larry gets a little nick over his eye? Does the fact of the blood and the wound help account for certain reactions to the incident?

5. What elements in the story make it more than a joke? If your answer includes "characterization," explain what you mean.

TICKETS, PLEASE

D. H. Lawrence

THERE is in the Midlands a single-line tramway system which boldly leaves the country town and plunges off into the black, industrial countryside, up hill and down dale, through the long, ugly villages of workmen's houses, over canals and railways, past churches perched high and nobly over the smoke and shadows, through stark, grimy, cold little market-places, tilting away in a rush past cinemas and shops down to the hollow where the collieries are, then up again, past a little rural church, under the ash trees, on in a rush to the terminus, the last little ugly place of industry, the cold little town that shivers on the edge of the wild, gloomy country beyond. There the green and creamy colored tram-car seems to pause and purr with curious satisfaction. But in a few minutes—the clock on the turret of the Co-operative Wholesale Society's Shops gives the time—away it starts once more on the adventure. Again there are the reckless swoops downhill, bouncing the loops:

again the chilly wait in the hill-top market-place: again the breathless slithering round the precipitous drop under the church: again the patient halts at the loops, waiting for the outcoming car: so on and on, for two long hours, till at last the city looms beyond the fat gas-works, the narrow factories draw near, we are in the sordid streets of the great town, once more we sidle to a standstill at our terminus, abashed by the great crimson and cream-coloured city cars, but still perky, jaunty, somewhat dare-devil, green as a jaunty sprig of parsley out of a black colliery garden.

To ride on these cars is always an adventure. Since we are in wartime, the drivers are men unfit for active service: cripples and hunchbacks. So they have the spirit of the devil in them. The ride becomes a steeple-chase. Hurray! we have leapt in a clear jump over the canal bridges—now for the four-lane corner. With a shriek and a trail of sparks we are clear again. To be sure, a tram often leaps the rails—but what matter! It sits in a ditch till other trams come to haul it out. It is quite common for a car, packed with one solid mass of living people, to come to a dead halt in the midst of unbroken blackness, the heart of nowhere on a dark night, and for the driver and the girl conductor to call, "All get off—car's on fire!" Instead, however, of rushing out in a panic, the passengers stolidly reply: "Get on—get on! We're not coming out. We're stopping where we are. Push on, George." So till flames actually appear.

The reason for this reluctance to dismount is that the nights are howlingly cold, black, and windswept, and a car is a haven of refuge. From village to village the miners travel, for a change of cinema, of girl, of pub. The trams are desperately packed. Who is going to risk himself in the black gulf outside, to wait perhaps an hour for another tram, then to see the forlorn notice "Depot Only," because there is something wrong! or to greet a unit of three bright cars all so tight with people that they sail past with a howl of derision. Trams that pass in the night.

This, the most dangerous tram-service in England, as the authorities themselves declare, with pride, is entirely conducted by girls, and driven by rash young men, a little crippled, or by delicate young men, who creep forward in terror. The girls are fearless young hussies. In their ugly blue uniform, skirts up to their knees, shapeless old peaked caps on their heads, they have all the sang-froid of an old non-commissioned officer. With a tram packed with howling colliers, roaring hymns downstairs and a sort of antiphony of obscenities upstairs, the lasses are perfectly at their ease. They pounce on the youths who try to evade their ticket-machine. They push off the men at the end of their distance. They are not going to be done in the eye—not they. They fear nobody—and everybody fears them.

"Hello, Annie!"

"Hello, Ted!"

"Oh, mind my corn, Miss Stone. It's my belief you've got a heart of stone, for you've trod on it again."

"You should keep it in your pocket," replies Miss Stone, and she goes sturdily upstairs in her high boots.

"Tickets, please."

She is peremptory, suspicious, and ready to hit first. She can hold her own against ten thousand. The step of that tram-car is her Thermopylae.

Therefore, there is a certain wild romance aboard these cars—and in the sturdy bosom of Annie herself. The time for soft romance is in the morning, between ten o'clock and one, when things are rather slack: that is, except market-day and Saturday. Thus Annie has time to look about her. Then she often hops off her car and into a shop where she has spied something, while the driver chats in the main road. There is very good feeling between the girls and the drivers. Are they not companions in peril, shipments aboard this careering vessel of a tram-car, for ever rocking on the waves of a stormy land.

Then, also, during the easy hours, the inspectors are most in evidence. For some reason, everybody employed in this tram-service is young: there are no grey heads. It would not do. Therefore the inspectors are of the right age, and one, the chief, is also good-looking. See him stand on a wet, gloomy morning, in his long oilskin, his peaked cap well down over his eyes, waiting to board a car. His face is ruddy, his small brown moustache is weathered, he has a faint impudent smile. Fairly tall and agile, even in his waterproof, he springs aboard a car and greets Annie.

"Hello, Annie! Keeping the wet out?"

"Trying to."

There are only two people in the car. Inspecting is soon over. Then for a long and impudent chat on the footboard, a good, easy, twelve-mile chat.

The inspector's name is John Thomas Raynor—always called John Thomas, except sometimes, in malice, Coddy. His face sets in fury when he is addressed, from a distance, with this abbreviation. There is considerable scandal about John Thomas in half a dozen villages. He flirts with the girl conductors in the morning and walks out with them in the dark night, when they leave their tram-car at the depot. Of course, the girls quit the service frequently. Then he flirts and walks out with the newcomer: always providing she is sufficiently attractive, and that she will consent to walk. It is remarkable, however, that most of the girls are quite comely, they are all young, and this roving life aboard the car gives them a sailor's dash and recklessness. What 'matter how they behave when the ship is in port. Tomorrow they will be aboard again.

Annie, however, was something of a Tartar, and her sharp tongue had kept John Thomas at arm's length for many months. Perhaps, therefore, she liked him all the more: for he always came up smiling, with impudence. She watched him vanquish one girl, then another. She could tell by the movement of his mouth and eyes, when he flirted with her in the morning, that he had been walking out with this lass, or the other, the night before. A fine cock-of-the-walk he was. She could sum him up pretty well.

In this subtle antagonism they knew each other like old friends, they were as shrewd with one another almost as man and wife. But Annie had always kept him sufficiently at arm's length. Besides, she had a boy of her own.

The Statutes fair, however, came in November, at Bestwood. It happened that Annie had the Monday night off. It was a drizzling ugly night, yet she dressed herself up and went to the fair ground. She was alone, but she expected soon to find a pal of some sort.

The roundabouts were veering round and grinding out their music, the side shows were making as much commotion as possible. In the cocoanut shies there were no cocoanuts, but artificial war-time substitutes, which the lad declared were fastened into the irons. There was a sad decline in brilliance and luxury. None the less, the ground was muddy as ever, there was the same crush, the press of faces lighted up by the flares and the electric lights, the same smell of naphtha and a few fried potatoes, and of electricity.

Who should be the first to greet Miss Annie, on the show ground, but John Thomas. He had a black overcoat buttoned up to his chin, and a tweed cap pulled down over his brows, his face between was ruddy and smiling and handy as ever. She knew so well the way his mouth moved.

She was very glad to have a "boy." To be at the Statutes without a fellow was no fun. Instantly, like the gallant he was, he took her on the Dragons, grim-toothed, roundabout switchbacks. It was not nearly so exciting as a tram-car actually. But, then, to be seated in a shaking green dragon, uplifted above the sea of bubble faces, careering in a rickety fashion in the lower heavens, whilst John Thomas leaned over her, his cigarette in his mouth, was after all the right style. She was a plump, quick, alive little creature. So she was quite excited and happy.

John Thomas made her stay on for the next round. And therefore she could hardly for shame repulse him when he put his arm round her and drew her a little nearer to him, in a very warm and cuddly manner. Besides, he was fairly discreet, he kept his movement as hidden as possible. She looked down and saw that his red, clean hand was out of sight of the crowd. And they knew each other so well. So they warmed up to the fair.

After the dragons they went on the horses. John Thomas paid each time, so she could but be complaisant. He, of course, sat astride on the outer horse—named "Black Bess"—and she sat sideways, towards him, on the inner horse—named "Wildfire." But of course John Thomas was not going to sit discreetly on "Black Bess," holding the brass bar. Round they spun and heaved, in the light. And round he swung on his wooden steed, flinging one leg across her mount, and perilously tipping up and down, across the space, half lying back, laughing at her. He was perfectly happy; she was afraid her hat was on one side, but she was excited.

He threw quoits on a table and won for her two large, pale-blue hat-pins. And then, hearing the noise of the cinemas, announcing another performance, they climbed the boards and went in.

Of course, during these performances pitch darkness falls from time to time, when the machine goes wrong. Then there is a wild whooping, and a loud smacking of simulated kisses. In these moments John Thomas drew Annie towards him. After all, he had a wonderfully warm, cosy way of holding a girl with his arm, he seemed to make such a nice fit. And after all, it was pleasant to be so held: so very comforting and cosy and nice. He leaned over her and she felt his breath on her hair; she knew he wanted to kiss her on the lips. And after all, he was so warm and she fitted in to him so softly. After all, she wanted him to touch her lips.

But the light sprang up; she also started electrically, and put her hat straight. He left his arm lying nonchalantly behind her. Well, it was fun, it was exciting to be at the Statutes with John Thomas.

When the cinema was over they went for a walk across the dark, damp fields. He had all the arts of love-making. He was especially good at holding a girl, when he sat with her on a stile in the black, drizzling darkness. He seemed to be holding her in space, against his own warmth and gratification. And his kisses were soft and slow and searching.

So Annie walked out with John Thomas, though she kept her own boy dangling in the distance. Some of the tram-girls chose to be huffy. But there, you must take things as you find them, in this life.

There was no mistake about it, Annie liked John Thomas a good deal. She felt so rich and warm in herself whenever he was near. And John Thomas really liked Annie more than usual. The soft, melting way in which she could flow into a fellow, as if she melted into his very bones, was something rare and good. He fully appreciated this.

But with a developing acquaintance there began a developing intimacy. Annie wanted to consider him a person, a man; she wanted to take an intelligent interest in him, and to have an intelligent response. She did not want a mere nocturnal presence, which was what he was so far. And she prided herself that he could not leave her.

Here she made a mistake. John Thomas intended to remain a nocturnal presence; he had no idea of becoming an all-round individual to her. When she started to take an intelligent interest in him and his life and his character, he sheered off. He hated intelligent interest. And he knew that the only way to stop it was to avoid it. The possessive female was aroused in Annie. So he left her.

It is no use saying she was not surprised. She was at first startled, thrown out of her count. For she had been so *very* sure of holding him. For a while she was staggered, and everything became uncertain to her. Then she wept with fury, indignation, desolation, and misery. Then she had a spasm of despair. And then, when he came, still impudently, on to her car, still familiar, but letting her see by the movement of his head that he had gone away to somebody else for the time being and was enjoying pastures new, then she determined to have her own back.

She had a very shrewd idea what girls John Thomas had taken out. She went to Nora Purdy. Nora was a tall, rather pale, but well-built girl, with beautiful yellow hair. She was rather secretive.

"Hey!" said Annie, accosting her, then softly, "Who's John Thomas on with now?"

"I don't know," said Nora.

"Why tha does," said Annie, ironically lapsing into dialect. "Tha knows as well as I do."

"Well, I do, then," said Nora. "It isn't me, so don't bother."

"It's Cissy Meakin, isn't it?"

"It is, for all I know."

"Hasn't he got a face on him!" said Annie. "I don't half like his cheek. I could knock him off the footboard when he comes round at me."

"He'll get dropped-on one of these days," said Nora.

"Ay, he will when somebody makes up their mind to drop it on him. I should like to see him taken down a peg or two, shouldn't you?"

"I shouldn't mind," said Nora.

"You've got quite as much cause to as I have," said Annie. "But we'll drop on him one of these days, my girl. What? Don't you want to?"

"I don't mind," said Nora.

But as a matter of fact, Nora was much more vindictive than Annie.

One by one Annie went the round of the old flames. It so happened that Cissy Meakin left the tramway service in quite a short time. Her mother made her leave. Then John Thomas was on the qui-vive. He cast his eyes over his old flock. And his eyes lighted on Annie. He thought she would be safe now. Besides, he liked her.

She arranged to walk home with him on Sunday night. It so happened that her car would be in the depot at half-past nine: the last car would come in at ten-fifteen. So John Thomas was to wait for her there.

At the depot the girls had a little waiting-room of their own. It was quite rough, but cosy, with a fire and an oven and a mirror, and table and wooden chairs. The half dozen girls who knew John Thomas only too well had arranged to take service this Sunday afternoon. So, as the cars began to come in, early, the girls dropped into the waiting-room. And instead of hurrying off home, they sat around the fire and had a cup of tea. Outside was the darkness and lawlessness of war-time.

John Thomas came on the car after Annie, at about a quarter to ten. He poked his head easily into the girls' waiting-room.

"Prayer-meeting?" he asked.

"Ay," said Laura Sharp. "Ladies only."

"That's me!" said John Thomas. It was one of his favourite exclamations.

"Shut the door, boy," said Muriel Baggaley.

"On which side of me?" said John Thomas.

"Which tha likes," said Polly Birkin.

He had come in and closed the door behind him. The girls moved in their circle, to make a place for him near the fire. He took off his great-coat and pushed back his hat.

"Who handles the teapot?" he said.

Nora Purdy silently poured him out a cup of tea.

"Want a bit o' my bread and drippin'?" said Muriel Baggaley to him.

"Ay, give us a bit."

And he began to eat his piece of bread.

"There's no place like home, girls," he said.

They all looked at him as he uttered this piece of impudence. He seemed to be sunning himself in the presence of so many damsels.

"Especially if you're not afraid to go home in the dark," said Laura Sharp.

"Me! By myself I am."

They sat till they heard the last tram come in. In a few minutes Emma Houselay entered.

"Come on, my old duck!" cried Polly Birkin.

"It *is* perishing," said Emma, holding her fingers to the fire.

"But—I'm afraid to, go home in, the dark," sang Laura Sharp, the tune having got into her mind.

"Who're you going with tonight, John Thomas?" asked Muriel Baggaley, coolly.

"Tonight?" said John Thomas. "Oh, I'm going home by myself tonight—all on my lonely-O."

"That's me!" said Nora Purdy, using his own ejaculation.

The girls laughed shrilly.

"Me as well, Nora," said John Thomas.

"Don't know what you mean," said Laura.

"Yes, I'm toddling," said he, rising and reaching for his overcoat.

"Nay," said Polly. "We're all here waiting for you."

"We've got to be up in good time in the morning," he said in the benevolent official manner.

They all laughed.

"Nay," said Muriel. "Don't leave us all lonely, John Thomas. Take one!"

"I'll take the lot, if you like," he responded gallantly.

"That you won't, either," said Muriel. "Two's company; seven's too much of a good thing."

"Nay—take one," said Laura. "Fair and square, all above board, and say which."

"Ay," cried Annie, speaking for the first time. "Pick, John Thomas; let's hear thee."

"Nay," he said. "I'm going home quiet tonight. Feeling good, for once."

"Whereabouts?" said Annie. "Take a good un, then, But tha's got to take one of us!"

"Nay, how can I take one," he said, laughing uneasily. "I don't want to make enemies."

"You'd only make *one*," said Annie.

"The chosen *one*," added Laura.

"Oh, my! Who said girls!" exclaimed John Thomas, again turning, as if to escape. "Well—good-night."

"Nay, you've got to make your pick," said Muriel. "Turn your face to the wall and say which one touches you. Go on—we shall only just touch your back—one of us. Go on—turn your face to the wall, and don't look, and say which one touches you."

He was uneasy, mistrusting them. Yet he had not the courage to break away. They pushed him to a wall and stood him there with his face to it. Behind his back they all grimaced, tittering. He looked so comical. He looked around uneasily.

"Go on!" he cried.

"You're looking—you're looking!" they shouted.

He turned his head away. And suddenly, with a movement like a swift cat, Annie went forward and fetched him a box on the side of the head that set his cap flying, and himself staggering. He started round.

But at Annie's signal they all flew at him, slapping him, pinching him, pulling his hair, though more in fun than in spite or anger. He, however, saw red. His blue eyes flamed with strange fear as well as fury, and he butted through the girls to the door. It was locked. He wrenched at it. Roused, alert, the girls stood round and looked at him. He faced them, at bay. At that moment they were rather horrifying to him, as they stood in their short uniforms. He was distinctly afraid.

"Come on, John Thomas! Come on! Choose!" said Annie.

"What are you after? Open the door," he said.

"We sha'n't—not till you've chosen!" said Muriel.

"Chosen what?" he said.

"Chosen the one you're going to marry," she replied.

He hesitated a moment.

"Open the blasted door," he said, "and get back to your senses." He spoke with official authority.

"You've got to choose!" cried the girls.

"Come on!" cried Annie, looking him in the eye. "Come on! Come on!"

He went forward, rather vaguely. She had taken off her belt, and swinging it, she fetched him a sharp blow over the head with the buckle end. He sprang and seized her. But immediately the other girls rushed upon him, pulling and tearing and beating him. Their blood was now thoroughly up. He was their sport now. They were going to have their own back, out of him. Strange, wild creatures, they hung on him and rushed at him to bear him down. His tunic was torn right up the back, Nora had hold at the back of his collar, and was actually strangling him. Luckily the button burst. He struggled in a wild frenzy of fury and terror, almost mad terror. His tunic was simply torn off his back, his shirt-sleeves were torn away, his arms were naked. The girls rushed at him, clenched their hands on him and pulled at him: or they rushed at him and pushed him, butted him with all their might: or they struck him wild blows. He ducked and cringed and struck sideways. They became more intense.

At last he was down. They rushed on him, kneeling on him. He had neither breath nor strength to move. His face was bleeding with a long scratch, his brow was bruised.

Annie knelt on him, the other girls knelt and hung on to him. Their faces were flushed, their hair wild, their eyes were all glittering strangely. He lay at last quite still, with face averted, as an animal lies when it is defeated and at the mercy of the captor. Sometimes his eye glanced back at the wild faces of the girls. His breast rose heavily, his wrists were torn.

"Now, then, my fellow!" gasped Annie at length. "Now then—now—"

At the sound of her terrifying, cold triumph, he suddenly started to struggle as an animal might, but the girls threw themselves upon him with unnatural strength and power, forcing him down.

"Yes—now, then!" gasped Annie at length.

And there was a dead silence, in which the thud of heart-beating was to be heard. It was a suspense of pure silence in every soul.

"Now you know where you are," said Annie.

The sight of his white, bare arm maddened the girls. He lay in a kind of trance of fear and antagonism. They felt themselves filled with supernatural strength.

Suddenly Polly started to laugh—to giggle wildly—helplessly—and Emma and Muriel joined in. But Annie and Nora and Laura remained the same, tense, watchful, with gleaming eyes. He winced away from these eyes.

"Yes," said Annie, in a curious low tone, secret and deadly. "Yes! You've got it now! You know what you've done, don't you? You know what you've done."

He made no sound nor sign, but lay with bright, averted eyes, and averted, bleeding face.

"You ought to be *killed*, that's what you ought," said Annie tensely. "You ought to be *killed*." And there was a terrifying lust in her voice.

Polly was ceasing to laugh, and giving long-drawn oh-h-hs and sighs as she came to herself.

"He's got to choose," she said vaguely.

"Oh, yes, he has," said Laura, with vindictive decision.

"Do you hear—do you hear?" said Annie. And with a sharp movement that made him wince, she turned his face to her.

"Do you hear?" she repeated, shaking him.

But he was quite dumb. She fetched him a sharp slap on the face. He started, and his eyes widened. Then his face darkened with defiance, after all.

"Do you hear?" she repeated.

He only looked at her with hostile eyes.

"Speak!" she said, putting her face devilishly near his.

"What?" he said, almost overcome.

"You've got to *choose!*" she cried, as if it were some terrible menace, and as if it hurt her that she could not exact more.

"What?" he said in fear.

"Choose your girl, Coddy. You've got to choose her now. And you'll get your neck broken if you play any more of your tricks, my boy. You're settled now."

There was a pause. Again he averted his face. He was cunning in his overthrow. He did not give in to them really—no, not if they tore him to bits.

"All right, then," he said, "I choose Annie." His voice was strange and full of malice. Annie let go of him as if he had been a hot coal.

"He's chosen Annie!" said the girls in chorus.

"Me!" cried Annie. She was still kneeling, but away from him. He was still lying prostrate, with averted face. The girls grouped uneasily around.

"Me!" repeated Annie, with a terrible bitter accent.

Then she got up, drawing away from him with strange disgust and bitterness.

"I wouldn't touch him," she said.

But her face quivered with a kind of agony, she seemed as if she would fall. The other girls turned aside. He remained lying on the floor, with his torn clothes and bleeding, averted face.

"Oh, if he's chosen—" said Polly.

"I don't want him—he can choose again," said Annie, with the same rather bitter hopelessness.

"Get up," said Polly, lifting his shoulder. "Get up."

He rose slowly, a strange, ragged, dazed creature. The girls eyed him from a distance, curiously, furtively, dangerously.

"Who wants him?" cried Laura roughly.

"Nobody," they answered with contempt. Yet each one of them waited for him to look at her, hoped he would look at her. All except Annie, and something was broken in her.

He, however, kept his face closed and averted from them all. There was a silence of the end. He picked up the torn pieces of his tunic, without knowing what to do with them. The girls stood about uneasily, flushed, panting, tidying their hair and their dress unconsciously, and watching him. He looked at none of them. He espied his cap in a corner and went and picked it up. He put it on his head, and one of the girls burst into a shrill, hysteric laugh at the sight he presented. He, however, took no heed but went straight to where his overcoat hung on a peg. The girls moved away from contact with him as if he had been an electric wire. He put on his coat and buttoned it down. Then he rolled his tunic-rags into a bundle, and stood before the locked door, dumbly.

"Open the door, somebody," said Laura.

"Annie's got the key," said one.

Annie silently offered the key to the girls. Nora unlocked the door.

"Tit for tat, old man," she said. "Show yourself a man, and don't bear a grudge."

But without a word or sign he had opened the door and gone, his face closed, his head dropped.

"That'll learn him," said Laura.

"Coddy!" said Nora.

"Shut up, for God's sake!" cried Annie fiercely, as if in torture.

"Well, I'm about ready to go, Polly. Look sharp!" said Muriel.

The girls were all anxious to be off. They were tidying themselves hurriedly, with mute, stupefied faces.

DISCUSSION

The plot of this story is quite simple. One of the young inspectors of the tram line, John Thomas, begins to go out with Annie, one of the girl conductors. He drops her when he realizes that she is taking his attentions seriously. Annie arranges a meeting with the other girls whom he has treated in this fashion, and they join her in roughing him up. They do not seriously hurt him, though they get in some blows and they tear his tunic. John Thomas leaves, and the girls find themselves nonplussed at what they have done, a little dazed, and even a little frightened.

Though the story presents a good deal of action, even violent action, not very much has been resolved. Presumably John Thomas and Annie will continue to go their separate ways. Indeed, the story ends on a note of uneasy irresolution. The superficial reader may even be baffled by the ending of the story and so dismiss it.

Other readers, however, may feel that the internal action is important. Indeed, the very debacle of the ending points toward an exciting psychological development. The girls have got in over their depth and find that their emotions toward John Thomas are in excess of, and indeed widely different from, the rather tomboyish triumph of their revenge. As the author tells us in the last sentence, after John Thomas's departure, the girls wear "mute, stupified faces."

The story derives much of its richness from the fact that it succeeds in dramatizing what may be called the "doubleness" of love—its strange mixture of aggressiveness and passivity, of cruelty and tenderness, of possessiveness and surrender. All the characters in the story experience something of these contradictory feelings, but the author has properly kept the focus upon one particular character, Annie, who is more deeply involved than the others, and who therefore not only feels the experience more intensely but is also the more intensely subject to the contradictory impulses within the experience.

What is it that Annie wants from the trick to be played on John Thomas? On the conscious level, presumably no more than the humiliation that he will suffer at facing all the girls together and the taunts that they mean to hurl at him. But unconsciously Annie must have wanted much more—if we are to judge from what actually happens in the latter part of the story. Certainly she must have wanted the specific confrontation with him—including the physical contact. She must also have wanted a chance to pour out some of her feelings of hurt and anger; the prank will afford her a kind of justification for doing so. Secretly, perhaps she wanted to hear him name her as his choice—if only to have the chance to tell him she has no interest in him. But it is plain that neither Annie nor the rest of the girls have really thought out just what they expect the prank to accomplish or to mean.

The last point comes out clearly when we see that nobody knows just how to end the joke. Once they have got into it, their actions are emotional and compulsive, sexual in fact, and sexual in a way that puzzles and even frightens the girls. They have worked themselves in a wild frenzy that they cannot understand and that might conceivably end in extreme violence. Annie gives John Thomas a box on the side of the head that is probably much harder than she had first meant to strike. At this signal the girls fly at John Thomas "more in fun than in spite or anger." But soon they have their "blood . . . up" and are attacking in frenzy. When John Thomas stops resisting, the girls find themselves waiting for something to happen, not knowing what to do next, and repeating illogically and "vaguely" that he has "got to choose." Indeed, some of the girls, beginning "to giggle wildly," are obviously on the verge of hysteria.

There is, of course, no way for the episode to end satisfactorily for any of the girls—least of all for the leader of the prank, Annie, whose relation to John Thomas is so emotionally ambiguous. The only satisfactory ending for such a mixture of feelings—and of feelings waked to such intensity by the physical struggle—is possession and marriage. But this is the solution that the tomboy prank has made impossible. (To Annie at least it will now *seem* so.) It is as if Annie's revenge has made John Thomas more desirable, and yet the forcing of his admission that, having to choose, he would indeed choose her, has made that choice in fact impossible. The very frustration of the prank she has engineered has revealed to her things about herself that she had not surmised.

1. Why is it with "bitter hopelessness" that Annie says "I don't want him"?

2. What is meant by the author's saying of Annie that "something was broken in her"?

3. What are Annie's feelings toward John Thomas at the end of the story?

4. What are John Thomas's feelings toward Annie?

5. Has the author put too much emphasis upon John Thomas's emotions, particularly in the last half of the story? Or too little emphasis?

6. Note that the author is constantly telling us what the characters think and what certain of their actions mean: for example, "He was uneasy, mistrusting them" and "yet each one of them . . . hoped he would look at her." Even so, the story is vivid in its presentation and remains "dramatic." Why don't the author's comments and interpretations kill the immediacy of this story?

7. Observe the tone of the story for the first several pages. The effect in describing the course of the tram is harum-scarum and comic. In fact, until John Thomas drops Annie, the general effect is comic, or at least detached, as is even the beginning of the get-even scene. What is implied in the sudden shift at this point? How is the shift of tone central to the meaning of the story? Is the event one that any individual girl might have imagined possible? Is there an element of self-discovery, even a frightening one, that comes out of the episode?

HAIRCUT

Ring Lardner

I GOT another barber that comes over from Carterville and helps me out Saturdays, but the rest of the time I can get along all right alone. You can see for yourself that this ain't no New York City and besides that, the most of the boys works all day and don't have no leisure to drop in here and get themselves prettied up.

You're a newcomer, ain't you? I thought I hadn't seen you round before. I hope you like it good enough to stay. As I say, we ain't no New York City or Chicago, but we have pretty good times. Not as good, though, since Jim Kendall got killed. When he was alive, him and Hod Meyers used to keep this town in an uproar. I bet they was more laughin' done here than any town its size in America.

Jim was comical, and Hod was pretty near a match for him. Since Jim's gone, Hod tries to hold his end up just the same as ever, but it's tough goin' when you ain't got nobody to kind of work with.

They used to be plenty fun in here Saturdays. This place is jam-packed Saturdays, from four o'clock on. Jim and Hod would show up right after their supper round six o'clock. Jim would set himself down in that big chair, nearest the blue spitoon. Whoever had been settin' in that chair, why, they'd get up when Jim come in and give it to him.

You'd of thought it was a reserved seat like they have sometimes in a theaytre. Hod would generally always stand or walk up and down or some Saturdays, of course, he'd be settin' in this chair part of the time, gettin' a haircut.

Well, Jim would set there a w'ile without openin' his mouth only to spit, and then finally he'd say to me, "Whitey,"—my right name, that is, my right first name, is Dick, but everybody round here calls me Whitey—Jim would say, "Whitey, your nose looks like a rosebud tonight. You must of been drinkin' some of your aw de cologne."

So I'd say, "No, Jim, but you look like you'd been drinkin' somethin' of that kind or somethin' worse."

Jim would have to laugh at that, but then he'd speak up and say, "No, I ain't had nothin' to drink, but that ain't sayin' I wouldn't like somethin'. I wouldn't even mind if it was wood alcohol."

Then Hod Meyers would say, "Neither would your wife." That would set everybody to laughin' because Jim and his wife wasn't on very good terms. She'd of divorced him only they wasn't no chance to get alimony and she didn't have no way to take care of herself and the kids. She couldn't never understand Jim. He *was* kind of rough, but a good fella at heart.

Him and Hod had all kinds of sport with Milt Sheppard. I don't suppose you've seen Milt. Well, he's got an Adam's apple that looks more like a mushmelon. So I'd been shavin' Milt and when I'd start to shave down here on his neck, Hod would holler, "Hey, Whitey, wait a minute! Before you cut into it, let's make up a pool and see who can guess closest to the number of seeds."

And Jim would say, "If Milt hadn't of been so hoggish, he'd of ordered a half a cantaloupe instead of a whole one and it might not of stuck in his throat."

All the boys would roar at this and Milt himself would force a smile, though the joke was on him. Jim certainly was a card!

There's his shavin' mug, setting on the shelf, right next to Charley Vail's. "Charles M. Vail." That's the druggist. He comes in regular for his shave three times a week. And Jim's is the cup next to Charley's. "James H. Kendall." Jim won't need no shavin' mug no more, but I'll leave it there just the same for old time's sake. Jim certainly was a character!

Years ago, Jim used to travel for a canned goods concern over in Carterville. They sold canned goods. Jim had the whole northern half of the State and was on the road five days out of every week. He'd drop in here Saturdays and tell his experiences for that week. It was rich.

I guess he paid more attention to playin' jokes than makin' sales. Finally the concern let him out and he come right home here and told everybody he'd been fired instead of sayin' he'd resigned like most fellas would of.

It was a Saturday and the shop was full and Jim got up out of that chair and says, "Gentlemen, I got an important announcement to make. I been fired from my job."

Well, they asked him if he was in earnest and he said he was and nobody could think of nothin' to say till Jim finally broke the ice himself. He says, "I been sellin' canned goods and now I'm canned goods myself."

You see, the concern he'd been workin' for was a factory that made canned goods. Over in Carterville. And now Jim said he was canned himself. He was certainly a card!

Jim had a great trick that he used to play w'ile he was travelin'. For instance, he'd be ridin' on a train and they'd come to some little town like, well, like, well, like, we'll say, like Benton. Jim would look out the train window and read the signs on the stores.

For instance, they'd be a sign, "Henry Smith, Dry Goods." Well, Jim would write down the name and the name of the town and when he got to wherever he was goin' he'd mail back a postal card to Henry Smith at Benton and not sign no name to it, but he'd write on the card, well, somethin' like "Ask your wife about that book agent that spent the afternoon last week," or "Ask your Missus who kept her from gettin' lonesome the last time you was in Carterville." And he'd sign the card, "A Friend."

Of course, he never knew what really come of none of these jokes, but he could picture what *probably* happened and that was enough.

Jim didn't work very steady after he lost his position with the Carterville people. What he did earn, doin' odd jobs round town, why, he spent pretty near all of it on gin, and his family might of starved if the stores hadn't of carried them along. Jim's wife tried her hand at dressmakin', but they ain't nobody goin' to get rich makin' dresses in this town.

As I say, she'd of divorced Jim, only she seen that she couldn't support herself and the kids and she was always hopin' that some day Jim would cut out his habits and give her more than two or three dollars a week.

They was a time when she would go to whoever he was workin' for and ask them to give her his wages, but after she done this once or twice, he beat her to it by borrowin' most of his pay in advance. He told it all round town, how he had outfoxed his Missus. He certainly was a caution!

But he wasn't satisfied with just outwittin' her. He was sore the way she had acted, tryin' to grab off his pay. And he made up his mind he'd get even. Well, he waited till Evans's Circus was advertised to come to town. Then he told his wife and two kiddies that he was goin' to take them to the circus. The day of the circus, he told them he would get the tickets and meet them outside the entrance to the tent.

Well, he didn't have no intentions of bein' there or buyin' tickets or nothin'. He got full of gin and laid round Wright's poolroom all day. His wife and the kids waited and waited and of course he didn't show up. His wife didn't have a dime with her, or nowhere else, I guess. So she finally had to tell the kids it was all off and they cried like they wasn't never goin' to stop.

Well, it seems, w'ile they was cryin', Doc Stair come along and he asked what was the matter, but Mrs. Kendall was stubborn and wouldn't tell him, but the kids told him and he insisted on takin' them and their mother in the show. Jim found this out afterwards and it was one reason why he had it in for Doc Stair.

Doc Stair come here about a year and a half ago. He's a mighty handsome young fella and his clothes always look like he has them made to order. He goes to Detroit two or three times a year and w'ile he's there must have a tailor take his measure and then make him a suit to order. They cost pretty near twice as much, but they fit a whole lot better than if you just bought them in a store.

For a w'ile everybody was wonderin' why a young doctor like Doc Stair should come to a town like this where we already got old Doc Gamble and Doc Foote that's both been here for years and all the practice in town was always divided between the two of them.

Then they was a story got round that Doc Stair's gal had throwed him over, a gal up in the Northern Peninsula somewhere, and the reason he come here was to hide himself away and forget it. He said himself that he thought they wasn't nothin' like general practice in a place like ours to fit a man to be a good all round doctor. And that's why he'd came.

Anyways, it wasn't long before he was makin' enough to live on, though they tell me that he never dunned nobody for what they owed him, and the folks here certainly has got the owin' habit, even in my business. If I had all that was comin' to me for just shaves alone, I could go to Carterville and put up at the Mercer for a week and see a different picture every night. For instance, they's old George Purdy—but I guess I shouldn't ought to be gossipin'.

Well, last year, our coroner died, died of the flu. Ken Beatty, that was his name. He was the coroner. So they had to choose another man to be coroner in his place and they picked Doc Stair. He laughed at first and said he didn't want it, but they made him take it. It ain't no job that anybody would fight for and what a man makes out of it in a year would just about buy seeds for their garden. Doc's the kind, though, that can't say no to nothin' if you keep at him long enough.

But I was goin' to tell you about a poor boy we got here in town— Paul Dickson. He fell out of a tree when he was about ten years old. Lit on his head and it done somethin' to him and he ain't never been right. No harm in him, but just silly. Jim Kendall used to call him cuckoo; that's a name Jim had for anybody that was off their head, only he called people's head their bean. That was another of his gags, callin' head bean and callin' crazy people cuckoo. Only poor Paul ain't crazy, but just silly.

You can imagine that Jim used to have all kinds of fun with Paul.

He'd send him to the White Front Garage for a left-handed monkey wrench. Of course they ain't no such thing as a left-handed monkey wrench.

And once we had a kind of a fair here and they was a baseball game between the fats and the leans and before the game started Jim called Paul over and sent him away down to Schrader's hardware store to get a key for the pitcher's box.

They wasn't nothin' in the way of gags that Jim couldn't think up, when he put his mind to it.

Poor Paul was always kind of suspicious of people, maybe on account of how Jim had kept foolin' him. Paul wouldn't have much to do with anybody only his own mother and Doc Stair and a girl here in town named Julie Gregg. That is, she ain't a girl no more, but pretty near thirty or over.

When Doc first came to town, Paul seemed to feel like here was a real friend and he hung round Doc's office most of the w'ile; the only time he wasn't there was when he'd go home to eat or sleep or when he seen Julie Gregg doin' her shoppin'.

When he looked out Doc's window and seen her, he'd run downstairs and join her and tag along with her to the different stores. The poor boy was crazy about Julie and she always treated him mighty nice and made him feel like he was welcome, though of course it wasn't nothin' but pity on her side.

Doc done all he could to improve Paul's mind and he told me once that he really thought the boy was getting better, that they was times when he was as bright and sensible as anybody else.

But I was goin' to tell you about Julie Gregg. Old man Gregg was in the lumber business, but got to drinkin' and lost the most of his money and when he died, he didn't leave nothin' but the house and just enough insurance for the girl to skimp along on.

Her mother was a kind of a half invalid and didn't hardly ever leave the house. Julie wanted to sell the place and move somewheres else after the old man died, but the mother said she was born here and would die here. It was tough on Julie as the young people round this town—well, she's too good for them.

She'd been away to school and Chicago and New York and different places and they ain't no subject she can't talk on, where you take the rest of the young folks here and you mention anything to them outside of Gloria Swanson or Tommy Meighan and they think you're delirious. Did you see Gloria in *Wages of Virtue?* You missed somethin'!

Well, Doc Stair hadn't been here more than a week when he come in one day to get shaved and I recognized who he was, as he had been pointed out to me, so I told him about my old lady. She's been ailin' for a couple years and either Doc Gamble or Doc Foote, neither one, seemed to be helpin' her. So he said he would come out and see her, but if she was able to get out herself, it would be better to bring her to his office where he could make a completer examination.

So I took her to his office and w'ile I was waitin' for her in the reception room, in come Julie Gregg. When somebody comes in Doc Stair's office, they's a bell that rings in his inside office so as he can tell they's somebody to see him.

So he left my old lady inside and come out to the front office and that's the first time him and Julie met and I guess it was what they call love at first sight. But it wasn't fifty-fifty. This young fella was the slickest lookin' fella she'd ever seen in this town and she went wild over him. To him she was just a lady that wanted to see the doctor.

She'd came on about the same business I had. Her mother had been doctorin' for years with Doc Gamble and Doc Foote and without no results. So she'd heard they was a new doc in town and decided to give him a try. He promised to call and see her mother that same day.

I said a minute ago that it was love at first sight on her part. I'm not only judgin' by how she acted afterwards but how she looked at him that first day in his office. I ain't no mind reader, but it was wrote all over her face that she was gone.

Now Jim Kendall, besides bein' a jokesmith and a pretty good drinker, well, Jim was quite a lady-killer. I guess he run pretty wild durin' the time he was on the road for them Carterville people, and besides that, he'd had a couple little affairs of the heart right here in town. As I say, his wife would have divorced him, only she couldn't.

But Jim was like the majority of men, and women, too, I guess. He wanted what he couldn't get. He wanted Julie Gregg and worked his head off tryin' to land her. Only he'd of said bean instead of head.

Well, Jim's habits and his jokes didn't appeal to Julie and of course he was a married man, so he didn't have no more chance than, well, than a rabbit. That's an expression of Jim's himself. When somebody didn't have no chance to get elected or somethin', Jim would always say they didn't have no more chance than a rabbit.

He didn't make no bones about how he felt. Right in here, more than once, in front of the whole crowd, he said he was stuck on Julie and anybody that could get her for him was welcome to his house and his wife and kids included. But she wouldn't have nothin' to do with him; wouldn't even speak to him on the street. He finally seen he wasn't gettin' nowheres with his usual line so he decided to try the rough stuff. He went right up to her house one evenin' and when she opened the door he forced his way in and grabbed her. But she broke loose and before he could stop her, she run in the next room and locked the door and phoned to Joe Barnes. Joe's the marshal. Jim could hear who she was phonin' to and he beat it before Joe got there.

Joe was an old friend of Julie's pa. Joe went to Jim the next day and told him what would happen if he ever done it again.

I don't know how the news of this little affair leaked out. Chances is that Joe Barnes told his wife and she told somebody else's wife and they told their husband. Anyways, it did leak out and Hod Meyers had the nerve to kid Jim about it, right here in this shop. Jim didn't deny nothin' and kind of laughed it off and said for us all to wait; that lots of people had tried to make a monkey out of him, but he always got even.

Meanw'ile everybody in town was wise to Julie's bein' wild mad over the Doc. I don't suppose she had any idear how her face changed when him and her was together; of course she couldn't of, or she'd of kept away from him. And she didn't know that we was all noticin' how many times she made excuses to go up to his office or pass it on the other side of the street and look up in his window to see if he was there. I felt sorry for her and so did most other people.

Hod Meyers kept rubbin' it into Jim about how the Doc had cut him out. Jim didn't pay no attention to the kiddin' and you could see he was plannin' one of his jokes.

One trick Jim had was the knack of changin' his voice. He could make you think he was a girl talkin' and he could mimic any man's voice. To show you how good he was along this line, I'll tell you the joke he played on me once.

You know, in most towns of any size, when a man is dead and needs a shave, why, the barber that shaves him soaks him five dollars for the job; that is, he don't soak *him,* but whoever ordered the shave. I just charge three dollars because personally I don't mind much shavin' a dead person. They lay a whole lot stiller than live customers. The only thing is that you don't feel like talkin' to them and you get kind of lonesome.

Well, about the coldest day we ever had here, two years ago last winter, the phone rung at the house w'ile I was home to dinner and I answered the phone and it was a woman's voice and she said she was Mrs. John Scott and her husband was dead and would I come out and shave him.

Old John had always been a good customer of mine. But they live seven miles out in the country, on the Streeter road. Still I didn't see how I could say no.

So I said I would be there, but would have to come in a jitney and it might cost three or four dollars besides the price of the shave. So she, or the voice, it said that was all right, so I got Frank Abbott to drive me out to the place and when I got there, who should open the door but old John himself! He wasn't no more dead than, well, than a rabbit.

It didn't take no private detective to figure out who had played me this little joke. Nobody could of thought it up but Jim Kendall. He certainly was a card!

I tell you this incident just to show you how he could disguise his voice and make you believe it was somebody else talkin'. I'd of swore it was Mrs. Scott had called me. Anyways, some woman.

Well, Jim waited till he had Doc Stair's voice down pat; then he went after revenge.

He called Julie up on a night when he knew Doc was over in Carterville. She never questioned but what it was Doc's voice. Jim said he must see her that night; he couldn't wait no longer to tell her somethin'. She was all excited and told him to come to the house. But he said he was expectin' an important long distance call and wouldn't she please forget her manners for once and come to his office. He said they couldn't nothin' hurt her and nobody would see her and he just *must* talk to her a little w'ile. Well, poor Julie fell for it.

Doc always keeps a night light in his office, so it looked to Julie like they was somebody there.

Meanw'ile Jim Kendall had went to Wright's poolroom, where they was a whole gang amusin' themselves. The most of them had drank plenty of gin, and they was a rough bunch when sober. They was always strong for Jim's jokes and when he told them to come with him and see some fun they give up their card games and pool games and followed along.

Doc's office is on the second floor. Right outside his door they's a flight of stairs leadin' to the floor above. Jim and his gang hid in the dark behind these stairs.

Well, Julie come up to Doc's door and rung the bell and they was nothin' doin'. She rung it again and she rung it seven or eight times. Then she tried the door and found it locked. Then Jim made some kind of a noise and she heard it and waited a minute, and then she says, "Is that you, Ralph?" Ralph is Doc's first name.

They was no answer and it must of came to her all of a sudden that she'd been bunked. She pretty near fell downstairs and the whole gang after her. They chased her all the way home, hollerin', "Is that you, Ralph?" and "Oh, Ralphie, dear, is that you?" Jim says he couldn't holler it himself, as he was laughin' too hard.

Poor Julie! She didn't show up here on Main Street for a long, long time afterward.

And of course Jim and his gang told everybody in town, everybody but Doc Stair. They was scared to tell him, and he might of never knowed only for Paul Dickson. The poor cuckoo, as Jim called him, he was here in the shop one night when Jim was still gloatin' yet over what he'd done to Julie. And Paul took in as much of it he could understand and he run to Doc with the story.

It's a cinch Doc went up in the air and swore he'd make Jim suffer. But it was a kind of a delicate thing, because if it got out that he had beat Jim up, Julie was bound to hear of it and then she'd know that Doc knew and of course knowin' that he knew would make it worse for her than ever. He was goin' to do somethin', but it took a lot of figurin'.

Well, it was a couple days later when Jim was here in the shop again, and so was the cuckoo. Jim was goin' duck-shootin' the next day and had came in lookin' for Hod Meyers to go with him. I happened to know that Hod had went over to Carterville and wouldn't be home till the end of the week. So Jim said he hated to go alone and he guessed he would call it off. Then poor Paul spoke up and said if Jim would take him he would go along. Jim thought a w'ile and then he said, well, he guessed a half-wit was better than nothin'.

I suppose he was plottin' to get Paul out in the boat and play some joke on him, like pushin' him in the water. Anyways, he said Paul could go. He asked him had he ever shot a duck and Paul said no, he'd never even had a gun in his hands. So Jim said he could set in the boat and watch him and if he behaved himself, he might lend him his gun for a couple of shots. They made a date to meet in the mornin' and that's the last I seen of Jim alive.

Next mornin', I hadn't been open more than ten minutes when Doc

Stair come in. He looked kind of nervous. He asked me had I seen Paul Dickson. I said no, but I knew where he was, out duck-shootin' with Jim Kendall. So Doc says that's what he had heard, and he couldn't understand it because Paul had told him he wouldn't never have no more to do with Jim as long as he lived.

He said Paul had told him about the joke Jim had played on Julie. He said Paul had asked him what he thought of the joke and the Doc told him that anybody that would do a thing like that ought not to be let live.

·I said it had been a kind of a raw thing, but Jim just couldn't resist no kind of a joke, no matter how raw. I said I thought he was all right at heart, but just bubblin' over with mischief. Doc turned and walked out.

At noon he got a phone call from old John Scott. The lake where Jim and Paul had went shootin' is on John's place. Paul had came runnin' up to the house a few minutes before and said they'd been an accident. Jim had shot a few ducks and then give the gun to Paul and told him to try his luck. Paul hadn't never handled a gun and he was nervous. He was shakin' so hard that he couldn't control the gun. He let fire and Jim sunk back in the boat, dead.

Doc Stair, bein' the coroner, jumped in Frank Abbott's flivver and rushed out to Scott's farm. Paul and old John was down on the shore of the lake. Paul had rowed the boat to shore, but they'd left the body in it, waiting for Doc to come.

Doc examined the body and said they might as well fetch it back to town. They was no use leavin' it there or callin' a jury, as it was a plain case of accidental shootin'.

Personally I wouldn't never leave a person shoot a gun in the same boat I was in unless I was sure they knew somethin' about guns. Jim was a sucker to leave a new beginner have his gun, let alone a half-wit. It probably served Jim right, what he got. But still we miss him round here. He certainly was a card! Comb it wet or dry?

DISCUSSION

The main action here is the story of the "card," the practical joker. He has no shred of human perception or feeling, and his jokes are, naturally, brutal and stupid, only a way of inflating his own ego. In the end, one of his jokes backfires, and we have the moral satisfaction of seeing the biter bit, the joker caught in the destructive consequences of a joke whose destructive nature for other people he could never have understood or cared about. Assuming that the card is adequately characterized, that the setting of the small town is adequately rendered for us, and that the plot is logically worked out, we might still feel that this main action, taken by itself, is somewhat too simple and predictable, even too moralistic and too obviously an illustration of brutal arrogance being paid off. Anyway, it seems that Ring Lardner must have felt that a naked presentation of the main action, that is, the story told straight by the author, would be unsatisfactory, for he provides a narrator, the barber, who gives us his version of the business.

The use of the narrator does, for the first thing, make the story seem less bare and simple—though, of course, complication for the mere sake of complication scarcely justifies itself—and, for another thing, the barber does give us a sense of the town, of the blankness and brutality of the hangers-on at the shop. But what other positive values was Lardner aiming at in his use of the barber as the narrator? To answer this we may well begin by asking another question: what is the barber like: More specifically, what is his attitude toward the story he tells?

The barber, we quickly discover, thinks that life is pretty dull around town now that the card is gone. The barber has vicariously participated in the brutal jokes, and is, therefore, a kind of accomplice. So we have a deepening of the originally simple action—a sense of the spreading ripples of complicity always around the evil act.

There is, also, another kind of deepening, not in content but in presentation. Let us suppose that the narrator of the story had merely told us about people like the barber, people who had some tacit complicity with the card's jokes, and that he himself, the narrator, found such people reprehensible. Given this treatment, we would find ourselves in immediate agreement with his attitude. There would be no shock of the collision between the narrator's attitude and our own. But as things actually stand, there is a shock of collision between the narrator's attitude and our own, a growing need to repudiate his attitude, and a sense of tension and drama between the (good) us and the (bad) barber. In other words, Lardner has used an inverted and ironical method. The narrator represents neither the author's view nor our own. The barber is used to belie, as it were, the meaning of the story, and by so doing to irritate us to a fuller awareness of what is at stake in the story, even to stir our awareness of our own less obvious cruelties or obtusities.

If the story were told directly, or told by a narrator whose attitudes were congenial with our own, we should be inclined to say that the card, of course, is a brute, a louse, and that he got just what he deserved. But we might say it too easily, and be inclined to dismiss the whole business. As it is, we are compelled, in a greater or lesser degree, to take issue with the barber, and in taking issue we are drawn more deeply into the story.

The use of this kind of narrator is, then, a fairly simple device for provoking what we may call "reader participation"—for making the reader do some of the interpreting himself, for drawing him into the story by making him invert an apparent meaning (here the barber's valuations) or develop meaning beyond the point where the story actually comes to rest. Irony, *understatement* (see Glossary), withholding—these are ways to provoke the reader to reassess things, to reassess his own feelings, and thus enter more deeply into the process of the piece of fiction.

Here it might be well to consider the general problem of the *point of view* or the *focus of narration* (see Glossary). We have just seen how important it is that "Haircut" is presented through the mentality of the barber, and we have seen how the use of this point of view affects the whole story and our reception of the story. The point of view—the choice of the teller of the story—is a question of the greatest importance for any piece of fiction. The action has to come to us through words, but through whose words? On the answer to that question, all else may often hinge. So we have such subsidiary questions as these:

1. What does the narrator know of the total action lying beyond the story? What can he tell?

2. Does he tell all he knows? If not, why not? What accounts for his withholding any information or narrative? If there is withholding, is it reasonable and justifiable, or merely trickery and mystification?

3. Why does he tell what he does tell? What is his motivation as narrator?

4. What is the narrator's attitude toward what he tells?

Though there are many other important questions that may develop around the point of view of a piece of fiction, we can see from these that the point of view bears most important relations to the structure and meaning of fiction. Before we go into such relations, however, we should sort out what points of view are possible in fiction.

There is, obviously, the first person—the story told, as is "Haircut," by an "I," speaking in his own person and in his own language, telling only what he himself can be reasonably supposed to know and what he is interested in telling. We are immediately aware that the status of such a narrator varies from story to story. At one extreme, the "I" may be the main character, as in "Araby," who tells his own story, or, at the other extreme, the "I" may be a mere observer or auditor who has seen or heard about the action of a story but has taken no significant part in it, like the newspaperman in "The Man Who Would Be King," who is a sort of marginal narrator, reporting the real narrator. He is really an aspect of the "convincing background."

In between these extremes may be all sorts of shadings and relationships, from the narrator who is not central but is deeply involved, like Peachey, through the narrator like the barber, who is not involved in any direct sense but who has a moral connection with the action, to the narrator of "The District Doctor," who, though he does show a minimal human reaction to the story, is little more than a conduit, a listener and repeater.

The other general point of view from which a story may be told is the third person, an unidentified author speaking impersonally. At one extreme here is the purely objective record made by an "external" narrator, that is, one who tells only what can be seen and heard from the outside—as though he were a camera and sound machine. John Collier's "De Mortuis" is an almost perfect example of such *dramatic* method, the immediate reportorial method, without summary or psychological interpretation or any entering into the thoughts or feelings of characters.

At the other extreme in the third person is the subjective revelation that can be made by an omniscient narrator, who knows everything about everybody in a story. This method does let us into the thoughts and feelings of one or more characters, sometimes so intimately into them that the story is little more than the tracing of their reactions. "The Secret Life of Walter Mitty" is such a story. Mitty's dream world is the world of the story, and by being admitted into it, we make a judgment on it even as we enjoy its comedy. But an author may, of course, lead us into a character's consciousness, not to follow more or less sympathetically the flow of thought and feeling but to dissect, summarize, and analyze, as in the subjective passages of "The Necklace."

The four main kinds of point of view can be related as shown in the accompanying chart.

		Internal analysis of events		External analysis of events
First person (narrator as a character in story)	1.	Main character tells own story.	2.	Minor character tells main character's story.
Third person (narrator not a character in story—mere observer, but identified)	4.	Analytic or omniscient narrator tells story, entering thoughts and feelings.	3.	Narrator (unidentified, i.e., author) tells story as observer, with or without personal judgment and interpretation.

To return to our remarks about the relation of point of view to structure and meaning, we may take a backward glance at "The Man Who Would Be King." That story has not only one narrator, but two. There is the newspaperman who gives us the general narration in his own person, a sort of shadow of Kipling, but within his narration there is the action narrated by Peachey, again in the first person. What is the logic of Kipling's choice of method?

First, we may observe that by taking a first-person narrator, a certain naturalness may be gained. This is not to say that the reader is so innocent that he more readily "believes" a story told in the first person, but it is to say that certain things can be introduced into a story more informally and casually, even though we recognize that the first-person method itself is a *convention* (see Glossary), a fiction. In this particular story we need to know something about the strange world of India, and if that information were given in the third person the burden of mere exposition would be more apparent. As it is, the newspaperman can more or less casually and incidentally give us a fairly complete notion of his world; he can feed the expository material in without making us feel that it is labeled, for it is part of his life.

Second, the presence of a first-person narrator introduces naturally into a story a device for *selectivity* (see Glossary). Since the narrator can tell only what he has observed, heard, or reasonably surmised, a considerable body of material from the hypothetical underlying action is not available to him. If for a particular story the narrator is well chosen, then the deletions he must make will seem natural, and the selections significant. We feel that *what* he has to tell is what he *can* tell and *must* tell.

For example, in "The Man Who Would Be King" we are dealing with an action that, taken in itself, is potentially a novel—the conquest of

Kafiristan. Kipling is, however, interested in only one thing—the idea of kingship, godhood, and manhood—and he wants to render only so much of the general action as is needed to make vivid and credible the development of Dravot. By the time Dravot's story is filtered through Peachey and the newspaperman only vivid and telling strokes are left. A piece of action that might require pages if given any ordinary development comes down to a sentence or two—for example, the taking of the four mules in the mountains. The scale of treatment can be controlled in terms of the narrator's presence—he tells it in his way, he makes the emphasis. *Selection, foreshortening, summary*—these things are natural to all fiction, but with the first-person narrator we have, as it were, a built-in device for controlling them. In other words, the plot of a story and the scale of the episodes—that is, the structure of action as it is actually presented to us—depend on the point of view.

Not only does structure depend on point of view. Let us take Peachey again. He is useful in the way we have said, as a narrator of events, the giver of the structure, but he is also a mirror to Dravot's development, a device of interpretation as well as of control. We can ask not merely what he knows of the action, but what he knows of the meaning of the action. We sense immediately that Dravot is the powerful one of the pair, the one with ambition and imagination, the one who starts the great scheme of looting a kingdom. Peachey is content to follow at an admiring distance. This same relationship prevails as Dravot begins his spiritual journey from mere looter up to the point that he achieves in the end. Each new phase of his development is played off against Peachey, the unimaginative follower who, if left alone, would be perfectly content to be merely the self-indulgent loafer and looter. It is through Peachey's blundering account and not entirely comprehending response that we sense the depth of experience represented by Dravot. We may say that Peachey, with his blunt lack of sensitivity and his simplicity of mind, is a device of irony and understatement. The fact that the spiritual significance of the theme comes through the man who, except for his association with Dravot, would remain loafer and looter, gives an ironical contrast—though the irony here, unlike that in "Haircut," makes us think not worse, but better, of the narrator. The meaning of Dravot's story, as filtered to us through Peachey, is understated: the full significance is not offered. Peachey is, as it were, a guide for our response, though a rather limping one. But in the end it is he who, in his delirium in the mountains, presents the image of the godlike Dravot who can hold up the peaks. Peachey's simplicity of mind makes it possible for us to accept the image. We accept the thematic truth of it and at the same time, because it comes from the delirium of Peachey's simple mind, accept the plausibility of it.

We have by now perhaps said enough to indicate something of the importance of point of view for both structure and meaning. In light of that, consider these questions:

1. How is the point of view of "De Mortuis" related to the tone of the story? Suppose the doctor were the narrator, or one of his friends. What new problems would have to be faced?

2. Suppose that the whole of "The Man Who Would Be King" were narrated by the newspaperman, with only his paraphrases and summaries of Peachey's account of what happened to him and Dravot. How would the story be different?

3. What would be lost if "The Drunkard" were set in the third person?

4. Could Annie, in "Tickets, Please," have told her own story? As Lawrence, the author, tells it, does Annie really grasp the full meaning of her own story? Should she?

We have seen how closely the development or revelation of character is related to the matter of point of view. It is related with equal intimacy to the matter of *style* (see Glossary). When a story is told in the first person, this relationship is most obvious: a man's language is the man. (Peachey is not the narrator of "The District Doctor," but try to imagine how different it would be if he were—how much the dialogue would change in his language; how little, even, he could understand of such a story.) Similarly, there are intimate relations between style and character in stories told in the third person. We have already remarked what we regard as defects of style in "The Furnished Room" and "Tennessee's Partner": inflation and poeticism that do not match the material, that are inappropriate to the context of the stories. But consider, in contrast, the appropriateness of style of "Araby," for instance. It is the style that at once informs the sensitive reader that though the story is one of painful adolescent love, it was not written or spoken by any adolescent boy. Rather it presents that painful experience as recollected, assimilated, judged, and set in true perspective by a man grown to maturity.

This is not the place to analyze a number of stylistic questions, but it is the place to insist on the fact that the style of the story that a character inhabits does have an essential relation to him, and to the attitude of author and reader toward him. In one sense, the style of the story is his world—and himself.

4
What Theme Reveals

In discussing the stories we have read thus far we have continually referred to the theme, the idea, the meaning. We cannot very long consider the actions or characters of a story without coming to some concern with theme of a story, for insofar as it is a good story, it is, as we have insisted, an organic unity in which all the vital elements have interrelations. Each element implies all the other elements, and implies them in motion toward a significant end.

Now, as we turn to a more systematic treatment of theme in fiction, let us review some of our notions. For one thing, the theme of a piece of fiction is not to be thought of as merely the topic of the story—though the word is sometimes loosely used in this sense. For instance, we may say that two stories shortly to be encountered, "The Killers," by Ernest Hemingway, and "The Man Who Was Almost a Man," by Richard Wright, have the same topic: growing up, the initiation into manhood. The titles of another pair—"Love" by Guy de Maupassant, and "Love" by Jess Stuart—proclaim the same topic, but even though we shall find considerable similarity in treatment, we shall also find significant differences in meaning and differences in the very "feel" of the stories. *The theme, then, is what is made of the topic.* It is what amounts to the comment of the idea *implied* in the process of the story.

The theme is what a piece of fiction stacks up to. It is the idea, the significance, the interpretation of persons and events, the pervasive and unifying view of life embodied in the total narrative. It is what we are to make of the human experience rendered in the story—always involving, directly or indirectly, some comment on values in human nature and conduct.

This last remark may provoke two objections. Some may feel that it makes fiction a kind of mere moralizing, with illustrations. Others may feel that it gives no accommodation to stories that are gay, lighthearted, and comic. Both objections are well taken, and deserve discussion.

Let us take an indirect approach to the first. When we read a good piece of fiction we may be caught by any number of interests, in different degrees. We may simply find a character attractive, and relish his company as we would that of a friend in real life. Or we may find our curiosity stimulated by strange backgrounds or events—the satisfaction of the same desire that leads us to travel. Or we may be held by suspense, the anxiety to know what comes next. We may even be caught by the writer's personality, his charm of spirit, his sprightliness of observation on life, or his poetic expression. Or we may enjoy daydreaming into experiences that we can never have in our humdrum lives. We may, in fact, be caught by any combination of things.

177

But in the end there is always the question "What does it add up to? what does it mean?" If we do not feel that things work out to some moment of significant stability, we feel defrauded. And we should not forget that the question every person, sooner or later, asks about life is "What does it mean?" If a story does not deal with this question, in some way or other, we are left dissatisfied.

One reason for such dissatisfaction is our simple human craving to have things put into order. We like to observe a story working itself out into a unity—just as we feel a need to have our own lives make sense. We demand the logic of cause and effect in fiction, and reasonable motivation, in the same way we demand it in life. We demand that there be a logic of theme—a thematic structure into which the various elements are drawn into unity. Thus, *no theme, no story*.

That is one approach to the objection that our discussion of theme seems to make fiction mere moralizing with illustrations. Another approach is related, but dissimilar. Let us examine the word *illustration* in this connection.

Fiction is not illustration, even though it sometime's pretends to be—as we see when we read "The Man Who Would Be King," which pretends to be an illustration of its motto: "Brother to a Prince and fellow to a begger if he be found worthy." Fiction is not illustration, because with illustration we are always aware that the idea being illustrated comes first in importance, that the content of the illustration is always being dictated by the nature of the thing—the "idea"—being illustrated. The illustration is an explanation, then, not a discovery developed from life.

But with fiction, insofar as it is successful, the imagination creates a world that exists, as it were, in its own right. With great masterpieces, this reality, in all aspects, is so compelling that it often seems closer to us than things we know to be hard facts. Hamlet, let us say, is more vivid to us than George Washington or the man next door. But even fiction that is merely good, not great, carries with it some degree of this illusion of independent existence.

How does this question of independent existence bear on the question of theme? Simply, thus: in a successful piece of fiction, out of this sense of an independent world, as the characters act and are acted upon, as one event leads to another, we become more and more aware of the significance of the whole. That is, *we gradually sense the development of a theme, the growth of significance*. We feel ourselves caught up in a vital process in which meaning emerges from experience. It is such a sense that, in the end, makes our own lives, insofar as we live above a brute level, interesting to us: the sense of deepening discovery in experience. Fiction, then, is never the mere illustration of an idea. *It is the created image of the very life process by which we feel ourselves moving toward meaning in our own experience.*

Let us turn, at long last, to the second objection, the objection that our emphasis on the place of theme in fiction leaves little play for the gay or comic. A full discussion of this would take us far into an analysis of the comic in itself, but it should be enough to say here that we are aware of the comic only by an implied contrast, however remote, with the serious, that the laughter of comedy always has in it some element of escape from the urgency—even the pain—of life.

If we look back at the comic stories read thus far—say, "The Secret Life of Walter Mitty" and "The Drunkard"—we readily see that always a slight shift of emphasis would plunge us into a world entirely different from that of the story. Comedy, including even warm humor, as well as savage satire, has to do with disappointment and surprise, the criticism and defeat of aspirations, contrasts of pretension and actuality, inability to adjust to the changing demands of life. The top-hatted man with his nose in the air who slips on a banana peel is the image behind all comedy—but the fall that rebukes vanity may sometimes break a neck. The distance between a good laugh and the need to call an ambulance is not very great.

At this point another question may be asked. Since theme is a comment on human values, how can we appreciate a story whose theme we cannot accept? There is no use in trying to evade this question by taking refuge in nice generalities, and no use in denying its importance or the difficulty of trying to give an honest answer.

To begin, let us forget fiction altogether, and think of our relations with other people. We live with a variety of people, and with most of them, we have, at some point or another, serious differences in opinion, tastes, and values. With Susie we disagree violently on literary matters, and every time we go to a movie with her we have an argument. With John Jacobs we disagree on politics; with Jim Kobeck, on how to play a hand of bridge. And we take a very dim view of Mary Moffet's intelligence. But—and here is the point—we may be good friends with all of them. We may even fall in love with, and marry, one of them. In other words, we recognize in any one of them, some particular qualities that we value despite disagreements. More important, we may recognize an underlying good will, and an honest attempt to make sense of things and to achieve decency. On recognizing such things, we may discover in ourselves some tolerance and some power of sympathetic imagination. In this process we realize that the world is complicated, and is the richer for the fact. We find that to live fruitfully we must modify our dogmatic attitudes and beliefs.

This is not to say that one thing is as good as another. Each of us has to work out his own scale of values and live by it. But what we have been saying *does* mean that when we encounter differences, we must try to understand their nature, and try to find the underlying common ground that makes human respect possible.

But how does this apply to fiction? In this way: we can think of the authors of stories as we think of friends and associates; we can make, even in disagreement, the imaginative effort to realize what underlies their logic, the logic by which a theme unfolds.

What, then, of the common ground? The common ground is the understanding of the fact that, insofar as a theme is coherently developed through a story, we are, as we read, witnessing and taking part in the great human effort to achieve meaning through experience. A story, as we have said, is an image of the life process.

We must here be prepared to make a concession. We must simply recognize that some writers, and some stories, offend us at so deep a level that we simply cannot find the common ground. We reject a story as we reject a person in real life, as an offense to our basic values.

Sometimes, however, we reject a story not because it offends us by its theme. We may reject it simply because it is unconvincing—even though we agree with the theme. The story fails in its logic of motivation, in its presentation of character, in the attempt to make the idea develop from the action. Or perhaps the story with the acceptable theme is merely sentimental, and the emotional and logical response demanded is not really justified by the characters and events. In such a case, the author has made the idea we believe in seem too easy to come by, too mechanical; so we reject his story because we know that any valuable idea is really related to life and demands some depth of scrutiny. To sum up such objections, the story fails to convince us because it is not *coherent*. The parts do not hang together.

This leads us back to our opening comments in section 1, where we discuss the *truth of correspondence* and the *truth of coherence*. If we reject a story because the theme offends us, we are appealing to what we take to be the truth about life and values. If we reject a story because of the other reasons given—if, as we usually put it, it is "unconvincing"—we are appealing to the truth of coherence. The story does not hang together on its own terms and therefore whatever meaning it may claim to offer does not really come out of the experience of the story. Most of our problems with fiction spring from problems of coherence.

The notion of coherence leads to the notion that the meaning—the theme—of a good story is general and pervasive. If a story shows organic unity, all parts contribute to the meaning. We live, of course, in an imperfect world, and few stories perfectly digest all their material. Nevertheless, let us assume that a story is coherent until we have given it a fair inspection. One way to give this inspection is to try to find what idea, what feeling, what attitude consistently develops in the process of the story.

We can look at what kinds of characters and what kind of world are presented. That is a starting point, for it tells us something of the interests of the writer and his range of experience and sympathy. We can ask what is at stake for a character—or characters—and what discoveries develop in the end. We can look at the pattern of plot and try to see what significant issues emerge, and what patterns seem important. We can ask what is the tone of the story, what is the pervasive feeling. Is it ironical, cold, reportorial, sympathetically analytic, pathetic, comic, angry? We can ask about the validity of the speech of the characters and try to judge the style of the author. And always, we are asking if the story is coherent. Only then are we really ready to pass a final judgment on the theme.

Our examination of the stories that follow is not to be taken as an exercise in moral hunting. It is not even to be taken, primarily, as an exercise in giving a general statement to the themes of the various stories—although the attempt to make such statements is a necessary part of our study. More important than framing such general statements are these two considerations:

First, to see how the theme of a story, if it is a good story, *necessarily* develops from the experience as presented in the story. Here, of course, we are dealing with problems of coherence.

Second, to see how the theme is *uniquely* developed. To do this means that we must try to see how a theme—even supposing we are able to state it in general terms—may be, in fact, qualified and modified by the actual treatment in the story, so that what the story "says" finally becomes something more special, uniquely applicable. And this, of course, is the most difficult of our problems.

The stories in this section employ various methods in the presentation of their themes. There may be general statements. There may be *allegory* and *symbolism* (see Glossary). There may be realistic dramatic situation. *But we must always remember that the total story, including its general atmosphere, is the embodiment of the theme.* As we have said in discussing plot in section 2, we must think of the whole story as an image, however shadowy, of the meaning of experience. It may be thought of as a massive symbol of the theme.

LOVE: THREE PAGES FROM A SPORTSMAN'S BOOK

Guy de Maupassant

I HAVE just read among the general news in one of the papers a drama of passion. He killed her and then he killed himself, so he must have loved her. What matters He or She? Their love alone matters to me, and it does not interest me because it moves me or astonishes me or because it softens me or makes me think, but because it recalls to my mind a remembrance of my youth, a strange recollection of a hunting adventure where Love appeared to me, as the Cross appeared to the early Christians, in the midst of the heavens.

I was born with all the instincts and the senses of primitive man, tempered by the arguments and the restraints of a civilized being. I am passionately fond of shooting, yet the sight of the wounded animal, of the blood on its feathers and on my hands, affects my heart so as almost to make it stop.

That year the cold weather set in suddenly toward the end of autumn, and I was invited by one of my cousins, Karl de Rauville, to go with him and shoot ducks on the marshes at daybreak.

My cousin was a jolly fellow of forty with red hair, very stout and bearded, a country gentleman, an amiable semibrute of a happy disposition and endowed with that Gallic wit which makes even mediocrity agreeable. He lived in a house, half farmhouse, half château, situated in a broad valley through which a river ran. The hills right and left were covered with woods, old manorial woods where magnificent trees still remained and where the rarest feathered game in that part of France was to be found. Eagles were shot there occasionally, and birds of passage, such as rarely venture into our overpopulated part of the country, invariably lighted amid these giant oaks as if they knew or recognized some little corner of a primeval forest which had remained there to serve them as a shelter during these short nocturnal halts.

In the valley there were large meadows watered by trenches and separated by hedges; then, further on, the river, which up to that point had been kept between banks, expanded into a vast marsh. That marsh was the best shooting ground I ever saw. It was my cousin's chief care, and he kept it as a preserve. Through the rushes that covered it, and made it rustling and rough, narrow passages had been cut, through which the flat-bottomed boats, impelled and steered by poles, passed along silently over dead water, brushing up against the reeds and making the swift fish take refuge in the weeds and the wild fowl, with their pointed black heads, dive suddenly.

I am passionately fond of the water: of the sea, though it is too vast, too full of movement, impossible to hold; of the rivers which are so beautiful but which pass on and flee away; and above all of the marshes, where the whole unknown existence of aquatic animals palpitates. The marsh is an entire world in itself on the world of earth—a different world which has its own life, its settled inhabitants and its passing travelers, its voices, its noises and above all its mystery. Nothing is more impressive, nothing more disquieting, more terrifying occasionally, than a fen. Why should a vague terror hang over these low plains covered with water? Is it the low rustling of the rushes, the strange will-o'-the-wisp lights, the silence which prevails on calm nights, the still mists which hang over the surface like a shroud; or is it the almost inaudible splashing, so slight and so gentle, yet sometimes more terrifying than the cannons of men or the thunders of the skies, which make these marshes resemble countries one has dreamed of, terrible countries holding an unknown and dangerous secret?

No, something else belongs to it—another mystery, perhaps the mystery of the creation itself! For was it not in stagnant and muddy water, amid the heavy humidity of moist land under the heat of the sun, that the first germ of life pulsated and expanded to the day?

I arrived at my cousin's in the evening. It was freezing hard enough to split the stones.

During dinner, in the large room whose sideboards, walls and ceiling were covered with stuffed birds with wings extended or perched on branches to which they were nailed—hawks, herons, owls, nightjars, buzzards, tercels, vultures, falcons—my cousin, who, dressed in a sealskin jacket, himself resembled some strange animal from a cold country, told me what preparations he had made for that same night.

We were to start at half-past three in the morning so as to arrive at the place which he had chosen for our watching place at about half-past four. On that spot a hut had been built of lumps of ice so as to shelter us somewhat from the trying wind which precedes daybreak, a wind so cold as to tear the flesh like a saw, cut it like the blade of a knife, prick it like a poisoned sting, twist it like a pair of pincers, and burn it like fire.

My cousin rubbed his hands. "I have never known such a frost," he said; "it is already twelve degrees below zero at six o'clock in the evening."

I threw myself onto my bed immediately after we had finished our meal and went to sleep by the light of a bright fire burning in the grate.

At three o'clock he woke me. In my turn I put on a sheepskin and found my cousin Karl covered with a bearskin. After having each swallowed two cups of scalding coffee, followed by glasses of liqueur brandy, we started, accompanied by a gamekeeper and our dogs, Plongeon and Pierrot.

From the first moment that I got outside I felt chilled to the very marrow. It was one of those nights on which the earth seems dead with cold. The frozen air becomes resisting and palpable, such pain does it cause; no breath of wind moves it, it is fixed and motionless; it bites you, pierces through you, dries you, kills the trees, the plants, the insects, the small birds themselves, who fall from the branches onto the hard ground and become stiff themselves under the grip of the cold.

The moon, which was in her last quarter and was inclining all to one side, seemed fainting in the midst of space, so weak that she was unable to wane, forced to stay up yonder, seized and paralyzed by the severity of the weather. She shed a cold mournful light over the world, that dying and wan light which she gives us every month at the end of her period.

Karl and I walked side by side, our backs bent, our hands in our pockets and our guns under our arms. Our boots, which were wrapped in wool so that we might be able to walk without slipping on the frozen river, made no sound, and I looked at the white vapor which our dogs' breath made.

We were soon on the edge of the marsh and entered one of the lanes of dry rushes which ran through the low forest.

Our elbows, which touched the long ribbonlike leaves, left a slight noise behind us, and I was seized, as I had never been before, by the powerful and singular emotion which marshes cause in me. This one was dead, dead from cold, since we were walking on it in the middle of its population of dried rushes.

Suddenly, at the turn of one of the lanes, I perceived the ice hut which had been constructed to shelter us. I went in, and as we had nearly an hour to wait before the wandering birds would awake I rolled myself up in my rug in order to try and get warm. Then, lying on my back, I began to look at the misshapen moon, which had four horns through the vaguely transparent walls of this polar house. But the frost of the frozen marshes, the cold of these walls, the cold from the firmament penetrated me so terribly that I began to cough. My cousin Karl became uneasy.

"No matter if we do not kill much today," he said. "I do not want you to catch cold; we will light a fire." And he told the gamekeeper to cut some rushes.

We made a pile in the middle of our hut, which had a hole in the middle of the roof to let out the smoke, and when the red flames rose up to the clear crystal blocks, they began to melt, gently, imperceptibly, as if they were sweating. Karl, who had remained outside, called out to me: "Come and look here!" I went out of the hut and remained struck with astonishment. Our hut, in the shape of a cone, looked like an enormous diamond with a heart of fire which had been suddenly planted there in the midst of the frozen water of the marsh. And inside we saw two fantastic forms, those of our dogs, who were warming themselves at the fire.

But a peculiar cry, a lost, a wandering cry, passed over our heads, and the light from our hearth showed us the wild birds. Nothing moves one so much as the first clamor of a life which one does not see, which passes through the somber air so quickly and so far off, just before the first streak of a winter's day appears on the horizon. It seems to me, at this glacial hour of dawn, as if that passing cry which is carried away by the wings of a bird is the sigh of a soul from the world!

"Put out the fire," said Karl "it is getting daylight."

The sky was, in fact, beginning to grow pale, and the flights of ducks made long rapid streaks which were soon obliterated on the sky.

A stream of light burst out into the night; Karl had fired, and the two dogs ran forward.

And then nearly every minute now he, now I, aimed rapidly as soon as the shadow of a flying flock appeared above the rushes. And Pierrot and Plongeon, out of breath but happy, retrieved the bleeding birds whose eyes still, occasionally, looked at us.

The sun had risen, and it was a bright day with a blue sky, and we were thinking of taking our departure, when two birds with extended necks and outstretched wings glided rapidly over our heads. I fired, and one of them fell almost at my feet. It was a teal with a silver breast, and then, in the blue space above me, I heard a voice, the voice of a bird. It was short, repeated heart-rending lament; and the bird, the little animal that had been spared, began to turn round in the blue sky over our heads, looking at its dead companion which I was holding in my hand.

Karl was on his knees, his gun to his shoulder, watching it eagerly until it should be within shot. "You have killed the duck," he said, "and the drake will not fly away."

He certainly did not fly away; he circled over our heads continually and continued his cries. Never have any groans of suffering pained me so much as that desolate appeal, as that lamentable reproach of this poor bird which was lost in space.

Occasionally he took flight under the menace of the gun which followed his movements and seemed ready to continue his flight alone, but as he could not make up his mind to this he returned to find his mate.

"Leave her on the ground," Karl said to me; "he will come within shot by and by." And he did indeed come near us, careless of danger, infatuated by his animal love, by his affection for his mate which I had just killed.

Karl fired, and it was as if somebody had cut the string which held the bird suspended. I saw something black descend, and I heard the noise of a fall among the rushes. And Pierrot brought it to me.

I put them—they were already cold—into the same gamebag, and I returned to Paris the same evening.

DISCUSSION

1. State the theme of this story.

2. What do you make of the first paragraph? Why does the story interest the narrator?

3. What is the significance of the second paragraph? What conflict is there in the story?

4. Does the characterization of the cousin serve any purpose in relation to the theme?

5. What is the value, if any, of the long atmospheric description of the marshes?

6. What do you make of the last sentence of the story?

Love

Jesse Stuart

YESTERDAY when the bright sun blazed down on the wilted corn my father and I walked around the edge of the new ground to plan a fence. The cows kept coming through the chestnut oaks on the cliff and running over the young corn. They bit off the tips of the corn and trampled down the stubble.

My father walked in the cornbalk. Bob, our collie, walked in front of my father. We heard a ground squirrel whistle down over the bluff among the dead treetops at the clearing's edge. "Whoop, take him, Bob," said my father. He lifted up a young stalk of corn, with wilted dried roots, where the ground squirrel had dug it up for the sweet grain of corn left on its tender roots. This has been a dry spring and the corn has kept well in the earth where the grain has sprouted. The ground squirrels love this corn. They dig up rows of it and eat the sweet grains. The young corn stalks are killed and we have to replant the corn.

I can see my father keep sicking Bob after the ground squirrel. He jumped over the corn rows. He started to run toward the ground squirrel. I, too, started running toward the clearing's edge where Bob was jumping and barking. The dust flew in tiny swirls behind our feet. There was a cloud of dust behind us.

"It's a big bull blacksnake," said my father. "Kill him, Bob! Kill him, Bob!"

Bob was jumping and snapping at the snake so as to make it strike and throw itself off guard. Bob had killed twenty-eight copperheads this spring. He knows how to kill a snake. He doesn't rush to do it. He takes his time and does the job well.

"Let's don't kill the snake," I said. "A blacksnake is a harmless snake. It kills poison snakes. It kills the copperhead. It catches more mice from the fields than a cat."

I could see the snake didn't want to fight the dog. The snake wanted to get away. Bob wouldn't let it. I wondered why it was crawling toward a heap of black loamy earth at the bend of the hill. I wondered why it had

185

come from the chestnut oak sprouts and the matted greenbriars on the cliff. I looked as the snake lifted its pretty head in response to one of Bob's jumps. "It's not a bull blacksnake," I said. "It's a she-snake. Look at the white on her throat."

"A snake is an enemy to me," my father snapped. "I hate a snake. Kill it, Bob. Go in there and get that snake and quit playing with it!"

Bob obeyed my father. I hated to see him take this snake by the throat. She was so beautifully poised in the sunlight. Bob grabbed the white patch on her throat. He cracked her long body like an ox whip in the wind. He cracked it against the wind only. The blood spurted from her fine-curved throat. Something hit against my legs like pellets. Bob threw the snake down. I looked to see what had struck my legs. It was snake eggs. Bob had slung them from her body. She was going to the sand heap to lay her eggs, where the sun is the setting-hen that warms them and hatches them.

Bob grabbed her body there on the earth where the red blood was running down on the gray-piled loam. Her body was still writhing in pain. She acted like a green weed held over a new-ground fire. Bob slung her viciously many times. He cracked her limp body against the wind. She was now limber as a shoestring in the wind. Bob threw her riddled body back on the sand. She quivered like a leaf in the lazy wind, then her riddled body lay perfectly still. The blood colored the loamy earth around the snake.

"Look at the eggs, won't you?" said my father. We counted thirty-seven eggs. I picked an egg up and held it in my hand. Only a minute ago there was life in it. It was an immature seed. It would not hatch. Mother sun could not incubate it on the warm earth. The egg I held in my hand was almost the size of a quail's egg. The shell on it was thin and tough and the egg appeared under the surface to be a watery egg.

"Well, Bob, I guess you see now why this snake couldn't fight," I said. "It is life. Weaker devour the stronger even among human beings. Dog kills snake. Snake kills birds. Birds kill the butterflies. Man conquers all. Man, too, kills for sport."

Bob was panting. He walked ahead of us back to the house. His tongue was out of his mouth. He was tired. He was hot under his shaggy coat of hair. His tongue nearly touched the dry dirt and white flecks of foam dripped from it. We walked toward the house. Neither my father nor I spoke. I still thought about the dead snake. The sun was going down over the chestnut ridge. A lark was singing. It was late for a lark to sing. The red evening clouds floated above the pine trees on our pasture hill. My father stood beside the path. His black hair was moved by the wind. His face was red in the blue wind of day. His eyes looked toward the sinking sun.

"And my father hates a snake," I thought.

I thought about the agony women know of giving birth. I thought about how they will fight to save their children. Then, I thought of the snake. I thought it was silly for me to think such thoughts.

This morning my father and I got up with the chickens. He says one has to get up with the chickens to do a day's work. We got the posthole digger, ax, spud, measuring pole and the mattock. We started for the clearing's edge. Bob didn't go along.

The dew was on the corn. My father walked behind with the posthole digger across his shoulder. I walked in front. The wind was blowing. It was a good morning wind to breathe and a wind that makes one feel like he can get under the edge of a hill and heave the whole hill upside down.

I walked out the corn row where we had come yesterday afternoon. I looked in front of me. I saw something. I saw it move. It was moving like a huge black rope winds around a windlass. "Steady," I says to my father. "Here is the bull blacksnake." He took one step up beside me and stood. His eyes grew wide apart.

"What do you know about this," he said.

"You have seen the bull blacksnake now," I said. "Take a good look at him! He is lying beside his dead mate. He has come to her. He, perhaps, was on her trail yesterday."

The male snake had trailed her to her doom. He had come in the night, under the roof of stars, as the moon shed rays of light on the quivering clouds of green. He had found his lover dead. He was coiled beside her, and she was dead.

The bull blacksnake lifted his head and followed us as we walked around the dead snake. He would have fought us to his death. He would have fought Bob to his death. "Take a stick," said my father, "and throw him over the hill so Bob won't find him. Did you ever see anything to beat that? I've heard they'd do that. But this is my first time to see it." I took a stick and threw him over the bank into the dewy sprouts on the cliff.

DISCUSSION

1. This story is clearly very similar to "Love" by Maupassant, but the general "feel" of the treatment is different. What difference do you think this makes in the meaning?

2. Wherein does the conflict lie in this story?

3. What change, if any, comes about in the story?

4. Why did the author choose to tell this story in the first person? If the story were told in the third person what problems of exposition might arise that do not now appear?

THE KILLERS

Ernest Hemingway

THE door of Henry's lunchroom opened and two men came in. They sat down at the counter.

"What's yours?" George asked them.

"I don't know," one of the men said. "What do you want to eat, Al?"

"I don't know," said Al. "I don't know what I want to eat."

Outside it was getting dark. The street light came on outside the window. The two men at the counter read the menu. From the other end of the counter Nick Adams watched them. He had been talking to George when they came in.

"I'll have a roast pork tenderloin with apple sauce and mashed potatoes," the first man said.

"It isn't ready yet."

"What the hell do you put it on the card for?"

"That's the dinner," George explained. "You can get that at six o'clock."

George looked at the clock on the wall behind the counter.

"It's five o'clock."

"The clock says twenty minutes past five," the second man said.

"It's twenty minutes fast."

"Oh, to hell with the clock," the first man said, "What have you got to eat?"

"I can give you any kind of sandwiches," George said. "You can have ham and eggs, bacon and eggs, liver and bacon, or a steak."

"Give me chicken croquettes with green peas and cream sauce and mashed potatoes."

"That's the dinner."

"Everything we want's the dinner, eh? That's the way you work it."

"I can give you ham and eggs, bacon and eggs, liver—"

"I'll take ham and eggs," the man called Al said. He wore a derby hat and a black overcoat buttoned across the chest. His face was small and white and he had tight lips. He wore a silk muffler and gloves.

"Give me bacon and eggs," said the other man. He was about the same size as Al. Their faces were different, but they were dressed like twins. Both wore overcoats too tight for them. They sat leaning forward, their elbows on the counter.

"Got anything to drink?" Al asked.

"Silver beer, bevo, ginger ale." George said.

"I mean you got anything to *drink?*"

"Just those I said."

"This is a hot town," said the other. "What do they call it?"

"Summit."

"Ever hear of it?" Al asked his friend.

"No," said the friend.

"What do you do here nights?" Al asked.

"They eat the dinner," his friend said. "They all come here and eat the big dinner."

"That's right," George said.

"So you think that's right?" Al asked George.

"Sure."

"You're a pretty bright boy, aren't you?"

"Sure," said George.

"Well, you're not," said the other little man. "Is he, Al?"

"He's dumb," said Al. He turned to Nick. "What's your name?"

"Adams."

"Another bright boy," Al said. "Ain't he a bright boy, Max?"

"The town's full of bright boys," Max said.

George put the two platters, one of ham and eggs, the other of bacon and eggs, on the counter. He set down two side dishes of fried potatoes and closed the wicket into the kitchen.

"Which is yours?" he asked Al.

"Don't you remember?"

"Ham and eggs."

"Just a bright boy," Max said. He leaned forward and took the ham and eggs. Both men ate with their gloves on. George watched them eat.

"What are *you* looking at?" Max looked at George.

"Nothing."

"The hell you were. You were looking at me."

"Maybe the boy meant it for a joke, Max," Al said.

George laughed.

"*You* don't have to laugh," Max said to him. "*You* don't have to laugh at all, see?"

"All right," said George.

"So he thinks it's all right." Max turned to Al. "He thinks it's all right. That's a good one."

"Oh, he's a thinker," Al said. They went on eating.

"What's the bright boy's name down the counter?" Al asked Max.

"Hey, bright boy," Max said to Nick. "You go around on the other side of the counter with your boy friend."

"What's the idea?" Nick asked.

"There isn't any idea."

"You better go around, bright boy," Al said. Nick went around behind the counter.

"What's the idea?" George asked.

"None of your damn business," Al said. "Who's out in the kitchen?"

"The nigger."

"What do you mean the nigger?"

"The nigger that cooks."

"Tell him to come in."

"What's the idea?"

"Tell him to come in."

"Where do you think you are?"

"We know damn well where we are," the man called Max said, "Do we look silly?"

"You talk silly," Al said to him. "What the hell do you argue with this kid for? Listen," he said to George, "tell the nigger to come out here."

"What are you going to do to him?"

"Nothing. Use your head, bright boy. What would we do to a nigger?"

George opened the slit that opened back into the kitchen. "Sam," he called. "Come in here a minute."

The door to the kitchen opened and the nigger came in. "What was it?" he asked. The two men at the counter took a look at him.

"All right, nigger. You stand right there," Al said.

Sam, the nigger, standing in his apron, looked at the two men sitting at the counter. "Yes, sir," he said. Al got down from his stool.

"I'm going back to the kitchen with the nigger and bright boy," he said. "Go on back to the kitchen, nigger. You go with him, bright boy." The little man walked after Nick and Sam, the cook, back into the kitchen. The door shut after them. The man called Max sat at the counter opposite George. He didn't look at George but looked in the mirror that ran along back of the counter. Henry's had been made over from a saloon into a lunch counter.

"Well, bright boy," Max said, looking into the mirror, "why don't you say something?"

"What's it all about?"

"Hey, Al," Max called, "bright boy wants to know what it's all about."

"Why don't you tell him?" Al's voice came from the kitchen.

"What do you think it's all about?"

"I don't know."

"What do you think?"

Max looked into the mirror all the time he was talking.

"I wouldn't say."

"Hey, Al, bright boy says he wouldn't say what he thinks it's all about."

"I can hear you, all right," Al said from the kitchen. He had propped open the slit that dishes passed through into the kitchen with a catsup bottle. "Listen, bright boy," he said from the kitchen to George. "Stand a little further along the bar. You move a little to the left, Max." He was like a photographer arranging for a group picture.

"Talk to me, bright boy," Max said. "What do you think's going to happen?"

George did not say anything.

"I'll tell you," Max said. "We're going to kill a Swede. Do you know a big Swede named Ole Andreson?"

"Yes."

"He comes here to eat every night, don't he?"

"Sometimes he comes here."

"He comes here at six o'clock, don't he?"

"If he comes."

"We know all that, bright boy," Max said. "Talk about something else. Ever go to the movies?"

"Once in a while."

"You ought to go to the movies more. The movies are fine for a bright boy like you."

"What are you going to kill Ole Andreson for? What did he ever do to you?"

"He never had a chance to do anything to us. He never even seen us."

"And he's only going to see us once," Al said from the kitchen.

"What are you going to kill him for, then?" George asked.

"We're killing him for a friend. Just to oblige a friend, bright boy."

"Shut up," said Al from the kitchen. "You talk too goddamn much."

"Well, I got to keep bright boy amused. Don't I, bright boy?"

"You talk too damn much," Al said. "The nigger and my bright boy are amused by themselves. I got them tied up like a couple of girl friends in a convent."

"I suppose you were in a convent."

"You never know."

"You were in a kosher convent. That's where you were."

George looked up at the clock.

"If anybody comes in you tell them the cook is off, and if they keep after it, you tell them you'll go back and cook yourself. Do you get that, bright boy?"

"All right," George said. "What you going to do with us afterward?"

"That'll depend," Max said. "That's one of those things you never know at the time."

George looked up at the clock. It was a quarter past six. The door from the street opened. A street-car motorman came in.

"Hello, George," he said. "Can I get supper?"

"Sam's gone out," George said. "He'll be back in about half an hour."

"I'd better go up the street," the motorman said. George looked at the clock. It was twenty minutes past six.

"That was nice, bright boy," Max said. "You're a regular little gentleman." At six-fifty-five George said: "He's not coming."

Two other people had been in the lunchroom. Once George had gone out to the kitchen and made a ham-and-egg sandwich "to go" that a man wanted to take with him. Inside the kitchen he saw Al, his derby hat tipped back, sitting on a stool beside the wicket with the muzzle of a sawed-off shotgun resting on the ledge. Nick and the cook were back to back in the corner, a towel tied in each of their mouths. George had cooked the sandwich, wrapped it up in oiled paper, put it in a bag, brought it in, and the man had paid for it and gone out.

"Bright boy can do everything," Max said. "He can cook and everything. You'd make some girl a nice wife, bright boy."

"Yes?" George said. "Your friend, Ole Andreson, isn't going to come."

"We'll give him ten minutes," Max said.

Max watched the mirror and the clock. The hands of the clock marked seven o'clock, and then five minutes past seven.

"Come on, Al," said Max. "We better go. He's not coming."

"Better give him five minutes," Al said from the kitchen.

In the five minutes a man came in, and George explained that the cook was sick.

"Why the hell don't you get another cook?" the man asked. "Aren't you running a lunch counter?" He went out.

"Come on, Al," Max said.

"What about the two bright boys and the nigger?"

"They're all right."

"You think so?"

"Sure. We're through with it."

"I don't like it," said Al. "It's sloppy. You talk too much."

"Oh, what the hell," said Max. "We got to keep amused, haven't we?"

"You talk too much, all the same," Al said. He came out from the kitchen. The cut-off barrels of the shotgun made a slight bulge under the waist of his too tight-fitting overcoat. He straightened his coat with his gloved hands.

"So long, bright boy," he said to George. "You got a lot of luck."

"That's the truth," Max said. "You ought to play the races, bright boy."

The two of them went out the door. George watched them, through the window, pass under the arc light and cross the street. In their tight overcoats and derby hats they looked like a vaudeville team. George went back through the swinging door into the kitchen and untied Nick and the cook.

"I don't want any more of that," said Sam, the cook. "I don't want any more of that."

Nick stood up. He had never had a towel in his mouth before.

"Say," he said. "What the hell?" He was trying to swagger it off.

"They were going to kill Ole Andreson," George said. "They were going to shoot him when he came in to eat."

"Ole Andreson?"

"Sure."

The cook felt the corners of his mouth with his thumbs.

"They all gone?" he asked.

"Yeah," said George. "They're gone now."

"I don't like it," said the cook. "I don't like any of it at all."

"Listen," George said to Nick. "You better go see Ole Andreson."

"All right."

"You better not have anything to do with it at all," Sam, the cook, said. "You better stay way out of it."

"Don't go if you don't want to," George said.

"Mixing up in this ain't going to get you anywhere," the cook said. "You stay out of it."

"I'll go see him," Nick said to George. "Where does he live?"

The cook turned away.

"Little boys always know what they want to do," he said.

"He lives up at Hirsch's rooming house," George said to Nick.

"I'll go up there."

Outside the arc light shone through the bare branches of a tree. Nick walked up the street beside the car tracks and turned at the next arc light down a side street. Three houses up the street was Hirsch's rooming house. Nick walked up the two steps and pushed the bell. A woman came to the door.

"Is Ole Andreson here?"

"Do you want to see him?"

"Yes, if he's in."

Nick followed the woman up a flight of stairs and back to the end of a corridor. She knocked on the door.

"Who is it?"

"It's somebody to see you, Mr. Andreson," the woman said.

"It's Nick Adams."

"Come in."

Nick opened the door and went into the room. Ole Andreson was lying on the bed with all his clothes on. He had been a heavyweight prize fighter and he was too long for the bed. He lay with his head on two pillows. He did not look at Nick.

"What was it?" he asked.

"I was up at Henry's," Nick said, "and two fellows came in and tied up me and the cook, and they said they were going to kill you."

It sounded silly when he said it. Ole Andreson said nothing.

"They put us out in the kitchen," Nick went on. "They were going to shoot you when you came in to supper."

Ole Andreson looked at the wall and did not say anything.

"George thought I better come and tell you about it."

"There isn't anything I can do about it," Ole Andreson said.

"I'll tell you what they were like."

"I don't want to know what they were like," Ole Andreson said. He looked at the wall. "Thanks for coming to tell me about it."

"That's all right."

Nick looked at the big man lying on the bed.

"Don't you want me to go and see the police?"

"No," Ole Andreson said. "That wouldn't do any good."

"Isn't there something I could do?"

"No. There ain't anything to do."

"Maybe it was just a bluff."

"No. It ain't just a bluff."

Ole Andreson rolled over toward the wall.

"The only thing is," he said, talking toward the wall, "I just can't make up my mind to go out. I been in here all day."

"Couldn't you get out of town?"

"No," Ole Andreson said. "I'm through with all that running around."

He looked at the wall.

"There ain't anything to do now."

"Couldn't you fix it up some way?"

"No. I got in wrong." He talked in the same flat voice. "There ain't anything to do. After a while I'll make up my mind to go out."

"I better go back and see George," Nick said.

"So long," said Ole Andreson. He did not look toward Nick. "Thanks for coming around."

Nick went out. As he shut the door he saw Ole Andreson with all his clothes on, lying on the bed looking at the wall.

"He's been in his room all day," the landlady said downstairs. "I guess he don't feel well. I said to him: 'Mr. Andreson, you ought to go out and take a walk on a nice fall day like this,' but he didn't feel like it."

"He doesn't want to go out."

"I'm sorry he don't feel well," the woman said. "He's an awfully nice man. He was in the ring, you know."

"I know it."

"You'd never know it except from the way his face is," the woman said. They stood talking just inside the street door. "He's just as gentle."

"Well, good-night, Mrs. Hirsch," Nick said.

"I'm not Mrs. Hirsch," the woman said. "She owns the place. I just look after it for her. I'm Mrs. Bell."

"Well, good-night, Mrs. Bell," Nick said.

"Good-night," the woman said.

Nick walked up the dark street to the corner under the arc light, and then along the car tracks to Henry's eating house. George was inside, back of the counter.

"Did you see Ole?"

"Yes," said Nick. "He's in his room and he won't go out."

The cook opened the door from the kitchen when he heard Nick's voice.

"I don't even listen to it," he said and shut the door.

"Did you tell him about it?" George asked.

"Sure. I told him but he knows what it's all about."

"What's he going to do?"

"Nothing."

"They'll kill him."

"I guess they will."

"He must have got mixed up in something in Chicago."

"I guess so," said Nick.

"It's a hell of a thing."

"It's an awful thing," Nick said.

They did not say anything. George reached down for a towel and wiped the counter.

"I wonder what he did?" Nick said.

"Double-crossed somebody. That's what they kill them for."

"I'm going to get out of this town," Nick said.

"Yes," said George. "That's a good thing to do."

"I can't stand to think about him waiting in the room and knowing he's going to get it. It's too damned awful."

"Well," said George, "you better not think about it."

DISCUSSION

There are certain fairly obvious points to be made about the technique of this story. It breaks up into one long scene and three short scenes. Indeed, the method is so thoroughly scenic that not over three or four sentences are required to make the transitions. The focus of narration is objective throughout; practically all information is conveyed in simple realistic dialogue. In the first scene the revelation of the mission of the gangsters is accomplished through a few significant details—the fact that the gangsters eat with gloves (to avoid leaving fingerprints), the fact that they keep their eyes on the mirror behind the bar, the fact that, after Nick and the cook have been tied up, the gangster who has the shotgun at the service window stations his friend and George out front "like a photographer arranging for a group picture"—all of this before the specific nature of their mission is made clear.

Other observations concerning the technique of the story could be made—the cleverness of composition, the subtlety with which the suspense is maintained in the first scene by the banter of the gangsters, and then is transferred to another level in the second scene. But such observations, though they are worth making, do not answer the question that first comes (or should come) to the reader's mind: what is the story about?

The importance of giving an early answer to this question can be seen by considering two readers who have typical but different reactions to the story. One reader, upon first acquaintance with the story, is inclined to feel that it is exhausted in the first scene, and in fact that the first scene itself does not come to focus—does not have a "point." The other reader sees that the first scene, with its lack of resolution, is really being used to "charge" the second scene. He finds his point in Ole Andreson's decision not to try to escape the gangsters—to stop "all that running around." This reader feels that the story should end here. He sees no relevance in the last several pages of the story, and wonders why the author has flattened his effect. The first reader, we may say, feels that "The Killers" is the gangsters' story—a story of action that does not come off. The second and more sophisticated reader interprets it as Andreson's story, though perhaps with some wonder that Andreson's story has been approached so indirectly and is allowed to trail off so irrelevantly.

In other words, the second reader is inclined to transpose the question "What is the story about?" into the question, "Whose story is it?" When he states the question in this way, he confronts the fact that Hemingway has left the story focused not on the gangsters, nor on Andreson, but on the boys at the lunchroom. Consider the last sentences of the story:

> "I'm going to get out of this town," Nick said.
> "Yes," said George. "That's a good thing to do."
> "I can't stand to think about him waiting in the room and knowing he's going to get it. It's too damned awful."
> "Well," said George, "you better not think about it."

So, of the two boys, it is obviously Nick on whom the impression has been made. George has managed to come to terms with the situation. By this line of reasoning, it is Nick's story. And the story is about the discovery of evil.

This definition of the theme of the story, even if it appears acceptable, must, of course, be tested against the detailed structure. In evaluating the story, as well as in understanding it, the skill with which the theme has been assimilated must be taken into account. For instance, to put a concrete question: does the last paragraph of the story illuminate for the reader certain details that had, at their first appearance, seemed to be merely casual, realistic items?

If we take the theme to be the boy's discovery of evil, several such details do find their meaning. Nick had been bound and gagged by the gangsters, and has been released by George. To quote: "Nick stood up. He had never had a towel in his mouth before. 'Say,' he said. 'What the hell?' He was trying to swagger it off." Being gagged was something you read about in a thriller and not something that happened to you; and the first effect is one of excitement, almost pleasurable, certainly an excuse for a manly pose. (It may be worth noting in this connection that Hemingway uses the specific word *towel* and not the general word *gag*. It is true that the word *towel* has a certain sensory advantage over the word *gag*—because it suggests the coarseness of the fabric and the unpleasant drying effect on the membranes of the mouth. But this advantage in immediacy is probably overshadowed by another: the towel is sanctified in the thriller as the gag, and here the cliché of the thriller has come true.) The way the whole incident is given—"He had *never* had a towel in his mouth *before*"—charges the apparently realistic detail as a pointer to the final discovery.

Another pointer appears in the gangster's wisecrack about the movies: "You ought to go to the movies more. The movies are fine for a bright boy like you." In one sense, of course, the iterated remarks about the movies, coming just after the gangsters have made their arrangements in the lunchroom, serve as a kind of indirect exposition: the reader knows the standard reason and procedure for gang killings. But at another level, these remarks emphasize the discovery that the unreal clichés of the newspaper and movie have become a reality.

The boy to whom the gangster speaks understands the allusion to the movies, for he immediately asks: "What are you going to kill Ole Andreson for? What did he ever do to you?" "He never had a chance to do anything to us. He never even seen us," the gangster replies.

The gangster accepts, and even glories a little in, the terms by which he lives—terms that transcend the small-town world. He lives, as it were, by a code, which lifts him above questions of personal likes or personal animosities. This unreal code—unreal because it denies the ordinary personal elements of life—has, like the gag, suddenly been discovered as real. This unreal and theatrical quality is reflected in the description of the gangsters as, after leaving the lunchroom, they go out under the arc light and cross the street: "In their tight overcoats and derby hats they looked like a vaudeville team." It even permeates their dialogue. The dialogue itself has the sleazy quality of mechanized gag and wisecrack, a kind of stereotyped banter that is always *a priori* to the situation and overrides the situation. On this level the comparison to the vaudeville team is a kind of explicit summary of details that have been presented more indirectly and dramatically. On another level, the weary and artificial quality of their wit has a grimmer implication. It is an index to the professional casualness with which they accept a situation that to the boys is shocking. They are contemptuous and even bored, with the contempt and boredom of the initiated when confronted by callow lay observers. This code, which has suddenly been transferred from the artificial world of the movie thriller into reality, is shocking enough, but even more shocking to Nick is the fact that Ole Andreson, the hunted man, accepts the code too. Confronted by the news that Nick brings, he rejects all the responses the boy would consider normal: he will not call the police; he will not regard the thing as a mere bluff; he will not leave town. "Couldn't you fix it up some way?" the boy asks. "No. I got in wrong."

As we observed earlier, for one type of reader this is the high point of the story, and the story should end here. If we are to convince such a reader that the author is right in proceeding, we are obliged to answer his question "What is the significance of the rather tame, and apparently irrelevant, little incident that follows, the conversation with Mrs. Bell?" It is sometimes said that Mrs. Bell serves to give a bit of delayed exposition or even to point the story by gaining sympathy for Andreson, who is, to her, "an awfully nice man," not at all like her idea of a pugilist. But this is not enough to satisfy the keen reader, and he is right in refusing to be satisfied with this. Mrs. Bell is, really, the Porter at Hell Gate in *Macbeth*. She is the world of normality, which is shocking now from the very fact that life continues to flow on in its usual course. To her, Ole Andreson is just a nice man, despite the fact that he has been in the ring; he ought to go out and take his walk on such a nice day. She points to his ordinary individuality, which is in contrast to the demands of the mechanical code. Even if the unreal horror of the movie thriller has become real, even if the hunted man lies upstairs on his bed trying to make up his mind to go out, Mrs. Bell is still Mrs. Bell. She is not Mrs. Hirsch. Mrs. Hirsch owns the place, she just looks after it for Mrs. Hirsch. She is Mrs. Bell: normal life.

At the door of the rooming house Nick has met Mrs. Bell—normality unconscious of the ironical contrast it presents. Back at the lunchroom, Nick returns to the normal scene, but the normal scene conscious of the impingement of horror. It is the same old lunchroom, with George and the cook going about their business. But they, unlike Mrs. Bell, know what has happened. Yet even they are scarcely deflected from their ordinary routine. George and the cook represent two different levels of response to the situation. The cook, from the first, has wanted no part of it. When he hears Nick's voice, on his return, he says, "I don't even listen to it." And he shuts the door. But George had originally suggested that Nick go see Andreson, telling him, however, "Don't go if you don't want to." After Nick has told his story, George can comment, "It's a hell of a thing," but George, in one sense at least, has accepted the code, too. When Nick says, "I wonder what he did?" George replies, with an echo of the killers' own casualness: "Double-crossed somebody. That's what they kill them for." In other words, the situation is shocking to the cook only insofar as it involves his own safety. George is aware of other implications but can dismiss them. Neither of them makes a discovery of evil in the situation. But Nick does, for he has not yet learned to take George's adult advice: "Well, you better not think about it."

Aside from such structural concerns as the relations among incidents and the attitudes of the characters, other interesting questions can be raised. What is Hemingway's attitude toward his material? How does this attitude find its expression?

Perhaps the simplest approach to these questions may be through a consideration of the kinds of situations and characters that Hemingway wrote about. The situations are usually violent ones: the hard-drinking and sexually promiscuous world of the *The Sun Also Rises;* the chaotic and brutal world of war in *A Farewell to Arms, For Whom the Bell Tolls,* and "A Way You'll Never Be"; the dangerous and exciting world of the bull ring or the prize ring in *The Sun Also Rises, Death in the Afternoon,* "The Undefeated," and "Fifty Grand"; the world of crime in "The Killers," *To Have and to Have Not,* and "The Gambler, the Nun, and the Radio." Hemingway's typical characters are usually tough men, experienced in the hard worlds they inhabit, and apparently insensitive: Lieutenant Henry in *A Farewell to Arms,* the big-game hunter in "The Snows of Kilimanjaro," Robert Jordan in *For Whom the Bell Tolls,* or even Ole Andreson. They are, also, usually defeated men. Out of their practical defeat, however, they have managed to salvage something. And here we come upon Hemingway's basic interest in such situations and such characters. They are not defeated except upon their own terms; some of them have even courted defeat; certainly, they have maintained, even in the practical defeat, an ideal of themselves, formulated or unformulated, by which they have lived.

Hemingway's attitude is, in a sense, like that of Robert Louis Stevenson, as Stevenson states it in one of his essays, "Pulvis et Umbra":

> Poor soul, here for so little, cast among so many hardships, filled with desires so incommensurate and so inconsistent, savagely surrounded, savagely descended, irremediably condemned to prey upon his fellow lives: who should have blamed him had he been of a piece with his destiny and a being merely barbarous? And we look and behold him instead filled with imperfect virtues: . . . an ideal of decency, to which he would rise if it were possible; a limit of shame, below which, if it be possible, he will not stoop. . . . Man is indeed marked for failure in his efforts to do right. But where the best consistently miscarry, how tenfold more remarkable that all should continue to strive; and surely we should find it both touching and inspiriting, that in a field from which success is banished, our race should not cease to labor. . . . It matters not where we look, under what climate we observe him, in what stage of society, in what depth of ignorance, burthened with what erroneous morality; by campfires in Assiniboia, the snow powdering his shoulders, the wind plucking his blanket, as he sits, passing the ceremonial calumet and uttering his grave opinions like a Roman senator; in ships at sea, a man inured to hardship and vile pleasures, his brightest hope a fiddle in a tavern and a bedizened trull who sells herself to rob him, and he for all that, simple, innocent, cheerful, kindly like a child, constant to toil, brave to drown, for others; . . . in the brothel, the discard of society, living mainly on strong drink, fed with affronts, a fool, a thief, the comrade of thieves, and even here keeping the point of honor and the touch of pity, often repaying the world's scorn with service, often standing firm upon a scruple, and at a certain cost, rejecting riches;—everywhere some virtue cherished or affected, everywhere some decency of thought and carriage, everywhere the ensign of man's ineffectual goodness! . . . under every circumstance of failure, without hope, without health, without thanks, still obscurely fighting the lost fight of virtue, still clinging, in the brothel or on the scaffold, to some rag of honor, the poor jewel of their souls! They may seek to escape, and yet they cannot; it is not alone their privilege and glory, but their doom, they are condemned to some nobility . . .

For Stevenson, the world in which this drama is played out is, objectively considered, a violent and meaningless world: "our rotary island loaded with predatory life and more drenched with blood . . . than ever mutinied ship, scuds through space." This is Hemingway's world, too. But its characters, at least those whose stories Hemingway cares to tell, make one gallant effort to redeem the incoherence and meaninglessness of this world: they attempt to impose some form upon the disorder of their lives, the technique of the bullfighter or sportsman, the discipline of the soldier, the code of the gangster, which, even though brutal and dehumanizing, has its own ethic. (Ole Andreson is willing to take his medicine without whining. Or the dying Mexican in "The Gambler, the Nun, and the Radio" refuses to squeal, despite the detective's argument: "One can, with honor, denounce one's assailant.") The form is never quite adequate to subdue the world, but the fidelity to it is part of the gallantry of defeat.

We have said that the typical Hemingway hero is tough and, apparently, insensitive. But only apparently, for the fidelity to a code, to a discipline, may be an index to a sensitivity that allows his characters to see, at moments, their true plight. At times, and usually at times of stress, it is the tough man—for Hemingway, the disciplined man—who actually is aware of pathos or tragedy. The individual toughness (which may be taken to be the private discipline demanded by the world), may find itself in conflict with some more natural and spontaneous human emotion; in contrast with this, the discipline may, even, seem to be inhuman; but the Hemingway hero, though he is aware of the claims of this spontaneous human emotion, is afraid to yield to those claims because he has learned that the only way to hold on to "honor," to individuality, to the human order as against the brute chaos of the world, is to live by his code. This is the irony of the situation in which the hero finds himself. Hemingway's heroes are aristocrats in the sense that they are the initiate, and practice a lonely virtue.

Hemingway's heroes utter themselves, not in rant and bombast, but in terms of ironic understatement. This understatement, stemming from the contrast between the toughness and the sensitivity, the violence and the sensitivity, is a constant aspect of Hemingway's method, an aspect that was happily caught in a cartoon in the *New Yorker* some years ago. The cartoonist showed a brawny, hairy forearm and a muscled hand clutching a little rose. The cartoon was entitled "The Soul of Ernest Hemingway." Just as there is a margin of victory in the defeat of the Hemingway characters, so there is a little margin of sensibility in their brutal and violent world.

Ole Andreson, as we have noted, fits into this pattern. Andreson won't whimper. But Ole Andreson's story is buried in the larger story, which is focused on Nick. How does Nick Adams fit into the pattern? Hemingway, as a matter of fact, is accustomed to treat his basic situation at one or the other of two levels. There is the story of the person who is already initiated, who has already adopted his appropriate code, or discipline, in the world that otherwise he cannot cope with. (One finds examples in Jake and Brett in *The Sun Also Rises,* Jordan and Pilar in *For*

Whom the Bell Tolls, the bullfighter in "The Undefeated," and many other stories.) There is also the story of the process of the initiation, the discovery of evil and disorder, and the first step toward the mastery of the discipline. This is Nick's story. (The same basic situation occurs in many other stories by Hemingway, for example, "Up in Michigan," "Indian Camp," and "The Three-Day Blow.")

Besides being tough and apparently insensitive, the typical Hemingway character is also, usually, simple. The impulse that led Hemingway to the simple character is akin to that that led the Romantic poet Wordsworth to the same choice. Wordsworth felt that peasants or children, who are the characters of so many of his poems, were more honest in their responses than the cultivated man, and therefore more poetic. Instead of Wordsworth's typical peasant we find in Hemingway's work the bullfighter, the soldier, the revolutionist, the sportsman, and the gangster; instead of Wordsworth's children, we find young men like Nick. There are, of course, differences between the approach of Wordsworth and that of Hemingway, but there is little difference on the point of marginal sensibility.

The main difference between the two writers depends on the difference in their two worlds. Hemingway's world is a more disordered world, and more violent, than the simple and innocent world of Wordsworth. Therefore, the sensibility of Hemingway's characters is in sharper contrast to the nature of his world. This creates an irony not found in the work of Wordsworth. Hemingway plays down the sensibility as such, and sheathes it in the code of toughness. Gertrude Stein once wrote of Hemingway: "Hemingway is the shyest and proudest and sweetest-smelling storyteller of my reading." When she refers to his "shyness" she was, apparently, thinking of his use of irony and understatement. The typical character is sensitive, but his sensitivity is never insisted upon; he may be worthy of pity, but he never demands it. The underlying attitude in Hemingway's work may be stated like this: pity is valid only when it is wrung from a man who has been seasoned by experience, and is only earned by a man who never demands it. Therefore, a premium is placed upon the fact of violent experience.

A further question suggests itself. How is Hemingway's style related to his basic fictional concerns? In "The Killers," as in many of his other stories, the style is simple even to the point of monotony. The characteristic sentence is simple, or compound; and if compound, there is no implied subtlety in the coordination of the clauses. The paragraph structure is, characteristically, based on simple sequence.[1] First, we can observe that there is an obvious relation between this style and the characters and situations with which the author is concerned: unsophisticated

---

[1]In some of Hemingway's work, especially in the novels, there are examples of a more fluent, lyrical style than is found in "The Killers." But even in such examples, one can observe that the fluency and the lyrical effect is based on the conjunction *and*—that there is no process of subordination but rather a process of sequence in terms of direct perceptions. The lyrical quality of such examples is to be taken as a manifestation of the "marginal sensibility," as can be demonstrated by an analysis of the situations in which the lyrical passages occur.

characters and simple, fundamental situations are rendered in an uncomplicated style.

There is another, and more interesting, aspect of the question of style, involving not the sensibility of the characters but the sensibility of the author himself. The short simple rhythms, the succession of coordinate clauses, and the general lack of subordination—all suggest a dislocated and ununified world. Hemingway was apparently trying to suggest in his style the direct experience—things as seen and felt, one·after another, and not as the mind arranges and analyzes them. A style that involves subordination and complicated shadings of emphasis, a style that tends toward complex sentences with many qualifying clauses and phrases, implies an exercise of critical discrimination—the sifting of experience through the intellect. But Hemingway, apparently, was primarily concerned with giving the immediate impact of experience rather than with analyzing and evaluating it in detail. (We can notice, in this connection, that in his work he rarely indulges in any psychological analysis, and is rarely concerned with the detailed development of a character.) His very style, then, seems to imply that the use of the intellect, with its careful discriminations, may blur the rendering of experience and may falsify it; and this style, in connection with his basic concern for the character of marginal sensibility, may be taken as implying a distrust of the intellect in solving man's basic problems. Despite the application of the human intellect to the problems of the world, he seems to be saying, the world is still a disorderly and brutal mess. And it is hard to find any sure scale of values. Therefore, it is well to remember the demands of fundamental situations—those involving sex, love; danger, and death, in which the instinctive life is foremost—because they are frequently glossed over or falsified by social conventions or sterile intellectuality. It is well to remember the simple virtues of courage, honesty, fidelity, discipline.

But is all of this a way of saying that Hemingway is really writing innocently, without calculation, crudely? Now, as a matter of fact, his style is a result of calculation, and is not, strictly speaking, spontaneous and naive at all. His style is, then, a dramatic device, developed because of its appropriateness to the total effect he intends to give. A writer who was in point of fact uninstructed and spontaneous would probably not be able to achieve the impression of spontaneity and immediacy found in Hemingway's best work, the work in which his basic attitude and subject matter can be functionally coordinated.

In our comment on this story we have tried, among other and more obvious concerns, to relate the style of the story to the theme and then to relate the various qualities of this story to the general body of Hemingway's work and his attitude toward his world. Ordinarily we have been studying stories taken individually, but it is time for us to realize that the various (and often quite different) stories done by a good writer always have some fundamental unifying attitudes—for a man can be only himself. Since this is true, we can nearly always enter more deeply into a piece of fiction and understand it more fully when we are prepared to relate it to the writer's other work. A good writer does not offer us, for instance, a glittering variety of themes. He probably treats, over and over, those few themes that seem to him most important in his actual living and observation of life.

Suppose you had read "The District Doctor" or "The Drunkard" without knowing the author and had been told it was by Hemingway. Would you have believed this? If not, why not?

DEATH IN THE WOODS

Sherwood Anderson

SHE was an old woman and lived on a farm near the town in which I lived. All country and small-town people have seen such old women, but no one knows much about them. Such an old woman comes into town driving an old worn-out horse or she comes afoot carrying a basket. She may own a few hens and have eggs to sell. She brings them in a basket and takes them to a grocer. There she trades them in. She gets some salt pork and some beans. Then she gets a pound or two of sugar and some flour.

Afterwards she goes to the butcher's and asks for some dog meat. She may spend ten or fifteen cents, but when she does she asks for something. Formerly the butchers gave liver to anyone who wanted to carry it away. In our family we were always having it. Once one of my brothers got a whole cow's liver at the slaughterhouse near the fairgrounds in our town. We had it until we were sick of it. It never cost a cent. I have hated the thought of it ever since.

The old farm woman got some liver and a soupbone. She never visited with anyone, and as soon as she got what she wanted she lit out for home. It made quite a load for such an old body. No one gave her a lift. People drive right down a road and never notice an old woman like that.

There was such an old woman who used to come into town past our house one summer and fall when I was a young boy and was sick with what was called inflammatory rheumatism. She went home later carrying a heavy pack on her back. Two or three large gaunt-looking dogs followed at her heels.

The old woman was nothing special. She was one of the nameless ones that hardly anyone knows, but she got into my thoughts. I have just suddenly now, after all these years, remembered her and what happened. It is a story. Her name was Grimes, and she lived with her husband and son in a small unpainted house on the bank of a small creek four miles from town.

The husband and son were a tough lot. Although the son was but twenty-one, he had already served a term in jail. It was whispered about that the woman's husband stole horses and ran them off to some other county. Now and then, when a horse turned up missing, the man had also disappeared. No one ever caught him. Once, when I was loafing at Tom Whitehead's livery barn, the man came there and sat on the bench in front. Two or three other men were there, but no one spoke to him. He sat for a few minutes and then got up and went away. When he was leaving he turned around and stared at the men. There was a look of defiance in his eyes. "Well, I have tried to be friendly. You don't want to talk to me. It has been so wherever I have gone in this town. If, some day, one of your fine horses turns up missing, well, then what?" He did not say anything actually. "I'd like to bust one of you on the jaw," was about what his eyes said. I remember how the look in his eyes made me shiver.

The old man belonged to a family that had had money once. His name was Jake Grimes. It all comes back clearly now. His father, John Grimes, had owned a sawmill when the country was new, and had made money. Then he got to drinking and running after women. When he died there wasn't much left.

Jake blew in the rest. Pretty soon there wasn't any more lumber to cut and his land was nearly all gone.

He got his wife off a German farmer, for whom he went to work one June day in the wheat harvest. She was a young thing then and scared to death. You see, the farmer was up to something with the girl—she was, I think a bound girl and his wife had her suspicions. She took it out on the girl when the man wasn't around. Then, when the wife had to go off to town for supplies, the farmer got after her. She told young Jake that nothing really ever happened, but he didn't know whether to believe it or not.

He got her pretty easy himself, the first time he was out with her. He wouldn't have married her if the German farmer hadn't tried to tell him where to get off. He got her to go riding with him in his buggy one night when he was threshing on the place, and then he came for her the next Sunday night.

She managed to get out of the house without her employer's seeing, but when she was getting into the buggy he showed up. It was almost dark, and he just popped up suddenly at the horse's head. He grabbed the horse by the bridle and Jake got out his buggy whip.

They had it out all right! The German was a tough one. Maybe he didn't care whether his wife knew or not. Jake hit him over the face and shoulders with the buggy whip, but the horse got to acting up and he had to get out.

Then the two men went for it. The girl didn't see it. The horse started to run away and went nearly a mile down the road before the girl got him stopped. Then she managed to tie him to a tree beside the road. (I wonder how I know all this. It must have stuck in my mind from small-town tales when I was a boy.) Jake found her there after he got through with the German. She was huddled up in the buggy seat, crying, scared to death. She told Jake a lot of stuff, how the German had tried to get her, how he chased her once into the barn, how another time, when they happened to be alone in the house together, he tore her dress open clear down the front. The German, she said, might have got her that time if he hadn't heard his old woman drive in at the gate. She had been off to town for supplies. Well, she would be putting the horse in the barn. The German managed to sneak off to the fields without his wife seeing. He told the girl he would kill her if she told. What could she do? She told a lie about ripping her dress in the barn when she was feeding the stock. I remember now that she was a bound girl and did not know where her father and mother were. Maybe she did not have any father. You know what I mean.

Such bound children were often enough cruelly treated. They were children who had no parents, slaves really. There were very few orphan homes then. They were legally bound into some home. It was a matter of pure luck how it came out.

II

She married Jake and had a son and a daughter, but the daughter died.

Then she settled down to feed stock. That was her job. At the German's place she had cooked the food for the German and his wife. The wife was a strong woman with big hips and worked most of the time in the fields with her husband. She fed them and fed the cows in the barn, fed the pigs, the horses and the chickens. Every moment of every day, as a young girl, was spent feeding something.

Then she married Jake Grimes and he had to be fed. She was a slight thing, and when she had been married for three or four years, and after the two children were born, her slender shoulders became stooped.

Jake always had a lot of big dogs around the house, that stood near the unused sawmill near the creek. He was always trading horses when he wasn't stealing something and had a lot of poor bony ones about. Also he kept three or four pigs and a cow. They were all pastured in the few acres left of the Grimes place and Jake did little enough work.

He went into debt for a threshing outfit and ran it for several years, but it did not pay. People did not trust him. They were afraid he would steal the grain at night. He had to go a long way off to get work and it cost too much to get there. In the winter he hunted and cut a little firewood, to be sold in some nearby town. When the son grew up he was just like the father. They got drunk together. If there wasn't anything to eat in the house when they came home the old man gave his old woman a cut over the head. She had a few chickens of her own and had to kill one of them in a hurry. When they were all killed she wouldn't have any eggs to sell when she went to town, and then what would she do?

She had to scheme all her life about getting things fed, getting the pigs fed so they would grow fat and could be butchered in the fall. When they were butchered her husband took most of the meat off to town and sold it. If he did not do it first, the boy did. They fought sometimes and when they fought the old woman stood aside trembling.

She had got the habit of silence anyway—that was fixed. Sometimes, when she began to look old—she wasn't forty yet—and when the husband and son were both off, trading horses or drinking or hunting or stealing, she went around the house and the barnyard muttering to herself.

How was she going to get everything fed?—that was her problem. The dogs had to be fed. There wasn't enough hay in the barn for the horses and the cow. If she didn't feed the chickens how could they lay eggs? Without eggs to sell how could she get things in town, things she had to have to keep the life of the farm going? Thank heaven, she did not have to feed her husband—in a certain way. That hadn't lasted long after their marriage and after the babies came. Where he went on his long trips she did not know. Sometimes he was gone from home for weeks, and after the boy grew up they went off together.

They left everything at home for her to manage and she had no money. She knew no one. No one ever talked to her in town. When it was winter she had to gather sticks of wood for her fire, had to try to keep the stock fed with very little grain.

The stock in the barn cried to her hungrily, the dogs followed her about. In the winter the hens laid few enough eggs. They huddled in the corners of the barn and she kept watching them. If a hen lays an egg in the barn in the winter and you do not find it, it freezes and breaks.

One day in winter the old woman went off to town with a few eggs and the dogs followed her. She did not get started until nearly three o'clock and the snow was heavy. She hadn't been feeling very well for several days and so she went muttering along, scantily clad, her shoulders stooped. She had an old grain bag in which she carried her eggs, tucked away down in the bottom. There weren't many of them, but in winter the price of eggs is up. She would get a little meat in exchange for the eggs, some salt pork, a little sugar, and some coffee perhaps. It might be the butcher would give her a piece of liver.

When she had got to town and was trading in her eggs the dogs lay by the door outside. She did pretty well, got the things she needed, more than she had hoped. Then she went to the butcher and he gave her some liver and some dog meat.

It was the first time anyone had spoken to her in a friendly way for a long time. The butcher was alone in his shop when she came in and was annoyed by the thought of such a sick-looking old woman out on such a day. It was bitter cold and the snow, that had let up during the afternoon, was falling again. The butcher said something about her husband and her son, swore at them, and the old woman stared at him, a look of mild surprise in her eyes as he talked. He said that if either the husband or the son were going to get any of the liver or the heavy bones with scraps of meat hanging to them that he had put into the grain bag, he'd see him starve first.

Starve, eh? Well, things had to be fed. Men had to be fed, and the horses that weren't any good but maybe could be traded off, and the poor thin cow that hadn't given any milk for three months.

Horses, cows, pigs, dogs, men.

III

The old woman had to get back before darkness came if she could. The dogs followed at her heels, sniffing at the heavy grain bag she had fastened on her back. When she got to the edge of town she stopped by a fence and tied the bag on her back with a piece of rope she had carried in her dress pocket for just that purpose. That was an easier way to carry it. Her arms ached. It was hard when she had to crawl over fences and once she fell over and landed in the snow. The dogs went frisking about. She had to struggle to get to her feet again, but she made it. The point of climbing over the fences was that there was a short cut over a hill and through a woods. She might have gone around by the road, but it was a mile farther that way. She was afraid she couldn't make it. And then, besides, the stock had to be fed. There was a little hay left and a little corn. Perhaps her husband and son would bring some home when they came. They had driven off in the only buggy the Grimes family had, a rickety thing, a rickety horse hitched to the buggy, two other rickety horses led by halters. They were going to trade horses, get a little money if they could. They might come home drunk. It would be well to have something in the house when they came back.

The son had an affair on with a woman at the county seat, fifteen miles away. She was a rough enough woman, a tough one. Once, in the summer, the son had brought her to the house. Both she and the son had been drinking. Jake Grimes was away and the son and his woman ordered the old woman about like a servant. She didn't mind much; she was used to it. Whatever happened she never said anything. That was her way of getting along. She had managed that way when she was a young girl at the German's and ever since she had married Jake. That time her son brought his woman to the house they stayed all night, sleeping together just as though they were married. It hadn't shocked the old woman, not much. She had got past being shocked early in life.

With the pack on her back she went painfully along across an open field, wading in the deep snow, and got into the woods.

There was a path, but it was hard to follow. Just beyond the top of the hill, where the woods was thickest, there was a small clearing. Had someone once thought of building a house there? The clearing was as large as a building lot in town, large enough for a house and a garden. The path ran along the side of the clearing, and when she got there the old woman sat down to rest at the foot of a tree.

It was a foolish thing to do. When she got herself placed, the pack against the tree's trunk, it was nice, but what about getting up again? She worried about that for a moment and then quietly closed her eyes.

She must have slept for a time. When you are about so cold you can't get any colder. The afternoon grew a little warmer and the snow came thicker than ever. Then after a time the weather cleared. The moon even came out.

There were four Grimes dogs that had followed Mrs. Grimes into town, all tall gaunt fellows. Such men as Jake Grimes and his son always keep just such dogs. They kick and abuse them, but they stay. The Grimes dogs, in order to keep from starving, had to do a lot of foraging for themselves, and they had been at it while the old woman slept with her back to the tree at the side of the clearing. They had been chasing rabbits in the woods and in adjoining fields and in their ranging had picked up three other farm dogs.

After a time all the dogs came back to the clearing. They were excited about something. Such nights, cold and clear and with a moon, do things to dogs. It may be that some old instinct, come down from the time when they were wolves and ranged the woods in packs on winter nights, comes back into them.

The dogs in the clearing, before the old woman, had caught two or three rabbits and their immediate hunger had been satisfied. They began to play, running in circles in the clearing. Round and round they ran, each dog's nose at the tail of the next dog. In the clearing, under the snow-laden trees and under the wintry moon they made a strange picture, running thus silently, in a circle their running had beaten in the soft snow. The dogs made no sound. They ran around and around in the circle.

It may have been that the old woman saw them doing that before she died. She may have awakened once or twice and looked at the strange sight with dim old eyes.

She wouldn't be very cold now, just drowsy. Life hangs on a long time. Perhaps the old woman was out of her head. She may have dreamed of her girlhood, at the German's, and before that, when she was a child and before her mother lit out and left her.

Her dreams couldn't have been very pleasant. Not many pleasant things have happened to her. Now and then one of the Grimes dogs left the running circle and came to stand before her. The dog thrust his face close to her face. His red tongue was hanging out.

The running of the dogs may have been a kind of death ceremony. It may have been that the primitive instinct of the wolf, having been aroused in the dogs by the night and the running, made them somehow afraid.

"Now we are no longer wolves. We are dogs, the servants of men. Keep alive, man! When man dies we become wolves again."

When one of the dogs came to where the old woman sat with her back against the tree and thrust his nose close to her face he seemed satisfied and went back to run with the pack. All the Grimes dogs did it at some time during the evening, before she died. I knew all about it afterward, when I grew to be a man, because once in a woods in Illinois, on another winter night, I saw a pack of dogs act just like that. The dogs were waiting for me to die as they had waited for the old woman that night when I was a child, but when it happened to me I was a young man and had no intention whatever of dying.

The old woman died softly and quietly. When she was dead and when one of the Grimes dogs had come to her and had found her dead all the dogs stopped running.

They gathered about her.

Well, she was dead now. She had fed the Grimes dogs when she was alive, what about now?

There was the pack on her back, the grain bag containing the piece of salt pork, the liver the butcher had given her, the dog meat, the soup-bones. The butcher in town, having been suddenly overcome with a feeling of pity, had loaded her grain bag heavily. It had been a big haul for the old woman.

It was a big haul for the dogs now.

IV

One of the Grimes dogs sprang suddenly out from among the others and began worrying the pack on the old woman's back. Had the dogs really been wolves, that one would have been the leader of the pack. What he did, all the others did.

All of them sank their teeth into the grain bag the old woman had fastened with ropes to her back.

They dragged the old woman's body out into the open clearing. The worn-out dress was quickly torn from her shoulders. When she was found, a day or two later, the dress had been torn from her body clear to the hips, but the dogs had not touched her body. They had got the meat out of the grain bag, that was all. Her body was frozen stiff when it was found, and the shoulders were so narrow and the body so slight that in death it looked like the body of some charming young girl.

Such things happened in towns of the Middle West, on farms near town, when I was a boy. A hunter out after rabbits found the old woman's body and did not touch it. Something, the beaten round path in the little snow-covered clearing, the silence of the place, the place where the dogs had worried the body trying to pull the grain bag away or tear it open—something startled the man and he hurried off to town.

I was in Main Street with one of my brothers who was town newsboy and who was taking the afternoon papers to the stores. It was almost night.

The hunter came into a grocery and told his story. Then he went to a hardware shop and into a drugstore. Men began to gather on the sidewalks. Then they started out along the road to the place in the woods.

My brother should have gone on about his business of distributing papers but he didn't. Everyone was going to the woods. The undertaker went and the town marshal. Several men got on a dray and rode out to where the path left the road and went into the woods, but the horses weren't very sharply shod and slid about on the slippery roads. They made no better time than those of us who walked.

The town marshal was a large man whose leg had been injured in the Civil War. He carried a heavy cane and limped rapidly along the road. My brother and I followed at his heels, and as we went other men and boys joined the crowd.

It had grown dark by the time we got to where the old woman had left the road, but the moon had come out. The marshal was thinking there might have been a murder. He kept asking the hunter questions. The hunter went along with his gun across his shoulders, a dog following at his heels. It isn't often a rabbit hunter has a chance to be so conspicuous. He was taking full advantage of it, leading the procession with the town marshal. "I didn't see any wounds. She was a beautiful young girl. Her face was buried in the snow. No, I didn't know her." As a matter of fact, the hunter had not looked closely at the body. He had been frightened. She might have been murdered and someone might spring out from behind a tree and murder him. In a woods, in the late afternoon, when the trees are all bare and there is white snow on the ground, when all is silent, something creepy steals over the mind and body. If something strange or uncanny has happened in the neighborhood all you think about is getting away from there as fast as you can.

The crowd of men and boys had got to where the old woman had crossed the field and went, following the marshal and the hunter, up the slight incline and into the woods.

My brother and I were silent. He had his bundle of papers in a bag slung across his shoulder. When he got back to town he would have to go on distributing his papers before he went home to supper. If I went along, as he had no doubt already determined I should, we would both be late. Either Mother or our older sister would have to warm our supper.

Well, we would have something to tell. A boy did not get such a chance very often. It was lucky we just happened to go into the grocery when the hunter came in. The hunter was a country fellow. Neither of us had ever seen him before.

Now the crowd of men and boys had got to the clearing. Darkness comes quickly on such winter nights, but the full moon made everything clear. My brother and I stood near the tree beneath which the old woman had died.

She did not look old, lying there in that light, frozen and still. One of the men turned her over in the snow and I saw everything. My body trembled with some strange mystical feeling and so did my brother's. It might have been the cold.

Neither of us had ever seen a woman's body before. It may have been the snow, clinging to the frozen flesh, that made it look so white and lovely, so like marble. No woman had come with the party from town; but one of the men, he was the town blacksmith, took off his overcoat and spread it over her. Then he gathered her into his arms and started off to town, all the others following silently. At that time no one knew who she was.

V

I had seen everything, had seen the oval in the snow, like a miniature race track, where the dogs had run, had seen how the men were mystified, had seen the white bare young-looking shoulders, had heard the whispered comments of the men.

The men were simply mystified. They took the body to the undertaker's and when the blacksmith, the hunter, the marshal and several others had got inside they closed the door. If Father had been there perhaps he could have got in, but we boys couldn't.

I went with my brother to distribute the rest of his papers and when we got home it was my brother who told the story.

I kept silent and went to bed early. It may have been I was not satisfied with the way he told it.

Later, in the town, I must have heard other fragments of the old woman's story. She was recognized the next day and there was an investigation.

The husband and son were found somewhere and brought to town and there was an attempt to connect them with the woman's death, but it did not work. They had perfect enough alibis.

However, the town was against them. They had to get out. Where they went I never heard.

I remember only the picture there in the forest, the men standing about, the naked girlish-looking figure, face down in the snow, the tracks made by the running dogs and the clear cold winter sky above. White fragments of clouds were drifting across the sky. They went racing across the little open space among the trees.

The scene in the forest had become for me, without my knowing it, the foundation for the real story I am now trying to tell. The fragments, you see, had to be picked up slowly, long afterward.

Things happened. When I was a young man I worked on the farm of a German. The hired girl was afraid of her employer. The farmer's wife hated her.

I saw things at that place. Once later, I had a half-uncanny, mystical adventure with dogs in an Illinois forest on a clear, moonlit winter night. When I was a schoolboy, and on a summer day, I went with a boy friend out along a creek some miles from town and came to the house where the old woman had lived. No one had lived in the house since her death. The doors were broken from the hinges; the window lights were all broken. As the boy and I stood in the road outside, two dogs, just roving farm dogs no doubt, came running around the corner of the house. The dogs were tall, gaunt fellows and came down to the fence and glared through at us, standing in the road.

The whole thing, the story of the old woman's death, was to me as I grew older like music heard from far off. The notes had to be picked up slowly one at a time. Something had to be understood.

The woman who died was one destined to feed animal life. Anyway, that is all she ever did. She was feeding animal life before she was born, as a child, as a young woman working on the farm of the German, after she married, when she grew old, and when she died. She fed animal life in cows, in chickens, in pigs, in horses, in dogs, in men. Her daughter had died in childhood and with her one son she had no articulate relations. On the night when she died she was hurrying homeward, bearing on her body food for animal life.

She died in the clearing in the woods and even after her death continued feeding animal life.

You see, it is likely that when my brother told the story that night when we got home and my mother and sister sat listening I did not think he got the point. He was too young and so was I. A thing so complete has its own beauty.

I shall not try to emphasize the point. I am only explaining why I was dissatisfied then and have been ever since. I speak of that only that you may understand why I have been impelled to try to tell the simple story over again.

DISCUSSION

1. Is the theme more specific in "Young Goodman Brown" or in "Death in the Woods"?

2. On the same ground, compare "Death in the Woods" with "Crossing into Poland" and "The Killers."

3. Suppose the dogs were omitted from this story. How different would be the meaning and effect?

4. How important is tone—a prevailing emotion and attitude—in this story?

5. What is the theme of this story? What does the boy, the narrator, discover by the event? What is gained by the fact that the story is told long after the actual event? What could you say is the dominant emotion of the story?

THE MAN WHO WAS ALMOST A MAN

Richard Wright

DAVE struck out across the fields, looking homeward through paling light. Whut's the use talkin wid em niggers in the field? Anyhow, his mother was putting supper on the table. Them niggers can't understan nothing. One of these days he was going to get a gun and practice shooting, then they couldn't talk to him as though he were a little boy. He slowed, looking at the ground. Shucks, Ah ain scareda them even ef they are biggern me! Aw, Ah know whut Ahma do. Ahm going to ol Joe's sto n git that Sears Roebuck catlog n look at them guns. Mebbe Ma will lemme buy one when she gits mah pay from ol man Hawkins. Ahma beg her t gimme some money. Ahm ol ernough to hava gun. Ahm seventeen. Almost a man. He strode, feeling his long loose-jointed limbs. Shucks, a man oughta hava little gun aftah he done worked hard all day.

He came in sight of Joe's store. A yellow lantern glowed on the front porch. He mounted steps and went through the screen door, hearing it bang behind him. There was a strong smell of coal oil and mackerel fish. He felt very confident until he saw fat Joe walk in through the rear door, then his courage began to ooze.

"Howdy, Dave! Whutcha want?"

"How yuh, Mistah Joe? Aw, Ah don wanna buy nothing. Ah jus wanted t see if yuhd lemme look at tha catlog erwhile."

"Sure! You wanna see it here?"

"Nawsuh. Ah wans t take it home wid me. Ah'll bring it back termorrow when Ah come in from the fiels."

"You plannin on buying something?"

"Yessuh."

"Your ma lettin you have your own money now?"

"Shucks. Mistah Joe, Ahm gittin t be a man like anybody else!"

Joe laughed and wiped his greasy white face with a red bandanna.

"Whut you plannin on buyin?"

Dave looked at the floor, scratched his head, scratched his thigh, and smiled. Then he looked up shyly.

"Ah'll tell yuh, Mistah Joe, ef yuh promise yuh won't tell."

"I promise."

"Waal, Ahma buy a gun."

"A gun? Whut you want with a gun?"

"Ah wanna keep it."

"You ain't nothing but a boy. You don't need a gun."

"Aw, lemme have the catlog, Mistah Joe. Ah'll bring it back."

Joe walked through the rear door. Dave was elated. He looked around at barrels of sugar and flour. He heard Joe coming back. He craned his neck to see if he were bringing the book. Yeah, he's got it. Gawddog, he's got it!

"Here, but be sure you bring it back. It's the only one I got."

"Sho, Mistah Joe."

"Say, if you wanna buy a gun, why don't you buy one from me? I gotta gun to sell."

"Will it shoot?"

"Sure it'll shoot."

"Whut kind is it?"

"Oh, it's kinda old . . . a left-hand Wheeler. A pistol. A big one."

"Is it got bullets in it?"

"It's loaded."

"Kin Ah see it?"

"Where's your money?"

"Whut yuh wan fer it?"

"I'll let you have it for two dollars."

"Just two dollahs? Shucks, Ah could buy tha when Ah git mah pay."

"I'll have it here when you want it."

"Awright, suh. Ah be in fer it."

He went through the door, hearing it slam again behind him. Ahma git some money from Ma n buy me a gun! Only two dollahs! He tucked the thick catalogue under his arm and hurried.

"Where yuh been, boy?" His mother held a steaming dish of black-eyed peas.

"Aw, Ma, Ah jus stopped down the road t talk wid the boys."

"Yuh know bettah t keep suppah waitin."

He sat down, resting the catalogue on the edge of the table.

"Yuh git up from there and git to the well n wash yoself! Ah ain feedin no hogs in mah house!"

She grabbed his shoulder and pushed him. He stumbled out of the room, then came back to get the catalogue.

"Whut this?"

"Aw, Ma, it's jusa catlog."

"Who yuh git it from?"

"From Joe, down at the sto."

"Waal, thas good. We kin use it in the outhouse."

"Naw, Ma." He grabbed for it. "Gimme ma catlog, Ma."

She held onto it and glared at him.

"Quit hollerin at me! Whut's wrong wid yuh? Yuh crazy?"

"But Ma, please. It ain mine! It's Joe's! He tol me t bring it back t im termorrow."

She gave up the book. He stumbled down the back steps, hugging the thick book under his arm. When he had splashed water on his face and hands, he groped back to the kitchen and fumbled in a corner for the towel. He bumped into a chair; it clattered to the floor. The catalogue sprawled at his feet. When he had dried his eyes he snatched up the book and held it again under his arm. His mother stood watching him.

"Now, ef yuh gonna act a fool over that ol book, Ah'll take it n burn it up."

"Naw, Ma, please."

"Waal, set down n be still!"

He sat down and drew the oil lamp close. He thumbed page after page, unaware of the food his mother set on the table. His father came in. Then his small brother.

"Whutcha got there, Dave?" his father asked.

"Jusa catlog," he answered, not looking up.

"Yeah, here they is!" His eyes glowed at blue-and-black revolvers. He glanced up, feeling sudden guilt. His father was watching him. He eased the book under the table and rested it on his knees. After the blessing was asked, he ate. He scooped up peas and swallowed fat meat without chewing. Buttermilk helped to wash it down. He did not want to mention money before his father. He would do much better by cornering his mother when she was alone. He looked at his father uneasily out of the edge of his eye.

"Boy, how come yuh don quit foolin wid tha book n eat yo suppah?"

"Yessuh."

"How you n ol man Hawkins gitten erlong?"

"Suh?"

"Can't yuh hear? Why don yuh lissen? Ah ast yu how wuz yuh n ol man Hawkins gittin erlong?"

"Oh, swell, Pa. Ah plows mo lan than anybody over there."

"Waal, yuh oughta keep yo mind on whut yuh doin."

"Yessuh."

He poured his plate full of molasses and sopped it up slowly with a chunk of cornbread. When his father and brother had left the kitchen, he still sat and looked again at the guns in the catalogue, longing to muster courage enough to present his case to his mother. Lawd, ef Ah only had tha pretty one! He could almost feel the slickness of the weapon with his fingers. If he had a gun like that he would polish it and keep it shining so it would never rust. N Ah'd keep it loaded, by Gawd!

"Ma?" His voice was hesitant.

"Hunh?"

"Ol man Hawkins give yuh mah money yit?"

"Yeah, but ain no usa yuh thinking bout throwin nona it erway. Ahm keepin tha money sos yuh kin have cloes t go to school this winter."

He rose and went to her side with the open catalogue in his palms. She was washing dishes, her head bent low over a pan. Shyly he raised the book. When he spoke, his voice was husky, faint.

"Ma, Gawd knows Ah wans one of these."

"One of whut?" she asked, not raising her eyes.

"One of these," he said again, not daring even to point. She glanced up at the page, then at him with wide eyes.

"Nigger, is yuh gone plumb crazy?"

"Aw, Ma—"

"Git outta here! Don yuh talk t me bout no gun! Yuh a fool!"

"Ma, Ah kin buy one fer two dollahs."

"Not ef Ah knows it, yuh ain!"

"But yuh promised me one—"

"Ah don care whut Ah promised! Yuh ain nothing but a boy yit!"

"Ma, ef yuh lemme buy one Ah'll *never* ast yuh fer nothing no mo."

"Ah tol yuh t git outta here! Yuh ain gonna toucha penny of tha money fer no gun! Thas how come Ah has Mistah Hawkins t pay yo wages t me, cause Ah knows yuh ain got no sense."

"But, Ma, we needa gun. Pa ain got no gun. We needa gun in the house. Yuh kin never tell whut might happen."

"Now don yuh try to maka fool outta me, boy! Ef we did hava gun, yuh wouldn't have it!"

He laid the catalogue down and slipped his arm around her waist.

"Aw, Ma, Ah done worked hard alla summer n ain ast yuh fer nothin, is Ah, now?"

"Thas whut yuh spose t do!"

"But Ma, Ah wans a gun. Yuh kin lemme have two dollahs outta mah money. Please, Ma. I kin give it to Pa . . . Please, Ma! Ah loves yuh, Ma."

When she spoke her voice came soft and low.

"What yu wan wida gun, Dave? Yuh don need no gun. Yuh'll git in trouble. N ef yo pa jus thought Ah let yuh have money t buy a gun he'd hava fit."

"Ah'll hide it, Ma. It ain but two dollahs."

"Lawd, chil, whut's wrong wid yuh?"

"Ain nothin wrong, Ma. Ahm almos a man now. Ah wans a gun."

"Who gonna sell yuh a gun?"

"Ol Joe at the sto."

"N it don cos but two dollahs?"

"Thas all, Ma. Jus two dollahs. Please, Ma."

She was stacking the plates away; her hands moved slowly, reflectively. Dave kept an anxious silence. Finally, she turned to him.

"Ah'll let yuh git tha gun ef yuh promise me one thing."

"Whut's tha, Ma?"

"Yuh bring it straight back t me, yuh hear? It be fer Pa."

"Yessum! Lemme go now, Ma."

She stooped, turned slightly to one side raised the hem of her dress, rolled down the top of her stocking, and came up with a slender wad of bills.

"Here," she said. "Lawd knows yuh don need no gun. But yer pa does. Yuh bring it right back t me, yuh hear? Ahma put it up. Now ef yuh don, Ahma have yuh pa lick yuh so hard yuh won fergit it."

"Yessum."

He took the money, ran down the steps, and across the yard.

"Dave! Yuuuuuh Daaaaave!"

He heard, but he was not going to stop now. "Naw, Lawd!"

The first movement he made the following morning was to reach under his pillow for the gun. In the gray light of dawn he held it loosely, feeling a sense of power. Could kill a man with a gun like this. Kill anybody, black or white. And if he were holding his gun in his hand, nobody could run over him; they would have to respect him. It was a big gun, with a long barrel and a heavy handle. He raised and lowered it in his hand, marveling at its weight.

He had not come straight home with it as his mother had asked; instead he had stayed out in the fields, holding the weapon in his hand, aiming it now and then at some imaginary foe. But he had not fired it; he had been afraid that his father might hear. Also he was not sure he knew how to fire it.

To avoid surrendering the pistol he had not come into the house until he knew that they were all asleep. When his mother had tiptoed to his bedside late that night and demanded the gun, he had first played possum; then he had told her that the gun was hidden outdoors, that he would bring it to her in the morning. Now he lay turning it slowly in his hands. He broke it, took out the cartridges, felt them, and then put them back.

He slid out of bed, got a long strip of old flannel from a trunk, wrapped the gun in it, and tied it to his naked thigh while it was still loaded. He did not go in to breakfast. Even though it was not yet daylight, he started for Jim Hawkins' plantation. Just as the sun was rising he reached the barns where the mules and plows were kept.

"Hey! That you, Dave?"

He turned. Jim Hawkins stood eying him suspiciously.

"What're yuh doing here so early?"

"Ah didn't know Ah wuz gittin up so early, Mistah Hawkins. Ah wuz fixin t hitch up ol Jenny n take her t the fiels."

"Good. Since you're so early, how about plowing that stretch down by the woods?"

"Suits me, Mistah Hawkins."

"O.K. Go to it!"

He hitched Jenny to a plow and started across the fields. Hot dog! This was just what he wanted. If he could get down by the woods, he could shoot his gun and nobody would hear. He walked behind the plow, hearing the traces creaking, feeling the gun tied tight to his thigh.

When he reached the woods, he plowed two whole rows before he decided to take out the gun. Finally, he stopped, looked in all directions, then untied the gun and held it in his hand. He turned to the mule and smiled.

"Know whut this is, Jenny? Naw, yuh wouldn know! Yuhs jusa ol mule! Anyhow, this is a gin, n it kin shoot, by Gawd!"

He held the gun at arm's length. Whut t hell, Ahma shoot this thing! He looked at Jenny again.

"Lissen here, Jenny! When Ah pull this ol trigger, Ah don wan yuh t run n acka fool now!"

Jenny stood with head down, her short ears pricked straight. Dave walked off about twenty feet, held the gun far out from him at arm's length, and turned his head. Hell, he told himself, Ah ain afraid. The gun felt loose in his fingers; he waved it wildly for a moment. Then he shut his eyes and tightened his forefinger. Bloom! A report half deafened him and he thought his right hand was torn from his arm. He heard Jenny whinnying and galloping over the field, and he found himself on his knees, squeezing his fingers hard between his legs. His hand was numb; he jammed it into his mouth, trying to warm it, trying to stop the pain. The gun lay at his feet. He did not quite know what had happened. He stood up and stared at the gun as though it were a living thing. He gritted his teeth and kicked the gun. Yuh almos broke mah arm! He turned to look for Jenny; she was far over the fields, tossing her head and kicking wildly.

"Hol on there, ol mule!"

When he caught up with her she stood trembling, walling her big white eyes at him. The plow was far away; the traces had broken. Then Dave stopped short, looking, not believing. Jenny was bleeding. Her left side was red and wet with blood. He went closer. Lawd, have mercy! Wondah did Ah shoot this mule? He grabbed for Jenny's mane. She flinched, snorted, whirled, tossing her head.

"Hol on now! Hol on."

Then he saw the hole in Jenny's side, right between the ribs. It was round, wet, red. A crimson stream streaked down the front leg, flowing fast. Good Gawd! Ah wuzn't shootin at tha mule. He felt panic. He knew he had to stop that blood, or Jenny would bleed to death. He had never seen so much blood in all his life. He chased the mule for half a mile, trying to catch her. Finally she stopped, breathing hard, stumpy tail half arched. He caught her mane and led her back to where the plough and gun lay. Then he stooped and grabbed handfuls of damp black earth and tried to plug the bullet hole. Jenny shuddered, whinnied, and broke from him.

"Hol on! Hol on now!"

He tried to plug it again, but blood came anyhow. His fingers were hot and sticky. He rubbed dirt into his palms, trying to dry them. Then again he attempted to plug the bullet hole, but Jenny shied away, kicking her heels high. He stood helpless. He had to do something. He ran at Jenny; she dodged him. He watched a red stream of blood flow down Jenny's leg and form a bright pool at her feet.

"Jenny . . . Jenny," he called weakly.

His lips trembled. She's bleeding t death! He looked in the direction of home, wanting to go back, wanting to get help. But he saw the pistol lying in the damp black clay. He had a queer feeling that if he only did something, this would not be; Jenny would not be there bleeding to death.

When he went to her this time, she did not move. She stood with sleepy, dreamy eyes; and when he touched her she gave a low-pitched whinny and knelt to the gound, her front knees slopping in blood.

"Jenny . . . Jenny . . ." he whispered.

For a long time she held her neck erect; then her head sank, slowly. Her ribs swelled with a mighty heave and she went over.

Dave's stomach felt empty, very empty. He picked up the gun and held it gingerly between his thumb and forefinger. He buried it at the foot of a tree. He took a stick and tried to cover the pool of blood with dirt—but what was the use? There was Jenny lying with her mouth open and her eyes walled and glassy. He could not tell Jim Hawkins he had shot his mule. But he had to tell something. Yeah, Ah'll tell em Jenny started gitting wil n fell on the joint of the plow. . . . But that would hardly happen to a mule. He walked across the field slowly, head down.

It was sunset. Two of Jim Hawkins' men were over near the edge of the woods digging a hole in which to bury Jenny. Dave was surrounded by a knot of people, all of whom were looking down at the dead mule.

"I don't see how in the world it happened," said Jim Hawkins for the tenth time.

The crowd parted and Dave's mother, father, and small brother pushed into the center.

"Where Dave?" his mother called.

"There he is," said Jim Hawkins.

His mother grabbed him.

"Whut happened, Dave? Whut yuh done?"

"Nothin."

"C mon, boy, talk," his father said.

Dave took a deep breath and told the story he knew nobody believed.

"Waal," he drawled. "Ah brung ol Jenny down here sos Ah could do mah plowin. Ah plowed bout two rows, just like yu see." He stopped and pointed at the long rows of upturned earth. "Then somethin musta been wrong wid ol Jenny. She wouldn ack right a-tall. She started snortin n kickin her heels. Ah tried t hol her, but she pulled erway, rearin n goin in. Then when the point of the plow was stickin up in the air, she swung erroun n twisted herself back on it . . . She stuck herself n started t bleed. N fo Ah could do anything, she wuz dead."

"Did you ever hear of anything like that in all your life?" asked Jim Hawkins.

There were white and black standing in the crowd. They murmured. Dave's mother came close to him and looked hard into his face. "Tell the truth, Dave," she said.

"Looks like a bullet hole to me," said one man.

"Dave, whut yuh do wid the gun?" his mother asked.

The crowd surged in, looking at him. He jammed his hands into his pockets, shook his head slowly from left to right, and backed away. His eyes were wide and painful.

"Did he hava gun?" asked Jim Hawkins.

"By Gawd, Ah tol yuh tha wuz a gun wound," said a man, slapping his thigh.

His father caught his shoulders and shook him till his teeth rattled.

"Tell whut happened, yuh rascal! Tell whut . . ."

Dave looked at Jenny's stiff legs and began to cry.

"Whut yuh do wid tha gun?" his mother asked.

"Whut wuz he doin wida gun?" his father asked.

"Come on and tell the truth," said Hawkins. "Ain't nobody going to hurt you . . ."

His mother crowded close to him.

"Did yuh shoot tha mule, Dave?"

Dave cried, seeing blurred white and black faces.

"Ahh ddinn gggo tt sshooot hher . . . Ah ssswear ffo Gawd Ahh ddin. . . . Ah wuz a-tryin t sssee ef the old gggun would sshoot—"

"Where yuh get the gun from?" his father asked.

"Ah got it from Joe, at the sto."

"Where yuh git the money?"

"Ma give it t me."

"He kept worryin me, Bob. Ah had t. Ah tol im t bring the gun right back t me . . . It was fer yug, the gun."

"But how yuh happen to shoot that mule?" asked Jim Hawkins.

"Ah wuzn shootin at the mule, Mistah Hawkins. The gun jumped when Ah pulled the trigger . . . N fo Ah knowed anythin Jenny was there a-bleedin."

Somebody in the crowd laughed. Jim Hawkins walked close to Dave and looked into his face.

"Well, looks like you have bought you a mule, Dave."

"Ah swear fo Gawd, Ah didn go t kill the mule, Mistah Hawkins!"

"But you killed her!"

All the crowd was laughing now. They stood on tiptoe and poked heads over one another's shoulders.

"Well, boy, looks like yuh done bought a dead mule! Hahaha!"

"Ain tha ershame."

"Hohohohoho."

Dave stood, head down, twisting his feet in the dirt.

"Well, you needn't worry about it, Bob," said Jim Hawkins to Dave's father. "Just let the boy keep on working and pay me two dollars a month."

"Whut yuh wan fer yo mule, Mistah Hawkins?"

Jim Hawkins screwed up his eyes.

"Fifty dollars."

"Whut yuh do wid tha gun?" Dave's father demanded.

Dave said nothing.

"Yuh wan me t take a tree n beat yuh till yuh talk!"

"Nawsuh!"

"Whut yuh do wid it?"

"Ah throwed it erway."

"Where?"

"Ah . . . Ah throwed it in the creek."

"Waal, c mon home. N firs thing in the mawnin git to tha creek n fin tha gun."

"Yessuh."

"Whut yuh pay fer it?"

"Two dollahs."

"Take tha gun n git yo money back n carry it t Mistah Hawkins, yuh hear? N don fergit Ahma lam you black bottom good fer this! Now march yosef on home, suh!"

Dave turned and walked slowly. He heard people laughing. Dave glared, his eyes welling with tears. Hot anger bubbled in him. Then he swallowed and stumbled on.

That night Dave did not sleep. He was glad that he had gotten out of killing the mule so easily, but he was hurt. Something hot seemed to turn over inside him each time he remembered how they had laughed. He tossed on his bed, feeling his hard pillow. N Pa says he's gonna beat me . . . He remembered other beatings, and his back quivered. Naw, naw, Ah sho don wan im t beat me tha way no mo. Dam em all! Nobody ever gave him anything. All he did was work. They treat me like a mule, n then they beat me. He gritted his teeth. N Ma had to tell on me.

Well, if he had to, he would take old man Hawkins that two dollars. But that meant selling the gun. And he wanted to keep that gun. Fifty dollars for a dead mule.

He turned over, thinking how he had fired the gun. He had an itch to fire it again. Ef other men kin shoota gun, by Gawd, Ah kin! He was still, listening. Mebbe they all sleepin now. The house was still. He heard the soft breathing of his brother. Yes, now! He would go down and get that gun and see if he could fire it! He eased out of bed and slipped into overalls.

The moon was bright. He ran almost all the way to the edge of the woods. He stumbled over the ground, looking for the spot where he had buried the gun. Yeah, here it is. Like a hungry dog scratching for a bone, he pawed it up. He puffed his black cheeks and blew dirt from the trigger and barrel. He broke it and found four cartridges unshot. He looked around; the fields were filled with silence and moonlight. He clutched the gun stiff and hard in his fingers. But, as soon as he wanted to pull the trigger, he shut his eyes and turned his head. Naw, Ah can't shoot wid mah eyes closed n mah head turned. With effort he held his eyes open; then he squeezed. *Blooooom!* He was stiff, not breathing. The gun was still in his hands. Dammit, he'd done it! He fired again. *Blooooom!* He smiled *Blooooom! Blooooom! Click, click.* There! It was empty. If anybody could shoot a gun, he could. He put the gun into his hip pocket and started across the fields.

When he reached the top of a ridge he stood straight and proud in the moonlight, looking at Jim Hawkins' big white house, feeling the gun sagging in his pocket. Lawd, ef Ah had just one mo bullet. Ah'd taka shot at tha house. Ah'd like t scare ol man Hawkins jusa little . . . Jusa enough t let im know Dave Saunders is a man.

To his left the road curved, running to the tracks of the Illinois Central. He jerked his head, listening. From far off came a faint *hoooof-hoooof; hoooof-hoooof; hoooof-hoooof. . . .* He stood rigid. Two dollahs a mont. Less see now . . . Tha means it'll take bout two years. Shucks! Ah'll be dam!

He started down the road, toward the tracks. Yeah, here she comes! He stood beside the track and held himself stiffly. Here she comes, er-roun the ben . . . C mon, yuh slow poke! C mon! He had his hand on his gun; something quivered in his stomach. Then the train thundered past, the gray and brown box cars rumbling and clinking. He gripped the gun tightly; then he jerked his hand out of his pocket. Ah betcha Bill wouldn't do it! Ah betcha . . . The cars slid past, steel grinding upon steel. Ahm ridin yuh ternight, so hep me Gawd! He was hot all over. He hesitated just a moment; then he grabbed, pulled atop of a car, and lay flat. He felt his pocket; the gun was still there. Ahead the long rails were glinting in the moonlight, stretching away, away to somewhere, some-where where he could be a man . . .

DISCUSSION

As in "Araby," "The District Doctor," "The Killers," and other stories in this collection, the subject here is growing up, initiation. "Araby" and "The District Doctor" are concerned with initiation into love, but this story, like "The Killers," deals with a youth's introduction into a more general kind of maturity. But here, though sex does not explicitly enter the story, the pistol may be taken as a mark of maturity and manhood.

It is clear from the general situation that Dave, the son of a black plantation tenant in Mississippi some half century ago, sees even his father as less than a man and finds his father a mere instrument of the plantation owner. And more generally speaking, he feels himself vic-timized as a mere "boy" by the other and older field hands.

Once he has the pistol he feels a surge of power. He can "kill any-body, black or white"—and so the hidden motive creeps out. The white man is his subconscious target. At the end of the story, before Dave catches the freight train, his last fantasy is to fire a shot at the big white house of Mr. Hawkins, the owner. No, not to hit him, he tells himself, only to scare him "jusa enough t let im know Dave Saunders is a man"—but he subconsciously knows he has at last found his logical target.

1. When Dave hops the freight train with his pistol, is he riding to-ward "freedom" and maturity or toward a new kind of bondage?

2. While the mule is being buried, Dave is made the butt of the jokes of other field hands in the crowd. What is the significance of this? How does this relate to the basic theme of the story? What is the motive behind the jokes of the other hands?

3. Why does Dave explain to himself that if he could fire at the white house he wouldn't really want to hit Mr. Hawkins? What is the impulse behind this reservation?

4. How do you define the theme of this story?

A ROSE FOR EMILY

William Faulkner

I

WHEN Miss Emily Grierson died, our whole town went to her funeral: the men through a sort of respectful affection for a fallen monument, the women mostly out of curiosity to see the inside of her house, which no one save an old manservant—a combined gardener and cook—had seen in at least ten years.

It was a big, squarish frame house that had once been white, decorated with cupolas and spires and scrolled balconies in the heavily lightsome style of the seventies, set on what had once been our most select street. But garages and cotton gins had encroached and obliterated even the august names of that neighborhood; only Miss Emily's house was left, lifting its stubborn and coquettish decay above the cotton wagons and the gasoline pumps—an eyesore among eyesores. And now Miss Emily had gone to join the representatives of those august names where they lay in the cedar-bemused cemetery among the ranked and anonymous graves of Union and Confederate soldiers who fell at the battle of Jefferson.

Alive, Miss Emily had been a tradition, a duty, and a care; a sort of hereditary obligation upon the town, dating from that day in 1894 when Colonel Sartoris, the mayor—he who fathered the edict that no Negro woman should appear on the streets without an apron—remitted her taxes, the dispensation dating from the death of her father on into perpetuity. Not that Miss Emily would have accepted charity. Colonel Sartoris invented an involved tale to the effect that Miss Emily's father had loaned money to the town, which the town, as a matter of business, preferred this way of repaying. Only a man of Colonel Sartoris' generation and thought could have invented it, and only a woman could have believed it.

When the next generation, with its more modern ideas, became mayors and aldermen, this arrangment created some little dissatisfaction. On the first of the year they mailed her a tax notice. February came, and there was no reply. They wrote her a formal letter, asking her to call at the sheriff's office at her convenience. A week later the mayor wrote her himself, offering to call or to send his car for her, and received in reply a note on paper of an archaic shape, in a thin, flowing calligraphy in faded ink, to the effect that she no longer went out at all. The tax notice was also enclosed, without comment.

They called a special meeting of the Board of Aldermen. A deputation waited upon her, knocked at the door through which no visitor had passed since she ceased giving china-painting lessons eight or ten years earlier. They were admitted by the old Negro into a dim hall from which a stairway mounted into still more shadow. It smelled of dust and disuse—a close, dank smell. The Negro led them into the parlor. It was furnished in heavy, leather-covered furniture. When the Negro opened the blinds of one window, a faint dust rose sluggishly about their thighs, spinning with slow motes in the single sun-ray. On a tarnished gilt easel before the fireplace stood a crayon portrait of Miss Emily's father.

They rose when she entered—a small, fat woman in black, with a thin gold chain descending to her waist and vanishing into her belt, leaning on an ebony cane with a tarnished gold head. Her skeleton was small and spare; perhaps that was why what would have been merely plumpness in another was obesity in her. She looked bloated, like a body long submerged in motionless water, and of that pallid hue. Her eyes, lost in the fatty ridges of her face, looked like two small pieces of coal pressed into a lump of dough as they moved from one face to another while the visitors stated their errand.

She did not ask them to sit. She just stood in the door and listened quietly until the spokesman came to a stumbling halt. Then they could hear the invisible watch ticking at the end of the gold chain.

Her voice was dry and cold. "I have no taxes in Jefferson. Colonel Sartoris explained it to me. Perhaps one of you can gain access to the city records and satisfy yourselves."

"But we have. We are the city authorities, Miss Emily. Didn't you get a notice from the sheriff, signed by him?"

"I received a paper, yes," Miss Emily said. "Perhaps he considers himself the sheriff. . . . I have no taxes in Jefferson."

"But there is nothing on the books to show that, you see. We must go by the—"

"See Colonel Sartoris. I have no taxes in Jefferson."

"But, Miss Emily—"

"See Colonel Sartoris." (Colonel Sartoris had been dead almost ten years.) "I have no taxes in Jefferson. Tobe!" The Negro appeared. "Show these gentlemen out."

II

So she vanquished them, horse and foot, just as she had vanquished their fathers thirty years before about the smell. That was two years after her father's death and a short time after her sweetheart—the one we believed would marry her—had deserted her. After her father's death she went out very little; after her sweetheart went away, people hardly saw her at all. A few of the ladies had the temerity to call, but were not received, and the only sign of life about the place was the Negro man—a young man then—going in and out with a market basket.

"Just as if a man—any man—could keep a kitchen properly," the ladies said; so they were not surprised when the smell developed. It was another link between the gross, teeming world and the high and mighty Griersons.

A neighbor, a woman, complained to the mayor, Judge Stevens, eighty years old.

"But what will you have me do about it, madam?" he said.

"Why, send her word to stop it," the woman said. "Isn't there a law?"

"I'm sure that won't be necessary," Judge Stevens said. "It's probably just a snake or a rat that nigger of hers killed in the yard. I'll speak to him about it."

The next day he received two more complaints, one from a man who came in diffident deprecation. "We really must do something about it, Judge. I'd be the last one in the world to bother Miss Emily, but we've got to do something." That night the Board of Aldermen met—three graybeards and one younger man, a member of the rising generation.

"It's simple enough," he said. "Send her word to have her place cleaned up. Give her a certain time to do it in, and if she don't . . ."

"Dammit, sir," Judge Stevens said, "will you accuse a lady to her face of smelling bad?"

So the next night, after midnight, four men crossed Miss Emily's lawn and slunk about the house like burglars, sniffing along the base of the brickwork and at the cellar openings while one of them performed a regular sowing motion with his hand out of a sack slung from his shoulder. They broke open the cellar door and sprinkled lime there, and in all the outbuildings. As they recrossed the lawn, a window that had been dark was lighted and Miss Emily sat in it, the light behind her, and her upright torso motionless as that of an idol. They crept quietly across the lawn and into the shadow of the locusts that lined the street. After a week or two the smell went away.

That was when people had begun to feel really sorry for her. People in our town, remembering how old lady Wyatt, her great-aunt, had gone completely crazy at last, believed that the Griersons held themselves a little too high for what they really were. None of the young men were quite good enough for Miss Emily and such. We had long thought of them as a tableau; Miss Emily a slender figure in white in the background, her father a spraddled silhouette in the foreground, his back to her and clutching a horsewhip, the two of them framed by the back-flung front door. So when she got to be thirty and was still single, we were not pleased exactly, but vindicated; even with insanity in the family she wouldn't have turned down all of her chances if they had really materialized.

When her father died, it got about that the house was all that was left to her; and in a way, people were glad. At last they could pity Miss Emily. Being left alone, and a pauper, she had become humanized. Now she too would know the old thrill and the old despair of a penny more or less.

The day after his death all the ladies prepared to call at the house and offer condolence and aid, as is our custom. Miss Emily met them at the door, dressed as usual and with no trace of grief on her face. She told them that her father was not dead. She did that for three days, with the ministers calling on her, and the doctors, trying to persuade her to let them dispose of the body. Just as they were about to resort to law and force, she broke down, and they buried her father quickly.

We did not say she was crazy then. We believed she had to do that. We remembered all the young men her father had driven away, and we knew that with nothing left, she would have to cling to that which had robbed her, as people will.

III

She was sick for a long time. When we saw here again, her hair was cut short, making her look like a girl, with a vague resemblance to those angels in colored church windows—sort of tragic and serene.

The town had just let the contracts for paving the sidewalks, and in the summer after her father's death they began to work. The construction company came with niggers and mules and machinery, and a foreman named Homer Barron, a Yankee—a big, dark, ready man, with a big voice and eyes lighter than his face. The little boys would follow in groups to hear him cuss the niggers, and the niggers singing in time to the rise and fall of picks. Pretty soon he knew everybody in town. Whenever you heard a lot of laughing anywhere about the square, Homer Barron would be in the center of the group. Presently we began to see him and Miss Emily on Sunday afternoons driving in the yellow-wheeled buggy and the matched team of bays from the livery stable.

At first we were glad that Miss Emily would have an interest, because the ladies all said, "Of course a Grierson would not think seriously of a Northerner, a day laborer." But there were still others, older people, who said that even grief could not cause a real lady to forget *noblesse oblige*—without calling it *noblesse oblige*. They just said, "Poor Emily. Her kinsfolk should come to her." She had some kin in Alabama; but years ago her father had fallen out with them over the estate of old lady Wyatt, the crazy woman, and there was no communication between the two families. They had not even been represented at the funeral.

And as soon as the old people said, "Poor Emily," the whispering began. "Do you suppose it's really so?" they said to one another. "Of course it is. What else could . . ." This behind their hands; rustling of craned silk and satin behind jalousies closed upon the sun of Sunday afternoon as the thin, swift clop-clop-clop of the matched team passed: "Poor Emily."

She carried her head high enough—even when we believed that she was fallen. It was as if she demanded more than ever the recognition of her dignity as the last Grierson; as if it had wanted that touch of earthiness to reaffirm her imperviousness. Like when she bought the rat poison, the arsenic. That was over a year after they had begun to say "Poor Emily," and while the two female cousins were visiting her.

"I want some poison," she said to the druggist. She was over thirty then, still a slight woman, though thinner than usual, with cold, haughty black eyes in a face the flesh of which was strained across the temples and about the eyesockets as you imagine a lighthouse-keeper's face ought to look. "I want some poison," she said.

"Yes, Miss Emily. What kind? For rats and such? I'd recom—"

"I want the best you have. I don't care what kind."

The druggist named several. "They'll kill anything up to an elephant. But what you want is—"

"Arsenic," Miss Emily said. "Is that a good one?"

"Is . . . arsenic? Yes ma'am. But what you want—"

"I want arsenic."

The druggist looked down at her. She looked back at him, erect, her face like a strained flag. "Why, of course," the druggist said. "If that's what you want. But the law requires you to tell what you are going to use it for."

Miss Emily just stared at him, her head tilted back in order to look him eye for eye, until he looked away and went and got the arsenic and wrapped it up. The Negro delivery boy brought her the package; the druggist didn't come back. When she opened the package at home there was written on the box, under the skull and bones: "For rats."

IV

So the next day we all said, "She will kill herself"; and we said it would be the best thing. When she had first begun to be seen with Homer Barron, we had said, "She will marry him." Then we said, "She will persuade him yet," because Homer himself had remarked—he liked men, and it was known that he drank with the younger men in the Elk's Club—that he was not a marrying man. Later we said, "Poor Emily," behind the jalousies as they passed on Sunday afternoon in the glittering buggy, Miss Emily with her head high and Homer Barron with his hat cocked and a cigar in his teeth, reins and whip in a yellow glove.

Then some of the ladies began to say that it was a disgrace to the town and a bad example to the young people. The men did not want to interfere, but at last the ladies forced the Baptist minister—Miss Emily's people were Episcopal—to call upon her. He would never divulge what happened during that interview, but he refused to go back again. The next Sunday they again drove about the streets, and the following day the minister's wife wrote to Miss Emily's relations in Alabama.

So she had blood-kin under her roof again and we sat back to watch developments. At first nothing happened. Then we were sure that they were to be married. We learned that Miss Emily had been to the jeweler's and ordered a man's toilet set in silver, with the letters H.B. on each piece. Two days later we learned that she had brought a complete outfit of men's clothing, including a nightshirt, and we said, "They are married." We were really glad. We were glad because the two female cousins were even more Grierson than Miss Emily had ever been.

So we were not surprised when Homer Barron—the streets had been finished some time since—was gone. We were a little disappointed that there was not a public blowing-off, but we believed that he had gone on to prepare for Miss Emily's coming, or to give her a chance to get rid of the cousins. (By that time it was a cabal, and we were all Miss Emily's allies to help circumvent the cousins.) Sure enough, after another week they departed. And, as we had expected all along, within three days Homer Barron was back in town. A neighbor saw the Negro man admit him at the kitchen door at dusk one evening.

And that was the last we saw of Homer Barron. And of Miss Emily for some time. The Negro man went in and out with the market basket, but the front door remained closed. Now and then we would see her at a window for a moment, as the men did that night when they sprinkled the lime, but for almost six months she did not appear on the streets. Then we knew that this was to be expected too; as if that quality of her father which had thwarted her woman's life so many times had been too viru- lent and too furious to die.

When we next saw Miss Emily, she had grown fat and her hair was turning gray. During the next few years it grew grayer and grayer until it attained an even pepper-and-salt iron-gray, when it ceased turning. Up to the day of her death at seventy-four it was still the vigorous iron-gray, like the hair of an active man.

From that time on her front door remained closed, save for a period of six or seven years, when she was about forty, during which she gave lessons in china-painting. She fitted up a studio in one of the downstairs rooms, where the daughters and granddaughters of Colonel Sartoris' contemporaries were sent to her with the same regularity and in the same spirit that they were sent on Sundays with a twenty-five cent piece for the collection plate. Meanwhile her taxes had been remitted.

Then the newer generation became the backbone and the spirit of the town, and the painting pupils grew up and fell away and did not send their children to her with boxes of color and tedious brushes and pic- tures cut from the ladies' magazines. The front door closed upon the last one and remained closed for good. When the town got free postal deliv- ery Miss Emily alone refused to let them fasten the metal numbers above her door and attach a mailbox to it. She would not listen to them.

Daily, monthly, yearly we watched the Negro grow grayer and more stooped, going in and out with the market basket. Each December we sent her a tax notice, which would be returned by the post office a week later, unclaimed. Now and then we would see her in one of the downstairs windows—she had evidently shut up the top floor of the house—like the carven torso of an idol in a niche, looking or not looking at us, we could never tell which. Thus she passed from generation to generation—dear, inescapable, impervious, tranquil, and perverse.

And so she died. Fell ill in the house filled with dust and shadows, with only a doddering Negro man to wait on her. We did not even know she was sick; we had long since given up trying to get any information from the Negro. He talked to no one, probably not even to her, for his voice had grown harsh and rusty, as if from disuse.

She died in one of the downstairs rooms, in a heavy walnut bed with a curtain, her gray head propped on a pillow yellow and moldy with age and lack of sunlight.

V

The Negro met the first of the ladies at the front door and let them in with their hushed, sibilant voices and their quick, curious glances, and then he disappeared. He walked right through the house and out the back and was not seen again.

The two female cousins came at once. They held the funeral on the second day, with the town coming to look at Miss Emily beneath a mass of bought flowers, with the crayon face of her father musing profoundly above the bier and the ladies sibilant and macabre; and the very old men—some in their brushed Confederate uniforms—on the porch and the lawn, talking of Miss Emily as if she had been a contemporary of theirs, believing that they had danced with her and courted her perhaps, confusing time with its mathematical progression, as the old do, to whom all the past is not a diminishing road, but, instead, a huge meadow which no winter ever quite touches, divided from them now by the narrow bottleneck of the most recent decade of years.

Already we knew that there was one room in that region above stairs which no one had seen in forty years, and which would have to be forced. They waited until Miss Emily was decently in the ground before they opened it.

The violence of breaking down the door seemed to fill this room with pervading dust. A thin, acid pall as of the tomb seemed to lie everywhere upon this room decked and furnished as for a bridal: upon the valance curtains of faded rose color, upon the rose-shaded lights, upon the dressing table, upon the delicate array of crystal and the man's toilet things backed with tarnished silver, silver so tarnished that the monogram was obscured. Among them lay a collar and tie, as if they had just been removed, which, lifted, left upon the surface a pale crescent in the dust. Upon a chair hung the suit, carefully folded; beneath it the two mute shoes and the discarded socks.

The man himself lay in the bed.

For a long while we just stood there, looking down at the profound and fleshless grin. The body had apparently once lain in the attitude of an embrace, but now the long sleep that outlasts love, that conquers even the grimace of love, had cuckolded him. What was left of him, rotted beneath what was left of the nightshirt, had become inextricable from the bed in which he lay; and upon him and upon the pillow beside him lay that even coating of the patient and biding dust.

Then we noticed that in the second pillow was the indentation of a head. One of us lifted something from it, and leaning forward, that faint and invisible dust dry and acrid in the nostrils, we saw a long strand of iron-gray hair.

DISCUSSION

This is a story of horror. We have a decaying mansion in which the protagonist, shut away from the world, grows into something monstrous, and becomes as divorced from humanity as some fungus growing in the dark on a damp wall. Miss Emily Grierson remains in voluntary isolation (or perhaps fettered by some inner compulsion) away from the bustle and dust and sunshine of the human world of normal affairs, and what in the end is found in the upstairs room gives perhaps a sense of penetrating and gruesome horror.

Has this sense of horror been conjured up for its own sake? If not, then why has the author contrived to insert so much of the monstrous into the story? In other words, does the horror contribute to the theme of Faulkner's story? Is the horror meaningful?

In order to answer this question, we shall have to examine rather carefully some of the items earlier in the story. In the first place, why does Miss Emily commit her monstrous act? Is she supplied with a proper motivation? Faulkner has, we can see, been rather careful to prepare for his denouement. Miss Emily, it becomes obvious fairly early in the story, is one of those persons for whom the distinction between reality and illusion has blurred. For example, she refuses to admit that she owes any taxes. When the mayor protests, she does not recognize him as mayor. Instead, she refers the committee to Colonel Sartoris, who, as the reader is told, has been dead for nearly ten years. For Miss Emily, apparently, Colonel Sartoris is still alive. Most specific preparation of all, when her father dies, she denies to the townspeople for three days that he is dead: "Just as they were about to resort to law and force, she broke down, and they buried her father quickly."

Miss Emily is obviously a pathological case. The narrator indicates plainly enough that people felt that she was crazy. All of this explanation prepares us for what Miss Emily does in order to hold her lover—the dead lover is in one sense still alive for her—the realms of reality and appearance merge. But having said this, we have got no nearer to justifying the story: for, if Faulkner is merely interested in relating a case history of abnormal psychology, the story lacks meaning and justification as a story and we are back to fiction as "clinical report," which we spoke of in connection with "The Occurrence at Owl Creek Bridge" in section 2. If the story is to be justified, there must be what may be called a moral significance, a meaning in moral terms—not merely psychological terms.

Incidentally, it is very easy to misread the story as merely a horrible case history, presented in order to titillate the reader. Faulkner has been frequently judged to be doing nothing more than this in his work.

The lapse of the distinction between illusion and reality, between life and death, is important, therefore, in helping to account for Miss Emily's motivation, but merely to note this lapse is not fully to account for the theme of the story.

Suppose we approach the motivation again in terms of character. What is Miss Emily like? What are the mainsprings of her character? What causes the distinction between illusion and reality to blur for her? She is obviously a woman of tremendous firmness of will. In the matter of the taxes, crazed though she is, she is never at a loss. She is utterly composed. She dominates the rather frightened committee of officers who see her. In the matter of her purchase of the poison, she completely overawes the clerk. She makes no pretense. She refuses to tell him what she wants the poison for. And yet this firmness of will and this iron pride have not kept her from being thwarted and hurt. Her father has run off the young men who came to call upon her, and the townspeople think of Miss Emily and her father as a tableau: "Miss Emily a slender figure in white in the background, her father a spraddled silhouette in the foreground, his back to her and clutching a horsewhip, the two of them framed by the backflung front door." Whether the picture is a remembered scene, or merely a symbolical construct, this is the picture that remains in the storyteller's mind.

Miss Emily's pride is connected with her contempt for public opinion. This comes to the fore, of course, when she rides around about the town with the foreman whom everybody believes is beneath her. And it is her proud refusal to admit an external set of codes, or conventions, or other wills in contradiction to her own, that makes her capable at the end of keeping her lover from going away. Confronted with his jilting her, she tries to override not only his will and the opinion of other people but the laws of death and decay themselves.

But this, still, hardly gives the meaning of the story. For in all that has been said thus far, we are still merely accounting for a psychological aberration—we are still merely dealing with a case history in abnormal psychology. In order to make a case for the story as "meaningful," we shall have to tie Miss Emily's thoughts and actions back into the normal life of the community, and establish some sort of relationship between them. And just here one pervasive element in the narration suggests a clue. The story is told by one of the townspeople. And in it, as a constant factor, is the reference to what the community thought of Miss Emily. Continually through the story it is what "we" said, and then what "we" did, and what seemed true to "us," and so on. The narrator puts the matter even more sharply still. It is said, in the course of the story, that to the community Miss Emily seemed "dear, inescapable, impervious, tranquil, and perverse." Each of the adjectives is important and meaningful. In a sense, Miss Emily because of her very fact of isolation and perversity belongs to the whole community. She is even something treasured by it. Ironically, because of Emily's perversion of an aristocratic independence of mores and because of her contempt for "what people say," her life is public, even communal. And various phrases used by the narrator underline this view of her position. For example, her face looks "as you imagine a lighthouse-keeper's face ought to look," like the face of a person who lives in the kind of isolation imposed on a lighthouse-keeper, who looks out into the blackness and whose light serves a public function. Or, again, after her father's death, she becomes very ill, and when she appears after the illness, she had "a vague resemblance to those angels in colored church windows—sort of tragic and serene." Whatever we make of these descriptions, certainly the author is trying to suggest a kind of calm and dignity that is supermundane, unearthly, or "over-earthly," such as an angel might possess.

Miss Emily, then, is a combination of idol and scapegoat for the community. On the one hand, the community feels admiration for Miss Emily—she represents something in the past of the community that the community is proud of. They feel a sort of awe of her, as is illustrated by the behavior of the mayor and the committee in her presence. On the other hand, her queerness, the fact that she cannot compete with them in their ordinary life, the fact that she is hopelessly out of touch with the modern world—all of these things make them feel superior to her, and also to the past that she represents. It is, then, Miss Emily's complete detachment that gives her actions their special meaning for the community.

Miss Emily, since she is the conscious aristocrat, since she is consciously "better" than other people, since she is above and outside their canons of behavior, can, at the same time, be worse than other people;

and she is worse, horribly so. She is worse than other people, but at the same time, as the narrator implies, she remains somehow admirable. This raises a fundamental question: why is this true?

Perhaps the horrible and the admirable aspects of Miss Emily's final deed arise from the same basic fact of her character: she insists on meeting the world on her own terms. She never cringes, she never begs for sympathy, she refuses to shrink into an amiable old maid, she never accepts the community's ordinary judgments or values. This independence of spirit and pride can, and does in her case, twist the individual into a sort of monster, but, at the same time, this refusal to accept the herd values carries with it a dignity and courage. The community senses this, as we gather from the fact that the community carries out the decencies of the funeral before breaking in the door of the upper room. There is, as it were, a kind of secret understanding that she has won her right of privacy, until she herself has entered history. Furthermore, despite the fact that, as the narrator says, "already we knew that there was one room in that region above stairs which no one had seen in forty years, and which would have to be forced," her funeral is something of a state occasion, with "the very old men—some in their brushed Confederate uniforms—on the porch and the lawn, talking of Miss Emily as if she had been a contemporary of theirs, believing that they had danced with her and courted her perhaps." In other words, the community accepts her into its honored history. All of this works as a kind of tacit recognition of Miss Emily's triumph of will. The community, we are told earlier, had wanted to pity Miss Emily when she had lost her money, just as they had wanted to commiserate over her when they believed that she had actually become a fallen woman, but she had triumphed over their pity and commiseration and condemnation, just as she had triumphed over all their other attitudes.

But, still, it may be said that Miss Emily is mad. This may be true, but there are two things to consider in this connection. First, one must consider the special terms that her "madness" takes. Her madness is simply a development of her pride and her refusal to submit to ordinary standards of behavior. So, because of this fact, her "madness" is meaningful after all. It involves issues that in themselves are really important and have to do with the world of conscious moral choice. Second, the community interprets her "madness" as meaningful. They admire her, even if they are disappointed by her refusals to let herself be pitied, and the narrator, who is a spokesman for the community, recognizes the last grim revelation as an instance of her having carried her own values to their ultimate conclusion. She would marry the common laborer, Homer Barron, let the community think what it would. She would not be jilted. And she would hold him as a lover. But it would all be on her own terms. She remains completely dominant, and contemptuous of the day-to-day world.

It has been suggested by many critics that tragedy implies a hero who is completely himself, who insists on meeting the world on his own terms, who wants something so intensely, or lives so intensely, that he cannot accept any compromise. It cannot be maintained that this story is comparable to any of the great tragedies, such as *Hamlet* or *King Lear*, but it can be pointed out that this story, in its own way, involves some of the same basic elements. Certainly, Miss Emily's pride, isolation, and independence remind us of aspects in the character of the typical tragic hero. And it can be pointed out that, just as the horror of her deed lies outside the ordinary life of the community, so the magnificence of her independence lies outside its ordinary virtues.

1. What difficulties would arise if you tried to tell this story from the point of view of the third person?
2. Why is it significant that Miss Emily chooses for her lover a man who is scornfully regarded by the community as a "Northerner, a day laborer"?
3. Look back at "Young Goodman Brown" and "The Killers" in the light of their general symbolic significance. Can it be argued that the present story, like them, has a more general significance—that it is a symbolic commentary on our society? If so, how would you argue this point?

A GOOD MAN IS HARD TO FIND

Flannery O'Connor

THE grandmother didn't want to go to Florida. She wanted to visit some of her connections in east Tennessee and she was seizing at every chance to change Bailey's mind. Bailey was the son she lived with, her only boy. He was sitting on the edge of his chair at the table, bent over the orange sports section of the *Journal*. "Now look here, Bailey," she said, "see here, read this," and she stood with one hand on her thin hip and the other rattling the newspaper at his bald head. "Here this fellow that calls himself The Misfit is aloose from the Federal Pen and headed toward Florida and you read what it says he did to these people. Just you read it. I wouldn't take my children in any direction with a criminal like that aloose in it. I couldn't answer to my conscience if I did."

Bailey didn't look up from his reading so she wheeled around then and faced the children's mother, a young woman in slacks, whose face was as broad and innocent as a cabbage and was tied around with a green headkerchief that had two points on the top like rabbit's ears. She was sitting on the sofa, feeding the baby his apricots out of a jar. "The children have been to Florida before," the old lady said. "You all ought to take them somewhere else for a change so they would see different parts of the world and be broad. They never have been to east Tennessee."

The children's mother didn't seem to hear her but the eight-year-old boy, John Wesley, a stocky child with glasses, said, "If you don't want to go to Florida, why dontcha stay at home?" He and the little girl, June Star, were reading the funny papers on the floor.

"She wouldn't stay at home to be queen for a day," June Star said without raising her yellow head.

"Yes, and what would you do if this fellow, The Misfit, caught you?" the grandmother asked.

"I'd smack his face," John Wesley said.

"She wouldn't stay at home for a million bucks," June Star said. "Afraid she'd miss something. She has to go everywhere we go."

"All right, Miss," the grandmother said. "Just remember that the next time you want me to curl your hair."

June Star said her hair was naturally curly.

The next morning the grandmother was the first one in the car, ready to go. She had her big black valise that looked like the head of a hippopotamus in one corner, and underneath it she was hiding a basket with Pitty Sing, the cat, in it. She didn't intend for the cat to be left alone in the house for three days because he would miss her too much and she was afraid he might brush against one of the gas burners and accidentally asphyxiate himself. Her son, Bailey, didn't like to arrive at a motel with a cat.

She sat in the middle of the back seat with John Wesley and June Star on either side of her. Bailey and the children's mother and the baby sat in front and they left Atlanta at eight forty-five with the mileage on the car at 55890. The grandmother wrote this down because she thought it would be interesting to say how many miles they had been when they got back. It took them twenty minutes to reach the outskirts of the city.

The old lady settled herself comfortably, removing her white cotton gloves and putting them up with her purse on the shelf in front of the back window. The children's mother still had on slacks and still had her head tied up in a green kerchief, but the grandmother had on a navy blue straw sailor hat with a bunch of white violets on the brim and a navy blue dress with a small white dot in the print. Her collars and cuffs were white organdy trimmed with lace and at her neckline she had pinned a purple spray of cloth violets containing a sachet. In case of an accident, anyone seeing her dead on the highway would know at once that she was a lady.

She said she thought it was going to be a good day for driving, neither too hot nor too cold, and she cautioned Bailey that the speed limit was fifty-five miles an hour and that the patrolmen hid themselves behind billboards and small clumps of trees and sped out after you before you had a chance to slow down. She pointed out interesting details of the scenery: Stone Mountain; the blue granite that in some places came up to both sides of the highway; the brilliant red clay banks slightly streaked with purple; and the various crops that made rows of green lace-work on the ground. The trees were full of silver-white sunlight and the meanest of them sparkled. The children were reading comic magazines and their mother had gone back to sleep.

"Let's go through Georgia fast so we won't have to look at it much," John Wesley said.

"If I were a little boy," said the grandmother, "I wouldn't talk about my native state that way. Tennessee has the mountains and Georgia has the hills."

"Tennessee is just a hillbilly dumping ground," John Wesley said, "and Georgia is a lousy state too."

"You said it," June Star said.

"In my time," said the grandmother, folding her thin veined fingers, "children were more respectful of their native states and their parents and everything else. People did right then. Oh look at the cute little pickaninny!" she said and pointed to a Negro child standing in the door of a shack. "Wouldn't that make a picture, now?" she asked and they all turned and looked at the little Negro out of the back window. He waved.

"He didn't have any britches on," June Star said.

"He probably didn't have any," the grandmother explained. "Little niggers in the country don't have things like we do. If I could paint, I'd paint that picture," she said.

The children exchanged comic books.

The grandmother offered to hold the baby and the children's mother passed him over the front seat to her. She set him on her knee and bounced him and told him about the things they were passing. She rolled her eyes and screwed up her mouth and stuck her leathery thin face into his smooth bland one. Occasionally he gave her a faraway smile. They passed a large cotton field with five or six graves fenced in the middle of it, like a small island. "Look at the graveyard!" the grandmother said, pointing it out. "That was the old family burying ground. That belonged to the plantation."

"Where's the plantation?" John Wesley asked.

"Gone With the Wind," said the grandmother. "Ha. Ha."

When the children finished all the comic books they had brought, they opened the lunch and ate it. The grandmother ate a peanut butter sandwich and an olive and would not let the children throw the box and the paper napkins out the window. When there was nothing else to do they played a game by choosing a cloud and making the other two guess what shape it suggested. John Wesley took one the shape of a cow and June Star guessed a cow and John Wesley said, no, an automobile, and June Star said he didn't play fair, and they began to slap each other over the grandmother.

The grandmother said she would tell them a story if they would keep quiet. When she told a story, she rolled her eyes and waved her head and was very dramatic. She said once when she was a maiden lady she had been courted by a Mr. Edgar Atkins Teagarden from Jasper, Georgia. She said he was a very good-looking man and a gentleman and that he brought her a watermelon every Saturday afternoon with his initials cut in it, E.A.T. Well, one Saturday, she said, Mr. Teagarden brought the watermelon and there was nobody at home and he left it on the front porch and returned in his buggy to Jasper, but she never got the watermelon, she said, because a nigger boy ate it when he saw the initials, E.A.T.! This story tickled John Wesley's funny bone and he giggled and giggled but June Star didn't think it was any good. She said she wouldn't marry a man that just brought her a watermelon on Saturday. The grandmother said she would have done well to marry Mr. Teagarden because he was a gentleman and had bought Coca-Cola stock when it first came out and that he had died only a few years ago, a very wealthy man.

They stopped at the Tower for barbecued sandwiches. The Tower was a part stucco and part wood filling station and dance hall set in a clearing outside of Timothy. A fat man named Red Sammy Butts ran it and there were signs stuck here and there on the building and for miles up and down the highway saying, TRY RED SAMMY'S FAMOUS BARBECUE. NONE LIKE FAMOUS RED SAMMY'S! RED SAM! THE FAT BOY WITH THE HAPPY LAUGH. A VETERAN! RED SAMMY'S YOUR MAN!

Red Sammy was lying on the bare ground outside The Tower with his head under a truck while a gray monkey about a foot high, chained to a small chinaberry tree, chattered nearby. The monkey sprang back into the tree and got on the highest limb as soon as he saw the children jump out of the car and run toward him.

Inside, The Tower was a long dark room with a counter at one end and tables at the other and dancing space in the middle. They all sat down at a board table next to the nickelodeon and Red Sam's wife, a tall burnt-brown woman with hair and eyes lighter than her skin, came and took their order. The children's mother put a dime in the machine and played "The Tennessee Waltz," and the grandmother said that tune always made her want to dance. She asked Bailey if he would like to dance but he only glared at her. He didn't have a naturally sunny disposition like she did and trips made him nervous. The grandmother's brown eyes were very bright. She swayed her head from side to side and pretended she was dancing in her chair. June Star said play something she could tap to so the children's mother put in another dime and played a fast number and June Star stepped out onto the dance floor and did her tap routine.

"Ain't she cute?" Red Sam's wife said, leaning over the counter. "Would you like to come be my little girl?"

"No I certainly wouldn't," June Star said. "I wouldn't live in a broken-down place like this for a million bucks!" and she ran back to the table.

"Ain't she cute?" the woman repeated, stretching her mouth politely.

"Aren't you ashamed?" hissed the grandmother.

Red Sam came in and told his wife to quit lounging on the counter and hurry up with these people's order. His khaki trousers reached just to his hip bones and his stomach hung over them like a sack of meal swaying under his shirt. He came over and sat down at a table nearby and let out a combination sigh and yodel. "You can't win," he said. "You can't win," and he wiped his sweating red face off with a gray handkerchief. "These days you don't know who to trust," he said. "Ain't that the truth?"

"People are certainly not nice like they used to be," said the grand-mother.

"Two fellers come in here last week," Red Sammy said, "driving a Chrysler. It was a old beat-up car but it was a good one and these boys looked all right to me. Said they worked at the mill and you know I let them fellers charge the gas they bought? Now why did I do that?"

"Because you're a good man!" the grandmother said at once.

"Yes'm, I suppose so," Red Sam said as if he were struck with this answer.

His wife brought the orders, carrying the five plates all at once without a tray, two in each hand and one balanced on her arm. "It isn't a soul in this green world of God's that you can trust," she said. "And I don't count nobody out of that, not nobody," she repeated, looking at Red Sammy.

"Did you read about that criminal, The Misfit, that's escaped?" asked the grandmother.

"I wouldn't be a bit surprised if he didn't attack this place right here," said the woman. "If he hears about it being here, I wouldn't be none surprised to see him. If he hears it's two cent in the cash register, I wouldn't be at all surprised if he . . ."

"That'll do," Red Sam said. "Go bring these people their Co'-Colas," and the woman went off to get the rest of the order.

"A good man is hard to find," Red Sammy said. "Everything is getting terrible. I remember the day you could go off and leave your screen door unlatched. Not no more."

He and the grandmother discussed better times. The old lady said that in her opinion Europe was entirely to blame for the way things were now. She said the way Europe acted you would think we were made of money and Red Sam said it was no use talking about it, she was exactly right. The children ran outside into the white sunlight and looked at the monkey in the lacy chinaberry tree. He was busy catching fleas on himself and biting each one carefully between his teeth as if it were a delicacy.

They drove off again into the hot afternoon. The grandmother took cat naps and woke up every few minutes with her own snoring. Outside of Toombsboro she woke up and recalled an old plantation that she had visited in this neighborhood once when she was a young lady. She said the house had six white columns across the front and that there was an avenue of oaks leading up to it and two little wooden trellis arbors on either side in front where you sat down with your suitor after a stroll in the garden. She recalled exactly which road to turn off to get to it. She knew that Bailey would not be willing to lose any time looking at an old house, but the more she talked about it, the more she wanted to see it once again and find out if the little twin arbors were still standing. "There was a secret panel in this house," she said craftily, not telling the truth but wishing that she were, "and the story went that all the family silver was hidden in it when Sherman came through but it was never found . . ."

"Hey!" John Wesley said. "Let's go see it! We'll find it! We'll poke all the woodwork and find it! Who lives there? Where do you turn off at? Hey Pop, can't we turn off there?"

"We never have seen a house with a secret panel!" June Star shrieked. "Let's go to the house with the secret panel! Hey Pop, can't we go see the house with the secret panel!"

"It's not far from here, I know," the grandmother said. "It wouldn't take over twenty minutes."

Bailey was looking straight ahead. His jaw was as rigid as a horseshoe. "No," he said.

The children began to yell and scream that they wanted to see the house with the secret panel. John Wesley kicked the back of the front seat and June Star hung over her mother's shoulder and whined desperately into her ear that they never had any fun even on their vacation, that they could never do what THEY wanted to do. The baby began to scream and John Wesley kicked the back of the seat so hard that his father could feel the blows in his kidney.

"All right!" he shouted and drew the car to a stop at the side of the road. "Will you all shut up? Will you all just shut up for one second? If you don't shut up, we won't go anywhere."

"It would be very educational for them," the grandmother murmured.

"All right," Bailey said, "but get this: this is the only time we're going to stop for anything like this. This is the one and only time."

"The dirt road that you have to turn down is about a mile back," the grandmother directed. "I marked it when we passed."

"A dirt road," Bailey groaned.

After they had turned around and were headed toward the dirt road, the grandmother recalled other points about the house, the beautiful glass over the front doorway and the candle-lamp in the hall. John Wesley said that the secret panel was probably in the fireplace.

"You can't go inside this house," Bailey said. "You don't know who lives there."

"While you all talk to the people in front, I'll run around behind and get in a window," John Wesley suggested.

"We'll all stay in the car," his mother said.

They turned onto the dirt road and the car raced roughly along in a swirl of pink dust. The grandmother recalled the times when there were no paved roads and thirty miles was a day's journey. The dirt road was hilly and there were sudden washes in it and sharp curves on dangerous embankments. All at once they would be on a hill, looking down over the blue tops of trees for miles around, then the next minute, they would be in a red depression with the dust-coated trees looking down on them.

"This place had better turn up in a minute," Bailey said, "or I'm going to turn around."

The road looked as if no one had traveled on it in months.

"It's not much farther," the grandmother said and just as she said it, a horrible thought came to her. The thought was so embarrassing that she turned red in the face and her eyes dilated and her feet jumped up, upsetting her valise in the corner. The instant the valise moved, the newspaper top she had over the basket under it rose with a snarl and Pitty Sing, the cat, sprang onto Bailey's shoulder.

The children were thrown to the floor and their mother, clutching the baby, was thrown out the door onto the ground; the old lady was thrown into the front seat. The car turned over once and landed right-side-up in a gulch off the side of the road. Bailey remained in the driver's seat with the cat—gray-striped with a broad white face and an orange nose—clinging to his neck like a caterpillar.

As soon as the children saw they could move their arms and legs, they scrambled out of the car, shouting, "We've had an ACCIDENT!" The grandmother was curled up under the dashboard, hoping she was injured so that Bailey's wrath would not come down on her all at once. The horrible thought she had had before the accident was that the house she had remembered so vividly was not in Georgia but in Tennessee.

Bailey removed the cat from his neck with both hands and flung it out the window against the side of a pine tree. Then he got out of the car and started looking for the children's mother. She was sitting against the side of the red gutted ditch, holding the screaming baby, but she only had a cut down her face and a broken shoulder. "We've had an ACCI-DENT!" the children screamed in a frenzy of delight.

"But nobody's killed," June Star said with disappointment as the grandmother limped out of the car, her hat still pinned to her head but the broken front brim standing up at a jaunty angle and the violet spray hanging off the side. They all sat down in the ditch, except the children, to recover from the shock. They were all shaking.

"Maybe a car will come along," said the children's mother hoarsely.

"I believe I have an injured organ," said the grandmother, pressing her side, but no one answered her. Bailey's teeth were clattering. He had on a yellow sport shirt with bright blue parrots designed on it and his face was as yellow as the shirt. The grandmother decided that she would not mention that the house was in Tennessee.

The road was about ten feet above and they could see only the tops of the trees on the other side of it. Behind the ditch they were sitting in there were more woods, tall and dark and deep. In a few minutes they saw a car some distance away on top of a hill, coming slowly as if the occupants were watching them. The grandmother stood up and waved both arms dramatically to attract their attention. The car continued to come on slowly, disappeared around a bend and appeared again, moving even slower, on top of the hill they had gone over. It was a big black battered hearse-like automobile. There were three men in it.

It came to a stop just over them and for some minutes, the driver looked down with a steady expressionless gaze to where they were sitting, and didn't speak. Then he turned his head and muttered something to the other two and they got out. One was a fat boy in black trousers and a red sweat shirt with a silver stallion embossed on the front of it. He moved around on the right side of them and stood staring, his mouth partly open in a kind of loose grin. The other had on khaki pants and a blue striped coat and a gray hat pulled down very low, hiding most of his face. He came around slowly on the left side. Neither spoke.

The driver got out of the car and stood by the side of it, looking down at them. He was an older man than the other two. His hair was just beginning to gray and he wore silver-rimmed spectacles that gave him a scholarly look. He had a long creased face and didn't have on any shirt or undershirt. He had on blue jeans that were too tight for him and was holding a black hat and a gun. The two boys also had guns.

"We've had an ACCIDENT!" the children screamed.

The grandmother had the peculiar feeling that the bespectacled man was someone she knew. His face was as familiar to her as if she had known him all her life but she could not recall who he was. He moved away from the car and began to come down the embankment, placing his feet carefully so that he wouldn't slip. He had on tan and white shoes and no socks, and his ankles were red and thin. "Good afternoon," he said. "I see you all had you a little spill."

"We turned over twice!" said the grandmother.

"Oncet," he corrected. "We seen it happen. Try their car and see will it run, Hiram," he said quietly to the boy with the gray hat.

"What you got that gun for?" John Wesley asked. "Whatcha gonna do with that gun?"

"Lady," the man said to the children's mother, "would you mind calling them children to sit down by you? Children make me nervous. I want all you to sit down right together there where you're at."

"What are you telling US what to do for?" June Star asked.

Behind them the line of woods gaped like a dark open mouth. "Come here," said their mother.

"Look here now," Bailey began suddenly, "we're in a predicament! We're in . . ."

The grandmother shrieked. She scrambled to her feet and stood staring. "You're The Misfit!" she said. "I recognized you at once!"

"Yes'm," the man said, smiling slightly as if he were pleased in spite of himself to be known, "but it would have been better for all of you, lady, if you hadn't of reckernized me."

Bailey turned his head sharply and said something to his mother that shocked even the children. The old lady began to cry and The Misfit reddened.

"Lady," he said, "don't you get upset. Sometimes a man says things he don't mean. I don't reckon he meant to talk to you thataway."

"You wouldn't shoot a lady, would you?" the grandmother said and removed the clean handkerchief from her cuff and began to slap at her eyes with it.

The Misfit pointed the toe of his shoe into the ground and made a little hole and then covered it up again. "I would hate to have to," he said.

"Listen," the grandmother almost screamed, "I know you're a good man. You don't look a bit like you have common blood. I know you must come from nice people!"

"Yes mam," he said, "finest people in the world." When he smiled he showed a row of strong white teeth. "God never made a finer woman than my mother and my daddy's heart was pure gold," he said. The boy with the red sweat shirt had come around behind them and was standing with his gun at his hip. The Misfit squatted down on the ground. "Watch them children, Bobby Lee," he said. "You know they make me nervous." He looked at the six of them huddled together in front of him and he seemed to be embarrassed as if he couldn't think of anything to say. "Ain't a cloud in the sky," he remarked, looking up at it. "Don't see no sun but don't see no cloud neither."

"Yes, it's a beautiful day," said the grandmother. "Listen," she said, "you shouldn't call yourself The Misfit because I know you're a good man at heart. I can just look at you and tell."

"Hush!" Bailey yelled. "Hush! Everybody shut up and let me handle this!" He was squatting in the position of a runner about to sprint forward but he didn't move.

"I pre-chate that, lady," The Misfit said and drew a little circle in the ground with the butt of his gun.

"It'll take a half a hour to fix this here car," Hiram called, looking over the raised hood of it.

"Well, first you and Bobby Lee get him and that little boy to step over yonder with you," The Misfit said, pointing to Bailey and John Wesley. "The boys want to ask you something," he said to Bailey. "Would you mind stepping back in them woods there with them?"

"Listen," Bailey began, "we're in a terrible predicament! Nobody realizes what this is," and his voice cracked. His eyes were as blue and intense as the parrots on his shirt and he remained perfectly still.

The grandmother reached up to adjust her hat brim as if she were going to the woods with him but it came off in her hand. She stood staring at it and after a second she let it fall on the ground. Hiram pulled Bailey up by the arm as if he were assisting an old man. John Wesley caught hold of his father's hand and Bobby Lee followed. They went off toward the woods and just as they reached the dark edge, Bailey turned and supported himself against a gray naked pine trunk, he shouted, "I'll be back in a minute, Mamma, wait on me!"

"Come back this instant!" his mother shrilled but they all disappeared into the woods.

"Bailey Boy!" the grandmother called in a tragic voice but she found she was looking at The Misfit squatting on the ground in front of her. "I just know you're a good man," she said desperately. "You're not a bit common!"

"Nome, I ain't a good man," The Misfit said after a second as if.he had considered her statement carefully, "but I ain't the worst in the world neither. My daddy said I was a different breed of dog from my brothers and sisters. 'You know,' Daddy said, 'it's some that can live their whole life out without asking about it and it's others has to know why it is, and this boy is one of the latters. He's going to be into everything!' " He put on his black hat and looked up suddenly and then away deep into the woods as if he were embarrassed again. "I'm sorry I don't have on a shirt before you ladies," he said, hunching his shoulders slightly. "We buried our clothes that we had on when we escaped and we're just making do until we can get better. We borrowed these from some folks we met," he explained.

"That's perfectly all right," the grandmother said. "Maybe Bailey has an extra shirt in his suitcase."

"I'll look and see terrectly," The Misfit said.

"Where are they taking him?" the children's mother screamed.

"Daddy was a card himself," The Misfit said. "You couldn't put anything over on him. He never got in trouble with the Authorities though. Just had the knack of handling them."

"You could be honest too if you'd only try," said the grandmother. "Think how wonderful it would be to settle down and live a comfortable life and not have to think about somebody chasing you all the time."

The Misfit kept scratching in the ground with the butt of his gun as if he were thinking about it. "Yes'm, somebody is always after you," he murmured.

The grandmother noticed how thin his shoulder blades were just behind his hat because she was standing up looking down on him. "Do you ever pray?" she asked.

He shook his head. All she saw was the black hat wiggle between his shoulder blades. "Nome," he said.

There was a pistol shot from the woods, followed closely by another. Then silence. The old lady's head jerked around. She could hear the wind move through the tree tops like a long satisfied insuck of breath. "Bailey Boy!" she called.

"I was a gospel singer for a while," The Misfit said. "I been most everything. Been in the arm service, both land and sea, at home and abroad, been twict married, been an undertaker, been with the railroads, plowed Mother Earth, been in a tornado, seen a man burnt alive oncet," and he looked up at the children's mother and the little girl who were sitting close together, their faces white and their eyes glassy; "I even seen a woman flogged," he said.

"Pray, pray," the grandmother began, "pray, pray . . ."

"I never was a bad boy that I remember of," The Misfit said in an almost dreamy voice, "but somewheres along the line I done something wrong and got sent to the penitentiary. I was buried alive," and he looked up and held her attention to him by a steady stare.

"That's when you should have started to pray," she said. "What did you do to get sent to the penitentiary that first time?"

"Turn to the right, it was a wall," The Misfit said, looking up again at the cloudless sky. "Turn to the left, it was a wall. Look up it was a ceiling, look down it was a floor. I forget what I done, lady. I set there and set there, trying to remember what it was I done and I ain't recalled it to this day. Oncet in a while, I would think it was coming to me, but it never come."

"Maybe they put you in by mistake," the old lady said vaguely.

"Nome," he said. "it wasn't no mistake. They had the papers on me."

"You must have stolen something," she said.

The Misfit sneered slightly. "Nobody had nothing I wanted," he said. "It was a head-doctor at the penitentiary said what I had done was kill my daddy but I known that for a lie. My daddy died in nineteen ought nineteen of the epidemic flu and I never had a thing to do with it. He was buried in the Mount Hopewell Baptist churchyard and you can go there and see for yourself."

"If you would pray," the old lady said, "Jesus would help you."

"That's right," The Misfit said.

"Well then, why don't you pray?" she asked trembling with delight suddenly.

"I don't want no hep," he said. "I'm doing all right by myself."

Bobby Lee and Hiram came ambling back from the woods. Bobby Lee was dragging a yellow shirt with bright blue parrots in it.

"Throw me that shirt, Bobby Lee," The Misfit said. The shirt came flying at him and landed on his shoulder and he put it on. The grandmother couldn't name what the shirt reminded her of. "No, lady," The Misfit said while he was buttoning it up, "I found out the crime don't matter. You can do one thing or you can do another, kill a man or take a tire off his car, because sooner or later you're going to forget what it was you done and just be punished for it."

The children's mother had begun to make heaving noises as if she couldn't get her breath. "Lady," he asked, "would you and that little girl like to step off yonder with Bobby Lee and Hiram and join your husband?"

"Yes, thank you," the mother said faintly. Her left arm dangled helplessly and she was holding the baby, who had gone to sleep, in the other. "Hep that lady up, Hiram," The Misfit said as she struggled to climb out of the ditch, "And Bobby Lee, you hold onto that little girl's hand."

"I don't want to hold hands with him," June Star said. "He reminds me of a pig."

The fat boy blushed and laughed and caught her by the arm and pulled her off into the woods after Hiram and her mother.

Alone with The Misfit, the grandmother found that she had lost her voice. There was not a cloud in the sky nor any sun. There was nothing around her but woods. She wanted to tell him that he must pray. She opened and closed her mouth several times before anything came out. Finally she found herself saying, "Jesus, Jesus," meaning, Jesus will help you, but the way she was saying it, it sounded as if she might be cursing.

"Yes'm," The Misfit said as if he agreed. "Jesus thown everything off balance. It was the same case with Him as with me except He hadn't committed any crime and they could prove I had committed one because they had the papers on me. Of course," he said, "they never shown me my papers. That's why I sign myself now. I said long ago, you get you a signature and sign everything you do and keep a copy of it. Then you'll know what you done and you can hold up the crime to the punishment and see do they match and in the end you'll have something to prove you ain't been treated right. I call myself The Misfit," he said, "because I can't make what all I done wrong fit what all I gone through in punishment."

There was a piercing scream from the woods, followed closely by a pistol report. "Does it seem right to you, lady, that one is punished a heap and another ain't punished at all?"

"Jesus!" the old lady cried. "You've got good blood! I know you wouldn't shoot a lady! I know you come from nice people! Pray! Jesus, you ought not to shoot a lady. I'll give you all the money I've got!"

"Lady," The Misfit said, looking beyond her far into the woods, "there never was a body that give the undertaker a tip."

There were two more pistol reports and the grandmother raised her head like a parched old turkey hen crying for water and called, "Bailey Boy, Bailey Boy!" as if her heart would break.

"Jesus was the only One that ever raised the dead," The Misfit continued, "and He shouldn't have done it. He thown everything off balance. If He did what He said, then it's nothing for you to do but throw away everything and follow Him, and if He didn't, then it's nothing for you to do but enjoy the few minutes you got left the best way you can—by killing somebody or burning down his house or doing some other meanness to him. No pleasure but meanness," he said and his voice had become almost a snarl.

"Maybe He didn't raise the dead," the old lady mumbled, not knowing what she was saying and feeling so dizzy that she sank down in the ditch with her legs twisted under her.

"I wasn't there so I can't say He didn't," The Misfit said. "I wisht I had of been there," he said, hitting the ground with his fist. "It ain't right I wasn't there because if I had of been there I would of known. Listen lady," he said in a high voice, "if I had of been there I would of known and I wouldn't be like I am now." His voice seemed about to crack and the grandmother's head cleared for an instant. She saw the man's face twisted close to her own as if he were going to cry and she murmured, "Why you're one of my babies. You're one of my own children!" She reached out and touched him on the shoulder. The Misfit sprang back as if a snake had bitten him and shot her three times through the chest. Then he put his gun down on the ground and took off his glasses and began to clean them.

Hiram and Bobby Lee returned from the woods and stood over the ditch, looking down at the grandmother who half sat and half lay in a puddle of blood with her legs crossed under her like a child's and her face smiling up at the cloudless sky.

Without his glasses, The Misfit's eyes were red-rimmed and pale and defenseless-looking. "Take her off and thow her where you thown the others," he said, picking up the cat that was rubbing itself against his leg.

"She was a talker, wasn't she?" Bobby Lee said, sliding down the ditch with a yodel.

"She would of been a good woman," The Misfit said, "if it had been somebody there to shoot her every minute of her life."

"Some fun!" Bobby Lee said.

"Shut up, Bobby Lee," The Misfit said. "It's no real pleasure in life."

DISCUSSION

1. This story, like "A Rose for Emily," presents us with a shocking piece of pathology. Viewed objectively, the story is an account of how a homicidal maniac slaughters a family of ordinary, innocent people whom he happens to encounter on the road. How does the author interpret this special situation as a comment on general human values? (Of course, insofar as the story is coherent, everything in it will bear on the answer to this question, but especially important for an answer is the dialogue between the old lady and The Misfit. Study very carefully this dialogue and then try to make a statement about the theme of the story.)

2. What is the character of the old lady? Pleasant or unpleasant? Admirable or unadmirable? Selfish or unselfish? How does her character bear on the interpretation of the story?

3. The story can be said to be in two parts—the long first part dealing with the trip, and the second part after the encounter with The Misfit. What, if anything, holds these two parts together? How does this connection between the parts relate to the theme of the story? In connection with this we may say that the encounter is pure coincidence—The Misfit just happens to come along at the moment when the family has the accident. We have said that, in general, dependence on coincidence is a fault in fiction. What about this instance? Does the fact of the coincidence bear on the theme?

4. What is the significance, if any, of the scene at the highway restaurant?

5. What responsibility does the old lady have for the family's disaster? Can we detect a pattern here? If so, what does it mean?

6. Let us suppose that the old lady were of unusual intelligence and were a completely devout Christian. What effect would this change have on the irony of the conclusion? In thinking of this question go back to the dialogue between the old lady and The Misfit. Which of the two, the sane woman or the maniac, is the more deeply involved in the religious question?

7. What significance for the story lies in the fact that the old lady feels that she has come down socially?

8. What impression do you have of the family in general?

9. Write a brief character sketch of the old lady. How do you relate her to the theme of the story?

10. What is the significance of the old lady's last words to The Misfit? For plot? For theme?

5

The New Fiction

As we have remarked earlier, fiction seeks to create an imagined reality. The "John" in the story is not, we know, a John who has a certain Social Security number, lives on a certain street, and usually votes Republican at election time. "John" is real only in the imagination of the writer and, provided the story is sufficiently well written, real in the imagination of the reader.

Most fiction we now encounter makes its "John"—the imagined fellow—as much like the real Johns as possible—driving a Ford or a Cadillac, dressing like other men of his economic and social level, and speaking the current language of his age and class. That is, most current fiction is realistic. We are so accustomed to this fact that we often forget that any other kind exists.

At this point, however, let us go back to our introduction (page 1). The tales told by the cave man at his fire, and by his ancient descendants, such as the Greeks of Homer's time, often had elements of realism in them, but they were frequently fantasies of one kind or another, populated by gods, demigods, or monsters, or by heroes of superhuman strength—all of them images drawn from dreams of personal power or terror in a world that was not very clearly understood. It was a world in which gods and goddesses took part in human quarrels, or even loved or hated human beings—a world in which gods might beget children of mortal women or goddesses bear children to mortal men. Furthermore, for centuries fables, fairy tales, and folk tales continued to deny the limitations of the day-to-day world. Of course, elements of realism might be included also—descriptions of palaces and hovels, accounts of seamanship, references to all the paraphernalia of daily living.

So much for the content of this earlier fiction. It differed from our realistic fiction also in language, in style, and in the fact that it was usually written in verse. The fictive stories of Homer (*The Iliad* and *The Odyssey*, as his epics are called) were written in strictly metered verse; the emotional effect of the rhythm worked to sustain an "emotional" realism and to allow the reader's imagination to transcend the limitations of a down-to-earth realism. The response of the reader to highly imaginative verse epics such as *The Odyssey* or *The Song of Roland* was very different from that elicited by present-day fiction, in which the presence of a Ford or a Cadillac in the story is there to substantiate the actuality of the world presented.

Though most plays of our own time are written in prose, in earlier times they were, as a matter of course, written in verse—not only the tragedies of the ancient Greeks, but also those of the Elizabethan age—

Shakespeare's plays, for example. As late as the seventeenth century verse was the characteristic mode of serious drama. Though some prose narratives date from the Elizabethan period, they were not notably realistic. As for the novel, in this period it can scarcely be said to have existed.

In fact, the long prose narrative, which we call the novel, did not really develop until the modern world began to take shape, with the growth of urban life; the beginnings of modern science; the coming of the Industrial Revolution; and the rise of a prosperous middle class, which generated a wider literacy. The novel, written for an audience nurtured by this new, modern world, took its content, more or less, from the nature of that world. The novel was written in the standard prose of the time, even though personal and regional peculiarities might be employed to provide realistic or comic effect.

Now, for one additional important fact underlying many others: In the eighteenth and nineteenth centuries the age of mechanical science had developed and was generally accepted. The world was a big, tidy machine (perhaps operated by God, though at a distance). Science constituted the attempt to understand this big machine, and the novel was an attempt to understand, or report, at least, on man in society, society being the human aspect of the big machine that was the world.

This is not the place to discuss the world-shattering revolution in science that marks the twentieth century—matters such as the rise of quantum physics, the new definitions of matter and energy, the theory of relativity, the new conceptions of time and space, the probing of the universe by powerful telescopes, and the unimaginable inwardness laid bare by the electronic microscope. One should add to these events developments in psychology—the complication of motive and behavior revealed by psychoanalysis and related studies. Such new discoveries and theories have developed at great speed.

In other words, the twentieth century would seem to the eyes of people of earlier centuries a world crammed with strange, uncanny, and fantastic events. Out of this shocking and wildly improbable world, the form of narrative which we call "science fiction" arose early in this century—perhaps earlier still. Yet not only science fiction was marked by the influence of the new view of our world. Fiction in general was affected. Fiction began to concern itself more and more with different levels of psychological and objective reality. Writers of fiction began to treat time in far more complex ways than they had in previous simple narratives, where time is linear as measured by the clock, and to explore the newly discerned complexity of human motives and actions, including the nature of shock and trauma, sexuality, and cruelty—all of which are features of the so-called neo-Gothic fiction.[1]

In the stories of this section, we see some examples of the new experimental fiction. This new type has certainly not supplanted the more

---

[1]The term *Gothic* was applied in the late eighteenth century and for a time after to a shocking, terror-ridden, and sadistic fiction then popular. The work of Poe, for example, would be a fairly late example, in America.

characteristic older type, but it is a force to be reckoned with, has already made itself felt among writers and readers, and has scored some triumphs in its mode. It may turn out to be, of course, a peripheral development, and the deeper effects of modern science and philosophy may take a quite different form. In any case, our main point here is to illustrate the fact that even the remote intellectual developments in science and philosophy are never without their effects on the development of fictional method and content.

CONTINUITY OF PARKS

Julio Cortázar

HE had begun to read the novel a few days before. He had put it down because of some urgent business conferences, opened it again on his way back to the estate by train; he permitted himself a slowly growing interest in the plot, in the characterization. That afternoon, after writing a letter giving his power of attorney and discussing a matter of joint ownership with the manager of his estate, he returned to the book in the tranquillity of his study which looked out upon the park with its oaks. Sprawled in his favorite armchair, its back toward the door—even the possibility of an intrusion would have irritated him, had he thought of it—he let his left hand caress repeatedly the green velvet upholstery and set to reading the final chapters. He remembered effortlessly the names and his mental image of the characters; the novel spread its glamour over him almost at once. He tasted the almost perverse pleasure of disengaging himself line by line from the things around him, and at the same time feeling his head rest comfortably on the green velvet of the chair with its high back, sensing that the cigarettes rested within reach of his hand, that beyond the great windows the air of afternoon danced under the oak trees in the park. Word by word, licked up by the sordid dilemma of the hero and heroine, letting himself be absorbed to the point where the images settled down and took on color and movement, he was witness to the final encounter in the mountain cabin. The woman arrived first, apprehensive; now the lover came in, his face cut by the backlash of a branch. Admirably, she stanched the blood with her kisses, but he rebuffed her caresses, he had not come to perform again the ceremonies of a secret passion, protected by a world of dry leaves and furtive paths through the forest. The dagger warmed itself against his chest, and underneath liberty pounded, hidden close. A lustful, panting dialogue raced down the pages like a rivulet of snakes, and one felt it had all been decided from eternity. Even to those caresses which writhed about the lover's body, as though wishing to keep him there, to dissuade him from it; they sketched abominably the frame of that other body it was necessary to destroy. Nothing had been forgotten: alibis, unforeseen hazards, possible mistakes. From this hour on, each instant had its use minutely assigned. The cold-blooded, twice-gone-over reexamination of the details was barely broken off so that a hand could caress a cheek. It was beginning to get dark.

Not looking at one another now, rigidly fixed upon the task which awaited them, they separated at the cabin door. She was to follow the trail that led north. On the path leading in the opposite direction, he turned for a moment to watch her running, her hair loosened and flying. He ran in turn, crouching among the trees and hedges until, in the yellowish fog of dusk, he could distinguish the avenue of trees which led up to the house. The dogs were not supposed to bark, they did not bark. The estate manager would not be there at this hour, and he was not there. He went up the three porch steps and entered. The woman's words reached him over the thudding of blood in his ears: first a blue chamber, then a hall, then a carpeted stairway. At the top, two doors. No one in the first room, no one in the second. The door of the salon, and then, the knife in hand, the light from the great windows, the high back of an armchair covered in green velvet, the head of the man in the chair reading a novel.

DISCUSSION

In this story a sudden turn of plot calls into question the nature of reality. This sudden turn, when the world of the man in the study is invaded by the characters in the novel he is reading, depends upon a rejection of realistic conventions: in real life, of course, we do not expect the characters in a novel literally to come off the page. Although the world of a story need not obey the "rules" of the everyday world, it must, as we have remarked, obey its *own* rules if the story is to be coherent. Let us see what rules are established here.

"Continuity of Parks" employs realistic detail to establish its setting. The man who is reading lets "his left hand caress repeatedly the green velvet upholstery" of the chair in his study, from which he can see the park on the grounds of his estate. Such realistic detail is also used to characterize the man, who has just written a letter conveying power of attorney to his correspondent, and has had a discussion with the caretaker of his estate, presumably concerning the maintenance of the grounds. What is true of setting and characterization in the story is also true, until its climatic moment, of plot. There is nothing unusual in a story line that can be summarized as "Wealthy man sits down to read novel; novel follows two lovers planning murder." Nothing here suggests anything other than a realistic plot.

While it is clear that even the most fantastic of fictive worlds will have certain realistic elements, it is also clear that a story that invokes the fantastic to resolve its action must invoke conventions other than the realistic at some point *prior* to the climatic moment in order to get an imaginative coherence. That is, the fantastic must become an imaginative reality within the story's world, and its functional relationship to the other elements in this world must be established. A story in which all elements are realistic inferentially excludes and cannot credibly invoke the fantastic to resolve its action. Since this story does not prepare the reader for any but realistic events, the turn of plot in which the lovers come out of the novel to kill the reader of the novel does not, in the terms laid down, seem credible. In other words, the shock here is that the reality of the novel and that of the reader of the novel literally coincide. The story, then, is about the margins of reality, or the varieties of reality, and it asks what is the relation between varieties—the so-called "real" and the fantastic.

1. Among the details used to establish a realistic setting is the green velvet upholstery of the man's chair. How does the repetition of this detail contribute to the shock effect of the surprise ending?
2. Do you have an idea of the basic impulse of this story? Does it concern reality and illusion? If so, how? Or does it merely depend on a trick? If so, how does the trick differ from that of "Occurrence at Owl Creek Bridge"?

THE MEETING

Jorge Luis Borges

ANYONE leafing his way through the morning paper does so either to escape his surroundings or to provide himself with small talk for later in the day, so it is not to be wondered at that no one any longer remembers—or else remembers as in a dream—the famous and once widely discussed case of Maneco Uriarte and of Duncan. The event took place, furthermore, back around 1910, the year of the comet and the Centennial, and since then we have had and have lost so many things. Both protagonists are now dead; those who witnessed the episode solemnly swore silence. I, too, raised my hand for the oath, feeling the importance of the ritual with all the romantic seriousness of my nine or ten years. I do not know whether the others noticed that I had given my word; I do not know whether they kept theirs. Anyway, here is the story, with all the inevitable variations brought about by time and by good or bad writing.

My cousin Lafinur took me to a barbecue that evening at a country house called The Laurels, which belonged to some friends of his. I cannot fix its exact location; let us take any of those suburban towns lying just to the north, shaded and quiet, that slope down to the river and that have nothing in common with sprawling Buenos Aires and its surrounding prairie. The journey by train lasted long enough to seem endless to me, but time for children—as is well known—flows slowly. It was already dark when we passed through the villa's main gate. Here, I felt, were all the ancient, elemental things: the smell of meat cooking golden brown, the trees, the dogs, the kindling wood, and the fire that brings men together.

The guests numbered about a dozen; all were grown-ups. The eldest, I learned later, was not yet thirty. They were also—this I was soon to find out—well versed in matters about which I am still somewhat backward: race horses, the right tailors, motorcars, and notoriously expensive women. No one ruffled my shyness, no one paid any attention to me. The lamb, slowly and skillfully prepared by one of the hired men, kept us a long time in the big dining room. The dates of vintages were argued back and forth. There was a guitar; my cousin, if I remember correctly, sang a couple of Elías Regules' ballads about gauchos in the back country of Uruguay and some verses in dialect, in the incipient *lunfardo* of those days, about a knife fight in a brothel on Junín Street. Coffee and Havana cigars were brought in. Not a word about getting back. I felt (in the words of the poet Lugones) the fear of what is suddenly too late. I dared not look at the clock. In order to disguise my boyish loneliness among grown-ups, I put away—not really liking it—a glass or two of wine. Uriarte, in a loud voice, proposed to Duncan a two-handed game of poker. Someone objected that that kind of play made for a poor game and suggested a hand of four. Duncan agreed, but Uriarte, with a stubbornness that I did not understand and that I did not try to understand, insisted on the first scheme. Outside of *truco*—a game whose real aim is to pass time with mischief and verses—and of the modest mazes of solitaire, I never enjoyed cards. I slipped away without anyone's noticing. A rambling old house, unfamiliar and dark (only in the dining room was there light), means more to a boy than a new country means to a traveler. Step by step, I explored the rooms; I recall a billiard room, a long gallery with rectangular and diamond-shaped panes, a couple of rocking chairs, and a window from which you could just make out a summerhouse. In the darkness I lost my way; the owner of the house, whose name, as I recall after all these years, may have been Acevedo or Acebal, finally came across me somehow. Out of kindness or perhaps out of a collector's vanity, he led me to a display cabinet. On lighting a lamp, I saw the glint of steel. It was a collection of knives that had once been in the hands of famous fighters. He told me that he had a bit of land somewhere to the north around Pergamino, and that he had been picking up these things on his travels back and forth across the province. He opened the cabinet and, without looking at what was written on the tags, he began giving me accounts of each item; they were more or less the same except for dates and place names. I asked him whether among the weapons he might have the dagger of Juan Moreira, who was in that day the archetype of the gaucho, as later Martín Fierro and Don Segundo Sombra would be. He had to confess that he hadn't but that he could show me one like it, with a U-shaped crosspiece in the hilt. He was interrupted by the sound of angry voices. At once he shut the cabinet and turned to leave; I followed him.

Uriarte was shouting that his opponent had tried to cheat him. All the others stood around the two players. Duncan, I remember, was a taller man than the rest of the company, and was well built, though somewhat round-shouldered; his face was expressionless, and his hair was so light it was almost white. Maneco Uriarte was nervous, dark, with perhaps a touch of Indian blood, and wore a skimpy, petulant moustache. It was obvious that everybody was drunk; I do not know whether there were two or three emptied bottles on the floor or whether an excess of movies suggests this false memory to me. Uriarte's insults did not let up; at first sharp, they now grew obscene. Duncan appeared not to hear, but finally, as though weary, he got up and threw a punch. From the floor, Uriarte snarled that he was not going to take this outrage, and he challenged Duncan to fight.

Duncan said no, and added, as though to explain, "The trouble is I'm afraid of you."

Everybody howled with laughter.

Uriarte, picking himself up, answered, "I'm going to have it out with you, and right now."

Someone—may he be forgiven for it—remarked that weapons were not lacking.

I do not know who went and opened the glass cabinet. Maneco Uriarte picked out the showiest and longest dagger, the one with the U-shaped crosspiece; Duncan, almost absentmindedly, picked a wooden-handled knife with the stamp of a tiny tree on the blade. Someone else said it was just like Maneco to play it safe, to choose a sword. It astonished no one that his hand began shaking; what was astonishing is that the same thing happened with Duncan.

Tradition demands that men about to fight should respect the house in which they are guests, and step outside. Half on a spree, half seriously, we all went out into the damp night. I was not drunk—at least, not on wine—but I was reeling with adventure; I wished very hard that someone would be killed, so that later I could tell about it and always remember it. Maybe at that moment the others were no more adult than I was. I also had the feeling that an overpowering current was dragging us on and would drown us. Nobody believed the least bit in Maneco's accusation; everyone saw it as the fruit of an old rivalry, exacerbated by the wine.

We pushed our way through a clump of trees, leaving behind the summerhouse. Uriarte and Duncan led the way, wary of each other. The rest of us strung ourselves out around the edge of an opening of lawn. Duncan had stopped there in the moonlight and said, with mild authority, "This looks like the right place."

The two men stood in the center, not quite knowing what to do. A voice rang out: "Let go of all that hardware and use your hands!"

But the men were already fighting. They began clumsily, almost as if they were afraid of hurting each other; they began by watching the blades, but later their eyes were on one another. Uriarte had laid aside his anger, Duncan his contempt or aloofness. Danger, in some way, had transfigured them; these were now two men fighting, not boys. I had imagined the fight as a chaos of steel; instead, I was able to follow it, or almost follow it, as though it were a game of chess. The intervening years may, of course, have exaggerated or blurred what I saw. I do not know how long it lasted; there are events that fall outside the common measure of time.

Without ponchos to act as shields, they used their forearms to block each lunge of the knife. Their sleeves, soon hanging in shreds, grew black with blood. I thought that we had gone wrong in supposing that they knew nothing about this kind of fencing. I noticed right off that they handled themselves in different ways. Their weapons were unequal. Duncan, in order to make up for his disadvantage, tried to stay in close to the other man; Uriarte kept stepping back to be able to lunge out with long, low thrusts. The same voice that had called attention to the display cabinet shouted out now: "They're killing each other! Stop them!"

But no one dared break it up. Uriarte had lost ground; Duncan charged him. They were almost body to body now. Uriarte's weapon sought Duncan's face. Suddenly the blade seemed shorter, for it was piercing the taller man's chest. Duncan lay stretched out on the grass. It was at this point that he said, his voice very low, "How strange. All this is like a dream."

He did not shut his eyes, he did not move, and I had seen a man kill another man.

Maneco Uriarte bent over the body, sobbing openly, and begged to be forgiven. The thing he had just done was beyond him. I know now that he regretted less having committed a crime than having carried out a senseless act.

I did not want to look anymore. What I had wished for so much had happened, and it left me shaken. Lafinur told me later that they had had to struggle hard to pull out the weapon. A makeshift council was formed. They decided to lie as little as possible and to elevate this duel with knives to a duel with swords. Four of them volunteered as seconds, among them Acebal. In Buenos Aires anything can be fixed; someone always has a friend.

On top of the mahogany table where the men had been playing, a pack of English cards and a pile of bills lay in a jumble that nobody wanted to look at or to touch.

In the years that followed, I often considered revealing the story to some friend, but always I felt that there was a greater pleasure in being the keeper of a secret than in telling it. However, around 1929, a chance conversation suddenly moved me one day to break my long silence. The retired police captain, Don José Olave, was recalling stories about men from the tough riverside neigborhood of the Retiro who had been handy with their knives; he remarked that when they were out to kill their man, scum of this kind had no use for the rules of the game, and that before all the fancy playing with daggers that you saw now on the stage, knife fights were few and far between. I said I had witnessed one, and gave him an account of what had happened nearly twenty years earlier.

He listened to me with professional attention, then said, "Are you sure Uriarte and What's-His-Name never handled a knife before? Maybe they had picked up a thing or two around their fathers' ranches."

"I don't think so," I said. "Everybody there that night knew one another pretty well, and I can tell you they were all amazed at the way the two men fought."

Olave went on in his quiet manner, as if thinking aloud. "One of the weapons had a U-shaped crosspiece in the handle. There were two daggers of that kind which became quite famous—Moreira's and Juan Almada's. Almada was from down south, in Tapalquén."

Something seemed to come awake in my memory. Olave continued. "You also mentioned a knife with a wooden handle, one with the Little Tree brand. There are thousands of them, but there was one—"

He broke off for a moment, then said, "Señor Acevedo had a big property up around Pergamino. There was another of these famous toughs from up that way—Juan Almanza was his name. This was along about the turn of the century. When he was fourteen, he killed his first man with one of these knives. From then on, for luck, he stuck to the same one. Juan Almanza and Juan Almada had it in for each other, jealous of the fact that many people confused the two. For a long time they searched high and low for one another, but they never met. Juan Almanza was killed by a stray bullet during some election brawl or other. The other man, I think, died a natural death in a hospital bed in Las Flores."

Nothing more was said. Each of us was left with his own conclusions.

Nine or ten men, none of whom is any longer living, saw what my eyes saw—that sudden stab and the body under the night sky—but perhaps what we were really seeing was the end of another story, an older story. I began to wonder whether it was Maneco Uriarte who killed Duncan or whether in some uncanny way it could have been the weapons, not the men, which fought. I still remember how Uriarte's hand shook when he first gripped his knife, and the same with Duncan, as though the knives were coming awake after a long sleep side by side in the cabinet. Even after their gauchos were dust, the knives—the knives, not their tools, the men—knew how to fight. And that night they fought well.

Things last longer than people; who knows whether these knives will meet again, who knows whether the story ends here.

DISCUSSION

1. In this story the sudden turn that questions the nature of reality is the suggestion that the knives used by the duelists had wills of their own. How does this story avoid the possible objection raised to "Continuity of Parks" that there is no preparation for the shock when the novel and actuality coincide?

2. Would this story be more credible if the anecdote about the enmity between the fighters were more strongly suggested before the events at the party?

3. What similarity of technique do you find in the use made here of the description of the knives with that of the chair in "Continuity of Parks"?

4. Behind this story can you sense the very modern idea that in this age of technology man becomes more and more the creature of his machines? If you have read Coleridge's poem "The Rime of the Ancient

Mariner," can you see a similarity here? Why does the mariner shoot the albatross? Can it be that he does so merely because the crossbow is in his hand? How does his act relate to the age of technology?

THE SECRET ROOM

Alain Robbe-Grillet

To Gustave Moreau

THE first thing to be seen is a red stain, of a deep, dark, shiny red, with almost black shadows. It is in the form of an irregular rosette, sharply outlined, extending in several directions in wide outflows of unequal length, dividing and dwindling afterward into single sinuous streaks. The whole stands out against a smooth, pale surface, round in shape, at once dull and pearly, a hemisphere joined by gentle curves to an expanse of the same pale color—white darkened by the shadowy quality of the place: a dungeon, a sunken room, or a cathedral—glowing with a diffused brilliance in the semidarkness.

Farther back, the space is filled with the cylindrical trunks of columns, repeated with progressive vagueness in their retreat toward the beginning of a vast stone stairway, turning slightly as it rises, growing narrower and narrower as it approaches the high vaults where it disappears.

The whole setting is empty, stairway and colonnades. Alone, in the foreground, the stretched-out body gleams feebly, marked with the red stain—a white body whose full, supple flesh can be sensed, fragile, no doubt, and vulnerable. Alongside the bloody hemisphere another identical round form, this one intact, is seen at almost the same angle of view; but the haloed point at its summit, of darker tint, is in this case quite recognizable, whereas the other one is entirely destroyed, or at least covered by the wound.

In the background, near the top of the stairway, a black silhouette is seen fleeing, a man wrapped in a long, floating cape, ascending the last steps without turning around, his deed accomplished. A thin smoke rises in twisting scrolls from a sort of incense burner placed on a high stand of ironwork with a silvery glint. Nearby lies the milkwhite body, with wide streaks of blood running from the left breast, along the flank and on the hip.

It is a fully rounded woman's body, but not heavy, completely nude, lying on its back, the bust raised up somewhat by thick cushions thrown down on the floor, which is covered with Oriental rugs. The waist is very narrow, the neck long and thin, curved to one side, the head thrown back into a darker area where, even so, the facial features may be discerned, the partly opened mouth, the wide-staring eyes, shining with a fixed brilliance, and the mass of long, black hair spread out in a complicated wavy disorder over a heavily folded cloth, of velvet perhaps, on which also rest the arm and shoulder.

It is a uniformly colored velvet of dark purple, or which seems so in this lighting. But purple, brown, blue also seem to dominate in the colors of the cushions—only a small portion of which is hidden beneath the velvet cloth, and which protrude noticeably, lower down, beneath the bust and waist—as well as in the Oriental patterns of the rugs on the floor. Farther on, these same colors are picked up again in the stone of the paving and the columns, the vaulted archways, the stairs, and the less discernible surfaces that disappear into the farthest reaches of the room.

The dimensions of this room are difficult to determine exactly; the body of the young sacrificial victim seems at first glance to occupy a substantial portion of it, but the vast size of the stairway leading down to it would imply rather that this is not the whole room, whose considerable space must in reality extend all around, right and left, as it does toward the faraway browns and blues among the columns standing in line, in every direction, perhaps toward other sofas, thick carpets, piles of cushions and fabrics, other tortured bodies, other incense burners.

It is also difficult to say where the light comes from. No clue, on the columns or on the floor, suggests the direction of the rays. Nor is any window or torch visible. The milkwhite body itself seems to light the scene, with its full breasts, the curve of its thighs, the rounded belly, the full buttocks, the stretched-out legs, widely spread, and the black tuft of the exposed sex, provocative, proffered, useless now.

The man has already moved several steps back. He is now on the first steps of the stairs, ready to go up. The bottom steps are wide and deep, like the steps leading up to some great building, a temple or theater; they grow smaller as they ascend, and at the same time describe a wide, helical curve, so gradually that the stairway has not yet made a half-turn by the time it disappears near the top of the vaults, reduced then to a steep, narrow flight of steps without handrail, vaguely outlined, moreover, in the thickening darkness beyond.

But the man does not look in this direction, where his movement nonetheless carries him; his left foot on the second step and his right foot already touching the third, with his knee bent, he has turned around to look at the spectacle for one last time. The long, floating cape thrown hastily over his shoulders, clasped in one hand at his waist, has been whirled around by the rapid circular motion that has just caused his head and chest to turn in the opposite direction, and a corner of the cloth remains suspended in the air as if blown by a gust of wind; this corner, twisting around upon itself in the form of a loose S, reveals the red silk lining with its gold embroidery.

The man's features are impassive, but tense, as if in expectation—or perhaps fear—of some sudden event, or surveying with one last glance the total immobility of the scene. Though he is looking backward, his whole body is turned slightly forward, as if he were continuing up the stairs. His right arm—not the one holding the edge of the cape—is bent sharply toward the left, toward a point in space where the balustrade should be, if this stairway had one, an interrupted gesture, almost incomprehensible, unless it arose from an instinctive movement to grasp the absent support.

As to the direction of his glance, it is certainly aimed at the body of the victim lying on the cushions, its extended members stretched out in the form of a cross, its bust raised up, its head thrown back. But the face is perhaps hidden from the man's eyes by one of the columns, standing at the foot of the stairs. The young woman's right hand touches the floor just at the foot of this column. The fragile wrist is encircled by an iron bracelet. The arm is almost in darkness, only the hand receiving enough light to make the thin, outspread fingers clearly visible against the circular protrusion at the base of the stone column. A black metal chain running around the column passes through a ring affixed to the bracelet, binding the wrist tightly to the column.

At the top of the arm a rounded shoulder, raised up by the cushions, also stands out well lighted, as well as the neck, the throat, and the other shoulder, the armpit with its soft hair, the left arm likewise pulled back with its wrist bound in the same manner to the base of another column, in the extreme foreground; here the iron bracelet and the chain are fully displayed, represented with perfect clarity down to the slightest details.

The same is true, still in the foreground but at the other side, for a similiar chain, but not quite as thick, wound directly around the ankle, running twice around the column and terminating in a heavy iron ring embedded in the floor. About a yard farther back, or perhaps slightly farther, the right foot is identically chained. But it is the left foot, and its chain, that are the most minutely depicted.

The foot is small, delicate, finely modeled. In several places the chain has broken the skin, causing noticeable if not extensive depressions in the flesh. The chain links are oval, thick, the size of an eye. The ring in the floor resembles those used to attach horses; it lies almost touching the stone pavement to which it is riveted by a massive iron peg. A few inches away is the edge of a rug; it is grossly wrinkled at this point, doubtless as a result of the convulsive, but necessarily very restricted, movements of the victim attempting to struggle.

The man is still standing about a yard away, half leaning over her. He looks at her face, seen upside down, her dark eyes made larger by their surrounding eyeshadow, her mouth wide open as if screaming. The man's posture allows his face to be seen only in a vague profile, but one senses in it a violent exaltation, despite the rigid attitude, the silence, the immobility. His back is slightly arched. His left hand, the only one visible, holds up at some distance from the body a piece of cloth, some dark-colored piece of clothing, which drags on the carpet, and which must be the long cape with its gold-embroidered lining.

This immense silhouette hides most of the bare flesh over which the red stain, spreading from the globe of the breast, runs in long rivulets that branch out, growing narrower, upon the pale background of the bust and the flank. One thread has reached the armpit and runs in an almost straight, thin line along the arm; others have run down toward the waist and traced out, along one side of the belly, the hip, the top of the thigh, a more random network already starting to congeal. Three or four tiny veins have reached the hollow between the legs, meeting in a sinuous line, touching the point of the V formed by the outspread legs, and disappearing into the black tuft.

Look, now the flesh is still intact: the black tuft and the white belly, the soft curve of the hips, the narrow waist, and, higher up, the pearly breasts rising and falling in time with the rapid breathing, whose rhythm grows more accelerated. The man, close to her, one knee on the floor, leans farther over. The head, with its long, curly hair, which alone is free to move somewhat, turns from side to side, struggling; finally the woman's mouth twists open, while the flesh is torn open, the blood spurts out over the tender skin, stretched tight, the carefully shadowed eyes grow abnormally larger, the mouth opens wider, the head twists violently, one last time, from right to left, then more gently, to fall back finally and become still, amid the mass of black hair spread out on the velvet.

At the very top of the stone stairway, the little door has opened, allowing a yellowish but sustained shaft of light to enter, against which stands out the dark silhouette of the man wrapped in his long cloak. He has but to climb a few more steps to reach the threshold.

Afterward, the whole setting is empty, the enormous room with its purple shadows and its stone columns proliferating in all directions, the monumental staircase with no handrail that twists upward, growing narrower and vaguer as it rises into the darkness, toward the top of the vaults where it disappears.

Near the body, whose wound has stiffened, whose brilliance is already growing dim, the thin smoke from the incense burner traces complicated scrolls in the still air: first a coil turned horizontally to the left, which then straightens out and rises slightly, then returns to the axis of its point of origin, which it crosses as it moves to the right, then turns back in the first direction, only to wind back again, thus forming an irregular sinusoidal curve, more and more flattened out, and rising, vertically, toward the top of the canvas.

DISCUSSION

This story most strikingly departs from realistic convention in its handling of time. The temporal movement in the story's single scene is, as often as not, backward: the moment immediately following the slaughter is presented in the middle of the story, while the moment just before the murder and the murder itself are presented later; and all of these moments are described after the long introductory description of the victim's body and of the torture chamber, at which point the murderer is seen already in flight, ascending the stairs that lead out of the dungeon.

That the action within a scene in a story moves forward in time borrows, of course, from experience, and contributes to the realism of the rendered scene. The predominant reversal of temporal movement in "The Secret Room" establishes a different sort of reality for its single scene, a reality that the reader recognizes as artificial but that presumably conveys the "true" or significant relation among the scene's various moments. The reader thus looks to the narrative voice rather than to time as the organizing force *within* the scene, just as he looks to the narrative voice to organize transitions *between* scenes, and to make other editorial decisions in the presentation of action in other stories.

We must now ask whether "The Secret Room" fulfills the commitment implied by its rejection of realistic convention in its handling of time; whether, in fact, the significant relation among the various moments of the story's single scene comes clear as a result of their temporal reorganization. The answer to this question seems to be no. For example, we do not discover what were the motivations of the woman's killer—whether the murder was some form of ritual sacrifice or a grotesque retribution or simply an act of sadistic perversion. Neither do we discover who opens the door at the top of the stairs to let the killer out—this at the story's conclusion, when action had returned to the point of time at which it had begun. In other words, the story does not have a plot in the ordinary sense. It is basically pictorial, not action in a logical time sequence. What the story does offer is suggestive variations of action based on the same pictorial material. In a sense, the story asks the reader to explore imaginatively the pictorial suggestions—to turn into significant time the possibilities of time in the picture. By the way, the narrative is revealed to be a description of a painting by Gustave Moreau, a French artist of the late nineteenth century, whose work was often just a macabre and decadent as that of "The Secret Room," which is dedicated to Moreau. The story may be taken as an exploration of narrative and the emotional suggestions of the painting.

That the story describes a painting does not resolve its problems of ordinary coherence. By witholding this information until literally the last moment, the story implies an intention for its manipulation of time that it does not fulfill: this juggling of temporal moments, that is, encourages the reader to pursue a significant relation among the moments of the story's action, and this relation does not appear. Rather, the reader is finally told that the narrator, like a man who says he has found a manuscript in a bottle, is not responsible for the organization of the story he tells. Such an ending is, like that of "Continuity of Parks," a toying with the margins of reality.

1. Had you known that a painting was being described, what sort of questions would you have raised about the painter's motivations as you read the story?

2. What retroactive meaning is given to narrative remarks such as "It is . . . difficult to say where the light comes from"? By the revelation that the story describes a painting? Does this foreshadowing of the story's surprise ending help to validate the ending?

3. What is the difference between the kinds of surprise ending in "The Furnished Room" and "An Occurrence at Owl Creek Bridge," on the one hand, and in "Continuity of Parks" and "The Secret Room" on the other?

29 INVENTIONS

Joyce Carol Oates

1

"I am dying. I am disappearing. I think about death all the time. Falling asleep I seem to be falling into death . . . dying. . . . I can hear my heartbeat moving away from me. It is inside me and yet moving away. This is a fact. I wake up suddenly and it comes back to me, beating hard. I get out of bed to take away this prize, this beating. I try to get away very quietly so that *he* won't hear me wake up—if he hears me he sits up and says, *Where are you going? What do you want?* It is like an avalanche, the way he falls on me from his side of the bed."

2

I have not invented her, not all of her. Most of the words are hers. She is forever sitting forward in that chair— a canebacked chair, very old—with the window to her right, all that glaring filmed-over glass, almost opaque with dirt. She is forever leaning forward to talk to my friend, a psychiatrist. To her I am a stenographer, a nurse, I am another woman and therefore not important. She doesn't bother to look at me. She is forever there in the clinic, deep in Detroit, buildings lying in rubble on either side of that five-story relic. *I am dying. I am disappearing.*

3

I have to invent her face because most of it is gone. The shock of her—the closeness of her to my friend—this unnerved me. I thought there was more distance between a psychiatrist and his patient. I was in disguise as a technician, taking notes for Dr. Geddes. Her face: young and yet not youthful. Premature lines on the forehead from too much frowning, too much fear for her departing heartbeat. She did have very light, fine blond hair. I remember that. She did nothing with it, just brushed it back behind her ears. A nervous habit: her hand darting to her forehead to brush away strands of hair. Imaginary strands. At one time—when she was in high school, maybe—she had a big mane of hair, a head of thick blond hair that cascaded down over her shoulders. I was taking notes. I pretended to take notes but really I was drawing faces on a pad. Dr. Geddes had said to me a few days before. *Do you want to encounter real life? Or are you afraid of it?*

4

Afraid.

5

When she began talking I couldn't take notes. Her words rushed out—no shame—it was too direct for me. Her heartbeat began to sound in the room. I could feel its vibrations. Why is that room so small? We were too close together, the three of us. I stared at her large, stunned, black eyes, that were unseeing on me, and I couldn't take notes. It would have been a betrayal—one woman betraying another.

6

So I will invent most of her: her thinnness, her shoulder bones showing through a tight yellow sweater, her hair combed back and fastened with bobby pins (the wrong color—brown and not blond bobby pins), her bare legs and their prickly, flushed look, her toes in open sandals grimy and careless, her purse a soiled yellow (some synthetic material, fake leather), lipstick. . . . No, she wasn't wearing lipstick. Her mouth was small and colorless and it surprised me, opening so desperately, letting out those words I can't forget: *I think about death all the time. Falling asleep I seem to be falling into death.*

7

She is leaning forward earnestly. A trickle of saliva in the corner of her mouth. Staring at my friend's face, the doctor's face, paying no attention to me. She is the kind of woman who thinks other women don't matter; so she won't look at me, I am just a nurse, or a secretary, taking notes for the doctor. She never sees me. She only sees him—she stares at him hungrily, anxiously. She is younger than I am. She has a delicate, beautiful face, but the eyebrows are too blond, too faint, and the mouth colorless. It is a weak face, it is either shut tight in a frown or opened in a plea, pleading with the doctor: *If I could see my way clear to leave him. . . . He would like to kill me. . . .*

8

"He is always after me. He wants to make love every day, almost. I feel so tired. I want to get out of there. He lies on top of me and my head goes empty, my neck is ready to snap, I want to scream and scream. . . . And, oh, I always think of . . . I think of him dying too. . . . When he does that. . . . His face gets all twisted and I think of him dying and how I would be free then. . . . I think about running away and then maybe neither one of us would have to die. But I wake up at night and my heart is going like crazy. I'm all sweat and I'm so scared of dying, doctor, I'm scared of going crazy too—what if my heart stopped? It races fast and then it gets faint and goes away inside my ribs, it's like a radio station that is going away and you try to get it back again . . . "

9

Dr. Geddes: thirty-five years old, a knobby, oblong face, thick eyebrows, dark hair, dark, clever, shrewd, listening eyes.

10

I park my car in a parking lot on Gratiot. The sign for the lot says, PARK HERE 75¢. And then in very small letters it says "first half hour." I

take the ticket from the attendant, a big black man. The street is busy—
the sidewalks busy—people everywhere, cars, trucks, city buses, the
smell of the city confining and cozy. It is all so predictable. I park my car
and leave the keys inside, and hurry across to the building where he is
waiting for me. It is in a block that will be razed for urban renewal. A
new clinic will be built on top of all that rubble, lots of glass and concrete
and mosaic decorations and plastic lounge chairs and television sets
. . . in the center of it Dr. Geddes will stand with his arms folded, a saint.

11

I can see his face, but it is not the face I have described. It is not so
clear. He is a fairly tall man and he walks in long, urgent strides. Has he
any muscles? I don't know. His eyes are dark, yes. Shadowed and dark.
He is thirty-five, I think, though sometimes he looks older. The girl must
be ten years younger than he is, at least. Yet she stares at him so hungrily.

12

"If I could see my way clear to leave him. . . . "
She is vague, wispy, imploring. Her eyelids are strangely pink, there
are small flakes on them, mixed in with her blond eyelashes.
Silence.
"He is so heavy at night, in bed. I can't sleep. I think about dying,
about sinking into mud or something. . . . I can feel my heart going
away. . . . If he wakes up he gets mad."
Dr. Geddes at his desk. Smoking through all this. I am behind him,
against the inner wall, out of sight. The three of us are very close together though. The room has a high ceiling and it is cracked. A calendar
on the wall, but no one believes in the future. No one has bothered to
turn the page over; the end of the month was last Friday. Time yawns
here. Outside the window there is nothing. The girl's head moves sleepy
and confused. She brushes a strand of hair back from her face. Dr. Geddes, my friend, shakes ashes from his cigarette into a black plastic
ashtray.
He says, "And then what?"
"If he wakes up, you mean?"
"Yes, then what?"
"Oh, then . . . then we maybe argue . . . I don't know. . . . I pretend
I have to go to the bathroom and hide in there until he falls asleep again.
But if he doesn't fall asleep he gets up and. . . . I hate him, I wish he
would let me alone. . . . "
"Why?"
She blinks at him. There are tiny flakes of skin on her eyelashes; she
must have a skin infection of some kind. "Why what?"
"Why do you want him to leave you alone?"
"Because. . . . "

13

I saw her out on the street once, walking fast. Long legs, blond hair
bobbing about her face, lipstick, bracelets. In a hurry. She looked like a

stranger, a girl of about twenty-five. She didn't notice me, I was alone, she was alone. Dr. Geddes was not in the city—this wasn't his day for volunteer work, charity work. He was in his own private office in Grosse Pointe, miles away. The girl didn't notice me, but if she had she would not have remembered me, because a woman does not matter to another woman. Her face was tight with frowning, very pale. Her head was filled with wild ideas, like weeds. Her long flaring legs. Her short skirt—I think it was white, and not very clean—her sandals, dirty toes—hair washed and curled and bouncing about her face. This is the girl some man, a husband, burrows into at night and would like to kill.

"Doctor, he wants to kill me. He said if I left him he would find me and kill me."

"Why?"

"Why what?"

"Why do you think he wants to kill you?"

"Because. . . ."

14

At the street corner she paused and turned to look at me. A full, ironic stare. I had just come out the back way from Hudson's, carrying one of their dark gray-green packages. She stared at me and her eyes narrowed a little in recognition. That small careful mouth. The slight arching of her back, one woman showing off her body to another. She stared at me. I hesitated, but she stood there, unmoving, while the light turned green and people moved out around her . . . I couldn't turn away, couldn't pretend I was someone else. I had to walk near her. Her lips moved away from her teeth in a small ironic smile. She whispered, "He doesn't love you! He loves me!"

She reached out and took hold of my wrist and dug her hard little nails into it.

15

I follow her home. She is not the way I remembered her. No, she is not that young—she is probably my age, she is thirty or more. Her hair is bleached. Dark brown at the roots. No, no, that can't be right—she wouldn't have blond eyebrows then, and she does have blond eyebrows; I remember that. Too blond. Flimsy and anemic, that kind of blond. So the hair isn't bleached. Erase that. Change that. A trim, wiry little body, thin wrists and ankles, a long unclean neck. A noble neck. I saw her on the street. I followed her home at a distance. . . . She didn't see me. If she saw me she would not have recognized me. She is in love with Dr. Geddes and never sees me, the nurse. I follow her home now, walking fast as she, keeping in time with her steps, one two three, one two three, swinging her arms, my arms are not free to swing, but my legs are as long and as eager as hers to take her out of this neighborhood, across John R. and a few blocks over, and into an apartment building.

I follow her up the stairs. I float up behind her. I am inside her skull: behind those flaky little moronic eyes! I put the key in the lock, open the door slowly, stealthily, I look around the cluttered kitchen to see if anyone is there. . . . Break-ins in this neighborhood, kids looking for loose change. Kids on dope. She enters the kitchen but does not yet close the door. If someone is hiding in the other room she'll have to get out fast. . . . I paint the kitchen white and then splatter the ceiling and walls with grease. Grease and dust. Designs of dirt like constellations. I tack that calendar on the wall with the pastel Virgin Mary on it, heart exposed, hand lifted in a blessing. I brush the girl's hair for her until it is bristling with electricity. She is a pretty young woman in spite of the frown lines. I walk her into the bathroom where there is a mirror and show her this face, her face. She stares at herself. She touches her face. *I am disappearing*, she says aloud.

16

I don't follow her home.

I saw her on the street but I didn't follow her. I released her. My heart gave a lunge of hatred, seeing her. She is more than ten years younger than he is, too young for him. She stares at him with her face like a water color, asking him to touch her, to kiss her, to smear her with his fingers. "I've got to leave him. I've got to get a divorce," she said last time, on Tuesday. A plea for help. The doctor smoked, frowned, thought about it. No. Not yet. Mustn't break up your family. Mustn't change your life. Too fast. Not now. Regret it later. Talk it over with him. Explain. *Yes, but he shoves me–shoves the table–* Talk to him. Explain. You are sore, you say, your body is sore from him; explain. Take a long bath. Sit in the tub. Warm water. Warm soapy water. Rest. Relax. *Yes, but he gets so mad*—Talk to him. Explain. No divorce. No change of life during counseling. And what about the children?

17

I didn't mention the children—

I invented her with bracelets, even loops of gold in her ears on that day, sandals, a short white skirt, a red pullover blouse, clean hair. All right. But she had two kids with her. Two boys. They looked very thin, thin chests, narrow shoulders. She was walking them fast—why so fast?—the yellow purse pressed against her ribs and her hand on the smaller boy's upper arm, guiding him. He looked panicked, that boy. Why was his mother making him walk so fast? The other boy ran a little ahead of them, in and around people, around a pile of debris at the curb, jumping out onto the curb to avoid a group of black kids, looping out around a parking meter and jumping back onto the sidewalk. Why was she hurrying them? I followed the three of them for a block, then gave up. Let her go. Let her go home and climb the stairs and unlock the door and herd the panting kids inside and rush into the bathroom where she can be alone, pressing her hand to her heart. *I am disappearing*! she cries out at her reflection in the mirror.

18

"They'll come with me. I want them with me."

"How will you support them?"

"Go on ADC."

"You wouldn't qualify."

"Go on welfare then."

"What is the advantage of leaving your husband right now?"

She stares at Dr. Geddes. Thinking. Thinking.

"Why should you change your life so radically at this time? Aren't you making progress with me here?"

Staring at him. Thinking. Her eyes film over with panic. Dr. Geddes is wearing a white shirt with narrow blue stripes today, and a dark blue tie. He carries himself cautiously in this building, up the stairs with me—we never take the elevator.

"I don't know—I don't know—" the girl stammers, terrified.

If we got into the elevator together, the door would close upon us and we would be alone, alone together, in a box moving creakily up to the fourth floor of the Metropolitan Clinic. Alone together. No, it is better to take the stairs, which creak too.

Aren't you making progress with me here?

19

She isn't his only patient. I invented a vacuum around her, describing her as if she were his only patient. No. There are many more. I drive downtown on Tuesdays around ten, I go up to his office, I have been invited into his life. This office of his at the clinic is just a desk, a room with a desk, and in the corridor people are always milling around, most of them blacks. Most of his patients here are blacks, yes, but I wasn't interested in them. I picked the white woman to be interested in. I sat through an interview with a black of about forty, a black-purplish face, big nose, watery eyes, bad teeth. Dr. Geddes, fastidious and kind, behind his desk. The desk is small and battered. Other doctors use it. It is Dr. Geddes's on Tuesdays, until late afternoon; for all I know someone else comes in at night and uses it. The calendar isn't his—now someone has turned the page over. It is June. The black man with the bad teeth talked slowly, maddeningly, one morning back in April. I sat and listened. The note pad, the ball-point pen. I stared at my own feet. The man talked about his landlord and about a car he had bought. He kept repeating himself. I stopped listening and stared at my feet, afraid that Dr. Geddes would sense I wasn't listening. *Do you want to encounter real life?* he had said. Dr. Geddes (which is not his real name) has the sardonic, weary look of doctors around here—they can't cure anything, they can only wear themselves out; they turn sour at the age of forty. But the black man did not interest me. A woman came in next, a lightskinned black woman in her thirties—heavyset, perfumy, sociable. She wasn't right either. I wanted someone else. Next came the blond girl, washed-out face and hair, two kids, scrawny kids she'd brought along with her, dirt lodged beneath her nails, the odor of panic about her. . . .

20

"Aren't you making progress with me here?"

"I don't know—"

"What do you mean?"

"I thought it would be—different—I mean, I need some help with the law, if I get a divorce, I don't know what to do—Sometimes I slide out of bed and go into the bathroom to hide. I can't stop crying. I'm afraid I'll go crazy. The kids sleep in the front room so I can't go in there. Sometimes they wake up. Jeffy starts bawling and then *he* wakes up and gets mad as hell. I want to die, I guess. I don't want to live with him."

"But we're making progress here, aren't we?"

Progress here. Progress. Dr. Geddes eyes her suspiciously. He doesn't want her to leave that husband. He wants her *there* with him, in the bed, in the bathroom, barefoot at four in the morning, rubbing her fists into her sore pinkened eyes. . . .

21

Her husband showed up one day, ten minutes after she arrived.

His body was clumsy, propelled toward us. Somehow he had gotten by the girl downstairs. His face was clumsy, flushed, furious. "You the doctor?" he yelled.

Danger.

Real life.

Dr. Geddes got to his feet at once. "You're—?"

The girl began to scream.

"You shut up! Shut it!" the man said to her.

"You're not supposed to be here! You followed me! Oh, you—you —" the girl screamed.

Everything came undone.

I got out of the way, pressed back against the wall. The girl jumped up, tried to run past her husband. He grabbed her. Dr. Geddes said quickly, nervously, "Wait a minute, please. Please. Wait a minute."

"Get the hell out of here, you!" cried the girl.

"You shut up!"

He started to drag her out but then, for some reason, released her. Maybe her screaming frightened him. The guard from downstairs, a policeman, came running up the stairs.

"I think everything is all right now, officer," Dr. Geddes said quickly.

The policeman was a young man. He stared at the husband. A sour smell to that husband—a sports shirt of green and black, designs like tropical vegetation—dark trousers bulging at the stomach. He hadn't shaved for a few days.

This man makes love to her? . . .

"I think it's all right now. Mrs. Pelletier will finish her hour with me . . . Mr. Pelletier can wait for her downstairs. . . . "

The husband was breathing hard.

"Mr. Pelletier? . . . " said Dr. Geddes.

He looked around, baffled. He was not accustomed to that name. Big bulging eyes. He is partly bald and yet his wife is so young; this dismays me. They have two children. She is trapped. She will never get free of him, never.

22

Dr. Geddes and I, standing together, in someone's home. A Saturday evening. We are standing together as if by accident, drawn away from the rest of the party.

"That girl . . . I keep thinking about that girl . . . " he whispers.

"Mrs. Pelletier?"

"I think about her all the time. I wonder. . . . "

I stare at him, surprised. I am leaning forward, eager and vacant.

"I wonder how she can live with him? A son of a bitch like that. . . . "

I want to cross this out; erase these words.

"It's happened before, a few times," he says, avoiding my look. "Falling in love with one of them. They get stuck in your head, their faces, and you can't forget them. . . ."

Then why do you tell her to stay with her husband?

23

Dr. Geddes and his wife, who is his age but looks older. Saturday evening. We are drawn together as if by accident. She moves her wrist watch nervously around her wrist, around and around. She eyes me, assessing me. Dr. Geddes is strained tonight—uneasy at parties. His sardonic look has taken over. His wife is wearing something golden—a disguise. The gold cloth casts its light up on her face. A handsome woman glowing, gold, but aging. She stares at me. She has been drinking all afternoon. I don't have to invent her ironic glare, her loose wrist watch. Does she know about her husband and me?

She brings her hand around, balled into a fist, and strikes me on the shoulder!

I cry out. Everyone in the room is looking at us.

24

I park the car, take the ticket from the attendant, cross over to the clinic. Men are working next door. It is July, it is very hot. Dust explodes. Heat! Heat! It is a Tuesday. Girls in short dresses walk by slowly, looking at me: a white woman, maybe she has money in that purse? I hurry up the steps and into the foyer, holding my breath because of the smell—is it sewage? The girl at the desk recognizes me, the policeman recognizes me, everyone is very warm and tired. Up the stairs. To the landing: outside, another explosion of dust. Why am I here in this heat and confusion?

People are milling around. A baby is crying.

His wife didn't strike me that night, no. Nothing happened.

25

If you love her, why do you tell her to stay with her husband?

26

But he doesn't love her. I invented that. It is a plot if you imagine people in love—the lazy looping crisscrosses of love, blows, stares, tears.

No. It doesn't happen. No love. People meet, touch stare into one another's faces, shake their heads clear, move on, forget. It doesn't happen.

27

Yesterday he telephoned me. "Where were you on Tuesday?"

A man's attention, a man's stern staring eyes. A white shirt with narrow blue stripes. I run along the street with the two children, eager to be free, to get the hell away from everyone. . . . I will get a divorce. A divorce. All that talk about "divorce" was my own invention; the girl never said the word herself. They don't say that word. It is too legal for them, it means lawyers and the city courthouse and fees and papers, birth certificates, police, trouble. She wants to get the hell out but she doesn't want a divorce. I gave her the idea, the word. I was sitting there, blond and panicked, leaning forward but not staring at Dr. Geddes (who is an ordinary man) but at the woman sitting behind him taking notes. Was she a nurse? A secretary? That is the best chair in the room, back there. Outside there is an air hammer. It hammers inside your skull. It is like a heartbeat. But which heart is it—hers or mine? At first she complained about her heart beating too faintly, then too loudly. Which is which? Did I make it up, or did I forget something she said in between?

He telephoned me yesterday and said, "Are you coming tomorrow?"

I park the car, cross the street, go up the stairs. It is already after ten. The door is ajar and he is inside, at the desk. . . . I stand out in the corridor, watching him. Yes, an ordinary man. The face of a weak king. Sallow skin. Or is it the light? A baby is crying, a young white woman is talking sharply to the baby, rocking it in her arms. Do I love that man? Do I want to love him? I stand out in the corridor and my mind is wild with the noise from the baby and the construction next door and what sounds like an alarm clock ringing. It is only a telephone ringing, with a strange persistent ring. . . . Do I love him, am I jealous of him? Do I want him to die so that all this will be over? I am inventing him as I stand in the corridor, erasing one man and inventing another. I want to be free of him and of the girl and of her husband, who shoves her around.

Dr. Geddes glances up at me. He is startled. "What? . . . Come in!" he says, standing.

I enter the little office.

"She didn't show up today," he says, indicating the chair.

An empty chair facing him.

"She didn't telephone. Last time, you weren't here, she was talking pretty wild . . . I wonder what's going on. . . ."

"What did she say?"

"It was hard to make sense of it. One of her children got hit by a truck, he walked right into it—she said he was drugged, he was taking heroin. They took him to "Receiving and—"

"Taking heroin?"

"That's what she said. They took the boy to get stitched up, then on the the way home her husband started fighting with her. She came in here looking worn out, I think she's taking something herself . . . she could hardly keep her eyes open. . . . "

"Her son is taking heroin? At that age?"

A haze seems to pass before my eyes. Dr. Geddes keeps on talking but I can't hear him.

"But what are you going to do?" I ask him.

"Well. . . . "

"Should you send a policeman over or something?"

"Well, no. I'll wait."

"How long? She's twenty minutes late."

"I mean I'll wait until next week."

"You don't think it's dangerous?"

"Why?"

"I mean with her—"

"That she might get hurt? Or hurt herself? No."

"But how can you be sure?"

"I'm reasonably sure."

"Don't they ever kill themselves, your patients?"

He shrugs his shoulders irritably.

"How would it affect you, if a patient killed himself?" I ask him.

"They do. Occasionally."

"How did it affect you?"

"I survived."

He smiles bitterly.

Someone is coming in—but it must be a mistake, it is a black woman with a very old man. They gape at us, apologize, back out.

"Why don't you sit down?" says my friend. "It's very hot outside, isn't it?"

I sit in the patient's chair.

I look across the battered little desk at Dr. Geddes. From here he looks different—his face more oblong, his nose a little lumpy.

I am dying. I am disappearing. Help me, please!

28

The husband was picked up for murder. The wife was killed, stabbed with a kitchen knife. Dr. Geddes tells me all this when we meet by accident, months later. It is September. Dr. Geddes speaks quickly and professionally, as if he were dictating notes to me. *She never did come back*, he says. We stare over each other's shoulders. A terrible tension rises between us, stinging as sweat, but we do not acknowledge it. We do not look at each other. He goes on to talk about his busy, difficult schedule, and about the clinic. "Christ, it's one thing after another . . . . Did you read about the electricians' strike? The work will be held up indefinitely because of those goddamn unions."

29

September never came.

It is still July.

I sit in the patient's cane-backed chair and dream above the air hammer outside. One of the chair's legs is shorter than the others, or uneven somehow. The chair wobbles. Dr. Geddes and I stare at each other in silence. *I, I, I* could make you happy! I am the only woman who could make you happy! But it is not true. It is a lie I dream to myself, sitting here, alone with a man. . . . I will add five years to Dr. Geddes's face. Yes. He is really about forty; his youth is finished. Drained away. I will make his dark hair thinner, especially on the top. I will imagine small stiff whiskers in his ears, faunlike and coarse. Good. Look at that! He puts his hand against his chest, the upper part of his stomach. He has ulcers, this successful doctor. Psychiatrists' suicide rate is ten times that of the normal population. They die, they close their folders, they relinquish their practice to younger men, they die, they die, they stop listening, they stick their fingers in their ears and go deaf, the lights go out, the air hammer is disconnected, the electricians rush into the building and unhook everything, cut the wires, tear the telephone out by the roots.

The girl doesn't show up.

I sit in her chair and feel the heat all about me. I think.

Yes, I will erase Dr. Geddes too. It is a failure, our love. It didn't happen. No elevator; we always took the stairs, chastely. I will erase him too. He wasn't there that morning when I arrived, ten minutes late. The door to his office was closed and locked. I stood there, stunned. Why hadn't he come? He had just telephoned me the day before, to make sure I would meet him. What was wrong? . . . But he wasn't there. I wandered along the corridor, bewildered, hurt. I looked out the window at the skyline of Detroit, which is not a skyline but just buildings, gaseous and plain, pressed in close. Why hadn't he come? I stand there, alone, bewildered, feeling a little sick. . . .

No, he doesn't show up.

And the girl doesn't show up.

I wait a while. The corridor is noisy. A young man in shirt sleeves—one of the doctors—asks me whom I am waiting for. I am dressed too well for this place, but my manner is that of a victim.

Ten-thirty.

Quarter to eleven.

Well, it is finished. The end. My face is flushed with disappointment, humiliation. I am a woman who has been humiliated. I go downstairs and outside. I cross over to the parking lot and pay the attendant—he charges me $1.50, for nothing!—I get in my car. I sit there for a minute, staring over at the clinic. Maybe Dr. Geddes will appear, hurrying? . . .

Maybe the girl will appear? . . .

No one. Nothing. I am alone.

And so I erase them both, I kill them off. They are gone. They never existed. The next time I drive through this neighborhood the clinic itself will have been torn down: good riddance! In the sunlight the city itself is shimmering and unclear. The rubble vibrates, the pavement vibrates. Is that a crack in the street? The parking lot attendant's little cabin tilts suddenly, about a yard on one side. It is the end of this city. The city is caving in. The end of the world. I am erasing them all— erasing Detroit—the dust rises in puffing explosions to erase everything.

Myself, I am dying. I am disappearing. I can hear my heartbeat moving away from me. I am a process that is dying, disappearing, moving away.

Of all of us, only you remain.

DISCUSSION

This story exhibits a concern with what is illusory in the reality it creates. It calls attention to what is artificial in its organization. The narrator of this story has no artistic pretensions. Her manipulation of the categories of her narrative's reality is dependent on her psychological need rather than an aesthetic concern. The assertion that concludes the story—"Of all of us, only you remain"—is an effort to "hurt" the reader, to assert that while the narrator can free herself from the bounds of the world she has rendered, the reader, for whom the experience of reading the story has become an unalterable fact of his past, cannot.

The assertion, of course, is disingenuous; the narrator is not freed from the experience. Even as she changes the plot of the story she tells, certain factors are constants: the characters' emotional pain, and their isolation from each other. The sleight of hand, the "erasure" by which the narrator "cancels" her involvement, no more diminishes for her than for the reader the impact of experiences in which, however problematic her role as actor, the narrator *as* narrator has undeniably been a participant.

   1. How does the patient's digging her nails into the narrator's wrist serve to prepare the reader for the initial "erasure" by the narrator? How does it predispose the reader to accept this "erasure"?

   2. In what sense is the physical fate of the characters irrelevant to the story's concerns? Is this why the narrator leaves the question unresolved? Would she say it was unresolved? How do such questions point to the importance of keeping in mind the distinction between narrative and authorial intention?

   3. How does the condition of the city correspond to the emotional states of the people in the story? Is this picture of the city a distortion owing to the distorted consciousness of this narrator? The answer to this question is not simple and it illustrates the complexity of the story's intentions.

THE HAND OF EMMAGENE

Peter Taylor

   After highschool, she had come down from Hortonsburg
To find work in Nashville.
She stayed at our house.
And she began at once to take classes
In a secretarial school.

As a matter of fact, she wasn't *right* out of highschool.
She had remained at home two years, I think it was,
To nurse her old grandmother
Who was dying of Bright's disease.
So she was not just some giddy young country girl
With her head full of nonsense
About running around to Nashville nightspots
Or even about getting married
And who knew nothing about what it was to work.

From the very beginning, we had in mind
– My wife and I did –
That she ought to know some boys
Her own age. That was one of our first thoughts.
She was a cousin of ours, you see – or of Nancy's.
And she was from Hortonsburg
Which is the little country place
Thirty miles north of Nashville
Where Nancy and I grew up.
That's why we felt responsible
For her social life
As much as for her general welfare.
We always do what we can of course
For our kin when they come to town –
Especially when they're living under our roof.
But instead of trying to entertain Emmagene
At the Club
Or by having people in to meet her
Nancy felt
We should first find out what the girl's interests were.
We would take our cue from that.

Well, what seemed to interest her most in the world
Was work. I've never seen anything quite like it.
In some ways, this seemed the oddest thing about her.
When she first arrived, she would be up at dawn,
Before her "Cousin Nan" or I had stirred,
Cleaning the house – We would smell floor wax
Before we opened our bedroom door some mornings –
Or doing little repair jobs
On the table linen or bed linen
Or on my shirts or even Nancy's underwear.
Often as not she would have finished
The polishing or cleaning she had taken upon herself to do
Before we came down. But she would be in the living room
Or sun parlor or den or dining room
Examining the objects of her exertions, admiring them,
Caressing them even – Nancy's glass collection
Or the Canton china on the sideboard.

One morning we found her with pencil and paper
Copying the little geometrical animals
From one of the oriental rugs.

     Or some mornings she would be down in the kitchen cooking
Before the servants arrived.
(And of course she'd have the dishes she'd dirtied
All washed and put away again before the cook
Came in to fix breakfast.) What she was making
Down there in the pre-dawn hours,
Would be a cake or a pie for Nancy and me.
(She didn't eat sweets, herself)
Its aroma would reach us
Before we were out of bed or just as we started down the stairs.
But whether cleaning or cooking,
She was silent as a mouse those mornings.
We heard nothing. There were only the smells
Before we came down. And after we came down there'd be
Just the sense of her contentment.

     It was different at night. The washing machine
Would be going in the basement till the wee hours,
Or sometimes the vacuum cleaner
Would be running upstairs before we came up
Or running downstairs after we thought
We'd put the house to bed.
(We used to ask each other and even ask her
What she thought the cook and houseman
Were meant to do. Sometimes now we ask ourselves
What did they do during the time that Emmagene was here.)
And when she learned how much we liked to have fires
In the living room and den, she would lay them
In the morning, after cleaning out the old ashes.
But at night we'd hear her out in the back yard
Splitting a fireplace log, trying to get lightwood
Or wielding the ax to make kindling
Out of old crates or odd pieces of lumber.
More than once I saw her out there in the moonlight
Raising the ax high above her head
And coming down with perfect accuracy
Upon an up-ended log or a balanced two-by-four.

     There would be those noises at night
And then we noticed sometimes the phone would ring.
One of us would answer it from bed,
And there would be no one there.
Or there would be a click
And then another click which we knew in all likelihood
Was on the downstairs extension.

One night I called her name into the phone – "Emmagene?" –
Before the second click came, just to see if she were there.
But Emmagene said nothing.
There simply came the second click.

There were other times, too, when the phone rang
And there would be dead silence when we answered.
"Who is it" I would say. "Who are you calling?"
Or Nancy would say, "To whom do you wish to speak?"
Each of us, meanwhile, looking across the room at Emmagene.
For we already had ideas then, about it. We had already
Noticed cars that crept by the house
When we three sat on the porch in the late spring.
A car would mosey by, going so slow we thought surely it would stop.
But if Nancy or I stood up
And looked out over the shrubbery toward the street,
Suddenly there would be a burst of speed.
The driver would even turn on a cut-out as he roared away.

More than once the phone rang while we were at the supper table
On Sunday night. Emmagene always prepared that meal
And did up the dishes afterward since the servants were off
On Sunday night. And ate with us too, of course.
I suppose it goes without saying
She always ate at the table with us.
She rather made a point of that from the start,
Though it never would have occurred to us
For it to be otherwise.
You see, up in Hortonsburg
Her family and my wife's had been kin of course
But quite different sorts of people really.
Her folks had belonged to a hard bitten, fundamentalist sect
And Nancy's tended to be Cumberland Presbyterians
Or Congregationalists or Methodists, at worst
(Or Episcopalians, I suppose I might say, "at best.")
The fact was, Nancy's family – like my own –
Went usually to the nearest church, whatever it was.
Whereas Emmagene's travelled thirteen miles each Sunday morning
To a church of a denomination that seemed always
To be *changing* its name by the addition of some qualifying adjective.
Either that or seceding from one synod or joining another.
Or deciding just to go it alone
Because of some disputed point of scripture.

Religion aside, however, there were differences of style.
And Emmagene – very clearly – had resolved
Or been instructed before leaving home
To brook no condescension on our part.
"We're putting you in the guest room," Nancy said

Upon her arrival. And quick as a flash Emmagene added:
"And we'll take meals together?"
"Why of course, why of course," Nancy said
Placing an arm about Emmagene's shoulder.
"You'll have place of honored guest at our table."

Well, on Sunday nights it was more like we
Were the honored guests,
With the servants off, of course,
And with Emmagene electing to prepare our favorite
Country dishes for us, and serving everything up
Out in the pantry, where we always take that meal.
It was as though we were all back home in Hortonsburg.
But if the phone rang,
Emmagene was up from the table in a split second,
(It might have been her own house we were in.)
And answered the call on the wall phone in the kitchen.
I can see her now, and hear her, too.
She would say "Hello," and then just stand there, listening,
The receiver pressed to her ear, and saying nothing more at all.
At first, we didn't even ask her who it was.
We would only look at each other
And go back to our food –
As I've said, we were more like guests at her house
On Sunday night. And so we'd wait till later
To speak about it to each other.
We both supposed from the start
It was some boy friend of hers she was too timid to talk with
Before us. You see, we kept worrying
About her not having any boy friends
Or any girl friends, either.
We asked ourselves again and again
Who in our acquaintance we could introduce her to,
What nice Nashville boy we knew who would not mind
Her plainness or her obvious puritanical nature –
She didn't wear make-up, not even lipstick or powder,
And didn't do anything with her hair.
She wore dresses that were like maids' uniforms except
Without any white collars and cuffs.
Nancy and I got so we hesitated to take a drink
Or even smoke a cigarette
When she was present.
I soon began watching my language.

I don't know how many times we saw her
Answer the phone like that or heard the clickings
On the phone upstairs. At last I told Nancy
She ought to tell the girls she was free
To invite whatever friends she had to come to the house.

Nancy said she would have to wait for the opportunity;
You didn't just come out with suggestions like that
To Emmagene.

    One Sunday night the phone rang in the kitchen.
Emmagene answered it of course and stood listening for a time.
Finally, very deliberately, as always,
She returned the little wall phone to its hook.
I felt her looking at us very directly
As she always did when she put down the phone.
This time Nancy didn't pretend
To be busy with her food.
"Who *was* that, Emmagene?" she asked
In a very polite, indifferent tone.
"Well, I'll tell you," the girl began
As though she had been waiting forever to be asked.
"It's some boy or other I knew up home.
Or *didn't* know." She made an ugly mouth and shrugged.
"That's who it always is," she added, "in case you *care* to know."
There was a too obvious irony
In the way she said "*care* to know."
As though we ought to have asked her long before this.
"That's who it is in the cars, too," she informed us –
Again, as though she had been waiting only too long for us to ask.
"When they're off work and have nothing better to do
They ring up or drive by
Just to make a nuisance of themselves."
"How many of them are there?" Nancy asked.
"There's quite some few of them," Emmagene said with emphasis.
"Well, Emmagene," I suddenly joined in,
"You ought to make your choice
And maybe ask one or two of them to come to the house to see you."
She looked at me with something like rage.
"They are not a good sort," she said. "They're a bad lot.
You wouldn't want them to set foot on your front steps.
Much less your front porch or in your house."

    I was glad it was all coming out in the open and said,
"They can't all be all bad. A girl has to be selective."
She stood looking at me for a moment
In a kind of silence only she could keep.
Then she went into the kitchen and came back
Offering us second helpings from the pot of greens.
And before I could say more,
She had changed the subject and was talking about the sermon
She had heard that morning, quoting with evangelistic fervor,
Quoting the preacher and quoting the Bible.
It was as if she were herself hearing all over again
All she had heard that very morning

At that church of hers somewhere way over on the far side
of East Nashville. It was while she was going on
About the sermon that I began to wonder for the first time
How long Emmagene was going to stay here with us.
I found myself reflecting:
She hasn't got a job yet and she hasn't got a beau.

   It wasn't that I hadn't welcomed Emmagene as much as Nancy
And hadn't really liked having her in the house.
We're always having relatives from the country
Stay with us this way. If we had children
It might be different. This big house wouldn't
Seem so empty then. (I often think we keep the servants
We have, at a time when so few people have any servants at all,
Just because the servants help fill the house.)
Sometimes it's the old folks from Hortonsburg we have
When they're taking treatments
At the Hospital or at one of the clinics.
Or it may be a wife
Who has to leave some trifling husband for a while.
(Usually the couples in Hortonsburg go back together.)
More often than not it's one of the really close kin
Or a friend we were in school with or who was in our wedding.
We got Emmagene
Because Nancy heard she was all alone
Since her Grandma died
And because Emmagene's mother
Before *she* died
Had been a practical nurse and had looked after Nancy's mother
In her last days. It was that sort of thing.
And it was no more than that.
But we could see from the first how much she loved
Being here in this house and loved Nancy's nice things.
That's what's so satisfying about having them here,
Seeing how they appreciate living for a while
In a house like ours. But I don't guess
Any of them ever liked it better than Emmagene
Or tried harder to please both Nancy and me
And the servants, too. Often we would notice her
Even after she had been here for months
Just wandering from room to room
Allowing her rather large but delicately made hands
To move lightly over every piece of furniture she passed.
One felt that in the houses she knew around Hortonsburg
  – In her mother's and grandmother's houses –
There had not been pretty things – not things she loved to fondle.
It was heartbreaking to see her the day she broke
A pretty pink china vase that Nancy had set out in a new place
In the sun parlor. The girl hadn't seen it before.

She took it up in her strong right hand
To examine it. Something startled her –
A noise outside, I think. Maybe it was a car going by,
Maybe one of those boys. – Suddenly the vase crashed to the floor.
Emmagene looked down at the pieces, literally wringing her hands
As if she would wring them off, like chicken's necks, if she could.
I was not there. Nancy told me about it later.
She said that though there was not a sign of a tear in the girl's eye
She had never before seen such a look of regret and guilt
In a human face. And what the girl said
Was even stranger. Nancy and I
Have mentioned it to each other many times since.
"I despise my hand for doing that," she wailed.
"I wish – I do wish I could punish it in some way.
I ought to see it don't do anything useful for a week."

      One night on the porch
When one of those boys went by in his car
At a snail's pace
And kept tapping lightly on his horn,
I said to Emmagene, "Why don't you stand up and wave to him,
Just for fun, just to see what happens. I don't imagine
They mean any harm."
"Oh, you don't know!" she said.
"They're a mean lot.
They're not like some nice Nashville boy
That you and Cousin Nan might know."
Nancy and I sat quiet after that,
As if some home truth had been served up to us.
It wasn't just that she didn't want to know
Those Hortonsburg boys.
She *wanted* to know Nashville boys
Of a kind we might introduce her to and approve of.
I began to see – and so did Nancy, the same moment –
That Emmagene had got ideas about herself
Which it wouldn't be possible for her to realize.
She not only liked our things. She liked our life.
She meant somehow to stay. And of course
It would never do. The differences were too deep.
That is to say, she had no notion of changing herself.
She was just as sure now
About what one did and didn't do
As she had been when she came.
She still dressed herself without any ornamentation
Or any taste at all. And would have called it a sin to do so.
Levity of any kind seemed an offence to her.
There was only one Book anyone need read.
Dancing and drinking and all that
Was beyond even thinking about.

And yet the kind of luxury we had in our house
Had touched her. She felt perfectly safe, perfectly good
With it. It was a bad situation
And we felt ourselves somewhat to blame.
Yet what else could we do
But help her try to find a life of her own?
That had been our good intention from the outset.

      I investigated those boys who did the ringing up
And the horn blowing. In Nashville you have ways
Of finding out who's in town from your home town.
It's about like being in Paris or Rome
And wanting to know who's there from the U.S.A.
You ask around among those who speak the home tongue.
And so I asked about those boys.
They were, I had to acknowledge, an untamed breed.
But, still, I said to Nancy, "Who's to tame 'em
If not someone like Emmagene. It's been going on
Up there in Horton County for, I'd say – Well,
For a good many generations anyway."

      I don't know what got into us, Nancy and me.
We set about it more seriously, more in earnest
Trying to get her to see something of those boys.
I'm not sure what got into us. Maybe it was seeing Emmagene
Working her fingers to the bone
– For no reason at all. There was no necessity. –
And loving everything about it so.
Heading out to secretarial school each morning,
Beating the pavements in search of a job all afternoon,
Then coming home here and setting jobs for herself
That kept her up half the night.
Suddenly our house seemed crowded with her in it.
Not just to us, but to the servants, too.
I heard the cook talking to her one night in the kitchen.
"You ought to see some young folks your own age.
You ought to have yourself a nice fellow."
"What nice young fellow would I know?" Emmagene asked softly.
"I'm not sure there is such a fellow – not that I would know."
"Listen to her!" said the cook. "Do you think we don't see
Those fellows that go riding past here?"
"They're trash!" Emmagene said. "And not one of them
That knows what a decent girl is like!"
"Listen to her!" said the cook.
"I hear her," said the houseman, "and you hear her.
But she don't hear us. She don't hear nobody but herself."
"Ain't nobody good enough for you?" the cook said.
"I'd like to meet some boy
Who lives around here," the poor girl said.

And to this the cook said indignantly,
"Don't git above your raisin', honey."
Emmagene said no more. It was the most
Any of us would ever hear her say on that subject.
Presently she left the kitchen
And went up the back stairs to her room.

  Yet during this time she seemed happier than ever
To be with us. She even took to singing
While she dusted and cleaned. We'd hear
Familiar old hymns above the washer and the vacuum cleaner.
And such suppers as we got on Sunday night!
Why, she came up with country ham and hot sausage
That was simply not to be had in stores where Nancy traded.
And then she *did* find a job!
She finished her secretarial training
And she came up with a job
Nowhere else but in the very building
Where my own office is.
There was nothing for it
But for me to take her to work in my car in the morning
And bring her home at night.

  But there was a stranger coincidence than where her job was.
One of those boys from Hortonsburg turned out to run the elevator
In our building. Another of them brought up my car each night
In the parking garage. I hadn't noticed before
Who those young fellows were that always called me by name.
But then I noticed them speaking to her too
And calling her "Emmagene." I teased her about them a little
But not too much, I think. I knew to take it easy
And not spoil everything.

  Then one night the boy in the garage
When he was opening the car door for Emmagene, said,
"George over there wants you to let him carry you home."
This George was still another boy from Hortonsburg,
(Not one that worked in my building or in the garage)
And he saluted me across the ramp.
"Why don't you ride with him, Emmagene?" I said.
I said it rather urgently, I suppose.
Then without another word, before Emmagene could climb in beside
Me, the garage boy had slammed my car door.
And I pulled off, down the ramp –
With my tires screeching.

  At home, Nancy said I ought to have been ashamed.
But she only said it after an hour had passed
And Emmagene had not come in.

At last she did arrive, though,
Just as we were finishing dinner.
We heard a car door slam outside.
We looked at each other and waited.
Finally Emmagene appeared in the dining room doorway.
She looked at us questioningly,
First at Nancy's face, then at mine.
When she saw how pleased we were
She came right on in to her place at the table.
And she sat down, said her blessing.
And proceeded to eat her supper as though nothing unusual
                                        had happened.

     She never rode to or from work with me again.
There was always somebody out there
In the side driveway, blowing for her in the morning
And somebody letting her out in the driveway at night.
For some reason she always made them let her out
Near the back door, as though it would be wrong
For them to let her out at the front.
And then she would come on inside the house the back way.

     She went out evenings sometimes, too,
Though always in answer to a horn's blowing in the driveway
And never, it seemed, by appointment.
She would come to the living room door
And say to us she was going out for a little ride.
When we answered with our smiling countenances
She would linger a moment, as if to be sure
About what she read in our eyes
Or perhaps to relish what she could so clearly read.
Then she would be off
And she would be home again within an hour or two.

     It actually seemed as if she were still happier with us now
Than before. And yet something was different too.
We both noticed it. The hymn singing stopped.
And – almost incredible as it seemed to us –
She developed a clumsiness, began tripping over things
About the house, doing a little damage here and there
In the kitchen. The cook complained
That she'd all but ruined the meat grinder
Dropping it twice when she was unfastening it from the table.
She sharpened the wood ax on the knife sharpener – or tried to,
And bent the thing so the houseman insisted
We'd have to have another.
What seemed more carelessness than clumsiness
Was that she accidentally threw away
One of Nancy's good spoons, which the cook retrieved

From the garbage can. Nancy got so she would glance at me
As if to ask, "What will it be next? – poor child."
We noticed how nervous she was at the table
How she would drop her fork on her plate –
As if she intended to smash the Haviland –
Or spill something on a clean place mat.
Her hands would tremble, and she would look at us
As though she thought we were going to reprimand her
Or as if she hoped we would.
One day when she broke off the head of a little figurine
While dusting, she came to Nancy with the head
In one hand and the body in the other.
Her two hands were held so tense,
Clasping so tightly the ceramic pieces,
That blue veins stood out where they were usually
All creamy whiteness. Nancy's heart went out to her.
She seized the two hands in her own
And commenced massaging them
As if they were a child's, in from the snow.
She told the girl that the broken shepherd
Didn't matter at all,
That there was nothing we owned
That mattered *that* much.

    Meanwhile, the girl continued to get calls at night
On the telephone. She would speak a few syllables
Into the telephone now. Usually
We couldn't make out what it was she was she was saying.
And we tried not to hear. All I ever managed
To hear her say – despite my wish not to hear –
Were things like "Hush, George" or "Don't say such things."
Finally one night Nancy heard her say:
"I haven't got the kind of dress to wear to such a thing."

    That was all Nancy needed. She got it out of the girl
What the event was to be. And next morning
Nancy was downtown by the time the stores opened,
Buying Emmagene a sleeveless, backless evening gown.
It seemed for a time Nancy had wasted her money.
The girl said she wasn't going to go out anywhere
Dressed like that. "You don't think I'd put you in a dress
That wasn't proper to wear," said Nancy,
Giving it to her very straight.
"It isn't a matter of what you think
Is proper," Emmagene replied.
"It's what he would think it meant –
George, and maybe some of the others, too."
They were in the guest room, where Emmagene was staying
And now Nancy sat down on the twin bed opposite·

The one where Emmagene was sitting, and facing her.
"This boy George doesn't really misbehave with you
Does he, Emmagene?" Nancy asked her. "Because if he does,
Then you mustn't, after all, go out with him –
With him or with the others."
"You know I wouldn't let him do that, Cousin Nan," she said.
"Not really. Not the real thing, Cousin Nan."
"What do you mean?" Nancy asked in genuine bewilderment.
The girl looked down at her hands, which were folded in her lap.
"I mean, it's my hands he likes," she said.
And she quickly put both her hands behind her, out of sight.
"It's what they all like if they can't have it any other way."
And then she looked at Nancy the way she had looked
At both of us when we finally asked her who it was on the telephone,
As though she'd only been waiting for such questions.
And then, as before, she gave more
Than she had been asked for.
"Right from the start, it was the most disgusting kind of things
They all said to me on the telephone. And the language, the words.
You wouldn't have known the meaning, Cousin Nan."
When she had said this the girl stood up
As if to tell Nancy it was time she leave her alone.
And with hardly another word, Nancy came on to our room.
She was so stunned she was half the night
Putting it across to me just what the girl had told her
Or had tried to tell her.

Naturally, we thought we'd hear no more about the dress.
But, no, it was the very next night, after dinner,
That she came down to us in the living room
And showed herself to us in that dress Nancy had bought.
It can't properly be said she was wearing it,
But she had it on her like a night gown,
As if she didn't have anything on under it.
And her feet in a pair of black leather pumps –
No make-up of course, her hair pulled back as usual into a knot.
There was something about her, though, as she stood there
With her clean scrubbed face and her freshly washed hair
And in that attire so strange and unfamiliar to her
That made one see the kind of beauty she had,
For the first time. And somehow one knew what she was going to say.

"I'll be going out," she said, searching our faces
As she had got so she was always doing when she spoke to us.
Nancy rose and threw her needle work on the chair arm
And didn't try to stop it when it fell on to the floor.
Clearly, she too had perceived suddenly a certain beauty about the girl.
She went over to her at once and said,
"Emmagene, don't go out with George again.

It isn't wise." They stepped into the hall
With Nancy's arm about the girl's waist.
"I've got to go," Emmagene said.
And as she spoke a horn sounded in the driveway.
"George is no worse than the rest," she said.
"He's *better*. I've come to like things about him now."
There was more tapping on the horn,
Not loud but insistent.
"He's not the kind of fellow I'd have liked to like.
But I can't stop now. And you've gone and bought this dress."

Nancy didn't seem to hear her. "You mustn't go," she said.
"I couldn't live through this evening.
I'd never forgive myself." The horn kept it up outside,
And the girl drew herself away from Nancy.
Planting herself in the middle of the hall
She gave us the first line of preaching we'd ever heard from her:
"It is not for us to forgive ourselves. God forgives us."
Nancy turned and appealed to me. When I stood up
The girl said defiantly, "Oh, I'm going!"
She was speaking to both of us. "You can't stop me now!"
The car horn had begun a sort of rat-a-tat-tat.
"That's what he's like," she said, nodding her head
Toward the driveway where he was tapping the horn.
"You can't stop me now!
I'm free white and twenty-one.
That's what *he* says about me."
Still the horn kept on.
And there was nothing we could think to say or do.
Nancy did say, "Well, you'll have to have a wrap.
You can't go out like that in this weather."
She called to the cook, who came running
(She must have been waiting just beyond the hall door to the kitchen.)
And Nancy sent her to the closet on the landing
To fetch her velvet evening cape.
There was such a commotion
With the girl running out through the kitchen,
The cape about her shoulders and billowing out behind
Almost knocking over the brass umbrella stand,
I felt the best thing I could do was to sit down again.
Nancy and the cook were whispering to each other
In the hall. I could see their lips moving
And then suddenly I heard the groan or scream
That came from the kitchen and could be heard all over the house.

I went out through the dining room and the pantry
But the cook got there first by way of the back hall door.
The cook said she heard the back door slam.
I didn't hear it. Nancy said afterward she heard

The car door slam. We all heard the car roar down the driveway
In reverse gear. We heard the tires whining
As the car backed into the street and swung around
Into forward motion. None of that matters,
But that's the kind of thing you tend to recall later.
What we saw in the kitchen was the blood everywhere.
And the ax lying in the middle of the linoleum floor
With the smeary trail of blood it left
When she sent it flying. The houseman
Came up from the servants' bathroom in the basement
Just when the cook and I got there.
He came in through the back porch.
He saw what we saw of course
Except he saw more. I followed his eyes
As he looked down into that trash can at the end of the counter
And just inside the porch door. But he turned away
And ran out onto the back porch without lifting his eyes again.
And I could hear him being sick out there.

The cook and I looked at each other, to see who would go first.
I knew I had to do it, of course.
I said, "You keep Miss Nancy out of here,"
And saw her go back into the hall.
I went over to the trash can,
Stepping over the ax and with no thought in my head
But that I must look. When I did look,
My first thought was, "Why, that's a human hand."
I suppose it was ten seconds or so before I was enough myself
To own it was Emmagene's hand
She had cut off with the wood ax.
I did just what you would expect.
I ran out into the driveway, seeing the blood every step,
And then back inside, past the houseman still retching
                              over the bannister rail.
And telephoned the police on the kitchen telephone.
They were there in no time.

The boy who had been waiting for Emmagene
In the car, and making the racket with his horn
Used better judgment than a lot of people might have.
When she drew back the velvet cape and showed him
What she had done to herself
And then passed out on the seat,
He didn't hesitate, didn't think of bringing her back inside the house.
He lit out for the emergency room at the Hospital.
She was dead when he got her there,
Which no doubt was for the best
When you think about it.
But everybody congratulated the boy

– The police, and the doctors as well.
The police arrested him in the emergency waiting room,
But I went down to the Station that night
And we had him free by nine o'clock next morning.
He was just a big country boy really
Without any notion of what he was into.
We looked after arrangements for Emmagene of course
And accompanied the body up to Hortonsburg for burial.
The pastor from her church came to the town cemetery
And held a graveside service for her.
He and everybody else said a lot of consoling things to us.
They were kind in a way that only country people
Of their sort can be,
Reminding us of how hospitable we'd always been
To our kinfolks from up there
And saying Emmagene had always been
A queer sort of a girl, even before she left home.
Even that boy George's parents were at the service.
Nancy and I did our best to make them see
George wasn't to be blamed too much.
After all, you could tell from looking at his parents
He hadn't had many advantages.
He was a country boy who grew up kind of wild no doubt.
He had come down to Nashville looking for a job
And didn't have any responsible relatives here
To put restraints upon him
Or to give him the kind of advice he needed.
That might have made all the difference for such a boy,
Though of course it wasn't something you could say
To George's parents –
Not there at Emmagene's funeral, anyway.

DISCUSSION

Like the narrator in "29 Inventions," the narrator in this story is a literary amateur. But unlike the narrator in that story, the man who tells
Emmagene's story has no psychological investment in distorting it, or at
least he does not believe he has. His effort, then, is to tell the story
"straight," and such innovative techniques as he employs, most strikingly
the rendering of the story in a free-verse form, are intended to clarify
rather than obscure or make ambiguous.

"The Hand of Emmagene" is thus representative of many contemporary stories that employ the conventions of realism but that raise questions about the reality of the worlds in which their characters move. Certainly the realities that Emmagene accepts—the religious fanaticism, the
violence of sexual guilt, the notion of her sexual satisfaction—are not
those accepted by the average reader, any more than they are, more rel-
evantly, those accepted by the narrator and his wife, or by the boys

whom Emmagene dates. The action of the story describes the process of the narrator's discovery of the different world in which Emmagene lives, or rather the process of this difference's redefinition, for the narrator and his wife have all along felt (and made) differences between themselves and Emmagene. In analyzing this story, the reader should consider the extent to which the narrator and his wife are responsible for the terrible consequences of Emmagene's final acceptance of the differences between their worlds.

This story introduces an element so characteristic of much of the "new" fiction that it is sometimes considered a mark of the genre: a "Gothic" violence or sadistic element.

1. At what point in the story does the reader first begin to suspect that Emmagene may have psychotic tendencies?

2. What authorial intention may be served by dramatizing the moment early in the action at which the narrator sees Emmagene chopping firewood? How does this dramatization accomplish what is otherwise an unannounced transition to a list of foreshadowing "proofs" of Emmagene's strange relations with the boys from Hortonsburg?

3. The first words spoken by the narrator's wife tell the reader a good deal about her personality. Consider the use of dialogue in the story as a characterizing device.

4. What unintentional irony sounds in the narrator's use of the word *restraints* at the story's conclusion?

THE BALLOON

Donald Barthelme

THE balloon, beginning at a point on Fourteenth Street, the exact location of which I cannot reveal, expanded northward all one night, while people were sleeping, until it reached the Park. There, I stopped it; at dawn the northernmost edges lay over the Plaza; the free-hanging motion was frivolous and gentle. But experiencing a faint irritation at stopping, even to protect the trees, and seeing no reason the balloon should not be allowed to expand upward, over the parts of the city it was already covering, into the "air space" to be found there, I asked the engineers to see to it. This expansion took place throughout the morning, soft imperceptible sighing of gas through the valves. The balloon then covered forty-five blocks north-south on either side of the Avenue in some places. That was the situation, then.

But it is wrong to speak of "situations," implying sets of circumstances leading to some resolution, some escape of tension; there were no situations, simply the balloon hanging there—muted heavy grays and browns for the most part, contrasting with walnut and soft yellows. A deliberate lack of finish, enhanced by skillful installation, gave the surface a rough, forgotten quality; sliding weights on the inside, carefully adjusted, anchored the great, vari-shaped mass at a number of points. Now we have had a flood of original ideas in all media, works of singular beauty as well as significant milestones in the history of inflation, but at that moment there was only *this balloon,* concrete particular, hanging there.

There were reactions. Some people found the balloon "interesting." As a response this seemed inadequate to the immensity of the balloon, the suddenness of its appearance over the city; on the other hand, in the absence of hysteria or other societally induced anxiety, it must be judged a calm, "mature" one. There was a certain amount of initial argumentation about the "meaning" of the balloon; this subsided, because we have learned not to insist on meanings, and they are rarely even looked for now, except in cases involving the simplest, safest phenomena. It was agreed that since the meaning of the balloon could never be known absolutely, extended discussion was pointless, or at least less purposeful than the activities of those who, for example, hung green and blue paper lanterns from the warm gray underside, in certain streets, or seized the occasion to write messages on the surface, announcing their availability for the performance of unnatural acts, or the availability of acquaintances.

Daring children jumped, especially at those points where the balloon hovered close to a building, so that the gap between balloon and building was a matter of a few inches, or points where the balloon actually made contact, exerting an ever-so-slight pressure against the side of a building, so that balloon and building seemed a unity. The upper surface was so structured that a "landscape" was presented, small valleys as well as slight knolls, or mounds; once atop the balloon, a stroll was possible, or even a trip, from one place to another. There was pleasure in being able to run down an incline, then up the opposing slope, both gently graded, or in making a leap from one side to the other. Bouncing was possible, because of the pneumaticity of the surface, and even falling, if that was your wish. That all these varied motions, as well as others, were within one's possibilities, in experiencing the "up" side of the balloon, was extremely exciting for children, accustomed to the city's flat, hard skin. But the purpose of the balloon was not to amuse children.

Too, the number of people, children and adults, who took advantage of the opportunities described was not so large as it might have been: a certain timidity, lack of trust in the balloon, was seen. There was, furthermore, some hostility. Because we had hidden the pumps, which fed helium to the interior, and because the surface was so vast that the authorities could not determine the point of entry—that is, the point at which the gas was injected—a degree of frustration was evidenced by those city officers into whose province such manifestations normally fell. The apparent purposelessness of the balloon was vexing (as was the fact that it was "there" at all). Had we painted, in great letters, "LABORATORY TESTS PROVE" or "18% MORE EFFECTIVE!" on the sides of the balloon, this difficulty would have been circumvented. But I could not bear to do so. On the whole, these officers were remarkably tolerant, considering the dimensions of the anomaly, this tolerance being the result of, first, secret tests conducted by night that convinced them that little or nothing could be done in the way of removing or destroying the balloon, and, secondly, a public warmth that arose (not uncolored by touches of the aforementioned hostility) toward the balloon, from ordinary citizens.

As a single balloon must stand for a lifetime of thinking about balloons, so each citizen expressed, in the attitude he chose, a complex of attitudes. One man might consider that the balloon had to do with the notion *sullied*, as in the sentence *The big balloon sullied the otherwise clear and radiant Manhattan sky.* That is, the balloon was, in this man's view, an imposture, something inferior to the sky that had formerly been there, something interposed between the people and their "sky." But in fact it was January, the sky was dark and ugly; it was not a sky you could look up into, lying on your back in the street, with pleasure, unless pleasure, for you, proceeded from having been threatened, from having been misused. And the underside of the balloon was a pleasure to look up into, we had seen to that, muted grays and browns for the most part, contrasted with walnut and soft, forgotten yellows. And so, while this man was thinking *sullied*, still there was an admixture of pleasurable cognition in his thinking, struggling with the original perception.

Another man, on the other hand, might view the balloon as if it were part of a system of unanticipated rewards, as when one's employer walks in and says, "Here, Henry, take this package of money I have wrapped for you, because we have been doing so well in the business here, and I admire the way you bruise the tulips, without which bruising your department would not be a success, or at least not the success that it is." For this man the balloon might be a brilliantly heroic "muscle and pluck" experience, even if an experience poorly understood.

Another man might say, "Without the example of ——, it is doubtful that —— would exist today in its present form," and find many to agree with him, or to argue with him. Ideas of "bloat" and "float" were introduced, as well as concepts of dream and responsibility. Others engaged in remarkably detailed fantasies having to do with a wish either to lose themselves in the balloon, or to engorge it. The private character of these wishes, of their origins, deeply buried and unknown, was such that they were not much spoken of; yet there is evidence that they were widespread. It was also argued that what was important was what you felt when you stood under the balloon; some people claimed that they felt sheltered, warmed, as never before, while enemies of the balloon felt, or reported feeling, constrained, a "heavy" feeling.

Critical opinion was divided:

"monstrous pourings"

"harp"

XXXXXXX *"certain contrasts with darker portions"*
"inner joy"
"large, square corners"
"conservative eclecticism that has so far governed modern balloon design"
:::::::: *"abnormal vigor"*
"warm, soft, lazy passages"

> *"Has unity been sacrificed for a sprawling quality?"*
> *"Quelle catastrophe!"*
> *"munching"*

People began, in a curious way, to locate themselves in relation to aspects of the balloon: "I'll be at that place where it dips down into Forty-seventh Street almost to the sidewalk, near the Alamo Chile House," or, "Why don't we go stand on top, and take the air, and maybe walk about a bit, where it forms a tight, curving line with the façade of the Gallery of Modern Art—" Marginal intersections offered entrances with a given time duration, as well as "warm, soft, lazy passages" in which . . . But it is wrong to speak of "marginal intersections," each intersection was crucial, none could be ignored (as if, walking there, you might not find someone capable of turning your attention, in a flash, from old exercises to new exercises, risks and escalations). Each intersection was crucial, meeting of balloon and building, meeting of balloon and man, meeting of balloon and balloon.

It was suggested that what was admired about the balloon was finally this: that it was not limited, or defined. Sometimes a bulge, blister, or sub-section would carry all the way east to the river on its own initiative, in the manner of an army's movements on a map, as seen in a headquarters remote from the fighting. Then that part would be, as it were, thrown back again, or would withdraw into new dispositions; the next morning, that part would have made another sortie, or disappeared altogether. This ability of the balloon to shift its shape, to change, was very pleasing, especially to people whose lives were rather rigidly patterned, persons to whom change, although desired, was not available. The balloon, for the twenty-two days of its existence, offered the possibility, in its randomness, of mislocation of the self, in contradistinction to the grid of precise, rectangular pathways under our feet. The amount of specialized training currently needed, and the consequent desirability of long-term commitments, has been occasioned by the steadily growing importance of complex machinery, in virtually all kinds of operations; as this tendency increases, more and more people will turn, in bewildered inadequacy, to solutions for which the balloon may stand as a prototype, or "rough draft."

I met you under the balloon, on the occasion of your return from Norway; you asked if it was mine; I said it was. The balloon, I said, is a spontaneous autobiographical disclosure, having to do with the unease I felt at your absence, and with sexual deprivation, but now that your visit to Bergen has been terminated, it is no longer necessary or appropriate. Removal of the balloon was easy; trailer trucks carried away the depleted fabric, which is now stored in West Virginia, awaiting some other time of unhappiness, sometime, perhaps, when we are angry with one another.

DISCUSSION

In our discussions of other stories in this section we have repeatedly asked whether those stories that reject the conventions of realism make accessible to the reader's imagination the alternative principles that may govern their fictive worlds. We now ask this same question of the world created in "The Balloon."

In the story's first sentence the narrator asserts that he "cannot reveal" exactly where on Fourteenth Street in New York City the balloon was inflated. This assertion naturally stimulates the reader's curiosity. What considerations prevent the narrator from giving this information? The possibilities range from psychological incapacity to national security, and it is the reader's conviction that once he knows why the narrator withholds this information he will be on his way to knowing what the world of the narrator is like, what sorts of concerns will govern his presentation; in short, what the story is about.

The narrator never gives the reader a truly satisfactory answer. He offers all manner of information about the response of the city's populace to the presence of the balloon, but not until the last paragraph of the story (except teasingly and inconclusively, when observing in the middle of the story that "the purpose of the balloon was not to amuse children") does the narrator return to his own relation to the balloon, to his reasons for having it inflated, or for writing about it. The last paragraph of the story explains that the balloon is "a spontaneous autobiographical disclosure, having to do with the unease I felt at your absence, and with sexual deprivation." This is an answer, but it is not one the reader can understand. Neither is the explanation offered at a time when, even if it were comprehensible, the reader could make use of it in developing a sense of the narrator's relation to the story he tells.

Rather, as he reads, the reader gradually comes to feel that all questions about the principles of narrative governing the story, in fact all questions about the story's meaning, are best put to one side. The narrator has said as much early on: "It is wrong to speak of 'situations,' implying sets of circumstances leading to some resolution, some escape of tension; there were no situations, simply the balloon . . . concrete particular, hanging there." Later in the story the narrator returns to the question of meaning, remarking that "the balloon . . . offered the possibility, in its randomness, of mislocation of the self, in contradistinction to the grid of precise, rectangular pathways under our feet."

The argument of "The Balloon" is thus that all efforts to understand the story's predication, like all efforts to understand the balloon itself, are wrongheaded, and that the proper course for the reader is simply to "mislocate" his self for a while, to enter into the experience of the story merely for what it is, participating in the differing reactions of the citizenry, without any overarching sense of the reason for this "mislocation," that is, of why he is reading the story. It is consistent with the story's argument that the narrator's motivations in telling the story be problematic. Were these to be clear, the reader would have a sense not only of why the narrator is telling the story but inferentially of why he (the reader), at least from the narrator's point of view, should be reading it. The reader would lose his sense of the "randomness" of his involvement in the story.

In a closed system, which every fiction is, all elements are inevitably related to all other elements. The relation may be insignificant, or shifting, but it exists, and in some fashion contributes to the dynamic of the whole. In the present instance, the narrator's reasons for telling the story are unclear. What does become clear is that he has no significant relation to the story he tells. He has the balloon inflated for reasons that, when finally revealed, are seen to have nothing to do with the events he describes, and his next action is to have the balloon deflated (and subsequently trucked to West Virginia) when the "you" whose absence prompted the balloon's inflation returns from an unexplained trip to Norway. The narrator, although he is the owner of the balloon, has nothing to do with the reported action of the story, which is concerned not with the balloon's ownership but with the reactions of the citizenry to the balloon's presence. This combination of the narrator's problematic reasons for telling the story and his peripheral relation to the actions described causes the reader to shift his attention from why the story is being told to what the story is telling.

It can be argued that "The Balloon" is a chronicle of how New Yorkers respond to an inexplicable but unquestionable fact of their environment, the presence of the balloon. How they respond is to find in the balloon gratifications and meanings and relations that are arbitrary and personal. The reader responds to the story in exactly the same fashion. He moves from paragraph to paragraph, finding gratifications and meanings in and relations among the story's individual moments, all of this within the story's arbitrary given, which is the narrator's inexplicable resolve to tell the story in the first place.

This seems to bring us to an inconsistency in the story's intentions. The narrator's assertion that the balloon, which may be taken at one level to represent the story, should be seen as nothing more than a pleasant and temporary opportunity for "mislocation of the self" is contradicted by the remarks of the last paragraph and by the introductory invitation to the reader to consider the question of the narrator's motivations. His calling the story "a spontaneous autobiographical disclosure" and his subsequent remarks to the story's "you" give further legitimacy to the reader's raising objections. These might be phrased as follows: "This story gives me inadequate information about the narrator, about his personality and concerns, about the world in which he moves and the people who share it with him. Besides, between the first and last paragraphs the story has nothing to do with the narrator."

No reader with a realistic bias would find this argument persuasive. He would, rather, feel that it is the story's erosion of the reader's sense of relation between form and content that, paradoxically, gives the story unity, and that the teasingly obscure suggestions about the narrator's private reasons for telling the story unjustifiably mislead the reader, creating a false expectation about the nature of the story. But a reader without such a bias might accept the relationships, however fantastic or difficult to locate on a psychological ground. Such a reader gets satisfaction in toying with "reality" in accepting deceptions—provisionally, of course.

Nevertheless, even a reader with a realistic bias might be led to admit that this incoherence of narrative does not diminish many of the story's virtues. We can point, for example, to the story's telling perceptions about mass psychology (had the balloon been labeled "laboratory tests prove," the narrator remarks, its presence would have caused no disturbance) as well as to the accurate parody of the clichés and jargon of "critical opinion" in its list of reactions to the balloon by the city's intelligentsia. We can point, that is, to just such individual congruences within a pleasurable randomness as the story's proper formal intention lead us to expect at the same time realizing the element of satiric parody.

To state the whole matter more succinctly, we may say that the meaning of the story is that it has no meaning. It has only the shape and pretense of meaning. It is a serious joke, as it were, on our normal demand that fiction (and life) be logically and ethically fulfilled.

1. With the exception of the balloon itself, the world of "The Balloon" seems very much like the everyday world. Why is this necessary for the purposes of the story? Contrast "The Balloon" with "An Occurrence at Owl Creek Bridge."

2. Among the quotations of "critical opinion" of the balloon, the narrator lists "munching." Is this listing credible? Can it be seen as a sort of slapstick treatment of reactions that to this point the narrator has satirized more subtly? If so, what function is served by this change in technique? Keep in mind where in the list of opinions the word appears.

3. When people use the balloon as a reference point in making plans to meet, their speech sounds rather "arty." What makes this dialogue credible?

4. Can it be argued that there is no end to the number, and case, of such stories as this—stories that proclaim meaninglessness through an ingenuity of seeming to proclaim meaningfulness? If so, how many such stories do you yearn to read?

6

Fiction and Human Experience

How Three Stories Came to Be Written

When we read a piece of fiction, we move from the world where we, as people, live, into a world of imagination. But that world of imagination has been created by a writer out of the actual world in which he, as a person, lives. So there are three worlds involved here, our actual world, the writer's actual world, and the world he has created for us. The world that the writer has created is what we want to savor and enjoy, but sometimes we cannot properly appreciate it unless we comprehend its relevance to the other two worlds, the writers world and our world.

A story, if it is a good story, is more than a little mechanical contrivance of words and events, more than a clever trick the writer has learned to do to amuse others or make an honest penny. It is an attempt, however modest and limited, to make sense of experience, to understand how things hang meaningfully together. Therefore, in our attempt to read fiction more fully and enjoy it more deeply, it may be of use to see what three writers have to say of the origins of their stories. If what they have to say can suggest to us how the individual story grew out of the personal world of the writer, then we can see more clearly how the created world of fiction relates to the world of actuality, including our own particular personal one, whatever that may be. For in the end, what our imagination craves is not a flight from actuality, but an illumination of it, a new vision of it.

As their comments indicate, the last thing any of our three writers had in mind to tell us is "How to Write a Short Story." Writers, even moderately good writers anyway, are not concerned with rules and formulas as such. As Eudora Welty says, "Each story is going to open up a different prospect and pose a new problem," and the important question is always "How do I write *this* story?"—or to adjust the question to the needs of the reader of this book: "How do I read *this* story?"

Every serious writer regards each of his stories as a process of discovery: there is a vital experience with roots, more or less obscure, in his own experience that has to be brought into clarity and full meaning. Thus every story represents the author's effort to make sense of his world. By realizing this, we free our own imaginations to enter more fully the created world of fiction. For it becomes plain that the writer's effort to write his story is closely parallel to our effort to make sense of our own process of daily living. And if we enter the world of fiction with this realization, we can also see how the created world of fiction fundamentally relates to our own personal, day-to-day worlds.

Although none of the following accounts makes much reference to technical questions, all writers, we may be sure, would admit the fact that there are technical problems, that such things as exposition and denouement are parts of plot, and so on. Most of them would probably concede that the analytic study of fiction is a worthwhile endeavor and may lead to a fuller understanding of fiction, and would concede further that for such a process we need to use certain technical terms, with more or less fixed meanings. But all of them would emphasize the difference between the analytic process, with which we have been so often concerned in this book, and the creative process.

The analytic process is concerned with breaking fiction down into the component parts—plot, theme, character, exposition, atmosphere, and so on. The creative process is concerned with bringing things together; but we may add that, in general, *what it brings together is not even the same kind of elements that critical analysis distinguishes.* The writer does not say, "I shall put this plot with that theme," or this character with that atmosphere, or anything of the sort. He is not, in the end, trying to put things "together" at all. He is trying to attain to what Eudora Welty calls a "vision"—a vision of people alive and moving in a meaningful way in a certain world that we recognize as real and yet a world dominated by a certain feeling characteristic of the story. It is, too, a vision that must find its substance, finally, in words if it is to be shared with others and be, in fact, a story.

To share the writer's vision, the reader concerns himself with analysis, with breaking fiction into its component parts; but the good reader, of course, puts them back together again, reassembles them and even tries to forget that he ever thought analytically about them. For the analysis is for the sake of better understanding, so that when the parts once more come together, they form the "vision." The good reader ultimately attains to a sort of "vision" too.

Attaining to the vision depends on some free movement of mind, on letting the mind go loose, so that one thing leads to another, at random as it were. But this kind of association has, in the end, to be a responsible kind of irresponsibility. Logic has to develop in it, and meaning from it; or, to state the matter another way, as logic and meaning come clearer in the process, the vision will, in its subsequent stages, more and more manifest them and develop them.

Of five things, or a thousand, that come into the writer's head, only one may be useful—only one may catch on to the emerging line of logic and meaning. Therefore, as the items come into his head, from whatever source, memory or imagination or outside suggestion, the writer's power of veto is constantly being exercised. In exercising his veto the writer may be very critical and conscious, and may argue out with himself the reasons for rejecting a thing; or he may simply feel in his bones that something is wrong, and chuck it. Usually, as the logic and meaning in the developing story are discovered the writer grows surer and surer in his veto. Sometimes, however, he may have fooled himself. He may think he knows the logic and knows the meaning, and then finds that all the time, at another level, there has been developing another logic and another meaning. We know, for instance, that in certain famous pieces of fiction, the writer had, in the very middle of the process, changed his whole conception of, say, a character, even switching a piece of dialogue from one person to another, or transferring an action. The writer might, for example, be aware that the "feel" of the story demanded such a thing to be done or said at a certain point, and yet might not know until late in the process of composition just which character should say or do the thing.

If this discussion, for all its brevity, is a fair account of the creative process, then what becomes of our worry about technical matters and our attempts at analysis? Nothing becomes of them. They remain important for the story itself. The story exists in itself and has its own architecture, no matter whether the author was consciously "working" it out or not. As for the awareness of technical matters, a writer may hope in his business of composition that the technical considerations will be completely absorbed into his whole way of thinking and feeling. When on the football field a man takes a pass and sees three tacklers coming, he doesn't stop and review the fundamentals of broken field running. If he does stop to make the review, he is very apt to be in the hospital and the score is apt to look very bad. The player wants to be in motion, with the fundamentals safely stowed away in his nerve centers, where they belong. So with the writer; he wants the technique absorbed into himself, and deeply related to all the other considerations of his story. By the same general principle, technique can be so thoroughly absorbed into the personal manner of a writer that we so often find among good writers little individualities of technique, their special way of doing things, from the way of putting sentences together to the handling of exposition. We recognize the personal touch, the "signature" of style.

But how does a writer get his technique absorbed? One may learn instinctively from trial and error. One may think consciously about one's own process of trial and error. One may think about the work of other writers in the hope that this study will enter into one's own unconscious processes of creation and modify them. There is no other possible way.

No doubt the total absorption of technical considerations into the process of composition is the ideal situation for a writer. But a writer never lives very long, if ever, in an ideal situation, and so when the going gets rough he may very well have to stop and reflect quite consciously on technical questions. He may have to ask himself such questions as "Shall I put this piece of exposition in now?"—or "Shall I rewrite this passage describing the room because the atmosphere is not in keeping with my story?"—or "Will the very contrast be effective?" He may not argue the reasons. He may not even put the question into words. But he has to make a conscious decision. If it is merely shutting his eyes and taking a plunge, he has to be aware even of that and of the risk he is taking.

One of the writers presented here, Katherine Anne Porter does not speak of technical questions at all—yet she is famed as an accomplished technician. Instead, she is thinking, in a peculiarly fascinating way, of the deep, far-off origins in the world of childhood of a particular story. But the other two, Eudora Welty and Robert Penn Warren, do touch on technical questions—though not on such questions taken in isolation.

Eudora Welty tells us how she had a story in her head for a long time but couldn't get it to work until she happened to go to a certain place; then, when she thought of the story as happening in this place, with its strange atmosphere, the story came clear and could get itself written. Her discussion provides a very nice instance of how that quality that we technically call atmosphere is related to the way in which at least one story came into being.

In Miss Welty's discussion of her story, the question of atmosphere leads her to another technical consideration: point of view. The change of scene for the story leads, she tells us, to a new conception of how the story should be told. First, it led to putting a stranger into the story to look at the heroine, to give a kind of mirror for our knowledge of her. Second, it led to a new conception of how the whole story should be looked at—but that had best be left to the author's own words when we come to her discussion.

As for "Blackberry Winter," the writer tells us how, after the story had begun in certain casual recollections, he stumbled on a pattern that could be developed, that could be used as a kind of guideline in thinking about the other things that subsequently came into consciousness. He also says that he had a kind of pattern for the denouement long before he got to the actual writing of the end, or even knew what would happen there. That is, he had some sense of the structure of the story at that point, and a feeling associated with the structure, before he had a precise content.

A story may start from anything, from the death cry heard distantly by Katherine Anne Porter on a summer day, when she was a child in Texas, from a character observed or imagined, from an episode seen or an anecdote heard, from a feeling that seems to come from nowhere and is seeking an objective mooring in actuality, from the atmosphere of a place that seems to yearn for some special thing to happen there, from a historical event, from a family affection or hatred, from an idea, or from a moral conviction. It may stem from anything that will start the imagination on its characteristic job of putting things concretely together in a movement toward meaning—no, not putting them together, but creating a world in which they can grow naturally together in a movement toward meaning.

NO PLACE FOR YOU, MY LOVE

Eudora Welty

THEY were strangers to each other, both fairly well strangers to the place, now seated side by side at luncheon—a party combined in a free-and-easy way when the friends he and she were with recognized each other across Galatoire's. The time was a Sunday in summer—those hours of afternoon that seem Time Out in New Orleans.

The moment he saw her little blunt, fair face, he thought that here was a woman who was having an affair. It was one of those odd meetings when such an impact is felt that it has to be translated at once into some sort of speculation.

With a married man, most likely, he supposed, slipping quickly into a groove—he was long married—and feeling more conventional, then, in his curiosity as she sat there, leaning her cheek on her hand, looking no further before her than the flowers on the table, and wearing that hat.

He did not like her hat, any more than he liked tropical flowers. It was the wrong hat for her, thought this Eastern businessman who had no interest whatever in women's clothes and no eye for them; he thought the unaccustomed thing crossly.

It must stick out all over me, she thought, so people think they can love me or hate me just by looking at me. How did it leave us—the old, safe, slow way people used to know of learning how one another feels, and the privilege that went with it of shying away if it seemed best? People in love like me, I suppose, give away the short cuts to everybody's secrets.

Something, though, he decided, had been settled about her predicament—for the time being, anyway; the parties to it were all still alive, no doubt. Nevertheless, her predicament was the only one he felt so sure of here, like the only recognizable shadow in that restaurant, where mirrors and fans were busy agitating the light, as the very local talk drawled across and agitated the peace. The shadow lay between her fingers, between her little square hand and her cheek, like something always best carried about the person. Then suddenly, as she took her hand down, the secret fact was still there—it lighted her. It was a bold and full light, shot up under the brim of that hat, as close to them all as the flowers in the center of the table.

Did he dream of making her disloyal to that hopelessness that he saw very well she'd been cultivating down here? He knew very well that he did not. What they amounted to was two Northerners keeping each other company. She glanced up at the big gold clock on the wall and smiled. He didn't smile back. She had that naïve face that he associated, for no good reason, with the Middle West—because it said "Show me," perhaps. It was a serious, now-watch-out-everybody face, which orphaned her entirely in the company of these Southerners. He guessed

297

her age, as he could not guess theirs: thirty-two. He himself was further along.

Of all human moods, deliberate imperviousness may be the most quickly communicated—it may be the most successful, most fatal signal of all. And two people can indulge in imperviousness as well as in anything else. "You're not very hungry either," he said.

The blades of fan shadows came down over their two heads, as he saw inadvertently in the mirror, with himself smiling at her now like a villain. His remark sounded dominant and rude enough for everybody present to listen back a moment; it even sounded like an answer to a question she might have just asked him. The other women glanced at him. The Southern look—Southern mask—of life-is-a-dream irony, which could turn to pure challenge at the drop of a hat, he could wish well away. He liked naïveté better.

"I find the heat down here depressing," she said, with the heart of Ohio in her voice.

"Well—I'm in somewhat of a temper about it, too," he said.

They looked with grateful dignity at each other.

"I have a car here, just down the street," he said to her as the luncheon party was rising to leave, all the others wanting to get back to their houses and sleep. "If it's all right with— Have you ever driven down south of here?"

Out on Bourbon Street, in the bath of July, she asked at his shoulder, "South of New Orleans? I didn't know there was any south to *here*. Does it just go on and on?" She laughed, and adjusted the exasperating hat to her head in a different way. It was more than frivolous, it was conspicuous, with some sort of glitter or flitter tied in a band around the straw and hanging down.

"That's what I'm going to show you."

"Oh—you've been there?"

"No!"

His voice rang out over the uneven, narrow sidewalk and dropped back from the walls. The flaked-off, colored houses were spotted like the hides of beasts faded and shy, and were hot as a wall of growth that seemed to breathe flower-like down onto them as they walked to the car parked there.

"It's just that it couldn't be any worse—we'll see."

"All right, then," she said. "We will."

So, their actions reduced to amiability, they settled into the car—a faded-red Ford convertible with a rather threadbare canvas top, which had been standing in the sun for all those lunch hours.

"It's rented," he explained. "I asked to have the top put down, and was told I'd lost my mind."

"It's out of this world. *Degrading* heat," she said and added, "Doesn't matter."

The stranger in New Orleans always sets out to leave it as though following the clue in a maze. They were threading through the narrow and one-way streets, past the pale-violet bloom of tired squares, the brown steeples and statues, the balcony with the live and probably famous black monkey dipping along the railing as over a ballroom floor, past the grillwork and the lattice-work to all the iron swans painted flesh color on the front steps of bungalows outlying.

Driving, he spread his new map and put his finger down on it. At the intersection marked Arabi, where their road led out of the tangle and he took it, a small Negro seated beneath a black umbrella astride a box chalked "Shou Shine" lifted his pink-and-black hand and waved them languidly good-by. She didn't miss it, and waved back.

Below New Orleans there was a raging of insects from both sides of the concrete highway, not quite together, like the playing of separated marching bands. The river and the levee were still on her side, waste and jungle and some occasional settlements on his—poor houses. Families bigger than housefuls thronged the yards. His nodding, driving head would veer from side to side, looking and almost lowering. As time passed and the distance from New Orleans grew, girls ever darker and younger were disposing themselves over the porches and the porch steps, with jet-black hair pulled high, and ragged palm-leaf fans rising and falling like rafts of butterflies. The children running forth were nearly always naked ones.

She watched the road. Crayfish constantly crossed in front of the wheels, looking grim and bonneted, in a great hurry.

"How the Old Woman Got Home," she murmured to herself.

He pointed, as it flew by, at a saucepan full of cut zinnias which stood waiting on the open lid of a mailbox at the roadside, with a little note tied onto the handle.

They rode mostly in silence. The sun bore down. They met fishermen and other men bent on some local pursuits, some in sulphur-colored pants, walking and riding; met wagons, trucks, boats in trucks, autos, boats on top of autos—all coming to meet them, as though something of high moment were doing back where the car came from, and he and she were determined to miss it. There was nearly always a man lying with his shoes off in the bed of any truck otherwise empty—with the raw, red look of a man sleeping in the daytime, being jolted about as he slept. Then there was a sort of dead man's land, where nobody came. He loosened his collar and tie. By rushing through the heat at high speed, they brought themselves the effect of fans turned onto their cheeks. Clearing alternated with jungle and canebrake like something tried, tried again. Little shell roads led off on both sides; now and then a road of planks led into the yellow-green.

"Like a dance floor in there." She pointed.

He informed her, "In there's your oil, I think."

There were thousands, millions of mosquitoes and gnats—a universe of them, and on the increase.

A family of eight or nine people on foot strung along the road in the same direction the car was going, beating themselves with the wild palmettos. Heels, shoulders, knees, breasts, back of the heads, elbows, hands, were touched in turn—like some game, each playing it with himself.

He struck himself on the forehead, and increased their speed. (His wife would not be at her most charitable if he came bringing malaria home to the family.)

More and more crayfish and other shell creatures littered their path, scuttling or dragging. These little samples, little jokes of creation, persisted and sometimes perished, the more of them the deeper down the road went. Terrapins and turtles came up steadily over the horizons of the ditches.

Back there in the margins were worse—crawling hides you could not penetrate with bullets or quite believe, grins that had come down from the primeval mud.

"Wake up." Her Northern nudge was very timely on his arm. They had veered toward the side of the road. Still driving fast, he spread his map.

Like a misplaced sunrise, the light of the river flowed up; they were mounting the levee on a little shell road.

"Shall we cross here?" he asked politely.

He might have been keeping track over years and miles of how long they could keep that tiny ferry waiting. Now skidding down the levee's flank, they were the last-minute car, the last possible car that could squeeze on. Under the sparse shade of one willow tree, the small, amateurish-looking boat slapped the water, as, expertly, he wedged on board.

"Tell him we put him on hub cap!" shouted one of the numerous olive-skinned, dark-eyed young boys standing dressed up in bright shirts at the railing, hugging each other with delight that that last straw was on board. Another boy drew his affectionate initials in the dust of the door on her side.

She opened the door and stepped out, and, after only a moment's standing at bay, started up a little iron stairway. She appeared above the car, on the tiny bridge beneath the captain's window and the whistle.

From there, while the boat still delayed in what seemed a trance—as if it were too full to attempt the start—she could see the panlike deck below, separated by its rusty rim from the tilting, polished water.

The passengers walking and jostling about there appeared oddly amateurish, too—too amateur travelers. They were having such a good time. They all knew each other. Beer was being passed around in cans, bets were being loudly settled and new bets made, about local and special subjects on which they all doted. One red-haired man in a burst of wildness even tried to give away his truckload of shrimp to a man on the other side of the boat—nearly all the trucks were full of shrimp—causing taunts and then protests of "They good! They good!" from the giver. The young boys leaned on each other thinking of what next, rolling their eyes absently.

A radio pricked the air behind her. Looking like a great tomcat just above her head, the captain was digesting the news of a fine stolen automobile.

At last a tremendous explosion burst—the whistle. Everything shuddered in outline from the sound, everybody said something—everybody else.

They started with no perceptible motion, but her hat blew off. It went spiraling to the deck below, where he, thank heaven, sprang out of the car and picked it up. Everybody looked frankly up at her now, holding her hands to her head.

The little willow tree receded as its shade was taken away. The heat was like something falling on her head. She held the hot rail before her. It was like riding a stove. Her shoulders dropping, her hair flying, her skirt buffeted by the sudden strong wind, she stood there, thinking they all must see that with her entire self all she did was wait. Her set hands, with the bag that hung from her wrist and rocked back and forth—all three seemed objects bleaching there, belonging to no one; she could not feel a thing in the skin of her face; perhaps she was crying, and not knowing it. She could look down and see him just below her, his black shadow, her hat, and his black hair. His hair in the wind looked unreasonably long and rippling. Little did he know that from here it had a red undergleam like an animal's. When she looked up and outward, a vortex of light drove through and over the brown waves like a star in the water.

He did after all bring the retrieved hat up the stairs to her. She took it back—useless—and held it to her skirt. What they were saying below was more polite than their searchlight faces.

"Where you think he come from, that man?"

"I bet he come from Lafitte."

"Lafitte? What you bet, eh?"—all crouched in the shade of trucks, squatting and laughing.

Now his shadow fell partly across her; the boat had jolted into some other strand of current. Her shaded arm and shaded hand felt pulled out from the blaze of light and water, and she hoped humbly for more shade for her head. It had seemed so natural to climb up and stand in the sun.

The boys had a surprise—an alligator on board. One of them pulled it by a chain around the deck, between the cars and trucks, like a toy—a hide that could walk. He thought, Well they had to catch one sometime. It's Sunday afternoon. So they have him on board now, riding him across the Mississippi River. . . . The playfulness of it beset everybody on the ferry. The hoarseness of the boat whistle, commenting briefly, seemed part of the general appreciation.

"Who want to rassle him? Who want to, eh?" two boys cried, looking up. A boy with shrimp-colored arms capered from side to side, pretending to have been bitten.

What was there so hilarious about jaws that could bite? And what danger was there once in this repulsiveness—so that the last wordly evidence of some old heroic horror of the dragon had to be paraded in capture before the eyes of country clowns?

He noticed that she looked at the alligator without flinching at all. Her distance was set—the number of feet and inches between herself and it mattered to her.

Perhaps her measuring coolness was to him what his bodily shade was to her, while they stood pat up there riding the river, which felt like the sea and looked like the earth under them—full of the red-brown earth, charged with it. Ahead of the boat it was like an exposed vein of ore. The river seemed to swell in the vast middle with the curve of the earth. The sun rolled under them. As if in memory of the size of things, uprooted trees were drawn across their path, sawing at the air and tumbling one over the other.

When they reached the other side, they felt that they had been racing around an arena in their chariot, among lions. The whistle took and shook the stairs as they went down. The young boys, looking taller, had taken out colored combs and were combing their wet hair back in solemn pompadour above their radiant foreheads. They had been bathing in the river themselves not long before.

The cars and trucks, then the foot passengers and the alligator, waddling like a child to school, all disembarked and wound up the weed-sprung levee.

Both respectable and merciful, their hides, she thought, forcing herself to dwell on the alligator as she looked back. Deliver us all from the naked in heart. (As she had been told.)

When they regained their paved road, he heard her give a little sigh and saw her turn her straw-colored head to look back once more. Now that she rode with her hat in her lap, her earrings were conspicuous too. A little metal ball set with small pale stones danced beside each square, faintly downy cheek.

Had she felt a wish for someone else to be riding with them? He thought it was more likely that she would wish for her husband if she had one (his wife's voice) than for the lover in whom he believed. Whatever people liked to think, situations (if not scenes) were usually three-way—there was somebody else always. The one who didn't—couldn't—understand the two made the formidable third.

He glanced down at the map flapping on the seat between them, up at his wristwatch, out at the road. Out there was the incredible brightness of four o'clock.

On this side of the river, the road ran beneath the brow of the levee and followed it. Here was a heat that ran deeper and brighter and more intense than all the rest—its nerve. The road grew one with the heat as it was one with the unseen river. Dead snakes stretched across the concrete like markers—inlaid mosaic bands, dry as feathers, which their tires licked at intervals that began to seem clocklike.

No, the heat faced them—it was ahead. They could see it waving at them, shaken in the air above the white of the road, always at a certain distance ahead, shimmering finely as a cloth, with running edges of green and gold, fire and azure.

"It's never anything like this in Syracuse," he said.

"Or in Toledo, either," she replied with dry lips.

They were driving through greater waste down here, through fewer and even more insignificant towns. There was water under everything. Even where a screen of jungle had been left to stand, splashes could be heard from under the trees. In the vast open, sometimes boats moved inch by inch through what appeared endless meadows of rubbery flowers.

Her eyes overcome with brightness and size, she felt a panic rise, as sudden as nausea. Just how far below questions and answers, conceal-ment and revelation, they were running now—that was still a new ques-tion, with a power of its own, waiting. How dear—how costly—could this ride be?

"It looks to me like your road can't go much further," she remarked cheerfully. "Just over there, it's all water."

"Time out," he said, and with that he turned the car into a sudden road of white shells that rushed at them narrowly out of the left.

They bolted over a cattle guard, where some rayed and crested pur-ple flowers burst out of the vines in the ditch, and rolled onto a long, narrow, green, mowed clearing: a churchyard. A paved track ran be-tween two short rows of raised tombs, all neatly white-washed and now brilliant as faces against the vast flushed sky.

The track was the width of the car with a few inches to spare. He passed between the tombs slowly but in the manner of a feat. Names took their places on the walls slowly at a level with the eye, names as near as the eyes of a person stopping in conversation, and as far away in origin, and in all their music and dead longing, as Spain. At intervals were set packed bouquets of zinnias, oleanders, and some kind of purple flowers, all quite fresh, in fruit jars; like nice welcomes on bureaus.

They moved on into an open plot beyond, of violent-green grass, spread before the green-and-white frame church with worked flower beds around it, flowerless poinsettias growing up to the windowsills. Beyond was a house, and left on the doorstep of the house a fresh-caught catfish the size of a baby—a fish wearing whiskers and bleeding. On a clothesline in the yard, a priest's black gown on a hanger hung air-ing, swaying at man's height, in a vague, trainlike, lady-like sweep along an evening breath that might otherwise have seemed imaginary from the unseen, felt river.

With the motor cut off, with the raging of the insects about them, they sat looking out at the green and white and black and red and pink as they leaned against the sides of the car.

"What is your wife like?" she asked. His right hand came up and spread—iron, wooden, manicured. She lifted her eyes to his face. He looked at her like that hand.

Then he lit a cigarette, and the portrait, and the righthand testimo-nial it made, were blown away. She smiled, herself as unaffected as by some stage performance; and he was annoyed in the cemetery. They did not risk going on to her husband—if she had one.

Under the supporting posts of the priest's house, where a boat was, solid ground ended and palmettos and water hyacinths could not wait to begin; suddenly the rays of the sun, from behind the car, reached that lowness and struck the flowers. The priest came out onto the porch in his underwear, stared at the car a moment as if he wondered what time it was, then collected his robe off the line and his fish off the doorstep and returned inside. Vespers was next, for him.

After backing out between the tombs he drove on still south, in the sunset. They caught up with an old man walking in a sprightly way in their direction, all by himself, wearing a clean bright shirt printed with a pair of palm trees fanning green over his chest. It might better be a big colored woman's shirt, but she didn't have it. He flagged the car with gestures like hoops.

"You're coming to the end of the road," the old man told them. He pointed ahead, tipped his hat to the lady, and pointed again. "End of the road." They didn't understand that he meant, "Take me."

They drove on. "If we do go any further, it'll have to be by water—is that it?" he asked her, hesitating at this odd point.

"You know better than I do," she replied politely.

The road had for some time ceased to be paved; it was made of shells. It was leading into a small, sparse settlement like the others a few miles back, but with even more of the camp about it. On the lip of the clearing, directly before a green willow blaze with the sunset gone behind it, the row of houses and shacks faced out on broad, colored, moving water that stretched to reach the horizon and looked like an arm of the sea. The houses on their shaggy posts, patchily built, some with plank runways instead of steps, were flimsy and alike, and not much bigger than the boats tied up at the landing.

"Venice," she heard him announce, and he dropped the crackling map in her lap.

They coasted down the brief remainder. The end of the road—she could not remember ever seeing a road simply end—was a spoon shape, with a tree stump in the bowl to turn around by.

Around it, he stopped the car, and they stepped out, feeling put down in the midst of a sudden vast pause or subduement that was like a yawn. They made their way on foot toward the water, where at an idle-looking landing men in twos and threes stood with their backs to them.

The nearness of darkness, the still uncut trees, bright water partly under a sheet of flowers, shacks, silence, dark shapes of boats tied up, then the first sounds of people just on the other side of thin walls—all this reached them. Mounds of shells like day-old snow, pink-tinted, lay around a central shack with a beer sign on it. An old man up on the porch there sat holding an open newspaper, with a fat white goose sitting opposite him on the floor. Below, in the now shadowless and sunless open, another old man, with a colored pencil bright under his hat brim, was late mending a sail.

When she looked clear around thinking they had a fire burning somewhere now, out of the heat had risen the full moon. Just beyond the trees, enormous, tangerine-colored, it was going solidly up. Other lights just striking into view, looking farther distant, showed moss shapes hanging, or slipped and broke matchlike on the water that so encroached upon the rim of ground they were standing on.

There was a touch at her arm—his, accidental.

"We're at the jumping-off place," he said.

She laughed, having thought his hand was a bat, while her eyes rushed downward toward a great pale drift of water hyacinths—still partly open, flushed and yet moonlit, level with her feet—through which paths of water for the boats had been hacked. She drew her hands up to her face under the brim of her hat; her own cheeks felt like the hyacinths to her, all her skin still full of too much light and sky, exposed. The harsh vesper bell was ringing.

"I believe there must be something wrong with me, that I came on this excursion to begin with," she said, as if he had already said this and she were merely in hopeful, willing, maddening agreement with him.

He took hold of her arm, and said, "Oh, come on—I see we can get something to drink here, at least."

But there was a beating, muffled sound from over the darkening water. One more boat was coming in, making its way through the tenacious, tough, dark flower traps, by the shaken light of what first appeared to be torches. He and she waited for the boat, as if on each other's patience. As if borne in on a mist of twilight or a breath, a horde of mosquitoes and gnats came singing and striking at them first. The boat bumped, men laughed. Somebody was offering somebody else some shrimp.

Then he might have cocked his dark city head down at her: she did not look up at him, only turned when he did. Now the shell mounds, like the shacks and trees, were solid purple. Lights had appeared in the not-quite-true window squares. A narrow neon sign, the lone sign, had come out in bright blush on the beer shack's roof: "Baba's Place." A light was on on the porch.

The barnlike interior was brightly lit and unpainted, looking not quite finished, with a partition dividing this room from what lay behind. One of the four cardplayers at a table in the middle of the floor was the newspaper reader; the paper was in his pants pocket. Midway along the partition was a bar, in the form of a pass-through to the other room, with a varnished, second-hand fretwork overhang. They crossed the floor and sat, alone there, on wooden stools. An eruption of humorous signs, newspaper cutouts and cartoons, razor-blade cards, and personal messages of significance to the owner or his friends decorated the overhang, framing where Baba should have been but wasn't.

Through there came a smell of garlic and cloves and red pepper, a blast of hot cloud escaped from a cauldron they could see now on a stove at the back of the other room. A massive back, presumably female, with a twist of gray hair on top, stood with a ladle akimbo. A young man joined her and with his fingers stole something out of the pot and ate it. At Baba's they were boiling shrimp.

When he got ready to wait on them, Baba strolled out to the counter, young, black-headed, and in very good humor.

"Coldest beer you've got. And food— What will you have?"

"Nothing for me, thank you," she said. "I'm not sure I could eat, after all."

"Well, I could," he said, shoving his jaw out. Baba smiled. "I want a good solid ham sandwich."

"I could have asked him for some water," she said, after he had gone.

While they sat waiting, it seemed very quiet. The bubbling of the shrimp, the distant laughing of Baba, and the slap of cards, like the beating of moths on the screens, seemed to come in fits and starts. The steady breathing they heard came from a big rough dog asleep in the corner. But it was bright. Electric lights were strung riotously over the room from a kind of spider web of old wires in the rafters. One of the written messages tacked before them read, "Joe! At the boyy!!" It looked very yellow, older than Baba's Place. Outside, the world was pure dark.

Two little boys, almost the same size, and just cleaned up, dived into the room with a double bang of the screen door, and circled around the card game. They ran their hands into the men's pockets.

"Nickel for some pop!"

"Nickel for some pop!"

"Go 'way and let me play, you!"

They circled around and shrieked at the dog, ran under the lid of the counter and raced through the kitchen and back, and hung over the stools at the bar. One child had a live lizard on his shirt, clinging like a breast pin—like lapis lazuli.

Bringing in a strong odor of geranium talcum, some men had come in now—all in bright shirts. They drew near the counter, or stood and watched the game.

When Baba came out bringing the beer and sandwich, "Could I have some water?" she greeted him.

Baba laughed at everybody. She decided the woman back there must be Baba's mother.

Beside her, he was drinking his beer and eating his sandwich—ham, cheese, tomato, pickle, and mustard. Before he finished, one of the men who had come in beckoned from across the room. It was the old man in the palmtree shirt.

She lifted her head to watch him leave her, and was looked at, from all over the room. As a minute passed, no cards were laid down. In a far-off way, like accepting the light from Arcturus, she accepted it that she was more beautiful or perhaps more fragile than the women they saw every day of their lives. It was just this thought coming into a womman's face, and at this hour, that seemed familiar to them.

Baba was smiling. He had set an opened, frosted brown bottle before her on the counter, and a thick sandwich, and stood looking at her. Baba made her eat some supper, for what she was.

"What the old fellow wanted," said he when he came back at last, "was to have a friend of his apologize. Seems church is just out. Seems the friend made a remark coming in just now. His pals told him there was a lady present."

"I see you bought him a beer," she said.

"Well, the old man looked like he wanted *something*."

All at once the juke box interrupted from back in the corner, with the same old song as anywhere. The half-dozen slot machines along the wall were suddenly all run to like Maypoles, and thrown into action—taken over by further battalions of little boys.

There were three little boys to each slot machine. The local custom appeared to be that one pulled the lever for the friend he was holding up to put the nickel in, while the third covered the pictures with the flat of his hand as they fell into place, so as to surprise them all if fell into place, so as to surprise them all if anything happened.

The dog lay sleeping on in front of the raging juke box, his ribs working fast as a concertina's. At the side of the room a man with a cap on his white thatch was trying his best to open a side screen door, but it was stuck fast. It was he who had come in with the remark considered ribald; now he was trying to get out the other way. Moths as thick as ingots were trying to get in. The card players broke into shouts of derision, then joy, then tired derision among themselves; they might have been here all afternoon—they were the only ones not cleaned up and shaved. The original pair of little boys ran in once more, with the hyphenated bang. They got nickels this time, then were brushed away from the table like mosquitoes, and they rushed under the counter and on to the cauldron behind, clinging to Baba's mother there. The evening was at the threshold.

They were quite unnoticed now. He was eating another sandwich, and she, having finished part of hers, was fanning her face with her hat. Baba had lifted the flap of the counter and come out into the room. Behind his head there was a sign lettered in orange crayon: "Shrimp Dance Sun. PM." That was tonight, still to be.

And suddenly she made a move to slide down from her stool, maybe wishing to walk out into that nowhere down the front steps to be cool a moment. But he had hold of her hand. He got down from his stool, and, patiently, reversing her hand in his own—just as she had had the look of being about to give up, faint—began moving her, leading her. They were dancing.

"I get to thinking this is what we get—what you and I deserve," she whispered, looking past his shoulder into the room. "And all the time, it's real. It's a real place—away off down here . . ."

They danced gratefully, formally, to some song carried on in what must be the local patois, while no one paid any attention as long as they were together, and the children poured the family nickels steadily into the slot machines, walloping the handles down with regular crashes and troubling nobody with winning.

She said rapidly, as they began moving together too well, "One of those clippings was an account of a shooting right here. I guess they're proud of it. And that awful knife Baba was carrying . . . I wonder what he called me," she whispered in his ear.

"Who?"

"The one who apologized to you."

If they had ever been going to overstep themselves, it would be now as he held her closer and turned her, when she became aware that he could not help but see the bruise at her temple. It would not be six inches from his eyes. She felt it come out like an evil star. (Let it pay him back, then, for the hand he had stuck in her face when she'd tried once to be sympathetic, when she'd asked about his wife.) They danced on still as the record changed, after standing wordless and motionless, linked together in the middle of the room, for the moment between.

Then, they were like a matched team—like professional, Spanish dancers wearing masks—while the slow piece was playing.

Surely even those immune from the world, for the time being, need the touch of one another, or all is lost. Their arms encircling each other, their bodies circling the odorous, just-nailed-down floor, they were, at last, imperviousness in motion. They had found it, and had almost missed it: they had had to dance. They were what their separate hearts desired that day, for themselves and each other.

They were so good together that once she looked up and half smiled. "For whose benefit did we have to show off?"

Like people in love, they had a superstition about themselves almost as soon as they came out on the floor, and dared not think the words "happy" or "unhappy," which might strike them, one or the other, like lightning.

In the thickening heat they danced on while Baba himself sang with the mosquito-voiced singer in the chorus of "*Moi pas l'aimez ça*," enumerating the *ça's* with a hot shrimp between his fingers. He was counting over the platters the old woman now set on the counter, each heaped with shrimp in their shells boiled to iridescence, like mounds of honeysuckle flowers.

The goose wandered in from the back room under the lid of the counter and hitched itself around the floor among the table legs and people's legs, never seeing that it was neatly avoided by two dancers—who nevertheless vaguely thought of this goose as learned, having earlier heard an old man read to it. The children called it Mimi, and lured it away. The old thatched man was again drunkenly trying to get out by the stuck side door; now he gave it a kick, but was prevailed on to remain. The sleeping dog shuddered and snored.

It was left up to the dancers to provide nickels for the juke box; Baba kept a drawerful for every use. They had grown fond of all the selections by now. This was the music you heard out of the distance at night—out of the roadside taverns you fled past, around the late corners in cities half asleep, drifting up from the carnival over the hill, with one odd little strain always managing to repeat itself. This seemed a homey place.

Bathed in sweat, and feeling the false coolness that it brings, they stood finally on the porch in the lapping night air for a moment before leaving. The first arrivals of the girls were coming up the steps under the porch light—all flowered fronts, their black pompadours giving out breathlike feelers from sheer abundance. Where they'd resprinkled it since church, the talcum shone like mica on their downy arms. Smelling solidly of geranium, they filed across the porch with short steps and fingers joined, just timed to turn their smiles loose inside the room. He held the door open for them.

"Ready to go?" he asked her.

Going back, the ride was wordless, quiet except for the motor and the insects driving themselves against the car. The windshield was soon blinded. The headlights pulled in two other spinning storms, cones of flying things that, it seemed, might ignite at the last minute. He stopped the car and got out to clean the windshield thoroughly with his brisk, angry motions of driving. Dust lay thick and cratered on the roadside scrub. Under the now ash-white moon, the world traveled through very faint stars—very many slow stars, very high, very low.

It was a strange land, amphibious—and whether water-covered or grown with jungle or robbed entirely of water and trees, as now, it had the same loneliness. He regarded the great sweep—like steppes, like moors, like deserts (all of which were imaginary to him); but more than it was like any likeness, it was South. The vast, thin, wide-thrown, pale, unfocused star-sky, with its veil of lightning adrift, hung over this land as it hung over the open sea. Standing out in the night alone, he was struck as powerfully with recognition of the extremity of this place as if all other bearings had vanished—as if snow had suddenly started to fall.

He climbed back inside and drove. When he moved to slap furiously at his shirtsleeves, she shivered in the hot, licking night wind that their speed was making. Once the car lights picked out two people—a Negro couple, sitting on two facing chairs in the yard outside their lonely cabin—half undressed, each battling for self against the hot night, with long white rags in endless, scarflike motions.

In peopleless open places there were lakes of dust, smudge fires burning at their hearts. Cows stood in untended rings around them, motionless in the heat, in the night—their horns standing up sharp against that glow.

At length, he stopped the car again, and this time he put his arm under her shoulder and kissed her—not knowing ever whether gently or harshly. It was the loss of that distinction that told him this was now. Then their faces touched unkissing, unmoving, dark, for a length of time. The heat came inside the car and wrapped them still, and the mosquitoes had begun to coat their arms and even their eyelids.

Later, crossing a large open distance, he saw at the same time two fires. He had the feeling that they had been riding for a long time across a face—great, wide, and upturned. In its eyes and open mouth were those fires they had had glimpses of, where the cattle had drawn together: a face, a head, far down here in the South—south of South, below it. A whole giant body sprawled downward then, on and on, always, constant as a constellation or an angel. Flaming and perhaps falling, he thought.

She appeared to be sound asleep, lying back flat as a child, with her hat in her lap. He drove on with her profile beside his, behind his, for he bent forward to drive faster. The earrings she wore twinkled with their rushing motion in an almost regular beat. They might have spoken like tongues. He looked straight before him and drove on, at a speed that, for the rented, overheated, not at all new Ford car, was demoniac.

It seemed often now that a barnlike shape flashed by, roof and all outlined in lonely neon—a movie house at a cross roads. The long white flat road itself, since they had followed it to the end and turned around to come back, seemed able, this far up, to pull them home.

A thing is incredible, if ever, only after it is told—returned to the world it came out of. For their different reasons, he thought, neither of them would tell this (unless something was dragged out of them): that, strangers, they had ridden down into a strange land together and were getting safely back—by a slight margin, perhaps, but margin enough. Over the levee wall now, like an aurora borealis, the sky of New Orleans, across the river, was flickering gently. This time they crossed by bridge, high above everything, merging into a long light-stream of cars turned cityward.

For a time afterward he was lost in the streets, turning almost at random with the noisy traffic until he found his bearings. When he stopped the car at the next sign and leaned forward frowning to make it out, she sat up stright on her side. It was Arabi. He turned the car right around.

"We're all right now," he muttered, allowing himself a cigarette.

Something that must have been with them all along suddenly, then, was not. In a moment, tall as panic, it rose, cried like a human, and dropped back.

"I never got my water," she said.

She gave him the name of her hotel, he drove her there, and he said good night on the sidewalk. They shook hands.

"Forgive . . ." For, just in time, he saw she expected it of him.

And that was just what she did, forgive him. Indeed, had she waked in time from a deep sleep, she would have told him her story. She disappeared through the revolving door, with a gesture of smoothing her hair, and he thought a figure in the lobby, strolled to meet her. He got back in the car and sat there.

He was not leaving for Syracuse until early in the morning. At length, he recalled the reason; his wife had recommended that he stay where he was this extra day so that she could entertain some old, unmarried college friends without him underfoot.

As he started up the car, he recognized in the smell of exhausted, body-warm air in the streets, in which the flow of drink was an inextricable part, the signal that the New Orleans evening was just beginning. In Dickie Grogan's, as he passed, the well-known Josefina at her organ was charging up and down with "*Clair de lune*." As he drove the little Ford safely to its garage, he remembered for the first time in years when he was young and brash, a student in New York, and the shriek and horror and unholy smother of the subway had its original meaning for him as the lilt and expectation of love.

HOW I WRITE

Eudora Welty

"HOW do I write my stories?" is a blessedly open question. For the writer it is forever in the course of being studied through doing and new doing, and wouldn't last very long as a matter of self-observation, which could very well turn him to stone. Apart from what he's learned about his separate stories, out of passion, the renewable passion, of doing each in the smallest part better (at least nearer the way he wants it), he may or may not be a good judge of his work in the altogether. To him if a story is good enough to be called finished, as far as he can see, it is detached on the dot from the hand that wrote it, and the luster goes with it; what *is* attached is the new story. "How I wrote," past tense, may be seen into from this detachment, but not with the same insight—that too is gone, displaced. Looking backward can't compete with looking forward with the story in progress—that invites and absorbs and uses every grain of his insight, and his love and wits and curiosity and strength of purpose. "How do I write *this* story?" is really the question, the vital question; but its findings can be set down only in terms of the story's own—terms of fiction. (At least, ordinarily. Story writing and an independently operating power of critical analysis are separate gifts, like spelling and playing the flute, and one person proficient in both has been doubly endowed. But even he can't rise and do both at the same time.)

I feel myself that any *generalization* about writing is remote from anything I have managed to learn about it. I believe I can make one wide one, and others must have often nailed it down, but I shall have to hold my blow till I get there. The only things I feel I really know well are stuck to the stories, part of the animal. The main lesson I've learned from work so far is the simple one that each story is going to open up a different prospect and pose a new problem; no story bears on another or helps another, even if the writing mind had room for help and the wish that it would come. Help would be a blight. I could add that it's hard for me to think that a writer's stories are a unified whole in any respect except perhaps their lyric quality. I don't believe they are written in any typical, predictable, logically developing, or even chronological way (for all that a good writer's stories are, to the reader, so immediately identifiable as his)—or in any way that after enough solid tries guarantees him a certain measure of excellence, safety (spare the word!), or delight.

I do have the feeling that all stories by one writer tend to spring from the same source within him. However they differ in subject or approach, however they vary in excellence or fluctuate in their power to alter the mind or mood or move the heart, all of one writer's stories must take on their quality, carry their signature, because of one characteristic, lyrical impulse of his mind—the impulse to praise, to love, to call up, to prophesy. But then what countless stories share a common source! All writers write out of the same few, few and eternal—love, pity, terror do not change.

Sources of stories could be examined with less confusion, perhaps, not in the subjective terms of emotion, but through finding what in the outside world leads back to those emotions most directly and tautly and specifically. The surest clue is the pull on the line, the "inspiration," the outside signal that has startled or moved the creative mind to complicity and brought the story to active being: the irresistible, the magnetic, the alarming (pleasurable or disturbing), the overwhelming person, place, or thing.

Surely, for the writer this is the world where stories come from, and where their origins are living reference plain to his eyes. The dark changes of the mind and heart, where all in the world is constantly *becoming* something—the poetic, the moral, the passionate, hence the *shaping* idea—are not mapped and plotted yet, except as psychiatry has applied the healing or tidying hand, and their being so would make no change in their processes, or their climates, or their way of life and death (any more than a map hung on the wall changes the world); or schedule or pigeonhole or allot or substitute or predict the mysteries rushing unsubmissively through them by the minute; or explain a single work of art that came out the other side. The artist at work functions, while whoever likes to may explain how he does it (or failing that, why)—without, however, the least power of prevention or prophecy or even cure—for some alarmists say that literature has come out of a disease of society, as if stamping out the housefly would stop it, and I've heard there's another critic who says writing is nothing but the death wish. (Exactly where in all this *standards* come in I don't know.)

It is of course the *way* of writing that gives a story, however humble, its whole distinction and glory—something learned, and learned each writer for himself, by dint of each story's unique challenge and his work that rises to meet it—work scrupulous, questioning, unprecedented, ungeneralized, uncharted, and his own. It is the changeable outside world and the learnable way of writing that are the different quotients. Always different, always differing, from writer to writer and story to story, they are—or so I believe—most intimately connected with each other.

Like a good many other writers, I am myself touched off by place. The place where I am and the place I know, and other places that familiarity with and love for my own make strange and lovely and enlightening to look into, are what set me to writing my stories. To such writers I suppose place opens a door in the mind; either spontaneously or through beating it down, attrition. The impression of place as revealing something is an indelible one—which of course is not to say it isn't highly personal and very likely distorted. The imagination further and further informs and populates the impression according to present mood, intensification of feeling, beat of memory, accretion of idea, and by the blessing of being located—contained—a story so changed is now capable of being written.

The connection of this to what's called regional writing is clear but not much more informing; it does mean a lot of writers behave the same way. Regional writing itself has old deep roots; it is not the big root itself. Place is surely one of the most simple and obvious and direct sources of the short story, and one of the most ancient—as it is of lyric poetry—and, if I may presume to speak freely here for other regional writers too, the connection of story to place can go for ever so long not even conscious in the mind, because taken for granted. The regional writer's vision is as surely made of the local clay as any mud pie of his childhood was, and it's still the act of the imagination that makes the feast; only in the case of any art the feast is real, for the act of the imagination gives vision the substance and makes it last.

After we see the connection between our place and our writing, has anything changed for us? We aren't admonished in any way we weren't admonished already by pride of work, surely? Yes, something *has* changed for us; we learn that. I am the proud partisan I am of regional writing because this connection between place and story *is* deep, *does* take time, and its claims on us are deep; they, like our own mind's responsibilities, are for us to find out. To be a regional writer is not like belonging to a club or a political party; it is nothing you can take credit for—it's an endowment, but more than that. It's a touchstone when you write, and shows up, before anything else does, truth and mistakes. In a way place is your honor as it is your wisdom, and would make you responsible to it for what you put down for the truth.

Whatever the story a reader takes up, the road from origin on isn't any the plainer for the simplicity of the start. Sometimes a reader thinks he is "supposed" to see in a story (I judge from letters from readers when they can't find it in mine) a sort of plant-from-seed development, rising in the end to a perfect Christmas tree of symmetry, branch, and ornament, with a star at the top for neatness. The reader of more willing imagination, who has specified for something else, may find the branchings not what he's expecting either, and the fulfillment not a perfect match, not at all to the letter of the promise—rather to a degree—(and to a degree of pleasure) mysterious. This is one of the short story's finest attributes. The analyst, should the story come under his eye, may miss this gentle shock and this pleasure too, for he's picked up the story at once by its heels (as if it had swallowed a button) and is examining the writing as his own process in reverse, as though a story (or any system of feeling) could be the more accessible to understanding for being hung upside down. "Sweet Analytics, 'tis thou hast ravish'd me!"

Analysis, to speak generally, has to travel backwards; the path it goes, while paved with good intentions, is an ever-narrowing one, whose goal is the vanishing point, beyond which only "influences" lie. But writing, bound in the opposite direction, works further and further always into the open. The choices get freer and wider, apparently, as with everything else that has a life and moves. "This story promises me fear and joy and so I write it" has been the writer's honest beginning. Dr. Faustus, the critic, coming to the end of his trail, may call out the starting point he's found, but the writer long ago knew the starting point for what it was to him—the jumping off place. If they coincide, it's a coincidence. I think the writer's out-bound choices seem obstructive sometimes to analysts simply because they wouldn't be there if they weren't plain evidence that they were to the writer inevitable choices, not arguable; impelled, not manipulated; that they came with an arrow inside them. Indeed they have been *fiction's* choices: one-way and fateful; strict as art, obliged as feeling, powerful in their authenticity though for slightest illusion's sake; and reasonable (in the out-of-fiction sense) only last, and by the grace of, again, coincidence—always to be welcomed and shown consideration, but never to be courted or flattered.

Certainly a story and its analysis are not the mirror opposites of each other, for all their running off in opposite directions. Criticism can be an art too and may go deeper than its object, and more times around; it may pick up a story and waltz with it, so that it's never the same. In any case it's not a reflection. But I think that's exactly why it cannot be *used* as one, whoever holds it up, even the curious author; why it's a mistake to think you can stalk back a story by analysis's footprints and even dream that's the original coming through the woods. Besides the difference in the direction of the two, there's the difference in speeds, when one has fury; but the main difference is in world-surround. One surround is a vision and the other is a pattern for good visions (which—who knows!— fashion may have tweaked a little) or the nicest, carefullest black-and-white tracing that a breath of life would do for. Each, either, or neither may be a masterpiece of construction; but the products are not to be confused.

The story is a vision; while it's being written, all choices must be its choices, and as these multiply upon one another, their field is growing too. The choices remain inevitable, in fact, through moving in a growing maze of possibilities that the writer, far from being dismayed at his presence on unknown ground (which might frighten him as a critic) has learned to be grateful for, and excited by. The fiction writer has learned (and here is my generalization) that it is the very existence, the very multitude and clamor and threat and lure of *possibility*—all possibilities his work calls up for itself as it goes—that guide his story most delicately. In the act of writing he finds, if no explanation outside fiction for what he is doing, or the need of it, no mystery about it either. What he does know is the word comes surest out of too much, not too little—just as the most exacting and sometimes the simplest-appearing work is brought off (when it does not fail) on the sharp edge of experiment, not in dim, reneging safety. He is not at the end yet, but it was for this he left all he knew behind, at the jumping off place, when he started this new story.

II

I made the remark above that I believed the changeable outside world and the learnable way of writing are connected with each other. I think it is this connection that can be specifically looked at in any story, but maybe a regional story could give us the easiest time. I offer here the clearest example I could find among my own stories of the working point I am hoping to make, since place not only suggested how to write the story but repudiated a way I had already tried it.

What happened was that I was invited to drive with a friend down south of New Orleans one summer day, to see that country for the first (and only) time, and when I got back home I realized that without being aware of it at the time I had treated a story, which I was working on then, to my ride, and it had come into my head in an altogether new form. I set to work and wrote the new version from scratch, which resulted in my throwing away the first and using the second. I learned all the specific detail of this story from the ride, though I should add that the story in neither version had any personal connection with myself and there was no conscious "gathering of material" on a pleasant holiday.

As first written, the story told, from the inside, of a girl in a claustrophobic predicament: she was caught fast in the over-familiar, monotonous life of her small town, and immobilized further by a hopeless and inarticulate love, which she had to pretend was something else. This happens all the time. As a result of my ride I extracted her. But she had been well sealed inside her world, by nature and circumstance both, and even more closely by my knowing her too well (the story had gone on too long) and too confidently. Before I could prize her loose, I had to take a primary step of getting outside her mind. I made her a girl from the Middle West—she'd been what I knew best, a Southerner, before. I kept outside her by taking glimpses of her through the curious eyes of a stranger: instead of the half-dozen characters (I knew them too well too) from the first version, I put in one single new one—a man whom I brought into the story *to be* a stranger. I had double-locked the doors behind me—you never dream the essentials can be simple again, within one story.

But the vital thing that happened to the story came from writing, as I began the work. My first realization of what it was came when I looked back and recognized that country (the once-submerged, strange land of "south from South" that had so stamped itself upon my imagination) as the image to me of the story's predicament come to life. This pointed out to me, as I wrote into the story, where the real point of view belonged. Once I was outside, I saw *it* was outside—suspended, hung in the air between the two people, fished alive from the surrounding scene, where as it carried the story along it revealed itself (I hoped) as more real, more essential, than the characters were or had any cause to be. In effect there'd come to be a sort of third character present—an identity, rather: the relationship between the two and between the two and the world. It was what grew up between them meeting as strangers, went on the trip with them, nodded back and forth from one to the other—listening, watching, persuading or denying them, enlarging or diminishing them, forgetful sometimes of who they were or what they were doing here, helping or betraying them along. Its role was that of hypnosis—it was what a relationship *does*, be it however brief, tentative, potential, happy or sinister, ordinary or extraordinary. I wanted to suggest that its being took shape as the strange, compulsive journey itself, was palpable as its climate and mood, the heat of the day—but was its spirit too, a spirit that held territory—what's seen fleeting past by two vulnerable people who might seize hands on the run. There are times in the story when I say neither "she felt" nor "he felt" but "they felt." All this is something that *doesn't* happen all the time. It merely could, or almost could, as here.

This is to grant that I rode out of the old story on the back of the girl and then threw away the girl; but I saved the story, for entirely different as the second version was, it was what I wanted to say. My subject was out in the open, provided at the same time with a place to happen and a way to say it was happening. All I had had to do was recognize it, which I did a little late.

Anyone who has visited the actual scene of this story has a chance of recognizing it when he meets it here, for the story is visual and the place is out of the ordinary. The connection between a story and its setting may not always be so plain. A reader may not see the slightest excuse for a given story after a personal inspection of the scene that called it up; the chances are good that he may not recognize it at all, and about 100 per cent that he will feel he would certainly have written something of a different sort himself. The point is, of course, that no matter whether the "likeness" is there for all to see or not, the place, once entered into the writer's mind in a story, is, in the course of writing the story, *functional*.

I wanted to make it seen and believed what was to me, in my story's grip, literally apparent—that secret and shadow are taken away in this country by the merciless light that prevails there, by the river that is like an exposed vein of ore, the road that descends as one with the heat—its nerve (these are all terms in the story), and that the heat is also a visual illusion, shimmering and dancing over the waste that stretches ahead. I was writing of a real place; but doing so in order to write about my subject. I was writing of exposure, and the shock of the world; in the end I tried to make the story's inside outside and then throw away the shell.

The vain courting of imperviousness in the face of exposure is this little story's plot. Deliver us all from the naked in heart, the girl thinks (this is what I kept of her). "So strangeness gently steels us," I read today in a poem of Richard Wilbur's. Riding down together into strange country is danger, a play at danger, secretly poetic, and the characters, in attempting it as a mutual feat, admit nothing to each other except the wicked heat and its comical inconvenience; the only time they will yield or touch is while they are dancing in the crowd that to them is comically unlikely (hence insulating, non-conducting) or taking a kiss outside time. Nevertheless it happens that they go along aware, from moment to moment, as one: as my third character, the straining, hallucinatory eyes and ears, the roused up sentiment being of that place. Exposure begins in intuition and has its end in showing the heart that has expected, while it dreads, that exposure. Writing it as I'd done before as a story of concealment, in terms of the hermetic and the familiar, had somehow resulted in my effective concealment of what I meant to say.

(I might say, for what interest it has here, that the original image of the story's first version came from an object—a grandiose, dusty, empty punch bowl of cut glass surrounded by its ring of cups, standing typically in the poor, small-town hardware store window where such things go unsold for ever, surrounded by the axes and halters, and tin mailboxes and shotguns of the country trade. Even as I write it's still provocative to me—as it is probably, also, still there in the window, still $13.75.)

In my second effort to show the story happen, the place had suggested to me that something demoniac was called for—the speed of the ride pitted against the danger of an easy or ignorant or tempting sympathy, too pressing, too acute, in the face of an inimical world, the heat that in itself drives on the driver. Something wilder than ordinary communication between well-disposed strangers, and more ruthless and more tender than their automatic, saving ironies and graces, I felt, and do so often feel, has to come up against a world like that.

I did my best to merge, rather to identify, the abstract with the concrete, it being so happily possible in this story—however the possibilities may have been realized—where setting, characters, mood, and method of writing all appeared parts of the same thing and subject to related laws and conditionings. I cut out some odd sentences that occurred, not because they were odd—for the story is that—but because they would tantalize some cooling explanations out of the mind if they stayed in. The story had to be self-evident and hold its speed—which I think of as racing, though it may not seem so to the reader. Above all I had no wish to sound mystical, but I did expect to sound mysterious now and then, if I could: this was a circumstantial, realistic story in which the reality *was* mystery. The cry that rose up at the story's end was, I hope unmistakably, the cry of the fading relationship—personal, individual, psychic— admitted in order to be denied, a cry that the characters were first able (and prone) to listen to, and then able in part to ignore. The cry was authentic to my story and so I didn't care if it did seem a little odd: the end of a journey *can* set up a cry, the shallowest provocation to sympathy and loves does hate to give up the ghost. A relationship of the most fleeting kind has the power inherent to loom like a genie—to become vocative at the last, as it has already become present and taken up room; as it has spread out as a destination however makeshift; as it has, more faintly, more sparsely, glimmered and rushed by in the dark and dust outside. Relationship *is* pervading and changing mystery; it is not words that make it so in life, but words have to make it so in a story. Brutal or lovely, the mystery waits for people wherever they go, whatever extreme they run to. I had got back at the end of the new story to suggesting what I had started with at the beginning of the old, but there was no question in my mind which story was nearer the mark.

This may not reflect very well on the brightness of the author; it may only serve to prove that for some writers a story has to rescue itself. This may be so, but I think it might show too what alone in the actual writing process may have interest for others besides the writer: that subject, method, form, style, all wait upon—indeed hang upon—a sort of double thunderclap at the author's ears: the break of the living world upon what is stirring inside the mind, and the answering impulse that in a moment of high consciousness fuses impact and image and fires them off together. There really never was a sound, but the impact is always recognizable, granting the author's sensitivity and sense, and if the impulse so projected is to some degree fulfilled it may give some pleasure out of reason to writer and reader. The living world remains just the same as it always was, and luckily enough for the story, among other things, for it can test and talk back to the story any day in the week.

NOON WINE

Katherine Anne Porter

Time: 1896–1905
Place: Small South Texas Farm

THE two grubby small boys with tow-colored hair who were digging among the ragweed in the front yard sat back on their heels and said, "Hello," when the tall bony man with straw-colored hair turned in at their gate. He did not pause at the gate; it had swung back, conveniently half open, long ago, and was now sunk so firmly on its broken hinges no one thought of trying to close it. He did not even glance at the small boys, much less give them good-day. He just clumped down his big square dusty shoes one after the other steadily, like a man following a plow, as if he knew the place well and knew where he was going and what he would find there. Rounding the right-hand corner of the house under the row of chinaberry trees, he walked up to the side porch where Mr. Thompson was pushing a big swing churn back and forth.

Mr. Thompson was a tough weather-beaten man with stiff black hair and a week's growth of black whiskers. He was a noisy proud man who held his neck so straight his whole face stood level with his Adam's apple, and the whiskers continued down his neck and disappeared into a black thatch under his open collar. The churn rumbled and swished like the belly of a trotting horse, and Mr. Thompson seemed somehow to be driving a horse with one hand, reining it in and urging it forward; and every now and then he turned halfway around and squirted a tremendous spit of tobacco juice out over the steps. The door stones were brown and gleaming with fresh tobacco juice. Mr. Thompson had been churning quite a while and he was tired of it. He was just fetching a mouthful of juice to squirt again when the stranger came around the corner and stopped. Mr. Thompson saw a narrow-chested man with blue eyes so pale they were almost white, looking and not looking at him from a long gaunt face, under white eyebrows. Mr. Thompson judged him to be another of these Irishmen, by his long upper lip.

"Howdy do, sir," said Mr. Thompson politely, swinging his churn.

"I need work," said the man, clearly enough but with some kind of foreign accent Mr. Thompson couldn't place. It wasn't Cajun and it wasn't Nigger and it wasn't Dutch, so it had him stumped. "You need a man here?"

Mr. Thompson gave the churn a great shove and it swung back and forth several times on its own momentum. He sat on the steps, shot his quid into the grass, and said, "Set down. Maybe we can make a deal. I been kinda lookin' round for somebody. I had two niggers but they got into a cutting scrape up the creek last week, one of 'em dead now and the other in the hoosegow at Cold Springs. Neither one of 'em worth killing, come right down to it. So it looks like I'd better get somebody. Where'd you work last?"

"North Dakota," said the man, folding himself down on the other end of the steps, but not as if he were tired. He folded up and settled down as if it would be a long time before he got up again. He never had looked at Mr. Thompson, but there wasn't anything sneaking in his eye, either. He didn't seem to be looking anywhere else. His eyes sat in his head and let things pass by them. They didn't seem to be expecting to see anything worth looking at. Mr. Thompson waited a long time for the man to say something more, but he had gone into a brown study.

"North Dakota," said Mr. Thompson, trying to remember where that was. "That's a right smart distance off, seems to me."

"I can do everything on farm," said the man; "cheap. I need work."

Mr. Thompson settled himself to get down to business. "My name's Thompson, Mr. Royal Earle Thompson," he said.

"I'm Mr. Helton," said the man, "Mr. Olaf Helton." He did not move.

"Well, now," said Mr. Thompson in his most carrying voice, "I guess we'd better talk turkey."

When Mr. Thompson expected to drive a bargain he always grew very hearty and jovial. There was nothing wrong with him except that he hated like the devil to pay wages. He said so himself. "You furnish grub and a shack," he said, "and then you got to pay 'em besides. It ain't right. Besides the wear and tear on your implements," he said, "they just let everything go to rack and ruin." So he began to laugh and shout his way through the deal.

"Now, what I want to know is, how much you fixing to gouge outa me?" he brayed, slapping his knee. After he had kept it up as long as he could, he quieted down, feeling a little sheepish, and cut himself a chew. Mr. Helton was staring out somewhere between the barn and the orchard, and seemed to be sleeping with his eyes open.

"I'm good worker," said Mr. Helton as from the tomb. "I get dollar a day."

Mr. Thompson was so shocked he forgot to start laughing again at the top of his voice until it was nearly too late to do any good. "Haw, haw," he bawled. "Why, for a dollar a day I'd hire out myself. What kinda work is it where they pay you a dollar a day?"

"Wheatfields, North Dakota," said Mr. Helton, not even smiling.

Mr. Thompson stopped laughing. "Well, this ain't any wheatfield by a long shot. This is more of a dairy farm," he said, feeling apologetic. "My wife, she was set on a dairy, she seemed to like working around with cows and calves, so I humored her. But it was a mistake," he said. "I got nearly everything to do, anyhow. My wife ain't very strong. She's sick today, that's a fact. She's been porely for the last few days. We plant a little feed, and a corn patch, and there's the orchard, and a few pigs and chickens, but our main hold is the cows. Now just speakin' as one man to another, there ain't any money in it. Now I can't give you no dollar a day because ackshally I don't make that much out of it. No, sir, we get along on a lot less than a dollar a day, I'd say, if we figger up everything in the long run. Now, I paid seven dollars a month to the two niggers, three-fifty each, and grub, but what I say is, one middlin'-good white man ekals a whole passel of niggers any day in the week, so I'll give you seven dollars and you eat at the table with us, and you'll be treated like a white man, as the feller says—"

"That's all right," said Mr. Helton. "I take it."

"Well, now I guess we'll call it a deal, hey?" Mr. Thompson jumped up as if he had remembered important business. "Now, you just take hold of that churn and give it a few swings, will you, while I ride to town on a coupla little errands. I ain't been able to leave the place all week. I guess you know what to do with butter after you get it, don't you?"

"I know," said Mr. Helton without turning his head. "I know butter business." He had a strange drawling voice, and even when he spoke only two words his voice waved slowly up and down and the emphasis was in the wrong place. Mr. Thompson wondered what kind of foreigner Mr. Helton could be.

"Now just where did you say you worked last?" he asked, as if he expected Mr. Helton to contradict himself.

"North Dakota," said Mr. Helton.

"Well, one place is good as another once you get used to it," said Mr. Thompson, amply. "You're a forriner, ain't you?"

"I'm a Swede," said Mr. Helton, beginning to swing the churn.

Mr. Thompson let forth a booming laugh, as if this was the best joke on somebody he'd ever heard. "Well, I'll be damned," he said at the top of his voice. "A Swede: well, now I'm afraid you'll get pretty lonesome around here. I never seen any Swedes in this neck of the woods."

"That's all right," said Mr. Helton. He went on swinging the churn as if he had been working on the place for years.

"In fact, I might as well tell you, you're practically the first Swede I ever laid eyes on."

"That's all right," said Mr. Helton.

Mr. Thompson went into the front room where Mrs. Thompson was lying down, with the green shades drawn. She had a bowl of water by her on the table and a wet cloth over her eyes. She took the cloth off at the sound of Mr. Thompson's boots and said, "What's all the noise out there? Who is it?"

"Got a feller out there says he's a Swede, Ellie," said Mr. Thompson; "says he knows how to make butter."

"I hope it turns out to be the truth," said Mrs. Thompson. "Looks like my head never will get any better."

"Don't you worry," said Mr. Thompson. "You fret too much. Now I'm gointa ride into town and get a little order of groceries."

"Don't you linger, now, Mr. Thompson," said Mrs. Thompson. "Don't go to the hotel." She meant the saloon; the proprietor also had rooms for rent upstairs.

"Just a coupla little toddies," said Mr. Thompson, laughing loudly, "never hurt anybody."

"I never took a dram in my life," said Mrs. Thompson, "and what's more I never will."

"I wasn't talking about the womenfolks," said Mr. Thompson.

The sound of the swinging churn rocked Mrs. Thompson first into a gentle doze, then a deep drowse from which she waked suddenly knowing that the swinging had stopped a good while ago. She sat up shading her weak eyes from the flat strips of late summer sunlight between the sill and the lowered shades. There she was, thank God, still alive, with supper to cook but no churning on hand, and her head still bewildered, but easy. Slowly she realized she had been hearing a new sound even in her sleep. Somebody was playing a tune on the harmonica, not merely shrilling up and down making a sickening noise, but really playing a pretty tune, merry and sad.

She went out through the kitchen, stepped off the porch, and stood facing the east, shading her eyes. When her vision cleared and settled, she saw a long, pale-haired man in blue jeans sitting in the doorway of the hired man's shack, tilted back in a kitchen chair, blowing away at the harmonica with his eyes shut. Mrs. Thompson's heart fluttered and sank. Heavens, he looked lazy and worthless, he did, now. First a lot of no-count fiddling darkies and then a no-count white man. It was just like Mr. Thompson to take on that kind. She did wish he would be more considerate, and take a little trouble with his business. She wanted to believe in her husband, and there were too many times when she couldn't. She wanted to believe that tomorrow, or at least the day after, life, such a battle at best, was going to be better.

She walked past the shack without glancing aside, stepping carefully, bent at the waist because of the nagging pain in her side, and went to the springhouse, trying to harden her mind to speak very plainly to that new hired man if he had not done his work.

The milk house was only another shack of weather-beaten boards nailed together hastily years before because they needed a milk house; it was meant to be temporary, and it was; already shapeless, leaning this way and that over a perpetual cool trickle of water that fell from a little grot, almost choked with pallid ferns. No one else in the whole countryside had such a spring on his land. Mr. and Mrs. Thompson felt they had a fortune in that spring, if ever they got around to doing anything with it.

Rickety wooden shelves clung at hazard in the square around the small pool where the larger pails of milk and butter stood, fresh and sweet in the cold water. One hand supporting her flat, pained side, the other shading her eyes, Mrs. Thompson leaned over and peered into the pails. The cream had been skimmed and set aside, there was a rich roll of butter, the wooden molds and shallow pans had been scrubbed and scalded for the first time in who knows when, the barrel was full of buttermilk ready for the pigs and the weanling calves, the hard packed-dirt floor had been swept smooth. Mrs. Thompson straightened up again, smiling tenderly. She had been ready to scold him, a poor man who needed a job, who had just come there and who might not have been expected to do things properly at first. There was nothing she could do to make up for the injustice she had done him in her thoughts but to tell him how she appreciated his good clean work, finished already, in no time at all. She ventured near the door of the shack with her careful steps; Mr. Helton opened his eyes, stopped playing, and brought his chair down straight, but did not look at her, or get up. She was a little frail woman with long thick brown hair in a braid, a suffering patient mouth and diseased eyes which cried easily. She wove her fingers into an eyeshade, thumbs on temples, and, winking her tearful lids, said with a polite little manner, "Howdy do, sir. I'm Miz Thompson, and I wanted to tell you I think you did real well in the milk house. It's always been a hard place to keep."

He said, "That's all right," in a slow voice, without moving.

Mrs. Thompson waited a moment. "That's a pretty tune you're playing. Most folks don't seem to get much music out of a harmonica."

Mr. Helton sat humped over, long legs sprawling, his spine in a bow, running this thumb over the square mouth-stops; except for his moving hand he might have been asleep. The harmonica was a big shiny new one, and Mrs. Thompson, her gaze wandering about, counted five others, all good and expensive, standing in a row on the shelf beside his cot. "He must carry them around in his jumper pocket," she thought, and noted there was not a sign of any other possession lying about. "I see you're mighty fond of music," she said. "We used to have an old accordion, and Mr. Thompson could play it right smart, but the little boys broke it up."

Mr. Helton stood up rather suddenly, the chair clattered under him, his knees straightened though his shoulders did not, and he looked at the floor as if he were listening carefully. "You'd better set them harmonicas on a high shelf or they'll be after them. They're great hands for getting into things. I try to learn 'em, but it don't do much good."

Mr. Helton, in one wide gesture of his long arms, swept his harmonicas up against his chest, and from there transferred them in a row to the ledge where the roof joined to the wall. He pushed them back almost out of sight.

"That'll do, maybe," said Mrs. Thompson. "Now I wonder," she said, turning and closing her eyes helplessly against the stronger western light, "I wonder what became of them little tads. I can't keep up with them." She had a way of speaking about her children as if they were rather troublesome nephews on a prolonged visit.

"Down by the creek," said Mr. Helton, in his hollow voice. Mrs. Thompson, pausing confusedly, decided he had answered her question. He stood in silent patience, not exactly waiting for her to go, perhaps, but pretty plainly not waiting for anything else. Mrs. Thompson was perfectly accustomed to all kinds of men full of all kinds of cranky ways. The point was, to find out just how Mr. Helton's crankiness was different from any other man's, and then get used to it, and let him feel at home. Her father had been cranky, her brothers, and uncles had all been set in their ways and none of them alike; and every hired man she'd ever seen had quirks and crotchets of his own. Now here was Mr. Helton, who was a Swede, who wouldn't talk, and who played the harmonica besides.

"They'll be needing something to eat," said Mrs. Thompson in a vague friendly way, "pretty soon. Now I wonder what I ought to be thinking about for supper? Now what do you like to eat, Mr. Helton? We always have plenty of good butter and milk and cream, that's a blessing. Mr. Thompson says we ought to sell all of it, but I say my family comes first." Her little face went all out of shape in a pained blind smile.

"I eat anything," said Mr. Helton, his words wandering up and down.

He *can't* talk, for one thing, thought Mrs. Thompson, it's a shame to keep at him when he don't know the language good. She took a slow step away from the shack, looking back over her shoulder. "We usually have cornbread except on Sundays," she told him. "I suppose in your part of the country you don't get much good cornbread."

Not a word from Mr. Helton. She saw from her eye-corner that he had sat down again, looking at his harmonica, chair tilted. She hoped he would remember it was getting near milking time. As she moved away, he started playing again, the same tune.

Milking time came and went. Mrs. Thompson saw Mr. Helton going back and forth between the cow barn and the milk house. He swung along in an easy lope, shoulders bent, head hanging, the big buckets balancing like a pair of scales at the ends of his bony arms. Mr. Thompson rode in from town sitting straighter than usual, chin in, a tow-sack full of supplies swung behind the saddle. After a trip to the barn, he came into the kitchen full of good will, and gave Mrs. Thompson a hearty smack on the cheek after dusting her face off with his tough whiskers. He had been to the hotel, that was plain. "Took a look around the premises, Ellie," he shouted. "That Swede sure is grinding out the labor. But he is the closest mouthed feller I ever met up with in all my days. Looks like he's scared he'll crack his jaw if he opens his front teeth."

Mrs. Thompson was stirring up a big bowl of buttermilk cornbread. "You smell like a toper, Mr. Thompson," she said with perfect dignity. "I wish you'd get one of the little boys to bring me in an extra load of firewood. I'm thinking about baking a batch of cookies tomorrow."

Mr. Thompson, all at once smelling the liquor on his own breath, sneaked out, justly rebuked, and brought in the firewood himself. Arthur and Herbert, grubby from thatched head to toes, from skin to shirt, came stamping in yelling for supper. "Go wash your faces and comb your hair," said Mrs. Thompson, automatically. They retired to the porch. Each one put his hand under the pump and wet his forelock, combed it down with his fingers, and returned at once to the kitchen, where all the fair prospects of life were centered. Mrs. Thompson set an extra plate and commanded Arthur, the eldest, eight years old, to call Mr. Helton for supper.

Arthur, without moving from the spot, bawled like a bull calf, "Saaaaaay, Helllllllton, suuuuuupper's ready!" and added in a lower voice, "You big Swede!"

"Listen to me," said Mrs. Thompson, "that's no way to act. Now you go out there and ask him decent, or I'll get your daddy to give you a good licking."

Mr. Helton loomed, long and gloomy, in the doorway. "Sit right there," boomed Mr. Thompson, waving his arm. Mr. Helton swung his square shoes across the kitchen in two steps, slumped onto the bench and sat. Mr. Thompson occupied his chair at the head of the table, the two boys scrambled into place opposite Mr. Helton, and Mrs. Thompson sat at the end nearest the stove. Mrs. Thompson clasped her hands, bowed her head and said aloud hastily, "Lord, for all these and Thy other blessings we thank Thee in Jesus' name, amen," trying to finish before Herbert's dusty little paw reached the nearest dish. Otherwise she would be dutybound to send him away from the table, and growing children need their meals. Mr. Thompson and Arthur always waited, but Herbert, aged six, was too young to take training yet.

Mr. and Mrs. Thompson tried to engage Mr. Helton in conversation, but it was a failure. They tried first the weather, and then the crops, and then the cows, but Mr. Helton simply did not reply. Mr. Thompson then told something funny he had seen in town. It was about some of the other old grangers at the hotel, friends of his, giving beer to a goat, and the goat's subsequent behavior. Mr. Helton did not seem to hear. Mrs. Thompson laughed dutifully, but she didn't think it was very funny. She had heard it often before, though Mr. Thompson, each time he told it, pretended it had happened that self-same day. It must have happened years ago if it ever happened at all, and it had never been a story that Mrs. Thompson thought suitable for mixed company. The whole thing came of Mr. Thompson's weakness for a dram too much now and then, though he voted for local option at every election. She passed the food to Mr. Helton, who took a helping of everything, but not much, not enough to keep him up to his full powers if he expected to go on working the way he had started.

At last he took a fair-sized piece of cornbread, wiped his plate up as clean as if it had been licked by a hound dog, stuffed his mouth full, and, still chewing, slid off the bench and started for the door.

"Good night, Mr. Helton," said Mrs. Thompson, and the other Thompsons took it up in a scattered chorus. "Good night, Mr. Helton!"

"Good night," said Mr. Helton's wavering voice grudgingly from the darkness.

"Gude not," said Arthur, imitating Mr. Helton.

"Gude not," said Herbert, the copy-cat.

"You don't do it right," said Arthur. "Now listen to me. Guuuuuude naht," and he ran a hollow scale in a luxury of successful impersonation. Herbert almost went into a fit with joy.

"Now you *stop* that," said Mrs. Thompson. "He can't help the way he talks. You ought to be ashamed of yourselves, both of you, making fun of a poor stranger like that. How'd you like to be a stranger in a strange land?"

"I'd like it," said Arthur. "I think it would be fun."

"They're both regular heathens, Ellie," said Mr. Thompson. "Just plain ignoramuses." He turned the face of awful fatherhood upon his young. "You're both going to get sent to school next year, and that'll knock some sense into you."

"I'm going to get sent to the 'formatory when I'm old enough," piped up Herbert. "That's where I'm goin'."

"Oh, you are, are you?" asked Mr. Thompson. "Who says so?"

"The Sunday School Superintendant," said Herbert, a bright boy showing off.

"You see?" said Mr. Thompson, staring at his wife. "What did I tell you?" He became a hurricane of wrath. "Get to bed, you two," he roared until his Adam's apple shuddered. "Get now before I take the hide off you!" They got, and shortly from their attic bedroom the sounds of scuffling and snorting and giggling and growling filled the house and shook the kitchen ceiling.

Mrs. Thompson held her head and said in a small uncertain voice, "It's no use picking on them when they're so young and tender. I can't stand it."

"My goodness, Ellie," said Mr. Thompson, "we've got to raise 'em. We can't just let 'em grow up hog wild."

She went on in another tone. "That Mr. Helton seems all right, even if he can't be made to talk. Wonder how he comes to be so far from home."

"Like I said, he isn't no whamper-jaw," said Mr. Thompson, "but he sure knows how to lay out the work. I guess that's the main thing around here. Country's full of fellers trampin' round looking for work."

Mrs. Thompson was gathering up the dishes. She now gathered up Mr. Thompson's plate from under his chin. "To tell you the honest truth," she remarked, "I think it's a mighty good change to have a man round the place who knows how to work and keep his mouth shut. Means he'll keep out of our business. Not that we've got anything to hide, but it's convenient."

"That's a fact," said Mr. Thompson. "Haw, haw," he shouted suddenly. "Means you can do all the talking, huh?"

"The only thing," went on Mrs. Thompson, "is this: he don't eat hearty enough to suit me. I like to see a man set down and relish a good meal. My granma used to say it was no use putting dependence on a man who won't set down and make out his dinner. I hope it won't be that way this time."

"Tell *you* the truth, Ellie," said Mr. Thompson, picking his teeth with a fork and leaning back in the best of good humors, "I always thought your granma was a ter'ble ole fool. She'd just say the first thing that popped into her head and call it God's wisdom."

"My granma wasn't anybody's fool. Nine times out of ten she knew what she was talking about. I always say, the first thing you think is the best thing you can say."

"Well," said Mr. Thompson, going into another shout, "you're so *ree*fined about that goat story, you just try speaking out in mixed comp'ny sometime! You just try it. S'pose you happened to be thinking about a hen and a rooster, hey? I reckon you'd shock the Babtist preacher!" He gave her a good pinch on her thin little rump. "No more meat on you than a rabbit," he said, fondly. "Now I like 'em cornfed."

Mrs. Thompson looked at him opened-eyed and blushed. She could see better by lamplight. "Why, Mr. Thompson, sometimes I think you're the evilest-minded man that ever lived." She took a handful of hair on the crown of his head and gave it a good, slow pull. "That's to show you how it feels, pinching so hard when you're supposed to be playing," she said, gently.

In spite of his situation in life, Mr. Thompson had never been able to outgrow his deep conviction that running a dairy and chasing after chickens was woman's work. He was fond of saying that he could plow a furrow, cut sorghum, shuck corn, handle a team, build a corn crib, as well as any man. Buying and selling, too, were man's work. Twice a week he drove the spring wagon to market with the fresh butter, a few eggs, fruits in their proper season, sold them, pocketed the change, and spent it as seemed best, being careful not to dig into Mrs. Thompson's pin money.

But from the first the cows worried him, coming up regularly twice a day to be milked, standing there reproaching him with their smug female faces. Calves worried him, fighting the rope and strangling themselves until their eyes bulged, trying to get at the teat. Wrestling with a calf unmanned him, like having to change a baby's diaper. Milk worried him, coming bitter sometimes, drying up, turning sour. Hens worried him, cackling, clucking, hatching out when you least expected it and leading their broods into the barnyard where the horses could step on them; dying of roup and wryneck and getting plagues of chicken lice; laying eggs all over God's creation so that half of them were spoiled before a man could find them, in spite of a rack of nests Mrs. Thompson had set out for them in the feed room. Hens were a blasted nuisance.

Slopping hogs was hired man's work, in Mr. Thompson's opinion. Killing hogs was a job for the boss, but scraping them and cutting them up was for the hired man again; and again woman's proper work was dressing meat, smoking, pickling, and making lard and sausage. All his carefully limited fields of activity were related somehow to Mr. Thompson's feeling for the appearance of things, his own appearance in the sight of God and man. "It don't *look* right," was his final reason for not doing anything he did not wish to do.

It was his dignity and his reputation that he cared about, and there were only a few kinds of work manly enough for Mr. Thompson to undertake with his own hands. Mrs. Thompson, to whom so many forms of work would have been becoming, had simply gone down on him early. He saw, after a while, how short-sighted it had been of him to expect much from Mrs. Thompson; he had fallen in love with her delicate waist and lace-trimmed petticoats and big blue eyes, and, though all those charms had disappeared, she had in the meantime become Ellie to him, not at all the same person as Miss Ellen Bridges, popular Sunday School teacher in the Mountain City First Baptist Church, but his dear wife, Ellie, who was not strong. Deprived as he was, however, of the main support in life which a man might expect in marriage, he had almost without knowing it resigned himself to failure. Head erect, a prompt payer of taxes, yearly subscriber to the preacher's salary, land owner and father of a family, employer, a hearty good fellow among men, Mr. Thompson knew, without putting it into words, that he had been going steadily down hill. God amighty, it did look like somebody around the place might take a rake in hand now and then and clear up the clutter around the barn and the kitchen steps. The wagon shed was so full of broken-down machinery and ragged harness and old wagon wheels and battered milk pails and rotting lumber you could hardly drive in there any more. Not a soul on the place would raise a hand to it, and as for him, he had all he could do with his regular work. He would sometimes in the slack season sit for hours worrying about it, squrting tobacco on the ragweeds growing in a thicket against the wood pile, wondering what a fellow could do, handicapped as he was. He looked forward to the boys growing up soon; he was going to put them through the mill just as his own father had done with him when he was a boy; they were going to learn how to take hold and run the place right. He wasn't going to overdo it, but those two boys were going to earn their salt, or he'd know why. Great big lubbers sitting around whittling! Mr. Thompson sometimes grew quite enraged with them, when imagining their possible future, big lubbers sitting around whittling or thinking about fishing trips. Well, he'd put a stop to that, mighty damn quick.

As the seasons passed, and Mr. Helton took hold more and more, Mr. Thompson began to relax in his mind a little. There seemed to be nothing the fellow couldn't do, all in the day's work and as a matter of course. He got up at five o'clock in the morning, boiled his own coffee and fried his own bacon and was out in the cow lot before Mr. Thompson had even begun to yawn, stretch, groan, roar and thump around looking for his jeans. He milked the cows, kept the milk house, and churned the butter; rounded the hens up and somehow persuaded them to lay in the nests, not under the house and behind the haystacks; he fed them regularly and they hatched out until you couldn't set a foot down for them. Little by little the piles of trash around the barns and house disappeared. He carried buttermilk and corn to the hogs, and curried cockleburs out of the horses' manes. He was gentle with the calves, if a little grim with the cows and hens; judging by his conduct, Mr. Helton had never heard of the difference between man's and woman's work on a farm.

In the second year, he showed Mr. Thompson the picture of a cheese press in a mail order catalogue, and said, "This is a good thing. You buy this, I make cheese." The press was bought and Mr. Helton did make cheese, and it was sold, along with the increased butter and the crates of eggs. Sometimes Mr. Thompson felt a little contemptuous of Mr. Helton's ways. It did seem kind of picayune for a man to go around picking up half a dozen ears of corn that had fallen off the wagon on the way from the field, gathering up fallen fruit to feed to the pigs, storing up old nails and stray parts of machinery, spending good time stamping a fancy pattern on the butter before it went to market. Mr. Thompson, sitting up high on the spring-wagon seat, with the decorated butter in a five-gallon lard can wrapped in wet towsack, driving to town, chirruping to the horses and snapping the reins over their backs, sometimes thought that Mr. Helton was a pretty meeching sort of fellow; but he never gave way to these feelings, he knew a good thing when he had it. It was a fact the hogs were in better shape and sold for more money. It was a fact that Mr. Thompson stopped buying feed, Mr. Helton managed the crops so well. When beef- and hog-slaughtering time came, Mr. Helton knew how to save the scraps that Mr. Thompson had thrown away, and wasn't above scraping guts and filling them with sausages that he made by his own methods. In all, Mr. Thompson had no grounds for complaint. In the third year, he raised Mr. Helton's wages, though Mr. Helton had not asked for a raise. The fourth year, when Mr. Thompson was not only out of debt but had a little cash in the bank, he raised Mr. Helton's wages again, two dollars and a half a month each time.

"The man's worth it, Ellie," said Mr. Thompson, in a glow of self-justification for his extravagance. "He's made this place pay, and I want him to know I appreciate it."

Mr. Helton's silence, the pallor of his eyebrows and hair, his long, glum jaw and eyes that refused to see anything, even the work under his hands, had grown perfectly familiar to the Thompsons. At first, Mrs. Thompson complained a little. "It's like sitting down at the table with a disembodied spirit," she said. "You'd think he'd find something to say, sooner or later."

"Let him alone," said Mr. Thompson. "When he gets ready to talk, he'll talk."

The years passed, and Mr. Helton never got ready to talk. After his work was finished for the day, he would come up from the barn or the milk house or the chicken house, swinging his lantern, his big shoes clumping like pony hoofs on the hard path. They, sitting in the kitchen in the winter, or on the back porch in the summer, would hear him drag out his wooden chair, hear the creak of it tilted back, and then for a little while he would play his single tune on one or another of his harmonicas. The harmonicas were in different keys, some lower and sweeter than the others, but the same changeless tune went on, a strange tune, with sudden turns in it, night after night, and sometimes even in the afternoons when Mr. Helton sat down to catch his breath. At first the Thompsons liked it very much, and always stopped to listen. Later there came a time when they were fairly sick of it, and began to wish to each other that he would learn a new one. At last they did not hear it any more, it was as natural as the sound of the wind rising in the evenings, or the cows lowing, or their own voices.

Mrs. Thompson pondered now and then over Mr. Helton's soul. He didn't seem to be a church-goer, and worked straight through Sunday as if it were any common day of the week. "I think we ought to invite him to go to hear Dr. Martin," she told Mr. Thompson. "It isn't very Christian of us not to ask him. He's not a forward kind of man. He'd wait to be asked."

"Let him alone," said Mr. Thompson. "The way I look at it, his religion is every man's own business. Besides, he ain't got any Sunday clothes. He wouldn't want to go to church in them jeans and jumpers of his. I don't know what he does with his money. He certainly don't spend it foolishly."

Still, once the notion got into her head, Mrs. Thompson could not rest until she invited Mr. Helton to go to church with the family next Sunday. He was pitching hay into neat little piles in the field back of the orchard. Mrs. Thompson put on smoked glasses and a sunbonnet and walked all the way down there to speak to him. He stopped and leaned on his pitchfork, listening, and for a moment Mrs. Thompson was almost frightened at his face. The pale eyes seemed to glare past her, the eyebrows frowned, the long jaw hardened. "I got work," he said bluntly, and lifting his pitchfork he turned from her and began to toss the hay. Mrs. Thompson, her feelings hurt, walked back thinking that by now she should be used to Mr. Helton's ways, but it did seem like a man, even a foreigner, could be just a little polite when you gave him a Christian invitation. "He's not polite, that's the only thing I've got against him," she said to Mr. Thompson. "He just can't seem to behave like other people. You'd think he had a grudge against the world," she said. "I sometimes don't know what to make of it."

In the second year something had happened that made Mrs. Thompson uneasy, the kind of thing she could not put into words, hardly into thoughts, and if she had tried to explain to Mr. Thompson it would have sounded worse than it was, or not bad enough. It was that kind of queer thing that seems to be giving a warning, and yet, nearly always nothing comes of it. It was on a hot, still spring day, and Mrs. Thompson had been down to the garden patch to pull some new carrots and green onions and string beans for dinner. As she worked, sunbonnet low over her eyes, putting each kind of vegetable in a pile by itself in her basket, she noticed how neatly Mr. Helton weeded, and how rich the soil was. He had spread it all over with manure from the barns, and worked it in, in the fall, and the vegetables were coming up fine and full. She walked back under the nubby little fig trees where the unpruned branches leaned almost to the ground, and the thick leaves made a cool screen. Mrs. Thompson was always looking for shade to save her eyes. So she, looking idly about, saw through the screen a sight that struck her as very strange. If it had been a noisy spectacle, it would have been quite natural. It was the silence that struck her. Mr. Helton was shaking Arthur by the shoulders, ferociously, his face most terribly fixed and pale. Arthur's head snapped back and forth and he had not stiffened in resistance, as he did when Mrs. Thompson tried to shake him. His eyes were rather frightened, but surprised, too, probably more surprised than anything else. Herbert stood by meekly, watching. Mr. Helton dropped Arthur, and seized Herbert, and shook him with the same methodical ferocity, the same face of hatred. Herbert's mouth crumpled as if he would cry, but he made no sound. Mr. Helton let him go, turned and strode into the shack, and the little boys ran, as if for their lives, without a word. They disappeared around the corner to the front of the house.

Mrs. Thompson took time to set her basket on the kitchen table, to push her sunbonnet back on her head and draw it forward again, to look in the stove and make certain the fire was going, before she followed the boys. They were sitting huddled together under a clump of chinaberry trees in plain sight of her bedroom window, as if it were a safe place they had discovered.

"What are you doing?" asked Mrs. Thompson.

They looked hang-dog from under their foreheads and Arthur mumbled, "Nothin'."

"Nothing *now*, you mean," said Mrs. Thompson, severely. "Well, I have plenty for you to do. Come right in here this minute and help me fix vegetables. This minute."

They scrambled up very eagerly and followed her close. Mrs. Thompson tried to imagine what they had been up to; she did not like the notion of Mr. Helton taking it on himself to correct her little boys, but she was afraid to ask them for reasons. They might tell her a lie, and she would have to overtake them in it, and whip them. Or she would have to pretend to believe them, and they would get in the habit of lying. Or they might tell her the truth, and it would be something she would have to whip them for. The very thought of it gave her a headache. She supposed she might ask Mr. Helton, but it was not her place to ask. She would wait and tell Mr. Thompson, and let him get at the bottom of it. While her mind ran on, she kept the little boys hopping. "Cut those carrot tops closer, Herbert, you're just being careless. Arthur, stop breaking up the beans so little. They're little enough already. Herbert, you go get an armload of wood. Arthur, you take these onions and wash them under the pump. Herbert, as soon as you're done here, you get a broom and sweep out this kitchen. Arthur, you get a shovel and take up the ashes. Stop picking your nose, Herbert. How often must I tell you? Arthur, you go look in the top drawer of my bureau, lefthand side, and bring me the vaseline for Herbert's nose. Herbert, come here to me. . . . "

They galloped through their chores, their animal spirits rose with activity, and shortly they were out in the front yard again, engaged in a wrestling match. They sprawled and fought, scrambled, clutched, rose and fell shouting, as aimlessly, noisily, monotonously as two puppies. They imitated various animals, not a human sound from them, and their dirty faces were streaked with sweat. Mrs. Thompson, sitting at her window, watched them with baffled pride and tenderness, they were so sturdy and healthy and growing so fast; but uneasily, too, with her pained little smile and the tears rolling from her eyelids that clinched themselves against the sunlight. They were so idle and careless, as if they had no future in this world, and no immortal souls to save, and oh, what had they been up to that Mr. Helton had shaken them, with his face positively dangerous?

In the evening before supper, without a word to Mr. Thompson of the curious fear the sight had caused her, she told him that Mr. Helton had shaken the little boys for some reason. He stepped out to the shack and spoke to Mr. Helton. In five minutes he was back, glaring at his young. "He says them brats been fooling with his harmonicas, Ellie, blowing in them and getting them all dirty and full of spit and they don't play good."

"Did he say all that?" asked Mrs. Thompson. "It doesn't seem possible."

"Well, that's what he meant, anyhow," said Mr. Thompson. "He didn't say it just that way. But he acted pretty worked up about it."

"That's a shame," said Mrs. Thompson, "a perfect shame. Now we've got to do something so they'll remember they mustn't go into Mr. Helton's things."

"I'll tan their hides for them," said Mr. Thompson. "I'll take a calf rope to them if they don't look out."

"Maybe you'd better leave the whipping to me," said Mrs. Thompson. "You haven't got a light enough hand for children."

"That's just what's the matter with them now," shouted Mr. Thompson, "rotten spoiled and they'll wind up in the penitentiary. You don't half whip 'em. Just little love taps. My pa used to knock me down with a stick of stove wood or anything else that came handy."

"Well, that's not saying it's right," said Mrs. Thompson. "I don't hold with that way of raising children. It makes them run away from home. I've seen too much of it."

"I'll break every bone in 'em," said Mr. Thompson, simmering down, "if they don't mind you better and stop being so bull-headed."

"Leave the table and wash your face and hands," Mrs. Thompson commanded the boys, suddenly. They slunk out and dabbled at the pump and slunk in again, trying to make themselves small. They had learned long ago that their mother always made them wash when there was trouble ahead. They looked at their plates. Mr. Thompson opened up on them.

"Well, now, what you got to say for yourselves about going into Mr. Helton's shack and ruining his harmonicas?"

The two little boys wilted, their faces drooped into the grieved hopeless lines of children's faces when they are brought to the terrible bar of blind adult justice; their eyes telegraphed each other in panic, "Now we're really going to catch a licking"; in despair, they dropped their buttered cornbread on their plates, their hands lagged on the edge of the table.

"I ought to break your ribs," said Mr. Thompson, "and I'm a good mind to do it."

"Yes, sir," whispered Arthur, faintly.

"Yes, sir," said Herbert, his lip trembling.

"Now, papa," said Mrs. Thompson in a warning tone. The children did not glance at her. They had no faith in her good will. She had betrayed them in the first place. There was no trusting her. Now she might save them and she might not. No use depending on her.

"Well, you ought to get a good thrashing. You deserve it, don't you, Arthur?"

Arthur hung his head. "Yes, sir."

"And the next time I catch either of you hanging around Mr. Helton's shack, I'm going to take the side off *both* of you, you hear me, Herbert?"

Herbert mumbled and choked, scattering his cornbread. "Yes, sir."

"Well, now sit up and eat your supper and not another word out of you," said Mr. Thompson, beginning on his own food. The little boys perked up somewhat and started chewing, but every time they looked around they met their parents' eyes, regarding them steadily. There was no telling when they would think of something new. The boys ate warily, trying not to be seen or heard, the cornbread sticking, the buttermilk gurgling, as it went down their gullets.

"And something else, Mr. Thompson," said Mrs. Thompson after a pause. "Tell Mr. Helton he's to come straight to us when they bother him, and not to trouble shaking them himself. Tell him we'll look after that."

"They're so mean," answered Mr. Thompson, staring at them. "It's a wonder he don't just kill 'em off and be done with it." But there was something in the tone that told Arthur and Herbert that nothing more worth worrying about was going to happen this time. Heaving deep sighs, they sat up, reaching for the food nearest them.

"Listen," said Mrs. Thompson, suddenly. The little boys stopped eating. "Mr. Helton hasn't come for his supper. Arthur, go and tell Mr. Helton he's late for supper. Tell him nice, now."

Arthur, miserably depressed, slid out of his place and made for the door, without a word.

There were no miracles of fortune to be brought to pass on a small dairy farm. The Thompsons did not grow rich, but they kept out of the poor house, as Mr. Thompson was fond of saying, meaning he had got a little foothold in spite of Ellie's poor health, and unexpected weather, and strange declines in market prices, and his own mysterious handicaps which weighed him down. Mr. Helton was the hope and the prop of the family, and all the Thompsons became fond of him, or at any rate they ceased to regard him as in any way peculiar, and looked upon him, from a distance they did not know how to bridge, as a good man and a good friend. Mr. Helton went his way, worked, played his tune. Nine years passed. The boys grew up and learned to work. They could not remember the time when Ole Helton hadn't been there: a grouchy cuss, Brother Bones; Mr. Helton, the dairymaid; that Big Swede. If he had heard them, he might have been annoyed at some of the names they called him. But he did not hear them and besides they meant no harm—or at least such harm as existed was all there, in the names; the boys referred to their father as the Old Man, or the Old Geezer, but not to his face. They lived through by main strength all the grimy, secret, oblique phases of growing up and got past the crisis safely if anyone does. Their parents could see they were good solid boys with hearts of gold in spite of their rough ways. Mr. Thompson was relieved to find that, without knowing how he had done it, he had succeeded in raising a set of boys who were not trifling whittlers. They were such good boys Mr. Thompson began to believe they were born that way, and that he had never spoken a harsh word to them in their lives, much less thrashed them. Herbert and Arthur never disputed his word.

Mr. Helton, his hair wet with sweat, plastered to his dripping forehead, his jumper streaked dark and light blue and clinging to his ribs, was chopping a little firewood. He chopped slowly, struck the ax into the end of the chopping log, and piled the wood up neatly. He then disappeared round the house into his shack, which shared with the wood pile a good shade from a row of mulberry trees. Mr. Thompson was lolling in a swing chair on the front porch, a place he had never liked. The chair was new, and Mrs. Thompson had wanted it on the front porch, though the side porch was the place for it, being cooler; and Mr. Thompson wanted to sit in the chair, so there he was. As soon as the new wore off of it, and Ellie's pride in it was exhausted, he would move it round to the side porch. Meantime the August heat was almost unbearable, the air so thick you could poke a hole in it. The dust was inches thick on everything, though Mr. Helton sprinkled the whole yard regularly every night. He even shot the hose upward and washed the tree tops and the roof of the house. They had laid waterpipes to the kitchen and an outside faucet. Mr. Thompson must have dozed, for he opened his eyes and shut his mouth just in time to save his face before a stranger who had driven up to the front gate. Mr. Thompson stood up, put on his hat, pulled up his jeans, and watched while the stranger tied his team, attached to a light spring wagon, to the hitching post. Mr. Thompson recognized the team and wagon. They were from a livery stable in Buda. While the stranger was opening the gate, a strong gate that Mr. Helton had built and set firmly on its hinges several years back, Mr. Thompson strolled down the path to greet him and find out what in God's world a man's business might be that would bring him out at this time of day, in all this dust and welter.

He wasn't exactly a fat man. He was more like a man who had been fat recently. His skin was baggy and his clothes were too big for him, and he somehow looked like a man who should be fat, ordinarily, but who might have just got over a spell of sickness. Mr. Thompson didn't take to his looks at all, he couldn't say why.

The stranger took off his hat. He said in a loud hearty voice, "Is this Mr. Thompson, Mr. Royal Earle Thompson?"

"That's my name," said Mr. Thompson, almost quietly, he was so taken back by the free manner of the stranger.

"My name is Hatch," said the stranger. "Mr. Homer T. Hatch, and I've come to see you about buying a horse."

"I reckon you've been misdirected," said Mr. Thompson. "I haven't got a horse for sale. Usually if I've got anything like that to sell," he said, "I tell the neighbors and tack up a little sign on the gate."

The fat man opened his mouth and roared with joy, showing rabbit teeth brown as shoeleather. Mr. Thompson saw nothing to laugh at, for once. The stranger shouted, "That's just an old joke of mine." He caught one of his hands in the other and shook hands with himself heartily. "I always say something like that when I'm calling on a stranger, because I've noticed that when a feller says he's come to buy something nobody takes him for a suspicious character. You see? Haw, haw, haw."

His joviality made Mr. Thompson nervous, because the expression in the man's eyes didn't match the sounds he was making. "Haw, haw," laughed Mr. Thompson obligingly, still not seing the joke. "Well, that's all wasted on me because I never take any man for a suspicious character 'til he shows hisself to be one. Says or does something," he explained. "Until that happens, one man's as good as another, so far's *I'm* concerned."

"Well," said the stranger, suddenly very sober and sensible, "I ain't come neither to buy nor sell. Fact is, I want to see you about something that's of interest to us both. Yes, sir, I'd like to have a little talk with you, and it won't cost you a cent."

"I guess that's fair enough," said Mr. Thompson, reluctantly. "Come on around the house where there's a little shade."

They went round and seated themselves on two stumps under a chinaberry tree.

"Yes, sir, Homer T. Hatch is my name and America is my nation," said the stranger. "I reckon you must know the name? I used to have a cousin named Jameson Hatch lived up the country a ways."

"Don't think I know the name," said Mr. Thompson. "There's some Hatchers settled somewhere around Mountain City."

"Don't know the old Hatch family," cried the man in deep concern. He seemed to be pitying Mr. Thompson's ignorance "Why, we came over from Georgia fifty years ago. Been here long yourself?"

"Just all my whole life," said Mr. Thompson, beginning to feel peevish. "And my pa and my grampap before me. Yes, sir, we've been right here all along. Anybody wants to find a Thompson knows where to look for him. My grampap immigrated in 1836."

"From Ireland, I reckon?" said the stranger.

"From Pennsylvania," said Mr. Thompson. "Now what makes you think we came from Ireland?"

The stranger opened his mouth and began to shout with merriment, and he shook hands with himself as if he hadn't met himself for a long time. "Well, what I always says is, a feller's got to come from *somewhere*, ain't he?"

While they were talking, Mr. Thompson kept glancing at the face near him. He certainly did remind Mr. Thompson of somebody, or maybe he really had seen the man himself somewhere. He couldn't just place the features. Mr. Thompson finally decided it was just that all rabbit-teethed men looked alike.

"That's right," acknowledged Mr. Thompson, rather sourly, "but what I always say is, Thompsons have been settled here for so long it don't make much difference any more *where* they come from. Now a course, this is the slack season, and we're all just laying round a little, but nevertheless we've all got our chores to do, and I don't want to hurry you, and so if you've come to see me on business maybe we'd better get down to it."

"As I said, it's not in a way, and again in a way it is," said the fat man. "Now I'm looking for a man named Helton, Mr. Olaf Eric Helton, from North Dakota, and I was told up around the country a ways that I might find him here, and I wouldn't mind having a little talk with him. No, siree, I sure wouldn't mind, if it's all the same to you."

"I never knew his middle name," said Mr. Thompson, "but Mr. Helton is right here, and been here now for going on nine years. He's a mighty steady man, and you can tell anybody I said so."

"I'm glad to hear that," said Mr. Homer T. Hatch. "I like to hear of a feller mending his ways and settling down. Now when I knew Mr. Helton he was pretty wild, yes, sir, wild is what he was, he didn't know his own mind atall. Well, now, it's going to be a great pleasure to me to meet up with an old friend and find him all settled down and doing well by hisself."

"We've all got to be young once," said Mr. Thompson. "It's like the measles, it breaks out all over you, and you're a nuisance to yourself and everybody else, but it don't last, and it usually don't leave no ill effects." He was so pleased with this notion he forgot and broke into a guffaw. The stranger folded his arms over his stomach and went into a kind of fit, roaring until he had tears in his eyes. Mr. Thompson stopped shouting and eyed the stranger uneasily. Now he liked a good laugh as well as any man, but there ought to be a little moderation. Now this feller laughed like a perfect lunatic, that was a fact. And he wasn't laughing because he really thought things were funny, either. He was laughing for reasons of his own. Mr. Thompson fell into a moody silence, and waited until Mr. Hatch settled down a little.

Mr. Hatch got out a very dirty blue cotton bandanna and wiped his eyes. "That joke just about caught me where I live," he said, almost apologetically. "Now I wish I could think up things as funny as that to say. It's a gift. It's . . ."

"If you want to speak to Mr. Helton, I'll go and round him up," said Mr. Thompson, making motions as if he might get up. "He may be in the milk house and he may be setting in his shack this time of day." It was drawing towards five o'clock. "It's right around the corner," he said.

"Oh, well, there ain't no special hurry," said Mr. Hatch. "I've been wanting to speak to him for a good long spell now and I guess a few minutes more won't make no difference. I just more wanted to locate him, like. That's all."

Mr. Thompson stopped beginning to stand up, and unbuttoned one more button of his shirt, and said, "Well, he's here, and he's this kind of man, that if he had any business with you he'd like to get it over. He don't dawdle, that's one thing you can say for him."

Mr. Hatch appeared to sulk a little at these words. He wiped his face with the bandanna and opened his mouth to speak, when round the house there came the music of Mr. Helton's harmonica. Mr. Thompson raised a finger. "There he is," said Mr. Thompson. "Now's your time."

Mr. Hatch cocked an ear towards the east side of the house and listened for a few seconds, a very strange expression on his face.

"I know that tune like I know the palm of my own hand," said Mr. Thompson, "but I never heard Mr. Helton say what it was."

"That's a kind of Scandahoovian song," said Mr. Hatch. "Where I come from they sing it a lot. In North Dakota, they sing it. It says something about starting out in the morning feeling so good you can't hardly stand it, so you drink up all your likker before noon. All the likker, y' understand, that you was saving for the noon lay-off. The words ain't much, but it's a pretty tune. It's a kind of drinking song." He sat there drooping a little, and Mr. Thompson didn't like his expression. It was a satisfied expression, but it was more like the cat that et the canary.

"So far as I know," said Mr. Thompson, "he ain't touched a drop since he's been on the place, and that's nine years this coming September. Yes, sir, nine years, so far as I know, he ain't wetted his whistle once. And that's more than I can say for myself," he said, meekly proud.

"Yes, that's a drinking song," said Mr. Hatch. "I used to play 'Little Brown Jug' on the fiddle when I was younger than I am now," he went on, "but this Helton, he just keeps it up. He just sits and plays it by himself."

"He's been playing it off and on for nine years right here on the place," said Mr. Thompson, feeling a little proprietary.

"And he was certainly singing it as well, fifteen years before that, in North Dakota," said Mr. Hatch. "He used to sit up in a straitjacket, practically, when he was in the asylum—"

"What's that you say?" said Mr. Thompson. "What's that?"

"Shucks, I didn't mean to tell you," said Mr. Hatch, a faint leer of regret in his drooping eyelids. "Shucks, that just slipped out. Funny, now I'd made up my mind I wouldn't say a word, because it would just make a lot of excitement, and what I say is, if a man has lived harmless and quiet for nine years it don't matter if he *is* loony, does it? So long's he keeps quiet and don't do nobody harm."

"You mean they had him in a straitjacket?" asked Mr. Thompson, uneasily. "In a lunatic asylum?"

"They sure did," said Mr. Hatch. "That's right where they had him, from time to time."

"They put my Aunt Ida in one of them things in the State asylum," said Mr. Thompson. "She got vi'lent, and they put her in one of these jackets with long sleeves and tied her to an iron ring in the wall, and Aunt Ida got so wild she broke a blood vessel and when they went to look after her she was dead. I'd think one of them things was dangerous."

"Mr. Helton used to sing his drinking song when he was in a straitjacket," said Mr. Hatch. "Nothing ever bothered him, except if you tried to make him talk. That bothered him, and he'd get vi'lent, like your Aunt Ida. He'd get vi'lent and then they'd put him in the jacket and go off and leave him, and he'd lay there perfickly contented, so far's you could see, singing his song. Then one night he just disappeared. Left, you might say, just went, and nobody ever saw hide or hair of him again. And then I come along and find him here," said Mr. Hatch, "all settled down and playing the same song."

"He never acted crazy to me," said Mr. Thompson. "He always acted like a sensible man, to me. He never got married, for one thing, and he works like a horse, and I bet he's got the first cent I paid him when he landed here, and he don't drink, and he never says a word, much less swear, and he don't waste time runnin' around Saturday nights, and if he's crazy," said Mr. Thompson, "why, I think I'll go crazy myself for a change."

"Haw, ha," said Mr. Hatch, "heh, he, that's good! Ha, ha, ha, I hadn't thought of it jes like that. Yeah, that's right! Let's all go crazy and get rid of our wives and save our money, hey?" He smiled unpleasantly, showing his little rabbit teeth.

Mr. Thompson felt he was being misunderstood. He turned around and motioned toward the open window back of the honeysuckle trellis.

"Let's move off down here a little," he said. "I oughta thought of that before." His visitor bothered Mr. Thompson. He had a way of taking the words out of Mr. Thompson's mouth, turning them around and mixing them up until Mr. Thompson didn't know himself what he had said. "My wife's not very strong," said Mr. Thompson. "She's been kind of invalid now goin' on fourteen years. It's mighty tough on a poor man, havin' sickness in the family. She had four operations," he said proudly, "one right after the other, but they didn't do any good. For five years hand-runnin', I just turned every nickel I made over to the doctors. Upshot is, she's a mightly delicate woman."

"My old woman," said Mr. Homer T. Hatch, "had a back like a mule, yes, sir. That woman could have moved the barn with her bare hands if she'd ever took the notion. I used to say, it was a good thing she didn't know her own stren'th. She's dead now, though. That kind wear out quicker than the puny ones. I never had much use for a woman always complainin'. I'd get rid of her mighty quick, yes, sir, mighty quick. It's just as you say: a dead loss, keepin' one of 'em up."

This was not at all what Mr. Thompson had heard himself say; he had been trying to explain that a wife as expensive as his was a credit to a man. "She's a mighty reasonable woman," said Mr. Thompson, feeling baffled, "but I wouldn't answer for what she'd say or do if she found out we'd had a lunatic on the place all this time." They moved away from the window; Mr. Thompson took Mr. Hatch the front way, because if he went the back way they would have to pass Mr. Helton's shack. For some reason he didn't want the stranger to see or talk to Mr. Helton. It was strange, but that was the way Mr. Thompson felt.

Mr. Thompson sat down again, on the chopping log, offering his guest another tree stump. "Now, I mighta got upset myself at such a thing, once," said Mr. Thompson, "but now I *deefy* anything to get me lathered up." He cut himself an enormous plug of tobacco with his horn-handled pocketknife, and offered it to Mr. Hatch, who then produced his own plug and, opening a huge bowie knife with a long blade sharply whetted, cut off a large wad and put it in his mouth. They then compared plugs and both of them were astonished to see how different men's ideas of good chewing tobacco were.

"Now, for instance," said Mr. Hatch, "mine is lighter colored. That's because, for one thing, there ain't any sweetenin' in this plug. I like it dry, natural leaf, medium strong."

"A little sweetenin' don't do no harm so far as I'm concerned," said Mr. Thompson, "but it's got to be mighty little. But with me, now, I want a strong leaf, I want it heavy-cured, as the feller says. There's a man near here, named Williams, Mr. John Morgan Williams, who chews a plug—well, sir, it's black as your hat and soft as melted tar. It fairly drips with molasses, jus' plain molasses, and it chews like licorice. Now, I don't call that a good chew."

"One man's meat," said Mr. Hatch, "is another man's poison. Now, such a chew would simply gag me. I couldn't begin to put it in my mouth."

"Well," said Mr. Thompson, a tinge of apology in his voice, "I jus' barely tasted it myself, you might say. Just took a little piece in my mouth and spit it out again."

"I'm dead sure I couldn't even get that far," said Mr. Hatch. "I like a dry natural chew without any artificial flavorin' of any kind."

Mr. Thompson began to feel that Mr. Hatch was trying to make out he had the best judgment in tobacco, and was going to keep up the argument until he proved it. He began to feel seriously annoyed with the fat man. After all, who was he and where did he come from? Who was he to go around telling other people what kind of tobacco to chew?

"Artificial flavorin'," Mr. Hatch went on, doggedly, "is jes put in to cover up a cheap leaf and make a man think he's gettin' somethin' more than he *is* gettin'. Even a little sweetenin' is a sign of a cheap leaf, you can mark my words."

"I've always paid a fair price for my plug," said Mr. Thompson, stiffly. "I'm not a rich man and I don't go round settin' myself up for one, but I'll say this, when it comes to such things as tobacco, I buy the best on the market."

"Sweetenin', even a little," began Mr. Hatch, shifting his plug and squirting tobacco juice at a dry-looking little rose bush that was having a hard enough time as it was, standing all day in the blazing sun, its roots clenched in the baked earth, "is the sign of—"

"About this Mr. Helton, now," said Mr. Thompson, determinedly, "I don't see no reason to hold it against a man because he went loony once or twice in his lifetime and so I don't expect to take no steps about it. Not a step. I've got nothin' against the man, he's always treated me fair. They's things and people," he went on," 'nough to drive any man loony. The wonder to me is, more men don't wind up in straitjackets, the way things are going these days and times."

"That's right," said Mr. Hatch, promptly, entirely too promptly, as if he were turning Mr. Thompson's meaning back on him. "You took the words right out of my mouth. There ain't every man in a straitjacket that ought to be there. Ha, ha, you're right all right. You got the idea."

Mr. Thompson sat silent and chewed steadily and stared at a spot on the ground about six feet away and felt a slow muffled resentment climbing from somewhere deep down in him, climbing and spreading all through him. What was this fellow driving at? What was he trying to say? It wasn't so much his words, but his looks and his way of talking: that droopy look in the eye, that tone of voice, as if he was trying to mortify Mr. Thompson about something. Mr. Thompson didn't like it, but he couldn't get hold of it either. He wanted to turn around and shove the fellow off the stump, but it wouldn't look reasonable. Suppose something happened to the fellow when he fell off the stump, just for instance, if he fell on the ax and cut himself, and then someone should ask Mr. Thompson why he shoved him, and what could a man say? It would look mighty funny, it would sound mighty strange to say, Well, him and me fell out over a plug of tobacco. He might just shove him anyhow and then tell people he was a fat man not used to the heat and while he was talking he got dizzy and fell off by himself, or something like that, and it wouldn't be the truth either, because it wasn't the heat and it wasn't the tobacco. Mr. Thompson made up his mind to get the fellow off the place pretty quick, without seeming to be anxious, and watch him sharp till he was out of sight. It doesn't pay to be friendly with strangers from another part of the country. They're always up to something, or they'd stay at home where they belong.

"And they's some people," said Mr. Hatch, "would jus' as soon have a loonatic around their house as not, they can't see no difference between them and anybody else. I always say, if that's the way a man feels, don't care who he associates with, why, why, that's his business, not mine. I don't wanta have a thing to do with it. Now back home in North Dakota, we don't feel that way. I'd like to a seen anybody hiring a loonatic there, aspecially after what he done."

"I didn't understand your home was North Dakota," said Mr. Thompson. "I thought you said Georgia."

"I've got a married sister in North Dakota," said Mr. Hatch, "married a Swede, but a white man if ever I saw one. So I say *we* because we got into a little business together out that way. And it seems like home, kind of."

"What did he do?" asked Mr. Thompson, feeling very uneasy again.

"Oh, nothin' to speak of," said Mr. Hatch, jovially, "jus' went loony one day in the hayfield and shoved a pitchfork right square through his brother, when they was makin' hay. They was goin' to execute him, but they found out he had went crazy with the heat, as the feller says, and so they put him in the asylum. That's all he done. Nothin' to get lathered up about, ha, ha, ha!" he said, and taking out his sharp knife he began to slice off a chew as carefully as if he were cutting cake.

"Well," said Mr. Thompson, "I don't deny that's news. Yes, sir, news. But I still say somethin' must have drove him to it. Some men make you feel like giving 'em a good killing just by lookin' at you. His brother may a been a mean ornery cuss."

"Brother was going to get married," said Mr. Hatch; "used to go courtin' his girl nights. Borrowed Mr. Helton's harmonica to give her a serenade one evenin', and lost it. Brand new harmonica."

"He thinks a heap of his harmonicas," said Mr. Thompson. "Only money he ever spends, now and then he buys hisself a new one. Must have a dozen in that shack, all kinds and sizes."

"Brother wouldn't buy him a new one," said Mr. Hatch, "so Mr. Helton just ups, and I says, and runs his pitchfork through his brother. Now you know he musta been crazy to get all worked up over a little thing like that."

"Sounds like it," said Mr. Thompson, reluctant to agree in anything with this intrusive and disagreeable fellow. He kept thinking he couldn't remember when he had taken such a dislike to a man on first sight.

"Seems to me you'd get pretty sick of hearin' the same tune year in, year out," said Mr. Hatch.

"Well, sometimes I think it wouldn't do no harm if he learned a new one," said Mr. Thompson, "but he don't, so there's nothin' to be done about it. It's a pretty good tune, though."

"One of the Scandahoovians told me what it meant, that's how I come to know," said Mr. Hatch. "Especially that part about getting so gay you jus' go ahead and drink up all the likker you got on hand before noon. It seems like up in them Swede countries a man carries a bottle of wine around with him as a matter of course, at least that's the way I understood it. Those fellers will tell you anything, though—" He broke off and spat.

The idea of drinking any kind of liquor in this heat made Mr. Thompson dizzy. The idea of anybody feeling good on a day like this, for instance, made him tired. He felt he was really suffering from the heat. The fat man looked as if he had grown to the stump; he slumped there in his damp, dark clothes too big for him, his belly slack in his pants, his wide black felt hat pushed off his narrow forehead red with prickly heat. A bottle of good cold beer, now, would be a help, thought Mr. Thompson, remembering the four bottles sitting deep in the pool at the springhouse, and his dry tongue squirmed in his mouth. He wasn't going to offer this man anything, though, not even a drop of water. He wasn't even going to chew any more tobacco with him. He shot out his quid suddenly, and wiped his mouth on the back of his hand, and studied the head near him attentively. The man was no good, and he was there for no good, but what was he up to? Mr. Thompson made up his mind he'd give him a little more time to get his business, whatever it was, with Mr. Helton over, and then if he didn't get off the place he'd kick him off.

Mr. Hatch, as if he suspected Mr. Thompson's thoughts, turned his eyes, wicked and pig-like, on Mr. Thompson. "Fact is," he said, as if he had made up his mind about something, "I might need your help in the little matter I've got on hand, but it won't cost you any trouble. Now, this Mr. Helton here, like I tell you, he's a dangerous escaped loonatic, you might say. Now fact is, in the last twelve years or so I musta rounded up twenty-odd escaped loonatics, besides a couple of escaped convicts that I just run into by accident, like I don't make a business of it, but if there's a reward, and there usually is a reward, of course, I get it. It amounts to a tidy little sum in the long run, but that ain't the main question. Fact is, I'm for law and order, I don't like to see lawbreakers and loonatics at large. It ain't the place for them. Now I reckon you're bound to agree with me on that, aren't you?"

Mr. Thompson said, "Well, circumstances alters cases, as the feller says. Now, what I know of Mr. Helton, he ain't dangerous, as I told you." Something serious was going to happen, Mr. Thompson could see that. He stopped thinking about it. He'd just let this fellow shoot off his head and then see what could be done about it. Without thinking he got out his knife and plug and started to cut a chew, then remembered himself and put them back in his pocket.

"The law," said Mr. Hatch, "is solidly behind me. Now this Mr. Helton, he's been one of my toughest cases. He's kept my record from being practically one hundred per cent. I knew him before he went loony, and I know the fam'ly, so I undertook to help out rounding him up. Well, sir, he was gone slick as a whistle, for all we knew the man was as good as dead long while ago. Now we never might have caught up with him, but do you know what he did? Well, sir, about two weeks ago his old mother gets a letter from him, and in that letter, what do you reckon she found? Well, it was a check on that little bank in town for eight hundred and fifty dollars, just like that; the letter wasn't nothing much, just said he was sending her a few little savings, she might need something, but there it was, name, postmark, date, everything. The old woman practically lost her mind with joy. She's gettin' childish, and it looked like she kinda forgot that her only living son killed his brother and went loony. Mr. Helton said he was getting along all right, and for her not to tell nobody. Well, natchally, she couldn't keep it to herself, with that check to cash and everything. So that's how I come to know." His feelings got the better of him. "You coulda knocked me down with a feather." He shook hands with himself and rocked, wagging his head, going "Heh, heh," in his throat. Mr. Thompson felt the corners of his mouth turning down. Why, the dirty low-down hound, sneaking around spying into other people's business like that. Collecting blood money, that's what it was! Let him talk!

"Yea, well, that musta been a surprise all right," he said, trying to hold his voice even. "I'd say a surprise."

"Well, siree," said Mr. Hatch, "the more I got to thinking about it, the more I just come to the conclusion that I'd better look into the matter a little, and so I talked to the old woman. She's pretty decrepit, now, half blind and all, but she was all for taking the first train out and going to see her son. I put it up to her square—how she was too feeble for the trip, and all. So, just as a favor to her, I told her for my expenses I'd come down and see Mr. Helton and bring her back all the news about him. She gave me a new shirt she made herself by hand, and a big Swedish kind of cake to bring to him, but I musta mislaid them along the road somewhere. It don't reely matter, though, he prob'ly ain't in any state of mind to appreciate 'em."

Mr. Thompson sat up and turning round on the log looked at Mr. Hatch and asked as quietly as he could, "And now what are you aiming to do? That's the question."

Mr. Hatch slouched up to his feet and shook himself. "Well, I come all prepared for a little scuffle," he said. "I got the handcuffs," he said, "but I don't want no violence if I can help it. I didn't want to say nothing around the countryside, making an uproar. I figured the two of us could overpower him." He reached into his big inside pocket and pulled them out. Handcuffs, for God's sake, thought Mr. Thompson. Coming round on a peaceable afternoon worrying a man, making trouble, and fishing handcuffs out of his pocket on a decent family homestead, as if it was all in the day's work.

Mr. Thompson, his head buzzing, got up too. "Well," he said, roundly, "I want to tell you I think you've got a mighty sorry job on hand, you sure must be hard up for something to do, and now I want to give you a good piece of advice. You just drop the idea that you're going to come here and make trouble for Mr. Helton, and the quicker you drive that hired rig away from my front gate the better I'll be satisfied."

Mr. Hatch put one handcuff in his outside pocket, the other dangling down. He pulled his hat down over his eyes, and reminded Mr. Thompson of a sheriff, somehow. He didn't seem in the least nervous, and didn't take up Mr. Thompson's words. He said, "Now listen just a minute, it ain't reasonable to suppose that a man like yourself is going to stand in the way of getting an escaped loonatic back to the asylum where he belongs. Now I know it's enough to throw you off, coming sudden like this, but fact is I counted on your being a respectable man and helping me out to see that justice is done. Now a course, if you won't help, I'll have to look around for help somewhere else. It won't look very good to your neighbors that you was harboring an escaped loonatic who killed his own brother, and then you refused to give him up. It will look mighty funny."

Mr. Thompson knew almost before he heard the words that it would look funny. It would put him in a mighty awkward position. He said, "But I've been trying to tell you all along that the man ain't loony now. He's been perfectly harmless for nine years. He's—he's—"

Mr. Thompson couldn't think how to describe how it was with Mr. Helton. "Why, he's been like one of the family," he said, "the best standby a man ever had." Mr. Thompson tried to see his way out. It was a fact Mr. Helton might go loony again any minute, and now this fellow talking around the country would put Mr. Thompson in a fix. It was a terrible position. He couldn't think of any way out. "You're crazy," Mr. Thompson roared suddenly, "you're the crazy one around here, you're crazier than he ever was! You get off this place or I'll handcuff you and turn you over to the law. You're trespassing," shouted Mr. Thompson. "Get out of here before I knock you down!"

He took a step towards the fat man, who backed off, shrinking, "Try it, try it, go ahead!" and then something happened that Mr. Thompson tried hard afterwards to piece together in his mind, and in fact it never did come straight. He saw the fat man with his long bowie knife in his hand, he saw Mr. Helton come round the corner on the run, his long jaw dropped, his arms swinging, his eyes wild. Mr. Helton came in between them, fists doubled up, then stopped short, glaring at the fat man, his big frame seemed to collapse, he trembled like a shied horse; and then the fat man drove at him, knife in one hand, handcuffs in the other. Mr. Thompson saw it coming, he saw the blade going into Mr. Helton's stomach, he knew he had the ax out of the log in his own hands, felt his arms go up over his head and bring the ax down on Mr. Hatch's head as if he were stunning a beef.

Mrs. Thompson had been listening uneasily for some time to the voices going on, one of them strange to her, but she was too tired at first to get up and come out to see what was going on. The confused shouting that rose so suddenly brought her up to her feet and out across the front porch without her slippers, hair half-braided. Shading her eyes, she saw first Mr. Helton, running all stooped over through the orchard, running like a man with dogs after him; and Mr. Thompson supporting himself on the ax handle was leaning over shaking by the shoulder a man Mrs. Thompson had never seen, who lay doubled up with the top of his head smashed and the blood running away in a greasy-looking puddle. Mr. Thompson without taking his hand from the man's shoulder, said in a thick voice, "He killed Mr. Helton, he killed him, I saw him do it. I had to knock him out," he called loudly, "but he won't come to."

Mrs. Thompson said in a faint scream, "Why, yonder goes Mr. Helton," and she pointed. Mrs. Thompson sat down slowly against the side of the house and began to slide forward on her face; she felt as if she were drowning, she couldn't rise to the top somehow, and her only thought was she was glad the boys were not there, they were out, fishing at Halifax, oh, God, she was glad the boys were not there.

Mr. and Mrs. Thompson drove up to their barn about sunset. Mr. Thompson handed the reins to his wife, got out to open the big door, and Mrs. Thompson guided old Jim in under the roof. The buggy was gray with dust and age, Mrs. Thompson's face was gray with dust and weariness, and Mr. Thompson's face, as he stood at the horse's head and began unhitching, was gray except for the dark blue of his freshly shaven jaws and chin, gray and blue and caved in, but patient, like a dead man's face.

Mrs. Thompson stepped down to the hard packed manure of the barn floor, and shook out her light flower-sprigged dress. She wore her smoked glasses, and her wide shady leghorn hat with the wreath of exhausted pink and blue forget-me-nots hid her forehead, fixed in a knot of distress.

The horse hung his head, raised a huge sigh and flexed his stiffened legs. Mr. Thompson's words came up muffled and hollow. "Poor ole Jim," he said, clearing his throat, "he looks pretty sunk in the ribs. I guess he's had a hard week." He lifted the harness up in one piece, slid it off and Jim walked out of the shafts halting a little. "Well, this is the last time," Mr. Thompson said, still talking to Jim. "Now you can get a good rest."

Mrs. Thompson closed her eyes behind her smoked glasses. The last time, and high time, and they should never have gone at all. She did not need her glasses any more, now the good darkness was coming down again, but her eyes ran full of tears steadily, though she was not crying, and she felt better with the glasses, safer, hidden away behind them. She took out her handkerchief with her hands shaking as they had been shaking ever since *that day*, and blew her nose. She said, "I see the boys have lighted the lamps. I hope they've started the stove going."

She stepped along the rough path holding her thin dress and starched petticoats around her, feeling her way between the sharp small stones, leaving the barn because she could hardly bear to be near Mr. Thompson, advancing slowly towards the house because she dreaded going there. Life was all one dread, the faces of her neighbors, of her boys, of her husband, the face of the whole world, the shape of her own house in the darkness, the very smell of the grass and the trees were horrible to her. There was no place to go, only one thing to do, bear it somehow—but how? She asked herself that question often. How was she going to keep on living now? Why had she lived at all? She wished now she had died one of those times when she had been so sick, instead of living on for this.

The boys were in the kitchen; Herbert was looking at the funny pictures from last Sunday's newspapers, the Katzenjammer Kids and Happy Hooligan. His chin was in his hands and his elbows on the table, and he was really reading and looking at the pictures, but his face was unhappy. Arthur was building the fire, adding kindling a stick at a time, watching it catch and blaze. His face was heavier and darker than Herbert's, but he was a little sullen by nature; Mrs. Thompson thought, he takes things harder, too. Arthur said, "Hello, Momma," and went on with his work. Herbert swept the papers together and moved over on the bench. They were big boys—fifteen and seventeen, and Arthur as tall as his father. Mrs. Thompson sat down beside Herbert, taking off her hat. She said, "I guess you're hungry. We were late today. We went the Log Hollow road, it's rougher than ever." Her pale mouth drooped with a sad fold on either side.

"I guess you saw the Mannings, then," said Herbert.

"Yes, and the Fergusons, and the Allbrights, and that new family McClellan."

"Anybody say anything?" asked Herbert.

"Nothing much, you know how it's been all along, some of them keeps saying, yes, they know it was a clear case and a fair trial and they say how glad they are your papa came out so well, and all that, some of 'em do, anyhow, but it looks like they don't really take sides with him. I'm about wore out," she said, the tears rolling again from under her dark glasses. "I don't know what good it does, but your papa can't seem to rest unless he's telling how it happened. I don't know."

"I don't think it does any good, not a speck," said Arthur, moving away from the stove. "It just keeps the whole question stirred up in people's minds. Everybody will go round telling what he heard, and the whole thing is going to get worse mixed up than ever. It just makes matters worse. I wish you could get Papa to stop driving round the country talking like that."

"Your papa knows best," said Mrs. Thompson. "You oughtn't to criticize him. He's got enough to put up with without that."

Arthur said nothing, his jaw stubborn. Mr. Thompson came in, his eyes hollowed out and dead-looking, his thick hands gray white and seamed from washing them clean every day before he started out to see the neighbors to tell them his side of the story. He was wearing his Sunday clothes, a thick pepper-and-salt-colored suit with a black string tie.

Mrs. Thompson stood up, her head swimming. "Now you-all get out of the kitchen, it's too hot in here and I need room. I'll get us a little bite of supper, if you'll just get out and give me some room."

They went as if they were glad to go, the boys outside, Mr. Thompson into his bedroom. She heard him groaning to himself as he took off his shoes, and heard the bed creak as he lay down. Mrs. Thompson opened the icebox and felt the sweet coldness flow out of it; she had never expected to have an icebox, much less did she hope to afford to keep it filled with ice. It still seemed like a miracle, after two or three years. There was the food, cold and clean, all ready to be warmed over. She would never have had that icebox if Mr. Helton hadn't happened along one day, just by the strangest luck; so saving, and so managing, so good, thought Mrs. Thompson, her heart swelling until she feared she would faint again, standing there with the door open and leaning her head upon it. She simply could not bear to remember Mr. Helton, with his long sad face and silent ways, who had always been so quiet and harmless, who had worked so hard and helped Mr. Thompson so much, running through the hot fields and woods, being hunted like a mad dog, everybody turning out with ropes and guns and sticks to catch and tie him. Oh, God, said Mrs. Thompson in a long dry moan, kneeling before the icebox and fumbling inside for the dishes, even if they did pile mattresses all over the jail floor and against the walls, and five men there to hold him to keep him from hurting himself any more, he was already hurt too badly, he couldn't have lived anyway. Mr. Barbee, the sheriff, told her about it. He said, well, they didn't aim to harm him but they had to catch him, he was crazy as a loon; he picked up rocks and tried to brain every man that got near him. He had two harmonicas in his jumper pocket, said the sheriff, but they fell out in the scuffle, and Mr. Helton tried to pick 'em up again, and that's when they finally got him. "They *had* to be rough, Miz Thompson, he fought like a wildcat." Yes, thought Mrs. Thompson, again with the same bitterness, of course, they had to be rough. They always have to be rough. Mr. Thompson can't argue with a man and get him off the place peaceably, she thought, standing up and shutting the icebox, he has to kill somebody, he has to be a murderer and ruin his boys' lives and cause Mr. Helton to be killed like a mad dog.

Her thoughts stopped with a little soundless explosion, cleared and began again. The rest of Mr. Helton's harmonicas were still in the shack, his tune ran in Mrs. Thompson's head at certain times of the day. She missed it in the evenings. It seemed so strange she had never known the name of that song, nor what it meant, until after Mr. Helton was gone. Mrs. Thompson, trembling in the knees, took a drink of water at the sink and poured the red beans into the baking dish, and began to roll the pieces of chicken in flour to fry them. There was a time, she said to herself, when I thought I had neighbors and friends, there was a time when we could hold up our heads, there was a time when my husband hadn't killed a man and I could tell the truth to anybody about anything.

Mr. Thompson, turning on his bed, figured that he had done all he could, he'd just try to let the matter rest from now on. His lawyer, Mr. Burleigh, had told him right at the beginning, "Now you keep calm and collected. You've got a fine case, even if you haven't got witnesses. Your wife must sit in court, she'll be a powerful argument with the jury. You just plead not guilty and I'll do the rest. The trial is going to be a mere formality, you haven't got a thing to worry about. You'll be clean out of this before you know it." And to make talk Mr. Burleigh had got to telling about all the men he knew around the country who for one reason or another had been forced to kill somebody, always in self-defense, and there just wasn't anything to it at all. He even told about how his own father in the old days had shot and killed a man just for setting foot inside his gate when he told him not to. "Sure, I shot the scoundrel," said

Mr. Burleigh's father, "in self-defense; I *told* him I'd shoot him if he set his foot in my yard, and he did, and I did." There had been bad blood between them for years, Mr. Burleigh said, and his father had waited a long time to catch the other fellow in the wrong, and when he did he certainly made the most of his opportunity.

"But Mr. Hatch, as I told you," Mr. Thompson had said, "made a pass at Mr. Helton with his bowie knife. That's why I took a hand."

"All the better," said Mr. Burleigh. "That stranger hadn't any right coming to your house on such an errand. Why, hell," said Mr. Burleigh, "that wasn't even manslaughter you committed. So now you just hold your horses and keep your shirt on. And don't say one word without I tell you."

Wasn't even manslaughter. Mr. Thompson had to cover Mr. Hatch with a piece of wagon canvas and ride to town to tell the sheriff. It had been hard on Ellie. When they got back, the sheriff and the coroner and two deputies, they found her sitting beside the road, on a low bridge over a gulley, about half a mile from the place. He had taken her up behind his saddle and got her back to the house. He had already told the sheriff that his wife had witnessed the whole business, and now he had time, getting her to her room and in bed, to tell her what to say if they asked anything. He had left out the part about Mr. Helton being crazy all along, but it came out at the trial. By Mr. Burleigh's advice Mr. Thompson had pretended to be perfectly ignorant; Mr. Hatch hadn't said a word about that. Mr. Thompson pretended to believe that Mr. Hatch had just come looking for Mr. Helton to settle old scores, and the two members of Mr. Hatch's family who had come down to try to get Mr. Thompson convicted didn't get anywhere at all. It hadn't been much of a trial, Mr. Burleigh saw to that. He had charged a reasonable fee, and Mr. Thompson had paid him and felt grateful, but after it was over Mr. Burleigh didn't seem pleased to see him when he got to dropping into the office to talk it over, telling him things that had slipped his mind at first: trying to explain what an ornery low hound Mr. Hatch had been, anyhow. Mr. Burleigh seemed to have lost his interest; he looked sour and upset when he saw Mr. Thompson at the door. Mr. Thompson kept saying to himself that he'd got off, all right, just as Mr. Burleigh had predicted, but, but—and it was right there that Mr. Thompson's mind stuck, squirming like an angleworm on a fishhook: he had killed Mr. Hatch, and he was a murderer. That was the truth about himself that Mr. Thompson couldn't grasp, even when he said the word to himself. Why, he had not even once *thought* of killing anybody, much less Mr. Hatch, and if Mr. Helton hadn't come out so unexpectedly, hearing the row, why, then—but then, Mr. Helton had come on the run that way to help him. What he couldn't understand was what happened next. He had seen Mr. Hatch go after Mr. Helton with the knife, he had seen the point, blade up, go into Mr. Helton's stomach and slice up like you slice a hog, but when they finally caught Mr. Helton there wasn't a knife scratch on him. Mr. Thompson knew he had the ax in his own hands and felt himself lifting it, but he couldn't remember hitting Mr. Hatch. He couldn't remember it. He couldn't. He remembered only that he had been determined to stop Mr. Hatch from cutting Mr. Helton. If he was given a chance he could explain the whole matter. At the trial they hadn't let him talk. They just asked questions and he answered yes or no, and they never did get to the core of the matter. Since the trial, now, every day for a week he had washed and shaved and put on his best clothes and had taken Ellie with him to tell every neighbor he had that he never killed Mr. Hatch on purpose, and what good did it do? Nobody believed him. Even when he turned to Ellie and said, "You was there, you saw it, didn't you?" and Ellie spoke up, saying, "Yes, that's the truth. Mr. Thompson was trying to save Mr. Helton's life," and he added, "If you don't believe me, you can believe my wife. She won't lie," Mr. Thompson saw something in all their faces that disheartened him, made him feel empty and tired out. They didn't believe he was not a murderer.

Even Ellie never said anything to comfort him. He hoped she would say finally, "I remember now, Mr. Thompson, I really did come round the corner in time to see everything. It's not a lie, Mr. Thompson. Don't you worry." But as they drove together in silence, with the days still hot and dry, shortening for fall, day after day, the buggy jolting in the ruts, she said nothing; they grew to dread the sight of another house, and the people in it: all houses looked alike now, and the people—old neighbors or new—had the same expression when Mr. Thompson told them why he had come and began his story. Their eyes looked as if someone had pinched the eyeball at the back; they shriveled and the light went out of them. Some of them sat with fixed tight smiles trying to be friendly. "Yes, Mr. Thompson, we know how you must feel. It must be terrible for you, Mrs. Thompson. Yes, you know, I've about come to the point where I believe in such a thing as killing in self-defense. Why, certainly, we believe you, Mr. Thompson, why shouldn't we believe you? Didn't you have a perfectly fair and above-board trial? Well, now, natchally, Mr. Thompson, we think you done right."

Mr. Thompson was satisfied they didn't think so. Sometimes the air around him was so thick with their blame he fought and pushed with his fists, and the sweat broke out all over him, he shouted his story in a dust-choked voice, he would fairly bellow at last: "My wife, here, you know her, she was there, she saw and heard it all, if you don't believe me, ask her, she won't lie!" and Mrs. Thompson, with her hands knotted together, aching, her chin trembling, would never fail to say: "Yes, that's right, that's the truth—"

The last straw had been laid on today, Mr. Thompson decided. Tom Allbright, an old beau of Ellie's, why, he had squired Ellie around a whole summer, had come out to meet them when they drove up, and standing there bareheaded had stopped them from getting out. He had looked past them with an embarrassed frown on his face, telling them his wife's sister was there with a raft of young ones, and the house was pretty full and everything upset, or he'd ask them to come in. "We've been thinking of trying to get up to your place one of these days," said Mr. Allbright, moving away trying to look busy, "we've been mighty occupied up here of late." So they had to say, "Well, we just happened to be driving this way," and go on. "The Allbrights," said Mrs. Thompson, "always was fair-weather friends." "They look out for number one, that's a fact," said Mr. Thompson. But it was cold comfort to them both.

Finally Mrs. Thompson had given up. "Let's go home," she said. "Old Jim's tired and thirsty, and we've gone far enough."

Mr. Thompson said, "Well, while we're out this way, we might as well stop at the McClellans'." They drove in, and asked a little cotton-haired boy if his mamma and papa were at home. Mr. Thompson wanted to see them. The little boy stood gazing with his mouth open, then galloped into the house shouting, "Mommer, Popper, come out hyah. That man that kilt Mr. Hatch has come ter see yer!"

The man came out in his sock feet, with one gallus up, the other broken and dangling, and said, "Light down, Mr. Thompson, and come in. The ole woman's washing, but she'll git here." Mrs. Thompson, feeling her way, stepped down and sat in a broken rocking-chair on the porch that sagged under her feet. The woman of the house, barefooted, in a calico wrapper, sat on the edge of the porch, her fat sallow face full of curiosity. Mr. Thompson began, "Well, as I reckon you happen to know, I've had some strange troubles lately, and, as the feller says, it's not the kind of trouble that happens to a man every day in the year, and there's some things I don't want no misunderstanding about in the neighbors' minds, so—" He halted and stumbled forward, and the two listening faces took on a mean look, a greedy, despising look, a look that said plain as day, "My, you must be a purty sorry feller to come round worrying about what *we* think, *we* know you wouldn't be here if you had anybody else to turn to—my, I wouldn't lower myself that much, myself." Mr. Thompson was ashamed of himself, he was suddenly in a rage, he'd like to knock their dirty skunk heads together, the low-down white trash—but he held himself down and went on to the end. "My wife will tell you," he said, and this was the hardest place, because Ellie always without moving a muscle seemed to stiffen as if somebody had threatened to hit her; "ask my wife, she won't lie."

"It's true, I saw it—"

"Well, now," said the man, drily, scratching his ribs inside his shirt, "that sholy is too bad. Well, now, I kaint see what we've got to do with all this here, however. I kaint see no good reason for us to git mixed up in these murder matters, I shore kaint. Which ever way you look at it, it ain't none of my business. However, it's mighty nice of you-all to come around and give us the straight of it, fur we've heerd some mighty queer yarns about it, mighty queer, I golly you couldn't hardly make head ner tail of it."

"Evvybody goin' round shootin' they heads off," said the woman. "Now we don't hold with killin'; the Bible says—"

"Shet yer trap," said the man, "and keep it shet 'r I'll shet it fer yer. Now it shore looks like to me—"

"We mustn't linger," said Mrs. Thompson, unclasping her hands. "We've lingered too long now. It's getting late, and we've far to go." Mr. Thompson took the hint and followed her. The man and the woman lolled against their rickety porch poles and watched them go.

Now lying on his bed, Mr. Thompson knew the end had come. Now, this minute, lying in the bed where he had slept with Ellie for eighteen years; under this roof where he had laid the shingles when he was waiting to get married; there as he was with his whiskers already sprouting since his shave that morning; with his fingers feeling his bony chin, Mr. Thompson felt he was a dead man. He was dead to his other life, he had got to the end of something without knowing why, and he had to make a fresh start, he did not know how. Something different was going to begin, he didn't know what. It was in some way not his business. He didn't feel he was going to have much to do with it. He got up, aching, hollow, and went out to the kitchen where Mrs. Thompson was just taking up the supper.

"Call the boys," said Mrs. Thompson. They had been down to the barn, and Arthur put out the lantern before hanging it on a nail near the door. Mr. Thompson didn't like their silence. They had hardly said a word about anything to him since that day. They seemed to avoid him, they ran the place together as if he wasn't there, and attended to everything without asking him for any advice. "What you boys been up to?" he asked, trying to be hearty. "Finishing your chores?"

"No, sir," said Arthur, "there ain't much to do. Just greasing some axles." Herbert said nothing. Mrs. Thompson bowed her head: "For these and all Thy blessings. . . . Amen," she whispered weakly, and the Thompsons sat there with their eyes down and their faces sorrowful, as if they were at a funeral.

Every time he shut his eyes, trying to sleep, Mr. Thompson's mind started up and began to run like a rabbit. It jumped from one thing to another, trying to pick up a trail here or there that would straighten out what had happened that day he killed Mr. Hatch. Try as he might, Mr. Thompson's mind would not go anywhere that it had not already been, he could not see anything but what he had seen once, and he knew that was not right. If he had not seen straight that first time, then everything about his killing Mr. Hatch was wrong from start to finish, and there was nothing more to be done about it, he might just as well give up. It still seemed to him that he had done, maybe not the right thing, but the only thing he could do, that day, but had he? *Did he have to kill Mr. Hatch?* He had never seen a man he hated more, the minute he laid eyes on him. He knew in his bones the fellow was there for trouble. What seemed so funny now was this: Why hadn't he just told Mr. Hatch to get out before he ever even got in?

Mrs. Thompson, her arms crossed on her breast, was lying beside him, perfectly still, but she seemed awake, somehow. "Asleep, Ellie?"

After all, he might have got rid of him peaceably, or maybe he might have had to overpower him and put those handcuffs on him and turn him over to the sheriff for disturbing the peace. The most they could have done was to lock Mr. Hatch up while he cooled off for a few days, or fine him a little something. He would try to think of things he might have said to Mr. Hatch. Why, let's see, I could just have said, Now look here, Mr. Hatch, I want to talk to you as man to man. But his brain would go empty. What could he have said or done? But if he *could* have done anything else almost except kill Mr. Hatch, then nothing would have happened to Mr. Helton. Mr. Thompson hardly ever thought of Mr. Helton. His mind just skipped over him and went on. If he stopped to think about Mr. Helton he'd never in God's world get anywhere. He tried to imagine how it might all have been, this very night even, if Mr. Helton were still safe and sound out in his shack playing his tune about feeling so good in the morning, drinking up all the wine so you'd feel even better; and Mr. Hatch safe in jail somewhere, mad as hops, maybe, but out of harm's way and ready to listen to reason and to repent of his meanness, the dirty, yellow-livered hound coming around persecuting an innocent man and ruining a whole family that never harmed him! Mr. Thompson felt the veins of his forehead start up, his fists clutched as if they seized an ax handle, the sweat broke out on him, he bounded up from the bed with a yell smothered in his throat, and Ellie started up after him, crying out, "Oh, oh, don't! Don't! Don't!" as if she were having a nightmare. He stood shaking until his bones rattled in him, crying hoarsely, "Light the lamp, light the lamp, Ellie."

Instead, Mrs. Thompson gave a shrill weak scream, almost the same scream he had heard on that day she came around the house when he was standing there with the ax in his hand. He could not see her in the dark, but she was on the bed, rolling violently. He felt for her in horror, and his groping hands found her arms, up, and her own hands pulling her hair straight out from her head, her neck strained back, and the tight screams strangling her. He shouted out for Arthur, for Herbert. "Your mother!" he bawled, his voice cracking. As he held Mrs. Thompson's arms, the boys came tumbling in, Arthur with the lamp above his head. By this light Mr. Thompson saw Mrs. Thompson's eyes, wide open, staring dreadfully at him, the tears pouring. She sat up at sight of the boys, and held out one arm towards them, the hand wagging in a crazy circle, then dropped on her back again, and suddenly went limp. Arthur set the lamp on the table and turned on Mrs. Thompson. "She's scared," he said, "she's scared to death." His face was in a knot of rage, his fists were doubled up, he faced his father as if he meant to strike him. Mr. Thompson's jaw fell, he was so surprised he stepped back from the bed. Herbert went to the other side. They stood on each side of Mrs. Thompson and watched Mr. Thompson as if he were a dangerous wild beast. "What did you do to her?" shouted Arthur, in a grown man's voice. "You touch her again and I'll blow your heart out!" Herbert was pale and his cheek twitched, but he was on Arthur's side; he would do what he could to help Arthur.

Mr. Thompson had no fight left in him. His knees bent as he stood, his chest collapsed. "Why, Arthur," he said, his words crumbling and his breath coming short. "She's fainted again. Get the ammonia." Arthur did not move. Herbert brought the bottle, and handed it, shrinking, to his father.

Mr. Thompson held it under Mrs. Thompson's nose. He poured a little in the palm of his hand and rubbed it on her forehead. She gasped and opened her eyes and turned her head away from him. Herbert began a doleful hopeless sniffling. "Mamma," he kept saying, "Mamma, don't die."

"I'm all right," Mrs. Thompson said. "Now don't you worry around. Now Herbert, you mustn't do that. I'm all right." She closed her eyes. Mr. Thompson began pulling on his best pants; he put on his socks and shoes. The boys sat on each side of the bed, watching Mrs. Thompson's face. Mr. Thompson put on his shirt and coat. He said, "I reckon I'll ride over and get the doctor. Don't look like all this fainting is a good sign. Now you just keep watch until I get back." They listened, but said nothing. He said, "Don't you get any notions in your head. I never did your mother any harm in my life, on purpose." He went out, and, looking back, saw Herbert staring at him from under his brows, like a stranger. "You'll know how to look after her," said Mr. Thompson.

Mr. Thompson went through the kitchen. There he lighted the lantern, took a thin pad of scratch paper and a stub pencil from the shelf where the boys kept their schoolbooks. He swung the lantern on his arm and reached into the cupboard where he kept the guns. The shotgun was there to his hand, primed and ready, a man never knows when he may need a shotgun. He went out of the house without looking around, or looking back when he had left it, passed his barn without seeing it, and struck out to the farthest end of his fields, which ran for half a mile to the east. So many blows had been struck at Mr. Thompson and from so many directions he couldn't stop any more to find out where he was hit. He walked on, over plowed ground and over meadow, going through barbed wire fences cautiously, putting his gun through first; he could almost see in the dark, now his eyes were used to it. Finally he came to the last fence; here he sat down, back against a post, lantern at his side, and, with the pad on his knee, moistened the stub pencil and began to write:

"Before Almighty God, the great judge of all before who I am about to appear, I do hereby solemnly swear that I did not take the life of Mr. Homer T. Hatch on purpose. It was done in defense of Mr. Helton. I did not aim to hit him with the ax but only to keep him off Mr. Helton. He aimed a blow at Mr. Helton who was not looking for it. It was my belief at that time that Mr. Hatch would of taken the life of Mr. Helton if I did not interfere. I have told all this to the judge and the jury and they let me off but nobody believes it. This is the only way I can prove I am not a cold blooded murderer like everybody seems to think. If I had been in Mr. Helton's place he would of done the same for me. I still think I done the only thing there was to do. My wife—"

Mr. Thompson stopped here to think a while. He wet the pencil point with the tip of his tongue and marked out the last two words. He sat a while blacking out the words until he had made a neat oblong patch where they had been, and started again:

"It was Mr. Homer T. Hatch who came to do wrong to a harmless man. He caused all this trouble and he deserved to die but I am sorry it was me who had to kill him."

He licked the point of his pencil again, and signed his full name carefully, folded the paper and put it in his outside pocket. Taking off his right shoe and sock, he set the butt of the shotgun along the ground with the twin barrels pointed towards his head. It was very awkward. He thought about this a little, leaning his head against the gun mouth. He was trembling and his head was drumming until he was deaf and blind, but he lay down flat on the earth on his side, drew the barrel under his chin and fumbled for the trigger with his great toe. That way he could work it.

"NOON WINE": THE SOURCES

Katherine Anne Porter

THIS short novel, "Noon Wine," exists so fully and wholly in its own right in my mind, that when I attempt to trace its growth from the beginning, to follow all the clues to their sources in my memory, I am dismayed; because I am confronted with my own life, the whole society in which I was born and brought up, and the facts of it. My aim is to find the truth in it, and to this end my imagination works and re-works its recollections in a constant search for meanings. Yet in this endless remembering which surely must be the main occupation of the writer, events are changed, reshaped, interpreted again and again in different ways, and this is right and natural because it is the intention of the writer to write fiction, after all—real fiction, not a *roman à clef*, or a thinly disguised personal confession which better belongs to the psychoanalyst's séance. By the time I wrote "Noon Wine" it had become "real" to me almost in the sense that I felt not as if I had made that story out of my own memory of real events and imagined consequences, but as if I were quite simply reporting events I had heard or witnessed. This is not in the least true: the story is fiction; but it is made up of thousands of things that did happen to living human beings in a certain part of the country, at a certain time of my life, things that are still remembered by others as single incidents; not as I remembered them, floating and moving with their separate life and reality, meeting and parting and mingling in my thoughts until they established their relationship. I could see and feel very clearly that all these events, episodes—hardly that, sometimes, but just mere glimpses and flashes here and there of lives strange or moving or astonishing to me—were forming a story, almost of themselves, it seemed; out of their apparent incoherence, unrelatedness, they grouped and clung in my mind in a form that gave a meaning to the whole that the individual parts had lacked. So I feel that this story is "true" in the way that a work of fiction should be true, created out of all the scattered particles of life I was able to absorb and combine and to shape into a living new being.

But why did this particular set of memories and early impressions combine in just this way to make this particular story? I do not in the least know. And though it is quite true that I intended to write fiction, this story wove itself in my mind for years before I ever intended to write it; there were many other stories going on in my head at once, some of them evolved and were written, more were not. Why? This to me is the most interesting question, because I am sure there is an answer, but nobody knows it yet.

When the moment came to write this story, I knew it; and I had to make quite a number of practical arrangements to get the time free for it, without fear of interruptions. I wrote it as it stands except for a few pen corrections in just seven days of trance-like absorption in a small room in an inn in rural Pennsylvania, from the early evening of November 7 to November 14, 1936. Yet I had written the central part, the scene between Mr. Hatch and Mr. Thompson, which leads up to the murder, in Basel, Switzerland, in the summer of 1932.

I had returned from Europe only fifteen days before I went to the inn in Pennsylvania: this was the end, as it turned out, of my living abroad, except for short visits back to Paris, Brittany, Rome, Belgium: but meantime I had, at a time of great awareness and active energy, spent nearly fourteen years of my life out of this country: in Mexico, Bermuda, various parts of Europe, but mostly by choice, Paris. Of my life in these places I felt then, and feel now, that it was all entirely right, timely, appropriate, exactly where I should have been and what doing at that very time. I did not feel exactly at home; I knew where home was; but the time had come for me to see the world for myself, and so I did, almost as naturally as a bird taking off on his new wingfeathers. In Europe, things were not so strange; sometimes I had a pleasant sense of having here and there touched home-base; if I was not at home, I was sometimes with friends. And all the time, I was making notes on stories—stories of my own place, my South—for my part of Texas was peopled almost entirely by Southerners from Virginia, Tennessee, the Carolinas, Kentucky—and I was almost instinctively living in a sustained state of mind and feeling, quietly and secretly, comparing one thing with another, always remembering and remembering; and all sorts of things were falling into their proper places, taking on their natural shapes and sizes, and going back and back clearly into right perspective—right for me as artist, I simply mean to say; and it was like breathing—I did not have consciously to urge myself to think about it. So my time in Europe served me in a way I had not dreamed of, even, besides its own charm and goodness; it gave me back my past and my own house and my own people—the native land of my heart.

This summer country of my childhood, this space and memory is filled with landscapes shimmering in light and color, moving with sounds and shapes I hardly ever describe or put in my stories in so many words; they form only the living background of what I am trying to tell, so familiar to my characters they would hardly notice them; the sound of mourning doves in the live-oaks, the childish voices of parrots chattering on every back porch in the little town, the hoverings of buzzards in the high blue air—all the life of that soft blackland farming country, full of fruits and flowers and birds, with good hunting and good fishing; with plenty of water, many little and big rivers. I shall name just a few of the rivers I remember—the San Antonio, the San Marcos, the Trinity, the Neuces, the Rio Grande, the Colorado, and the small clear branch of the Colorado—full of colored pebbles—Indian Creek, the place where I was born. The colors and tastes all had their smells, as the sounds have now their echoes: the bitter whiff of air over a sprawl of animal skeleton after the buzzards were gone; the smells and flavors of roses and melons, and peach bloom and ripe peaches, of cape jessamine in hedges blooming like popcorn, and the sickly sweetness of chinaberry florets; of honeysuckle in great swags on a trellised gallery; heavy tomatoes dead ripe and warm with the midday sun, eaten there, at the vine; the delicious milky green corn, and savory hot corn bread eaten with still-warm sweet milk; and the clinging brackish smell of the muddy little ponds where we caught, and boiled crawfish—in a discarded lard can—and ate them, then and there, we children, in the company of an old Negro who had once been my grandparents' slave, as I have told in another story. He was by our time only a servant, and a cantankerous old cuss very sure of his place in the household.

Uncle Jimbilly, for that was his name, was not the only one who knew exactly where he stood, and just about how far he could go in maintaining the right, privileges, exemptions of his status so long as he performed its duties. At this point, I want to give a rather generalized view of the society of that time and place as I remember it, and as talks with my elders since confirm it. (Not long ago I planned to visit a very wonderful old lady who was a girlhood friend of my mother. I wrote to my sister that I could not think of being a burden to Miss Cora, and would therefore stop at the little hotel in town and call on her. And my sister wrote back air-mail on the very day saying: "For God's sake, don't mention the word hotel to Miss Cora—she'll think you've lost your raising!") The elders all talked and behaved as if the final word had gone out long ago on manners, morality, religion, even politics: nothing was ever to change, they said, and even as they spoke, everything was changing, sliding, disappearing. This had been happening in fact ever since they were born; the greatest change, the fatal dividing change in this country, the war between the states, was taking place even as most of my father's generation were coming into the world. But it was the grandparents who still ruled in daily life; and they showed plainly in acts, words, and even looks—an enormously handsome generation they seemed to have been I remember—all those wonderful high noses with a diamond shaped bony structure in the bridge!—the presence of good society, very well based on traditional Christian beliefs. These beliefs were mainly Protestant but not yet petty middle-class puritanism: there remained still an element fairly high stepping and wide gestured in its personal conduct. The petty middle class of fundamentalists who saw no difference between wine-drinking, dancing, card-playing, and adultery, had not yet got altogether the upper hand—in fact, never did except in certain limited areas; but it was making a brave try. It was not really a democratic society; if everybody had his place, sometimes very narrowly defined, at least he knew where it was, and so did everybody else. So too, the higher laws of morality and religion were defined; if a man offended against the one, or sinned against the other, he knew it, and so did his neighbors, and they called everything by its right name.

This firm view applied also to social standing. A man who had humble ancestors had a hard time getting away from them and rising in the world. If he prospered and took to leisurely ways of living, he was merely "getting above his raising." If he managed to marry into one of the good old families, he had simply "outmarried himself." If he went away and made a success somewhere else, when he returned for a visit he was still only "that Jimmerson boy who went No'th." There is—was, perhaps I should say—a whole level of society of the South where it was common knowledge that the mother's family outranked the father's by half, at least. This might be based on nothing more tangible than that the mother's family came from Richmond or Charleston, while the father's may have started out somewhere from Pennsylvania, or to have got bogged down one time or another in Arkansas. If they turned out well, the children of these matches were allowed their mother's status, for good family must never be denied, but father remained a member of the Plain People to the end. Yet there was nothing against any one hinting at better lineage, and a family past more dignified than the present, no matter how humble his present circumstances, nor how little proof he could offer for his claim. Aspiration to higher and better things was natural to all men, and a sign of proper respect for true blood and birth. Pride and hope may be denied to no one.

In this society of my childhood there were all sorts of tender ways of feeling and thinking, subtle understanding between people in matters of ritual and ceremony; I think in the main a civilized society, and yet, with the underlying, perpetual ominous presence of violence; violence potential that broke through the smooth surface almost without warning, or maybe just without warning to children one learned later to know the signs. There were old cruel customs, the feud, for one, gradually dying out among the good families, never in fact prevalent among them—the men of that class fought duels, and abided—in theory at least—on the outcome; and country life, ranch life, was rough, in Texas, at least. I remember tall bearded booted men striding about with clanking spurs; and carrying loaded pistols inside their shirts next to their ribs, even to church. It was quite matter of course that you opened a closet door in a bedroom and stared down into the cold eyes of shotguns and rifles, stacked there because there was no more room in the gun closet. In the summer, in that sweet smelling flowery country, we children with our father or some grown-up in charge, spent long afternoons on a range, shooting at fixed targets or clay pigeons with the ordinary domestic firearms, pistols, rifles of seven calibers, shotguns single and double. I never fired a shotgun, but I knew the sounds and could name any round of fire I heard, even at great distances.

Some one asked me once where I had ever heard that conversation in "Noon Wine" between two men about chewing tobacco—that apparently aimless talk between Mr. Hatch and Mr. Thompson which barely masks hatred and is leading towards a murder. It seems that I *must* have heard something of the sort somewhere, some time or another; I do not in the least remember it. But that whole countryside was full of tobacco-chewing men, whittling men, hard-working farming men perched on fences with their high heels caught on a rail, or squatting on their toes, gossiping idly and comfortably for hours at a time. I often wondered what they found to say to each other, day in day out year after year; but I should never have dared go near enough to listen profitably; yet I surely picked up something that came back whole and free as air that summer in Basel, Switzerland, when I thought I was studying only the life of Erasmus and the Reformation. And I have seen them, many a time, take out their razor-sharp long-bladed knives and slice a "chew" as delicately and precisely as if they were cutting a cake. These knives were so keen, often I have watched my father, shelling pecans for me, cut off the ends of the hard shells in a slow circular single gesture; then split them down the sides in four strips and bring out the nut meat whole. This fascinated me, but it did not occur to me to come near the knife, or offer to touch it. In our country life, in summers, we were surrounded by sharpened blades—hatchets, axes, ploughshares, carving knives, bowie knives, straight razors. We were taught so early to avoid all these, I do not remember ever being tempted to take one in my hand. Living as we did among loaded guns and dangerous cutting edges, four wild, adventurous children always getting hurt in odd ways, we none of us were ever injured seriously. The worst thing that happened was, my elder sister got a broken collar bone from a fall, not as you might expect from a horse, for we almost lived on horseback, but from a three-foot fall off a fence where she had climbed to get a better view of a battle between two bulls. But these sharp blades slicing tobacco—did I remember it because it was an unusual sight? I think not. I must have seen it, as I remember it, dozens of times—but one day I really *saw* it: and it became part of Mr. Thompson's hallucinated vision when he killed Mr. Hatch, and afterward could not live without justifying himself.

There is an early memory, not the first, but certainly before my third year, always connected with this story, "Noon Wine"; it is the source, if there could be only one. I was a very small child. I know this by the remembered vastness of the world around me, the giant heights of grown-up people; a chair something to be scaled like a mountain; a table top to be peered over on tiptoe. It was late summer and near sunset, for the sky was a clear green-blue with long streaks of burning rose in it, and the air was full of the mournful sound of swooping bats. I was all alone in a wide grassy plain—it was the lawn on the east side of the house—and I was in that state of instinctive bliss which children only know, when there came like a blow of thunder echoing and rolling in that green sky, the explosion of a shotgun, not very far away; for it shook the air. There followed at once a high, thin, long-drawn scream, a sound I had never heard, but I knew what it was—it was the sound of death in the voice of a man. How did I know it was a shotgun? How should I not have known? How did I know it was death? We are born knowing death.

Let me examine this memory a little, which though it is of an actual event, is like a remembered dream; but then all my childhood is that; and if in parts of this story I am trying to tell you, I use poetic terms, it is because in such terms do I remember many things, and the feeling is valid, it cannot be left out, or denied.

In the first place, could I have been alone when this happened? It is most unlikely. I was one of four children, brought up in a houseful of adults of ripening age; a grandmother, a father, several Negro servants, among them two aged, former slaves; visiting relatives, uncles, aunts, cousins; grandmother's other grandchildren older than we, with always an ill-identified old soul or two, male or female, who seemed to be guests but helped out with stray chores. The house, which seemed so huge to me, was probably barely adequate to the population it accommodated; but of one thing I am certain—nobody was ever alone except for the most necessary privacies, and certainly no child at any time. Children had no necessary privacies. We were watched and herded and monitored and followed and spied upon and corrected and lectured and scolded (and kissed, let's be just, loved tenderly, and prayed over!) all day, every day, through the endless years of childhood—endless, but where did they go? So the evidence all points to the fact that I was not, could not have been, bodily speaking, alone in that few seconds when for the first time I heard the sound of murder. Who was with me? What did she say—for it was certainly one of the care-taking women around the house. Could I have known by instinct, of which I am so certain now, or did some one speak words I cannot remember which nonetheless told me what had happened? There is nothing more to tell, all speculations are useless; this memory is a spot of clear light and color and sound, of immense, mysterious illumination of feeling against a horizon of total darkness.

Yet, was it the next day? next summer? In that same place, that grassy shady yard, in broad daylight I watched a poor little funeral procession creeping over the stony ridge of the near horizon, the dusty road out of town which led also to the cemetery. The hearse was just a spring wagon decently roofed and curtained with black oil cloth, poverty indeed, and some members of our household gathered on the front gallery to watch it pass, said, "Poor Pink Hodges—old man A—— got him just like he said he would." Had it been Pink Hodges, then, I had heard screaming death in the blissful sunset? And who was old man A, whose name I do not remember, and what became of him, I wonder? I'll never know. I remember only that the air of our house was full of pity for Pink Hodges, for his harmlessness, his helplessness, "so pitiful, poor thing," they said; and, "It's just not right," they said. But what did they do to bring old man A to justice, or at least a sense of his evil? Nothing, I am afraid. I began to ask all sorts of questions, and was silenced invariably by some elder who told me I was too young to understand such things.

Yet here I am coming to something quite clear, of which I am entirely certain. It happened in my ninth year, and again in that summer house in the little town near the farm, with the yard full of roses and irises and honeysuckle and hackberry trees, and the vegetable garden and the cow barn in back. It was already beginning to seem not so spacious to me; it went on dwindling year by year to the measure of my growing up.

One hot moist day after a great thunderstorm and heavy long rain, I saw a strange horse and buggy standing at the front gate. Neighbors and kin in the whole countryside knew each other's equipages as well as they did their own, and this outfit was not only strange, but not right; don't ask me why. It was not a good horse, and the buggy was not good, either. There was something wrong with the whole thing, and I went full of curiosity to see why such strangers as would drive such a horse and buggy would be calling on my grandmother. (At this point say anything you please about the snobbism of children and dogs. It is real. As real as the snobbism of their parents and owners, and much more keen and direct.)

I stood just outside the living room door, unnoticed for a moment by my grandmother, who was sitting rather stiffly, with an odd expression on her face: a doubtful smiling mouth, brows knitted in painful inquiry. She was a woman called upon for decisions, many decisions every day, wielding justice among her unruly family. Once she struck, justly or unjustly, she dared not retract—the whole pack would have torn her in pieces. They did not want justice in any case, but revenge, each in his own favor. But this situation had nothing to do with her family, and there she sat, worried, undecided. I had never seen her so, and it dismayed me.

Then I saw first a poor sad pale beaten-looking woman in a faded cotton print dress and a wretched little straw hat with a wreath of wilted forget-me-nots. She looked as if she had never eaten a good dinner, or slept in a comfortable bed, the mark of life-starvation was all over her. Her hands were twisted tight in her lap and she was looking down at them in shame. Her eyes were covered with dark glasses. While I stared at her, I heard the man sitting near her almost shouting in a coarse, roughened voice: "I swear, it was in self-defense! His life or mine! If you don't believe me, ask my wife here. She saw it. My wife won't lie!" Every time he repeated these words, without lifting her head or moving, she would say in a low voice, "Yes, that's right. I saw it."

In that moment, or in another moment later as this memory sank in and worked in my feelings and understanding, it was quite clear to me, and seems now to have been clear from the first, that he expected her to lie, was indeed forcing her to tell a lie; that she did it unwillingly and unlovingly in bitter resignation to the double disgrace of her husband's crime and her own sin; and that he, stupid, dishonest, soiled as he was, was imploring her as his only hope, somehow to make his lie a truth.

I used this scene in "Noon Wine," but the man in real life was not lean and gaunt and blindly, foolishly proud, like Mr. Thompson; no, he was just a great loose-faced, blabbing man full of guilt and fear, and he was bawling at my grandmother, his eyes bloodshot with drink and tears, "Lady, if you don't believe me, ask my wife! She won't lie!" At this point my grandmother noticed my presence and sent me away with a look we children knew well and never dreamed of disobeying. But I heard part of the story later, when my grandmother said to my father, with an unfamiliar coldness in her voice, for she had made her decision about this affair, too: "I was never asked to condone a murder before. Something new." My father said, "Yes, and a cold-blooded murder too if ever there was one."

So, there was the dreary tale of violence again, this time with the killer out on bail, going the rounds of the countryside with his wretched wife, telling his side of it—whatever it was; I never knew the end. In the meantime, in one summer or another, certainly before my eleventh year, for that year we left that country for good, I had two other memorable glimpses. My father and I were driving from the farm to town, when we met with a tall black-whiskered man on horseback, sitting so straight his chin was level with his Adam's apple, dressed in clean mended blue denims, shirt open at the throat, a big devil-may-care black felt hat on the side of his head. He gave us a lordly gesture of greeting, caused his fine black horse to curvet and prance a little, and rode on, grandly. I asked my father who that could be, and he said, "That's Ralph Thomas, the proudest man in seven counties." I said, "What is he proud of?" And my father said, "I suppose the horse. It's a very fine horse," in a good-humored, joking tone, which made the poor man quite ridiculous, and yet not funny, but sad in some way I could not understand.

On another of these journeys I saw a bony, awkward, tired-looking man, tilted in a kitchen chair against the wall of his comfortless shack, set back from the road under the thin shade of hackberry trees, a thatch of bleached-looking hair between his eyebrows, blowing away at a doleful tune on his harmonica, in the hot dull cricket-whirring summer day: the very living image of loneliness. I was struck with pity for this stranger, his eyes closed against the alien scene, consoling himself with such poor music. I was told he was someone's Swedish hired man.

In time—when? how? Pink Hodges, whom I never knew except in the sound of his death-cry, merged with my glimpse of the Swedish hired man to become the eternal Victim; the fat bullying whining man in my grandmother's living room became the Killer. But nothing can remain so simple as that, this was only a beginning. Helton too, the Victim in my story, is also a murderer, with the dubious innocence of the madman; but no less a shedder of blood. Everyone in this story contributes, one way or another directly, or indirectly, to murder, or death by violence; even the two young sons of Mr. Thompson who turn on him in their fright and ignorance and side with their mother, who does not need them; they are guiltless, for they meant no harm, and they do not know what they have contributed to; indeed in their innocence they believe they are doing, not only right, but the only thing they could possibly do in the situation as they understand it: they must defend their mother. . . .

And here I am brought to a pause, for almost without knowing it, I have begun to write about these characters in a story of mine as though they were real persons exactly as I have shown them. And these fragments of memory on which the story is based now seem to have a random look; they nowhere contain in themselves, together or separately, the story I finally wrote out of them; a story of the most painful moral and emotional confusions, in which every one concerned, yes, in his crooked way, even Mr. Hatch, is trying to do right.

It is only in the varying levels of quality in the individual nature that we are able finally more or less to measure the degree of virtue in each man. Mr. Thompson's motives are most certainly mixed, yet not ignoble; he helps some one who helps him in turn; while acting in defense of what he sees as the good in his own life, the thing worth trying to save at almost any cost, he is trying at the same time to defend another life—the life of Mr. Helton, who has proved himself the bringer of good, the present help, the true friend. Mr. Helton would have done as much for me, Mr. Thompson says, and he is right. Yet he hated Mr. Hatch on sight, wished to injure him before he had a reason: could it not be a sign of virtue in Mr. Thompson that he surmised and resisted at first glance the evil in Mr. Hatch? The whole countryside, let us remember, for this is most important, the relations of a man to his society, agrees with Mr. Burleigh the lawyer, and the jury and the judge that Mr. Thompson's deed was justifiable homicide: but this did not, as his neighbors confirmed, make it any less a murder. Mr. Thompson was not an evil man, he was only a poor sinner doing his best according to his lights, lights somewhat dimmed by his natural aptitude for Pride and Sloth. He still had his virtues, even if he did not quite know what they were, and so gave himself credit for some few that he had not.

But Hatch was the doomed man, evil by nature, a lover and do-er of evil, who did no good thing for any one, not even, in the long run, himself. He was evil in the most dangerous, irremediable way: one who works safely within the law, and has reasoned himself into believing that his motives, if not good, are at least no worse than any one else's: for he believes quite simply and naturally that the motives of others are no better than his own; and putting aside all nonsense about good, he will always be found on the side of custom and common sense and the letter of the law. When challenged he has his defense pat and ready, and there is nothing much wrong with it—it only lacks human decency, of which he has no conception beyond a faint hearsay. Mr. Helton is, by his madness, beyond good and evil, his own victim as well as the victim of others. Mrs. Thompson is a woman of the sort produced in numbers in that time, that place, that code: so trained to the practice of her prescribed womanly vocation of virtue as such—manifest, unrelenting, sacrificial, stupifying—she has almost lost her human qualities, and her spiritual courage and insight, to boot. She commits the, to her, dreadful unforgivable sin of lying; moreover, lying to shield a criminal, even if that criminal is her own husband. Having done this, to the infinite damage, as she sees it, of her own soul (as well as her self-respect which is founded on her feeling of irreproachability) she lacks the courage and the love to see her sin through to its final good purpose; to commit it with her whole heart and with perfect acceptance of her guilt; to say to her husband the words that might have saved them both, soul and body—might have, I say only. I do not know and shall never know. Mrs. Thompson was not that robust a character, and this story, given all, must end as it does end . . . there is nothing in any of these beings tough enough to work the miracle of redemption in them.

Suppose I imagine now that I really saw all of these persons in the flesh at one time or another? I saw what I have told you, a few mere flashes of a glimpse here and there, one time or another; but I do know why I remembered them, and why in my memory they slowly took on their separate lives in a story. It is because there radiated from each one of those glimpses of strangers some element, some quality that arrested my attention at a vital moment of my own growth, and caused me, a child, to stop short and look outward, away from myself; to look at another human being with that attention and wonder and speculation which ordinarily, and very naturally, I think, a child lavishes only on himself. Is it not almost the sole end of civilized education of all sorts to teach us to be more and more highly, sensitively conscious of the reality of the existence, the essential being, of others, those around us so very like us and yet so bafflingly, so mysteriously different? I do not know whether my impressions were on the instant, as I now believe, or did they draw to their magnet gradually with time and confirming experience? That man on the fine horse, with his straight back, straight neck, shabby and unshaven, riding like a cavalry officer, "the proudest man in seven counties—" I saw him no doubt as my father saw him, absurd, fatuous, but with some human claim on respect and not to be laughed at, for all his simple vanity.

The woman I have called Mrs. Thompson—I never knew her name—showed me for the first time I am certain the face of pure shame; humiliation so nearly absolute it could not have been more frightening if she had grovelled in the floor; and I knew that whatever the cause, it was mortal and beyond help. In that bawling sweating man with the loose mouth and staring eyes, I saw the fear that is moral cowardice and I knew he was lying. In that yellow-haired, long-legged man playing his harmonica I felt almost the first glimmer of understanding and sympathy for any suffering not physical. Most certainly I had already done my share of weeping over lost or dying pets, or beside some one I loved who was very sick, or my own pains and accidents; but *this* was a spiritual enlightenment, some tenderness, some first wakening of charity in my self-centered heart. I am using here some very old fashioned noble words in their prime sense. They have perfect freshness and reality to me, they are the irreplaceable names of Realities. I know well what they mean, and I need them here to describe as well as I am able what happens to a child when the human feelings and the moral sense and the sense of charity are unfolding, and are touched once and for all in that first time when the soul is prepared for them; and I know that the all-important things in that way have all taken place long and long before we know the words for them.

BLACKBERRY WINTER
Robert Penn Warren

IT was getting into June and past eight o'clock in the morning, but there was a fire—even if it wasn't a big fire, just a fire of chunks—on the hearth of the big stone fireplace in the living room. I was standing on the hearth, almost into the chimney, hunched over the fire, working my bare toes slowly on the warm stone. I relished the heat which made the skin of my bare legs warp and creep and tingle, even as I called to my mother, who was somewhere back in the dining room or kitchen and said: "But it's June, I don't have to put them on!"

"You put them on if you are going out," she called.

I tried to assess the degree of authority and conviction in the tone, but at that distance it was hard to decide. I tried to analyze the tone, and then I thought what a fool I had been to start out the back door and let her see that I was barefoot. If I had gone out the front door or the side door she would never have known, not till dinner time anyway, and by then the day would have been half gone and I would have been all over the farm to see what the storm had done and down to the creek to see the flood. But it had never crossed my mind that they would try to stop you from going barefoot in June, no matter if there had been a gully-washer and a cold spell.

Nobody had ever tried to stop me in June as long as I could remember, and when you are nine years old, what you remember seems forever; for you remember everything and everything is important and stands big and full and fills up Time and is so solid that you can walk around and around it like a tree and look at it. You are aware that time passes, that there is a movement in time, but that is not what Time is. Time is not a movement, a flowing, a wind then, but is, rather, a kind of climate in which things are, and when a thing happens it begins to live and keeps on living and stands solid in Time like the tree that you can walk around. And if there is a movement, the movement is not Time itself, no more than a breeze is climate, for all the breeze does is to shake a little the leaves on the tree which is alive and solid. When you are nine, you know that there are things that you don't know, but you know that when you know something you know it. You know how a thing has been and you know that you can go barefoot in June. You do not understand that voice from back in the kitchen which says that you cannot go barefoot outdoors and run to see what has happened and rub your feet over the wet shivery grass and make the perfect mark of your foot in the smooth, creamy, red mud and then muse upon it as though you had suddenly come upon that single mark on the glistening auroral beach of the world. You have never seen a beach, but you have read the book and how the footprint was there.

The voice had said what it had said, and I looked savagely at the black stockings and the strong, scuffed brown shoes which I had brought from my closet as far as the hearth rug. I called once more, "But it's June," and waited.

"It's June," the voice replied from far away, "but it's blackberry winter."

I had lifted my head to reply to that, to make one more test of what was in that tone, when I happened to see the man.

The fireplace in the living room was at the end; for the stone chimney was built, as in so many of the farmhouses in Tennessee, at the end of a gable, and there was a window on each side of the chimney. Out of the window on the north side of the fireplace I could see the man. When I saw the man I did not call out what I had intended, but, engrossed by the strangeness of the sight, watched him, still far off, come along the path by the edge of the woods.

What was strange was that there should be a man there at all. That path went along the yard fence, between the fence and the woods which came right down to the yard, and then on back past the chicken runs and on by the woods until it was lost to sight where the woods bulged out and cut off the back field. There the path disappeared into the woods. It led on back, I knew, through the woods and to the swamp, skirted the swamp where the big trees gave way to sycamores and water oaks and willows and tangled cane, and then led on to the river. Nobody ever went back there except people who wanted to gig frogs in the swamp or to fish in the river or to hunt in the woods, and those people, if they didn't have a standing permission from my father, always stopped to ask permission to cross the farm. But the man whom I now saw wasn't, I could tell even at that distance, a sportsman. And what would a sportsman have been doing down there after a storm? Besides, he was coming from the river, and nobody had gone down there that morning. I knew that for a fact, because if anybody had passed, certainly if a stranger had passed, the dogs would have made a racket and would have been out on him. But this man was coming up from the river and had come up through the woods. I suddenly had a vision of him moving up the grassy path in the woods, in the green twilight under the big trees, not making any sound on the path, while now and then, like drops off the eaves, a big drop of water would fall from a leaf or bough and strike a stiff oak leaf lower down with a small, hollow sound like a drop of water hitting tin. That sound, in the silence of the woods, would be very significant.

When you are a boy and stand in the stillness of woods, which can be so still that your heart almost stops beating and makes you want to stand there in the green twilight until you feel your very feet sinking into and clutching the earth like roots and your body breathing slow through its pores like the leaves—when you stand there and wait for the next drop to drop with its small, flat sound to a lower leaf, that sound seems to measure out something, to put an end to something, to begin something, and you cannot wait for it to happen and are afraid it will not happen, and then when it has happened, you are waiting again, almost afraid.

But the man whom I saw coming through the woods in my mind's eye did not pause and wait, growing into the ground and breathing with the enormous, soundless breathing of the leaves. Instead, I saw him moving in the green twilight inside my head as he was moving at that very moment along the path by the edge of the woods, coming toward the house. He was moving steadily, but not fast, with his shoulders hunched a little and his head thrust forward, like a man who has come a long way and has a long way to go. I shut my eyes for a couple of seconds, thinking that when I opened them he would not be there at all. There was no place for him to have come from, and there was no reason for him to come where he was coming, toward our house. But I opened my eyes, and there he was, and he was coming steadily along the side of the woods. He was not yet even with the back chicken yard.

"Mama," I called.

"You put them on," the voice said.

"There's a man coming," I called, "out back."

She did not reply to that, and I guessed that she had gone to the kitchen window to look. She would be looking at the man and wondering who he was and what he wanted, the way you always do in the country, and if I went back there now she would not notice right off whether or not I was barefoot. So I went back to the kitchen.

She was standing by the window. "I don't recognize him," she said, not looking around at me.

"Where could he be coming from?" I asked.

"I don't know," she said.

"What would he be doing down at the river? At night? In the storm?"

She studied the figure out the window, then said, "Oh, I reckon maybe he cut across from the Dunbar place."

That was, I realized, a perfectly rational explanation. He had not been down at the river in the storm, at night. He had come over this morning. You could cut across from the Dunbar place if you didn't mind breaking through a lot of elder and sassafras and blackberry bushes which had about taken over the old cross path, which nobody ever used any more. That satisfied me for a moment, but only for a moment. "Mama," I asked, "What would he be doing over at the Dunbar place last night?"

Then she looked at me, and I knew I had made a mistake, for she was looking at my bare feet. "You haven't got your shoes on," she said.

But I was saved by the dogs. That instant there was a bark which I recognized as Sam, the collie, and then a heavier, churning kind of bark which was Bully, and I saw a streak of white as Bully tore round the corner of the back porch and headed out for the man. Bully was a big, bone-white bull dog, the kind of dog that they used to call a farm bull dog but that you don't see any more, heavy chested and heavy headed, but with pretty long legs. He could take a fence as light as a hound. He had just cleared the white paling fence toward the woods when my mother ran out to the back porch and began calling, "Here you, Bully! Here you!"

Bully stopped in the path, waiting for the man, but he gave a few more of those deep, gargling, savage barks that reminded you of something down a stone-lined well. The red clay mud, I saw, was splashed up over his white chest and looked exciting, like blood.

The man, however, had not stopped walking even when Bully took the fence and started at him. He had kept right on coming. All he had done was to switch a little paper parcel which he carried from the right hand to the left, and then reach into his pants pocket to get something. Then I saw the glitter and knew that he had a knife in his hand, probably the kind of mean knife just made for devilment and nothing else, with a blade as long as the blade of a frog-sticker, which will snap out ready when you press a button in the handle. That knife must have had a button in the handle, or else how could he have had the blade out glittering so quick and with just one hand?

Pulling his knife against the dogs was a funny thing to do, for Bully was a big, powerful brute and fast, and Sam was all right. If those dogs had meant business, they might have knocked him down and ripped him before he got a stroke in. He ought to have picked up a heavy stick, something to take a swipe at them with and something which they could see and respect when they came at him. But he apparently did not know much about dogs. He just held the knife blade close against the right leg, low down, and kept on moving down the path.

Then my mother had called, and Bully had stopped. So the man let the blade of the knife snap back into the handle, and dropped it into his pocket, and kept on coming. Many women would have been afraid with the strange man who they knew had that knife in his pocket. That is, if they were alone in the house with nobody but a nine-year-old boy. And my mother was alone, for my father had gone off, and Dellie, the cook, was down at her cabin because she wasn't feeling well. But my mother wasn't afraid. She wasn't a big woman, but she was clear and brisk about everything she did and looked everybody and everything right in the eye from her own blue eyes in her tanned face. She had been the first woman in the country to ride a horse astride (that was back when she was a girl and long before I was born), and I have seen her snatch up a pump gun and go out and knock a chicken hawk out of the air like a busted skeet when he came over her chicken yard. She was a steady and self-reliant woman, and when I think of her now after all the years she has been dead, I think of her brown hands, not big, but somewhat square for a woman's hands, with square-cut nails. They looked, as a matter of fact, more like a young boy's hands than a grown woman's. But back then it never crossed my mind that she would ever be dead.

She stood on the back porch and watched the man enter the back gate, where the dogs (Bully had leaped back into the yard) were dancing and muttering and giving sidelong glances back to my mother to see if she meant what she had said. The man walked right by the dogs, almost brushing them, and didn't pay them any attention. I could see now that he wore old khaki pants, and a dark wool coat with stripes in it, and a gray felt hat. He had on a gray shirt with blue stripes in it, and no tie. But I could see a tie, blue and reddish, sticking in his side coat-pocket. Everything was wrong about what he wore. He ought to have been wearing blue jeans or overalls, and a straw hat or an old black felt hat, and the coat, granting that he might have been wearing a wool coat and not a jumper, ought not to have had those stripes. Those clothes, despite the fact that they were old enough and dirty enough for any tramp, didn't belong there in our back yard, coming down the path, in Middle Tennessee, miles away from any big town, and even a mile off the pike.

When he got almost to the steps, without having said anything, my mother, very matter-of-factly, said, "Good morning."

"Good morning," he said, and stopped and looked her over. He did not take off his hat, and under the brim you could see the perfectly unmemorable face, which wasn't old and wasn't young, or thick or thin. It was grayish and covered with about three days of stubble. The eyes were a kind of nondescript, muddy hazel, or something like that, rather bloodshot. His teeth, when he opened his mouth, showed yellow and uneven. A couple of them had been knocked out. You knew that they had been knocked out, because there was a scar, not very old, there on the lower lip just beneath the gap.

"Are you hunting work?" my mother asked him.

"Yes," he said—not "yes, mam"—and still did not take off his hat.

"I don't know about my husband, for he isn't here," she said, and didn't mind a bit telling the tramp, or whoever he was, with the mean knife in his pocket, that no man was around, "but I can give you a few things to do. The storm has drowned a lot of my chicks. Three coops of them. You can gather them up and bury them. Bury them deep so the dogs won't get at them. In the woods. And fix the coops the wind blew over. And down yonder beyond that pen by the edge of the woods are some drowned poults. They got out and I couldn't get them in. Even after it started to rain hard. Poults haven't got any sense."

"What are them things—poults?" he demanded, and spat on the brick walk. He rubbed his foot over the spot, and I saw that he wore a black, pointed-toe low shoe, all cracked and broken. It was a crazy kind of shoe to be wearing in the country.

"Oh, they're young turkeys," my mother was saying. "And they haven't got any sense. I oughtn't to try to raise them around here with so many chickens, anyway. They don't thrive near chickens, even in separate pens. And I won't give up my chickens." Then she stopped herself and resumed briskly on the note of business. "When you finish that, you can fix my flower beds. A lot of trash and mud and gravel has washed down. Maybe you can save some of my flowers if you are careful."

"Flowers," the man said, in a low, impersonal voice which seemed to have a wealth of meaning, but a meaning which I could not fathom. As I think back on it, it probably was not pure contempt. Rather, it was a kind of impersonal and distant marveling that he should be on the verge of grubbing in a flower bed. He said the word, and then looked off across the yard.

"Yes, flowers," my mother replied with some asperity, as though she would have nothing said or implied against flowers. "And they were very fine this year." Then she stopped and looked at the man. "Are you hungry?" she demanded.

"Yeah," he said.

"I'll fix you something," she said, "before you get started." She turned to me. "Show him where he can wash up," she commanded, and went into the house.

I took the man to the end of the porch where a pump was and where a couple of wash pans sat on a low shelf for people to use before they went into the house. I stood there while he laid down his little parcel wrapped in newspaper and took off his hat and looked around for a nail to hang it on. He poured the water and plunged his hands into it. They were big hands, and strong looking, but they did not have the creases and the earth-color of the hands of men who work outdoors. But they were dirty, with black dirt ground into the skin and under the nails. After he had washed his hands, he poured another basin of water and washed his face. He dried his face, and with the towel still dangling in his grasp, stepped over to the mirror on the house wall. He rubbed one hand over the stubble on his face. Then he carefully inspected his face, turning first one side and then the other, and stepped back and settled his striped coat down on his shoulders. He had the movements of a man who had just dressed up to go to church or a party—the way he settled his coat and smoothed it and scanned himself in the mirror.

Then he caught my glance on him. He glared at me for an instant out of the bloodshot eyes, then demanded in a low, harsh voice, "What you looking at?"

"Nothing," I managed to say, and stepped back a step from him.

He flung the towel down, crumpled, on the shelf, and went toward the kitchen door and entered without knocking.

My mother said something to him which I could not catch. I started to go in again, then thought about my bare feet, and decided to go back of the chicken yard, where the man would have to come to pick up the dead chicks. I hung around behind the chicken house until he came out.

He moved across the chicken yard with a fastidious, not quite finicking motion, looking down at the curdled mud flecked with bits of chicken-droppings. The mud curled up over the soles of his black shoes. I stood back from him some six feet and watched him pick up the first of the drowned chicks. He held it up by one foot and inspected it.

There is nothing deader looking than a drowned chick. The feet curl in that feeble, empty way which back when I was a boy, even if I was a country boy who did not mind hog-killing or frog-gigging, made me feel hollow in the stomach. Instead of looking plump and fluffy, the body is stringy and limp with the fluff plastered to it, and the neck is long and loose like a little string of rag. And the eyes have that bluish membrane over them which makes you think of a very old man who is sick about to die.

The man stood there and inspected the chick. Then he looked all around as though he didn't know what to do with it.

"There's a great big old basket in the shed," I said, and pointed to the shed attached to the chicken house.

He inspected me as though he had just discovered my presence, and moved toward the shed.

"There's a spade there, too," I added.

He got the basket and began to pick up the other chicks, picking each one up slowly by a foot and then flinging it into the basket with a nasty, snapping motion. Now and then he would look at me out of the bloodshot eyes. Every time he seemed on the verge of saying something, but he did not. Perhaps he was building up to say something to me, but I did not wait that long. His way of looking at me made me so uncomfortable that I left the chicken yard.

Besides, I had just remembered that the creek was in flood, over the bridge, and that people were down there watching it. So I cut across the farm toward the creek. When I got to the big tobacco field I saw that it had not suffered much. The land lay right and not many tobacco plants had washed out of the ground. But I knew that a lot of tobacco round the country had been washed right out. My father had said so at breakfast.

My father was down at the bridge. When I came out of the gap in the osage hedge into the road, I saw him sitting on his mare over the heads of the other men who were standing around, admiring the flood. The creek was big here, even in low water; for only a couple of miles away it ran into the river, and when a real flood came, the red water got over the pike where it dipped down to the bridge, which was an iron bridge, and high over the floor and even the side railings of the bridge. Only the upper iron work would show, with the water boiling and frothing red and white around it. That creek rose so fast and so heavy because a few miles back it came down out of the hills, where the gorges filled up with water in no time when a rain came. The creek ran in a deep bed with limestone bluffs along both sides until I got within three quarters of a mile of the bridge, and when it came out from between those bluffs in flood it was boiling and hissing and steaming like water from a fire house.

Whenever there was a flood, people from half the county would come down to see the sight. After a gully-washer there would not be any work to do anyway. If it didn't ruin your crop, you couldn't plow and you felt like taking a holiday to celebrate it. If it did ruin your crop, there wasn't anything to do except to try to take your mind off the mortgage, if you were rich enough to have a mortgage, and if you couldn't afford a mortgage you needed something to take your mind off how hungry you would be by Christmas. So people would come down to the bridge and look at the flood. It made something different from the run of days.

There would not be much talking after the first few minutes of trying to guess how high the water was this time. The men and kids just stood around, or sat their horses or mules, as the case might be, or stood up in the wagon beds. They looked at the strangeness of the flood for an hour or two, and then somebody would say that he had better be getting on home to dinner and would start walking down the gray, puddled limestone pike, or would touch heel to his mount and start off. Everybody always knew what it would be like when he got down to the bridge, but people always came. It was like church or a funeral. They always came, that is, if it was summer and the flood unexpected. Nobody ever came down in winter to see high water.

When I came out of the gap in the bowdock hedge, I saw the crowd, perhaps fifteen or twenty men and a lot of kids, and saw my father sitting his mare, Nellie Gray. He was a tall, limber man and carried himself well.

I was always proud to see him sit a horse, he was so quiet and straight, and when I stepped through the gap of the hedge that morning, the first thing that happened was, I remember, the warm feeling I always had when I saw him up on a horse, just sitting. I did not go toward him, but skirted the crowd on the far side, to get a look at the creek. For one thing, I was not sure what he would say about the fact that I was barefoot. But the first thing I knew, I heard his voice calling, "Seth!"

I went toward him, moving apologetically past the men, who bent their large, red or thin, sallow faces above me. I knew some of the men, and knew their names, but because those I knew were there in a crowd, mixed with the strange faces, they seemed foreign to me, and not friendly. I did not look up at my father until I was almost within touching distance of his heel. Then I looked up and tried to read his face, to see if he was angry about my being barefoot. Before I could decide anything from that impassive, high-boned face, he had leaned over and reached a hand to me. "Grab on," he commanded.

I grabbed on and gave a little jump, and he said, "Up-see-daisy!" and whisked me, light as a feather, up to the pommel of his McClellan saddle.

"You can see better up here," he said, slid back on the cantle a little to make me more comfortable, and then, looking over my head at the swollen, tumbling water, seemed to forget all about me. But his right hand was laid on my side, just above my thigh, to steady me.

I was sitting there as quiet as I could, feeling the faint stir of my father's chest against my shoulders as it rose and fell with his breath, when I saw the cow. At first, looking up the creek, I thought it was just another big piece of driftwood steaming down the creek in the ruck of water, but all at once a pretty good-size boy who had climbed part way up a telephone pole by the pike so that he could see better yelled out, "Golly-damn, look at that-air cow!"

Everybody looked. It was a cow all right, but it might just as well have been driftwood; for it was dead as a chunk, rolling and rolling down the creek, appearing and disappearing, feet up or head up, it didn't matter which.

The cow started up the talk again. Somebody wondered whether it would hit one of the clear places under the top girder of the bridge and get through or whether it would get tangled in the drift and trash that had piled against the upright girders and braces. Somebody remembered how about ten years before so much driftwood had piled up on the bridge that it was knocked off its foundations. Then the cow hit. It hit the edge of the drift against one of the girders, and hung there. For a few seconds it seemed as though it might tear loose, but then we saw that it was really caught. It bobbed and heaved on its side there in a slow, grinding, uneasy fashion. It had a yoke around its neck, the kind made out of a forked limb to keep a jumper behind fence.

"She shore jumped one fence," one of the men said.

And another: "Well, she done jumped her last one, fer a fack."

Then they began to wonder about whose cow it might be. They decided it must belong to Milt Alley. They said that he had a cow that was a jumper, and kept her in a fenced-in piece of ground up the creek. I had never seen Milt Alley, but I knew who he was. He was a squatter and lived up the hills a way, on a shirt-tail patch of set-on-edge land, in a cabin. He was pore white trash. He had lots of children. I had seen the children at school, when they came. They were thin-faced, with straight, sticky-looking, dough-colored hair, and they smelled something like old sour buttermilk, not because they drank so much buttermilk but because that is the sort of smell which children out of those cabins tend to have. The big Alley boy drew dirty pictures and showed them to the little boys at school.

That was Milt Alley's cow. It looked like the kind of cow he would have, a scrawny, old, sway-backed cow, with a yoke around her neck. I wondered if Milt Alley had another cow.

"Poppa," I said, "do you think Milt Alley has got another cow?"

"You say 'Mr. Alley,' " my father said quietly.

"Do you think he has?"

"No telling," my father said.

Then a big gangly boy, about fifteen, who was sitting on a scraggly little old mule with a piece of croker sack thrown across the saw-tooth spine, and who had been staring at the cow, suddenly said to nobody in particular, "Reckin anybody ever et drownt cow?"

He was the kind of boy who might just as well as not have been the son of Milt Alley, with his faded and patched overalls ragged at the bottom of the pants and the mud-stiff brogans hanging off his skinny, bare ankles at the level of the mule's belly. He had said what he did, and then looked embarrassed and sullen when all the eyes swung at him. He hadn't meant to say it, I am pretty sure now. He would have been too proud to say it, just as Milt Alley would have been too proud. He had just been thinking out loud, and the words had popped out.

There was an old man standing there on the pike, an old man with a white beard. "Son," he said to the embarrassed and sullen boy on the mule, "you live long enough and you'll find a man will eat anything when the time comes."

"Time gonna come fer some folks this year," another man said.

"Son," the old man said, "in my time I et things a man don't like to think on. I was a sojer and I rode with Gin'l Forrest, and them things we et when the time come. I tell you. I et meat what got up and run when you taken out yore knife to cut a slice to put on the fire. You had to knock it down with a carbeen butt, it was so active. That-air meat would jump like a bullfrog, it was so full of skippers."

But nobody was listening to the old man. The boy on the mule turned his sullen sharp face from him, dug a heel into the side of the mule and went off up the pike with a motion which made you think that any second you would hear mule bones clashing inside that lank and scrofulous hide.

"Cy Dundee's boy," a man said, and nodded toward the figure going up the pike on the mule.

"Reckin Cy Dundee's young-uns seen times they'd settle fer drownt cow," another man said.

The old man with the beard peered at them both from his weak, slow eyes, first at one and then at the other. "Live long enough," he said, "and a man will settle fer what he kin git."

Then there was silence again, with the people looking at the red, foam-flecked water.

My father lifted the bridle rein in his left hand, and the mare turned and walked around the group and up the pike. We rode on up to our big gate, where my father dismounted to open it and let me myself ride Nellie Gray through. When he got to the lane that led off from the drive about two hundred yards from our house, my father said, "Grab on." I grabbed on, and he let me down to the ground. "I'm going to ride down and look at my corn," he said. "You go on." He took the lane, and I stood there on the drive and watched him ride off. He was wearing cowhide boots and an old hunting coat, and I thought that that made him look very military, like a picture. That and the way he rode.

I did not go the house. Instead, I went by the vegetable garden and crossed behind the stables, and headed down for Dellie's cabin. I wanted to go down and play with Jebb, who was Dellie's little boy about two years older than I was. Besides, I was cold. I shivered as I walked, and I had goose-flesh. The mud which crawled up between my toes with every step I took was like ice. Dellie would have a fire, but she wouldn't make me put on shoes and stockings.

Dellie's cabin was of logs, with one side, because it was on a slope, set on limestone chunks, with a little porch attached to it, and had a little whitewashed fence around it and a gate with plow-points on a wire to clink when somebody came in, and had two big white oaks in the yard and some flowers and a nice privy in the back with some honeysuckle growing over it. Dellie and Old Jebb, who was Jebb's father and who lived with Dellie and had lived with her for twenty-five years even if they never had got married, were careful to keep everything nice around their cabin. They had the name all over the community for being clean and clever Negroes. Dellie and Jebb were what they used to call "white-folks' niggers." There was a big difference between their cabin and the other two cabins farther down where the other tenants lived. My father kept the other cabins weatherproof, but he couldn't undertake to go down and pick up after the litter they strewed. They didn't take the trouble to have a vegetable patch like Dellie and Jebb or to make preserves from wild plum, and jelly from crab apple the way Dellie did. They were shiftless, and my father was always threatening to get shed of them. But he never did. When they finally left, they just up and left on their own, for no reason, to go and be shiftless somewhere else. Then some more came. But meanwhile they lived down there, Matt Rawson and his family, and Sid Turner and his, and I played with their children all over the farm when they weren't working. But when I wasn't around they were mean sometimes to Little Jebb. That was because the other tenants down there were jealous of Dellie and Jebb.

I was so cold that I ran the last fifty yards to Dellie's gate. As soon as I had entered the yard, I saw that the storm had been hard on Dellie's flowers. The yard was, as I have said, on a slight slope, and the water running across had gutted the flower beds and washed out all the good black woods-earth which Dellie had brought in. What little grass there was in the yard was plastered sparsely down on the ground, the way the drainage water had left it. It reminded me of the way the fluff was plastered down on the skin of the drowned chicks that the strange man had been picking up, up in my mother's chicken yard.

I took a few steps up the path to the cabin, and then I saw that the drainage water had washed a lot of trash and filth out from under Dellie's house. Up toward the porch, the ground was not clean any more. Old pieces of rag, two or three rusted cans, pieces of rotten rope, some hunks of old dog dung, broken glass, old paper, and all sorts of things like that had washed out from under Dellie's house to foul her clean yard. It looked just as bad as the yards of the other cabins, or worse. It was worse, as a matter of fact, because it was a surprise. I had never thought of all that filth being under Dellie's house. It was not anything against Dellie that the stuff had been under the cabin. Trash will get under any house. But I did not think of that when I saw the foulness which had washed out on the ground which Dellie sometimes used to sweep with a twig broom to make nice and clean.

I picked my way past the filth, being careful not to get my bare feet on it, and mounted to Dellie's door. When I knocked, I heard her voice telling me to come in.

It was dark inside the cabin, after the daylight, but I could make out Dellie piled up in bed under a quilt, and Little Jebb crouched by the hearth, where a low fire simmered. "Howdy," I said to Dellie, "how you feeling?"

Her big eyes, the whites surprising and glaring in the black face, fixed on me as I stood there, but she did not reply. It did not look like Dellie, or act like Dellie, who would grumble and bustle around our kitchen, talking to herself, scolding me or Little Jebb, clanking pans, making all sorts of unnecessary noises and mutterings like an old-fashioned black steam thrasher engine when it has got up an extra head of steam and keeps popping the governor and rumbling and shaking on its wheels. But now Dellie just lay there on the bed, under the patchwork quilt, and turned the black face, which I scarcely recognized, and the glaring white eyes to me.

"How you feeling?" I repeated.

"I'se sick," the voice said croakingly out of the strange black face which was not attached to Dellie's big, squat body, but stuck out from under a pile of tangled bedclothes. Then the voice added: "Mighty sick."

"I'm sorry," I managed to say.

The eyes remained fixed on me for a moment, then they left me and the head rolled back on the pillow. "Sorry," the voice said, in a flat way which wasn't question or statement of anything. It was just the empty word put into the air with no meaning or expression, to float off like a feather or a puff of smoke, while the big eyes, with the whites like the peeled white of hard-boiled eggs, stared at the ceiling.

"Dellie," I said after a minute, "there's a tramp up at the house. He's got a knife."

She was not listening. She closed her eyes.

I tiptoed over to the hearth where Jebb was and crouched beside him. We began to talk in low voices. I was asking him to get out his train and play train. Old Jebb had put spool wheels on three cigar boxes and put wire links between the boxes to make a train for Jebb. The box that was the locomotive had the top closed and a length of broom stick for a smoke stack. Jebb didn't want to get the train out, but I told him I would go home if he didn't. So he got out the train, and the colored rocks, and fossils of crinoid stems, and other junk he used for the load, and we began to push it around, talking the way we thought trainmen talked, making a chuck-chucking sound under the breath for the noise of the locomotive and now and then uttering low, cautious toots for the whistle. We got so interested in playing train that the toots got louder. Then, before he thought, Jebb gave a good, loud *toot-toot*, blowing for a crossing.

"Come here," the voice said from the bed.

Jebb got up slow from his hands and knees, giving me a sudden, naked, inimical look.

"Come here!" the voice said.

Jebb went to the bed. Dellie propped herself weakly up on one arm, muttering, "Come closer."

Jebb stood closer.

"Last thing I do, I'm gonna do it," Dellie said. "Done tole you to be quiet."

Then she slapped him. It was an awful slap, more awful for the kind of weakness which it came from and brought to focus. I had seen her slap Jebb before, but the slapping had always been the kind of easy slap you would expect from a good-natured, grumbling Negro woman like Dellie. But this was different. It was awful. It was so awful that Jebb didn't make a sound. The tears just popped out and ran down his face, and his breath came sharp, like gasps.

Dellie fell back. "Cain't even be sick," she said to the ceiling. "Git sick and they won't even let you lay. They tromp all over you. Cain't even be sick." Then she closed her eyes.

I went out of the room. I almost ran getting to the door, and I did run across the porch and down the steps and across the yard, not caring whether or not I stepped on the filth which had washed out from under the cabin. I ran almost all the way home. Then I thought about my mother catching me with the bare feet. So I went down to the stables.

I heard a noise in the crib, and opened the door. There was Big Jebb, sitting on an old nail keg, shelling corn into a bushel basket. I went in, pulling the door shut behind me, and crouched on the floor near him. I crouched there for a couple of minutes before either of us spoke, and watched him shelling the corn.

He had very big hands, knotted and grayish at the joints, with callused palms which seemed to be streaked with rust with the rust coming up between the fingers to show from the back. His hands were so strong and tough that he could take a big ear of corn and rip the grains right off the cob with the palm of his hand, all in one motion, like a machine. "Work long as me," he would say, "and the good Lawd'll give you a hand lak cass-ion won't nuthin' hurt." And his hands did look like cast iron, old cast iron streaked with rust.

He was an old man, up in his seventies, thirty years or more older than Dellie, but he was strong as a bull. He was a squat sort of man, heavy in the shoulders, with remarkably long arms the kind of build they say the river natives have on the Congo from paddling so much in their boats. He had a round bullet-head, set on powerful shoulders. His skin was very black, and the thin hair on his head was now grizzled like tufts of old cotton batting. He had small eyes and a flat nose, not big, and the kindest and wisest old face in the world, the blunt, sad, wise face of an old animal peering tolerantly out on the goings-on of the merely human creatures before him. He was a good man, and I loved him next to my mother and father. I crouched there on the floor of the crib and watched him shell corn with the rusty cast-iron hands, while he looked down at me out of the little eyes set in the blunt face.

"Dellie says she's mighty sick," I said.

"Yeah," he said.

"What's she sick from?"

"Woman-mizry," he said.

"What's woman-mizry?"

"Hit comes on 'em," he said. "Hit just comes on 'em when the time comes."

"What is it?"

"Hit is the change," he said. "Hit is the change of life and time."

"What changes?"

"You too young to know."

"Tell me."

"Time come and you find out everything."

I knew that there was no use in asking him any more. When I asked him things and he said that, I always knew that he would not tell me. So I continued to crouch there and watch him. Now that I had sat there a little while, I was cold again.

"What you shiver fer?" he asked me.

"I'm cold. I'm cold because it's blackberry winter," I said.

"Maybe 'tis and maybe 'tain't," he said.

"My mother says it is."

"Ain't sayen Miss Sallie doan know and ain't sayen she do. But folks doan know everything."

"Why isn't it blackberry winter?"

"Too late fer blackberry winter. Blackberries done bloomed."

"She said it was."

"Blackberry winter just a leetle cold spell. Hit come and then hit go away, and hit is growed summer of a sudden lak a gunshot. Ain't no tellen hit will go way this time."

"It's June," I said.

"June," he replied with great contempt. "That what folks say. What June mean? Maybe hit is come cold to stay."

"Why?"

"Cause this-here old yearth is tahrd. Hit is tahrd and ain't gonna perduce. Lawd let hit come rain one time forty days and forty nights, 'cause He was tahrd of sinful folks. Maybe this-here old yearth say to the Lawd, Lawd, I done plum tahrd. Lawd, lemme rest. And Lawd say,

Yearth, you done yore best, you give 'em cawn and you give 'em taters, and all they think on is they gut, and, Yearth, you kin take a rest."

"What will happen?"

"Folks will eat up everything. The yearth won't perduce no more. Folks cut down all the trees and burn 'em cause they cold, and the yearth won't grow no more. I been tellen 'em. I been tellen folks. Sayen, maybe this year, hit is the time. But they doan listen to me, how the yearth is tahrd. Maybe this year they find out."

"Will everything die?"

"Everything and everybody, hit will be so."

"This year?"

"Ain't no tellen. Maybe this year."

"My mother said it is blackberry winter," I said confidently, and got up.

"Ain't sayen nuthin' agin Miss Sallie," he said.

I went to the door of the crib. I was really cold. Running, I had got up a sweat and now I was worse.

I hung on the door, looking at Jebb, who was shelling corn again.

"There's a tramp came to the house," I said. I had almost forgotten the tramp.

"Yeah."

"He came by the back way. What was he doing down there in the storm?"

"They comes and they goes," he said, "ain't no tellen."

"He had a mean knife."

"The good ones and the bad ones, they comes and they goes. Storm or sun, light or dark. They is folks and they comes and they goes lak folks."

I hung on the door, shivering.

He studied me a moment, then said, "You git on to the house. You ketch yore death. Then what yore mammy say?"

I hesitated.

"You git," he said.

When I came to the back yard, I saw that my father was standing by the back porch and the tramp was walking toward him. They began talking before I reached them, but I got there just as my father was saying, "I'm sorry, but I haven't got any work. I got all the hands on the place I need now. I won't need any extra until wheat thrashing."

The stranger made no reply, just looked at my father.

My father took out his leather coin purse, and got out a half-dollar. He held it toward the man. "This is for half a day," he said.

The man looked at the coin, and then at my father, making no motion to take the money. But that was the right amount. A dollar a day was what you paid them back in 1910. And the man hadn't even worked half a day.

Then the man reached out and took the coin. He dropped it into the right side pocket of his coat. Then he said, very slowly and without feeling: "I didn't want to work on your —— farm."

He used the word which they would have frailed me to death for using.

I looked at my father's face and it was streaked white under the sunburn. Then he said, "Get off this place. Get off this place or I won't be responsible."

The man dropped his right hand into his pants pocket. It was the pocket where he kept the knife. I was just about to yell to my father about the knife when the hand came back out with nothing in it. The man gave a kind of twisted grin, showing where the teeth had been knocked out above the new scar. I thought that instant how maybe he had tried before to pull a knife on somebody else and had got his teeth knocked out.

So now he just gave that twisted, sickish grin out of the unmemorable, grayish face, and then spat on the brick path. The glob landed just about six inches from the toe of my father's right boot. My father looked down at it, and so did I. I thought that if that glob had hit my father's boot something would have happened. I looked down and saw the bright glob, and on one side of it my father's strong cowhide boots, with the brass eyelets and the leather thongs, heavy boots splashed with good red mud and set solid on the bricks, and on the other side the pointed-toe, broken, black shoes, on which the mud looked so sad and out of place. Then I saw one of the black shoes move a little, just a twitch first, then a real step backward.

The man moved in a quarter circle to the end of the porch, with my father's steady gaze upon him all the while. At the end of the porch, the man reached up to the shelf where the wash pans were to get his little newspaper-wrapped parcel. Then he disappeared around the corner of the house and my father mounted the porch and went into the kitchen without a word.

I followed around the house to see what the man would do. I wasn't afraid of him now, no matter if he did have the knife. When I got around in front, I saw him going out the yard gate and starting up the drive toward the pike. So I ran to catch up with him. He was sixty yards or so up the drive before I caught up.

I did not walk right up even with him at first, but trailed him, the way a kid will, about seven or eight feet behind, now and then running two or three steps in order to hold my place against his longer stride. When I first came up behind him, he turned to give me a look, just a meaningless look, and then fixed his eyes up the drive and kept on walking.

When we had got around the bend in the drive which cut the house from sight, and were going along by the edge of the woods, I decided to come up even with him. I ran a few steps, and was by his side, or almost, but some feet off to the right. I walked along in this position for a while, and he never noticed me. I walked along until we got within sight of the big gate that let on the pike.

Then I said: "Where did you come from?"

He looked at me then with a look which seemed almost surprised that I was there. Then he said, "It ain't none of yore business."

We went on another fifty feet.

Then I said, "Where are you going?"

He stopped, studied me dispassionately for a moment, then suddenly took a step toward me and leaned his face down at me. The lips jerked back, but not in any grin, to show where the teeth were knocked out and to make the scar on the lower lip come white with the tension.

He said: "Stop following me. You don't stop following me and I cut yore throat, you little son-of-a-bitch."

Then he went on to the gate, and up the pike.

That was thirty-five years ago. Since that time my father and mother have died. I was still a boy: but a big boy, when my father got cut on the blade of a mowing machine and died of lockjaw. My mother sold the place and went to town to live with her sister. But she never took hold after my father's death, and she died within three years, right in middle life. My aunt always said, "Sallie just died of a broken heart, she was so devoted." Dellie is dead, too, but she died, I heard, quite a long time after we sold the farm.

As for Little Jebb, he grew up to be a mean and ficey Negro. He killed another Negro in a fight and got sent to the penitentiary, where he is yet, the last I heard tell. He probably grew up to be mean and ficey from just being picked on so much by the children of the other tenants, who were jealous of Jebb and Dellie for being thrifty and clever and being white-folks' niggers.

Old Jebb lived forever. I saw him ten years ago and he was about a hundred then, and not looking much different. He was living in town then, on relief—that was back in the Depression—when I went to see him. He said to me: "Too strong to die. When I was a young feller just comen on and seen how things wuz, I prayed the Lawd. I said, Oh, Lawd, gimme strength and make me strong fer to do and in-dure. The Lawd hearkened to my prayer. He give me strength. I was in-duren proud fer being strong and me much man. The Lawd give me my prayer and my strength. But now He done gone off and fergot me and left me alone with my strength. A man doan know what to pray fer, and him mortal."

Jebb is probably living yet, as far as I know.

That is what has happened since the morning when the tramp leaned his face down at me and showed his teeth and said: "Stop following me. You don't stop following me and I cut yore throat, you little son-of-a-bitch." That was what he said, for me not to follow him. But I did follow him, all the years.

"BLACKBERRY WINTER": A RECOLLECTION

Robert Penn Warren

I REMEMBER with peculiar distinctness the writing of this story, especially the balance, tension, interplay—or what you will—between a sense of compulsion, a sense that the story was writing itself, and the flashes of self-consciousness and self-criticism. I suppose that in all attempts at writing there is some such balance, or oscillation, but here the distinction between the two aspects of the process was peculiarly marked, between the ease and the difficulty, between the elation and, I am tempted to say, the pain. But the pain, strangely enough, seemed to be attached to the compulsion, as though in some way I did not want to go into that remembered world, and the elation attached to the critical effort I had to make to ride herd on the wrangle of things that came milling into my head. Or perhaps the truth is that the process was more complicated than that and I shall never know the truth, even in the limited, provisional way the knowing of truth is possible in such matters.

It crosses my mind that the vividness with which I have always remembered the writing of this story may have something to do with the situation in which it was written. It was the fall or winter of 1945–46 just after the war, and even if one had had no hand in the blood-letting, there was the sense that the world, and one's own life, would never be the same again. I was then reading Herman Melville's poetry, and remember being profoundly impressed by "The Conflict of Convictions," a poem about the coming of the American Civil War. Whatever the rights and wrongs of the matter, the war, Melville said, would show "the slimed foundations" of the world. There was the sense in 1945, even with victory, that we had seen the slimed foundations, and as I now write this, the image that comes into my mind is the homely one from my story— the trash washed by the storm from under Dellie's cabin to foul her pridefully clean yard. And I should not be surprised if the picture in the story had its roots in the line from Melville as well as in such a fact, seen a hundred times in my rural boyhood. So the mixed feelings I had in our moment of victory in 1945, Melville's poem, and not only the image of Dellie's cabin, but something of the whole import of my little story, belong, it seems, in the same package.

For a less remote background, I had just finished two long pieces of work, a novel called *All the King's Men* and a critical study of Coleridge's poem *The Ancient Mariner*, both of which had been on my mind for years. Both those things were impersonal, about as impersonal as the work of any man's hand can be said to be. Even though much of my personal feeling had been drawn into both projects, they belonged to worlds very different from my own. At that time, too, I was living in a very cramped apartment over a garage, in a big, modern, blizzard-bit northern city, again a place very different from the world of my story.

In my daily life, I certainly was not thinking about and remembering that world. I suppose I was living in some anxiety about the fate of the two forthcoming pieces of work, on which I had staked much, and in the unspoken, even denied, conviction that some sort of watershed of life and experience was being approached. For one thing, the fortieth birthday, lately passed, and the sense of let-down after the long period of intense work, could account, in part at least, for that feeling.

Out of this situation the story began, but it began by a kind of accident. Some years earlier, I had written a story about a Tennessee sharecropper, a bad story that had never been published. Now I thought I saw a way to improve it. I don't know whether I actually sat down to rewrite the story that was to have the new avatar of "The Patented Gate and the Mean Hamburger," or whether I got sidetracked into "Blackberry Winter" first. In any case, I was going back into a primal world of recollection. I was fleeing, if you wish. Hunting old bearings and benchmarks, if you wish. Trying to make a fresh start, if you wish. Whatever people do in their doubleness of living in a present and a past.

I recollect the particular thread that led me back into that past: the feeling you have when, after vacation begins, you are allowed to go barefoot. Not that I ever liked to go barefoot, not with my bony feet. But the privilege itself was important, a declaration of independence from the tyranny of winter and school and, even, your own family. It was like what the anthropologists call a rite of passage. But it had another meaning, too. It carried you back into a dream of nature, the woods not the house was now your natural habitat, the stream not the street. Looking out into the snow-banked alley of that iron latitude where I now lived, I had a vague, nostalgic feeling and wondered if spring would ever come. (It finally came—and then on May 5 there was again snow, and the heavy-headed blooms of lilac were beautiful with their hoods of snow and beards of ice.)

With the recollection of going barefoot came another, which had been recurrent over the years: the childhood feeling of betrayal when early summer gets turned upside-down, and all its promises are revoked by the cold-spell, the gully-washer. So by putting those two recollections together, the story got started. I had no idea where it was going, if anywhere. Sitting at the typewriter was merely a way of indulging nostalgia. But something has to happen in a story, if there is to be more than a dreary lyric poem posing as a story to promote the cause of universal boredom and deliquescent prose. Something had to happen, and the simplest thing ever to have happen is to say: *Enter, mysterious stranger.* And so he did.

The tramp who thus walked into the story had been waiting a long time in the wings of my imagination—an image drawn, no doubt, from a dozen unremembered episodes of childhood, the city bum turned country tramp, suspicious, resentful, contemptuous of hick dumbness, bringing his own brand of violence into a world where he half-expected to find another kind, enough unlike his own to make him look over his shoulder down the empty lane as dusk came on, a creature altogether lost and pitiful, a dim image of what, in one perspective, our human condition is. But then, at that moment, I was merely thinking of the impingement of his loose-footedness and lostness on a stable and love-defined world of childhood.

Before the tramp actually appeared, I had, however, known he was coming, and without planning I began to write the fourth paragraph of the story, about the difference between what time is when we have grown up and what it was when we stood on what, in my fancy phrase in the story, I called the glistening auroral beach of the world—a phrase which belonged, by the way, to an inland boy who had never seen a beach but whose dreams were all of the sea. Now the tramp came up, not merely out of the woods, but out of the darkening grown-up world of time.

The tramp had, literally, come up through the river woods, and so in the boy's literal speculations he sees the tramp coming through the woods. By now, however, the natural thematic distinction touched on in relation to time is moving into a pattern, the repetition in fiction of the established notion in a new guise. So when the boy sees the mental image of the tramp coming through the woods, there is the distinction set up between the way a man, particularly such a man as this, would go through woods, and the way a boy can stand in the woods in absolute quiet, almost taking root and growing moss on himself, trying to catch the rhythm, as it were, of that vegetative life, trying to breathe himself into that mode of being.

But what would this other, woodland, vegetative world of being carry with it in human terms—in terms, that is, of what a story must be about? I can promise that the passage was written on impulse, but an impulse conditioned by the idea that there had to be an expressed difference between boy-in-woods and tramp-in-woods, the tramp who doesn't know what a poult is and thinks the final degradation is to mess with a flower bed. And so here we are back to the contrast between the tramp's world and that of childhood innocence appearing in some sense of a rapport between the child and nature, his feeling that he himself might enter that very life of nature.

As soon as the passage was written I knew its import; I was following my nose, trusting, for what they were worth, my powers of association, hoping that those powers would work in relation to a pattern that had begun to emerge as a series of contrasts. And it was natural, therefore, after a few paragraphs about the strangeness and fish-out-of-waterness of the tramp, his not knowing about dogs for example, to have the mother's self-sufficiency set against the tramp's rude, resentful uncertainty, and then have her portrait at the time of the episode set against the time when she would be dead, and only a memory—though back then, of course, in the secure world of changelessness and timelessness, it had never crossed the boy's mind that "she would ever be dead."

The instant I wrote that clause I knew, not how the story would end, for I was still writing by guess and by God, but on what perspective of feeling it would end. I knew that it would end with a kind of detached summary of the work of time, some hint of the adult's grim orientation toward that fact. From now on, the items that came on the natural wash of recollection came not only with their, to me, nostalgic quality, but also with the freighting of the grimmer possibilities of change—the flood, which to the boy is only an exciting spectacle but which will mean hunger to others, the boy's unconscious contempt for poor white-trash like Milt Alley, the recollection of hunger by the old man who had ridden with Forrest, Dellie suffering in her "woman mizry." But before I had got to Dellie, I already had Old Jebb firmly in mind, with some faint sense of the irony of having his name remind one—or at least me—of the dashing Confederate cavalryman killed at Yellow Tavern.

Perhaps what I finally did with Dellie stemmed, in fact, from the name I gave Old Jebb. Even if the boy would see no irony in that echo of J. E. B. Stuart's fame, he would get a shock when Dellie slapped her beloved son, and would sense that that blow was, in some deep way, a blow at him. I knew this, for I knew the inside of that prideful cabin, and the shock of early recognition that beneath mutual kindliness and regard some dark, tragic, unresolved something lurked. And with that scene with Dellie, I felt I was forecasting the role of the tramp in the story. The story, to put it in another way, was now shifting emphasis from the lyricism of nostalgia to a concern with the jags and injustices of human relationships. What had earlier come in unconsciously, reportorially, in regard to Milt Alley now got a conscious formulation.

I have said that the end was by now envisaged as a kind of summary of the work of time on the human relationships. But it could not afford to be a mere summary: I wanted some feeling for the boy's family and Jebb's family to shine through the flat surface. Now it struck me that I might build this summary with Jebb as a kind of pilot for the feeling I wanted to get; that is, by accepting, in implication at least, something of Jebb's feeling about his own life, we might become aware of our human communion. I wanted the story to give some notion that out of change and loss a human recognition may be redeemed, more precious for being no longer innocent. So I wrote the summary.

When I had finished the next to the last paragraph I still did not know what to do with my tramp. He had already snarled at the boy, and gone, but I sensed that in the pattern of things his meaning would have to coalesce with the meaning I hoped to convey in the summary about the characters. Then, for better or worse, there it was. In his last anger and frustration, the tramp had said to the boy: "You don't stop following me and I cut yore throat, you little son-of-a-bitch."

Had the boy then stopped or not? Yes, of course, literally, in the muddy lane. But at another level—no. Insofar as later he had grown up, had really learned something of the meaning of life, he had been bound to follow the tramp all his life, in the imaginative recognition, with all the responsibility which such a recognition entails, of this lost, mean, defeated, cowardly, worthless, bitter being as somehow a man.

So what had started out for me as, perhaps, an act of escape, of fleeing back into the simplicities of childhood, had turned, as it always must if we accept the logic of our lives, into an attempt to bring something meaningfully out of that simple past into the complication of the present. And what had started out as a personal indulgence had tried to be, in the end, an impersonal generalization about experience, as a story must always try to be if it accepts the logic of fiction. And now, much later, I see that the story and the novel which I had then only lately finished, as well as the study of Coleridge, all bore on the same end.

I would give a false and foolish impression if I were to imply that I think this to be the only way a story should be written, or that this is the only way I myself have ever written stories. As a matter of fact, most of my stories and all of my novels (except two unpublished ones) have started very differently, from some objective situation or episode, observed or read about, something that caught my eye and imagination so that feeling and interpretation began to flow in. And I sometimes think it strange that the last story I ever wrote and presumably the last I shall ever write (for poems are great devourers of stories) should have sprung so instinctively from the world of simple recollection—not a blackberry winter at all, but a kind of Indian summer.

I would give a false impression, too, if I were to imply that this story is autobiographical. It is not. I never knew these particular people, only that world and people like them. And no tramp ever leaned down at me and said for me to stop following him or he would cut my throat. But if one had, I hope that I might have been able to follow him anyway, in the way the boy in the story does.

7

Stories for Reading

These stories are here primarily to be enjoyed—and to give to the reader additional examples of the almost infinite variety of short fiction. But if enjoyment is to be had at its fullest, the reader must first grasp that in reading fiction, as in most things in life—for instance, playing tennis or running a bank or raising a family—intelligent participation, not passivity, stimulates enjoyment.

Specifically, here the reader should try to arrive at the fullest possible understanding as an aspect of the fullest possible imaginative participation in the stories. One is not possible without the other. You should ask your self leading questions and try seriously to answer them. And these questions should involve not only meaning but *method*; for, as we have long since seen, these two things are intimately related—are, in fact, often aspects of the same thing, the story itself. But beyond this, the effort to exercise imaginative feeling in dealing with character and action is necessary. When you read a story, you are playing a role—or several roles.

FERN

Jean Toomer

FACE flowed into her eyes. Flowed in soft cream foam and plaintive ripples, in such a way that wherever your glance may momentarily have rested, it immediately thereafter wavered in the direction of her eyes. The soft suggestion of down slightly darkened, like the shadow of a bird's wing might, the creamy brown color of her upper lip. Why, after noticing it, you sought her eyes, I cannot tell you. Her nose was aquiline, Semitic. If you have heard a Jewish cantor sing, if he has touched you and made your own sorrow seem trivial when compared with his, you will know my feeling when I follow the curves of her profile, like mobile rivers, to their common delta. They were strange eyes. In this, that they sought nothing—that is, nothing that was obvious and tangible and that one could see, and they gave the impression that nothing was to be denied. When a woman seeks, you will have observed, her eyes deny. Fern's eyes desired nothing that you could give her; there was no reason why they should withhold. Men saw her eyes and fooled themselves. Fern's eyes said to them that she was easy. When she was young, a few men took her, but got no joy from it. And then, once done, they felt bound to her (quite unlike their hit and run with other girls), felt as though it would take them a lifetime to fulfill an obligation which they could find no name for. They became attached to her, and hungered after finding the barest trace of what she might desire. As she grew up, new men who came to town felt as almost everyone did who ever saw her: that they would not be denied. Men were everlastingly bringing her their bodies. Something inside of her got tired of them, I guess, for I am certain that for the life of her she could not tell why or how she began to turn them off. A man in fever is no trifling thing to send away. They began to leave her, baffled and ashamed, yet vowing to themselves that some day they would do some fine thing for her: send her candy every week and not let her know whom it came from, watch out for her wedding-day and give her a magnificent something with no name on it, buy a house and deed it to her, rescue her from some unworthy fellow who had tricked her into marrying him. As you know, men are apt to idolize or fear that which they cannot understand, especially if it be a woman. She did not deny them, yet the fact was that they were denied. A sort of superstition crept into their consciousness of her being somehow above them. Being above them meant that she was not to be approached by anyone. She became a virgin. Now a virgin in a small southern town is by no means the usual thing, if you will believe me. That the sexes were made to mate is the practice of the South. Particularly, black folks were made to mate. And it is black folks whom I have been talking about thus far. What white men thought of Fern I can arrive at only by analogy. They let her alone.

Anyone, of course, could see her, could see her eyes. If you walked up the Dixie Pike most any time of day, you'd be most like to see her resting listless-like on the railing of her porch, back propped against a post, head tilted a little forward because there was a nail in the porch post just where her head came which for some reason or other she never took the trouble to pull out. Her eyes, if it were sunset, rested idly where the sun, molten and glorious, was pouring down between the fringe of pines. Or maybe they gazed at the gray cabin on the knoll from which an evening folk-song was coming. Perhaps they followed a cow that had been turned loose to roam and feed on cotton-stalks and corn leaves. Like as not they'd settle on some vague spot above the horizon, though hardly a trace of wistfulness would come to them. If it were dusk, then they'd wait for the search-light of the evening train which you could see miles up the track before it flared across the Dixie Pike, close to her home. Wherever they looked you'd follow them and then waver back. Like her face, the whole countryside seemed to flow into her eyes. Flowed into them with the soft listless cadence of Georgia's South. A young Negro, once, was looking at her, spellbound, from the road. A white man passing in a buggy had to flick him with his whip if he was to get by without running him over. I first saw her on her porch. I was passing with a fellow whose crusty numbness (I was from the North and suspected of being prejudiced and stuck-up) was melting as he found me warm. I asked him who she was. "That's Fern," was all that I could get from him. Some folks already thought that I was given to nosing around; I let it go at that, so far as questions were concerned. But at first sight of her I felt as if I heard a Jewish cantor sing. As if his singing rose above the unheard chorus of a folk-song. And I felt bound to her. I too had my dreams: something I would do for her. I have knocked about from town to town too much not to know the futility of mere change of place. Besides, picture if you can, this cream-colored solitary girl sitting at a tenement window looking down on the indifferent throngs of Harlem. Better that she listen to folk-songs at dusk in Georgia, you would say, and so would I. Or, suppose she came up North and married. Even a doctor or a lawyer, say, one who would be sure to get along—that is, make money. You and I know who have had experience in such things, that love is not a thing like prejudice which can be bettered by change of town. Could men in Washington, Chicago, or New York, more than the men of Georgia, bring her something left vacant by the bestowal of their bodies? You and I know men in these cities will have to say, they could not. See her out and out a prostitute along State Street in Chicago. See her move into a southern town where white men are more aggressive. See her become a white man's concubine . . . Something I must do for her. There was myself. What could I do for her? Talk, of course. Push back the fringe of pines upon new horizons. To what purpose? and what for? Her? Myself? Men in her case seem to lose their selfishness. I lost mine before I touched her. I ask you, friend (it makes no difference if you sit in the Pullman or the Jim Crow as the train crosses her road), what thoughts would come to you—that is, after you'd finished all the thoughts that leap into men's minds at the sight of a pretty woman who will not deny them; what thoughts would come to you, had you seen her in a quick flash, keen and intuitively, as she sat there on her porch when your train thundered by? Would you have got off at the next station and come back for her to take her where? Would you have completely forgotten her as soon as you reached Macon, Atlanta, Augusta, Pasadena, Madison, Chicago, Boston, or New Orleans? Would you tell your wife or sweetheart about a girl you saw? Your thoughts can help me, and I would like to know. Something I would do for her.

One evening I walked up the Pike on purpose, and stopped to say hello. Some of her family were about, but they moved away to make room for me. Damn if I knew how to begin. Would you? Mr. and Miss So-and-So, people, the weather, the crops, the new preacher, the frolic, the church benefit, rabbit and possum hunting, the new soft drink they had at Old Pap's store, the schedule of the trains, what kind of town Macon was, Negro's migration North, bollweevils, syrup, the Bible—to all these things she gave a yassur or nassur, without further comment. I began to wonder if perhaps me own emotional sensibility had played one of its tricks on me. "Let's take a walk," I at last ventured. The suggestion, coming after so long an isolation, was novel enough, I guess, to surprise. But it wasn't that. Something told me that men before me had said just that as a prelude to the offering of their bodies. I tried to tell her with my eyes. I think she understood. The thing from her that made my throat catch, vanished. Its passing left her visible in a way I'd thought, but never seen. We walked down the Pike with people on all the porches gaping at us. "Doesnt it make you mad?" She meant the row of petty gossiping people. She meant the world. Through a canebrake that was ripe for cutting, the branch was reached. Under a sweet-gum tree, and where reddish leaves had dammed the creek a little, we sat down. Dusk, suggesting the almost imperceptible procession of giant trees, settled with a purple haze about the cane. I felt strange, as I always do in Georgia, particularly at dusk. I felt that things unseen to men were tangibly immediate. It would not have surprised me had I had vision. People have them in Georgia more often than you would suppose. A black woman once saw the mother of Christ and drew her in charcoal on the courthouse wall . . . When one is on the soil of one's ancestors, most anything can come to one. . . From force of habit, I suppose, I held Fern in my arms—that is, without at first noticing it. Then my mind came back to her. Her eyes, unusually weird and open, held me. Held God. He flowed in as I've seen the countryside flow in. Seen men. I must have done something—what, I dont know, in the confusion of my emotion. She sprang up. Rushed some distance from me. Fell to her knees, and began swaying, swaying. Her body was tortured with something it could not let out. Like boiling sap it flooded arms and fingers till she shook them as if they burned her. It found her throat, and spattered inarticulately in plaintive, convulsive sounds, mingled with calls to Christ Jesus. And then she sang, brokenly. A Jewish cantor singing with a broken voice. A child's voice, uncertain, or an old man's. Dusk hid her; I could hear only her song. It seemed to me as though she were pounding her head in anguish upon the ground. I rushed to her. She fainted in my arms.

There was talk about her fainting with me in the canefield. And I got one or two ugly looks from town men who'd set themselves up to protect her. In fact, there was talk of making me leave town. But they never did. They kept a watch-out for me, though. Shortly after, I came back North. From the train window I saw her as I crossed her road. Saw her on her porch, head tilted a little forward where the nail was, eyes vaguely focused on the sunset. Saw her face flow into them, the countryside and something that I call God, flowing into them. . . Nothing ever really happened. Nothing ever came to Fern, not even I. Something I would do for her. Some fine unnamed thing. . . And, friend, you? She is still living, I have reason to know. Her name, against the chance that you might happen down that way, is Fernie May Rosen.

THE BATTLE ROYAL

Ralph Ellison

IT goes a long way back, some twenty years. All my life I had been looking for something, and everywhere I turned someone tried to tell me what it was. I accepted their answers too, though they were often in contradiction and even self-contradictory. I was naïve. I was looking for myself and asking everyone except myself questions which I, and only I, could answer. It took me a long time and much painful boomeranging of my expectations to achieve a realization everyone else appears to have been born with: That I am nobody but myself. But first I had to discover that I am an invisible man!

And yet I am no freak of nature, nor of history. I was in the cards, other things having been equal (or unequal) eighty-five years ago. I am not ashamed of my grandparents for having been slaves. I am only ashamed of myself for having at one time been ashamed. About eighty-five years ago they were told that they were free, united with others of our country in everything pertaining to the common good, and, in everything social, separate like the fingers of the hand. And they believed it. They exulted in it. They stayed in their place, worked hard, and brought up my father to do the same. But my grandfather is the one. He was an odd old guy, my grandfather, and I am told I take after him. It was he who caused the trouble. On his deathbed he called my father to him and said, "Son, after I'm gone I want you to keep up the good fight. I never told you, but our life is a war and I have been a traitor all my born days, a spy in the enemy's country ever since I give up my gun back in the Reconstruction. Live with your head in the lion's mouth. I want you to overcome 'em with yeses, undermine 'em with grins, agree 'em to death and destruction, let 'em swoller you till they vomit or bust wide open." They thought the old man had gone out of his mind. He had been the meekest of men. The younger children were rushed from the room, the shades drawn and the flame of the lamp turned so low that it sputtered on the wick like the old man's breathing. "Learn it to the younguns," he whispered fiercely; then he died.

But my folks were more alarmed over his last words than over his dying. It was as though he had not died at all, his words caused so much anxiety. I was warned emphatically to forget what he had said and, indeed, this is the first time it has been mentioned outside the family circle. It had a tremendous effect upon me, however. I could never be sure of what he meant. Grandfather had been a quiet old man who never made any trouble, yet on his deathbed he had called himself a traitor and a spy, and he had spoken of his meekness as a dangerous activity. It became a constant puzzle which lay unanswered in the back of my mind. And whenever things went well for me I remembered my grandfather and felt guilty and uncomfortable. It was as though I was carrying out his advice in spite of myself. And to make it worse, everyone loved me for it. I was praised by the most lily-white men of the town. I was considered an example of desirable conduct—just as my grandfather had been. And what puzzled me was that the old man had defined it as *treachery*. When I was praised for my conduct I felt a guilt that in some way I was doing something that was really against the wishes of the white folks, that if they had understood they would have desired me to act just the opposite, that I should have been sulky and mean, and that that really would have been what they wanted, even though they were fooled and thought they wanted me to act as I did. It made me afraid that some day they would look upon me as a traitor and I would be lost. Still I was more afraid to act any other way because they didn't like that at all. The old man's words were like a curse. On my graduation day I delivered an oration in which I showed that humility was the secret, indeed, the very essence of progress. (Not that I believed this—how could I, remembering my grandfather?—I only believed that it worked.) It was a great success. Everyone praised me and I was invited to give the speech at a gathering of the town's leading white citizens. It was a triumph for our whole community.

It was in the main ballroom of the leading hotel. When I got there I discovered that it was on the occasion of a smoker, and I was told that since I was to be there anyway I might as well take part in the battle royal to be fought by some of my schoolmates as part of the entertainment. The battle royal came first.

All of the town's big shots were there in their tuxedoes, wolfing down the buffet foods, drinking beer and whiskey and smoking black cigars. It was a large room with a high ceiling. Chairs were arranged in neat rows around three sides of a portable boxing ring. The fourth side was clear, revealing a gleaming space of polished floor. I had some misgivings over the battle royal, by the way. Not from a distaste for fighting, but because I didn't care too much for the other fellows who were to take part. They were tough guys who seemed to have no grandfather's curse worrying their minds. No one could mistake their toughness. And besides, I suspected that fighting a battle royal might detract from the dignity of my speech. In those pre-invisible days I visualized myself as a potential Booker T. Washington. But the other fellows didn't care too much for me either, and there were nine of them. I felt superior to them in my way, and I didn't like the manner in which we were all crowded together into the servants' elevator. Nor did they like my being there. In fact, as the warmly lighted floors flashed past the elevator we had words over the fact that I, by taking part in the fight, had knocked one of their friends out of a night's work.

We were led out of the elevator through a rococo hall into an anteroom and told to get into our fighting togs. Each of us was issued a pair of boxing gloves and ushered out into the big mirrored hall, which we entered looking cautiously about us and whispering, lest we might accidentally be heard above the noise of the room. It was foggy with cigar smoke. And already the whiskey was taking effect. I was shocked to see some of the most important men of the town quite tipsy. They were all there—bankers, lawyers, judges, doctors, fire chiefs, teachers, merchants. Even one of the more fashionable pastors. Something we could not see was going on up front. A clarinet was vibrating sensuously and the men were standing up and moving eagerly forward. We were a small tight group, clustered together, our bare upper bodies touching and shining with anticipatory sweat; while up front the big shots were becoming increasingly excited over something we still could not see. Suddenly I heard the school superintendent, who had told me to come, yell, "Bring up the shines, gentlemen! Bring up the little shines!"

We were rushed up to the front of the ballroom, where it smelled even more strongly of tobacco and whiskey. Then we were pushed into place. I almost wet my pants. A sea of faces, some hostile, some amused, ringed around us, and in the center, facing us, stood a magnificent blonde—stark naked. There was a dead silence. I felt a blast of cold air chill me. I tried to back away, but they were behind me and around me. Some of the boys stood with lowered heads trembling. I felt a wave of irrational guilt and fear. My teeth chattered, my skin turned to goose flesh, my knees knocked. Yet I was strongly attracted and looked in spite of myself. Had the price of looking been blindness, I would have looked. The hair was yellow like that of a circus kewpie doll, the face heavily powdered and rouged, as though to form an abstract mask, the eyes hollow and smeared a cool blue, the color of a baboon's butt. I felt a desire to spit upon her as my eyes brushed slowly over her body. Her breasts were firm and round as the domes of East Indian temples, and I stood so close as to see the fine skin texture and beads of pearly perspiration glistening like dew around the pink and erected buds of her nipples. I wanted at one and the same time to run from the room, to sink through the floor, or go to her and cover her from my eyes and the eyes of the others with my body; to feel the soft thighs, to caress her and destroy her, to love her and murder her, to hide from her, and yet to stroke where below the small American flag tattooed upon her belly her thighs formed a capital V. I had a notion that of all in the room she saw only me with her impersonal eyes.

And then she began to dance, a slow sensuous movement; the smoke of a hundred cigars clinging to her like the thinnest of veils. She seemed like a fair bird-girl girdled in veils calling to me from the angry surface of some gray and threatening sea. I was transported. Then I became aware of the clarinet playing and the big shots yelling at us. Some threatened us if we looked and others if we did not. On my right I saw one boy faint. And now a man grabbed a silver pitcher from a table and stepped close as he dashed ice water upon him and stood him up and forced two of us to support him as his head hung and moans issued from his thick bluish lips. Another boy began to plead to go home. He was the largest of the group, wearing dark red fighting trunks much too small to conceal the erection which projected from him as though in answer to the insinuating low-registered moaning of the clarinet. He tried to hide himself with his boxing gloves.

And all the while the blonde continued dancing, smiling faintly at the big shots who watched her with fascination, and faintly smiling at our fear. I noticed a certain merchant who followed her hungrily, his lips loose and drooling. He was a large man who wore diamond studs in a shirtfront which swelled with the ample paunch underneath, and each time the blonde swayed her undulating hips he ran his hand through the thin hair of his bald head and, with his arms upheld, his posture clumsy like that of an intoxicated panda, wound his belly in a slow and obscene grind. This creature was completely hypnotized. The music had quickened. As the dancer flung herself about with a detached expression on her face, the men began reaching out to touch her. I could see their beefy fingers sink into the soft flesh. Some of the others tried to stop them and she began to move around the floor in graceful circles, as they gave chase, slipping and sliding over the polished floor. It was mad. Chairs went crashing, drinks were spilt, as they ran laughing and howling after her. They caught her just as she reached a door, raised her from the floor, and tossed her as college boys are tossed at a hazing, and above her red, fixed-smiling lips I saw the terror and disgust in her eyes, almost like my own terror and that which I saw in some of the other boys. As I watched, they tossed her twice and her soft breasts seemed to flatten against the air and her legs flung wildly as she spun. Some of the more sober ones helped her to escape. And I started off the floor, heading for the anteroom with the rest of the boys.

Some were still crying and in hysteria. But as we tried to leave we were stopped and ordered to get into the ring. There was nothing to do but what we were told. All ten of us climbed under the ropes and allowed ourselves to be blindfolded with broad bands of white cloth. One of the men seemed to feel a bit sympathetic and tried to cheer us up as we stood with our backs against the ropes. Some of us tried to grin. "See that boy over there?" one of the men said. "I want you to run across at the bell and give it to him right in the belly. If you don't get him, I'm going to get you. I don't like his looks." Each of us was told the same. The blindfolds were put on. Yet even then I had been going over my speech. In my mind each word was as bright as flame. I felt the cloth pressed into place, and frowned so that it would be loosened when I relaxed.

But now I felt a sudden fit of blind terror. I was unused to darkness. It was as though I had suddenly found myself in a dark room filled with poisonous cottonmouths. I could hear the bleary voices yelling insistently for the battle royal to begin.

"Get going in there!"

"Let me at the big nigger!"

I strained to pick up the school superintendent's voice, as though to squeeze some security out of that slightly more familiar sound.

"Let me at those black sonsabitches!" someone yelled.

"No, Jackson, no!" another voice yelled. "Here somebody, help me hold Jack."

"I want to get at that ginger-colored nigger. Tear him limb from limb," the first voice yelled.

I stood against the ropes trembling. For in those days I was what they called ginger-colored, and he sounded as though he might crunch me between his teeth like a crisp ginger cookie.

Quite a struggle was going on. Chairs were being kicked about and I could hear voices grunting as with a terrific effort. I wanted to see, to see more desperately than ever before. But the blindfold was as tight as a thick skin-puckering scab and when I raised my gloved hands to push the layers of white aside a voice yelled, "Oh, no you don't, black bastard! Leave that alone!"

"Ring the bell before Jackson kills him a coon!" someone boomed in the sudden silence. And I heard the bell clang and the sound of feet scuffling forward.

A glove smacked against my head. I pivoted, striking out stiffy as someone went past, and felt the jar ripple along the length of my arm to my shoulder. Then it seemed as though all nine of the boys had turned upon me at once. Blows pounded me from all sides while I struck out as best I could. So many blows landed upon me that I wondered if I were not the only blindfolded fighter in the ring, or if the man called Jackson hadn't succeeded in getting me after all.

Blindfolded, I could no longer control my motions. I had no dignity. I stumbled about like a baby or a drunken man. The smoke had become thicker and with each new blow it seemed to sear and further restrict my lungs. My saliva became like a hot bitter glue. A glove connected with my head, filling my mouth with warm blood. It was everywhere. I could not tell if the moisture I felt upon my body was sweat or blood. A blow landed hard against the nape of my neck. I felt myself going over my head hitting the floor. Streaks of blue light filled the black world behind the blindfold. I lay prone, pretending that I was knocked out, but felt myself seized by hands and yanked to my feet. "Get going, black boy! Mix it up!" My arms were like lead, my head smarting from blows. I managed to feel my way to the ropes and held on, trying to catch my breath. A glove landed in my midsection and I went over again, feeling as though the smoke had become a knife jabbed into my guts. Pushed this way and that by the legs milling around me, I finally pulled erect and discovered that I could see the black, sweat-washed forms weaving in the smoky-blue atmosphere like drunken dancers weaving to the rapid drum-like thuds of blows.

Everone fought hysterically. It was complete anarchy. Everybody fought everybody else. No group fought together for long. Two, three, four, fought one, then turned to fight each other, were themselves attacked. Blows landed below the belt and in the kidney, with the gloves open as well as closed, and with my eye partly open now there was not so much terror. I moved carefully, avoiding blows, although not too many to attract attention, fighting from group to group. The boys groped about like blind, cautious crabs crouching to protect their mid-sections, their heads pulled in short against their shoulders, their arms stretched nervously before them, with their fists testing the smoke-filled air like the knobbed feelers of hypersensitive snails. In one corner I glimpsed a boy violently punching the air and heard him scream in pain as he smashed his hand against a ring post. For a second I saw him bent over holding his hand, then going down as a blow caught his unprotected head. I played one group against the other, slipping in and throwing a punch then stepping out of range while pushing the others into the melee to take the blows blindly aimed at me. The smoke was agonizing and there were no rounds, no bells at three minute intervals to relieve our exhaustion. The room spun round me, a swirl of lights, smoke, sweating bodies surrounded by tense white faces. I bled from both nose and mouth, the blood spattering upon my chest.

The men kept yelling, "Slug him, black boy! Knock his guts out!"

"Uppercut him! Kill him! Kill that big boy!"

Taking a fake fall, I saw a boy going down heavily beside me as though we were felled by a single blow, saw a sneaker-clad foot shoot into his groin as the two who had knocked him down stumbled upon him. I rolled out of range, feeling a twinge of nausea.

The harder we fought the more threatening the men became. And yet, I had begun to worry about my speech again. How would it go? Would they recognize my ability? What would they give me?

I was fighting automatically when suddenly I noticed that one after another of the boys was leaving the ring. I was surprised, filled with panic, as though I had been left alone with an unknown danger. Then I understood. The boys had arranged it among themselves. It was the custom for the two men left in the ring to slug it out for the winner's prize. I discovered this too late. When the bell sounded two men in tuxedoes leaped into the ring and removed the blindfold. I found myself facing Tatlock, the biggest of the gang. I felt sick at my stomach. Hardly had the bell stopped ringing in my ears than it clanged again and I saw him moving swiftly toward me. Thinking of nothing else to do I hit him smash on the nose. He kept coming, bringing the rank sharp violence of stale sweat. His face was a black blank of a face, only his eyes alive—with hate of me and aglow with a feverish terror from what had happened to us all. I became anxious. I wanted to deliver my speech and he came at me as though he meant to beat it out of me. I smashed him again and again, taking his blows as they came. Then on a sudden impulse I struck him lightly and as we clinched, I whispered, "Fake like I knocked you out, you can have the prize."

"I'll break your behind," he whispered hoarsely.

"For *them?*"

"For *me*, sonofabitch."

They were yelling for us to break it up and Tatlock spun me half around with a blow, and as a joggled camera sweeps in a reeling scene, I saw the howling red faces crouching tense beneath the cloud of blue-gray smoke. For a moment the world wavered, unraveled, flowed, then my head cleared and Tatlock bounced before me. That fluttering shadow before my eyes was his jabbing left hand. Then falling forward, my head against his damp shoulder, I whispered,

"I'll make it five dollars more."

"Go to hell!"

But his muscles relaxed a trifle beneath my pressure and I breathed, "Seven?"

"Give it to your ma,". he said, ripping me beneath the heart.

And while I still held him I butted him and moved away. I felt myself bombarded with punches. I fought back with hopeless desperation. I wanted to deliver my speech more than anything else in the world, because I felt only these men could judge truly my ability, and now this stupid clown was ruining my chances. I began fighting carefully now, moving in to punch him and out again with my greater speed. A lucky blow to his chin and I had him going too—until I heard a loud voice yell, "I got my money on the big boy."

Hearing this, I almost dropped my guard. I was confused: Should I try to win against the voice out there? Would not this go against my speech, and was not this a moment for humility, for nonresistance? A blow to my head as I danced about sent my right eye popping like a jack-in-the-box and settled my dilemma. The room went red as I fell. It was a dream fall, my body languid and fastidious as to where to land, until the floor became impatient and smashed up to meet me. A moment later I came to. An hypnotic voice said FIVE emphatically. And I lay there, hazily watching a dark red spot of my own blood shaping itself into a butterfly, glistening and soaking into the soiled gray world of the canvas.

When the voice drawled TEN I was lifted up and dragged to a chair. I sat dazed. My eye pained and swelled with each throb of my pounding heart and I wondered if now I would be allowed to speak. I was wringing wet, my mouth still bleeding. We were grouped along the wall now. The other boys ignored me as they congratulated Tatlock and speculated as to how much they would be paid. One boy whimpered over his smashed hand. Looking up front, I saw attendants in white jackets rolling the portable ring away and placing a small square rug in the vacant space surrounded by chairs. Perhaps, I thought, I will stand on the rug to deliver my speech.

Then the M.C. called to us, "Come on up here boys and get your money."

We ran forward to where the men laughed and talked in their chairs, waiting. Everyone seemed friendly now.

"There it is on the rug," the man said. I saw the rug covered with coins of all dimensions and a few crumpled bills. But what excited me, scattered here and there, were the gold pieces.

"Boys, it's all yours," the man said. "You get all you grab."

"That's right, Sambo," a blond man said, winking at me confidentially.

I trembled with excitement, forgetting my pain. I would get the gold and the bills, I thought. I would use both hands. I would throw my body against the boys nearest me to block them from the gold.

"Get down around the rug now," the man commanded, "and don't anyone touch it until I give the signal."

"This ought to be good," I heard.

As told, we got around the square rug on our knees. Slowly the man raised his freckled hand as we followed it upward with our eyes.

I heard, "These niggers look like they're about to pray!"

Then, "Ready," the man said. "Go!"

I lunged for a yellow coin lying on the blue design of the carpet, touching it and sending a surprised shriek to join those rising around me. I tried frantically to remove my hand but could not let go. A hot, violent force tore through my body, shaking me like a wet rat. The rug was electrified. The hair bristled up on my head as I shook myself free. My muscles jumped, my nerves jangled, writhed. But I saw that this was not stopping the other boys. Laughing in fear and embarrassment, some were holding back and scooping up the coins knocked off by the painful contortions of the others. The men roared above us as we struggled.

"Pick it up, goddamnit, pick it up!" someone called like a bass-voiced parrot. "Go on, get it!"

I crawled rapidly around the floor, picking up the coins, trying to avoid the coppers and to get greenbacks and the gold. Ignoring the shock by laughing, as I brushed the coins off quickly, I discovered that I could contain the electricity—a contradiction, but it works. Then the men began to push us onto the rug. Laughing embarrassedly, we struggled out of their hands and kept after the coins. We were all wet and slippery and hard to hold. Suddenly I saw a boy lifted into the air, glistening with sweat like a circus seal, and dropped, his wet back landing flush upon the charged rug, heard him yell and saw him literally dance upon his back, his elbows beating a frenzied tattoo upon the floor, his muscles twitching like the flesh of a horse stung by many flies. When he finally rolled off, his face was gray and no one stopped him when he ran from the floor amid booming laughter.

"Get the money," the M.C. called. "That's good hard American cash!"

And we snatched and grabbed, snatched and grabbed. I was careful not to come too close to the rug now, and when I felt the hot whiskey breath descend upon me like a cloud of foul air I reached out and grabbed the leg of a chair. It was occupied and I held on desperately.

"Leggo nigger! Leggo!"

The huge face wavered down to mine as he tried to push me free. But my body was slippery and he was too drunk. It was Mr. Colcord, who owned a chain of movie houses and "entertainment palaces." Each time he grabbed me I slipped out of his hands. It became a real struggle. I feared the rug more than I did the drunk, so I held on, surprising myself for a moment by trying to topple *him* upon the rug. It was such an enormous idea that I found myself actually carrying it out. I tried not to be obvious, yet when I grabbed his leg, trying to tumble him out of the chair, he raised up roaring with laughter, and looking at me with soberness dead in the eye, kicked me viciously in the chest. The chair leg flew out of my hand and I felt myself going and rolled. It was as though I had rolled through a bed of hot coals. It seemed a whole century would pass before I would roll free, a century in which I was seared through the deepest levels of my body to the fearful breath within me and the breath seared and heated to the point of explosion. It'll all be over in a flash, I thought as I rolled clear. It'll all be over in a flash.

But not yet, the men on the other side were waiting, red faces swollen as though from apoplexy as they bent forward in their chairs. Seeing their fingers coming toward me I rolled away as a fumbled football rolls off the receiver's fingertips, back into the coals. That time I luckily sent the rug sliding out of place and heard the coins ringing against the floor and the boys scuffling to pick them up and the M.C. calling, "All right, boys, that's all. Go get dressed and get your money."

I was limp as a dish rag. My back felt as though it had been beaten with wires.

When we had dressed the M.C. came in and gave us each five dollars, except Tatlock, who got ten for being last in the ring. Then he told us to leave. I was not to get a chance to deliver my speech, I thought. I was going out into the dim alley in despair when I was stopped and told to go back. I returned to the ballroom, where the men were pushing back their chairs and gathering in groups to talk.

The M.C. knocked on a table for quiet. "Gentlemen," he said, "we almost forgot an important part of the program. A most serious part, gentlemen. This boy was brought here to deliver a speech which he made at his graduation yesterday . . ."

"Bravo!"

"I'm told that he is the smartest boy we've got out there in Greenwood. I'm told that he knows more big words than a pocket-sized dictionary."

Much applause and laughter.

"So now, gentlemen, I want you to give him your attention."

There was still laughter as I faced them, my mouth dry, my eye throbbing. I began slowly, but evidently my throat was tense, because they began shouting, "Louder! Louder!"

"We of the younger generation extol the wisdom of that great leader and educator," I shouted, "who first spoke these flaming words of wisdom: 'A ship lost at sea for many days suddenly sighted a friendly vessel. From the mast of the unfortunate vessel was seen a signal: "Water, water; we die of thirst!" The answer from the friendly vessel came back: "Cast down your bucket where you are." The captain of the distressed vessel, at last heeding the injunction, cast down his bucket, and it came up full of fresh sparkling water from the mouth of the Amazon River.' And like him I say, and in his words, "To those of my race who depend upon bettering their condition in a foreign land, or who underestimate the importance of cultivating friendly relations with Southern white man, who is his next-door neighbor, I would say: "Cast down your bucket where you are"—cast it down in making friends in every manly way of the people of all races by whom we are surrounded. . . .'"

I spoke automatically and with such fervor that I did not realize that the men were still talking and laughing until my dry mouth, filling up with blood from the cut, almost strangled me. I coughed, wanting to stop and go to one of the tall brass, sand-filled spittoons to relieve myself, but a few of the men, especially the superintendent, were listening and I was afraid. So I gulped it down, blood, saliva and all, and continued. (What powers of endurance I had during those days! What enthusiasm! What a belief in the rightness of things!) I spoke even louder in spite of the pain. But still they talked and still they laughed, as though deaf with cotton in dirty ears. So I spoke with greater emotional emphasis. I closed my ears and swallowed blood until I was nauseated. The speech seemed a hundred times as long as before, but I could not leave out a single word. All had to be said, each memorized nuance considered, rendered. Nor was that all. Whenever I uttered a word of three or more syllables a group of voices would yell for me to repeat it. I used the phrase "social responsibility" and they yelled:

"What's that word you say, boy?"

"Social responsibility," I said.

"What?"

"Social . . ."

"Louder."

". . . responsibility."

"More!"

"Respon—"

"Repeat!"

"—sibility."

The room filled with the uproar of laughter until, no doubt, distracted by having to gulp down my blood, I made a mistake and yelled a phrase I had often seen denounced in newspaper editorials, heard debated in private.

"Social . . "

"What?" they yelled.

". . . equality—"

The laughter hung smokelike in the sudden stillness. I opened my eyes, puzzled. Sounds of displeasure filled the room. The M.C. rushed forward. They shouted hostile phrases at me. But I did not understand.

A small dry mustached man in the front row blared out, "Say that slowly, son!"

"What sir?"

"What you just said!"

"Social responsibility, sir," I said.

"You weren't being smart, were you boy?" he said, not unkindly.

"No, sir!"

"You sure that about 'equality' was a mistake?"

"Oh, yes, sir," I said. "I was swallowing blood."

"Well, you had better speak more slowly so we can understand. We mean to do right by you, but you've got to know your place at all times. All right, now, go on with your speech."

I was afraid. I wanted to leave but I wanted also to speak and I was afraid they'd snatch me down.

"Thank you sir," I said, beginning where I had left off, and having them ignore me as before.

Yet when I finished there was a thunderous applause. I was surprised to see the superintendent come forth with a package wrapped in white tissue paper, and, gesturing for quiet, address the men.

"Gentlemen, you see that I did not overpraise this boy. He makes a good speech and some day he'll lead his people in the proper paths. And I don't have to tell you that this is important in these days and times. This is a good, smart boy, and so to encourage him in the right direction, in the name of the Board of Education I wish to present him a prize in the form of this . . . "

He paused, removing the tissue paper and revealing a gleaming calfskin brief case.

". . . . in the form of this first-class article from Shad Whitmore's shop."

"Boy," he said, addressing me, "take this prize and keep it well. Consider it a badge of office. Prize it. Keep developing as you are and some day it will be filled with important papers that will help shape the destiny of your people."

I was so moved that I could hardly express my thanks. A rope of bloody saliva forming a shape like an undiscovered continent drooled upon the leather and I wiped it quickly away. I felt an importance that I had never dreamed.

"Open it and see what's inside," I was told.

My fingers a-tremble, I complied, smelling the fresh leather and finding an official-looking document inside. It was a scholarship to the state college for Negroes. My eyes filled with tears and I ran awkwardly off the floor.

I was overjoyed; I did not even mind when I discovered that the gold pieces I had scrambled for were brass pocket tokens advertising a certain make of automobile.

When I reached home everyone was excited. Next day the neighbors came to congratulate me. I even felt safe from grandfather, whose death-bed curse usually spoiled my triumphs. I stood beneath his photograph with my brief case in hand and smiled triumphantly into his stolid black peasant's face. It was a face that fascinated me. The eyes seemed to follow everywhere I went.

That night I dreamed I was at a circus with him and that he refused to laugh at the clowns no matter what they did. Then later he told me to open my brief case and read what was inside and I did, finding an official envelope stamped with the state seal; and inside the envelope I found another and another, endlessly, and I thought I would fall of weariness. "Them's years," he said. "Now open that one." And I did and in it I found an engraved document containing a short message in letters of gold. "Read it," my grandfather said. "Out loud."

"To Whom it May Concern," I intoned. "Keep This Nigger-Boy Running."

I awoke with the old man's laughter ringing in my ears.

(It was a dream I was to remember and dream again for many years after. But at that time I had no insight into its meaning. First I had to attend college.)

THE FAR AND THE NEAR

Thomas Wolfe

ON the outskirts of a little town upon a rise of land that swept back from the railway there was a tidy little cottage of white boards, trimmed vividly with green blinds. To one side of the house there was a garden neatly patterned with plots of growing vegetables, and an arbor for the grapes which ripened late in August. Before the house there were three mighty oaks which sheltered it in their clean and massive shade in summer, and to the other side there was a border of gay flowers. The whole place had an air of tidiness, thrift, and modest comfort.

Every day, a few minutes after two o'clock in the afternoon, the limited express between two cities passed this spot. At that moment the great train, having halted for a breathing-space at the town near by, was beginning to lengthen evenly into its stroke, but it had not yet reached the full drive of its terrific speed. It swung into view deliberately, swept past with a powerful swaying motion of the engine, a low smooth rumble of its heavy cars upon pressed steel, and then it vanished in the cut. For a moment the progress of the engine could be marked by heavy bellowing puffs of smoke that burst at spaced intervals above the edges of the meadow grass, and finally nothing could be heard but the solid clacking tempo of the wheels receding into the drowsy stillness of the afternoon.

Every day for more than twenty years, as the train had approached this house, the engineer had blown on the whistle, and every day, as soon as she heard this signal, a woman had appeared on the back porch of the little house and waved to him. At first she had a small child clinging to her skirts, and now this child had grown to full womanhood, and every day she, too, came with her mother to the porch and waved.

The engineer had grown old and gray in service. He had driven his great train, loaded with its weight of lives, across the land ten thousand times. His own children had grown up and married, and four times he had seen before him on the tracks the ghastly dot of tragedy converging like a cannon ball to its eclipse of horror at the boiler head—a light spring wagon filled with children, with its clustered row of small stunned faces; a cheap automobile stalled upon the tracks, set with the wooden figures of people paralyzed with fear; a battered hobo walking by the rail, too deaf and old to hear the whistle's warning; and a form flung past his window with a scream—all this the man had seen and known. He had known all the grief, the joy, the peril and the labor such a man could know; he had grown seamed and weathered in his loyal service, and now, schooled by the qualities of faith and courage and humbleness that attended his labor, he had grown old, and had the grandeur and the wisdom these men have.

But no matter what peril or tragedy he had known, the vision of the little house and the women waving to him with a brave free motion of the arm had become fixed in the mind of the engineer as something beautiful and enduring, something beyond all change and ruin, and something that would always be the same, no matter what mishap, grief or error might break the iron schedule of his days.

The sight of the little house and of these two women gave him the most extraordinary happiness he had ever known. He had seen them in a thousand lights, a hundred weathers. He had seen them through the harsh bare light of wintry gray across the brown and frosted stubble of the earth, and he had seen them again in the green luring sorcery of April.

He felt for them and for the little house in which they lived such tenderness as a man might feel for his own children, and at length the picture of their lives was carved so sharply in his heart that he felt that he knew their lives completely, to every hour and moment of the day, and he resolved that one day, when his years of service should be ended, he would go and find these people and speak at last with them whose lives had been so wrought into his own.

That day came. At last the engineer stepped from a train onto the station platform of the town where these two women lived. His years upon the rail had ended. He was a pensioned servant of his company, with no more work to do. The engineer walked slowly through the station and out into the streets of the town. Everything was as strange to him as if he had never seen this town before. As he walked on, his sense of bewilderment and confusion grew. Could this be the town he had passed ten thousand times? Were these the same houses he had seen so often from the high windows of his cab? It was all as unfamiliar, as disquieting as a city in a dream, and the perplexity of his spirit increased as he went on.

Presently the houses thinned into the straggling outposts of the town, and the street faded into a country road—the one on which the women lived. And the man plodded on slowly in the heat and dust. At length he stood before the house he sought. He knew at once that he had found the proper place. He saw the lordly oaks before the house, the flower beds, the garden and the arbor, and farther off, the glint of rails.

Yes, this was the house he sought, the place he had passed so many times, the destination he had longed for with such happiness. But now that he had found it, now that he was here, why did his hand falter on the gate; why had the town, the road, the earth, the very entrance to this place he loved turned unfamiliar as the landscape of some ugly dreams? Why did he now feel this sense of confusion, doubt, and hopelessness?

At length he entered by the gate, walked slowly up the path and in a moment more had mounted three short steps that led up to the porch, and was knocking at the door. Presently he heard steps in the hall, the door was opened, and a woman stood facing him.

And instantly, with a sense of bitter loss and grief, he was sorry he had come. He knew at once that the woman who stood there looking at him with a mistrustful eye was the same woman who had waved to him so many thousand times. But her face was harsh and pinched and meager; the flesh sagged wearily in sallow folds, and the small eyes peered at him with timid suspicion and uneasy doubt. All the brave freedom, the warmth and the affection that he had read into her gesture, vanished in the moment that he saw her and heard her unfriendly tongue.

And now his own voice sounded unreal and ghastly to him as he tried to explain his presence, to tell her who he was and the reason he had come. But he faltered on, fighting subbornly against the horror of regret, confusion, disbelief that surged up in his spirit, drowning all his former joy and making his act of hope and tenderness seem shameful to him.

At length the woman invited him almost unwillingly into the house, and called her daughter in a harsh shrill voice. Then, for a brief agony of time, the man sat in an ugly little parlor, and he tried to talk while the two women stared at him with a dull, bewildered hostility, a sullen, timorous restraint.

And finally, stammering a crude farewell, he departed. He walked away down the path and then along the road toward town, and suddenly he knew that he was an old man. His heart, which had been brave and confident when it looked along the familiar vista of the rails, was now sick with doubt and horror as it saw the strange and unsuspected visage of an earth which had always been within a stone's throw of him, and which he had never seen or known. And he knew that all the magic of that bright lost way, the vista of that shining line, the imagined corner of that small good universe of hope's desire, was gone forever, could never be got back again.

THE BITCH

Colette

WHEN the sergeant arrived in Paris on leave, he found his mistress not at home. He was nevertheless greeted with tremulous cries of surprise and joy, embraced and covered with wet kisses. His bitch, Vorace, the sheep-dog whom he had left with his young sweetheart, enveloped him like a flame and licked him with a tongue pale with emotion. Meanwhile, the charwoman was making as much noise as the dog and kept exclaiming:

"Of all the bad luck! Madame's just gone to Marlotte for a couple of days to shut up her house there. Madame's tenants have just left and she's going through the inventory of the furniture. Fortunately, it isn't all that far away! Will Monsieur write out a telegram for Madame? If it goes immediately, Madame will be here tomorrow morning before lunch. Monsieur must sleep here. Shall I turn on the geyser?"

"My good Lucie, I had a bath at home. Soldiers on leave are pretty good at washing!"

He eyed his reflection in the glass; he was both bluish and ruddy, like the granite rocks of Brittany. The Briard sheep-dog, standing close to him in a reverent silence, was trembling in every hair. He laughed because she looked so like him, gray and blue and shaggy.

"Vorace!"

She raised her head and looked lovingly at her master, and the sergeant's heart turned over as he suddenly thought of his mistress Jeannine, so young and so gay—a little too young and often too gay.

During dinner the dog faithfully observed all the ritual of their former life, catching the pieces of bread he tossed for her and barking at certain words. So ardent was the worship in which she was rooted that the moment of return abolished for her the months of absence.

"I've missed you a lot," he told her in a low voice. "Yes, you too!"

He was smoking now, half lying on the divan. Crouching like a greyhound on a tombstone, the dog was pretending to be asleep, her ears quite still. Only her eyebrows, twitching at the slightest noise, revealed that she was on the alert.

Worn out as he was, the silence gradually lulled the man, until his hand which held the cigarette slid down the cushion, scorching the silk. He roused himself, opened a book, fingered a few new knick-knacks and a photograph, which he had not seen before, of Jeannine in a short skirt, with bare arms, in the country.

"An amateur snapshot . . . How charming she looks!"

On the back of the unmounted print he read:

" 'June the fifth 1916.' Where was I on June the fifth? . . . Oh, I know, over in the direction of Arras. June the fifth. I don't know the writing."

He sat down again and was overcome by a sleep which drove all thought away. Ten o'clock struck; he was still just sufficiently awake to smile at the rich and solemn sound of the little clock whose voice, Jeannine used to say, was bigger than its stomach. But as it struck ten the dog got up.

"Quiet!" said the sleepy sergeant. "Lie down!"

But Vorace did not lie down. She snorted and stretched her paws which, for a dog, is the same as putting on a hat to go out. She went up to her master and her yellow eyes asked plainly:

"Well?"

"Well," he answered, "What's the matter with you?"

Out of respect she dropped her ears while he was speaking, raising them again immediately.

"Oh, what a bore you are!" sighed the sergeant. "You're thirsty. D'you want to go out?"

At the words "go out," Vorace grinned and began to pant gently, showing her beautiful teeth and the fleshy petal of her tongue.

"All right, then, we'll go out. But not for long, because I'm absolutely dropping with sleep."

In the road Vorace was so excited that she barked like a wolf, jumped right up to her master's neck, charged a cat and spun round playing "inner circle" with her tail. Her master scolded her tenderly and she did all her tricks for him. Finally, she sobered down again and walked along sedately. The sergeant suited his pace to hers, enjoying the warm night and making a little song out of two or three idle thoughts:

"I'll see Jeannine tomorrow morning . . . I'm going to sleep in a comfy bed . . . I've got seven more days to spend here . . . "

He became aware that his dog, who had trotted ahead, was waiting for him under a gas lamp with the same look of impatience. Her eyes, her wagging tail and her whole body asked:

"Well? Are you coming?"

As soon as he caught up with her, she turned the corner at a determined trot. It was then that he realized she was going somewhere.

"Perhaps," he thought to himself, "the charwoman usually . . . Or Jeannine . . . "

He stood still for a moment, then went on again, following the dog, without even noticing that he had, all at once, stopped feeling tired, and sleepy, and happy. He quickened his pace and the delighted dog went before, like a good guide.

"Go on, go on!" ordered the sergeant from time to time.

He looked at the name of a road, then went on again. They passed gardens with lodges at the gates; the road was dimly lit and they met no one. On her excitement, the dog pretended to bite the hand that hung at his side, and he had to restrain a brutal impulse, which he could not explain, in order not to beat her.

At last she stopped, as though saying: "Well, here we are!" before an old, broken-down railing protecting the garden of a little low house smothered in vines and bignonia, a timid shrouded little house.

"Well, why don't you open it?' said the dog, who had taken up a position before the wooden wicket-gate.

The sergeant lifted his hand to the latch and let it fall again. He bent down to the dog, pointed with his finger to a thread of light along the closed shutters, and asked her in a low voice:

"Who's there? . . . Jeannine?"

The dog gave a shrill "Hi!" and barked.

"Shhh!" breathed the sergeant, clapping his hands over her cool wet mouth.

Once more he stretched out a hesitant arm towards the door and the dog bounded forward. But he held her back by her collar and led her to the opposite pavement, whence he gazed at the unknown house and the thread of rosy light. He sat down on the pavement beside the dog. He had not yet gathered together all those images and thoughts which spring up round a possible betrayal, but he felt singularly alone, and weak.

"Do you love me?" he murmured in the dog's ear.

She licked his cheek.

"Come on; let's go away."

They set off, he in front this time. And when they were once more in the little sitting-room, she saw that he was putting his linen and slippers in a sack that she knew well. Desperate but respectful, she followed all his movements, while tears, the color of gold, trembled in her yellow eyes. He laid his hand on her neck to reassure her:

"You're coming too. You're not going to leave me any more. Next time you won't be able to tell me what happened 'after.' Perhaps I'm mistaken. Perhaps I haven't understood you properly. But you mustn't stay here. Your soul wasn't meant to guard any secrets but mine."

And while the dog shivered, still uncertain, he held her head in his hands, saying to her in a low voice:

"Your soul . . . Your doggy soul . . . Your beautiful soul . . . "

THE MAGIC BARREL

Bernard Malamud

NOT long ago there lived in uptown New York, in a small, almost meager room, though crowded with books, Leo Finkle, a rabbinical student in the Yeshivah University. Finkle, after six years of study, was to be ordained in June and had been advised by an acquaintance that he might find it easier to win himself a congregation if he were married. Since he had no present prospects of marriage, after two tormented days of turning it over in his mind, he called in Pinye Salzman, a marriage broker whose two-line advertisement he had read in the *Forward*.[1]

The matchmaker appeared one night out of the dark fourth-floor hallway of the graystone rooming house where Finkle lived, grasping a black, strapped portfolio that had been worn thin with use. Salzman, who had been long in the business, was of slight but dignified build, wearing an old hat, and an overcoat too short and tight for him. He smelled frankly of fish, which he loved to eat, and although he was missing a few teeth, his presence was not displeasing, because of an amiable manner curiously contrasted with mournful eyes. His voice, his lips, his wisp of beard, his bony fingers were animated, but give him a moment of repose and his mild blue eyes revealed a depth of sadness, a characteristic that put Leo a little at ease although the situation, for him, was inherently tense.

He at once informed Salzman why he had asked him to come, explaining that his home was in Cleveland, and that but for his parents, who had married comparatively late in life, he was alone in the world. He had for six years devoted himself almost entirely to his studies, as a result of which, understandably, he had found himself without time for a social life and the company of young women. Therefore he thought it the better part of trial and error—of embarrassing fumbling—to call in an experienced person to advise him on these matters. He remarked in passing that the function of the marriage broker was ancient and honorable, highly approved in the Jewish community, because it made practical the necessary without hindering joy. Moreover, his own parents had been brought together by a matchmaker. They had made, if not a financially profitable marriage—since neither had possessed any worldly goods to speak of—at least a successful one in the sense of their everlasting devotion to each other. Salzman listened in embarrassed surprise, sensing a sort of apology. Later, however, he experienced a glow of pride in his work, an emotion that had left him years ago, and he heartily approved of Finkle.

The two went to their business. Leo had led Salzman to the only clear place in the room, a table near a window that overlooked the lamplit city. He seated himself at the matchmaker's side but facing him, at-

[1]*Jewish Daily Forward*, influential Yiddish-language newspaper with a famous advice column (romantic and otherwise)—"Brintel Brief."

tempting by an act of will to suppress the unpleasant tickle in his throat. Salzman eagerly unstrapped his portfolio and removed a loose rubber band from a thin packet of much-handled cards. As he flipped through them, a gesture and sound that physically hurt Leo, the student pretended not to see and gazed steadfastly out the window. Although it was still February, winter was on its last legs, signs of which he had for the first time in years begun to notice. He now observed the round white moon, moving high in the sky through a cloud menagerie, and watched with half-open mouth as it penetrated a huge hen, and dropped out of her like an egg laying itself. Salzman, though pretending through eyeglasses he had just slipped on, to be engaged in scanning the writing on the cards, stole occasional glances at the young man's distinguished face, noting with pleasure the long, severe scholar's nose, brown eyes heavy with learning, sensitive yet ascetic lips, and a certain, almost hollow quality of the dark cheeks. He gazed around at shelves upon shelves of books and let out a soft, contented sigh.

When Leo's eyes fell upon the cards, he counted six spread out in Salzman's hand.

"So few?" he asked in disappointment.

"You wouldn't believe me how much cards I got in my office," Salzman replied. "The drawers are already filled to the top, so I keep them now in a barrel, but is every girl good for a new rabbi?"

Leo blushed at this, regretting all he had revealed of himself in a curriculum vitae he had sent to Salzman. He had thought it best to acquaint him with his strict standards and specifications, but in having done so, felt he had told the marriage broker more than was absolutely necessary.

He hesitantly inquired, "Do you keep photographs of your clients on file?"

"First comes family, amount of dowry, also what kind promises," Salzman replied, unbuttoning his tight coat and settling himself in the chair. "After comes pictures, rabbi."

"Call me Mr. Finkle. I'm not yet a rabbi."

Salzman said he would, but instead called him doctor, which he changed to rabbi when Leo was not listening too attentively.

Salzman adjusted his horn-rimmed spectacles, gently cleared his throat and read in an eager voice the contents of the top card:

"Sophie P. Twenty-four years. Widow one year. No children. Educated high school and two years college. Father promises eight thousand dollars. Has wonderful wholesale business. Also real estate. On the mother's side comes teachers, also one actor. Well known on Second Avenue."

Leo gazed up in surprise. "Did you say a widow?"

"A widow don't mean spoiled, rabbi. She lived with her husband maybe four months. He was a sick boy she made a mistake to marry him."

"Marrying a widow has never entered my mind."

"This is because you have no experience. A widow, especially if she is young and healthy like this girl, is a wonderful person to marry. She will be thankful to you the rest of her life. Believe me, if I was looking now for a bride, I would marry a widow."

Leo reflected, then shook his head.

Salzman hunched his shoulders in an almost imperceptible gesture of disappointment. He placed the card down on the wooden table and began to read another:

"Lily H. High school teacher. Regular. Not a substitute. Has savings and new Dodge car. Lived in Paris one year. Father is successful dentist thirty-five years. Interested in professional man. Well Americanized family. Wonderful opportunity."

"I knew her personally," said Salzman. "I wish you could see this girl. She is a doll. Also very intelligent. All day you could talk to her about books and theyater and what not. She also knows current events."

"I don't believe you mentioned her age?"

"Her age?" Salzman said, raising his brows. "Her age is thirty-two years."

Leo said after a while, "I'm afraid that seems a little too old."

Salzman let out a laugh. "So how old are you, rabbi?"

"Twenty-seven."

"So what is the difference, tell me, between twenty-seven and thirty-two? My own wife is seven years older than me. So what did I suffer?— Nothing. If Rothschild's daughter wants to marry you, would you say on account her age, no?"

"Yes," Leo said dryly.

Salzman shook off the no in the eyes. "Five years don't mean a thing. I give you my word that when you will live with her for one week you will forget her age. What does it mean five years—that she lived more and knows more than somebody who is younger? On this girl, God bless her, years are not wasted. Each one that it comes makes better the bargain."

"What subject does she teach in high school?"

"Languages. If you heard the way she speaks French, you will think it is music. I am in the business twenty-five years, and I recommend her with my whole heart. Believe me, I know what I'm talking, rabbi."

"What's on the next card?" Leo said abruptly.

Salzman reluctantly turned up the third card:

"Ruth K. Nineteen years. Honor student. Father offers thirteen thousand cash to the right bridegroom. He is a medical doctor. Stomach specialist with marvelous practice. Brother in law owns own garment business. Particular people."

Salzman looked as if he had read his trump card.

"Did you say nineteen?" Leo asked with interest.

"On the dot."

"Is she attractive?" He blushed. "Pretty?"

Salzman kissed his finger tips. "A little doll. On this I give you my word. Let me call the father tonight and you will see what means pretty."

But Leo was troubled. "You're sure she's that young?"

"This I am positive. The father will show you the birth certificate."

"Are you positive there isn't something wrong with her?" Leo insisted.

"Who says there is wrong?"

"I don't understand why an American girl her age should go to a marriage broker."

A smile spread over Salzman's face.

"So for the same reason you went, she comes."

Leo flushed. "I am pressed for time."

Salzman, realizing he had been tactless, quickly explained. "The father came, not her. He wants she should have the best, so he looks around himself. When we will locate the right boy he will introduce him and encourage. This makes a better marriage than if a young girl without experience takes for herself. I don't have to tell you this."

"But don't you think this young girl believes in love?" Leo spoke uneasily.

Salzman was about was about to guffaw but caught himself and said soberly, "Love comes with the right person, not before."

Leo parted dry lips but did not speak. Noticing that Salzman had snatched a glance at the next card, he cleverly asked, "How is her health?"

"Perfect," Salzman said, breathing with difficulty. "Of course, she is a little lame on her right foot from an auto accident that it happened to her when she was twelve years, but nobody notices on account she is so brilliant and also beautiful."

Leo got up heavily and went to the window. He felt curiosly bitter and upbraided himself for having called in the marriage broker. Finally, he shook his head.

"Why not?" Salzman persisted, the pitch of his voice rising.

"Because I detest stomach specialists."

"So what do you care what is his business? After you marry her do you need him? Who says he must come every Friday night in your house?"

Ashamed of the way the talk was going, Leo dismissed Salzman, who went home with heavy, melancholy eyes.

Though he had felt only relief at the marriage broker's departure, Leo was in low spirits the next day. He explained it as arising from Salzman's failure to produce a suitable bride for him. He did not care for his type of clientele. But when Leo found himself hesitating whether to seek out another matchmaker, one more polished than Pinye, he wondered if it could be—protestations to the contrary, and although he honored his father and mother—that he did not, in essence, care for the matchmaking institution? This thought he quickly put out of mind yet found himself still upset. All day he ran around in the woods—missed an important appointment, forgot to give out his laundry, walked out of a Broadway cafeteria without paying and had to run back with the ticket in his hand; had even not recognized his landlady in the street when she passed with a friend and courteously called out, "A good evening to you, Doctor Finkle." By nightfall, however, he had regained sufficient calm to sink his nose into a book and there found peace from his thoughts.

Almost at once there came a knock on the door. Before Leo could say enter, Salzman, commercial cupid, was standing in the room. His face was gray and meager, his expression hungry, and he looked as if he would expire on his feet. Yet the marriage broker managed, by some trick of the muscles to display a broad smile

"So good evening. I am invited?"

Leo nodded, disturbed to see him again, yet unwilling to ask the man to leave.

Beaming still, Salzman laid his portfolio on the table. "Rabbi, I got for you tonight good news."

"I've asked you not to call me rabbi. I'm still a student."

"Your worries are finished. I have for you a first-class bride."

"Leave me in peace concerning this subject." Leo pretended lack of interest.

"The world will dance at your wedding."

"Please, Mr. Salzman, no more."

"But first must come back my strength," Salzman said weakly. He fumbled with the portfolio straps and took out of the leather case an oily paper bag, from which he extracted a hard, seeded roll and a small, smoked white fish. With a quick motion of his hand he stripped the fish out of its skin and began ravenously to chew. "All day in a rush," he muttered.

Leo watched him eat.

"A sliced tomato you have maybe?" Salzman hesitantly inquired.

"No."

The marriage broker shut his eyes and ate. When he had finished he carefully cleaned up the crumbs and rolled up the remains of the fish, in the paper bag. His spectacled eyes roamed the room until he discovered, amid some piles of books, a one-burner gas stove. Lifting his hat he humbly asked, "A glass of tea you got, rabbi?"

Conscience-stricken, Leo rose and brewed the tea. He served it with a chunk of lemon and two cubes of lump sugar, delighting Salzman.

After he had drunk his tea, Salzman's strength and good spirits were restored.

"So tell me rabbi," he said amiably, "you considered some more the three clients I mentioned yesterday?"

"There was no need to consider."

"Why not?"

"None of them suits me."

"What then suits you?"

Leo let it pass because he could give only a confused answer.

Without waiting for a reply, Salzman asked, "You remember this girl I talked to you—the high school teacher?"

"Age thirty-two?"

But surprisingly, Salzman's face lit in a smile. "Age twenty-nine."

Leo shot him a look. "Reduced from thirty-two?"

"A mistake," Salzman avowed. "I talked today with the dentist. He took me to his safety deposit box and showed me the birth certificate. She was twenty-nine years last August. They made her a party in the mountains where she went for her vacation. When her father spoke to me the first time I forgot to write the age and I told you thirty-two, but now I remember this was a different client, a widow."

"The same one you told me about? I thought she was twenty-four?"

"A different. Am I responsible that the world is filled with widows?"

"No, but I'm not interested in them, nor for that matter, in school teachers."

Salzman pulled his clasped hand to his breast. Looking at the ceiling he devoutly exclaimed, "Yiddishe kinder,[2] what can I say to somebody that he is not interested in high school teachers? So what then you are interested?"

Leo flushed but controlled himself.

"In what else will you be interested," Salzman went on, "if you not interested in this fine girl that she speaks four languages and has personally in the bank ten thousand dollars? Also her father guarantees further twelve thousand. Also she has a new car, wonderful clothes, talks on all subjects, and she will give you a first-class home and children. How near do we come in our life to paradise?"

"If she's so wonderful, why wasn't she married ten years ago?"

"Why?" said Salzman with a heavy laugh. "—Why? Because she is *partikiler*. This is why. She wants the *best*."

Leo was silent, amused at how he had entangled himself. But Salzman had aroused his interest in Lily H., and he began seriously to consider calling on her. When the marriage broker observed how intently Leo's mind was at work on the facts he had supplied, he felt certain they would soon come to an agreement.

Late Saturday afternoon, conscious of Salzman, Leo Finkle walked with Lily Hirschorn along Riverside Drive. He walked briskly and erectly, wearing with distinction the black fedora he had that morning taken with trepidation out of the dusty hat box on his closet shelf, and the heavy black Saturday coat he had throughly whisked clean. Leo also owned a walking stick, a present from a distant relative, but quickly put temptation aside and did not use it. Lily, petite and not unpretty, had on something signifing the approach of spring. She was au courant, animatedly, with all sorts of subjects, and he weighed her words and found her surprisingly sound—score another for Salzman, whom he uneasily sensed to be somewhere around, hiding perhaps high in a tree along the street, flashing the lady signals with a pocket mirror; or perhaps a cloven-hoofed Pan, piping nuptial ditties as he danced his invisible way before them, strewing wild buds on the walk and purple grapes in their path, symbolizing fruit of a union, though there was of course still none.

Lily startled Leo by remarking, "I was thinking of Mr. Salzman, a curious figure, wouldn't you say?"

Not certain what to answer, he nodded.

She bravely went on, blushing, "I for one am grateful for his introducing us. Aren't you?"

He courteously replied, "I am."

"I mean," she said with a little laugh—and it was all in good taste, to

---

[2] "Jewish children!"

at least gave the effect of being not in bad—"do you mind that we came together so?"

He was not displeased with her honesty, recognizing that she meant to set the relationship aright, and understanding that it took a certain amount of experience in life, and courage, to want to do it quite that way. One had to have some sort of past to make that kind of beginning.

He said that he did not mind. Salzman's function was traditional and honorable—valuable for what it might achieve, which, he pointed out, was frequently nothing.

Lily agreed with a sigh. They walked on for a while and she said after a long silence, again with a nervous laugh, "Would you mind if I asked you something a little bit personal? Frankly, I find the subject fascinating." Although Leo shrugged, she went on half embarrassedly, "How was it that you came to your calling? I mean was it a sudden passionate inspiration?"

Leo, after a time, slowly replied. "I was always interested in the Law."

"You saw revealed in it the presence of the Highest?"

He nodded and changed the subject. "I understand that you spent a little time in Paris, Miss Hirschorn?"

"Oh, did Mr. Salzman tell you, Rabbi Finkle?" Leo winced but she went on, "It was ages ago and almost forgotten. I remember I had to return for my sister's wedding."

And Lily would not be put off. "When," she asked in a trembly voice, "did you become enamored of God?"

He stared at her. Then it came to him that she was talking not about Leo Finkle, but of a total stranger, some mystical figure, perhaps even passionate prophet that Salzman had dreamed up for her—no relation to the living or dead. Leo trembled with rage and weakness. The trickster had obviously sold her a bill of goods, just as he had him, who'd expected to become acquainted with a young lady of twenty-nine, only to behold, the moment he laid eyes upon her strained and anxious face, a woman past thirty-five and aging rapidly. Only his self control had kept him this long in her presence.

"I am not," he said gravely, "a talented religious person," and in seeking words to go on, found himself possessed by shame and fear. "I think," he said in a strained manner, "that I came to God not because I loved Him, but because I did not."

This confession he spoke harshly because its unexpectedness shook him.

Lily wilted. Leo saw a profusion of loaves of bread go flying like ducks high over his head, not unlike the winged loaves by which he had counted himself to sleep last night. Mercifully, then, it snowed, which he would not put past Salzman's machinations.

He was infuriated with the marriage broker and swore he would throw him out of the room the minute he reappeared. But Salzman did not come that night, and when Leo's anger had subsided, an unaccountable despair grew in its place. At first he thought this was caused by his disappointment in Lily, but before long it became evident that he had involved himself with Salzman without a true knowledge of his own intent. He gradually realized—with an emptiness that seized him with six hands—that he had called in the broker to find him a bride because he was incapable of doing it himself. This terrifying insight he had derived as a result of his meeting and conversation with Lily Hirschorn. Her probing questions had somehow irritated him into revealing—to himself more than her—the true nature of his relationship to God, and from that it had come upon him, with shocking force, that apart from his parents, he had never loved anyone. Or perhaps it went the other way, that he did not love God so well as he might, because he had not loved man. It seemed to Leo that his whole life stood starkly revealed and he saw himself for the first time as he truly was—unloved and loveless. This bitter but somehow not fully unexpected revelation brought him to a point of panic, controlled only by extraordinary effort. He covered his face with his hands and cried.

The week that followed was the worst of his life. He did not eat and lost weight. His beard darkened and grew ragged. He stopped attending seminars and almost never opened a book. He seriously considered leaving the Yeshivah, although he was deeply troubled at the thought of the loss of all his years of study—saw them like pages torn from a book, strewn over the city—and at the devastating effect of this decision upon his parents. But he had lived without knowledge of himself, and never in the Five Books[3] and all the Commentaries—mea culpa—had the truth been revealed to him. He did not know where to turn, and in all this desolating loneliness there was no *to whom*, although he often thought of Lily but not once could bring himself to go downstairs and make the call. He became touchy and irritable, especially with his landlady, who asked him all manner of personal questions; on the other hand sensing his own disagreeableness, he waylaid her on the stairs and apologized abjectly, until mortified, she ran from him. Out of this, however, he drew the consolation that he was a Jew and that a Jew suffered. But gradually, as the long and terrible week drew to a close, he regained his composure and some idea of purpose in life to go on as planned. Although he was imperfect, the ideal was not. As for his quest of a bride, the thought of continuing afflicted him with anxiety and heartburn, yet perhaps with this new knowledge of himself he would be more successful than in the past. Perhaps love would now come to him and a bride to that love. And for this sanctified seeking who needed a Salzman?

The marriage broker, a skeleton with haunted eyes, returned that very night. He looked, withal, the picture of frustrated expectancy—as if he had steadfastly waited the week at Miss Lily Hirschorn's side for a telephone call that never came.

Casually coughing, Salzman came immediately to the point: "So how did you like her?"

Leo's anger rose and he could not refrain from chiding the matchmaker: "Why did you lie to me, Salzman?"

---

[3]The Torah, or five books of Moses (the Pentateuch): Genesis, Exodus, Leviticus, Numbers, Deuteronomy.

Salzman's pale face went dead white, the world had snowed on him.

"Did you not state that she was twenty-nine?" Leo insisted.

"I give you my word—"

"She was thirty-five, if a day. *At least* thirty-five."

"Of this don't be too sure. Her father told me—"

"Never mind. The worst of it was that you lied to her."

"How did I lie to her, tell me?"

"You told her things about me that weren't true. You made out to be more, consequently less than I am. She had in mind a totally different person, a sort of semi-mystical Wonder Rabbi."

"All I said, you was a religious man."

"I can imagine."

Salzman sighed. "This is my weakness that I have," he confessed. "My wife says to me I shouldn't be a salesman, but when I have.two fine people that they would be wonderful to be married, I am so happy that I talk too much." He smiled wanly. "This is why Salzman is a poor man."

Leo's anger left him. "Well, Salzman, I'm afraid that's all."

The marriage broker fastened hungry eyes on him.

"You don't want any more a bride?"

"I do," said Leo, "but I have decided to seek her in a different way. I am no longer interested in an arranged marriage. To be frank, I now admit the necessity of premarital love. That is, I want to be in love with the one I marry."

"Love?" said Salzman, astounded. After a moment he remarked "For us, our love is our life, not for the ladies. In the ghetto they—"

"I know, I know," said Leo. "I've thought of it often. Love, I have said to myself, should be a by-product of living and worship rather than its own end. Yet for myself I find it necessary to establish the level of my need and fulfill it."

Salzman shrugged but answered, "Listen, rabbi, if you want love, this I can find for you also. I have such beautiful clients that you will love them the minute your eyes will see them."

Leo smiled unhappily. "I'm afraid you don't understand."

But Salzman hastily unstrapped his portfolio and withdrew a manila packet from it.

"Pictures," he said, quickly laying the envelope on the table.

Leo called after him to take the pictures away, but as if on the wings of the wind, Salzman had disappeared.

March came. Leo had returned to his regular routine. Although he felt not quite himself yet—lacked energy—he was making plans for a more active social life. Of course it would cost something, but he was an expert in cutting corners; and when there were no corners left he would make circles rounder. All the while Salzman's pictures had lain on the table, gathering dust. Occasionally as Leo sat studying, or enjoying a cup of tea, his eyes fell on the manila envelope, but he never opened it.

The days went by and no social life to speak of developed with a member of the opposite sex—it was difficult, given the circumstances of his situation. One morning Leo toiled up the stairs to his room and stared out the window at the city. Although the day was bright his view of it was dark. For some time he watched the people in the street below hurrying along and then turned with a heavy heart to his little room. On the table was the packet. With a sudden relentless gesture he tore it open. For a half-hour he stood by the table in a state of excitement, examining the photographs of the ladies Salzman had included. Finally, with a deep sigh he put them down. There were six, of varying degree of attractiveness, but look at them long enough and they all became Lily Hirschorn: all past their prime, all starved behind bright smiles, not a true personality in the lot. Life, despite their frantic yoohooings, had passed them by; they were pictures in a brief case that stank of fish. After a while, however, as Leo attempted to return the photographs into the envelope, he found in it another, a snapshot of the type taken by a machine for a quarter. He gazed at it a moment and let out a cry.

Her face deeply moved him. Why, he could at first not say. It gave him the impression of youth—spring flowers, yet age—a sense of having been used to the bone, wasted; this came from the eyes, which were hauntingly familiar, yet absolutely strange. He had a vivid impression that he had met her before, but try as he might he could not place her although he could almost recall her name, as if he had read it in her own handwriting. No, this couldn't be; he would have remembered her. It was not, he affirmed, that she had an extraordinary beauty—no, though her face was attractive enough; it was that *something* about her moved him. Feature for feature, even some of the ladies of the photographs could do better; but she leaped forth to his heart—had *lived*, or wanted to—more than just wanted, perhaps regretted how she had lived—had somehow deeply suffered: it could be seen in the depths of those reluctant eyes, and from the way the light enclosed and shone from her, and within her, opening realms of possibility: this was her own. Her he desired. His head ached and eyes narrowed with the intensity of his gazing, then as if an obscure fog had blown up in the mind, he experienced fear of her and was aware that he had received an impression, somehow, of evil. He shuddered, saying softly, it is thus with us all. Leo brewed some tea in a small pot and sat sipping it without sugar, to calm himself. But before he had finished drinking, again with excitement he examined the face and found it good: good for Leo Finkle. Only such a one could understand him and help him seek whatever he was seeking. She might, perhaps, love him. How she had happened to be among the discards in Salzman's barrel he could never guess, but he knew he must urgently go find her.

Leo rushed downstairs, grabbed up the Bronx telephone book, and searched for Salzman's home address. He was not listed, nor was his office. Neither was he in the Manhattan book. But Leo remembered having written down the address on a slip of paper after he had read Salzman's advertisement in the "personals" column of the *Forward*. He ran up to his room and tore through his papers, without luck. It was exasperating. Just when he needed the matchmaker he was nowhere to be found. Fortunately Leo remembered to look in his wallet. There on a card he found his name written and a Bronx address. No phone number was listed, the reason—Leo now recalled—he had originally communicated with Salzman by letter. He got on his coat, put a hat on over his skull cap and hurried to the subway station. All the way to the far end of the Bronx he sat on the edge of his seat. He was more than once tempted to take out the picture and see if the girl's face was as he remembered it, but he refrained, allowing the snapshot to remain in his inside coat pocket, content to have her so close. When the train pulled into the station he was waiting at the door and bolted out. He quickly located the street Salzman had advertised.

The building he sought was less than a block from the subway, but it was not an office building, nor even a loft, nor a store in which one could rent office space. It was a very old tenement house. Leo found Salzman's name in pencil on a soiled tag under the bell and climbed three dark flights to his apartment. When he knocked, the door was opened by a thin, asthmatic, gray-haired woman in felt slippers.

"Yes?" she said, expecting nothing. She listened without listening. He could have sworn he had seen her, too, before but knew it was an illusion.

"Salzman—does he live here? Pinye Salzman," he said, "the matchmaker?"

She stared at him a long minute. "Of course."

He felt embarrassed. "Is he in?"

"No." Her mouth, though left open, offered nothing more.

"The matter is urgent. Can you tell me where his office is?"

"In the air." She pointed upward.

"You mean he has no office?" Leo asked.

"In his socks."

He peered into the apartment. It was sunless and dingy, one large room divided by a half-open curtain, beyond which he could see a sagging metal bed. The near side of the room was crowded with rickety chairs, old bureaus, a three-legged table, racks of cooking utensils, and all the apparatus of a kitchen. But there was no sign of Salzman or his magic barrel, probably also a figment of the imagination. An odor of frying fish made Leo weak to the knees.

"Where is he?" he insisted. "I've got to see your husband."

At length she answered, "So who knows where he is? Every time he thinks a new thought he runs to a different place. Go home, he will find you."

"Tell him Leo Finkle."

She gave no sign she had heard.

He walked downstairs, depressed.

But Salzman, breathless, stood waiting at his door.

Leo was astounded and overjoyed. "How did you get here before me?"

"I rushed."

"Come inside."

They entered. Leo fixed tea, and a sardine sandwich for Salzman. As they were drinking he reached behind him for the packet of pictures and handed them to the marriage broker.

Salzman put down his glass and said expectantly, "You found somebody you like?"

"Not among these."

The marriage broker turned away.

"Here is the one I want." Leo held forth the snapshot.

Salzman slipped on his glasses and took the picture into his trembling hand. He turned ghastly and let out a groan.

"What's the matter?" cried Leo.

"Excuse me. Was an accident this picture. She isn't for you."

Salzman frantically shoved the manila packet into his portfolio. He thrust the snapshot into his pocket and fled down the stairs.

Leo, after momentary paralysis, gave chase and cornered the marriage broker in the vestibule. The landlady made hysterical outcries but neither of them listened.

"Give me back the picture, Salzman."

"No." The pain in his eyes was terrible.

"Tell me who she is then."

"This I can't tell you. Excuse me."

He made to depart, but Leo, forgetting himself, seized the matchmaker by his tight coat and shook him frenziedly.

"Please," sighed Salzman. "*Please.*"

Leo ashamedly let him go. "Tell me who she is," he begged. "It's very important for me to know."

"She is not for you. She is a wild one—wild, without shame. This is not a bride for a rabbi."

"What do you mean wild?"

"Like an animal. Like a dog. For her to be poor was a sin. This is why to me she is dead now."

"In God's name, what do you mean?"

"Her I can't introduce to you," Salzman cried.

"Why are you so excited?"

"Why, he asks," Salzman said, bursting into tears. "This is my baby, my Stella, she should burn in hell."

Leo hurried up to bed and hid under the covers. Under the covers he thought his life through. Although he soon fell asleep he could not sleep her out of his mind. He woke, beating his breast. Though he prayed to be rid of her, his prayers went unanswered. Through days of torment he endlessly struggled not to love her; fearing success, he escaped it. He then concluded to convert her to goodness, himself to God. The idea alternately nauseated and exalted him.

He perhaps did not know that he had come to a final decision until he encountered Salzman in a Broadway cafeteria. He was sitting alone at a rear table, sucking the bony remains of a fish. The marriage broker appeared haggard, and transparent to the point of vanishing.

Salzman looked up at first without recognizing him. Leo had grown a pointed beard and his eyes were weighted with wisdom.

"Salzman," he said, "love has at last come to my heart."

"Who can love from a picture?" mocked the marriage broker.

"It is not impossible."

"If you can love her, then you can love anybody. Let me show you some new clients that they just sent me their photographs. One is a little doll."

"Just her I want," Leo murmured.

"Don't be a fool, doctor Don't bother with her."

"Put me in touch with her, Salzman," Leo said humbly. "Perhaps I can be of service."

Salzman had stopped eating and Leo understood with emotion that it was now arranged.

Leaving the cafeteria, he was, however, afflicted by a tormenting suspicion that Salzman had planned it all to happen this way.

Leo was informed by letter that she would meet him on a certain corner, and she was there one spring night, waiting under a street lamp. He appeared carrying a small bouquet of violets and rosebuds. Stella stood by the lamp post, smoking. She wore white with red shoes, which fitted his expectations, although in a troubled moment he had imagined the dress red, and only the shoes white. She waited uneasily and shyly. From afar he saw that her eyes—clearly her father's—were filled with desperate innocence. He pictured, in her, his own redemption. Violins and lit candles revolved in the sky. Leo ran forward with flowers out-thrust.

Around the corner, Salzman, leaning against a wall, chanted prayers for the dead.

Dermuche

Marcel Aymé

HE had murdered a family of three in order to get possession of a gramophone record which he had coveted for several years. The fiery eloquence of counsel for the prosecution was unnecessary, and that of the defending counsel unavailing. He was unanimously condemned to have his head cut off, and not a voice was raised in sympathy, in the courtroom or elsewhere. Heavy-shouldered and bull-necked, he had a huge, flat face, all jaw and no forehead, with small, half-closed, dull-staring eyes. Even had there been a doubt as to his guilt, his brutish aspect would have caused any sensitive jury to condemn him. Throughout the trial he stayed motionless, seemingly indifferent and uncomprehending.

"Dermuche," asked the presiding judge, "are you sorry for what you did?"

"Well, yes and no, your Honor," said Dermuche. "I am, and then again, I'm not."

"Try to make yourself more clear. Do you feel any remorse?"

"Pardon, your Honor?"

"Don't you know what the word 'remorse' means? Have you no feeling of distress when you think of your victims?"

"I feel all right, your Honor, thanking you all the same."

Only at one moment during the trial did Dermuche display any interest, and this was when the prosecution produced the gramophone record. Leaning over the edge of the dock he gazed at it steadfastly, and when the gramophone, set in motion by the clerk, ground out the refrain, a smile of great gentleness passed over his dull, heavy face.

In the condemned cell he waited calmly for the day of execution, seemingly untroubled by the prospect. He never spoke of it to the warders entering the cell. Indeed, he had no desire to talk to them, and merely replied politely to the questions put to him. His sole occupation was to hum the magical refrain that had driven him to murder, and he knew it badly. His was a very slow memory, and perhaps it was his exasperation at being unable to recapture it which had taken him, on a September evening, to the modest villa in Nogent-sur-Mare. Three persons of small independent means lived in the villa, two old maids and an uncle, decorated with the Legion of Honor, who felt the cold. Every Sunday, at the end of the midday meal, the elder of the two sisters wound up the gramophone. In fine weather they kept the dining-room window open, and for three years Dermuche had known enchanted summers. Crouched at the foot of the villa wall he listened to that Sunday melody which during the ensuing week he sought to fix wholly in his memory, without ever being completely successful in doing so. But with the onset of autumn the uncle who felt the cold caused the window to be shut, and thereafter the music sounded only for persons of independent means. For three years in succession Dermuche had lived through the long months of deprivation, without music and without rapture. Little by little the refrain escaped him, diminishing day by day, until by the end of winter nothing was left of it but the longing. The fourth year he could not endure the thought of that long period of waiting, and so he broke into the villa. The police found him there next morning, listening to the song of the gramophone record in company with the three dead bodies.

For a month he had it by heart, but by the time the trial came on he had forgotten it again. Now, in the condemned cell, he gathered together the fragments restored to him by the playing of the record during the trial, but which every day became more uncertain. *Tum-tum-ti-tum*, hummed the condemned man from morning till night.

The prison chaplain visited Dermuche and found him filled with good will. He would have liked it better, however, if the poor wretch had shown himself more receptive, so that the words of consolation entered his heart. Dermuche listened with the docility of a tree, but neither his brief replies nor his expressionless face afforded any evidence that he was interested in his soul's salvation, or even that he possessed a soul. Nevertheless, one day in December, when he was talking of the Holy Virgin and the angels, the chaplain thought he caught a little gleam of light in those dull eyes—so fugitive, however, that he was not sure if he had really seen it. At the end of the interview Dermuche asked abruptly: "And the little Jesus, is he still alive?" The chaplain did not hesitate. No doubt he should have replied that the infant Jesus had once lived, but that, since he had died on the cross at the age of thirty-three, it was not possible to speak of him in the present tense. But Dermuche was so thick-headed that it was difficult to get him to understand. The fable of the infant Jesus was more within his range and might open his heart to the light of the sacred truths. The chaplain told the story of how the Son of God had elected to be born in a stable, between the ox and the ass.

"You see, Dermuche, it was to show that he loved the poor and had come for their sake. He might equally well have chosen to be born in a prison, among the most unhappy of men."

"Yes, sir, I see. In fact, Jesus might have been born in this cell I'm in, but he wouldn't have wanted to be born in a villa."

The chaplain contented himself with a wag of the head. Dermuche's logic was unassailable, but it was related rather too narrowly to his own particular case, and seemed unlikely to lead him into the way of repentance. Having thus nodded non-committally, the chaplain went on to tell him about the magi, the slaughter of innocents, the flight, and finally how the infant Jesus, when his beard was grown, had died crucified between two thieves to open the gates of heaven to mankind.

"Only think, Dermuche. The soul of the good thief must have been the first of all human souls to enter Paradise, and that was not due to accident, it was because God wished to show us what every sinner may expect of His mercy. For Him even the greatest crimes are no more than the accidents of life. . . . "

But for some time past Dermuche had not been following the chaplain's narrative, and the story of the good thief seemed to him as obscure as the miracle of the loaves and fishes.

"And so then little Jesus went back to his manger?"

He could think only of the infant Jesus. The chaplain left the cell reflecting that this murderer possessed no more understanding than a child. He even questioned whether Dermuche could be held responsible for his crime, and he prayed God to have mercy on him.

"A child's soul in a laborer's body. . . . He killed those three old people without malice, just as a child cuts open its doll, or pulls off its legs. A child that doesn't know its own strength. An unhapppy child and nothing more. And the proof is that he believes in the infant Jesus."

A few days later, paying Dermuche another visit, the chaplain asked the warder who opened the cell door:

"What's that he's singing?"

The male voice of Dermuche, like a deep-toned bell, could be heard incessantly repeating, *tum-tum-ti-tum*.

"He never stops that *tum-tum-tum* of his," said the warder. "If only it sounded like something it wouldn't be so bad, but it isn't even a tune."

This apparent lightness of heart, on the part of a condemned man who had not yet come to terms with Heaven, was disturbing to the chaplain. He found Dermuche livelier than usual. His brutish face had an expression of gentle alertness, and through the half-closed lids there shone a gleam of laughter. Moreover, he was almost talkative.

"What's the weather like outside today, sir?"

"It's snowing, my son."

"Well, that doesn't matter. The snow won't stop him. A fat lot he cares about the snow."

Once again the chaplain talked of God's mercy and the light of repentance, but the condemned man constantly interrupted him with questions about the infant Jesus, so that his exhortations were without effect.

"Does little Jesus know everybody? Is little Jesus the boss in Paradise? Would you say, sir, that little Jesus likes music?"

The chaplain finally found himself unable to get a word in edgeways. As he turned towards the door Dermuche thrust into his hand a sheet of paper folded in four.

"It's my letter to little Jesus," he said with a smile.

The chaplain took it and read it a few minutes later.

"Dear little Jesus," the letter ran. "This is asking you a favor. My name is Dermuche. It will soon be Christmas. I know you don't mind about me doing those three old geezers in Nogent. You wouldn't have wanted to be born in the house of people like that. I'm not asking for anything here on earth, seeing it won't be long before I have my chips. All I ask is, when I get to Heaven can I have my gramophone record? Thanking you in advance, and good luck to you—Dermuche."

The priest was horrified by the letter, which revealed all too clearly how impervious the murderer was to the idea of repentance.

"It is true," he reflected, "that the man is an innocent possessing no more discernment than a newborn babe. The trust he places in the infant Jesus bears sufficient witness to his childlike simplicity. But when he appears at the Seat of Judgment with three murders on his conscience, and no vestige of repentance, even God will be able to do nothing for him. Yet his small soul is as pure as the waters of a spring."

That evening he went to the prison chapel, and after having prayed for Dermuche, placed his letter in the plaster cradle of the infant Jesus.

At dawn on the 24th December, Christmas Eve, a party of well-dressed gentlemen accompanied the warders into the condemned cell. Their eyes still heavy with sleep, stomachs rumbling and mouths suppressing yawns, they paused at a short distance from the bed, seeking in the pallid early light to make out the shape of a body stretched beneath the coverings. The blankets moved feebly and a faint wail came from the bed. The Public Prosecutor felt a shiver pass down his spine. The Governor of the prison straightened his black tie and moved apart from the group. Shooting his cuffs he sought a posture appropriate to the occasion, and with his head inclined forward, shoulders rounded and hands clasped in front of his fly-buttons, he said in a theatrical voice:

"You must be brave, Dermuche. Your appeal has failed."

Another wail answered him, louder and more insistent than the first, but Dermuche did not move. He seemed to be buried even to his hair, and nothing of him emerged from the blankets.

"Come, Dermuche, you mustn't keep us waiting," said the Governor. "Do show a little co-operation, just for once."

A warder moved forward to shake the condemned man. He bent over the bed, then straightened himself and turned to the Governor with an air of astonishment.

"Why, what's the matter?"

"I don't know, sir. The bedclothes are moving, and yet . . . "

A long wail of heart-rending poignancy came from the blankets. With an abrupt movement the warder stripped them off the bed and then uttered a sharp exclamation. The others, who had pressed forward, in their turn uttered a cry of stupefaction. In place of Dermuche, on the uncovered bed, lay an infant a few months old. It seemed pleased to find itself in the light, and gazed placidly smiling at the visitors.

"What does this mean?" shouted the Governor, turning to the chief warder. "Have you let the prisoner escape?"

"It's impossible, sir. I made my last round three-quarters of an hour ago, and I'm positive I saw Dermuche in his bed."

Purple with fury, the Governor abused his subordinates, threatening them with the direst sanctions. The chaplain, meanwhile, had sunk to his knees and was offering thanks to God, the Holy Virgin, St. Joseph, Providence and the infant Jesus. But no one paid any attention to him.

"God almighty," cried the Governor, bending over the child, "will you look at that? It's got the same tattoo-marks as Dermuche on its chest!"

The others leaned over in their turn. The child had two pictures tattooed on either side of his chest, a woman's head on one side and a dog's head on the other. Dermuche had had exactly the same, even to their relative size. The warders all confirmed it. There was a long silence.

"I am perhaps mistaken," said M. Leboeuf, the Public Prosecutor, "but the child seems to me to be as much like Dermuche as a child that age can be like a man of thirty-three. Look at the big head, the flat face, the low forehead, the small, slit-eyes and even the shape of the nose. Don't you agree?" And he turned to M. Bridon, counsel for the defense.

"There does certainly seem to be a resemblance," said M. Bridon.

"Dermuche had a brown birthmark on the back of one thigh," the chief warder said.

They examined the child's leg and found the same thing.

"Fetch me the condemned man's finger-prints," said the Governor. "We'll see how those compare."

The chief warder went off at the double. While they awaited his return the others sought to find some rational explanation for the metamorphosis of Dermuche, which none could any longer doubt. The Governor alone took no part in the conversation but paced nervously up and down the cell. When the infant, alarmed by the sound of voices, began to cry, he advanced to the bedside and said in a threatening voice:

"You wait, my lad. I'll give you something to cry about!"

M. Leboeuf, who had seated himself beside the child, looked up at him with an intrigued expression.

"Do you really think this is your murderer?" he asked.

"I hope so. In any case, we shall soon know."

Confronted by this exquisite miracle, the chaplain continued to give thanks to God, his eyes damp with tenderness as he gazed at the virtually divine infant lying between Leboeuf and the Governor. He wondered a little anxiously what was to happen now, but concluded with confidence, "It will be as if the infant Jesus decides."

When the comparison of finger-prints had confirmed the extraordinary metamorphosis the Governor gave a sigh of relief and rubbed his hands.

"Well, now let's get on with it," he said. "We've simply been wasting time. Come along, Dermuche. Come along."

A murmur of protest arose in the cell, and M. Bridon cried indignantly:

"You surely can't intend to execute a babe in arms! It would be a hideous thing to do, utterly monstrous. Even if we admit the fact of Dermuche's guilt, and that he deserved the death sentence, we have surely no need to plead the innocence of a newly born infant."

"I can't go into those details," answered the Governor. "Is this Dermuche, or isn't it? Did he murder three people in Nogent-sur-Marne? Was he condemned to death? The law applies to everyone and I don't want any trouble. The scaffold has been erected and the guillotine was set up more than an hour ago. This talk about the innocence of the newly born is merely tiresome. At that rate anyone could escape justice simply by turning themselves into an infant. It would be a bit too easy!"

The defending counsel, with a maternal gesture, had drawn the covers back over the dimpled body of his client. The infant, responding to the warmth, laughed and crowed with pleasure, and the Governor looked coldly at it, finding this manifestation of gaiety out of place.

"You note the cynicism," he said. "He means to brazen it out to the end."

"My dear Governor," said the chaplain, "is it possible that you cannot see in this episode the hand of God?"

"Perhaps, but that makes no difference. It's certainly nothing to do with me. It isn't God who gave me my job or who is responsible for my advancement. I've had my instructions, and I intend to carry them out." The Governor turned to the Public Prosecutor. "Don't you agree that I'm entirely right?"

M. Leboeuf took time for thought before giving his opinion.

"Undoubtedly your position is logically sound. It would be profoundly unjust for a murderer to be privileged to begin his life again instead of paying the just penalty of his crime. On the other hand, the execution of an infant is a rather ticklish matter. I think you would be wise to consult your superiors."

"I know them," said the Governor. "They'll be annoyed with me for putting them in an embarrassing position. However, I'll ring them up."

The high officials concerned had not yet arrived at the Ministry. The Governor had to ring up their homes. Being still only half awake they were not in the best of tempers. The metamorphosis of Dermuche seemed to them a treacherous stratagem aimed directly at themselves, and they were highly indignant. The fact remained, none the less, that the condemned man was now a babe in arms. But the times were harsh, and they feared for their advancement if they should be suspected of lenience. Having agreed among themselves they resolved that—"the fact that the murderer has somewhat shrunk beneath the burden of remorse, or from no matter what cause, can in no way be allowed to divert the course of Justice."

Accordingly the condemned man's toilet was proceeded with—that is to say, he was wrapped in one of the bed coverings and the soft down on the back of his neck was shaved off. The chaplain then took the precaution of baptising him. It was he who carried him in his arms to the machine erected in the prison courtyard.

As they returned from the place of execution he told counsel for the defense of Dermuche's letter to the infant Jesus.

"God could not allow a murderer entirely untouched by remorse to enter Paradise. But Dermuche had hope on his side, and his love of the infant Jesus. So God effaced his life as a sinner and restored him to the age of innocence."

"But if his life as a sinner was effaced, then Dermuche committed no crime and those people in Nogent were never murdered."

Wanting to be quite sure on this point, the Counsel immediately went to Nogent-sur-Marne. Upon arriving there he asked to be directed to the house where the crime had been committed, but no one had heard of any crime. He had no difficulty, however, in finding the house where the two Mademoiselles Bridaine lived with their uncle who suffered from the cold. The three old people received him at first with mistrust, and after being reassured, complained to him that that very night someone had stolen a gramophone record lying on the dining-room table.

THE BLACK MADONNA

Doris Lessing

THERE are some countries in which the arts, let alone Art, cannot be said to flourish. Why this should be so it is hard to say, although of course we all have our theories about it. For sometimes it is the most barren soil that sends up gardens of those flowers which we all agree are the crown and justification of life, and it is this fact which makes it hard to say, finally, why the soil of Zambesia should produce such reluctant plants.

Zambesia is a tough, sunburnt, virile, positive country contemptuous of subtleties and sensibility: yet there have been States with these qualities which have produced art, though perhaps with the left hand. Zambesia is, to put it mildly, unsympathetic to those ideas so long taken for granted in other parts of the world, to do with liberty, fraternity and the rest. Yet there are those, and some of the finest souls among them, who maintain that art is impossible without a minority whose leisure is guaranteed by a hard-working majority. And whatever Zambesia's comfortable minority may lack, it is not leisure.

Zambesia—but enough; out of respect for ourselves and for scientific accuracy, we should refrain from jumping to conclusions. Particularly when one remembers the almost wistful respect Zambesians show when an artist does appear in their midst.

Consider, for instance, the case of Michele.

He came out of the internment camp at the time when Italy was made a sort of honorary ally, during the Second World War. It was a time of strain for the authorities, because it is one thing to be responsible for thousands of prisoners of war whom one must treat according to certain recognized standards; it is another to be faced, and from one day to the next, with these same thousands transformed by some international legerdemain into comrades in arms. Some of the thousands stayed where they were in the camps; they were fed and housed there at least. Others went as farm labourers, though not many; for while the farmers were as always short of labour, they did not know how to handle farm labourers who were also white men: such a phenomenon had never happened in Zambesia before. Some did odd jobs around the towns, keeping a sharp eye out for the trade unions, who would neither admit them as members nor agree to their working.

Hard, hard, the lot of these men, but fortunately not for long, for soon the war ended and they were able to go home.

Hard, too, the lot of the authorities, as has been pointed out; and for that reason they were doubly willing to take what advantages they could from the situation; and that Michele was such an advantage there could be no doubt.

His talents were first discovered when he was still a prisoner of war. A church was built in the camp, and Michele decorated its interior. It became a show-place, that little tin-roofed church in the prisoners' camp, with its whitewashed walls covered all over with frescoes depicting swarthy peasants gathering grapes for the vintage, beautiful Italian girls dancing, plump dark-eyed children. Amid crowded scenes of Italian life, appeared the Virgin and her Child, smiling and beneficent, happy to move familiarly among her people.

Culture-loving ladies who had bribed the authorities to be taken inside the camp would say, "Poor thing, how homesick he must be." And they would beg to be allowed to leave half a crown for the artist. Some were indignant. He was a prisoner, after all, captured in the very act of fighting against justice and democracy, and what right had he to protest?—for they felt these paintings as a sort of protest. What was there in Italy that we did not have right here in Westonville, which was the capital and hub of Zambesia? Were there not sunshine and mountains and fat babies and pretty girls here? Did we not grow—if not grapes, at least lemons and oranges and flowers in plenty?

People were upset—the desperation of nostalgia came from the painted white walls of that simple church, and affected everyone according to his temperament.

But when Michele was free, his talent was remembered. He was spoken of as "that Italian artist." As a matter of fact, he was a bricklayer. And the virtues of those frescoes might very well have been exaggerated. It is possible they would have been overlooked altogether in a country where picture-covered walls were more common.

When one of the visiting ladies came rushing out to the camp in her own car, to ask him to paint her children, he said he was not qualified to do so. But at last he agreed. He took a room in the town and made some nice likenesses of the children. Then he painted the children of a great number of the first lady's friends. He charged ten shillings a time. Then one of the ladies wanted a portrait of herself. He asked ten pounds for it; it had taken him a month to do. She was annoyed, but paid.

And Michele went off to his room with a friend and stayed there drinking red wine from the Cape and talking about home. While the money lasted he could not be persuaded to do any more portraits.

There was a good deal of talk among the ladies about the dignity of labour, a subject in which they were well versed; and one felt they might almost go so far as to compare a white man with a kaffir, who did not understand the dignity of labour either.

He was felt to lack gratitude. One of the ladies tracked him down, found him lying on a camp-bed under a tree with a bottle of wine, and spoke to him severely about the barbarity of Mussolini and the fecklessness of the Italian temperament. Then she demanded that he should instantly paint a picture of herself in her new evening dress. He refused and she went home very angry.

It happened that she was the wife of one of our most important citizens, a General or something of that kind, who was at that time engaged in planning a military tattoo or show for the benefit of the civilian population. The whole of Westonville had been discussing this show for weeks. We were all bored to extinction by dances, fancy-dress balls, fairs, lotteries and other charitable entertainments. It is not too much to say that while some were dying for freedom, others were dancing for it. There comes a limit to everything. Though, of course, when the end of the war actually came and the thousands of troops stationed in the country had to go home—in short, when enjoying ourselves would no longer be a duty, many were heard to exclaim that life would never be the same again.

In the meantime, the Tattoo would make a nice change for us all. The military gentlemen responsible for the idea did not think of it in these terms. They thought to improve morale by giving us some idea of what war was really like. Headlines in the newspaper were not enough. And in order to bring it all home to us, they planned to destroy a village by shell-fire before our very eyes.

First, the village had to be built.

It appears that the General and his subordinates stood around in the red dust of the parade-ground under a burning sun for the whole of one day, surrounded by building materials, while hordes of African labourers ran around with boards and nails, trying to make something that looked like a village. It became evident that they would have to build a proper village in order to destroy it; and this would cost more than was allowed for the whole entertainment. The General went home in a bad temper, and his wife said what they needed was an artist, they needed Michele. This was not because she wanted to do Michele a good turn; she could not endure the thought of him lying around singing while there was work to be done. She refused to undertake any delicate diplomatic missions when her husband said he would be damned if he would ask favours of any little Wop. She solved the problem for him in her own way: a certain Captain Stocker was sent out to fetch him.

The Captain found him on the same camp-bed under the same tree, in rolled-up trousers, and an uncollared shirt; unshaven, mildly drunk, with a bottle of wine standing beside him on the earth. He was singing an air so wild, so sad, that the Captain was uneasy. He stood at ten paces from the disreputable fellow and felt the indignities of his position. A year ago, this man had been a mortal enemy to be shot at sight. Six months ago, he had been an enemy prisoner. Now he lay with his knees up, in an untidy shirt that had certainly once been military. For the Captain, the situation crystallised in a desire that Michele should salute him.

"Piselli!" he said sharply.

Michele turned his head and looked at the Captain from the horizontal. "Good morning," he said affably.

"You are wanted," said the Captain.

"Who?" said Michele. He sat up, a fattish, olive-skinned little man. His eyes were resentful.

"The authorities."

"The war is over?"

The Captain, who was already stiff and shiny enough in his laundered khaki, jerked his head back frowning, chin out. He was a large man, blond, and wherever his flesh showed, it was brick-red. His eyes were small and blue and angry. His red hands, covered all over with fine yellow bristles, clenched by his side. Then he saw the disappointment in Michele's eyes, and the hands unclenched. "No it is not over," he said. "Your assistance is required."

"For the war?"

"For the war effort. I take it you are interested in defeating the Germans?"

Michele looked at the Captain. The little dark-eyed artisan looked at the great blond officer with his cold eyes, his narrow mouth, his hands like bristle-covered steaks. He looked and said: "I am very interested in the end of the war."

"*Well?*" said the Captain between his teeth.

"The pay?" said Michele.

"You will be paid."

Michele stood up. He lifted the bottle against the sun, then took a gulp. He rinsed his mouth out with wine and spat. Then he poured what was left on to the red earth, where it made a bubbling purple stain.

"I am ready," he said. He went with the Captain to the waiting lorry, where he climbed in beside the driver's seat and not, as the Captain had expected, into the back of the lorry. When they had arrived at the parade-ground the officers had left a message that the Captain would be personally responsible for Michele and for the village. Also for the hundred or so labourers who were sitting around on the grass verges waiting for orders.

The Captain explained what was wanted. Michele nodded. Then he waved his hand at the Africans. "I do not want these," he said.

"You will do it yourself—a village?"

"Yes."

"With no help?"

Michele smiled for the first time. "I will do it."

The Captain hesitated. He disapproved on principle of white men doing heavy manual labour. He said: "I will keep six to do the heavy work."

Michele shrugged; and the Captain went over and dismissed all but six of the Africans. He came back with them to Michele.

"It is hot," said Michele.

"Very," said the Captain. They were standing in the middle of the parade-ground. Around its edge trees, grass, gulfs of shadow. Here, nothing but reddish dust, drifting and lifting in a low hot breeze.

"I am thirsty," said Michele. He grinned. The Captain felt his stiff lips loosen unwillingly in reply. The two pairs of eyes met. It was a moment of understanding. For the Captain, the little Italian had suddenly become human. "I will arrange it," he said, and went off down-town. By the time he had explained the position to the right people, filled in forms and made arrangements, it was late afternoon. He returned to the parade-ground with a case of Cape brandy, to find Michele and the six black men seated together under a tree. Michele was singing an Italian song to them, and they were harmonizing with him. The sight affected the Captain like an attack of nausea. He came up, and the Africans stood to attention. Michele continued to sit.

"You said you would do the work yourself?"

"Yes, I said so."

The Captain then dismissed the Africans. They departed with friendly looks towards Michele, who waved at them. The Captain was beef-red with anger. "You have not started yet?"

"How long have I?"

"Three weeks."

"Then there is plenty of time," said Michele, looking at the bottle of brandy in the Captain's hand. In the other were two glasses. "It is evening," he pointed out. The Captain stood frowning for a moment. Then he sat down on the grass, and poured out two brandies.

"Ciao," said Michele.

"Cheers," said the Captain. Three weeks, he was thinking, Three weeks with this damned little Itie! He drained his glass and refilled it, and set it in the grass. The grass was cool and soft. A tree was flowering somewhere close—hot waves of perfume came on the breeze.

"It is nice here," said Michele. "We will have a good time together. Even in a war, there are times of happiness. And of friendship. I drink to the end of the war."

Next day, the Captain did not arrive at the parade-ground until after lunch. He found Michele under the trees with a bottle. Sheets of ceiling board had been erected at one end of the parade-ground in such a way that they formed two walls and a part of a third, and a slant of steep roof supported on struts.

"What's that?" said the Captain, furious.

"The church," said Michele.

"Wha-at?"

"You will see. Later. It is very hot." He looked at the brandy bottle that lay on its side on the ground. The Captain went to the lorry and returned with the case of brandy. They drank. Time passed. It was a long time since the Captain had sat on grass under a tree. It was a long time, for that matter, since he had drunk so much. He always drank a great deal, but it was regulated to the times and seasons. He was a disciplined man. Here, sitting on the grass beside this little man whom he still could not help thinking of as an enemy, it was not that he let his self-discipline go, but that he felt himself to be something different: he was temporarily set outside his normal behaviour. Michele did not count. He listened to Michele talking about Italy, and it seemed to him he was listening to a savage speaking: as if he heard tales from the mythical South Sea islands where a man like himself might very well go just once in his life. He found himself saying he would like to make a trip to Italy after the war. Actually, he was attracted only by the North and by Northern people. He had visited Germany, under Hitler, and though it was not the time to say so, had found it very satisfactory. Then Michele sang him some Italian songs. He sang Michele some English songs. Then Michele took out photographs of his wife and children, who lived in a village in the mountains of North Italy. He asked the Captain if he were married. The Captain never spoke about his private affairs.

He had spent all his life in one or other of the African colonies as a policeman, magistrate, native commisssioner, or in some other useful capacity. When the war started, military life came easy to him. But he hated city life, and had his own reasons for wishing the war over. Mostly, he had been in bush-stations with one or two other white men, or by himself, far from the rigours of civilisation. He had relations with native women; and from time to time visited the city where his wife lived with her parents and the children. He was always tormented by the idea that she was unfaithful to him. Recently he had even appointed a private detective to watch her; he was convinced the detective was inefficient. Army friends coming from L——where his wife was, spoke of her at parties, enjoying herself. When the war ended, she would not find it so easy to have a good time. And why did he not simply live with her and be done with it? The fact was, he could not. And his long exile to remote bush-stations was because he needed the excuse not to. He could not bear to think of his wife for too long; she was that part of his life he had never been able, so to speak, to bring to heel.

Yet he spoke of her now to Michele, and of his favourite bush-wife, Nadya. He told Michele the story of his life, until he realized that the shadows from the trees they sat under had stretched right across the parade-ground to the grandstand. He got unsteadily to his feet, and said: "There is work to be done. You are being paid to work."

"I will show you my church when the light goes."

The sun dropped, darkness fell, and Michele made the Captain drive his lorry on to the parade-ground a couple of hundred yards away and switch on his lights. Instantly, a white church sprang up from the shapes and shadows of the bits of board.

"Tomorrow, some houses," said Michele cheerfully.

At the end of a week, the space at the end of the parade-ground had crazy gawky constructions of lath and board over it, that looked in the sunlight like nothing on this earth. Privately, it upset the Captain; it was like a nightmare that these skeleton-like shapes should be able to persuade him, with the illusions of light and dark, that they were a village. At night, the Captain drove up his lorry, switched on the lights, and there it was, the village, solid and real against a background of full green trees. Then, in the morning sunlight, there was nothing there, just bits of board stuck in the sand.

"It is finished," said Michele.

"You were engaged for three weeks," said the Captain. He did not want it to end, this holiday from himself.

Michele shrugged. "The army is rich," he said. Now, to avoid curious eyes, they sat inside the shade of the church, with the case of brandy between them. The Captain talked, talked endlessly, about his wife, about women. He could not stop talking.

Michele listened. Once he said: "When I go home—when I go home—I shall open my arms . . . " He opened them, wide. He closed his eyes. Tears ran down his cheeks. "I shall take my wife in my arms, and I shall ask nothing, nothing. I do not care. It is enough to be together. That is what the war has taught me. It is enough, it is enough. I shall ask no questions and I shall be happy."

The Captain stared before him, suffering. He thought how he dreaded his wife. She was a scornful creature, gray and hard, who laughed at him. She had been laughing at him ever since they married. Since the war, she had taken to calling him names like Little Hitler, and Storm-trooper. "Go ahead, my little Hitler," she had cried last time they met. "Go ahead, my Storm-trooper. If you want to waste your money on private detectives, go ahead. But don't think I don't know what *you* do when you're in the bush. I don't care what you do, but remember that I know it . . . "

The Captain remembered her saying it. And there sat Michele on his packing-case, saying: "It's a pleasure for the rich, my friend, detectives and the law. Even jealousy is a pleasure I don't want any more. Ah, my friend, to be together with my wife again, and the children, that is all I ask of life. That and wine and food and singing in the evenings." And the tears wetted his cheeks and splashed on to his shirt.

That a man should cry, good lord! thought the Captain. And without shame! He seized the bottle and drank.

Three days before the great occasion, some high-ranking officers came strolling through the dust, and found Michele and the Captain sitting together on the packing-case, singing. The Captain's shirt was open down the front, and there were stains on it.

The Captain stood to attention with the bottle in his hand, and Michele stood to attention too, out of sympathy with his friend. Then the officers drew the Captain aside—they were all cronies of his—and said, what the hell did he think he was doing? And why wasn't the village finished?

Then they went away.

"Tell them it is finished," said Michele. "Tell them I want to go."

"No," said the Captain, "no. Michele, what would you do if your wife . . . "

"This world is a good place. We should be happy—that is all."

"Michele . . ."

"I want to go. There is nothing to do. They paid me yesterday."

"Sit down, Michele. Three more days, and then it's finished."

"Then I shall paint the inside of the church as I painted the one in the camp."

The Captain laid himself down on some boards and went to sleep. When he woke, Michele was surrounded by the pots of paint he had used on the outside of the village. Just in front of the Captain was a picture of a black girl. She was young and plump. She wore a patterned blue dress and her shoulders came soft and bare out of it. On her back was a baby slung in a band of red stuff. Her face was turned towards the Captain and she was smiling.

"That's Nadya," said the Captain. Nadya . . ." He groaned loudly. He looked at the black child and shut his eyes. He opened them, and mother and child were still there. Michele was very carefully drawing thin yellow circles around the heads of the black girl and her child.

"Good God," said the Captain, "you can't do that."

"Why not?"

"You can't have a black Madonna."

"She was a peasant. This is a peasant. Black peasant Madonna for black country."

"This is a German village," said the Captain.

"This is my madonna," said Michele angrily. "Your German village and my Madonna. I paint this picture as an offering to the Madonna. She is pleased—I feel it."

The Captain lay down again. He was feeling ill. He went back to sleep. When he woke for the second time it was dark. Michele had brought in a flaring paraffin lamp, and by its light was working on the long wall. A bottle of brandy stood beside him. He painted until long after midnight, and the Captain lay on his side and watched, as passive as a man suffering a dream. Then they both went to sleep on the boards. The whole of the next day Michele stood painting black Madonnas, black saints, black angels. Outside, troops were practising in the sunlight, bands were blaring and motorcyclists roared up and down. But Michele painted on, drunk and oblivious. The Captain lay on his back, drinking and muttering about his wife. Then he would say "Nadya, Nadya," and burst into sobs.

Towards nightfall the troops went away. The officers came back, and the Captain went off with them to show how the village sprang into being when the great lights at the end of the parade-ground were switched on. They all looked at the village in silence. They switched the lights off, and there were only the tall angular boards leaning like gravestones in the moonlight. On went the lights—and there was the village. They were silent, as if suspicious. Like the Captain, they seemed to feel it was not right. Uncanny it certainly was, but *that* was not it. Unfair—that was the word. It was cheating. And profoundly disturbing.

"Clever chap, that Italian of yours," said the General.

The Captain, who had been woodenly correct until this moment, suddenly came rocking up to the General, and steadied himself by laying his hand on the august shoulder. "Bloody Wops," he said. "Bloody kaffirs. Bloody . . . Tell you what, though, there's one Itie that's some good. Yes, there is. I'm telling you. He's a friend of mine, actually."

The General looked at him. Then he nodded at his underlings. The Captain was taken away for disciplinary purposes. It was decided, however, that he must be ill, nothing else could account for such behaviour. He was put to bed in his own room with a nurse to watch him.

He woke twenty-four hours later, sober for the first time in weeks. He slowly remembered what had happened. Then he sprang out of bed and rushed into his clothes. The nurse was just in time to see him run down the path and leap into his lorry.

He drove at top speed to the parade-ground, which was flooded with light in such a way that the village did not exist. Everything was in full swing. The cars were three deep around the square, with people on the running-boards and even the roofs. The grandstand was packed. Women dressed up as gipsies, country girls, Elizabethan court dames, and so on, wandered about with trays of ginger beer and sausage-rolls and programmes at five shillings each in aid of the war effort. On the square, troops deployed, obsolete machine-guns were being dragged up and down, bands played, and motorcyclists roared through flames.

As the Captain parked the lorry, all this activity ceased, and the lights went out. The Captain began running around the outside of the square to reach the place where the guns were hidden in a mess of net and branches. He was sobbing with the effort. He was a big man, and unused to exercise, and sodden with brandy. He had only one idea in his mind—to stop the guns firing, to stop them at all costs.

Luckily, there seemed to be a hitch. The lights were still out. The unearthly graveyard at the end of the square glittered white in the moonlight. Then the lights briefly switched on, and the village sprang into existence for just long enough to show large red crosses all over a white building beside the church. Then moonlight flooded everything again, and the crosses vanished. "Oh, the bloody fool!" sobbed the Captain, running, running as if for his life. He was no longer trying to reach the guns. He was cutting across a corner of the square direct to the church. He could hear some officers cursing behind him: "Who put those red crosses there? Who? We can't fire on the Red Cross."

The Captain reached the church as the searchlights burst on. Inside, Michele was kneeling on the earth looking at his first Madonna. "They are going to kill my Madonna," he said miserably.

"Come away, Michele, come away."

"They're going to . . ."

The Captain grabbed his arm and pulled. Michele wrenched himself free and grabbed a saw. He began hacking at the ceiling board. There was a dead silence outside. They heard a voice booming through the loudspeakers: "The village that is about to be shelled is an English village, not as represented on the programme, a German village. Repeat, the village that is about to be shelled is . . ."

Michele had cut through two sides of a square around the Madonna.

"Michele," sobbed the Captain, "*get out of here.*"

Michele dropped the saw, took hold of the raw edges of the board and tugged. As he did so, the church began to quiver and lean. An irregular patch of board ripped out and Michele staggered back into the Captain's arms. There was a roar. The church seemed to dissolve around them into flame. Then they were running away from it, the Captain holding Michele tight by the arm. "Get down," he shouted suddenly, and threw Michele to the earth. He flung himself down beside him. Looking from under the crook of his arm, he heard the explosion, saw a great pillar of smoke and flame, and the village disintegrated in a flying mass of debris. Michele was on his knees gazing at his Madonna in the light from the flames. She was unrecognizable, blotted out with dust. He looked horrible, quite white, and a trickle of blood soaked from his hair down one cheek.

"They shelled my Madonna," he said.

"Oh, damn it, you can paint another one," said the Captain. His own voice seemed to him strange, like a dream voice. He was certainly crazy, as mad as Michele himself . . . He got up, pulled Michele to his feet, and marched him towards the edge of the field. There they were met by the ambulance people. Michele was taken off to hospital, and the Captain was sent back to bed.

A week passed. The Captain was in a darkened room. That he was having some kind of a breakdown was clear, and two nurses stood guard over him. Sometimes he lay quiet. Sometimes he muttered to himself. Sometimes he sang in a thick clumsy voice bits out of opera, fragments from Italian songs, and—over and over again—"There's a Long Long Trail." He was not thinking of anything at all. He shied away from the thought of Michele as if it were dangerous. When, therefore, a cheerful female voice announced that a friend had come to cheer him up, and it would do him good to have some company, and he saw a white bandage moving towards him in the gloom, he turned sharp over on to his side, face to the wall.

"Go away," he said. "Go away, Michele."

"I have come to see you," said Michele. "I have brought you a present."

The Captain slowly turned over. There was Michele, a cheerful ghost in the dark room. "You fool," he said. "You messed everything up. What did you paint those crosses for?"

"It was a hospital," said Michele. "In a village there is a hospital, and on the hospital the Red Cross, the beautiful Red Cross—no?"

"I was nearly court-martialled."

"It was my fault," said Michele. "I was drunk."

"I was responsible."

"How could you be responsible when I did it? But it is all over. Are you better?"

"Well, I suppose those crosses saved your life."

"I did not think," said Michele. "I was remembering the kindness of the Red Cross people when we were prisoners."

"Oh shut up, shut up, shut up."

"I have brought you a present."

The Captain peered through the dark. Michele was holding up a picture. It was of a native woman with a baby on her back smiling sideways out of the frame.

Michele said: "You did not like the haloes. So this time, no haloes. For the Captain—no Madonna." He laughed. "You like it? It is for you. I painted it for you."

"God damn you!" said the Captain.

"You do not like it?" said Michele, very hurt.

The Captain closed his eyes. "What are you going to do next?" he asked tiredly.

Michele laughed again. "Mrs. Pannerhurst, the lady of the General, she wants me to paint her picture in her white dress. So I paint it."

"You should be proud to."

"Silly bitch. She thinks I am good. They know nothing—savages. Barbarians. Not you, Captain, you are my friend. But these people they know nothing."

The Captain lay quiet. Fury was gathering in him. He thought of the General's wife. He disliked her, but he had known her well enough.

"These people," said Michele. "They do not know a good picture from a bad picture. I paint, I paint, this way, that way. There is the picture—I look at it and laugh inside myself." Michele laughed out loud. "They say, he is a Michelangelo, this one, and try to cheat me out of my price. Michele—Michelangelo—that is a joke, no?"

The Captain said nothing.

"But for you I painted this picture to remind you of our good times with the village. You are my friend. I will always remember you."

The Captain turned his eyes sideways in his head and stared at the black girl. Her smile at him was half innocence, half malice.

"Get out," he said suddenly.

Michele came closer and bent to see the Captain's face. "You wish me to go?" He sounded unhappy. "You saved my life. I was a fool that night. But I was thinking of my offering to the Madonna—I was a fool, I say it myself. I was drunk, we are fools when we are drunk."

"Get out of here," said the Captain again.

For a moment the white bandage remained motionless. Then it swept downwards in a bow.

Michele turned towards the door.

"And take that bloody picture with you."

Silence. Then, in the dim light, the Captain saw Michele reach out for the picture, his white head bowed in profound obeisance. He straightened himself and stood to attention, holding the picture with one hand, and keeping the other stiff down his side. Then he saluted the Captain.

"Yes, *sir*," he said, and he turned and went out of the door with the picture.

The Captain lay still. He felt—what did he feel? There was a pain under his ribs. It hurt to breathe. He realized he was unhappy. Yes, a terrible unhappiness was filling him, slowly, slowly. He was unhappy because Michele had gone. Nothing had ever hurt the Captain in all his life as much as that mocking *Yes, sir.* Nothing. He turned his face to the wall and wept. But silently. Not a sound escaped him, for the fear the nurses might hear.

A & P

John Updike

IN walks these three girls in nothing but bathing suits. I'm in the third checkout slot, with my back to the door, so I don't see them until they're over by the bread. The one that caught my eye first was the one in the plaid green two-piece. She was a chunky kid, with a good tan and a sweet broad soft-looking can with those two crescents of white just under it, where the sun never seems to hit at the top of the backs of her legs. I stood there with my hand on a box of HiHo crackers trying to remember if I rang it up or not. I ring it up again and the customer starts giving me hell. She's one of these cash-register-watchers, a witch about fifty with rouge on her cheekbones and no eyebrows, and I know it made her day to trip me up. She'd been watching cash registers for fifty years and probably never seen a mistake before.

By the time I got her feathers smoothed and her goodies into a bag—she gives me a little snort in passing, if she'd been born at the right time they would have burned her over in Salem—by the time I get her on her way the girls had circled around the bread and were coming back, without a pushcart, back my way along the counters, in the aisle between the checkouts and the Special bins. They didn't even have shoes on. There was this chunky one, with the two-piece—it was bright green and the seams on the bra were still sharp and her belly was still pretty pale so I guessed she just got it (the suit)—there was this one, with one of those chubby berry-faces, the lips all bunched together under her nose, this one, and a tall one, with black hair that hadn't quite frizzed right, and one of these sunburns right across under the eyes, and a chin that was too long—you know, the kind of girl other girls think is very "striking" and "attractive" but never quite makes it, as they very well know, which is why they like her so much—and then the third one, that wasn't quite so tall. She was the queen. She kind of led them, the other two peeking around and making their shoulders round. She didn't look around, not this queen, she just walked straight on slowly, on these long white prima-donna legs. She came down a little hard on her heels, as if she didn't walk in her bare feet that much, putting down her heels and then letting the weight move along to her toes as if she was testing the floor with every step, putting a little deliberate extra action into it. You never know for sure how girls' minds work (do you really think it's a mind in there or just a little buzz like a bee in a glass jar?) but you got the idea she had talked the other two into coming in here with her, and now she was showing them how to do it, walk slow and hold yourself straight.

She had on a kind of dirty-pink—beige maybe, I don't know—

bathing suit with a little nubble all over it and, what got me, the straps were down. They were off her shoulders looped loose around the cool tops of her arms, and I guess as a result the suit had slipped a little on her, so all around the top of the cloth there was this shining rim. If it hadn't been there you wouldn't have known there could have been anything whiter than those shoulders. With the straps pushed off, there was nothing between the top of the suit and the top of her head except just *her*, this clean bare plane of the top of her chest down from the shoulder bones like a dented sheet of metal tilted in the light. I mean, it was more than pretty.

She had sort of oaky hair that the sun and salt had bleached, done up in a bun that was unravelling, and a kind of prim face. Walking into the A & P with your straps down, I suppose it's the only kind of face you *can* have. She held her head so high her neck, coming up out of those white shoulders, looked kind of stretched, but I didn't mind. The longer her neck was, the more of her there was.

She must have felt in the corner of her eye me and over my shoulder Stokesie in the second slot watching, but she didn't tip. Not this queen. She kept her eyes moving across the racks, and stopped, and turned so slow it made my stomach rub the inside of my apron, and buzzed to the other two, who kind of huddled against her for relief, and then they all three of them went up the cat-and-dog-food-breakfast-cereal-macaroni-rice-raisins-seasonings-spreads-spaghetti-soft-drinks-crackers-and-cookies aisle. From the third slot I look stright up this aisle to the meat counter, and I watched them all the way. The fat one with the tan sort of fumbled with the cookies, but on second thought she put the package back. The sheep pushing their carts down the aisle—the girls were walking against the usual traffic (not that we have one-way signs or anything)—were pretty hilarious. You could see them, when Queenie's white shoulders dawned on them, kind of jerk, or hop, or hiccup, but their eyes snapped back to their own baskets and on they pushed. I bet you could set off dynamite in an A & P and the people would by and large keep reaching and checking oatmeal off their lists and muttering "Let me see, there was a third thing, began with A, asparagus, no, ah, yes, applesauce!" or whatever it is they do mutter. But there was no doubt, this jiggled them. A few houseslaves in pin curlers even looked around after pushing their carts past to make sure what they had seen was correct.

You know, it's one thing to have a girl in a bathing suit down on the beach, where what with the glare nobody can look at each other much anyway, and another thing in the cool of the A & P, under the fluorescent lights, against all those stacked packages, with her feet paddling along naked over our checkerboard green-and-cream rubber-tile floor.

"Oh Daddy," Stokesie said beside me. "I feel so faint."

"Darling," I said. "Hold me tight." Stokesie's married, with two babies chalked up on his fuselage already, but as far as I can tell that's the only difference. He's twenty-two, and I was nineteen this April.

"Is it done?" he asks, the responsible married man finding his voice. I forgot to say he thinks he's going to be manager some sunny day, maybe in 1990 when it's called the Great Alexandrov and Petrooshki Tea Company[1] or something.

What he meant was, our town is five miles from a beach, with a big summer colony out on the Point, but we're right in the middle of town, and the women generally put on a shirt or shorts or something before they get out of the car into the street. And anyway these are usually women with six children and varicose veins mapping their legs and no-body, including them, could care less. As I say, we're right in the middle of town, and if you stand at our front doors you can see two banks and the Congregational church and the newspaper store and three real-estate offices and about twenty-seven old freeloaders tearing up Central Street because the sewer broke again. It's not as if we're on the Cape; we're north of Boston and there's people in this town haven't seen the ocean for twenty years.

The girls had reached the meat counter and were asking McMahon something. He pointed, they pointed, and they shuffled out of sight be-hind a pyramid of Diet Delight peaches. All that was left for us to see was old McMahon patting his mouth and looking after them sizing up their joints. Poor kids, I began to feel sorry for them, they couldn't help it.

Now here comes the sad part of the story, at least my family says it's sad, but I don't think it's so sad myself. The store's pretty empty, it being Thursday afternoon, so there was nothing much to do except lean on the register and wait for the girls to show up again. The whole store was like a pinball machine and I didn't know which tunnel they'd come out of. After a while they come around out of the far aisle, around the light bulbs, records at discount of the Caribbean Six or Tony Martin Sings or some such gunk you wonder they waste the wax on, sixpacks of candy bars, and plastic toys done up in cellophane that fall apart when a kid looks at them anyway. Around they come, Queenie still leading the way, and holding a little gray jar in her hand. Slots Three through Seven are unmanned and I could see her wondering between Stokes and me, but Stokesie with his usual luck draws an old party in baggy gray pants who stumbles up with four giant cans of pineapple juice (what do these bums *do* with all that pineapple juice? I've often asked myself) so the girls come to me. Queenie puts down the jar and I take it into my fingers icy cold. Kingfish Fancy Herring Snacks in Pure Sour Cream; 49¢. Now her hands are empty, not a ring or a bracelet, bare as God made them, and I wonder where the money's coming from. Still with that prim look she lifts a folded dollar bill out of the hollow at the center of her nubbled pink top. The jar went heavy in my hand. Really, I thought that was so cute.

Then everybody's luck begins to run out. Lengel comes in from haggling with a truck full of cabbages on the lot and is about to scuttle into that door marked MANAGER behind which he hides all day when the girls touch his eye. Lengel's pretty dreary, teaches Sunday school and the rest, but he doesn't miss that much. He comes over and says, "Girls, this isn't the beach."

[1] "A & P" is actually an abbreviation of Great Atlantic and Pacific Tea Company.

Queenie blushes, though maybe it's just a brush of sunburn I was noticing for the first time, now that she was so close. "My mother asked me to pick up a jar of herring snacks." Her voice kind of startled me, the way voices do when you see the people first, coming out so flat and dumb yet kind of tony, too, the way it ticked over "pick up" and "snacks." All of a sudden I slid right down her voice into her living room. Her father and the other men were standing around in ice-cream coats and bow ties and the women were in sandals picking up herring snacks on toothpicks off a big glass plate and they were all holding drinks the color of water with olives and sprigs of mint in them. When my parents have somebody over they get lemonade and if it's a real racy affair Schlitz in tall glasses with "They'll Do It Every Time" cartoons stencilled on.

"That's all right," Lengel said. "But this isn't the beach." His repeating this struck me as funny, as if it had just occurred to him, and he had been thinking all these years that A & P was a great big dune and he was the head lifeguard. He didn't like my smiling—as I say he doesn't miss much—but he concentrates on giving the girls that sad Sunday-school-superintendent stare.

Queenie's blush is no sunburn now, and the plump one in plaid, that I liked better from the back—a really sweet can—pipes up, "We weren't doing any shopping. We just came in for the one thing."

"That makes no difference," Lengel tells her, and I could see from the way his eyes went that he hadn't noticed she was wearing a two-piece before. "We want you decently dressed when you come in here."

"We *are* decent," Queenie says suddenly, her lower lip pushing, getting sore now that she remembers her place, a place from which the crowd that runs the A & P must look pretty crummy. Fancy Herring Snacks flashed in her very blue eyes.

"Girls, I don't want to argue with you. After this come in here with your shoulders covered. It's our policy." He turns his back. That's policy for you. Policy is what the kingpins want. What the others want is juvenile delinquency.

All this while, the customers had been showing up with their carts but, you know, sheep, seeing a scene, they had all bunched up on Stokesie, who shook open a paper bag as gently as peeling a peach, not wanting to miss a word. I could feel in the silence everybody getting nervous, most of all Lengel, who asks me, "Sammy, have you rung up their purchase?"

I thought and said "No" but it wasn't about that I was thinking. I go through the punches, 4, 9, GROC, TOT—it's more complicated than you think, and after you do it often enough, it begins to make a little song, that you hear words to, in my case "Hello (*bing*) there, you (*gung*) hap-py *pee*-pul (*splat*)!"—the *splat* being the drawer flying out. I uncrease the bill, tenderly as you may imagine, it just having come from between the two smoothest scoops of vanilla I had ever known were there, and pass a half and a penny into her narrow pink palm, and nestle the herrings in a bag and twist its neck and hand it over, all the time thinking.

The girls, and who'd blame them, are in a hurry to get out, so I say "I quit" to Lengel quick enough for them to hear, hoping they'll stop and watch me, their unsuspected hero. They keep right on going, into the electric eye; the door flies open and they flicker across the lot to their car, Queenie and Plaid and Big Tall Goony-Goony (not that as raw material she was so bad), leaving me with Lengel and a kink in his eyebrow.

"Did you say something, Sammy?"

"I said I quit."

"I thought you did."

"You didn't have to embarrass them."

"It was they who were embarrassing us."

I started to say something that came out "Fiddle-de-doo." It's a saying of my grandmother's, and I know she would have been pleased.

"I don't think you know what you're saying," Lengel said.

"I know you don't," I said. "But I do." I pull the bow at the back of my apron and start shrugging it off my shoulders. A couple customers that had been heading for my slot begin to knock against each other, like scared pigs in a chute.

Lengel sighs and begins to look very patient and old and gray. He's been a friend of my parents for years. "Sammy, you don't want to do this to your Mom and Dad," he tells me. It's true, I don't. But it seems to me that once you begin a gesture it's fatal not to go through with it. I fold the apron, "Sammy" stitched in red on the pocket, and put it on the counter, and drop the bow tie on top of it. The bow tie is theirs, if you've ever wondered. "You'll feel this for the rest of your life," Lengel says, and I know that's true, too, but remembering how he made that pretty girl blush makes me so scrunchy inside I punch the No Sale tab and the machine whirs "pee-pul" and the drawer splats out. One advantage to this scene taking place in summer, I can follow this up with a clean exit, there's no fumbling around getting your coat and galoshes, I just saunter into the electric eye in my white shirt that my mother ironed the night before, and the door heaves itself open, and outside the sunshine is skating around on the asphalt.

I looked around for my girls, but they're gone, of course. There wasn't anybody but some young married screaming with her children about some candy they didn't get by the door of a powder-blue Falcon station wagon. Looking back in the big windows, over the bags of peat moss and aluminum lawn furniture stacked on the pavement, I could see Lengel in my place in the slot, checking the sheep through. His face was dark gray and his back stiff, as if he'd just had an injection of iron, and my stomach kind of fell as I felt how hard the world was going to be to me hereafter.

THE DEATH OF IVAN ILYCH

Leo Tolstoi

DURING an interval in the Melvinski trial in the large building of the Law Courts the members and public prosecutor met in Ivan Egorovich Shebek's private room, where the conversation turned on the celebrated Krasovski case. Fedor Vasilievich warmly maintained that it was not subject to their jurisdiction, Ivan Egorovich maintained the contrary, while Peter Ivanovich, not having entered into the discussion at the start, took no part in it but looked through the *Gazette* which had just been handed in.

"Gentlemen," he said, "Ivan Ilych has died!"

"You don't say so!"

"Here, read it yourself," replied Peter Ivanovich, handing Fedor Vasilievich the paper still damp from the press. Surrounded by a black border were the words: "Praskovya Fedorovna Golovina, with profound sorrow, informs relatives and friends of the demise of her beloved husband Ivan Ilych Golovin, Member of the Court of Justice, which occurred on February the 4th of this year 1882. The funeral will take place on Friday at one o'clock in the afternoon."

Ivan Ilych had been a colleague of the gentlemen present and was liked by them all. He had been ill for some weeks with an illness said to be incurable. His post had been kept open for him, but there had been conjectures that in case of his death Alexeev might receive his appointment, and that either Vinnikov or Shtabel would succeed Alexeev. So on receiving the news of Ivan Ilych's death the first thought of each of the gentlemen in that private room was of the changes and promotions it might occasion among themselves or their acquaintances.

"I shall be sure to get Shtabel's place or Vinnikov's," thought Fedor Vasilievich. "I was promised that long ago, and the promotion means an extra eight hundred rubles a year for me besides the allowance."

"Now I must apply for my brother-in-law's transfer from Kaluga," thought Peter Ivanovich. "My wife will be very glad, and then she won't be able to say that I never do anything for her relations."

"I thought he would never leave his bed again," said Peter Ivanovich aloud. "It's very sad."

"But what really was the matter with him?"

"The doctors couldn't say—at least they could, but each of them said something different. When last I saw him I thought he was getting better."

"And I haven't been to see him since the holidays. I always meant to go."

"Had he any property?"

"I think his wife had a little—but something quite trifling."

"We shall have to go to see her, but they live so terribly far away."

"Far away from you, you mean. Everything's far away from your place."

"You see, he never can forgive my living on the other side of the river," said Peter Ivanovich, smiling at Shebek. Then, still talking of the distances between different parts of the city, they returned to the Court.

Besides considerations as to the possible transfers and promotions likely to result from Ivan Ilych's death, the mere fact of the death of a near acquaintance aroused, as usual, in all who heard of it the complacent feeling that, "it is he who is dead and not I."

Each one thought or felt, "Well, he's dead but I'm alive!" But the more intimate of Ivan Ilych's acquaintances, his so-called friends, could not help thinking also that they would now have to fulfil the very tiresome demands of propriety by attending the funeral service and paying a visit of condolence to the widow.

Fedor Vasilievich and Peter Ivanovich had been his nearest acquaintances. Peter Ivanovich had studied law with Ivan Ilych and had considered himself to be under obligations to him.

Having told his wife at dinner-time of Ivan Ilych's death, and of his conjecture that it might be possible to get her brother transferred to their circuit, Peter Ivanovich sacrificed his usual nap, put on his evening clothes, and drove to Ivan Ilych's house.

At the entrance stood a carriage and two cabs. Leaning against the wall in the hall downstairs near the cloak-stand was a coffin lid covered with cloth of gold, ornamented with gold cord and tassels, that had been polished up with metal powder. Two ladies in black were taking off their fur cloaks. Peter Ivanovich recognized one of them as Ivan Ilych's sister, but the other was a stranger to him. His colleague Schwartz was just coming downstairs, but on seeing Peter Ivanovich enter he stopped and winked at him, as if to say: "Ivan Ilych has made a mess of things—not like you and me."

Schwartz's face with his Piccadilly whiskers, and his slim figure in evening dress, had as usual an air of elegant solemnity which contrasted with the playfulness of his character and had a special piquancy here, or so it seemed to Peter Ivanovich.

Peter Ivanovich allowed the ladies to precede him and slowly followed them upstairs. Schwartz did not come down but remained where he was, and Peter Ivanovich understood that he wanted to arrange where they should play bridge that evening. The ladies went upstairs to the widow's room, and Schwartz with seriously compressed lips but a playful look in his eyes, indicated by a twist of his eyebrows the room to the right where the body lay.

Peter Ivanovich, like everyone else on such occasions, entered feeling uncertain what he would have to do. All he knew was that at such times it is always safe to cross oneself. But he was not quite sure whether one should make obeisances while doing so. He therefore adopted a middle course. On entering the room he began crossing himself and made a slight movement resembling a bow. At the same time, as far as the motion of his head and arm allowed, he surveyed the room. Two young men—apparently nephews, one of whom was a high-school pupil—were leaving the room, crossing themselves as they did so. An old woman was standing motionless, and a lady with strangely arched eyebrows was saying something to her in a whisper. A vigorous, resolute Church Reader, in a frock-coat, was reading something in a loud voice with an expression that precluded any contradiction. The butler's assistant, Gerasim, stepping lightly in front of Peter Ivanovich, was strewing something on the floor. Noticing this, Peter Ivanovich was immediately aware of a faint odour of a decomposing body.

The last time he had called on Ivan Ilych, Peter Ivanovich had seen Gerasim in the study. Ivan Ilych had been particularly fond of him and he was performing the duty of a sick nurse.

Peter Ivanovich continued to make the sign of the cross slightly inclining his head in an intermediate direction between the coffin, the Reader, and the icons on the table in a corner of the room. Afterwards, when it seemed to him that this movement of his arm in crossing himself had gone on too long, he stopped and began to look at the corpse.

The dead man lay, as dead men always lie, in a specially heavy way, his rigid limbs sunk in the soft cushions of the coffin, with his head forever bowed on the pillow. His yellow waxen brow with bald patches over his sunken temples was thrust up in the way peculiar to the dead, the protruding nose seeming to press on the upper lip. He was much changed and had grown even thinner since Peter Ivanovich had last seen him, but, as is always the case with the dead, his face was handsomer and above all more dignified than when he was alive. The expression on the face said that what was necessary had been accomplished, and accomplished rightly. Besides this there was in that expression a reproach and a warning to the living. This warning seemed to Peter Ivanovich out of place, or at least not applicable to him. He felt a certain discomfort and so he hurriedly crossed himself once more and turned and went out of the door—too hurriedly and too regardless of propriety, as he himself was aware.

Schwartz was waiting for him in the adjoining room with legs spread wide apart and both hands toying with his top-hat behind his back. The mere sight of that playful, well-groomed, and elegant figure refreshed Peter Ivanovich. He felt that Schwartz was above all these happenings and would not surrender to any depressing influences. His very look said that this incident of a church service for Ivan Ilych could not be a sufficient reason for infringing the order of the session—in other words, that it would certainly not prevent his unwrapping a new pack of cards and shuffling them that evening while a footman placed four fresh candles on the table: in fact, that there was no reason for supposing that this incident would hinder their spending the evening agreeably. Indeed he said this in a whisper as Peter Ivanovich passed him, proposing that they should meet for a game at Fedor Vasilievich's. But apparently Peter Ivanovich was not destined to play bridge that evening. Praskovya Fedorovna (a short, fat woman who despite all efforts to the contrary had continued to broaden steadily from her shoulders downwards and who had the same extraordinarily arched eyebrows as the lady who had been standing by the coffin), dressed all in black, her head covered with lace, came out of her own room with some other ladies, conducted them to the room where the dead body lay, and said: "The service will begin immediately. Please go in."

Schwartz, making an indefinite bow, stood still, evidently neither accepting nor declining this invitation. Praskovya Fedorovna recognizing Peter Ivanovich, sighed, went close up to him, took his hand, and said: "I know you were a true friend to Ivan Ilych . . ." and looked at him awaiting some suitable response. And Peter Ivanovich knew that, just as it had been the right thing to cross himself in that room, so what he had to do here was to press her hand, sigh, and say, "Believe me . . . ." So he did all this and as he did it felt that the desired result had been achieved: that both he and she were touched.

"Come with me. I want to speak to you before it begins," said the widow. "Give me your arm."

Peter Ivanovich gave her his arm and they went to the inner rooms, passing Schwartz who winked at Peter Ivanovich compassionately.

"That does for our bridge! Don't object if we find another player. Perhaps you can cut in when you do escape," said his playful look.

Peter Ivanovich sighed still more deeply and despondently, and Praskovya Fedorovna pressed his arm gratefully. When they reached the drawing-room, upholstered in pink cretonne and lighted by a dim lamp, they sat down at the table—she on a sofa and Peter Ivanovich on a low pouffe, the springs of which yielded spasmodically under his weight. Praskovya Fedorovna had been on the point of warning him to take another seat, but felt that such a warning was out of keeping with her present condition and so changed her mind. As he sat down on the pouffe Peter Ivanovich recalled how Ivan Ilych had arranged this room and had consulted him regarding this pink cretonne with green leaves. The whole room was full of furniture and knick-knacks, and on her way to the sofa the lace of the widow's black shawl caught on the carved edge of the table. Peter Ivanovich rose to detach it, and the springs of the pouffe, relieved of his weight, rose also and gave him a push. The widow began detaching her shawl herself, and Peter Ivanovich again sat down, suppressing the rebellious springs of the pouffe under him. But the widow had not quite freed herself and Peter Ivanovich got up again, and again the pouffe rebelled and even creaked. When this was all over she took out a clean cambric handkerchief and began to weep. The episode with the shawl and the struggle with the pouffe had cooled Peter Ivanovich's emotions and he sat there with a sullen look on his face. This awkward situation was interrupted by Sokolov, Ivan Ilych's butler, who came to report that the plot in the cemetery that Praskovya Fedorovna had chosen would cost two hundred rubles. She stopped weeping and, looking at Peter Ivanovich with the air of a victim, remarked in French that it was very hard for her. Peter Ivanovich made a silent gesture signifying his full conviction that it must indeed be so.

"Please smoke," she said in a magnanimous yet crushed voice, and turned to discuss with Sokolov the price of the plot for the grave.

Peter Ivanovich while lighting his cigarette heard her inquiring very circumstantially into the prices of different plots in the cemetery and finally decide which she would take. When that was done she gave instructions about engaging the choir. Sokolov then left the room.

"I look after everything myself," she told Peter Ivanovich, shifting the albums that lay on the table: and noticing that the table was endangered by his cigarette-ash, she immediately passed him an ashtray, saying as she did so: "I consider it an affectation to say that my grief prevents my attending to practical affairs. On the contrary, if anything can—I won't say console me, but—distract me, it is seeing to everything concerning him." She again took out her handkerchief as if preparing to cry, but suddenly, as if mastering her feeling, she shook herself and began to speak calmly. "But there is something I want to talk to you about."

Peter Ivanovich bowed, keeping control of the springs of the pouffe, which immediately began quivering under him.

"He suffered terribly the last few days."

"Did he?" said Peter Ivanovich.

"Oh, terribly! He screamed unceasingly, not for minutes but for hours. For the last three days he screamed incessantly. It was unendurable. I cannot understand how I bore it; you could hear him three rooms off. Oh, what I have suffered!"

"Is it possible that he was conscious all that time?" asked Peter Ivanovich.

"Yes," she whispered. "To the last moment. He took leave of us a quarter of an hour before he died, and asked us to take Volodya away."

The thought of the sufferings of this man he had known so intimately, first as a merry little boy, then as a school-mate, and later as a grown-up colleague, suddenly struck Peter Ivanovich with horror, despite an unpleasant consciousness of his own and the woman's dissimulation. He again saw that brow, and that nose pressing down on the lip, and felt afraid for himself.

"Three days of frightful suffering and then death! Why, that might suddenly, at any time, happen to me," he thought, and for a moment felt terrified. But—he did not himself know how—the customary reflection at once occurred to him that this had happened to Ivan Ilych and not to him, and that it should not and could not happen to him, and that to think that it could would be yielding to depression which he ought not to do, as Schwartz's expression plainly showed. After which reflection Peter Ivanovich felt reassured, and began to ask with interest about the details of Ivan Ilych's death, as though death was an accident natural to Ivan Ilych but certainly not to himself.

After many details of the really dreadful physical sufferings Ivan Ilych had endured (which details he learnt only from the effect those sufferings had produced on Praskovya Fedorovna's nerves) the widow apparently found it necessary to get to business.

"Oh, Peter Ivanovich, how hard it is! How terribly, terribly hard!" and she again began to weep.

Peter Ivanovich sighed and waited for her to finish blowing her nose. When she had done so he said, "Believe me. . . ." and she again began talking and brought out what was evidently her chief concern with him—namely, to question him as to how she could obtain a grant of money from the government on the occasion of her husband's death. She made it appear that she was asking Peter Ivanovich's advice about her pension, but he soon saw that she already knew about that to the minutest detail, more even than he did himself. She knew how much could be got out of the government in consequence of her husband's death, but wanted to find out whether she could not possibly extract something more. Peter Ivanovich tried to think of some means of doing so, but after reflecting for a while and, out of propriety, condemning the government for its niggardliness, he said he thought that nothing more could be got. Then she sighed and evidently began to devise means of getting rid of her visitor. Noticing this, he put out his cigarette, rose, pressed her hand, and went out into the anteroom.

In the dining-room where the clock stood that Ivan Ilych had liked so much and had bought at an antique shop, Peter Ivanovich met a priest and a few acquaintances who had come to attend the service, and he recognized Ivan Ilych's daughter, a handsome young woman. She was in black and her slim figure appeared slimmer than ever. She had a gloomy, determined, almost angry expression, and bowed to Peter Ivanovich as though he were in some way to blame. Behind her, with the same offended look, stood a wealthy young man, an examining magistrate, whom Peter Ivanovich also knew and who was her fiancé, as he had heard. He bowed mournfully to them and was about to pass into the death-chamber, when from under the stairs appeared the figure of Ivan Ilych's schoolboy son, who was extremely like his father. He seemed a little Ivan Ilych, such as Peter Ivanovich remembered when they studied law together. His tear-stained eyes had in them the look that is seen in the eyes of boys of thirteen or fourteen who are not pure-minded. When he saw Peter Ivanovich he scowled morosely and shamefacedly. Peter Ivanovich nodded to him and entered the death-chamber. The service began: candles, groans, incense, tears, and sobs. Peter Ivanovich stood looking gloomily down at his feet. He did not look once at the dead man, did not yield to any depressing influence, and was one of the first to leave the room. There was no one in the anteroom, but Gerasim darted out of the dead man's room, rummaged with his strong hands among the fur coats to find Peter Ivanovich's and helped him on with it.

"Well, friend Gerasim," said Peter Ivanovich, so as to say something. "It's a sad affair, isn't it?"

"It's God's will. We shall all come to it some day," said Gerasim, displaying his teeth—the even, white teeth of a healthy peasant—and, like a man in the thick of urgent work, he briskly opened the front door, called the coachman, helped Peter Ivanovich into the sledge, and sprang back to the porch as if in readiness for what he had to do next.

Peter Ivanovich found the fresh air particularly pleasant after the smell of incense, the dead body, and carbolic acid.

"Where to, sir?" asked the coachman.

"It's not too late even now. . . . I'll call round on Fedor Vasilievich."

He accordingly drove there and found them just finishing the first rubber, so that it was quite convenient for him to cut in.

II

Ivan Ilych's life had been most simple and most ordinary and therefore most terrible.

He had been a member of the Court of Justice, and died at the age of forty-five. His father had been an official who after serving in various ministries and departments in Petersburg had made the sort of career which brings men to positions from which by reason of their long service they cannot be dismissed, though they are obviously unfit to hold any responsible position, and for whom therefore posts are specially created, which though fictitious carry salaries of from six to ten thousand rubles that are not fictitious, and in receipt of which they live on to a great age.

Such was the Privy Councillor and superfluous member of various superfluous institutions, Ilya Epimovich Golovin.

He had three sons, of whom Ivan Ilych was the second. The eldest son was following in his father's footsteps only in another department, and was already approaching that stage in the service at which a similar sinecure would be reached. The third son was a failure. He had ruined his prospects in a number of positions and was now serving in the railway department. His father and brothers, and still more their wives, not merely disliked meeting him, but avoided remembering his existence unless compelled to do so. His sister had married Baron Greff, a Petersburg official of her father's type. Ivan Ilych was *le phénix de la famille* as people said. He was neither as cold and formal as his elder brother nor as wild as the younger, but was a happy mean between them—an intelligent, polished, lively and agreeable man. He had studied with his younger brother at the School of Law, but the latter had failed to complete the course and was expelled when he was in the fifth class. Ivan Ilych finished the course well. Even when he was at the School of Law he was just what he remained for the rest of his life: a capable, cheerful, good-natured, and sociable man, though strict in the fulfilment of what he considered to be his duty: and he considered his duty to be what was so considered by those in authority. Neither as a boy nor as a man was he a toady, but from early youth was by nature attracted to people of high station as a fly is drawn to the light, assimilating their ways and views of life and establishing friendly relations with them. All the enthusiasms of childhood and youth passed without leaving much trace on him; he succumbed to sensuality, to vanity, and latterly among the highest classes to liberalism, but always within limits which his instinct unfailingly indicated to him as correct.

At school he had done things which had formerly seemed to him very horrid and made him feel disgusted with himself when he did them; but when later on he saw that such actions were done by people of good position and that they did not regard them as wrong, he was able not exactly to regard them as right, but to forget about them entirely or not be at all troubled at remembering them.

Having graduated from the School of Law and qualified for the tenth rank of the civil service, and having received money from his father for his equipment, Ivan Ilych ordered himself clothes at Scharmer's, the fashionable tailor, hung a medallion inscribed *respice finem* on his watch-chain, took leave of his professor and the prince who was patron of the school, had a farewell dinner with his comrades at Donon's first-class restaurant, and with his new and fashionable portmanteu, linen, clothes, shaving and other toilet appliances, and a travelling rug, all purchased at the best shops, he set off for one of the provinces, where, through his father's influence, he had been attached to the Governor as an official for special service.

In the province Ivan Ilych soon arranged as easy and agreeable a position for himself as he had had at the School of Law. He performed his official tasks, made his career, and at the same time amused himself pleasantly and decorously. Occasionally he paid official visits to country districts, where he behaved with dignity both to his superiors and in-

feriors, and performed the duties entrusted to him, which related chiefly
to the sectarians, with exactness and incorruptible honesty of which he
could not but feel proud.

In official matters, despite his youth and taste for frivolous gaiety,
he was exceedingly reserved, punctilious, and even severe; but in society
he was often amusing and witty, and always good-natured, correct in his
manner, and *bon enfant*, as the governor and his wife—with whom he
was like one of the family—used to say of him.

In the province he had an affair with a lady who made advances to
the elegant young lawyer, and there was also a milliner; and there were
carousals with aides-de-camp who visited the district, and after-supper
visits to a certain outlying street of doubtful reputation; and there was
too some obsequiousness to his chief and even to his chief's wife, but all
this was done with such a tone of good breeding that no hard names
could be applied to it. It all came under the heading of the French saying: *'Il faut que jeunesse se passe.'*[1] It was all done with clean hands, in clean
linen, with French phrases, and above all among people of the best society and consequently with the approval of people of rank.

So Ivan Ilych served for five years and then came a change in his
official life. The new and reformed judicial institutions were introduced,
and new men were needed. Ivan Ilych became such a new man. He was
offered the post of Examining Magistrate, and he accepted it though the
post was in another province and obliged him to give up the connexions
he had formed and to make new ones. His friends met to give him a
send-off; they had a group-photograph taken and presented him with a
silver cigarette-case, and he set off to his new post.

As examining magistrate Ivan Ilych was just as *comme il faut* and
decorous a man, inspiring general respect and capable of separating his
official duties from his private life, as he had been when acting as an official on special service. His duties now as examining magistrate were far
more interesting and attractive than before. In his former position it had
been pleasant to wear an undress uniform made by Scharmer, and to
pass through the crowd of petitioners and officials who were timorously
awaiting an audience with the governor, and who envied him as with
free and easy gait he went straight into his chief's private room to have a
cup of tea and a cigarette with him. But not many people had then been
directly dependent on him—only police officials and the sectarians when
he went on special missions—and he liked to treat them politely, almost
as comrades, as if he were letting them feel that he who had the power to
crush them was treating them in this simple, friendly way. There were
then but few such people. But now, as an examining magistrate, Ivan
Ilych felt that everyone without exception, even the most important and
self-satisfied, was in his power, and that he need only write a few words
on a sheet of paper with a certain heading, and this or that important,
self-satisfied person would be brought before him in the role of an accused person or a witness, and if he did not choose to allow him to sit
down, would have to stand before him and answer his questions. Ivan
Ilych never abused his power: he tried on the contrary to soften its ex-

[1]Youth must have its fling.

pression, but the consciousness of it and of the possibility of softening its effect, supplied the chief interest and attraction of his office. In his work itself, especially in his examinations, he very soon acquired a method of eliminating all considerations irrelevant to the legal aspect of the case, and reducing even the most complicated case to a form in which it would be presented on paper only in its externals, completely excluding his personal opinion of the matter, while above all observing every pre-scribed formality. The work was new and Ivan Ilych was one of the first men to apply the new Code of 1864.[2]

On taking up the post of examining magistrate in a new town, he made new acquaintances and connexions, placed himself on a new foot-ing, and assumed a somewhat different tone. He took up an attitude of rather dignified aloofness towards the provincial authorities, but picked out the best circle of legal gentlemen and wealthy gentry living in the town and assumed a tone of slight dissatisfaction with the government, of moderate liberalism, and of enlightened citizenship. At the same time, without at all altering the elegance of his toilet, he ceased shaving his chin and allowed his beard to grow as it pleased.

Ivan Ilych settled down very pleasantly in this new town. The society there, which inclined towards opposition to the Governor, was friendly, his salary was larger, and he began to play *vint* [a form of bridge], which he found added not a little to the pleasure of life, for he had a capacity for cards, played good-humouredly, and calculated rapidly and astutely, so that he usually won.

After living there for two years he met his future wife, Praskovya Fedorovna, and as relaxations from his labours as examining magistrate, Ivan Ilych established light and playful relations with her.

While he had been an official on special service he had been accus-tomed to dance, but now as an examining magistrate it was exceptional for him to do so. If he danced now, he did it as if to show that though he served under the reformed order of things, and had reached the fifth official rank, yet when it came to dancing he could do it better than most people. So at the end of an evening he sometimes danced with Praskovya Fedorovna, and it was chiefly during these dances that he captivated her. She fell in love with him. Ivan Ilych had at first no definite intention of marrying, but when the girl fell in love with him he said to himself: "Re-ally, why shouldn't I marry?"

Praskovya Fedorovna came of a good family, was not bad looking, and had some little property. Ivan Ilych might have aspired to a more brilliant match, but even this was good. He had his salary, and she, he hoped, would have an equal income. She was well connected, and was a sweet, pretty, and thoroughly correct young woman. To say that Ivan Ilych married because he fell in love with Praskovya Fedorovna and found that she sympathized with his views of life would be as incorrect as to say that he married because his social circle approved of the match. He was swayed by both these considerations: the marriage gave him per-

---

[2]After the emancipation of the serfs in 1861, judicial proceedings were reformed.

sonal satisfaction, and at the same time it was considered the right thing by the most highly placed of his associates.

So Ivan Ilych got married.

The preparations for marriage and the beginning of married life, with its conjugal caresses, the new furniture, new crockery, and new linen, were very pleasant until his wife became pregnant—so that Ivan Ilych had begun to think that marriage would not impair the easy, agreeable, gay and always decorous character of his life, approved of by society and regarded by himself as natural, but would even improve it. But from the first months of his wife's pregnancy, something new, unpleasant, depressing, and unseemly, and from which there was no way of escape, unexpectedly showed itself.

His wife, without any reason—*de gaieté de coeur* as Ivan Ilych expressed it to himself—began to disturb the pleasure and propriety of their life. She began to be jealous without any cause, expected him to devote his whole attention to her, found fault with everything, and made coarse and ill-mannered scenes.

At first Ivan Ilych hoped to escape from the unpleasantness of this state of affairs by the same easy and decorous relation to life that had served him heretofore: he tried to ignore his wife's disagreeable moods, continued to live in his usual easy and pleasant way, invited friends to his house for a game of cards, and also tried going out to his club or spending his evenings with friends. But one day his wife began upbraiding him so vigorously, using such coarse words, and continued to abuse him every time he did not fulfill her demands, so resolutely and with such evident determination not to give way till he submitted—that is, till he stayed at home and was bored just as she was—that he became alarmed. He now realized that matrimony—at any rate with Praskovya Fedorovna—was not always conducive to the pleasures and amenities of life but on the contrary often infringed both comfort and propriety, and that he must therefore entrench himself against such infringement. And Ivan Ilych began to seek for means of doing so. His official duties were the one thing that imposed upon Praskovya Fedorovna, and by means of his official work and the duties attached to it he began struggling with his wife to secure his own independence.

With the birth of their child, the attempts to feed it and the various failures in doing so, and with the real and imaginary illnesses of mother and child, in which Ivan Ilych's sympathy was demanded but about which he understood nothing, the need of securing for himself an existence outside his family life became still more imperative.

As his wife grew more irritable and exacting and Ivan Ilych transferred the centre of gravity of his life more and more to his official work, so did he grow to like his work better and became more ambitious than before.

Very soon, within a year of his wedding, Ivan Ilych had realized that marriage, though it may add some comforts to life, is in fact a very intricate and difficult affair towards which in order to perform one's duty, that is, to lead a decorous life approved of by society, one must adopt a definite attitude just as towards one's official duties.

And Ivan Ilych evolved such an attitude toward married life. He only required of it those conveniences—dinner at home, housewife, and bed—which it could give him, and above all that propriety of external forms required by public opinion. For the rest he looked for light-hearted pleasure and propriety, and was very thankful when he found them, but if he met with antagonism and querulousness he at once retired into his separate fenced-off world of official duties, where he found satisfaction.

Ivan Ilych was esteemed a good official, and after three years was made Assistant Public Prosecutor. His new duties, their importance, the possibility of indicting and imprisoning anyone he chose, the publicity his speeches received, and the success he had in all these things, made his work still more attractive.

More children came. His wife became more and more querulous and ill-tempered, but the attitude Ivan Ilych had adopted towards his home life rendered him almost impervious to her grumbling.

After seven years' service in that town he was transferred to another province as Public Prosecutor. They moved, but were short of money and his wife did not like the place they moved to. Though the salary was higher the cost of living was greater, besides which two of their children died and family life became still more unpleasant for him.

Praskovya Fedorovna blamed her husband for every inconvenience they encountered in their new home. Most of the conversations between husband and wife, especially as to the children's education, led to topics which recalled former disputes, and those disputes were apt to flare up again at any moment. There remained only those rare periods of amorousness which still came to them at times but did not last long. These were islets at which they anchored for a while and then again set out upon that ocean of veiled hostility which showed itself in their aloofness from one another. This aloofness might have grieved Ivan Ilych had he considered that it ought not to exist, but he now regarded the position as normal, and even made it the goal at which he aimed in family life. His aim was to free himself more and more from those unpleasantnesses and to give them a semblance of harmlessness and propriety. He attained this by spending less and less time with his family, and when obliged to be at home he tried to safeguard his position by the presence of outsiders. The chief thing however was that he had his official duties. The whole interest of his life now centred in the official world and that interest absorbed him. The consciousness of his power, being able to ruin anybody he wished to ruin, the importance, even the external dignity of his entry into court, or meetings with his subordinates, his success with superiors and inferiors, and above all his masterly handling of cases, of which he was conscious—all this gave him pleasure and filled his life, together with chats with his colleagues, dinners, and bridge. So that on the whole Ivan Ilych's life continued to flow as he considered it should do—pleasantly and properly.

So things continued for another seven years. His eldest daughter was already sixteen, another child had died, and only one son was left, a schoolboy and a subject of dissension. Ivan Ilych wanted to put him in the School of Law, but to spite him Praskovya Fedorovna entered him at the High School. The daughter had been educated at home and had turned out well: the boy did not learn badly either.

III

So Ivan Ilych lived for seventeen years after his marriage. He was already a Public Prosecutor of long standing, and had declined several proposed transfers while awaiting a more desirable post, when an unanticipated and unpleasant occurrence quite upset the peaceful course of his life. He was expecting to be offered the post of presiding judge in a University town, but Happe somehow came to the front and obtained the appointment instead. Ivan Ilych became irritable, reproached Happe, and quarrelled both with him and with his immediate superiors—who became colder to him and again passed him over when other appointments were made.

This was in 1880, the hardest year of Ivan Ilych's life. It was then that it became evident on the one hand that his salary was insufficient for them to live on, and on the other that he had been forgotten, and not only this, but that what was for him the greatest and most cruel injustice appeared to others a quite ordinary occurrence. Even his father did not consider it was his duty to help him. Ivan Ilych felt himself abandoned by everyone, and that they regarded his position with a salary of 3,500 rubles as quite normal and even fortunate. He alone knew that with the consciousness of the injustices done him, with his wife's incessant nagging, and with the debts he had contracted by living beyond his means, his position was far from normal.

In order to save money that summer he obtained leave of absence and went with his wife to live in the country at her brother's place.

In the country, without his work, he experienced *ennui* for the first time in his life, and not only *ennui* but intolerable depression, and he decided that it was impossible to go on living like that, and that it was necessary to take energetic measures.

Having passed a sleepless night pacing up and down the veranda, he decided to go to Petersburg and bestir himself, in order to punish those who had failed to appreciate him and to get transferred to another ministry.

Next day, despite many protests from his wife and her brother, he started for Petersburg with the sole object of obtaining a post with a salary of five thousand rubles a year. He was no longer bent on any particular department, or tendency, or kind of activity. All he now wanted was an appointment to another post with a salary of five thousand rubles, either in the administration, in the banks, with the railways, in one of the Empress Marya's Institutions, or even in the customs—but it had to carry with it a salary of five thousand rubles and be in a ministry other than that in which they had failed to appreciate him.

And this quest of Ivan Ilyich's was crowned with remarkable and unexpected success. At Kursk an acquaintance of his, F. I. Ilyin, got into the first-class carriage, sat down beside Ivan Ilych, and told him of a telegram just received by the Governor of Kursk announcing that a change was about to take place in the ministry: Peter Ivanovich was to be superseded by Ivan Semenovich.

The proposed change, apart from its significance for Russia, had a special significance for Ivan Ilych, because by bringing forward a new man, Peter Petrovich, and consequently his friend Zachar Ivanovich, it was highly favourable for Ivan Ilych, since Zachar Ivanovich was a friend and colleague of his.

In Moscow this news was confirmed, and on reaching Petersburg Ivan Ilych found Zachar Ivanovich and received a definite promise of an appointment in his former department of Justice.

A week later he telegraphed to his wife: "Zachar in Miller's place. I shall receive appointment on presentation of report."

Thanks to this change of personnel, Ivan Ilych had unexpectedly obtained an appointment in his former ministry which placed him two stages above his former colleagues besides giving him five thousand rubles salary and three thousand five hundred rubles for expenses connected with his removal. All his ill humour towards his former enemies and the whole department vanished, and Ivan Ilych was completely happy.

He returned to the country more cheerful and contented than he had been for a long time. Praskovya Fedorovna also cheered up and a truce was arranged between them. Ivan Ilych told of how he had been fêted by everybody in Petersburg, how all those who had been his enemies were put to shame and now fawned on him, how envious they were of his appointment, and how much everybody in Petersburg had liked him.

Praskovya Fedorovna listened to all this and appeared to believe it. She did not contradict anything, but only made plans for their life in the town to which they were going. Ivan Ilych saw with delight that these plans were his plans, that he and his wife agreed, and that, after a stumble, his life was regaining its due and natural character of pleasant lightheartedness and decorum.

Ivan Ilych had come back for a short time only, for he had to take up his new duties on the 10th of September. Moreover, he needed time to settle into the new place, to move all his belongings from the province, and to buy and order many additional things: in a word, to make such arrangements as he had resolved on, which were almost exactly what Praskovya Fedorovna too had decided on.

Now that everything had happened so fortunately, and that he and his wife were at one in their aims and moreover saw so little of one another, they got on together better than they had done since the first years of marriage. Ivan Ilych had thought of taking his family away with him at once, but the insistence of his wife's brother and her sister-in-law, who had suddenly become particularly amiable and friendly to him and his family, induced him to depart alone.

So he departed, and the cheerful state of mind induced by his success and by the harmony between his wife and himself, the one intensifying the other, did not leave him. He found a delightful house, just the thing both he and his wife had dreamt of. Spacious, lofty reception rooms in the old style, a convenient and dignified study, rooms for his wife and daughter, a study for his son—it might have been specially built for them. Ivan Ilych himself superintended the arrangements, chose the wallpapers, supplemented the furniture (preferably with antiques which he considered particularly *comme il faut*), and supervised the upholstering. Everything progressed and progressed and approached the ideal he had set himself: even when things were only half completed they exceeded his expectations. He saw what a refined and elegant character, free from vulgarity, it would all have when it was ready. On falling asleep he pictured to himself how the reception-room would look. Looking at the yet unfinished drawing-room he could see the fireplace, the screen, the what-not, the little chairs dotted here and there, the dishes and plates on the walls, and the bronzes, as they would be when everything was in place. He was pleased by the thought of how his wife and daughter, who shared his taste in this matter, would be impressed by it. They were certainly not expecting as much. He had been particularly successful in finding, and buying cheaply, antiques which gave a particularly artistocratic character to the whole place. But in his letters he intentionally understated everything in order to be able to surprise them. All this so absorbed him that his new duties—though he liked his official work—interested him less than he expected. Sometimes he even had moments of absent-mindedness during the Court Sessions, and would consider whether he should have straight or curved cornices for his curtains. He was so interested in it all that he often did things himself, rearranging the furniture, or rehanging the curtains. Once when mounting a stepladder to show the upholsterer, who did not understand, how he wanted the hangings draped, he made a false step and slipped, but being a strong and agile man he clung on and only knocked his side against the knob of the window frame. The bruised place was painful but the pain soon passed, and he felt particularly bright and well just then. He wrote: "I feel fifteen years younger." He thought he would have everything ready by September, but it dragged on till mid-October. But the result was charming not only in his eyes but to everyone who saw it.

In reality it was just what is usually seen in the houses of people of moderate means who want to appear rich, and therefore succeed only in resembling others like themselves: there were damasks, dark wood, plants, rugs, and dull and polished bronzes—all the things people of a certain class have in order to resemble other people of that class. His house was so like the others that it would never have been noticed, but to him it all seemed to be quite exceptional. He was very happy when he met his family at the station and brought them to the newly furnished house all lit up, where a footman in a white tie opened the door into the hall decorated with plants, and when they went on into the drawing-room and the study uttering exclamations of delight. He conducted them everywhere, drank in their praises eagerly, and beamed with pleasure. At tea that evening, when Praskovya Fedorovna among other things asked him about his fall, he laughed, and showed them how he had gone flying and had frightened the upholsterer.

"It's a good thing I'm a bit of an athlete. Another man might have been killed, but I merely knocked myself, just here; it hurts when it's touched, but it's passing off already—it's only a bruise."

So they began living in their new home—in which, as always happens, when they got thoroughly settled in they found they were just one room short—and with the increased income, which as always was just a little (some five hundred rubles) too little, but it was all very nice.

Things went particularly well at first, before everything was finally arranged and while something had still to be done: this thing bought, that thing ordered, another thing moved, and something else adjusted. Though there were some disputes between husband and wife, they were both so well satisfied and had so much to do that it all passed off without any serious quarrels. When nothing was left to arrange it became rather dull and something seemed to be lacking, but they were then making acquaintances, forming habits, and life was growing fuller.

Ivan Ilych spent his mornings at the law court and came home to dinner, and at first he was generally in a good humour, though he occasionally became irritable just on account of his house. (Every spot on the tablecloth or the upholstery, and every broken window-blind string, irritated him. He had devoted so much trouble to arranging it all that every disturbance of it distressed him.) But on the whole his life ran its course as he believed life should do: easily, pleasantly, and decorously.

He got up at nine, drank his coffee, read the paper, and then put on his undress uniform and went to the law courts. There the harness in which he worked had already been stretched to fit him and he donned it without a hitch: petitioners, inquiries at the chancery, the chancery itself, and the sittings public and administrative. In all this the thing was to exclude everything fresh and vital, which always disturbs the regular course of official business, and to admit only official relations with people, and then only on official grounds. A man would come, for instance, wanting some information. Ivan Ilych, as one in whose sphere the matter did not lie, would have nothing to do with him: but if the man had some business with him in his official capacity, something that could be expressed on officially stamped paper, he would do everything, positively everything he could within the limits of such relations, and in doing so would maintain the semblance of friendly human relations, that is, would observe the courtesies of life. As soon as the official relations ended, so did everything else. Ivan Ilych possessed this capacity to separate his real life from the official side of affairs and not mix the two, in the highest degree, and by long practice and natural aptitude had brought it to such a pitch that sometimes, in the manner of a virtuoso, he would even allow himself to let the human and official relations mingle. He let himself do this just because he felt that he could at any time he chose resume the strictly official attitude again and drop the human relation. And he did it all easily, pleasantly, correctly, and even artistically. In the intervals between the sessions he smoked, drank tea, chatted a little about politics, a little about general topics, a little about cards, but most of all about official appointments. Tired, but with the feelings of a virtuoso—one of the first violins who has played his part in an orchestra with precision—he would return home to find that his wife and daughter had been out paying calls, or had a visitor, and that his son had been to school, had done his homework with his tutor, and was duly learning what is taught at High Schools. Everything was as it should be. After dinner, if they had no visitors, Ivan Ilych sometimes read a book that was being much discussed at the time, and in the evening settled down to work, that is, read official papers, compared the depositions of witnesses, and noted paragraphs of the Code applying to them. This was neither dull nor amusing. It was dull when he might have been playing bridge, but if no bridge was available it was at any rate better than doing nothing or sitting with his wife. Ivan Ilych's chief pleasure was giving little dinners to which he invited men and women of good social position, and just as his drawing-room resembled all other drawing-rooms so did his enjoyable little parties resemble all other such parties.

Once they even gave a dance. Ivan Ilych enjoyed it and everything went off well, except that it led to a violent quarrel with his wife about the cakes and sweets. Praskovya Fedorovna had made her own plans, but Ivan Ilych insisted on getting everything from an expensive confectioner and ordered too many cakes, and the quarrel occurred because some of those cakes were left over and the confectioner's bill came to forty-five rubles. It was a great and disagreeable quarrel. Praskovya Fedorovna called him "a fool and an imbecile," and he clutched at his head and made angry allusions to divorce.

But the dance itself had been enjoyable. The best people were there, and Ivan Ilych had danced with Princess Trufonova, a sister of the distinguished founder of the Society "Bear my Burden."

The pleasures connected with his work were pleasures of ambition; his social pleasures were those of vanity; but Ivan Ilych's greatest pleasure was playing bridge. He acknowledged that whatever disagreeable incident happened in his life, the pleasure that beamed like a ray of light above everything else was to sit down to bridge with good players, not noisy partners, and of course to four-handed bridge (with five players it was annoying to have to stand out, though one pretended not to mind), to play a clever and serious game (when the cards allowed it) and then to have supper and drink a glass of wine. After a game of bridge, especially if he had won a little (to win a large sum was unpleasant), Ivan Ilych went to bed in specially good humour.

So they lived. They formed a circle of acquaintances among the best people and were visited by people of importance and by young folk. In their views as to their acquaintances, husband and wife and daughter were entirely agreed, and tacitly and unanimously kept at arm's length and shook off the various shabby friends and relations who, with much show of affection, gushed into the drawing-room with its Japanese plates on the walls. Soon these shabby friends ceased to obtrude themselves and only the best people remained in the Golovins' set.

Young men made up to Lisa, and Petrishchev, an examining magistrate and Dmitri Ivanovich Petrishchev's son and sole heir, began to be so attentive to her that Ivan Ilych had already spoken to Praskovya Fedorovna about it, and considered whether they should not arrange a party for them, or get up some private theatricals.

So they lived, and all went well, without change, and life flowed pleasantly.

IV

They were all in good health. It could not be called ill health if Ivan Ilych sometimes said that he had a queer taste in his mouth and felt some discomfort in his left side.

But this discomfort increased and, though not exactly painful, grew into a sense of pressure in his side accompanied by ill humour. And his irritability became worse and worse and began to mar the agreeable, easy, and correct life that had established itself in the Golovin family. Quarrels between husband and wife became more and more frequent, and soon the ease and amenity disappeared and even the decorum was barely maintained. Scenes again became frequent, and very few of those islets remained on which husband and wife could meet without an explosion. Praskovya Fedorovna now had good reason to say that her husband's temper was trying. With characteristic exaggeration she said he had always had a dreadful temper, and that it had needed all her good nature to put up with it for twenty years. It was true that now the quarrels were started by him. His bursts of temper always came just before dinner, often just as he began to eat his soup. Sometimes he noticed that a plate or dish was chipped, or the food was not right, or his son put his elbow on the table, or his daughter's hair was not done as he liked it, and for all this he blamed Praskovya Fedorovna. At first she retorted and said disagreeable things to him, but once or twice he fell into such a rage at the beginning of dinner that she realized it was due to some physical derangement brought on by taking food, and so she restrained herself and did not answer, but only hurried to get the dinner over. She regarded this self-restraint as highly praiseworthy. Having come to the conclusion that her husband had a dreadful temper and made her life miserable, she began to feel sorry for herself, and the more she pitied herself the more she hated her husband. She began to wish he would die; yet she did not want him to die because then his salary would cease. And this irritated her against him still more. She considered herself dreadfully unhappy just because not even his death could save her, and though she concealed her exasperation, that hidden exasperation of hers increased his irritation also.

After one scene in which Ivan Ilych had been particularly unfair and after which he had said in explanation that he certainly was irritable but that it was due to his not being well, she said that if he was ill it should be attended to, and insisted on his going to see a celebrated doctor.

He went. Everything took place as he had expected and as it always does. There was the usual waiting and the important air assumed by the doctor, with which he was so familiar (resembling that which he himself assumed in court), and the sounding and listening, and the questions which called for answers that were foregone conclusions and were evidently unnecessary, and the look of importance which implied that "if only you put yourself in our hands we will arrange everything—we know indubitably how it has to be done, always in the same way for everybody alike." It was all just as it was in the law courts. The doctor put on just the same air towards him as he himself put on towards an accused person.

The doctor said that so-and-so indicated that there was so-and-so inside the patient, but if the investigation of so-and-so did not confirm this, then he must assume that and that. If he assumed that and that, then . . . and so on. To Ivan Ilych only one question was important: was his case serious or not? But the doctor ignored that inappropriate question. From his point of view it was not the one under consideration, the real question was to decide between a floating kidney, chronic catarrh, or appendicitis. It was not a question of Ivan Ilych's life or death, but one between a floating kidney and appendicitis. And that question the doctor solved brilliantly, as it seemed to Ivan Ilych, in favour of the appendix, with the reservation that should an examination of the urine give fresh indications the matter would be reconsidered. All this was just what Ivan Ilych had himself brilliantly accomplished a thousand times in dealing with men on trial. The doctor summed up just as brilliantly, looking over his spectacles triumphantly and even gaily at the accused. From the doctor's summing up Ivan Ilych concluded that things were bad, but that for the doctor, and perhaps for everybody else, it was a matter of indifference, though for him it was bad. And this conclusion struck him painfully, arousing in him a great feeling of pity for himself and of bitterness towards the doctor's indifference to a matter of such importance.

He said nothing of this, but rose, placed the doctor's fee on the table, and remarked with a sigh: "We sick people probably often put inappropriate questions. But tell me, in general, is this complaint dangerous, or not? . . ."

The doctor looked at him sternly over his spectacles with one eye, as if to say: "Prisoner, if you will not keep to the questions put to you, I shall be obliged to have you removed from the court."

"I have already told you what I consider necessary and proper. The analysis may show something more." And the doctor bowed.

Ivan Ilych went out slowly, seated himself self disconsolately in his sledge, and drove home. All the way home he was going over what the doctor had said, trying to translate those complicated, obscure, scientific phrases into plain language and find in them an answer to the question: "Is my condition bad? Is it very bad? Or is there as yet nothing much wrong?" And it seemed to him that the meaning of what the doctor had said was that it was very bad. Everything in the streets seemed depressing. The cabmen, the houses, the passers-by, and the shops, were dismal. His ache, this dull gnawing ache that never ceased for a moment, seemed to have acquired a new and more serious significance from the doctor's dubious remarks. Ivan Ilych now watched it with a new and oppressive feeling.

He reached home and began to tell his wife about it. She listened, but in the middle of his account his daughter came in with her hat on, ready to go out with her mother. She sat down reluctantly to listen to this tedious story, but could not stand it long, and her mother too did not hear him to the end.

"Well, I am very glad," she said. "Mind now to take your medicine regularly. Give me the prescription and I'll send Gerasim to the chemist's." And she went to get ready to go out.

While she was in the room Ivan Ilych had hardly taken time to breathe, but he sighed deeply when she left it.

"Well," he thought, "perhaps it isn't so bad after all."

He began taking his medicine and following the doctor's directions, which had been altered after the examination of the urine. But then it happened that there was a contradiction between the indications drawn from the examination of the urine and the symptoms that showed themselves. It turned out that what was happening differed from what the doctor had told him, and that he had either forgotten, or blundered, or hidden something from him. He could not, however, be blamed for that, and Ivan Ilych still obeyed his orders implicitly and at first derived some comfort from doing so.

From the time of his visit to the doctor, Ivan Ilych's chief occupation was the exact fulfilment of the doctor's instructions regarding hygiene and the taking of medicine, and the observation of his pain and his excretions. His chief interests came to be people's ailments and people's health. When sickness, deaths, or recoveries, were mentioned in his presence, especially when the illness resembled his own, he listened with agitation which he tried to hide, asked questions, and applied what he heard to his own case.

The pain did not grow less, but Ivan Ilych made efforts to force himself to think that he was better. And he could do this so long as nothing agitated him. But as soon as he had any unpleasantness with his wife, any lack of success in his official work, or held bad cards at bridge, he was at once acutely sensible of his disease. He had formerly borne such mischances, hoping soon to adjust what was wrong, to master it and attain success, or make a grand slam. But now every mischance upset him and plunged him into despair. He would say to himself: "There now, just as I was beginning to get better and the medicine had begun to take effect, comes this accursed misfortune, or unpleasantness . . ." And he was furious with the mishap, or with the people who were causing the unpleasantness and killing him, for he felt that this fury was killing him but could not restrain it. One would have thought that it should have been clear to him that this exasperation with circumstances and people aggravated his illness, and that he ought therefore to ignore unpleasant occurrences. But he drew the very opposite conclusion: he said that he needed peace, and he watched for everything that might disturb it and became irritable at the slightest infringement of it. His condition was rendered worse by the fact that he read medical books and consulted doctors. The progress of his disease was so gradual that he could deceive himself when comparing one day with another—the difference was so slight. But when he consulted the doctors it seemed to him that he was getting worse, and even very rapidly. Yet despite this he was continually consulting them.

That month he went to see another celebrity, who told him almost the same as the first had done but put his questions rather differently, and the interview with this celebrity only increased Ivan Ilych's doubts and fears. A friend of a friend of his, a very good doctor, diagnosed his illness again quite differently from the others, and though he predicted recovery, his questions and suppositions bewildered Ivan Ilych still more and increased his doubts. A homoeopathist diagnosed the disease in yet another way, and prescribed medicine which Ivan Ilych took secretly for a week. But after a week, not feeling any improvement and having lost confidence both in the former doctor's treatment and in this one's, he became still more despondent. One day a lady acquaintance mentioned a cure effected by a wonder-working icon. Ivan Ilych caught himself listening attentively and beginning to believe that it had occurred. This incident alarmed him. "Has my mind really weakened to such an extent?" he asked himself. "Nonsense! It's all rubbish: I mustn't give way to nervous fears but having chosen a doctor must keep strictly to his treatment. That is what I will do. Now it's all settled. I won't think about it, but will follow the treatment seriously till summer, and then we shall see. From now there must be no more of this wavering!" This was easy to say but impossible to carry out. The pain in his side oppressed him and seemed to grow worse and more incessant, while the taste in his mouth grew stranger and stranger. It seemed to him that his breath had a disgusting smell, and he was conscious of a loss of appetite and strength. There was no deceiving himself: something terrible, new, and more important than anything before in his life, was taking place within him of which he alone was aware. Those about him did not understand or would not understand it, but thought everything in the world was going on as usual. That tormented Ivan Ilych more than anything. He saw that his household, especially his wife and daughter who were in a perfect whirl of visiting, did not understand anything of it and were annoyed that he was so depressed and exacting, as if he were to blame for it. Though they tried to disguise it he saw that he was an obstacle in their path, and that his wife had adopted a definite line in regard to his illness and kept to it regardless of anything he said or did. Her attitude was this: "You know," she would say to her friends, "Ivan Ilych can't do as other people do, and keep to the treatment prescribed for him. One day he'll take his drops and keep strictly to his diet and go to bed in good time, but the next day unless I watch him he'll suddenly forget his medicine, eat sturgeon—which is forbidden—and sit up playing cards until one o'clock in the morning."

"Oh, come, when was that?" Ivan Ilych would ask in vexation. "Only once at Peter Ivanovich's."

"And yesterday with Shebek."

"Well, even if I hadn't stayed up, this pain would have kept me awake."

"Be that as it may you'll never get well like that, but will always make us wretched."

Praskovya Fedorovna's attitude to Ivan Ilych's illness, as she expressed it both to others and to him, was that it was his own fault and was another of the annoyances he caused her. Ivan Ilych felt that this opinion escaped her involuntarily—but that did not make it easier for him.

At the law courts too, Ivan Ilych noticed, or thought he noticed, a strange attitude towards himself. It sometimes seemed to him that people were watching him inquisitively as a man whose place might soon be vacant. Then again, his friends would suddenly begin to chaff him in a friendly way about his low spirits, as if the awful, horrible, and unheard-of thing that was going on within him, incessantly gnawing at him and irresistably drawing him away, was a very agreeable subject for jests. Schwartz in particular irritated him by his jocularity, vivacity, and *savoir-faire*, which reminded him of what he himself had been ten years ago.

Friends came to make up a set and they sat down to cards. They dealt, bending the new cards to soften them, and he sorted the diamonds in his hand and found he had seven. His partner said "No trumps" and supported him with two diamonds. What more could be wished for? It ought to be jolly and lively. They would make a grand slam. But suddenly Ivan Ilych was conscious of that gnawing pain, that taste in his mouth, and it seemed ridiculous that in such circumstances he should be pleased to make a grand slam.

He looked at his partner Mikhail Mikhaylovich, who rapped the table with his strong hand and instead of snatching up the tricks pushed the cards courteously and indulgently towards Ivan Ilych that he might have the pleasure of gathering them up without the trouble of stretching out his hand for them. "Does he think I am too weak to stretch out my arm?" thought Ivan Ilych, and forgetting what he was doing he over-trumped his partner, missing the grand slam by three tricks. And what was most awful of all was that he saw how upset Mikhail Mikhaylovich was about it but did not himself care. And it was dreadful to realize why he did not care.

They all saw that he was suffering, and said: "We can stop if you are tired. Take a rest." Lie down? No, he was not at all tired, and he finished the rubber. All were gloomy and silent. Ivan Ilych felt that he had diffused this gloom over them and could not dispel it. They had supper and went away, and Ivan Ilych was left alone with the consciousness that his life was poisoned and was poisoning the lives of others, and that this poison did not weaken but penetrated more and more deeply into his whole being.

With this consciousness, and with physical pain besides the terror, he must go to bed, often to lie awake the greater part of the night. Next morning he had to get up again, dress, go to the law courts, speak, and write; or if he did not go out, spend at home those twenty-four hours a day each of which was a torture. And he had to live thus all alone on the brink of an abyss, with no one who understood or pitied him.

V

So one month passed and then another. Just before the New Year his brother-in-law came to town and stayed at their house. Ivan Ilych was at the law courts and Praskovya Fedorovna had gone shopping. When Ivan Ilych came home and entered his study he found his brother-in-law there—a healthy, florid man—unpacking his portmanteau himself. He raised his head on hearing Ivan Ilych's footsteps and looked up at him for a moment without a word. That stare told Ivan Ilych everything. His brother-in-law opened his mouth to utter an exclamation of surprise but checked himself, and that action confirmed all.

"I have changed, eh?"

"Yes, there is a change."

And after that, try as he would to get his brother-in-law to return to the subject of his looks, the latter would say nothing about it. Praskoyva Fedorovna came home and her brother went out to her. Ivan Ilych locked the door and began to examine himself in the glass, first full face, then in profile. He took up a portrait of himself taken with his wife, and compared it with what he saw in the glass. The change in him was immense. Then he bared his arms to the elbow, looked at them, drew the sleeves down again, sat down on an ottoman, and grew blacker than night.

"No, no, this won't do!" he said to himself, and jumped up, went to the table, took up some law papers and began to read them, but could not continue. He unlocked the door and went into the reception-room. The door leading to the drawing-room was shut. He approached it on tiptoe and listened.

"No, you are exaggerating!" Praskovya Fedorovna was saying.

"Exaggerating! Don't you see it? Why, he's a dead man! Look at his eyes—there's no light in them. But what is it that is wrong with him?"

"No one knows. Nikolaevich (that was another doctor) said something, but I don't know what. And Leschetitsky (this was the celebrated specialist) said quite the contrary . . . "

Ivan Ilych walked away, went to his own room, lay down, and began musing: "The kidney, a floating kidney." He recalled all the doctors had told him of how it detached itself and swayed about. And by an effort of imagination he tried to catch that kidney and arrest it and support it. So little was needed for this, it seemed to him. "No, I'll go to see Peter Ivanovich again." (That was the friend whose friend was a doctor.) He rang, ordered the carriage, and got ready to go.

"Where are you going, Jean?" asked his wife, with a specially sad and exceptionally kind look.

This exceptionally kind look irritated him. He looked morosely at her.

"I must go to see Peter Ivanovich."

He went to see Peter Ivanovich, and together they went to see his friend, the doctor. He was in, and Ivan Ilych had a long talk with him.

Reviewing the anatomical and psychological details of what in the doctor's opinion was going on inside him, he understood it all.

There was something, a small thing, in the vermiform appendix. It might all come right. Only stimulate the energy of one organ and check the activity of another, then absorption would take place and everything would come right. He got home rather late for dinner, ate his dinner, and conversed cheerfully, but could not for a long time bring himself to go back to work in his room. At last, however, he went to his study and did what was necessary, but the consciousness that he had put something aside—an important, intimate matter which he would revert to when his work was done—never left him. When he had finished his work he re-membered that this intimate matter was the thought of his vermiform appendix. But he did not give himself up to it, and went to the drawing-room for tea. There were callers there, including the examining magis-trate who was a desirable match for his daughter, and they were convers-ing, playing the piano and singing. Ivan Ilych, as Praskovya Fedorovna remarked, spent that evening more cheerfully than usual, but he never for a moment forgot that he had postponed the important matter of the appendix. At eleven o'clock he said good-night and went to his bedroom. Since his illness he had slept in a small room next to his study. He un-dressed and took up a novel by Zola, but instead of reading it he fell into thought, and in his imagination that desired improvement in the ver-miform appendix occurred. There was the absorption and evacuation and the reestablishment of normal activity. "Yes, that's it!" he said to him-self. "One need only assist nature, that's all." He remembered his medicine, rose, took it, and lay down on his back watching for the be-neficient action of the medicine and for it to lessen the pain. "I need only take it regularly and avoid all injurious influences. I am already feeling better, much better." He began touching his side: it was not painful to the touch. "There, I really don't feel it. It's much better already." He put out the light and turned on his side . . . "The appendix is getting better, absorption is occurring." Suddenly he felt the old, familiar, dull, gnaw-ing pain, stubborn and serious. There was the same familiar loathsome taste in his mouth. His heart sank and he felt dazed. "My God! My God!" he muttered. "Again, again! And it will never cease." And suddenly the matter presented itself in a quite different aspect. "Vermiform appendix! Kidney!" he said to himself. "It's not a question of appendix or kidney, but of life and . . . death. Yes, life was there and now it is going, going and I cannot stop it. Yes. Why deceive myself? Isn't it obvious to everyone but me that I'm dying, and that it's only a question of weeks, days . . . it may happen this moment. There was light and now there is darkness. I was here and now I'm going there! Where?" A chill came over him, his breathing ceased, and he felt only the throbbing of his heart.

"When I am not, what will there be? There will be nothing. Then where shall I be when I am no more? Can this be dying? No, I don't want to!" He jumped up and tried to light the candle, felt for it with trembling hands, dropped candle and candlestick on the floor, and fell back on his pillow.

"What's the use? It makes no difference," he said to himself, staring with wide-open eyes into the darkness. "Death. Yes, death. And none of them know or wish to know it, and they have no pity for me. Now they are playing." (He heard through the door the distant sound of a song and its accompaniment.) "It's all the same to them, but they will die too! Fools! I first, and they later, but it will be the same for them. And now they are merry . . . the beasts!"

Anger choked him and he was agonizingly, unbearably miserable. "It is impossible that all men have been doomed to suffer this awful hor-ror!" He raised himself.

"Something must be wrong. I must calm myself—must think it all over from the beginning." And he again began thinking. "Yes, the beginning of my illness: I knocked my side, but I was still quite well that day and the next. It hurt a little, then rather more. I saw the doctors, then followed despondency and anguish, more doctors, and I drew nearer to the abyss. My strength grew less and I kept coming nearer and nearer, and now I have wasted away and there is no light in my eyes. I think of the appendix—but this is death! I think of mending the appendix, and all the while here is death! Can it really be death?" Again terror seized him and he gasped for breath. He leant down and began feeling for the matches, pressing with his elbow on the stand beside the bed. It was in his way and hurt him, he grew furious with it, pressed on it still harder, and upset it. Breathless and in despair he fell on his back, expecting death to come immediately.

Meanwhile the visitors were leaving. Praskovya Fedorovna was seeing them off. She heard something fall and came in.

"What has happened?"

"Nothing. I knocked it over accidentally."

She went out and returned with a candle. He lay there panting heavily, like a man who has run a thousand yards, and stared upwards at her with a fixed look.

"What is it, Jean?"

"No . . . o . . . thing. I upset it." ("Why speak of it? She won't understand," he thought.)

And in truth she did not understand. She picked up the stand, lit the candle, and hurried away to see another visitor off. When she came back he still lay on his back, looking upwards.

"What is it? Do you feel worse?"

"Yes."

She shook her head and sat down.

"Do you know, Jean, I think we must ask Leshchetitsky to come and see you here."

This meant calling in the famous specialist, regardless of expense. He smiled malignantly and said "No." She remained a little longer and then went up to him and kissed his forehead.

While she was kissing him he hated her from the bottom of his soul and with difficulty refrained from pushing her away.

"Good-night. Please God you'll sleep."

"Yes."

VI

Ivan Ilych saw that he was dying, and he was in continual despair.

In the depth of his heart he knew he was dying, but not only was he not accustomed to the thought, he simply did not and could not grasp it.

The syllogism he had learnt from Kiezewetter's Logic: "Caius is a man, men are mortal, therefore Caius is mortal," had always seemed to him correct as applied to Caius, but certainly not as applied to himself. That Caius—man in the abstract—was mortal, was perfectly correct, but he was not Caius, not an abstract man, but a creature quite quite separate from all others. He had been little Vanya, with a mamma and a papa, with Mitya and Volodya, with the toys, a coachman and a nurse, afterwards with Katenka and with all the joys, griefs, and delights of childhood, boyhood, and youth. What did Caius know of the smell of that striped leather ball Vanya had been so fond of? Had Caius kissed his mother's hand like that, and did the silk of her dress rustle so for Caius? Had he rioted like that at school when the pastry was bad? Had Caius been in love like that? Could Caius preside at a session as he did? "Caius really was mortal, and it was right for him to die; but for me, little Vanya, Ivan Ilych, with all my thoughts and emotions, it's altogether a different matter. It cannot be that I ought to die. That would be too terrible."

Such was his feeling.

"If I had to die like Caius I should have known it was so. An inner voice would have told me so, but there was nothing of the sort in me and I and all my friends felt that our case was quite different from that of Caius. And now here it is!" he said to himself. "It can't be. It's impossible! But here it is. How is this? How is one to understand it?"

He could not understand it, and tried to drive this false, incorrect, morbid thought away and to replace it by other proper and healthy thoughts. But that thought, and not the thought only but the reality itself, seemed to come and confront him.

And to replace that thought he called up a succession of others, hoping to find in them some support. He tried to get back into the former current of thoughts that had once screened the thought of death from him. But strange to say, all that had formerly shut off, hidden, and destroyed, his consciousness of death, no longer had that effect. Ivan Ilych now spent most of his time in attempting to re-establish that old current. He would say to himself: "I will take up my duties again—after all I used to live by them." And banishing all doubts he would go to the law courts, enter into conversation with his colleagues, and sit carelessly as was his wont, scanning the crowd with a thoughtful look and leaning both his emaciated arms on the arms of his oak chair; bending over as usual to a colleague and drawing his papers nearer he would interchange whispers with him, and then suddenly raising his eyes and sitting erect would pronounce certain words and open the proceedings. But suddenly in the midst of those proceedings the pain in his side, regardless of the stage the proceedings had reached, would begin its own gnawing work. Ivan Ilych would turn his attention to it and try to drive the thought of it away, but without success. *It* would come and stand before him and look at him, and he would be petrified and the light would die out of his eyes, and he would again begin asking himself whether *It* alone was true. And his colleagues and subordinates would see with surprise and distress that he, the brilliant and subtle judge, was becoming confused and making mistakes. He would shake himself, try to pull himself together, manage somehow to bring the sitting to a close, and return home with the sorrowful consciousness that his judicial labours could not as formerly hide from him what he wanted them to hide, and could not deliver him from *It*. And what was worst of all was that *It* drew his attention to itself not in order to make him take some action but only that he should look at *It*, look it straight in the face: look at it and without doing anything, suffer inexpressibly.

And to save himself from this condition Ivan Ilych looked for consolations—new screens—and new screens were found and for a while seemed to save him, but then they immediately fell to pieces or rather became transparent, as if *It* penetrated them and nothing could veil *It*.

In these latter days he would go into the drawing-room he had arranged—that drawing-room where he had fallen and for the sake of which (how bitterly ridiculous it seemed) he had sacrificed his life—for he knew that his illness originated with that knock. He would enter and see that something had scratched the polished table. He would look for the cause of this and find that it was the bronze ornamentation of an album, that had got bent. He would take up the expensive album which he had lovingly arranged, and feel vexed with his daughter and her friends for their untidiness—for the album was torn here and there and some of the photographs turned upside down. He would put it carefully in order and bend the ornamentation back into position. Then it would occur to him to place all those things in another corner of the room, near the plants. He would call the footman, but his daughter or wife would come to help him. They would not agree, and his wife would contradict him, and she would dispute and grow angry. But that was all right, for then he did not think about *It*. *It* was invisible.

But then, when he was moving something himself, his wife would say: "Let the servants do it. You will hurt yourself again." And suddenly *It* would flash through the screen and he would see it. It was just a flash, and he hoped it would disappear, but he would involuntarily pay attention to his side. "It sits there as before, gnawing just the same." And he could no longer forget *It*, but could distinctly see it looking at him from behind the flowers. "What is it all for?"

"It really is so! I lost my life over that curtain as I might have done when storming a fort. Is that possible? How terrible and how stupid. It can't be true! It can't, but it is."

He would go to his study, lie down, and again be alone with *It*: face to face with *It*. And nothing could be done with *It* except to look at it and shudder.

VII

How it happened it is impossible to say because it came about step by step, unnoticed, but in the third month of Ivan Ilych's illness, his wife, his daughter, his son, his acquaintances, the doctors, the servants, and above all he himself, were aware that the whole interest he had for other people was whether he would soon vacate his place, and at least release the living from the discomfort caused by his presence and be himself released from his sufferings.

He slept less and less. He was given opium and hypodermic injections or morphine, but this did not relieve him. The dull depression he experienced in a somnolent condition at first gave him a little relief, but only as something new, afterwards it became as distressing as the pain itself or even more so.

Special foods were prepared for him by the doctor's orders, but all those foods became increasingly distasteful and disgusting to him.

For his excretions also special arrangements had to be made, and this was a torment to him every time—a torment from the uncleanliness, the unseemliness, and the smell, and from knowing that another person had to take part in it.

But just through this most unpleasant matter Ivan Ilych obtained comfort. Gerasim, the butler's young assistant, always came in to carry the things out. Gerasim was a clean, fresh peasant lad, grown stout on town food and always cheerful and bright. At first the sight of him, in his clean Russian peasant costume, engaged on that disgusting task embarrassed Ivan Ilych.

Once when he got up from the commode too weak to draw up his trousers, he dropped into a soft armchair and looked with horror at his bare, enfeebled thighs with the muscles so sharply marked on them.

Gerasim with a firm light tread, his heavy boots emitting a pleasant smell of tar and fresh winter air, came in wearing a clean Hessian apron, the sleeves of his print shirt tucked up over his strong bare young arms and refraining from looking at his sick master out of consideration for his feelings, and restraining the joy of life that beamed from his face, he went up to the commode.

"Gerasim!" said Ivan Ilych in a weak voice.

Gerasim started, evidently afraid he might have committed some blunder, and with a rapid movement turned his fresh, kind, simple young face which just showed the first downy signs of a beard.

"Yes, sir?"

"That must be very unpleasant for you. You must forgive me. I am helpless."

"Oh, why, sir," and Gerasim's eyes beamed and he showed his glistening white teeth, "what's a little trouble? It's a case of illness with you, sir."

And his deft strong hands did their accustomed task, and he went out of the room stepping lightly. Five minutes later he as lightly returned.

Ivan Ilych was still sitting in the same position in the armchair.

"Gerasim," he said when the latter had replaced the freshly-washed utensil. "Please come here and help me." Gerasim went up to him. "Lift me up. It is hard for me to get up, and I have sent Dmitri away."

Gerasim went up to him, grasped his master with his strong arms deftly but gently, in the same way that he stepped—lifted him, supported him with one hand, and with the other drew up his trousers and would have set him down again, but Ivan Ilych asked to be led to the sofa. Gerasim, without an effort and without apparent pressure, led him, almost lifting him, to the sofa and placed him on it.

"Thank you. How easily and well you do it all!"

Gerasim smiled again and turned to leave the room. But Ivan Ilych felt his presence such a comfort that he did not want to let him go.

"One thing more, please move up that chair. No, the other one—under my feet. It is easier for me when my feet are raised."

Gerasim brought the chair, set it down gently in place, and raised Ivan Ilych's legs on to it. It seemed to Ivan Ilych that he felt better while Gerasim was holding up his legs.

"It's better when my legs are higher," he said. "Place that cushion under them."

Gerasim did so. He again lifted the legs and placed them, and again Ivan Ilych felt better while Gerasim held his legs. When he set them down Ivan Ilych fancied he felt worse.

"Gerasim," he said. "Are you busy now?"

"Not at all, sir," said Gerasim, who had learnt from the townfolk how to speak to gentlefolk.

"What have you still to do?"

"What have I to do? I've done everything except chopping the logs for tomorrow."

"Then hold my legs up a bit higher, can you?"

"Of course I can. Why not?" And Gerasim raised his master's legs higher and Ivan Ilych thought that in that position he did not feel any pain at all.

"And how about the logs?"

"Don't trouble about that, sir. There's plenty of time."

Ivan Ilych told Gerasim to sit down and hold his legs, and began to talk to him. And strange to say it seemed to him that he felt better while Gerasim held his legs up.

After that Ivan Ilych would sometimes call Gerasim and get him to hold his legs on his shoulders, and he liked talking to him. Gerasim did it all easily, willingly, simply, and with a good nature that touched Ivan Ilych. Health, strength, and vitality in other people were offensive to him, but Gerasim's strength and vitality did not mortify but soothed him.

What tormented Ivan Ilych most was the deception, the lie, which for some reason they all accepted, that he was not dying but was simply ill, and that he only need keep quiet and undergo a treatment and then something very good would result. He however knew that do what they would nothing would come of it, only still more agonizing suffering and death. This deception tortured him—their not wishing to admit what they all knew and what he knew, but wanting to lie to him concerning his terrible condition, and wishing and forcing him to participate in that lie. Those lies—lies enacted over him on the eve of his death and destined to degrade this awful, solemn act to the level of their visitings, their curtains, their sturgeon for dinner—were a terrible agony for Ivan Ilych. And strangely enough, many times when they were going through their antics over him he had been within a hairbreadth of calling out to them: "Stop lying! You know and I know that I am dying. Then at least stop lying about it." But he had never had the spirit to do it. The awful terrible act of his dying was, he could see, reduced by those about him to the level of a casual, unpleasant, and almost indecorous incident (as if someone entered a drawing-room diffusing an unpleasant odor) and this was done by that very decorum which he had served all his life long. He saw that no one felt for him, because no one even wished to grasp his position. Only Gerasim recognized it and pitied him. And so Ivan Ilych felt at ease only with him. He felt comforted when Gerasim supported his legs (sometimes all night long) and refused to go to bed, saying: "Don't you worry, Ivan Ilych. I'll get sleep enough later on," or when he suddenly became familiar and exclaimed: "If you weren't sick it would be another matter, but as it is, why should I grudge a little trouble?" Gerasim alone did not lie; everything showed that he alone understood the facts of the case and did not consider it necessary to disguise them, but simply felt sorry for his emaciated and enfeebled master. Once when Ivan Ilych was sending him away he even said straight out: "We shall all of us die, so why should I grudge a little trouble?"—expressing the fact that he did not think his work burdensome, because he was doing it for a dying man and hoped someone would do the same for him when his time came.

Apart from this lying, or because of it, what most tormented Ivan Ilych was that no one pitied him as he wished to be pitied. At certain moments after prolonged suffering he wished most of all (though he would have been ashamed to confess it) for someone to pity him as a sick child is pitied. He longed to be petted and comforted. He knew he was an important functionary, that he had a beard turning grey, and that therefore what he longed for was impossible, but still he longed for it. And in Gerasim's attitude toward him there was something akin to what he wished for, and so that attitude comforted him. Ivan Ilych wanted to be petted and cried over, and then his colleague Shebek would come, and instead of weeping and being petted, Ivan Ilych would assume a serious, severe, and profound air, and by force of habit would express his opinion on a decision of the Court of Cassation and would stubbornly insist on that view. This falsity around him and within him did more than anything else to poison his last days.

VIII

It was morning. He knew it was morning because Gerasim had gone, and Peter the footman had come and put out the candles, drawn back one of the curtains, and began quietly to tidy up. Whether it was morning or evening, Friday or Sunday, made no difference, it was all just the same: the gnawing, unmitigated, agonizing pain, never ceasing for an instant, the consciousness of life inexorably waning but not yet extinguished, the approach of that ever dreaded and hateful Death which was the only reality, and always the same falsity. What were days, weeks, hours, in such a case?

"Will you have some tea, sir?"

"He wants things to be regular, and wishes the gentlefolk to drink tea in the morning," thought Ivan Ilych, and only said "No."

"Wouldn't you like to move onto the sofa, sir?"

"He wants to tidy up the room, and I'm in the way. I am uncleanliness and disorder," he thought, and said only:

"No leave me alone."

The man went on bustling about. Ivan Ilych stretched out his hand. Peter came up, ready to help.

"What is it, sir?"

"My watch."

Peter took the watch which was close at hand and gave it to his master.

"Half-past eight. Are they up?"

"No sir, except Vladimir Ivanich" (the son) "who has gone to school. Praskovya Fedorovna ordered me to wake her if you asked for her. Shall I do so?"

"No, there's no need to." "Perhaps I'd better have some tea," he thought and added aloud: "Yes, bring me some tea."

Peter went out. Left alone Ivan Ilych dreaded being left alone. "How can I keep him here? Oh yes, my medicine." "Peter, give me my medicine." "Why not? Perhaps it may still do me some good." He took a spoonful and swallowed it. "No, it won't help. It's all tomfoolery, all deception," he decided as soon as he became aware of the familiar, sickly, hopeless taste. "No, I can't believe in it any longer. But the pain, why this pain? If it would only cease just for a moment!" And he moaned. Peter turned towards him. "It's all right. Go and fetch me some tea."

Peter went out. Left alone Ivan Ilych groaned not so much with pain, terrible though that was, as from mental anguish. Always and for ever the same, always these endless days and nights. If only it would come quicker! If only *what* would come quicker? Death, darkness? . . . No, no! Anything rather than death!

When Peter returned with the tea on a tray, Ivan Ilych stared at him for a time in perplexity, not realizing who and what he was. Peter was disconcerted by that look and his embarrassment brought Ivan Ilych to himself.

"Oh, tea! All right, put it down. Only help me to wash and put on a clean shirt."

And Ivan Ilych began to wash. With pauses for rest, he washed his hands and then his face, cleaned his teeth, brushed his hair, and looked in the glass. He was terrified by what he saw, especially by the limp way in which his hair clung to his pallid forehead.

While his shirt was being changed he knew that he would be still more frightened at the sight of his body, so he avoided looking at it. Finally he was ready. He drew on a dressing-gown, wrapped himself in a plaid, and sat down in the armchair to take his tea. For a moment he felt refreshed, but as soon as he began to drink the tea he was again aware of the same taste, and the pain also returned. He finished it with an effort, and then lay down stretching out his legs, and dismissed Peter.

Always the same. Now a spark of hope flashes up, then a sea of despair rages, and always pain; always pain, always despair, and always the same. When alone he had a dreadful and distressing desire to call someone, but he knew beforehand that with others present it would be still worse. "Another dose of morphine—to lose consciousness. I will tell him, the doctor, that he must think of something else. It's impossible, impossible, to go on like this."

An hour and another pass like that. But now there is a ring at the door bell. Perhaps it's the doctor? It is. He comes in fresh, hearty, plump, and cheerful, with that look on his face that seems to say: "There now, you're in a panic about something, but we'll arrange it all for you directly!" The doctor knows this expression is out of place here, but he has put it on once for all and can't take it off—like a man who has put on a frock-coat in the morning to pay a round of calls.

The doctor rubs his hands vigorously and reassuringly.

"Brr! How cold it is! There's such a sharp frost: just let me warm myself!" he says, as if it were only a matter of waiting till he was warm, and then he would put everything right.

"Well now, how are you?"

Ivan Ilych feels that the doctor would like to say: "Well, how are our affairs?" but that even he feels that this would not do and says instead: "What sort of a night have you had?"

Ivan Ilych looks at him as much as to say: "Are you really never ashamed of lying?" But the doctor does not wish to understand this question, and Ivan Ilych says: "Just as terrible as ever. The pain never leaves me and never subsides. If only something . . ."

"Yes, you sick people are always like that. . . . There, now I think I am warm enough. Even Praskovya Fedorovna, who is so particular, could find no fault with my temperature. Well, now I can say good-morning," and the doctor presses his patient's hand.

Then, dropping his former playfulness, he begins with a most serious face to examine the patient, feeling his pulse and taking his temperature, and then begins the sounding and auscultation.

Ivan Ilych knows quite well and definitely that all this is nonsense and pure deception, but when the doctor, getting down on his knee, leans over him, putting his ear first higher then lower, and performs various gymnastic movements over him with a significant expression on his face, Ivan Ilych submits to it all as he used to submit to the speeches of the lawyers, though he knew very well that they were all lying and why they were lying.

The doctor, kneeling on the sofa, is still sounding him when Praskovya Fedorovna's silk dress rustles at the door and she is heard scolding Peter for not having let her know of the doctor's arrival.

She comes in, kisses her husband, and at once proceeds to prove that she has been up a long time already, and only owing to a misunderstanding failed to be there when the doctor arrived.

Ivan Ilych looks at her, scans her all over, sets against her the whiteness and plumpness and cleanness of her hands and neck, the gloss of her hair, and the sparkle of her vivacious eyes. He hates her with his whole soul. And the thrill of hatred he feels for her makes him suffer from her touch.

Her attitude towards him and his disease is still the same. Just as the doctor had adopted a certain relation to his patient which he could not abandon, so had she formed one towards him—that he was not doing something he ought to do and was himself to blame, and that she reproached him lovingly for this—and she could not now change that attitude.

"You see he doesn't listen to me and doesn't take his medicine at the proper time. And above all he lies in a position that is no doubt bad for him—with his legs up."

She described how he made Gerasim hold his legs up.

The doctor smiled with a contemptuous affability that said: "What's to be done? These sick people do have foolish fancies of that kind, but we must forgive them."

When the examination was over the doctor looked at his watch, and then Praskovya Fedorovna announced to Ivan Ilych that it was of course as he pleased, but she had sent to-day for a celebrated specialist who would examine him and have a consultation with Michael Danilovich (their regular doctor).

"Please don't raise any objections. I am doing this for my own sake," she said ironically, letting it be felt that she was doing it all for his sake and only said this to leave him no right to refuse. He remained silent, knitting his brows. He felt that he was so surrounded and involved in a mesh of falsity that it was hard to unravel anything.

Everything she did for him was entirely for her own sake, and she told him she was doing for herself what she actually was doing for herself, as if that was so incredible that he must understand the opposite.

At half-past eleven the celebrated specialist arrived. Again the sounding began and the significant conversations in his presence and in another room, about the kidneys and the appendix, and the questions and answers, with such an air of importance that again, instead of the real question of life and death which now alone confronted him, the question arose of the kidney and appendix which were not behaving as they ought to and would now be attacked by Michael Danilovich and the specialist and forced to amend their ways.

The celebrated specialist took leave of him with a serious though not hopeless look, and in reply to the timid question Ivan Ilych, with eyes glistening with fear and hope, put to him as to whether there was a chance of recovery, said that he could not vouch for it but there was a possibility. The look of hope with which Ivan Ilych watched the doctor out was so pathetic that Praskovya Fedorovna, seeing it, even wept as she left the room to hand the doctor his fee.

The gleam of hope kindled by the doctor's encouragement did not last long. The same room, the same pictures, curtains, wall-paper, medicine bottles, were all there, and the same aching suffering body, and Ivan Ilych began to moan. They gave him a subcutaneous injection and he sank into oblivion.

It was twilight when he came to. They brought his dinner and he swallowed some beef tea with difficulty, and then everything was the same again and night was coming on.

After dinner, at seven o'clock, Praskovya Fedorovna came into the room in evening dress, her full bosom pushed up by her corset, and with traces of powder on her face. She had reminded him in the morning that they were going to the theatre. Sarah Bernhardt was visiting the town and they had a box, which he had insisted on their taking. Now he had forgotten about it and her toilet offended him, but he concealed his vexation when he remembered that he had himself insisted on their securing a box and going because it would be an instructive and aesthetic pleasure for the children.

Praskovya Fedorovna came in, self-satisfied but yet with a rather guilty air. She sat down and asked how he was but, as he saw, only for the sake of asking and not in order to learn about it, knowing that there was nothing to learn—and then went on to what she really wanted to say: that she would not on any account have gone but that the box had been taken and Helen and their daughter were going, as well as Petrishchev (the examining magistrate, their daughter's fianceé) and that it was out of the question to let them go alone; but that she would have much preferred to sit with him for a while; and he must be sure to follow the doctor's orders while she was away.

"Oh, and Fedor Petrovich" (the fiancé) "would like to come in. May he? And Lisa?"

"All right."

Their daughter came in in full evening dress, her fresh young flesh exposed (making a show of that very flesh which in his own case caused so much suffering), strong, healthy, evidently in love, and impatient with illness, suffering, and death, because they interfered with her happiness.

Fedor Petrovich came in too, in evening dress, his hair curled *à la Capoul*, a tight stiff collar round his long sinewy neck, an enormous white shirt-front and narrow black trousers tightly stretched over his strong thighs. He had one white glove tightly drawn on, and was holding his opera hat in his hand.

Following him the schoolboy crept in unnoticed, in a new uniform, poor little fellow, and wearing gloves. Terribly dark shadows showed under his eyes, the meaning of which Ivan Ilych knew well.

His son had always seemed pathetic to him, and now it was dreadful to see the boy's frightened look of pity. It seemed to Ivan Ilych that Vasya was the only one besides Gerasim who understood and pitied him.

They all sat down and again asked how he was. A silence followed. Lisa asked her mother about the opera-glasses, and there was an altercation between mother and daughter as to who had taken them and where they had been put. This occasioned some unpleasantness.

Fedor Petrovich inquired of Ivan Ilych whether he had ever seen Sarah Bernhardt. Ivan Ilych did not at first catch the question, but then replied: "No, have you seen her before?"

"Yes, in *Adrienne Lecouvreur.*"

Praskovya Fedorovna mentioned some roles in which Sarah Bernhardt was particularly good. Her daughter disagreed. Conversation sprang up as to the elegance and realism of her acting—the sort of conversation that is always repeated and is always the same.

In the midst of the conversation Fedor Petrovich glanced at Ivan Ilych and became silent. The others also looked at him and grew silent. Ivan Ilych was staring with glittering eyes straight before him, evidently indignant with them. This had to be rectified, but it was impossible to do so. The silence had to be broken, but for a time no one dared to break it and they all became afraid that the conventional deception would suddenly become obvious and the truth become plain to all. Lisa was the first to pluck up courage and break that silence, but by trying to hide what everybody was feeling, she betrayed it.

"Well, if we are going it's time to start," she said, looking at her watch, a present from her father, and with a faint and significant smile at Fedor Petrovich relating to something known only to them. She got up with a rustle of her dress.

They all rose, said good-night, and went away.

When they had gone it seemed to Ivan Ilych that he felt better; the falsity had gone with them. But the pain remained—that same pain and that same fear that made everything monotonously alike, nothing harder and nothing easier. Everything was worse.

Again minute followed minute and hour followed hour. Everything remained the same and there was no cessation. And the inevitable end of it all became more and more terrible.

"Yes, send Gerasim here," he replied to a question Peter asked.

IX

His wife returned late at night. She came in on tiptoe, but he heard her, opened his eyes, and made haste to close them again. She wished to send Gerasim away and to sit with him herself, but he opened his eyes and said: "No, go away."

"Are you in great pain?"

"Always the same."

"Take some opium."

He agreed and took some. She went away.

Till about three in the morning he was in a state of stupified misery. It seemed to him that he and his pain were being thrust into a narrow, deep black sack, but though they were pushed further and further in they could not be pushed to the bottom. And this, terrible enough in itself, was accompanied by suffering. He was frightened yet wanted to fall through the sack, he struggled but yet co-operated. And suddenly he broke through, fell, and regained consciousness. Gerasim was sitting at the foot of the bed dozing quietly and patiently, while he himself lay with his emaciated stockinged legs resting on Gerasim's shoulders; the same shaded candle was there and the same unceasing pain.

"Go away, Gerasim," he whispered.

"It's all right, sir. I'll stay a while."

"No. Go away."

He removed his legs from Gerasim's shoulders, turned sideways onto his arm, and felt sorry for himself. He only waited till Gerasim had gone into the next room and then restrained himself no longer but wept like a child. He wept on account of his helplessness, his terrible loneliness, the cruelty of man, the cruelty of God, and the absence of God.

"Why hast Thou done all this? Why hast Thou brought me here? Why, why dost Thou torment me so terribly?"

He did not expect an answer and yet wept because there was no answer and could be none. The pain again grew more acute, but he did not stir and did not call. He said to himself: "Go on! Strike me! But what is it for? What have I done to Thee? What is it for?"

Then he grew quiet and not only ceased weeping but even held his breath and became all attention. It was as though he were listening not to an audible voice but to the voice of his soul, to the current of thoughts arising within him.

"What is it you want?" was the first clear conception capable of expression in words, that he heard.

"What do you want? What do you want?" he repeated to himself. "What do I want? To live and not to suffer," he answered.

And again he listened with such concentrated attention that even his pain did not distract him.

"To live? How?" asked his inner voice.

"Why, to live as I used to—well and pleasantly."

"As you lived before, well and pleasantly?" the voice repeated.

And in imagination he began to recall the best moments of his pleasant life. But strange to say none of those best moments of his pleasant life now seemed at all what they had then seemed—none of them except the first recollections of childhood. There, in childhood, there had been something really pleasant with which it would be possible to live if it could return. But the child who had experienced that happiness existed no longer, it was like a reminiscence of somebody else.

As soon as the period began which had produced the present Ivan Ilych, all that had then seemed joys now melted before his sight and turned into something trivial and often nasty.

And the further he departed from childhood and the nearer he came to the present the more worthless and doubtful were the joys. This began with the School of Law. A little that was really good was still found there—there was light-heartedness, friendship, and hope. But in the upper classes there had already been fewer of such good moments. Then during the first years of his official career, when he was in the service of the Governor, some pleasant moments again occurred: they were the memories of love for a woman. Then all became confused and there was still less of what was good; later on again there was still less that was good, and the further he went the less there was. His marriage, a mere accident, then the disenchantment that followed it, his wife's bad breath and the sensuality and hypocrisy: then that deadly official life and those preoccupations about money, a year of it, and two, and ten, and twenty, and always the same thing. And the longer it lasted the more deadly it became. "It is as if I had been going downhill while I imagined I was going up. And that is really what it was. I was going up in public opinion, but to the same extent life was ebbing away from me. And now it is all done and there is only death."

"Then what does it mean? Why? It can't be that life is so senseless and horrible. But if it really has been so horrible and senseless, why must I die and die in agony? There is something wrong!"

"Maybe I did not live as I ought to have done," it suddenly occurred to him. "But how could that be, when I did everything properly?" he replied, and immediately dismissed from his mind this, the sole solution of all the riddles of life and death, as something quite impossible.

"Then what do you want now? To live? Live how? Live as you lived in the law courts when the usher proclaimed "The judge is coming." The judge is coming, the judge!" he repeated to himself. "Here he is the judge. But I am not guilty!" he exclaimed angrily. "What is it for?" And he ceased crying, but turning his face to the wall continued to ponder on the same question: Why, and for what purpose, is there all this horror? But however much he pondered he found no answer. And whenever the thought occurred to him, as it often did, that it all resulted from his not having lived as he ought to have done, he at once recalled the correctness of his whole life and dismissed so strange an idea.

X

Another fortnight passed. Ivan Ilych now no longer left his sofa. He would not lie in bed but lay on the sofa, facing the wall nearly all the time. He suffered ever the same unceasing agonies and in his loneliness pondered always on the same insoluble question: "What is this? Can it be that it is Death?" And the inner voice answered: "Yes, it is Death."

"Why these sufferings?" And the voice answered, "For no reason—they just are so." Beyond and besides this there was nothing.

From the very beginning of his illness, ever since he had first been to see the doctor, Ivan Ilych's life had been divided between two contrary and alternating moods: now it was despair and the expectation of his un-comprehended and terrible death, and now hope and an intently interested observation of the functioning of his organs. Now before his eyes there was only a kidney or an intestine that temporarily evaded its duty, and now only that incomprehensible and dreadful death from which it was impossible to escape.

These two states of mind had alternated from the very beginning of his illness, but the further it progressed the more doubtful and fantastic became the conception of the kidney, and the more real the sense of impending death.

He had but to call to mind what he had been three months before and what he was now, to call to mind with what regularity he had been going downhill, for every possibility of hope to be shattered.

Latterly during that loneliness in which he found himself as he lay facing the back of the sofa, a loneliness in the midst of a populous town and surrounded by numerous acquaintances and relations but that yet could not have been more complete anywhere—either at the bottom of the sea or under the earth—during that terrible loneliness Ivan Ilych had lived only in memories of the past. Pictures of his past rose before him one after another. They always began with what was nearest in time and then went back to what was most remote—to his childhood—and rested there. If he thought of the stewed prunes that had been offered him that day, his mind went back to the raw shrivelled French plums of his childhood, their peculiar flavour and the flow of saliva when he sucked their stones, and along with the memory of that taste came a whole series of memories of those day: his nurse, his brother, and their toys. "No, I musn't think of that. . . . It is too painful," Ivan Ilych said to himself, and brought himself back to the present—to the button on the back of the sofa and the creases in its morocco. "Morocco is expensive, but it does not wear well: there had been a quarrel about it. It was a different kind of quarrel and a different kind of morocco that time when we tore father's portfolio and were punished, and mamma brought us some tarts. . . ."And again his thoughts dwelt on his childhood, and again it was painful and he tried to banish them and fix his mind on something else.

Then again together with that chain of memories another series passed through his mind—of how his illness had progressed and grown worse. There also the further back he looked the more life there had been. There had been more of what was good in life and more of life itself. The two merged together. "Just as the pain went on getting worse and worse so my life grew worse and worse," he thought. "There is one bright spot there at the back, at the beginning of life, and afterwards all becomes blacker and blacker and proceeds more and more rapidly—in inverse ratio to the square of the distance from death," thought Ivan Ilych. And the example of a stone falling downwards with increasing velocity entered his mind. Life, a series of increasing sufferings, flies further and further towards its end—the most terrible suffering. "I am flying. . . ." He shuddered, shifted himself, and tried to resist, but was already aware that resistance was impossible, and again with eyes weary of gazing but unable to cease seeing what was before them, he stared at the back of the sofa and waited—awaiting that dreadful fall and shock and destruction.

"Resistance is impossible!" he said to himself. "If I could only understand what it is all for! But that too is impossible. An explanation would be possible if it could be said that I have not lived as I ought to. But it is impossible to say that," and he remembered all the legality, correctitude, and propriety of his life. "That at any rate can certainly not be admitted," he thought, and his lips smiled ironically as if someone could see that smile and be taken in by it. "There is no explanation! Agony, death. . . . What for?"

XI

Another two weeks went by in this way and during that fortnight an event occurred that Ivan Ilych and his wife had desired. Petrishchev formally proposed. It happened in the evening. The next day Praskovya Fedorovna came into her husband's room considering how best to inform him of it, but that very night there had been a fresh change for the worse in his condition. She found him still lying on the sofa but in a different position. He lay on his back, groaning and staring fixedly straight in front of him.

She began to remind him of his medicines, but he turned his eyes towards her with such a look that she did not finish what she was saying; so great an animosity, to her in particular, did that look express.

"For Christ's sake let me die in peace!" he said.

She would have gone away, but just then their daughter came in and went up to say good morning. He looked at her as he had done at his wife, and in reply to her inquiry about his health said dryly that he would soon free them all of himself. They were both silent and after sitting with him for a while went away.

"Is it our fault?" Lisa said to her mother. "It's as if we were to blame! I am sorry for papa, but why should we be tortured?"

The doctor came at his usual time. Ivan Ilych answered "Yes" and "No," never taking his angry eyes from him, and at last said: "You know you can do nothing for me, so leave me alone."

"We can ease your sufferings."

"You can't even do that. Let me be."

The doctor went into the drawing-room and told Praskovya Fedorovna that the case was very serious and that the only resource left was opium to allay her husband's sufferings, which must be terrible.

It was true, as the doctor said, that Ivan Ilych's physical sufferings were terrible, but worse than the physical sufferings were his mental sufferings which were his chief torture.

His mental sufferings were due to the fact that that night, as he looked at Gerasim's sleepy, good-natured face with its prominent cheek-bones, the question suddenly occurred to him: "What if my whole life has really been wrong?"

It occurred to him that what had appeared perfectly impossible before, namely that he had not spent his life as he should have done, might after all be true. It occurred to him that his scarcely perceptible attempts to struggle against what was considered good by the most highly placed people, those scarcely noticeable impulses which he had immediately suppressed, might have been the real thing, and all the rest false. And his professional duties and the whole arrangement of his life and of his family, and all his social and official interests, might all have been false. He tried to defend all those things to himself and suddenly felt the weakness of what he was defending. There was nothing to defend.

"But if that is so," he said to himself, "and I am leaving this life with the consciousness that I have lost all that was given me and it is impossible to rectify it—what then?"

He lay on his back and began to pass his life in review in quite a new way. In the morning when he saw first his footman, then his wife, then his daughter, and then the doctor, their every word and movement confirmed to him the awful truth that had been revealed to him during the night. In them he saw himself—all that for which he had lived—and saw clearly that it was not real at all, but a terrible and huge deception which had hidden both life and death. This consciousness intensified his physical suffering tenfold. He groaned and tossed about, and pulled at his clothing which choked and stifled him. And he hated them on that account.

He was given a large dose of opium and became unconscious, but at noon his sufferings began again. He drove everybody away and tossed from side to side.

His wife came to him and said:

"Jean, my dear, do this for me. It can't do any harm and often helps. Healthy people often do it."

He opened his eyes wide.

"What? Take communion? Why? It's unnecessary! However. . . ."
She began to cry.

"Yes, do, my dear. I'll send for our priest. He is such a nice man."

"All right. Very well," he muttered.

When the priest came and heard his confession, Ivan Ilych was softened and seemed to feel a relief from his doubts and consequently from his sufferings, and for a moment there came a ray of hope. He again began to think of the vermiform appendix and the possibility of correcting it. He received the sacrament with tears in his eyes.

When they laid him down again afterwards he felt a moment's ease, and the hope that he might live awoke in him again. He began to think of the operation that had been suggested to him. "To live! I want to live!" he said to himself.

His wife came in to congratulate him after his communion, and when uttering the usual conventional words she added:

"You feel better, don't you?"

Without looking at her he said "Yes."

Her dress, her figure, the expression of her face, the tone of her voice, all revealed the same thing. "This is wrong, it is not as it should be. All you have lived for and still live for is falsehood and deception, hiding life and death from you." And as soon as he admitted that thought, his hatred and his agonizing physical suffering again sprang up, and with that suffering a consciousness of the unavoidable, approaching end. And to this was added a new sensation of grinding shooting pain and a feeling of suffocation.

The expression of his face when he uttered that "yes" was dreadful. Having uttered it, he looked her straight in the eyes, turned on his face with a rapidity extraordinary in his weak state and shouted:

"Go away! Go away and leave me alone!"

XII

From that moment the screaming began that continued for three days, and was so terrible that one could not hear it through two closed doors without horror. At the moment he answered his wife he realized that he was lost, that there was no return, that the end had come, the very end, and his doubts were still unsolved and remained doubts.

"Oh! Oh! Oh!" he cried in various intonations. He had begun by screaming "I won't!" and continued screaming on the letter "o."

For three whole days, during which time did not exist for him, he struggled in that black sack into which he was being thrust by an invisible, resistless force. He struggled as a man condemned to death struggles in the hands of the executioner, knowing that he cannot save himself. And every moment he felt that despite all his efforts he was drawing nearer and nearer to what terrified him. He felt that his agony was due to his being thrust into that black hole and still more to his not being able to get right into it. He was hindered from getting into it by his conviction that his life had been a good one. That very justification of his life held him fast and prevented his moving forward, and it caused him most torment of all.

Suddenly some force struck him in the chest and side, making it still harder to breathe, and he fell through the hole and there at the bottom was a light. What had happened to him was like the sensation one sometimes experiences in a railway carriage when one thinks one is going backwards while one is really going forwards and suddenly becomes aware of the real direction.

"Yes, it was all not the right thing," he said to himself, "but that's no matter. It can be done. But what *is* the right thing?" he asked himself, and suddenly grew quiet.

This occurred at the end of the third day, two hours before his death. Just then his schoolboy son had crept softly in and gone up to the bedside. The dying man was still screaming desperately and waving his arms. His hand fell on the boy's head, and the boy caught it, pressed it to his lips, and began to cry.

At that very moment Ivan Ilych fell through and caught sight of the light, and it was revealed to him that though his life had not been what it should have been, this could still be rectified. He asked himself, "What *is* the right thing?" and grew still, listening. Then he felt that someone was kissing his hand. He opened his eyes, looked at his son, and felt sorry for him. His wife came up to him and he glanced at her. She was gazing at him open-mouthed, with undried tears on her nose and cheek and a despairing look on her face. He felt sorry for her too.

"Yes, I am making them wretched," he thought. "They are sorry, but it will be better for them when I die." He wished to say this but had not the strength to utter it. "Besides, why speak? I must act," he thought. With a look at his wife he indicated his son and said: "Take him away . . . sorry for him . . . sorry for you too. . . ." He tried to add, "forgive me," but said "forego" and waved his hand, knowing that He whose understanding mattered would understand.

And suddenly it grew clear to him that what had been oppressing him and would not leave him was all dropping away at once from two sides, from ten sides, and from all sides. He was sorry for them, he must act so as not to hurt them: release them and free himself from these sufferings. "How good and how simple!" he thought. "And the pain?" he asked himself. "What has become of it? Where are you, pain?"

He turned his attention to it.

"Yes, here it is. Well, what of it? Let the pain be."

"And death . . . where is it?"

He sought his former accustomed fear of death and did not find it. "Where is it? What death?" There was no fear because there was no death.

In place of death there was light.

"So that's what it is!" he suddenly exclaimed aloud. "What joy!"

To him all this happened in a single instant, and the meaning of that instant did not change. For those present his agony continued for another two hours. Something rattled in his throat, his emaciated body twitched, then the gasping and rattle became less and less frequent.

"It is finished!" said someone near him.

He heard these words and repeated them in his soul.

"Death is finished," he said to himself. "It is no more!"

He drew in a breath, stopped in the midst of a sigh, stretched out, and died.

THE BRIDE COMES TO YELLOW SKY

Stephen Crane

I

THE great Pullman was whirling onward with such dignity of motion that a glance from the window seemed simply to prove that the plains of Texas were pouring eastward. Vast flats of green grass, dull-hued spaces of mesquit and cactus, little groups of frame houses, woods of light and tender trees, all were sweeping into the east, sweeping over the horizon, a precipice.

A newly married pair had boarded this coach at San Antonio. The man's face was reddened from many days in the wind and sun, and a direct result of his new black clothes was that his brick-coloured hands were constantly performing in a most conscious fashion. From time to time he looked down respectfully at his attire. He sat with a hand on each knee, like a man waiting in a barber's shop. The glances he devoted to other passengers were furtive and shy.

The bride was not pretty, nor was she very young. She wore a dress of blue cashmere, with small reservations of velvet here and there, and with steel buttons abounding. She continually twisted her head to regard her puff sleeves, very stiff, straight, and high. They embarrassed her. It was quite apparent that she had cooked, and that she expected to cook, dutifully. The blushes caused by the careless scrutiny of some passengers as she had entered the car were strange to see upon this plain, underclass countenance, which was drawn in placid, almost emotionless lines.

They were evidently very happy. "Ever been in a parlor-car before?" he asked, smiling with delight.

"No," she answered; "I never was. It's fine, ain't it?"

"Great! And then after a while we'll go forward to the diner, and get a big lay-out. Finest meal in the world. Charge a dollar."

"Oh, do they?" cried the bride. "Charge a dollar? Why, that's too much—for—us—ain't it, Jack?"

"Not this trip, anyhow," he answered bravely. "We're going to go the whole thing."

Later he explained to her about the trains. "You see, it's a thousand miles from one end of Texas to the other; and this train runs right across it, and never stops but four times." He had the pride of an owner. He pointed out to her the dazzling fittings of the coach; and in truth her eyes opened wider as she contemplated the sea-green figured velvet, the shining brass, silver, and glass, the wood that gleamed as darkly brilliant as the surface of a pool of oil. At one end a bronze figure sturdily held a support for a separated chamber, and at convenient places on the ceiling were frescos in olive and silver.

To the minds of the pair, their surroundings reflected the glory of their marriage that morning in San Antonio; this was the environment of their new estate; and the man's face in particular beamed with an elation that made him appear ridiculous to the Negro porter. This individual at times surveyed them from afar with an amused and superior grin. On other occasions he bullied them with skill in ways that did not make it exactly plain to them that they were being bullied. He subtly used all the manners of the most unconquerable kind of snobbery. He oppressed them; but on this oppression they had small knowledge, and they speedily forgot that infrequently a number of travellers covered them with stares of derisive enjoyment. Historically there was supposed to be something infinitely humorous in their situation.

"We are due in Yellow Sky at 3:42," he said, looking tenderly into her eyes.

"Oh, are we?" she said, as if she had not been aware of it. To evince surprise at her husband's statement was part of her wifely amiability. She took from a pocket a little silver watch; as she held it before her, and stared at it with a frown of attention, the new husband's face shone.

"I bought it in San Anton' from a friend of mine," he told her gleefully.

"It's seventeen minutes past twelve," she said, looking up at him with a kind of shy and clumsy coquetry. A passenger, noting this play, grew excessively sardonic, and winked at himself in one of the numerous mirrors.

At last they went to the dining-car. Two rows of Negro waiters, in glowing white suits, surveyed their entrance with the interest, and also the equanimity, of men who had been forewarned. The pair fell to the lot of a waiter who happened to feel pleasure in steering them through their meal. He viewed them with the manner of a fatherly pilot, his countenance radiant with benevolence. The patronage, entwined with the ordinary deference, was not plain to them. And yet, as they turned to their coach, they showed in their faces a sense of escape.

To the left, miles down a long purple slope, was a little ribbon of mist where moved the keening Rio Grande. The train was approaching it at an angle, and the apex was Yellow Sky. Presently it was apparent that, as the distance from Yellow Sky grew shorter, the husband became commensurately restless. His brick-red hands were more insistent in their prominence. Occasionally he was even rather absent-minded and far-away when the bride leaned forward and addressed him.

As a matter of truth, Jack Potter was beginning to find the shadow of a deed weigh upon him like a leaden slab. He, the town marshal of Yellow Sky, a man known, liked, and feared in his corner, a prominent person, had gone to San Antonio to meet a girl he believed he loved, and there, after the usual prayers, had actually induced her to marry him, without consulting Yellow Sky for any part of the transaction. He was now bringing his bride before an innocent and unsuspecting community.

Of course people in Yellow Sky married as it pleased them, in accordance with a general custom; but such was Potter's thought of his duty to his friends, or of their idea of his duty, or of an unspoken form which does not control men in these matters, that he felt he was heinous. He had committed an extraordinary crime. Face to face with this girl in San Antonio, and spurred by his sharp impulse, he had gone headlong over all the social hedges. At San Antonio he was like a man hidden in the dark. A knife to sever any friendly duty, any form, was easy to his hand in that remote city. But the hour of Yellow Sky—the hour of daylight—was approaching.

He knew full well that this marriage was an important thing to his town. It could only be exceeded by the burning of the new hotel. His friends could not forgive him. Frequently he had reflected on the advisability of telling them by telegraph, but a new cowardice had been upon him. He feared to do it. And now the train was hurrying him toward a scene of amazement, glee, and reproach. He glanced out of the window at the line of haze swinging slowly in toward the train.

Yellow Sky had a kind of brass band, which played painfully, to the delight of the populace. He laughed without heart as he thought of it. If the citizens could dream of his prospective arrival with his bride, they would parade the band at the station and escort them, amid cheers and laughing congratulations to his adobe home.

He resolved that he would use all the devices of speed and plainscraft in making the journey from the station to his house. Once within that safe citadel, he could issue some sort of vocal bulletin, and then not go among the citizens until they had time to wear off a little of their enthusiasm.

The bride looked anxiously at him. "What's worrying you, Jack?"

He laughed again, "I'm not worrying, girl; I'm only thinking of Yellow Sky."

She flushed in comprehension.

A sense of mutual guilt invaded their minds and developed a finer tenderness. They looked at each other with eyes softly aglow. But Potter often laughed the same nervous laugh; the flush upon the bride's face seemed quite permanent.

The traitor to the feelings of Yellow Sky narrowly watched the speeding landscape. "We're nearly there," he said.

Presently the porter came and announced the proximity of Potter's home. He held a brush in his hand, and, with all his airy superiority gone, he brushed Potter's new clothes as the latter slowly turned this way and that way. Potter fumbled out a coin and gave it to the porter, as he had seen others do. It was a heavy and muscle-bound business, as that of a man shoeing his first horse.

The porter took their bag, and as the train began to slow they moved forward to the hooded platform of the car. Presently the two engines and their long string of coaches rushed into the station of Yellow Sky.

"They have to take water here," said Potter, from a constricted throat and in mournful cadence, as one announcing death. Before the train stopped his eyes had swept the length of the platform, and he was glad and astonished to see there was none upon it but the station-agent, who, with a slightly hurried and anxious air, was walking toward the water-tanks. When the train had halted, the porter alighted first, and placed in position a little temporary step.

"Come on, girl," said Potter, hoarsely. As he helped her down they each laughed on a false note. He took the bag from the Negro, and bade his wife cling to his arm. As they slunk rapidly away, his hang-dog glance perceived that they were unloading the two trunks, and also that the station-agent, far ahead near the baggage-car, had turned and was running toward him, making gestures. He laughed, and groaned as he laughed, when he noted the first effect of his marital bliss upon Yellow Sky. He gripped his wife's arm firmly to his side, and they fled. Behind them the porter stood, chuckling fatuously.

II

The California express on the Southern Railway was due at Yellow Sky in twenty-one minutes. There were six men at the bar of the Weary Gentleman saloon. One was a drummer who talked a great deal and rapidly; three were Texans who did not care to talk at that time; and two were Mexican sheepherders, who did not talk as a general practice in the Weary Gentleman saloon. The barkeeper's dog lay on the board walk that crossed in front of the door. His head was on his paws, and he glanced drowsily here and there with the constant vigilance of a dog that is kicked on occasion. Across the sandy street were some vivid green grass-plots, so wonderful in appearance, amid the sands that burned near them in a blazing sun, that they caused a doubt in the mind. They exactly resembled the grass mats used to represent lawns on the stage. At the cooler end of the railway station, a man without a coat sat in a tilted chair and smoked his pipe. The fresh-cut bank of the Rio Grande circled near the town, and there could be seen beyond it a great plum-coloured plain of mesquit.

Save for the busy drummer and his companions in the saloon, Yellow Sky was dozing. The new-comer leaned gracefully upon the bar, and recited many tales with the confidence of a bard who has come upon a new field.

"—and at the moment that the old man fell downstairs with the bureau in his arms, the old woman was coming up with two scuttles of coal, and of course—"

The drummer's tale was interrupted by a young man who suddenly appeared in the open door. He cried: "Scratchy Wilson's drunk, and has turned loose with both hands." The two Mexicans at once set down their glasses and faded out of the rear entrance of the saloon.

The drummer, innocent and jocular, answered: "All right, old man. S'pose he has? Come in and have a drink, anyhow."

But the information had made such an obvious cleft in every skull in the room that the drummer was obliged to see its importance. All had become instantly solemn. "Say," said he, mystified, "what is this?" His three companions made the introductory gesture of eloquent speech; but the young man at the door forestalled them.

"It means, my friend," he answered, as he came into the saloon, "that for the next two hours this town won't be a health resort."

The barkeeper went to the door, and locked and barred it; reaching out of the window, he pulled in heavy wooden shutters, and barred them. Immediately a solemn, chapel-like gloom was upon the place. The drummer was looking from one to another.

"But say," he cried, "what is this, anyhow? You don't mean there is going to be a gun-fight?"

"Don't know whether there'll be a fight or not," answered one man, grimly; "but there'll be some shootin'—some good shootin'."

The young man who had warned them waved his hand. "Oh, there'll be a fight fast enough, if any one wants it. Anybody can get a fight out there in the street. There's a fight just waiting."

The drummer seemed to be swayed between the interest of a foreigner and a perception of personal danger.

"What did you say his name was?" he asked.

"Scratchy Wilson," they answered in chorus.

"And will he kill anybody? What are you going to do? Does this happen often? Does he rampage around like this once a week or so? Can he break in that door?"

"No; he can't break down that door," replied the barkeeper. "He's tried it three times. But when he comes you'd better lay down on the floor, stranger. He's dead sure to shoot at it, and a bullet may come through."

Thereafter the drummer kept a strict eye upon the door. The time had not yet been called for him to hug the floor, but, as a minor precaution, he sidled near to the wall. "Will he kill anybody?" he said again.

The man laughed low and scornfully at the question.

"He's out to shoot, and he's out for trouble. Don't see any good in experimentin' with him."

"But what do you do in a case like this? What do you do?"

A man responded: "Why, he and Jack Potter—"

"But," in chorus the other men interrupted, "Jack Potter's in San Anton'."

"Well, who is he? What's he got to do with it?"

"Oh, he's the town marshal. He goes out and fights Scratchy when he gets on one of these tears."

"Wow!" said the drummer, mopping his brow. "Nice job he's got."

The voices had toned away to mere whisperings. The drummer wished to ask further questions, which were born of an increasing anxiety and bewilderment; but when he attempted them, the men merely looked at him in irritation and motioned him to remain silent. A tense waiting hush was upon them. In the deep shadows of the room their eyes shone as they listened for sounds from the street. One man made three gestures at the barkeeper; and the latter, moving like a ghost, handed him a glass and a bottle. The man poured a full glass of whisky, and set down the bottle noiselessly. He gulped the whisky in a swallow, and turned again toward the door in immovable silence. The drummer saw that the barkeeper, without a sound, had taken a Winchester from beneath the bar. Later he saw this individual beckoning to him, so he tiptoed across the room.

"You better come with me back of the bar."

"No, thanks," said the drummer, perspiring; "I'd rather be where I can make a break for the back door."

Whereupon the man of bottles made a kindly but peremptory gesture. The drummer obeyed it, and, finding himself seated on a box with his head below the level of the bar, balm was laid upon his soul at sight of various zinc and copper fittings that bore a resemblance to armour-plate. The barkeeper took a seat comfortably upon an adjacent box.

"You see," he whispered, "this here Scratchy Wilson is a wonder with a gun—a perfect wonder; and when he goes on the war-trail, we hunt our holes—naturally. He's about the last one of the old gang that used to hang out along the river here. He's a terror when he's drunk. When he's sober he's all right—kind of simple—wouldn't hurt a fly—nicest fellow in town. But when he's drunk—whoo!"

There were periods of stillness. "I wish Jack Potter was back from San Anton'," said the barkeeper. "He shot Wilson up once—in the leg—and he would sail in and pull out the kinks in this thing."

Presently they heard from a distance the sound of a shot, followed by three wild yowls. It instantly removed a bond from the men in the darkened saloon. There was a shuffling of feet. They looked at each other. "Here he comes," they said.

III

A man in a maroon-colored flannel shirt, which had been purchased for purposes of decoration, and made principally by some Jewish women on the East Side of New York, rounded a corner and walked into the middle of the main street of Yellow Sky. In either hand the man held a long, heavy, blue-black revolver. Often he yelled, and these cries rang through a semblance of a deserted village, shrilly flying over the roofs in a volume that seemed to have no relation to the ordinary vocal strength of a man. It was as if the surrounding stillness formed the arch of a tomb over him. These cries of ferocious challenge rang against walls of silence. And his boots had red tops with gilded imprints, of the kind beloved in winter by little sledding boys on the hillsides of New England.

The man's face flamed in a rage begot of whisky. His eyes, rolling, and yet keen for ambush, hunted the still doorways and windows. He walked with the creeping movement of the midnight cat. As it occurred to him, he roared menacing information. The long revolvers in his hands were as easy as straws; they were moved with an electric swiftness. The little fingers of each hand played sometimes in a musician's way. Plain from the low collar of the shirt, the cords of his neck straightened and sank, straightened and sank, as passion moved him. The only sounds were his terrible invitations. The calm adobes preserved their demeanour at the passing of this small thing in the middle of the street.

There was no offer of fight—no offer of fight. The man called to the sky. There were no attractions. He bellowed and fumed and swayed his revolvers here and everywhere.

The dog of the barkeeper of the Weary Gentleman saloon had not appreciated the advance of events. He yet lay dozing in front of his master's door. At sight of the dog, the man paused and raised his revolver humorously. At sight of the man, the dog sprang up and walked diagonally away, with a sullen head and growling. The man yelled, and the dog broke into a gallop. As it was about to enter an alley, there was a loud noise, a whistling, and something spat the ground directly before it. The dog screamed, and, wheeling in terror, galloped headlong in a new direction. Again there was a noise, a whistling, and sand was kicked viciously before it. Fear-stricken, the dog turned and flurried like an animal in a pen. The man stood laughing, his weapons at his hips.

Ultimately the man was attracted by the closed door of the Weary Gentleman saloon. He went to it and, hammering with a revolver, demanded drink.

The door remained imperturbable, he picked a bit of paper from the walk, and nailed it to the framework with a knife. He then turned his back contemptuously upon this popular resort and, walking to the opposite side of the street and spinning there on his heel quickly and lithely, fired at the bit of paper. He missed it by a half-inch. He swore at himself, and went away. Later he comfortably fusilladed the windows of his most intimate friend. The man was playing with this town; it was a toy for him.

But still there was no offer of fight. The name of Jack Potter, his ancient antagonist, entered his mind, and he concluded that it would be a glad thing if he should go to Potter's house, and by bombardment induce him to come out and fight. He moved in the direction of his desire, chanting Apache scalp-music.

When he arrived at it, Potter's house presented the same still front as had the other adobes. Taking up a strategic position, the man howled a challenge. But this house regarded him as might a great stone god. It gave no sign. After a decent wait, the man howled further challenges, mingling with them wonderful epithets.

Presently there came the spectacle of a man churning himself into deepest rage over the immobility of a house. He fumed at it as the winter wind attacks a prairie cabin in the North. To the distance there should have gone the sound of a tumult like the fighting of two hundred Mexicans. As necessity bade him, he paused for breath or to reload his revolvers.

IV

Potter and his bride walked sheepishly and with speed. Sometimes they laughed together shamefacedly and low.

"Next corner, dear," he said finally.

They put forth the efforts of a pair walking bowed against a strong wind. Potter was about to raise a finger to point the first appearance of the new home when, as they circled the corner, they came face to face with a man in a maroon-colored shirt, who was feverishly pushing cartridges into a large revolver. Upon the instant the man dropped his revolver to the ground and, like lightning, whipped another from its holster. The second weapon was aimed at the bridegroom's chest.

There was a silence. Potter's mouth seemed to be merely a grave for his tongue. He exhibited an instinct to at once loosen his arm from the woman's grip, and he dropped the bag to the sand. As for the bride, her face had gone as yellow as old cloth. She was a slave to hideous rites, gazing at the apparitional snake.

The two men faced each other at a distance of three paces. He of the revolver smiled with a new and quiet ferocity.

"Tried to sneak up on me," he said. "Tried to sneak up on me!" His eyes grew more baleful. As Potter made a slight movement, the man thrust his revolver venomously forward. "No; don't you do it, Jack Potter. Don't you move a finger toward a gun just yet. Don't you move an eyelash. The time has come for me to settle with you, and I'm goin' to do it my own way, and loaf along with no interferin'. So if you don't want a gun bent on you, just mind what I tell you."

Potter looked at his enemy. "I ain't got a gun on me, Scratchy," he said. "Honest, I ain't." He was stiffening and steadying, but yet somewhere at the back of his mind a vision of the Pullman floated: the sea-green figured velvet, the shining brass, silver, and glass, the wood that gleamed as darkly brilliant as the surface of a pool of oil—all the glory of the marriage, the environment of the new estate. "You know I fight when it comes to fighting, Scratchy Wilson; but I ain't got a gun on me. You'll have to do all the shootin' yourself."

His enemy's face went livid. He stepped forward, and lashed his weapon to and fro before Potter's chest. "Don't you tell me you ain't got no gun on you, you whelp. Don't tell me no lie like that. There ain't a man in Texas ever seen you without no gun. Don't take me for no kid." His eyes blazed with light, and his throat worked like a pump.

"I ain't takin' you for no kid," answered Potter. His heels had not moved an inch backward. "I'm takin' you for a damn fool. I tell you I ain't got a gun, and I ain't. If you're goin' to shoot me up, you better begin now; you'll never get a chance like this again."

So much enforced reasoning had told on Wilson's rage; he was calmer. "If you ain't got a gun, why ain't you got a gun?" he sneered. "Been to Sunday-school?"

"I ain't got a gun because I've just come from San Anton' with my wife. I'm married," said Potter. "And if I'd thought there was going to be any galoots like you prowling around when I brought my wife home, I'd had a gun, and don't you forget it."

"Married!" said Scratchy, not at all comprehending.

"Yes, married. I'm married," said Potter, distinctly.

"Married?" said Scratchy. Seemingly for the first time, he saw the drooping, drowning woman at the other man's side. "No!" he said. He was like a creature allowed a glimpse of another world. He moved a pace backward, and his arm, with the revolver, dropped to his side. "Is this the lady?" he asked.

"Yes; this is the lady," answered Potter.

There was another period of silence.

"Well," said Wilson at last, slowly, "I s'pose it's all off now."

"It's all off if you say so, Scratchy. You know I didn't make the trouble," Potter lifted his valise.

"Well, I 'low it's off, Jack," said Wilson. He was looking at the ground. "Married!" He was not a student of chivalry; it was merely that in the presence of this foreign condition he was a simple child of the earlier plains. He picked up his starboard revolver, and, placing both weapons in their holsters, he went away. His feet made funnel-shaped tracks in the heavy sand.

WINTER DREAMS

F. Scott Fitzgerald

SOME of the caddies were poor as sin and lived in one-room houses with a neurasthenic cow in the front yard, but Dexter Green's father owned the second best grocery-store in Black Bear—the best one was "The Hub," patronized by the wealthy people from Sherry Island—and Dexter caddied only for pocket-money.

In the fall when the days became crisp and gray, and the long Minnesota winter shut down like the white lid of a box, Dexter's skis moved over the snow that hid the fairways of the gulf course. At these times the country gave him a feeling of profound melancholy—it offended him that the links should lie in enforced fallowness, haunted by ragged sparrows for the long season. It was dreary, too, that on the tees where the gay colors fluttered in summer there were now only the desolate sand-boxes knee-deep in crusted ice. When he crossed the hills the wind blew cold as misery, and if the sun was out he tramped with his eyes squinted up against the hard dimensionless glare.

In April the winter ceased abruptly. The snow ran down into Black Bear Lake scarcely tarrying for the early golfers to brave the season with red and black balls. Without elation, without an interval of moist glory, the cold was gone.

Dexter knew that there was something dismal about this Northern spring, just as he knew there was something gorgeous about the fall. Fall made him clinch his hands and tremble and repeat idiotic sentences to himself, and make brisk abrupt gestures of command to imaginary audiences and armies. October filled him with hope which November raised to a sort of ecstatic triumph, and in this mood the fleeting brilliant impressions of the summer at Sherry Island were ready grist to his mill. He became a golf champion and defeated Mr. T. A. Hedrick in a marvellous match played a hundred times over the fairways of his imagination, a match each detail of which he changed about untiringly—sometimes he won with almost laughable ease, sometimes he came up magnificently from behind. Again, stepping from a Pierce-Arrow automobile, like Mr.

Mortimer Jones, he strolled frigidly into the lounge of the Sherry Island Golf Club—or perhaps, surrounded by an admiring crowd, he gave an exhibition of fancy diving from the spring-board of the club raft. . . . Among those who watched him in open-mouthed wonder was Mr. Mortimer Jones.

And one day it came to pass that Mr. Jones—himself and not his ghost—came up to Dexter with tears in his eyes and said that Dexter was the —— —— best caddy in the club, and wouldn't he decide not to quit if Mr. Jones made it worth his while, because every other —— —— caddy in the club lost one ball a hole for him—regularly—

"No, sir," said Dexter decisively. "I don't want to caddy any more." Then, after a pause: "I'm too old."

"You're not more than fourteen. Why the devil did you decide just this morning that you wanted to quit? You promised that next week you'd go over to the state tournament with me."

"I decided I was too old."

Dexter handed in his "A Class" badge, collected what money was due him from the caddy master, and walked home to Black Bear Village.

"The best —— —— caddy I ever saw," shouted Mr. Mortimer Jones over a drink that afternoon. "Never lost a ball! Willing! Intelligent! Quiet! Honest! Grateful!"

The little girl who had done this was eleven—beautifully ugly as little girls are apt to be who are destined after a few years to be inexpressibly lovely and bring no end of misery to a great number of men. The spark, however, was perceptible. There was a general ungodliness in the way her lips twisted down at the corners when she smiled, and in the—Heaven help us!—in the almost passionate quality of her eyes. Vitality is born early in such women. It was utterly in evidence now, shining through her thin frame in a sort of glow.

She had come eagerly out on to the course at nine o'clock with a white linen nurse and five small new golf-clubs in a white canvas bag which the nurse was carrying. When Dexter first saw her she was standing by the caddy house, rather ill at ease and trying to conceal the fact by engaging her nurse in an obviously unnatural conversation graced by startling and irrelevant grimaces from herself.

"Well, it's certainly a nice day, Hilda," Dexter heard her say. She drew down the corners of her mouth, smiled, and glanced furtively around, her eyes in transit falling for an instant on Dexter.

Then to the nurse:

"Well, I guess there aren't very many people out here this morning, are there?"

The smile again—radiant, blatantly artificial—convincing.

"I don't know what we're supposed to do now," said the nurse, looking nowhere in particular.

"Oh, that's all right. I'll fix it up."

Dexter stood perfectly still, his mouth slightly ajar. He knew that if he moved forward a step his stare would be in her line of vision—if he moved backward he would lose his full view of her face. For a moment he had not realized how young she was. Now he remembered having seen her several times the year before—in bloomers.

Suddenly, involuntarily, he laughed, a short abrupt laugh—then, startled by himself, he turned and began to walk quickly away.

"Boy—"

Dexter stopped.

"Boy—"

Beyond question he was addressed. Not only that, but he was treated to that absurd smile, that preposterous smile—the memory of which at least a dozen men were to carry into middle age.

"Boy, do you know where the golf teacher is?"

"He's giving a lesson."

"Well, do you know where the caddy-master is?"

"He isn't here yet this morning."

"Oh." For a moment this baffled her. She stood alternately on her right and left foot.

"We'd like to get a caddy," said the nurse. "Mrs. Mortimer Jones sent us out to play golf, and we don't know how without we get a caddy."

Here she was stopped by an ominous glance from Miss Jones, followed immediately by the smile.

"There aren't any caddies here except me," said Dexter to the nurse, "and I got to stay here in charge until the caddy-master gets here."

"Oh."

Miss Jones and her retinue now withdrew, and at a proper distance from Dexter became involved in a heated conversation, which was concluded by Miss Jones taking one of the clubs and hitting it on the ground with violence. For further emphasis she raised it again and was about to bring it down smartly upon the nurse's bosom, when the nurse seized the club and twisted it from her hands.

"You damn little mean old *thing*!" cried Miss Jones wildly.

Another argument ensued. Realizing that the elements of the comedy were implied in the scene, Dexter several times began to laugh, but each time restrained the laugh before it reached audibility. He could not resist the monstrous conviction that the little girl was justified in beating the nurse.

The situation was resolved by the fortuitous appearance of the caddy-master, who was appealed to immediately by the nurse.

"Miss Jones is to have a little caddy, and this one says he can't go."

"Mr. McKenna said I was to wait here till you came," said Dexter quickly.

"Well, he's here now." Miss Jones smiled cheerfully at the caddy-master. Then she dropped her bag and set off at a haughty mince toward the first tee.

"Well?" The caddy-master turned to Dexter. "What you standing there like a dummy for? Go pick up the young lady's clubs."

"I don't think I'll go out to-day," said Dexter.

"You don't—"

"I think I'll quit."

The enormity of his decision frightened him. He was a favorite caddy, and the thirty dollars a month he earned through the summer were not to be made elsewhere around the lake. But he had received a strong emotional shock, and his perturbation required a violent and immediate outlet.

It is not so simple as that, either. As so frequently would be the case in the future, Dexter was unconsciously dictated to by his winter dreams.

II

Now, of course, the quality and the seasonability of these winter dreams varied, but the stuff of them remained. They persuaded Dexter several years later to pass up a business course at the state university— his father, prospering now, would have paid his way—for the precarious advantage of attending an older and more famous university in the East, where he was bothered by his scanty funds. But do not get the impression, because his winter dreams happened to be concerned at first with musings on the rich, that there was anything merely snobbish in the boy. He wanted not association with glittering things and glittering people—he wanted the glittering things themselves. Often he reached out for the best without knowing why he wanted it—and sometimes he ran up against the mysterious denials and prohibitions in which life indulges. It is with one of those denials and not with his career as a whole that this story deals.

He made money. It was rather amazing. After college he went to the city from which Black Bear Lake draws its wealthy patrons. When he was only twenty-three and had been there not quite two years, there were already people who liked to say: "Now *there's* a boy—" All about him rich men's sons were peddling bonds precariously, or investing patrimonies precariously, or plodding through the two dozen volumes of the "George Washington Commercial Course," but Dexter borrowed a thousand dollars on his college degree and his confident mouth, and bought a partnership in a laundry.

It was a small laundry when he went into it, but Dexter made a speciality of learning how the English washed fine woolen golf-stockings without shrinking them, and within a year he was catering to the trade that wore knickerbockers. Men were insisting that their Shetland hose and sweaters go to his laundry, just as they had insisted on a caddy who could find golf-balls. A little later he was doing their wives' lingerie as well—and running five branches in different parts of the city. Before he was twenty-seven he owned the largest string of laundries in his section of the country. It was then that he sold out and went to New York. But the part of his story that concerns us goes back to the days when he was making his first big success.

When he was twenty-three Mr. Hart—one of the gray-haired men who like to say "Now there's a boy"—gave him a guest card to the Sherry Island Golf Club for a week-end. So he signed his name one day on the register, and that afternoon played golf in a foursome with Mr. Hart and Mr. Sandwood and Mr. T. A. Hedrick. He did not consider it necessary to remark that he had once carried Mr. Hart's bag over this same links, and that he knew every trap and gully with his eyes shut—but he found himself glancing at the four caddies who trailed them, trying to catch a gleam or gesture that would remind him of himself, that would lessen the gap which lay between his present and his past.

It was a curious day, slashed abruptly with fleeting, familiar impressions. One minute he had the sense of being a trespasser—in the next he was impressed by the tremendous superiority he felt toward Mr. T. A. Hedrick, who was a bore and not even a good golfer any more.

Then, because of a ball Mr. Hart lost near the fifteenth green, an enormous thing happened. While they were searching the stiff grasses of the rough there was a clear call of "Fore!" from behind a hill in their rear. And as they all turned abruptly from their search a bright new ball sliced abruptly over the hill and caught Mr. T. A. Hendrick in the abdomen.

"By Gad!" cried Mr. T. A. Hedrick, "they ought to put some of these crazy women off the course. It's getting to be outrageous."

A head and a voice came up together over the hill:

"Do you mind if we go through?"

"You hit me in the stomach!" declared Mr. Hedrick wildly.

"Did I?" The girl approached the group of men. "I'm sorry. I yelled 'Fore!' "

Her glance fell casually on each of the men—then scanned the fairway for her ball.

"Did I bounce into the rough?"

It was impossible to determine whether this question was ingenuous or malicious. In a moment, however, she left no doubt, for as her partner came up over the hill she called cheerfully:

"Here I am! I'd have gone on the green except that I hit something."

As she took her stance for a short mashie shot, Dexter looked at her closely. She wore a blue gingham dress, rimmed at throat and shoulders with a white edging that accentuated her tan. The quality of exaggeration, of thinness, which had made her passionate eyes and down-turning mouth absurd at eleven, was gone now. She was arrestingly beautiful. The color in her cheeks was centred like the color in a picture—it was not a "high" color, but a sort of fluctuating and feverish warmth, so shaded that it seemed at any moment it would recede and disappear. This color and the mobility of her mouth gave a continual impression of flux, of intense life, of passionate vitality—balanced only partially by the sad luxury of her eyes.

She swung her mashie impatiently and without interest, pitching the ball into a sand-pit on the other side of the green. With a quick, insincere smile and a careless "Thank you!" she went on after it.

"That Judy Jones!" remarked Mr. Hedrick on the next tee, as they waited—some moments—for her to play on ahead. "All she needs is to be turned up and spanked for six months and then to be married off to an old-fashioned cavalry captain."

"My God, she's good-looking!" said Mr. Sandwood, who was just over thirty.

"Good-looking!" cried Mr. Hedrick contemptuously, "she always looks as if she wanted to be kissed! Turning those big cow-eyes on every calf in town!"

It was doubtful if Mr. Hedrick intended a reference to the maternal instinct.

"She'd play pretty good golf if she'd try," said Mr. Sandwood.

"She has no form," said Mr. Hedrick solemnly.

"She has a nice figure," said Mr. Sandwood.

"Better thank the Lord she doesn't drive a swifter ball," said Mr. Hart, winking at Dexter.

Later in the afternoon the sun went down with a riotous swirl of gold and varying blues and scarlets, and left the dry, rustling night of Western summer. Dexter watched from the veranda of the Golf Club, watched the even overlap of the waters in the little wind, silver molasses under the harvest-moon. Then the moon held a finger to her lips and the lake became a clear pool, pale and quiet. Dexter put on his bathing-suit and swam out to the farthest raft, where he stretched dripping on the wet canvas of the springboard.

There was a fish jumping and a star shining and the lights around the lake were gleaming. Over on a dark peninsula a piano was playing the songs of last summer and of summers before that—songs from "Chin-Chin" and "The Count of Luxemburg" and "The Chocolate Soldier"—and because the sound of a piano over a stretch of water had always seemed beautiful to Dexter he lay perfectly quiet and listened.

The tune the piano was playing at that moment had been gay and new five years before when Dexter was a sophomore at college. They had played it at a prom once when he could not afford the luxury of proms, and he had stood outside the gymnasium and listened. The sound of the tune precipitated in him a sort of ecstasy and it was with that ecstasy he viewed what happened to him now. It was a mood of intense appreciation, a sense that, for once, he was magnificently attune to life and that everything about him was radiating a brightness and a glamour he might never know again.

A low, pale oblong detached itself suddenly from the darkness of the Island, spitting forth the reverberate sound of a racing motorboat. Two white streamers of cleft water rolled themselves out behind it and almost immediately the boat was beside him, drowning out the hot tinkle of the piano in the drone of its spray. Dexter raising himself on his arms was aware of a figure standing at the wheel, of two dark eyes regarding him over the lengthening space of water—then the boat had gone by and was sweeping in an immense and purposeless circle of spray round and round in the middle of the lake. With equal eccentricity one of the circles flattened out and headed back toward the raft.

"Who's that?" she called, shutting off her motor. She was so near now that Dexter could see her bathing-suit, which consisted apparently of pink rompers.

The nose of the boat bumped the raft, and as the latter tilted rakishly he was precipitated toward her. With different degrees of interest they recognized each other.

"Aren't you one of those men we played through this afternoon?" she demanded.

He was.

"Well, do you know how to drive a motor-boat? Because if you do I wish you'd drive this one so I can ride on the surf-board behind. My name is Judy Jones"—she favored him with an absurd smirk—rather, what tried to be a smirk, for, twist her mouth as she might, it was not grotesque, it was merely beautiful—"and I live in a house over there on the Island, and in that house there is a man waiting for me. When he drove up at the door I drove out of the dock because he says I'm his ideal."

There was a fish jumping and a star shining and the lights around the lake were gleaming. Dexter sat beside Judy Jones and she explained how her boat was driven. Then she was in the water, swimming to the floating surfboard with a sinuous crawl. Watching her was without effort to the eye, watching a branch waving or a sea-gull flying. Her arms, burned to butternut, moved sinuously among the dull platinum ripples, elbow appearing first, casting the forearm back with a cadence of falling water, then reaching out and down, stabbing a path ahead.

They moved out into the lake; turning, Dexter saw that she was kneeling on the low rear of the now uptilted surfboard.

"Go faster," she called, "fast as it'll go."

Obediently he jammed the lever forward and the white spray mounted at the bow. When he looked around again the girl was standing up on the rushing board, her arms spread wide, her eyes lifted toward the moon.

"It's awful cold," she shouted. "What's your name?"

He told her.

"Well, why don't you come to dinner to-morrow night?" His heart turned over like the fly-wheel of the boat, and, for the second time, her casual whim gave a new direction to his life.

III

Next evening while he waited for her to come downstairs, Dexter peopled the soft deep summer room and the sun-porch that opened from it with the men who had already loved Judy Jones. He knew the sort of men they were—the men who when he first went to college had entered from the great prep schools with graceful clothes and the deep tan of healthy summers. He had seen that, in one sense, he was better than these men. He was newer and stronger. Yet in acknowledging to himself that he wished his children to be like them he was admitting that he was but the rough, strong stuff from which they eternally sprang.

When the time had come for him to wear good clothes, he had known who were the best tailors in America, and the best tailors in America had made him the suit he wore this evening. He had acquired that particular reserve peculiar to his university, that set it off from other universities. He recognized the value to him of such a mannerism and he had adopted it: he knew that to be careless in dress and manner required more confidence than to be careful. But carelessness was for his children. His mother's name had been Krimelich. She was a Bohemian of the peasant class and she had talked broken English to the end of her days. Her son must keep to the set patterns.

At a little after seven Judy Jones came down-stairs. She wore a blue silk afternoon dress, and he was disappointed at first that she had not put on something more elaborate. This feeling was accentuated when, after a brief greeting, she went to the door of a butler's pantry and pushing it open called: "You can serve dinner, Martha." He had rather expected that a butler would announce dinner, that there would be a cocktail. Then he put these thoughts behind him as they sat down side by side on a lounge and looked at each other.

"Father and mother won't be here," she said thoughtfully.

He remembered the last time he had seen her father, and he was glad the parents were not to be here to-night—they might wonder who he was. He had been born in Keeble, a Minnesota village fifty miles farther north, and he always gave Kebble as his home instead of Black Bear Village. Country towns were well enough to come from if they weren't inconveniently in sight and used as footstools by fashionable lakes.

They talked of his university, which she had visited frequently during the past two years, and of the near-by city which supplied Sherry Island with its patrons, and whether Dexter would return next day to his prospering laundries.

During dinner she slipped into a moody depression which gave Dexter a feeling of uneasiness. Whatever petulance she uttered in her throaty voice worried him. Whatever she smiled at—at him, at a chicken liver, at nothing—it disturbed him that her smile could have no root in mirth, or even in amusement. When the scarlet corners of her lips curved down, it was less a smile than an invitation to a kill.

Then, after dinner, she led him out on the dark sun-porch and deliberately changed the atmosphere.

"Do you mind if I weep a little?" she said.

"I'm afraid I'm boring you," he responded quickly.

"You're not. I like you. But I've just had a terrible afternoon. There was a man I cared about, and this afternoon he told me out of a clear sky that he was poor as a church-mouse. He'd never even hinted it before. Does this sound horribly mundane?"

"Perhaps he was afraid to tell you."

"Suppose he was," she answered. "He didn't start right. You see, if I'd thought of him as poor—well, I've been mad about loads of poor men, and fully intended to marry them all. But in this case, I hadn't thought of him that way, and my interest in him wasn't strong enough to survive the shock. As if a girl calmly informed her fiancé that she was a widow. He might not object to widows, but—"

"Let's start right," she interrupted herself suddenly. "Who are you, anyhow?"

For a moment Dexter hesitated. Then:

"I'm nobody," he announced. "My career is largely a matter of futures."

"Are you poor?"

"No," he said frankly, "I'm probably making more money than any man my age in the Northwest. I know that's an obnoxious remark, but you advised me to start right."

There was a pause. Then she smiled and the corners of her mouth drooped and an almost imperceptible sway brought her closer to him, looking up into his eyes. A lump rose in Dexter's throat, and he waited breathless for the experiment, facing the unpredictable compound that would form mysteriously from the elements of their lips. Then he saw—she communicated her excitement to him, lavishly, deeply, with kisses that were not a promise but a fulfillment. They aroused in him not hunger demanding renewal but surfeit that would demand more surfeit . . . kisses that were like charity, creating want by holding back nothing at all.

It did not take him many hours to decide that he had wanted Judy Jones ever since he was a proud, desirous little boy.

IV

It began like that—and continued, with varying shades of intensity, on such a note right up to the dénouement. Dexter surrendered a part of himself to the most direct and unprincipled personality with which he had ever come in contact. Whatever Judy wanted, she went after with the full pressure of her charm. There was no divergence of method, no jockeying for position or premeditation of effects—there was a very little mental side to any of her affairs. She simply made men conscious to the highest degree of her physical loveliness. Dexter had no desire to change her. Her deficiencies were knit up with a passionate energy that transcended and justified them.

When, as Judy's head lay against his shoulder that first night, she whispered, "I don't know what's the matter with me. Last night I thought I was in love with a man and to-night I think I'm in love with you—"—it seemed to him a beautiful and romantic thing to say. It was the exquisite excitability that for the moment he controlled and owned. But a week later he was compelled to view this same quality in a different light. She took him in her roadster to a picnic supper, and after supper she disappeared, likewise in her roadster, with another man. Dexter became enormously upset and was scarcely able to be decently civil to the other people present. When she assured him that she had not kissed the other man, he knew she was lying—yet he was glad that she had taken the trouble to lie to him.

He was, as he found before the summer ended, one of a varying dozen who circulated about her. Each of them had at one time been favored above all others—about half of them still basked in the solace of occasional sentimental revivals. Whenever one showed signs of dropping out through long neglect, she granted him a brief honeyed hour, which encouraged him to tag along for a year or so longer. Judy made these forays upon the helpless and defeated without malice, indeed half unconscious that there was anything mischievous in what she did.

When a new man came to town every one dropped out—dates were automatically cancelled.

The helpless part of trying to do anything about it was that she did it all herself. She was not a girl who could be "won" in the kinetic sense— she was proof against cleverness, she was proof against charm; if any of these assailed her too strongly she would immediately resolve the affair to a physical basis, and under the magic of her physical splendor the strong as well as the brilliant played her game and not their own. She was entertained only by the gratification of her desires and by the direct exercise of her own charm. Perhaps from so much youthful love, so many youthful lovers, she had come, in self-defense, to nourish herself wholly from within.

Succeeding Dexter's first exhilaration came restlessness and dissatisfaction. The helpless ecstasy of losing himself in her was opiate rather than tonic. It was fortunate for his work during the winter that those moments of ecstasy came infrequently. Early in their acquaintance it had seemed for a while that there was a deep and spontaneous mutual attraction—that first August, for example—three days of long evenings on her dusky veranda, of strange wan kisses through the late afternoon, in shadowy alcoves or behind the protecting trellises of the garden arbors, of mornings when she was fresh as a dream and almost shy at meeting him in the clarity of the rising day. There was all the ecstasy of an engagement about it, sharpened by his realization that there was no engagement. It was during those three days that, for the first time, he had asked her to marry him. She said "maybe some day," she said "kiss me," she said "I'd like to marry you," she said "I love you"—she said— nothing.

The three days were interrupted by the arrival of a New York man who visited at her house for half September. To Dexter's agony, rumor engaged them. The man was the son of the president of a great trust company. But at the end of a month it was reported that Judy was yawning. At a dance one night she sat all evening in a motor-boat with a local beau, while the New Yorker searched the club for her frantically. She told the local beau that she was bored with her visitor, and two days later he left. She was seen with him at the station, and it was reported that he looked very mournful indeed.

On this note the summer ended. Dexter was twenty-four, and he found himself increasingly in a position to do as he wished. He joined two clubs in the city and lived at one of them. Though he was by no means an integral part of the stag-lines at these clubs, he managed to be on hand at dances where Judy Jones was likely to appear. He could have gone out socially as much as he liked—he was an eligible young man, now, and popular with down-town fathers. His confessed devotion to Judy Jones had rather solidified his position. But he had no social aspirations and rather despised the dancing men who were always on tap for the Thursday or Saturday parties and who filled in at dinners with the younger married set. Already he was playing with the idea of going East to New York. He wanted to take Judy Jones with him. No disillusion as to the world in which she had grown up could cure his illusion as to her desirability.

Remember that—for only in the light of it can what he did for her be understood.

Eighteen months after he first met Judy Jones he became engaged to another girl. Her name was Irene Scheerer, and her father was one of the men who had always believed in Dexter. Irene was light-haired and sweet and honorable, and a little stout, and she had two suitors whom she pleasantly relinquished when Dexter formally asked her to marry him.

Summer, fall, winter, spring, another summer, another fall—so much he had given of his active life to the incorrigible lips of Judy Jones. She had treated him with interest, with encouragement, with malice, with indifference, with contempt. She had inflicted on him the innumerable little slights and indignities possible in such a case—as if in revenge for having ever cared for him at all. She had beckoned him and yawned at him and beckoned him again and he had responded often with bitterness and narrowed eyes. She had brought him ecstatic happiness and intolerable agony of spirit. She had caused him untold inconvenience and not a little trouble. She had insulted him, and she had ridden over him, and she had played his interest in her against his interest in his work—for fun. She had done everything to him except to criticise him—this she had not done—it seemed to him only because it might have sullied the utter indifference she manifested and sincerely felt toward him.

When autumn had come and gone again it occurred to him that he could not have Judy Jones. He had to beat this into his mind but he convinced himself at last. He lay awake at night for a while and argued it over. He told himself the trouble and the pain she had caused him, he enumerated her glaring deficiences as a wife. Then he said to himself that he loved her, and after a while he fell asleep. For a week, lest he imagine her husky voice over the telephone or her eyes opposite him at lunch, he worked hard and late, and at night he went to his office and plotted out his years.

At the end of a week he went to a dance and cut in on her once. For almost the first time since they had met he did not ask her to sit out with him or tell her that she was lovely. It hurt him that she did not miss these things—that was all. He was not jealous when he saw that there was a new man to-night. He had been hardened against jealousy long before.

He stayed late at the dance. He sat for an hour with Irene Scheerer and talked about books and about music. He knew very little about either. But he was beginning to be master of his own time now, and he had a rather priggish notion that he—the young and already fabulously successful Dexter Green—should know more about such things.

That was in October, when he was twenty-five. In January, Dexter and Irene became engaged. It was to be announced in June, and they were to be married three months later.

The Minnesota winter prolonged itself interminably, and it was almost May when the winds came soft and the snow ran down into Black Bear Lake at last. For the first time in over a year Dexter was enjoying a certain tranquillity of spirit. Judy Jones had been in Florida, and afterward in Hot Springs, and somewhere she had been engaged, and somewhere she had broken it off. At first, when Dexter had definitely given her up, it had made him sad that people still linked them together and asked for news of her, but when he began to be placed at dinner next to Irene Scheerer people didn't ask him about her any more—they told him about her. He ceased to be an authority on her.

May at last. Dexter walked the streets at night when the darkness was damp as rain, wondering that so soon, with so little done, so much of ecstasy had gone from him. May one year back had been marked by Judy's poignant, unforgivable, yet forgiven turbulence—it had been one of those rare times when he fancied she had grown to care for him. That old penny's worth of happiness he had spent for this bushel of content. He knew that Irene would be no more than a curtain spread behind him, a hand moving among gleaming teacups, a voice calling to children . . . fire and loveliness were gone, the magic of nights and the wonder of the varying hours and seasons . . . slender lips, down-turning, dropping to his lips and bearing him up into a heaven of eyes. . . . The thing was deep in him. He was too strong and alive for it to die lightly.

In the middle of May when the weather balanced for a few days on the thin bridge that led to deep summer he turned in one night at Irene's house. Their engagement was to be announced in a week now—no one would be surprised at it. And to-night they would sit together on the lounge at the University Club and look on for an hour at the dancers. It gave him a sense of solidity to go with her—she was so sturdily popular, so intensely "great."

He mounted the steps of the brownstone house and stepped inside.

"Irene," he called.

Mrs. Scheerer came out of the living-room to meet him.

"Dexter," she said, "Irene's gone up-stairs with a splitting headache. She wanted to go with you but I made her go to bed."

"Nothing serious, I—"

"Oh, no. She's going to play golf with you in the morning. You can spare her for just one night, can't you, Dexter?"

Her smile was kind. She and Dexter liked each other. In the living-room he talked for a moment before he said good-night.

Returning to the University Club, where he had rooms, he stood in the doorway for a moment and watched the dancers. He leaned against the door-post, nodded at a man or two—yawned.

"Hello, darling."

The familiar voice at his elbow startled him. Judy Jones had left a man and crossed the room to him—Judy Jones, a slender enamelled doll in cloth of gold: gold in a band at her head, gold in two slipper points at her dress's hem. The fragile glow of her face seemed to blossom as she smiled at him. A breeze of warmth and light blew through the room. His hands in the pockets of his dinner-jacket tightened spasmodically. He was filled with a sudden excitement.

"When did you get back?" he asked casually.

"Come here and I'll tell you about it."

She turned and he followed her. She had been away—he could have wept at the wonder of her return. She had passed through enchanted streets, doing things that were like provocative music. All mysterious happenings, all fresh and quickening hopes, had gone away with her, come back with her now.

She turned in the doorway.

"Have you a car here? If you haven't, I have."

"I have a coupé."

In then, with a rustle of golden cloth. He slammed the door. Into so many cars she had stepped—like this—like that—her back against the leather, so—her elbow resting on the door—waiting. She would have been soiled long since had there been anything to soil her—except herself—but this was her own self outpouring.

With an effort he forced himself to start the car and back into the street. This was nothing, he must remember. She had done this before, and he had put her behind him, as he would have crossed a bad account from his books.

He drove slowly down-town and, affecting abstraction, traversed the deserted streets of the business section, peopled here and there where a movie was giving out its crowd or where consumptive or pugilistic youth lounged in front of pool halls. The clink of glasses and the slap of hands on the bars issued from saloons, cloisters of glazed glass and dirty yellow light.

She was watching him closely and the silence was embarrassing, yet in this crisis he could find no casual word with which to profane the hour. At a convenient turning he began to zigzag back toward the University Club.

"Have you missed me?" she asked suddenly.

"Everybody missed you."

He wondered if she knew of Irene Scheerer. She had been back only a day—her absence had been almost contemporaneous with his engagement.

"What a remark!" Judy laughed sadly—without sadness. She looked at him searchingly. He became absorbed in the dashboard.

"You're handsomer than you used to be," she said thoughtfully. "Dexter, you have the most rememberable eyes."

He could have laughed at this, but he did not laugh. It was the sort of thing that was said to sophomores. Yet it stabbed at him.

"I'm awfully tired of everything, darling." She called everyone darling, endowing the endearment with careless, individual camaraderie. I wish you'd marry me."

The directness of this confused him. He should have told her now that he was going to marry another girl, but he could not tell her. He could as easily have sworn that he had never loved her.

"I think we'd get along," she continued, on the same note, "unless probably you've forgotten me and fallen in love with another girl."

Her confidence was obviously enormous. She had said, in effect, that she found such a thing impossible to believe, that if it were true he had merely committed a childish indiscretion—and probably to show off. She would forgive him, because it was not a matter of any moment but rather something to be brushed aside lightly.

"Of course you could never love anybody but me," she continued, "I like the way you love me. Oh, Dexter, have you forgotten last year?"

"No, I haven't forgotten."

"Neither have I!"

Was she sincerely moved—or was she carried along by the wave of her own acting?

"I wish we could be like that again," she said, and he forced himself to answer:

"I don't think we can."

"I suppose not. . . . I hear you're giving Irene Scheerer a violent rush."

There was not the faintest emphasis on the name, yet Dexter was suddenly ashamed.

"Oh, take me home," cried Judy suddenly; "I don't want to go back to that idiotic dance—with those children."

Then, as he turned up the street that led to the residence district, Judy began to cry quietly to herself. He had never seen her cry before.

The dark street lightened, the dwellings of the rich loomed up around them, he stopped his coupé in front of the great white bulk of the Mortimer Joneses' house, somnolent, gorgeous, drenched with the splendor of the damp moonlight. Its solidity startled him. The strong walls, the steel of the girders, the breadth and beam and pomp of it were there only to bring out the contrast with the young beauty beside him. It was sturdy to accentuate her slightness—as if to show what a breeze could be generated by a butterfly's wing.

He sat perfectly quiet, his nerves in wild clamor, afraid that if he moved he would find her irresistibly in his arms. Two tears had rolled down her wet face and trembled on her upper lip.

"I'm more beautiful than anybody else," she said brokenly, "why can't I be happy?" Her moist eyes tore at his stability—her mouth turned slowly downward with an exquisite sadness: "I'd like to marry you if you'll have me, Dexter. I suppose you think I'm not worth having, but I'll be so beautiful for you, Dexter."

A million phrases of anger, pride, passion, hatred, tenderness fought on his lips. Then a perfect wave of emotion washed over him, carrying off with it a sediment of wisdom, of convention, of doubt, of honor. This was his girl who was speaking, his own, his beautiful, his pride.

"Won't you come in?" He heard her draw in her breath sharply.

Waiting.

"All right," his voice was trembling, "I'll come in."

V

It was strange that neither when it was over nor a long time afterward did he regret that night. Looking at it from the perspective of ten years, the fact that Judy's flare for him endured just one month seemed of little importance. Nor did it matter that by his yielding he subjected himself to a deeper agony in the end and gave serious hurt to Irene

Scheerer and to Irene's parents, who had befriended him. There was nothing sufficiently pictorial about Irene's grief to stamp itself on his mind.

Dexter was at bottom hard-minded. The attitude of the city on his action was of no importance to him, not because he was going to leave the city, but because any outside attitude on the situation seemed superficial. He was completely indifferent to popular opinion. Nor, when he had seen that it was no use, that he did not possess in himself the power to move fundamentally or to hold Judy Jones, did he bear any malice toward her. He loved her, and he would love her until the day he was too old for loving—but he could not have her. So he tasted the deep pain that is reserved only for the strong, just as he had tasted for a little while the deep happiness.

Even the ultimate falsity of the grounds upon which Judy terminated the engagement that she did not want to "take him away" from Irene—Judy who had wanted nothing else—did not revolt him. He was beyond any revulsion or any amusement.

He went East in February with the intention of selling out his laundries and settling in New York—but the war came to America in March and changed his plans. He returned to the West, handed over the management of the business to his partner, and went into the first officers' training-camp in late April. He was one of those young thousands who greeted the war with a certain amount of relief, welcoming the liberation from webs of tangled emotion.

VI

This story is not his biography, remember, although things creep into it which have nothing to do with those dreams he had when he was young. We are almost done with them and with him now. There is only one more incident to be related here, and it happens seven years farther on.

It took place in New York, where he had done well—so well that there were no barriers too high for him. He was thirty-two years old, and except for one flying trip immediately after the war, he had not been West in seven years. A man named Devlin from Detriot came into his office to see him in a business way, and then and there this incident occurred, and closed out, so to speak, this particular side of his life.

"So you're from the Middle West," said the man Devlin with careless curiosity. "That's funny—I thought men like you were probably born and raised on Wall Street. You know—wife of one of my best friends in Detroit came from your city. I was an usher at the wedding."

Dexter waited with no apprehension of what was coming.

"Judy Simms," said Devlin with no particular interest; "Judy Jones she was once."

"Yes, I knew her." A dull impatience spread over him. He had heard, of course, that she was married—perhaps deliberately he had heard no more.

"Awfully nice girl," brooded Devlin meaninglessly, "I'm sort of sorry for her."

"Why?" Something in Dexter was alert, receptive, at once.

"Oh, Lud Simms has gone to pieces in a way. I don't mean he ill-uses her, but he drinks and runs around—"

"Doesn't she run around?"

"No. Stays at home with her kids."

"Oh."

"She's a little too old for him," said Devlin.

"Too old!" cried Dexter. "Why, man, she's only twenty-seven."

He was possessed with a wild notion of rushing out into the streets and taking a train to Detroit. He rose to his feet spasmodically.

"I guess you're busy," Devlin apologized quickly. "I didn't realize—"

"No, I'm not busy," said Dexter, steading his voice. "I'm not busy at all. Not busy at all. Did you say she was—twenty-seven? No, I said she was twenty-seven."

"Yes, you did," agreed Devlin dryly.

"Go on, then. Go on."

"What do you mean.?"

"About Judy Jones."

Devlin looked at him helplessly.

"Well, that's—I told you all there is to it. He treats her like the devil. Oh, they're not going to get divorced or anything. When he's particularly outrageous she forgives him. In fact, I'm inclined to think she loves him. She was a pretty girl when she first came to Detroit."

A pretty girl! The phrase struck Dexter as ludicrous.

"Isn't she—a pretty girl any more?"

"Oh, she's all right."

"Look here," said Dexter, sitting down suddenly. "I don't understand. You say she was a 'pretty girl' and now you say she's 'all right.' I don't understand what you mean—Judy Jones wasn't a pretty girl, at all. She was a great beauty. Why, I knew her, I knew her. She was—"

Devlin laughed pleasantly.

"I'm not trying to start a row," he said. "I think Judy's a nice girl and I like her. I can't understand how a man like Lud Simms could fall madly in love with her but he did." Then he added: "Most of the women like her."

Dexter looked closely at Devlin, thinking wildly that there must be a reason for this, some insensitivity in the man or some private malice.

"Lots of women fade just like *that*," Devlin snapped his fingers. "You must have seen it happen. Perhaps I've forgotten how pretty she was at her wedding. I've seen her so much since then, you see. She has nice eyes."

A sort of dullness settled down upon Dexter. For the first time in his life he felt like getting very drunk. He knew that he was laughing loudly at something Devlin had said, but he did not know what it was or why it was funny. When, in a few minutes, Devlin went he lay down on his lounge and looked out the window at the New York sky-line into which the sun was sinking in dull lovely shades of pink and gold.

He had thought that having nothing else to lose he was invulnerable at last—but he knew that he had just lost something more, as surely as if he had married Judy Jones and seen her fade away before his eyes.

The dream was gone. Something had been taken from him. In a sort of panic he pushed the palms of his hands into his eyes and tried to bring up a picture of the waters lapping on Sherry Island and the moonlit veranda, and gingham on the golf-links and the dry sun and the gold color of her neck's soft down. And her mouth damp to his kisses and her eyes plaintive with melancholy and her freshness like new fine linen in the morning. Why, these things were no longer in the world! They had existed and they existed no longer.

For the first time in years the tears were streaming down his face. But they were for himself now. He did not care about mouth and eyes and moving hands. He wanted to care, and he could not care. For he had gone away and he could never go back any more. The gates were closed, the sun was gone down, and there was no beauty but the gray beauty of steel that withstands all time. Even the grief he could have borne was left behind in the country of illusion, of youth, of the richness of life, where his winter dreams had flourished.

"Long ago," he said, "long ago, there was something in me, but now that thing is gone. Now that thing is gone, that thing is gone. I cannot cry. I cannot care. That thing will come back no more."

THE ROCKPILE

James Baldwin

ACROSS the street from their house, in an empty lot between two houses, stood the rockpile. It was a strange place to find a mass of natural rock jutting out of the ground; and someone, probably Aunt Florence, had once told them that the rock was there and could not be taken away because without it the subway cars underground would fly apart, killing all the people. This, touching on some natural mystery concerning the surface and the center of the earth, was far too intriguing an explanation to be challenged, and it invested the rockpile, moreover, with such mysterious importance that Roy felt it to be his right, not to say his duty, to play there.

Other boys were to be seen there each afternoon after school and all day Saturday and Sunday. They fought on the rockpile. Sure footed, dangerous, and reckless, they rushed each other and grappled on the heights, sometimes disappearing down the other side in a confusion of dust and screams and upended flying feet. "It's a wonder they don't kill themselves," their mother said, watching sometimes from the fire escape. "You children stay away from there, you hear me?" Though she said "children," she was looking at Roy, where he sat beside John on the fire escape. "The good Lord knows," she continued, "I don't want you to come home bleeding like a hog every day the Lord sends." Roy shifted impatiently, and continued to stare at the street, as though in this gazing he might somehow acquire wings. John said nothing. He had not really been spoken to: he was afraid of the rockpile and of the boys who played there.

Each Saturday morning John and Roy sat on the fire escape and watched the forbidden street below. Sometimes their mother sat in the room behind them, sewing, or dressing their younger sister, or nursing the baby, Paul. The sun fell across them and across the fire escape with a high, benevolent indifference; below them, men and women, and boys and girls, sinners all, loitered; sometimes one of the church-members passed and saw them and waved. Then, for the moment that they waved decorously back, they were intimidated. They watched the saint, man or woman, until he or she had disappeared from sight. The passage of one of the redeemed made them consider, however vacantly, the wickedness of the street, their own latent wickedness in sitting where they sat; and made them think of their father, who came home early on Saturdays and who would soon be turning this corner and entering the dark hall below them.

But until he came to end their freedom, they sat, watching and longing above the street. At the end of the street nearest their house was the bridge which spanned the Harlem River and led to a city called the Bronx; which was where Aunt Florence lived. Nevertheless, when they saw her coming, she did not come from the bridge, but from the opposite end of the street. This, weakly, to their minds, she explained by saying that she had taken the subway, not wishing to walk, and that, besides, she did not live in *that* section of the Bronx. Knowing that the Bronx was across the river, they did not believe this story ever, but, adopting toward her their father's attitude, assumed that she had just left some sinful place which she dared not name, as, for example, a movie palace.

In the summertime boys swam in the river diving off the wooden dock, or wading in from the garbage-heavy bank. Once a boy, whose name was Richard, drowned in the river. His mother had not known where he was; she had even come to their house, to ask if he was there. Then, in the evening, at six o'clock, they had heard from the street a woman screaming and wailing; and they ran to the windows and looked out. Down the street came the woman, Richard's mother, screaming, her face raised to the sky and tears running down her face. A woman walked beside her, trying to make her quiet and trying to hold her up. Behind them walked a man, Richard's father, with Richard's body in his arms. There were two white policemen walking in the gutter, who did not seem to know what should be done. Richard's father and Richard were wet, and Richard's body lay across his father's arms like a cotton baby. The woman's screaming filled all the street; cars slowed down and the people in the cars stared; people opened their windows and looked out and came rushing out of doors to stand in the gutter, watching. Then the small procession disappeared within the house which stood beside the rockpile. Then, *"Lord, Lord, Lord!"* cried Elizabeth, their mother, and slammed the window down.

One Saturday, an hour before his father would be coming home, Roy was wounded on the rockpile and brought screaming upstairs. He and John had been sitting on the fire escape and their mother had gone into the kitchen to sip tea with Sister McCandless. By and by Roy became bored and sat beside John in restless silence; and John began drawing into his schoolbook a newspaper advertisement which featured a new electric locomotive. Some friends of Roy passed beneath the fire escape and called him. Roy began to fidget, yelling down to them through the bars. Then a silence fell. John looked up. Roy stood looking at him.

"I'm going downstairs," he said.

"You better stay where you is, boy. You know Mama don't want you going downstairs."

"I be right *back*. She won't even know I'm gone, less you run and tell her."

"I ain't *got* to tell her. What's going to stop her from coming in here and looking out the window?"

"She's talking," Roy said. He started into the house.

"But Daddy's going to be home soon!"

"I be back before *that*. What you all the time got to be so *scared* for?" He was already in the house and he now turned, leaning on the window-sill, to swear impatiently, "I be back in *five* minutes."

John watched him sourly as he carefully unlocked the door and disappeared. In a moment he saw him on the sidewalk with his friends. He did not dare to go and tell his mother that Roy had left the fire escape because he had practically promised not to. He started to shout, *Remember, you said five minutes!* but one of Roy's friends was looking up at the fire escape. John looked down at his schoolbook: he became engrossed again in the problem of the locomotive.

When he looked up again he did not know how much time had passed, but now there was a gang fight on the rockpile. Dozens of boys fought each other in the harsh sun: clambering up the rocks and battling hand to hand, scuffed shoes sliding on the slippery rock; filling the bright air with curses and jubilant cries. They filled the air, too, with flying weapons: stones, sticks, tin cans, garbage, whatever could be picked up and thrown. John watched in a kind of absent amazement— until he remembered that Roy was still downstairs, and that he was one of the boys on the rockpile. Then he was afraid; he could not see his brother among the figures in the sun; and he stood up, leaning over the fire-escape railing. Then Roy appeared from the other side of the rocks; John saw that his shirt was torn; he was laughing. He moved until he stood at the very top of the rockpile. Then, something, an empty tin can, flew out of the air and hit him on the forehead, just above the eye. Immediately, one side of Roy's face ran with blood, he fell and rolled on his face down the rocks. Then for a moment there was no movement at all, no sound, the sun, arrested, lay on the street and the sidewalk and the arrested boys. Then someone screamed or shouted; boys began to run away, down the street, toward the bridge. The figure on the ground, having caught its breath and felt its own blood, began to shout. John cried, "Mama! Mama!" and ran inside.

"Don't fret, don't fret," panted Sister McCandless as they rushed down the dark, narrow, swaying stairs, "don't fret. Ain't a boy been born don't get his knocks every now and again. *Lord!*" they hurried into the sun. A man had picked Roy up and now walked slowly toward them. One or two boys sat silent on their stoops; at either end of the street there was a group of boys watching. "He ain't hurt bad," the man said, "Wouldn't be making this kind of noise if he was hurt real bad."

Elizabeth, trembling, reached out to take Roy, but Sister McCandless, bigger, calmer, took him from the man and threw him over her shoulder as she once might have handled a sack of cotton. "God bless you," she said to the man, "God bless you son," Roy was still screaming. Elizabeth stood behind Sister McCandless to stare at his bloody face.

"It's just a flesh wound," the man kept saying "just broke the skin, that's all." They were moving across the sidewalk, toward the house. John, not now afraid of the staring boys, looked toward the corner to see if his father was yet in sight.

Upstairs, they hushed Roy's crying. They bathed the blood away, to find, just above the left eyebrow, the jagged, superficial scar. "Lord, have mercy," murmured Elizabeth, "another inch and it would've been his eye." And she looked with apprehension toward the clock. "Ain't it the truth," said Sister McCandless, busy with bandages and iodine.

"When did he go downstairs?" his mother asked at last.

Sister McCandless now sat fanning herself in the easy chair at the head of the sofa where Roy lay, bound and silent. She paused for a moment to look sharply at John. John stood near the window, holding the newspaper advertisement and the drawing he had done.

"We was sitting on the fire escape," he said. "Some boys he knew called him."

"When?"

"He said he'd be back in five minutes."

"Why didn't you tell me he was downstairs?"

He looked at his hands, clasping his notebook, and did not answer.

"Boy," said Sister McCandless, "you hear your mother a-talking to you?"

He looked at his mother. He repeated:

"He said he'd be back in five minutes."

"He said he'd be back in five minutes," said Sister McCandless with scorn, "don't look to me like that's no right answer. You's the man of the house, you supposed to look after your baby brothers and sisters—you ain't supposed to let them run off and get half-killed. But I expect," she added, rising from the chair, dropping the cardboard fan, "your Daddy'll make you tell the truth. Your Ma's way too soft with you."

He did not look at her, but at the fan where it lay in the dark red, depressed seat where she had been. The fan advertised a pomade for the hair and showed a brown woman and her baby, both with glistening hair, smiling happily at each other.

"Honey," said Sister McCandless, "I got to be moving along. Maybe I drop in later tonight. I don't reckon you going to be at Tarry Service tonight?"

Tarry Service was the prayer meeting held every Saturday night at church to strengthen believers and prepare the church for the coming of the Holy Ghost on Sunday.

"I don't reckon," said Elizabeth. She stood up; she and Sister McCandless kissed each other on the cheek. "But you be sure to remember me in your prayers."

"I surely will do that." She paused, with her hand on the door knob, and looked down at Roy and laughed. "Poor little man," she said, "reckon he'll be content to sit on the fire escape *now*."

Elizabeth laughed with her. "It sure ought to be a lesson to him. You don't reckon," she asked nervously, still smiling, "he going to keep that scar, do you?"

"Lord, no," said Sister McCandless, "ain't nothing but a scratch. I declare, Sister Grimes, you worse than a child. Another couple of weeks and you won't be able to *see* no scar. No, you go on about your housework honey, and thank the Lord it weren't no worse." She opened the door; they heard the sound of feet on the stairs. "I expect that's the Reverend," said Sister McCandless, placidly, I *bet* he's going to raise cain."

"Maybe it's Florence," Elizabeth said. "Sometimes she get here about this time." They stood in the doorway, staring, while the steps reached the landing below and began again climbing to their floor. "No," said Elizabeth then, "that ain't her walk. That's Gabriel."

"Well, I'll just go on," said Sister McCandless, "and kind of prepare his mind." She pressed Elizabeth's hand as she spoke and started into the hall, leaving the door behind her slightly ajar. Elizabeth turned slowly back into the room. Roy did not open his eyes, or move; but she knew that he was not sleeping; he wished to delay until the last possible moment any contact with his father. John put his newspaper and his notebook on the table and stood, leaning on the table, staring at her.

"It wasn't my fault," he said, "I couldn't stop him from going downstairs."

"No," she said, "you ain't got nothing to worry about. You just tell your Daddy the truth."

He looked directly at her, and she turned to the window, staring into the street. What was Sister McCandless saying? Then from her bedroom she heard Delilah's thin wail and she turned, frowning, looking toward the bedroom and toward the still open door. She knew that John was watching her. Delilah continued to wail, she thought, angrily, *Now that girl's getting too big for that,* but she feared that Delilah would awaken Paul and she hurried into the bedroom. She tried to soothe Delilah back to sleep. Then she heard the front door open and close—too loud, Delilah raised her voice, with an exasperated sigh Elizabeth picked the child up. Her child and Gabriel's, her children and Gabriel's: Roy, Delilah, Paul. Only John was nameless and a stranger, living, unalterable testimony to his mother's days in sin.

"What happened?" Gabriel demanded. He stood, enormous, in the center of the room, his black lunchbox dangling from his hand, staring at the sofa where Roy lay. John stood just before him, it seemed to her astonished vision just below him, beneath his fist, his heavy shoe. The child stared at the man in fascination and terror—when a girl down home she had seen rabbits stand so paralyzed before the barking dog. She hurried past Gabriel to the sofa, feeling the weight of Delilah in her arms like the weight of a shield, and stood over Roy, saying:

"Now, ain't a thing to get upset about, Gabriel. This boy sneaked downstairs while I had my back turned and got hisself hurt a little. He's alright now."

Roy, as though in confirmation, now opened his eyes and looked gravely at his father. Gabriel dropped his lunchbox with a clatter and knelt by the sofa.

"How you feel, son? Tell your Daddy what happened?"

Roy opened his mouth to speak and then, relapsing into panic, began to cry. His father held him by the shoulder.

"You don't want to cry. You's Daddy's little man. Tell your Daddy what happened."

"He went downstairs," said Elizabeth, "where he didn't have no business to be, and got to fighting with them bad boys playing on that rockpile. That's what happened and it's a mercy it weren't nothing worse."

He looked up at her. "Can't you let this boy answer me for hisself?"

Ignoring this, she went on, more gently: "He got cut on the forehead, but it ain't nothing to worry about."

"You call a doctor? How you know it ain't nothing to worry about?"

"Is you got money to be throwing away on doctors? No, I ain't called no doctor. Ain't nothing wrong with my eyes that I can't tell whether he's hurt bad or not. He got a fright more'n anything else, and you ought to pray God it teaches him a lesson."

"You got a lot to say *now*," he said, "but I'll have *me* something to say in a minute. I'll be wanting to know when all this happened, what you was doing with your eyes *then*." He turned back to Roy, who had lain quietly sobbing eyes wide open and body held rigid: and who now, at his father's touch, remembered the height, the sharp, sliding rock beneath his feet, the sun, the explosion of the sun, his plunge into darkness and his salty blood; and recoiled, beginning to scream, as his father touched his forehead. "Hold still, hold still," crooned his father, shaking, "hold still. Don't cry. Daddy ain't going to hurt you, he just wants to see this bandage, see what they've done to his little man." But Roy continued to scream and would not be still and Gabriel dared not lift the bandage for fear of hurting him more. And he looked at Elizabeth in fury: "Can't you put that child down and help me with this boy? John, take your baby sister from your mother—don't look like neither of you got good sense."

John took Delilah and sat down with her in the easy chair. His mother bent over Roy, and held him still, while his father, carefully—but still Roy screamed—lifted the bandage and stared at the wound. Roy's sobs began to lessen. Gabriel readjusted the bandage. "You see," said Elizabeth, finally, "he ain't nowhere near dead."

"It sure ain't your fault that he ain't dead." He and Elizabeth considered each other for a moment in silence. "He came mightly close to losing an eye. Course, his eyes ain't as big as your'n, so I reckon you don't think it matters so much." At this her face hardened; he smiled. "Lord, have mercy," he said, "you think you ever going to learn to do right? Where was you when all this happened? Who let him go downstairs?"

"Ain't nobody let him go downstairs, he just went. He got a head just like his father, it got to be broken before it'll bow. I was in the kitchen."

"Where was Johnnie?"

"He was in here?"

"Where?"

"He was on the fire escape."

"Didn't he know Roy was downstairs?"

"I reckon."

"What you mean, you reckon? He ain't got your big eyes for nothing, does he?" He looked over at John. "Boy, you see your brother go downstairs?"

"Gabriel, ain't no sense in trying to blame Johnnie. You know right well if you have trouble making Roy behave, he ain't going to listen to his brother. He don't hardly listen to me."

"How come you didn't tell your mother Roy was downstairs?"

John said nothing, staring at the blanket which covered Delilah.

"Boy, you hear me? You want me to take a strap to you?"

"No, you ain't," she said. "You ain't going to take no strap to this boy, not today you ain't. Ain't a soul to blame for Roy's lying up there now but you—you because you done spoiled him so that he thinks he can do just anthing and get away with it. I'm here to tell you that ain't no way to raise no child. You don't pray to the Lord to help you do better than you been doing, you going to live to shed bitter tears that the Lord didn't take his soul today." And she was trembling. She moved, unseeing, toward John and took Delilah from his arms. She looked back at Gabriel, who had risen, who stood near the sofa, staring at her. And she found in his face not fury alone, which would not have surprised her; but hatred so deep as to become insupportable in its lack of personality. His eyes were struck alive, unmoving, blind with malevolence—she felt, like the pull of the earth at her feet, his longing to witness her perdition. Again, as though it might be propitiation, she moved the child in her arms. And at this his eyes changed, he looked at Elizabeth, the mother of his children, the helpmeet given by the Lord. Then her eyes clouded; she moved to leave the room; her foot struck the lunchbox lying on the floor.

"John," she said, "pick up your father's lunchbox like a good boy."

She heard, behind her, his scrambling movement as he left the chair, the scrape and jangle of the lunchbox as he picked it up, bending his dark head near the toe of his father's heavy shoe.

Glossary

ABSTRACT   Abstractions are qualities and characteristics isolated as pure ideas. A piece of *sugar* is a concrete substance with its own qualities but we may *abstract* (literally *draw away*) from it *whiteness, hardness, sweetness*. Literature characteristically deals with the concrete rather than the abstract, and also the specific rather than the general. All of which is not to say that ideas, which are capable of being stated abstractly—love, courage, justice—are not involved in literature, but such ideas rarely emerge as abstractions, rather, they are incorporated in the concrete elements—in the case of fiction, in the particular characters and situations and events. The general observations that one may abstract from the particulars of a story—observations about human nature or about life—are not to be taken as the equivalent of the story. The abstraction—and the generalization—are something less than—merely a part of—the concrete particularity of the story itself. See p. 176.

ACTION   A series of events having unity and significance. See pp. 33–34.

ACTION STORY   A story in which the principal interest lies in plot suspense, such as adventure or detective fiction. See pp. 3, 30, 33–34, 77–80.

ALLEGORICAL   See ALLEGORY.

ALLEGORY   An allegory is a kind of narrative in which the characters, objects, and events are to be taken, not as real but as standing for some set of ideas. That is, each item in the narrative is equated with some item among the ideas. For example, in Bunyan's *The Pilgrim's Progress*, the character Christian, who leaves his home to journey to the Celestial City, is to be taken as the type of all people who try to lead the Christian life, and each event that takes place on the journey stands for some problem in the spiritual life. See PARABLE, and see p. 30.

ALLITERATION   Repetition of consonants, particularly of initial consonants as in *lullaby* or "*l*evels of the *l*ake." See p. 19.

ANECDOTE   A brief narrative account of some incident or event. See p. 3.

ANTICLIMAX   A break in the climactic order of events or effects, a falling off from the expected intensification of effect. See CLIMAX and IRONY. See also p. 36.

ATMOSPHERE   The general pervasive feeling aroused by the various factors in a piece of fiction, such as setting, character, theme, and the like; the general effect of the handling of the total work. To be distinguished from SETTING and from TONE. Considerations of the metaphorical origin of the two terms, *atmosphere* and *tone*, may be helpful here. *Tone* is to be referred ultimately to the author's attitude (the tone of voice of a speaker as qualifying what he says) toward what is being presented, whereas *atmosphere* is to be referred to the general qualification provided by the materials themselves (an atmosphere of sunshine, of cheerfulness, an atmosphere of gloom, and the like). There is, however, a good deal of overlapping and vagueness about the use of these terms in ordinary discussion. The student, in referring to a particular case in fiction, should ask himself whether he wishes to emphasize the author's attitude or the mere effect of the materials as such. See pp. 35, 125, 296.

CLICHÉ   Usually used in reference to a phrase which has lost its force because of continual use; for example, "in the arms of Morpheus," or "a dull, sickening thud." But the term is also applied occasionally to fictional situations or events which have become hackneyed and stereotyped. The cliché represents one kind of appeal to a STOCK RESPONSE on the part of the reader. But, of course, clichés may be used justifiably by the author, for ironical effect, or because a certain kind of character would normally use clichés in his speech, or for other reasons. In general, it may be said that a cliché is bad when used with the intention of creating a vivid and memorable effect; it fails in such cases because it does not represent a fresh perception. See pp. 19, 119, 196.

CLIMAX   The highest point in an ascending series; in fiction, for example, the point at which the forces in conflict reach the highest intensification. See pp. 36, 78, 118.

COHERENCE   The hanging together—the interconnectedness—of the parts of a piece of fiction. TRUTH OF COHERENCE has to do with the internal consistency of a piece of literature. See pp. 38–39, 111, 180.

COINCIDENCE   An accidental coming together of certain events. (See SURPRISE ENDING.) The use of coincidence is, in one sense, unavoidable in fiction, for the original situation in any story may be defined as a coincidence. But the use of coincidence is, generally speaking, illegitimate when it functions to solve the fictional problem; that is, when the events which bring about the resolution of a plot have no logical connection with preceding events. See pp. 45–46, 55–56, 72, 243.

COMPLICATION   The interplay between character and event which builds up a tension and develops a problem out of the original situation given in the story. See pp. 36, 109.

CONCRETE   See ABSTRACT.

CONFLICT   All fiction involves, at one level or another, conflict. The characters struggle against environment or with each other (external conflict) or are engaged in struggles with themselves (internal conflict). One important approach to the understanding of any story is to determine the nature of the conflict involved and the pattern that the opposing forces assume. See pp. 34, 110.

CONNOTATION   See DENOTATION

CONVENTION   Any method, device, or rule that is accepted by explicit or tacit agreement. For example, the fact that the letter *t* shall have a certain consonantal value, or that a touchdown shall count for six points depends upon nothing intrinsic but is determined by convention. All the arts, including that of fiction, make use of *conventions*. For example, the omniscient author's ability to enter into the innermost thoughts of several of his characters depends upon a convention. The author continually makes use of traditional conventions handed down to him from the past. His work, however, is termed CONVENTIONAL in a bad sense when it fails to justify the conventional items it employs by relating them freshly to the new problem.

CONVENTIONAL   See CONVENTION.

CUTBACK   A passage in a narrative which breaks the chronological sequence to deal with earlier events. See p. 35.

DENOTATION   The exact thing or idea indicated by word. The denotation is not only the primary meaning, but it is the specific and abstract meaning. Scientific prose needs no more than the denotations of words, and the attempt to build up a scientific and technical language is in harmony with this situation. But the

CONNOTATIONS of a word are the things suggested by or associated with the word. These connotations, though necessarily vague and inexact (as compared with denotations) are nevertheless powerful and important, and the skillful writer whose intention is literary rather than scientific makes full use of them. See pp. 126–27.

DENOUEMENT   The final resolution or untying of the plot. It sometimes, but not always, coincides with the climax. See p. 36.

DISTANCE   The term is used to mean the degree of detachment with which the characters in a story are viewed.

DRAMATIC   Strictly speaking, fictional method is said to be dramatic when the author gives a purely OBJECTIVE rendering of his material, without indulging either in editorial comment and generalization of his own or in the analysis of the feelings and thoughts of his characters. The clearest case of such a method in this book is "The Killers" (p. 296). Where a dramatic method is used the reader must infer the inner situation from the external action and dialogue. But the term is used more loosely to indicate merely the presence of strong tension and sharp conflict in a story or novel; and it is used more loosely still to indicate concrete presentation as opposed to asbstract statement.

EPISODE   A separate incident in a larger piece of action.

EPISODIC   A piece of fiction is said to be *episodic* when there is not a strongly emphasized causal continuity between one episode and the next. Episodic structure is, logically, loose structure, in so far as plot is concerned.

EXPOSITION   The process of giving the reader necessary information concerning characters and events existing before the action proper of a story begins. See pp. 36, 107–8.

FABLE   A tale, usually rather simple and often illustrating some maxim about human nature. See pp. 6, 110.

FICTION   A narrative of an event or events that did not necessarily actually occur; a story produced by the imagination, the truth of which does not rest upon fact. The first 31 pages of this book attempt to suggest what the basic elements of fiction are.

FIRST-PERSON NARRATION   See FOCUS OF NARRATION. See also pp. 171–73.

FOCUS   The center around which the material of an imaginative work is concentrated. The focus may shift from moment to moment in a piece of fiction or it may remain constant. For example, the focus may be primarily upon character, upon an idea, upon a setting, or the like.

FOCUS OF CHARACTER   A piece of fiction is not merely a sequence of events. The events are of special concern to some person, or group of persons, involved in them, and the structure of the narrative depends, in one sense, upon the reference to the person or persons, most fundamentally concerned. See pp. 109, 195.

FOCUS OF NARRATION (POINT OF VIEW)   The focus of narration has to do with who tells the story. We may make four basic distinctions: (1) a character may tell his own story in the first person; (2) a character may tell, in the first person, a story which he has observed; (3) the author may tell what happens in the purely objective sense—deeds, words, gestures—without going into the minds of the characters and without giving his own comment; (4) the author may tell what happens with full liberty to go into the minds of characters and to give his own comment. These four types of narration may be called: (1) first-person, (2) first-person observer, (3) author-observer, and (4) omniscient author. Combinations of these methods are, of course, possible. See pp. 127, 171–73, 294.

FORESHADOWING   The process of giving the reader an intimation of some event which is to follow later in the action.

FORM   The arrangement of various elements in a work of literature; the organization of various materials (ideas, images, characters, setting, and the like) to give a single effect. It may be said that a story is successful—that it has achieved form—when all of the elements are functionally related to each other, when each part contributes to the intended effect. Form is not to be thought of merely as a sort of container for the story; it is, rather, the total principle of organization and affects every aspect of the composition. (See pp. 1–28, 645–46.) STRUCTURE and STYLE are also used to indicate the author's arrangement of his materials to give his effect. *Structure*, however, is usually used with more special reference to the ordering of the larger elements such as episodes, scenes, and details of action, in contrast to the arrangement of words, for which the term *style* is ordinarily employed. In the fullest sense, both the terms become synonymous with form, but in this book *style* is used merely to refer to the selection and ordering of language. See pp. 127–28, 176.

FUNCTIONAL   Having to do with the development of the total effect of a piece of fiction. The term is used in this book to denote those elements of a story which actually play a part in building up the complex and rich unity of a story in contrast to those used merely because they are fashionable, or feed some external interest, or are merely sensational or decorative or engaging.

IMAGERY   The representation of any sense experience. Imagery does not consist merely of "mental pictures," but may make an appeal to any of the senses. In keeping with its insistence upon the concrete and the particular, all literature, including fiction, makes much use of imagery, not only in obvious descriptive fashion but also in figurative language. The most common forms of figurative language are SIMILES and METAPHORS. A *simile* is a direct comparison between two things, and such a comparison is introduced by *like* or *as*. A *metaphor* does not announce the comparison and proceeds indirectly to indicate an identification of the two items involved. Although such details of style may seem trivial in fiction, their effects are subtle and important. Sometimes the fundamental attitude of an author (see TONE), and hence the fundamental meaning of a piece of fiction, may be largely conveyed in terms of such details. See pp. 126, 194. See also ATMOSPHERE.

IMAGINATION   The creative power that manifests itself in the making of literary fictions of all kinds—rich descriptions, striking metaphors and similes, lifelike characters, and credible dramas and narratives. One must distinguish between the adjectives *imaginary* and *imaginative*. The former stresses the quality of *unreality*. The latter refers to the accomplishment of the great literary artist. His fictions possess their own kind of truth in spite of the fact that they make no claim to give a verbatim report of actual events. This whole textbook is devoted to the accomplishments (and occasional failures) of the fiction writer's imagination as he attempts to present the truth about human life.

INEVITABILITY   The sense that the result presented is the only possible result of the situation previously given. It cannot be strictly maintained that inevitability in fiction is absolute, if one is to judge by realistic standards. The element of chance, or what appears as chance, in human affairs is too great to admit of such an interpretation. The term is simply used in most discussions to indicate a high degree of logic in the handling of the development of plot or character.

IRONICAL   See IRONY.

IRONY   Irony always involves contrast, a discrepancy between the expected and the actual, between the apparent and the real. Such contrast may appear in many forms. A speaker uses irony, for example, when he deliberately says something which he does not mean, but indicates by his tone what he does mean. UNDERSTATEMENT—the saying of less than what one feels the occasion would warrant—and PARADOX—the saying of something which is apparently untrue but which on examination proves to be true, or partially true—both of these are forms of irony. In addition to such forms of IRONY OF STATEMENT, there are also various forms of IRONY OF SITUATION. The irony of situation involves a discrepancy between what we expect the outcome of an action to be, or what would seem to be the fitting outcome, and the actual outcome. In dealing with this term, the student should always remember that there are a thousand subtle shadings of irony, and must, therefore, not take it in too restricted a sense, for example, in the sense of obvious sarcasm. See pp. 45, 50–51, 172, 229.

LOGIC   In fiction, the relation that exists between character and character, or character and setting. See pp. 36, 79. See also INEVITABILITY.

MELODRAMATIC   An effect is said to be melodramatic when the violent or the sensational seems to be used for its own sake without adequate reference to the motivation of the characters or to other elements in the story. But the mere fact of violence, it should be pointed out, does not constitute melodrama. If the violence is logical and meaningful, it is not melodramatic. See pp. 227–28.

METAPHOR   See IMAGERY.

MOTIVATION   The purpose, or mixture of purposes, or even the more or less unconscious impulses that determine the behavior of a character. See pp. 36, 43–44.

OBJECTIVE   In relation to fiction, the pair of terms OBJECTIVE and SUBJECTIVE, is used in two connections. In the first, they are used with reference to the author, and in the second they are used with reference to a character, or characters, in the work of fiction. In the first connection, an *objective* treatment by the author implies an attitude of detachment toward the material which is being presented, a refusal to comment and interpret directly. (See DISTANCE, DRAMATIC, and SCALE.) A *subjective* treatment, on the other hand, is one which is highly colored by the author's own feelings and beliefs. Of course, the amount of subjectivity or objectivity is always a matter of degree. Since all fiction involves, ultimately, the author's interpretations, feelings, judgments, and the like, there is strictly speaking no absolutely objective presentation, but we can say that, in terms of method the distinction can be made. In reference to the character, or characters, in a work of fiction, the terms can be applied more absolutely. When there is no direct presentation of the thoughts or feelings of a character, the treatment is said to be objective; when such presentation is made the treatment is said to be subjective. But most pieces of fiction tend to mix the two methods, some events being rendered objectively, some characters being treated objectively, and some subjectively.

PACE   The rate of speed with which the various parts of the story are made to move, ranging from summary to fully reported scene. See p. 73.

PARABLE   A story, usually simple, which makes an obvious point or has a rather obvious symbolic meaning. The method of parable is closely related to that of ALLEGORY, but the tendency is to use the term *allegory* to indicate a more systematic and complicated structure of equivalents. See pp. 5, 30–31, 110.

PARADOX   See IRONY.

PATHOS   The sense of pity. The author, however, must be on his guard to make sure that the pathos in a story emerges legitimately from the situation given. When there is no reasonable basis in character and situation for the pathos, one has an effect of SENTIMENTALITY. The quality of being *pathetic* is to be distinguished from that of being *tragic*. In a tragic sutuation the sense of pity is complicated by an effect of struggle and conflict. The pathetic effect may be given by the spectacle of a weak person suffering; the tragic effect requires that the sufferer have strength enough to struggle vigorously against his situation.

PERSONIFICATION   The attribution of the qualities of a person to an inanimate object or idea.

PLOT   The structure of action *as presented* in fiction or drama. Plot, as PLOT PATTERN, is one aspect of the total design of a story. See 1–31, 33–39.

POINT OF VIEW   This term is loosely used to refer to the author's basic attitudes and ideas; for example, one may speak of a detached point of view, a sympathetic point of view, a Christian point of view. More strictly, the term is used to refer to the teller of the story—to the mind through which the material of the story is presented. The story may be told in the first or in the third person, and the teller may be the mere observer or much more than that. See pp. 127–28, 171–73. See also FOCUS OF NARRATION.

PROPAGANDA   Propaganda literature is literature which tends to state its theme abstractly and tends to insist upon its "message" at the expense of other elements. Usually it can be said that such literature oversimplifies its material in order to emphasize a particular interpretation.

REALISM   See REALISTIC.

REALISTIC   Having a strong sense of fact or actuality. The term is used in this text to refer to the presentation of ordinary, easily observable details which give an impression of fidelity to experience. *Realistic* is to be contrasted with ROMANœ TIC, which implies the remote, the exotic, the exaggerated. (There is no attempt in this book to go into the distinction between *romantic* and *classic*.)

RHYTHM   Movement with a recurrent beat or stress. Though prose rhythms are not so marked as those in poetry, most of which is written in *verse*, the rhythms in a piece of prose are frequently important and may indeed be highly expressive.

SCALE   The relative amount of detail of treatment allowed to the various parts in a story. See p. 73.

SELECTION   The creation of a piece of fiction involves a constant process of selection from a multitude of possible events, images, tonalities, etc. The writer's choice of principles of structure and matters of detail will obviously depend upon what theme he is concerned to dramatize and on what aspects of the human predicament he wishes to explore. See also FORM and STYLE.

SELECTIVITY   See SELECTION.

SENTIMENTALITY   Emotional response in excess of the occasion; emotional response that has not been prepared for in the story in question. See pp. 46, 119–20, 127–28. See also TONE.

SETTING   The physical background, the element of place, in a story. See pp. 29, 125–26, 312–13.

SIMILE   See IMAGERY.

STOCK RESPONSE   The automatic or conventional or generally uncritical response of a reader to some word, phrase, situation, character, or subject in literature. See also CLICHÉ.

STRUCTURE   See FORM.

STYLE   See FORM.

SUBJECTIVE   See OBJECTIVE.

SURPRISE ENDING   An ending in a story that comes with some sense of shock to the reader. (For the grounds for distinguishing between legitimate and illegitimate surprise endings, see pp. 45–46, 56, 63–64, 72–73.) See also COINCIDENCE.

SYMBOL   An object, character, or incident that stands for something else, or suggests something else, is a *symbol* of that thing. See pp. 29, 105. But we need to distinguish between two kinds of symbols. The crown, like the cross or flag, is a *conventional* symbol. That is, men *have agreed* that the figure of the cross should stand for Christianity, that a flag of a certain design should stand for the United States of America, or that a circlet of gold should stand for the authority of kingship. Such conventional symbols occur in literature just as they occur in our daily speech, but the symbolism with which we are characteristically concerned as we read poems and stories is not conventional. It is special, and it is related to a particular context. Thus, in "The Man Who Would be King" (pp. 80–104), Dravot's crown of gold comes in the end to stand for something more admirable and more truly kingly than his power over the barbarous tribesmen of Kafiristan. Or consider "The Necklace" (pp. 66–72). The sparkling circlet has, at the end of the story, become in meaning more than just another piece of jewelry. It has become a symbol of the vanity for which human beings may sacrifice their lives. In literature, objects and events often become symbolic, possessing a wider significance and thus becoming expressive of the author's meaning. Since fiction is concrete and dramatic in its presentation, the author must necessarily make use of symbols at some level, for he does not "state" his meanings abstractly but renders them through the presentation of concrete particulars.

THEME   The "point" or "meaning" of a story or novel. See pp. 105, 195, 277–78.

TONE   The tone is the reflection in the story of the author's attitude toward his material and toward his audience. (It is to be distinguished from ATMOSPHERE, which see.) See pp. 18–19. See also SENTIMENTALITY.

TRAGEDY   See PATHOS. See also pp. 105, 229–30.

UNDERSTATEMENT   See IRONY. See also p. 172.

UNITY   The sense of wholeness or oneness. See pp. 34–36, 111.